An F. Scott Fitzgerald Encyclopedia

Robert L. Gale

Greenwood Press
Westport, Connecticut • London

Library of Congress Cataloging-in-Publication Data

Gale, Robert L., 1919–
An F. Scott Fitzgerald encyclopedia / Robert L. Gale.
p. cm.
Includes bibliographical references (p.) and index.
ISBN 0–313–30139–5 (alk. paper)
1. Fitzgerald, F. Scott (Francis Scott), 1896–1940—Encyclopedias.
2. Authors, American—20th century—Biography—Encyclopedias.
I. Title.
PS3511.I9Z6247 1998
813'.52—dc21
[B] 98–13976

British Library Cataloguing in Publication Data is available.

Library of Congress Catalog Card Number: 98–13976
ISBN: 0–313–30139–5

First published in 1998

Greenwood Press, 88 Post Road West, Westport, CT 06881
An imprint of Greenwood Publishing Group, Inc.

Printed in the United States of America

The paper used in this book complies with the Permanent Paper Standard issued by the National Information Standards Organization (Z39.48–1984).

10 9 8 7 6 5 4 3 2 1

To the Men of the Dartmouth College
Class of 1942—
Born mostly in Fitzgerald's Roaring Twenties,
We entered Dartmouth with the New England Hurricane of 1938
and continued into World War II

Contents

Preface ix

Chronology xiii

Abbreviations xvii

The Encyclopedia 1

Bibliography 471

Index 473

Preface

F. Scott Fitzgerald is internationally known as the author of *The Great Gatsby*, which is firmly established as a twentieth-century literary classic, and as the author of several short stories, notably ''Absolution,'' ''Babylon Revisited,'' ''Crazy Sunday,'' ''The Diamond as Big as the Ritz,'' ''May Day,'' ''The Rich Boy,'' and ''Winter Dreams,'' all of which have been widely anthologized. He is also celebrated as a symbol of the Jazz Age and an eponym of the Roaring Twenties, that grand, tragic, pathetic era in American history that lasted from 1918 until shortly after the Crash and the beginning of the Great Depression. Fitzgerald's wife, Zelda Sayre Fitzgerald, also participated in that gaudy age, which featured other attractive but dangerously irresponsible ''flappers.''

Less well known are Fitzgerald's other novels, including *This Side of Paradise*, which started his meteoric rise to sparkling prominence, and *Tender Is the Night*, which among other things dramatizes his fall, caused by his ruinous but sometimes delightful personality quirks.

Delightful, yes. As a freshman member of the Dartmouth College Class of 1942, I well remember waiting on the handsome Fitzgerald's table at the Hanover Inn during his alcoholic appearance at our Winter Carnival in February 1939. With chagrin, I also remember having to be told later who he was, because I did not know him from Walter Wanger or Budd Schulberg, also there from Hollywood. It was still later before I began to read, appreciate, and then revere his magic prose, somewhat after the Fitzgerald revival began in the 1950s. When I highlighted Fitzgerald in my undergraduate lecture course, titled ''The Roaring Twenties,'' beginning in the 1970s at the University of Pittsburgh, he was the most popular figure among the dozens we considered.

Still less well known is the fact that Fitzgerald, despite personal and professional difficulties, was almost constantly productive and that in a literary career effectively beginning in 1919, when he turned professional, and ending with his death only twenty-one years later, he wrote five novels, about 180 short stories (depending on inclusion of possible ''sketches''), numerous essays and reviews, much poetry, several plays, and some filmscripts. He was not merely the author of six or eight fictional masterpieces. It is also true that, even when he wrote hastily and perhaps bleary eyed, sustained by gin and coffee, the finished product almost always bears traces of his genius. He was much more versatile than many realize. Moreover, beneath all the roaring-age hoopla and glitter for which his prose is famous lies the realistic warning that, while personal recklessness can be dangerous, the romantic yearning of the heart toward love can be redemptive. Fitzgerald often aimed to preach to as well as entertain his readers. I think that no one who consults this encyclopedia can fail to be struck by Fitzgerald's bewilderingly numerous characters, almost always neatly etched, by his delightful imagination and surprising range, and by his often sobering, if whispered, little sermons.

This book presents the essential action in Fitzgerald's novels, short stories, plays, and narrative poems and summarizes the core meaning of his other works. All named fictional characters are identified, and their significance in works in which they appear is indicated. Brief biographical sketches of Fitzgerald's family members, friends, and professional associates are included. Ample proof is given that Fitzgerald the author could fall on his face once in a while, as with ''The Ants at Princeton'' and ''Strange Sanctuary,'' for example. Pieces merely attributed to Fitzgerald are not included, even when charming, for example, ''Ethel had her shot of brandy'' and ''Oui, le backfield est from Paris.'' For them, and other such omissions, the reader is invited to consult *F. Scott Fitzgerald in His Own Time, a Miscellany*, edited by Matthew J. Bruccoli and Jackson R. Bryer (New York: Popular Library, 1971).

To save space, I rarely mention discarded titles of works published under different titles, nor do I discuss revisions of texts. Despite our being at table together in 1939, I do not emulate some nervy biographers who refer to Fitzgerald as Scott. Please excuse my occasionally clipped syntax, also designed to cut wordage. To save still more space, I have tried to keep individual end-of-entry bibliographies to a minimum. Experienced Fitzgerald scholars will recognize my frequent use of facts and occasional use of insights gleaned from publications by others, most notably by the following experts on Fitzgerald's life and works: Matthew J. Bruccoli, John Kuehl, Bryant Mangum, Arthur Mizener, Alice Hall Petry, Stephen W. Potts, Jeffrey Meyers, Nancy Milford, and Andrew Turnbull. I hope my expression of thanks, here and now, to these scholarly pioneers will disarm any suspicions that I have ungraciously ''borrowed'' too much.

Although this encyclopedia aims primarily to be informational, a few critical judgments are implicit on occasion; and the bibliographies, emphasizing post-1990 material wherever pertinent, should prove useful to critically minded readers. To aid them, items are cross-referenced by being marked with an asterisk (*). Fitzgerald's titles and characters, which have individual entries, are not so marked.

Despite the detail included in this encyclopedia, it is not possible to do justice to the complexity of Fitzgerald's work here. My work is obviously designed to aid readers beginning to appreciate Fitzgerald, more experienced readers in high school, college, and university classes studying his works, and graduate students, seasoned teachers, and scholars seeking quick reviews of primary and secondary data or desiring to refresh their memories of previous readings. To appreciate Fitzgerald's style, verve, imagery, humor, and substantive depths, one must turn to his own pages and nothing else.

For kindness and encouragement I offer thanks to the following colleagues at the University of Pittsburgh: H. David Brumble III, Bruce Dobler, Frederick A. Hetzel, and Philip E. Smith. Also I owe much to several Pitt librarians, especially Laurie Cohen, Elizabeth A. Evans, Anne W. Gordon, Amy E. Knapp, and Marie Mazzocco Scipione. My editors George F. Butler and Betty C. Pessagno of Greenwood Press and copyeditor Lynn E. Wheeler have also been unfailingly helpful. Unique accolades must be accorded Matthew J. Bruccoli, for his *F. Scott Fitzgerald: A Descriptive Bibliography* (rev. ed., Pittsburgh: University of Pittsburgh Press, 1987), a monumental, standard-setting bibliography, without which no one can trace Fitzgerald's more elusive publications. Finally, much love and gratitude to my wife, Maureen, and our immediate family members—John, Jim, Christine, and Bill.

Chronology

1853	Fitzgerald's father Edward Fitzgerald* (1853–1931) born near Rockville, Montgomery County, Maryland.
1858	Fitzgerald's father-in-law Anthony Dickinson Sayre* born in Tuskegee, Alabama.
1860	Fitzgerald's mother Mary McQuillan Fitzgerald* (1860–1936) born in St. Paul, Minnesota, and his mother-in-law Minnie Buckner Mahen Sayre* born near Eddyville, Kentucky.
1890	Edward Fitzgerald and Mary McQuillan marry in Roman Catholic Church ceremony, in St. Paul.
1896	Francis Scott Key Fitzgerald (1896–1940) born 24 September in St. Paul.
1898	The family moves to Buffalo, New York, where Edward Fitzgerald works for Procter and Gamble.
1901	The family moves to Syracuse, New York, where Edward Fitzgerald continues with Procter and Gamble; Fitzgerald's sister Annabel Fitzgerald* born (1901–1987), who becomes Mrs. Clifton Sprague in 1932.
1903	The family returns to Buffalo, where Edward Fitzgerald continues with Procter and Gamble.
1908	The family returns to St. Paul, where Edward Fitzgerald works as a wholesale grocery salesman and Fitzgerald enrolls in St. Paul Academy (private boys' school).
1909	"The Mystery of the Raymond Mortgage," first story, published.
1910	Confirmed in Catholic Church.
1911	*The Girl from Lazy J*, first play, produced; enrolls in Newman School (private Catholic high school) in Hackensack, New Jersey.
1912	Meets Cyril Sigourney Webster Fay.*

1913 Enters Princeton University, as member of class of 1917; tries out for football team, becomes member of Triangle Club (social organization producing annual musical shows), does poorly in class work.

1914 Falls in love with Chicagoan Ginevra King,* rich and inaccessible; *Fie! Fie! Fi-Fi!*, first musical, produced.

1915 At Princeton, joins Cottage Club, is Triangle Club secretary, but withdraws from school because of poor health and poor grades; returns to St. Paul.

1916 Reenters Princeton, as member of class of 1918.

1917 Enters U.S. Army, commissioned as infantry second lieutenant, trains at Fort Leavenworth, Kansas, begins first novel (''The Romantic Egoist''), calls 1917 his last year as a formal Catholic.

1918 Transfers to Camp Taylor (Louisville, Kentucky), Camp Gordon (Georgia), Camp Sheridan (Montgomery, Alabama); meets Zelda Sayre (*see* Fitzgerald, Zelda Sayre) (1900–1948); novel rejected by Scribner's but with encouragement; reports to Camp Mills (Long Island).

1919 Returns to Camp Sheridan and is discharged; becomes engaged to Zelda; works in New York City advertising agency and revises novel (now called ''The Education of a Personage''), again rejected by Scribner's with encouragement. Zelda breaks engagement. Fitzgerald returns to parents' St. Paul home; completes novel (now *This Side of Paradise*), which Scribner's accepts; publishes ''Babes in the Woods,'' first commercial sale. Is engaged to Zelda again. Sells stories to *Smart Set, Scribner's, Saturday Evening Post*; hires Harold Ober* to act as literary agent.

1920 Lives briefly in New Orleans. *This Side of Paradise* published (March). Fitzgerald and Zelda marry in New York City (April) and rent a house in Westport, Connecticut. *Flappers and Philosophers* published (September). Fitzgeralds move to Manhattan. *The Chorus Girl's Romance*, first movie adaptation (from ''Head and Shoulders'') is produced.

1921 Fitzgeralds live in France and Italy, then in Montgomery and St. Paul. Daughter Frances Scott (''Scottie'') Fitzgerald* (Mrs. Samuel Jackson Lanahan, Mrs. Grove Smith) (1921–1986) born in St. Paul (26 October). Fitzgeralds move to St. Paul.

1922 *The Beautiful and Damned* and *Tales of the Jazz Age* published (March, September). Fitzgeralds move to Great Neck, Long Island.

1923 Fitzgerald's play *The Vegetable* published (April), produced in Atlantic City (November), fails.

1924 Fitzgeralds live in France. Zelda has affair with Edouard Jozan. Fitzgeralds move to Italy.

1925 *The Great Gatsby* published (April); Fitzgeralds return to France.

1926 Zelda displays mental instability. *All the Sad Young Men* published (February). Play version of *Gatsby* appears on Broadway. Fitzgeralds return to America.

1927	Fitzgerald works for United Artists in Hollywood. Fitzgeralds move to ''Ellerslie,'' outside Wilmington, Delaware. Zelda ambitious to become ballerina.
1928	Fitzgeralds spend summer in Paris, start to drink excessively, return to Delaware.
1929	Fitzgeralds return to Italy and France.
1930	Fitzgeralds travel in Africa. Zelda is hospitalized in French and Swiss clinics.
1931	Fitzgerald attends father's funeral in Maryland. Fitzgeralds live in France and Montgomery. Fitzgerald begins to work for Metro-Goldwyn-Mayer in Hollywood.
1932	Zelda is institutionalized in Baltimore, Maryland. Fitzgerald moves to Towson, Maryland. Zelda joins him but is soon hospitalized in Baltimore.
1933	Fitzgeralds live in Baltimore.
1934	Zelda is reinstitutionalized; *Tender Is the Night* is published (April).
1935	Fitzgerald lives in North Carolina, mostly in Asheville, and in Baltimore. *Taps at Reveille* published (March).
1936	Zelda is institutionalized in Asheville.
1937	Fitzgerald returns to North Carolina, writes in Hollywood for MGM (July 1937 to December 1938), meets Sheilah Graham,* works on script of *Three Comrades* (only screen credit).
1938	Fitzgerald vacations with Zelda at Virginia Beach, lives in Malibu Beach and Encino, California. Scottie enters Vassar College.
1939	Fitzgerald goes to Dartmouth College for MGM but is fired for drunkenness. Freelances in Hollywood for several movie studios; vacations with Zelda in Cuba.
1940	Continues freelancing for studios and for publication. Zelda lives briefly with her mother in Montgomery. Fitzgerald dies of heart attack on 21 December in Hollywood.
1941	*The Last Tycoon* published even though unfinished (October).
1945	*The Crack-Up* published (August).
1948	Zelda burns to death on 10 March in Asheville sanitarium.
1986	Scottie dies (15 June).

Abbreviations

Allen	Joan M. Allen. *Candles and Carnival Lights: The Catholic Sensibility of F. Scott Fitzgerald* (New York: New York University Press, 1978).
Bruccoli, *Gatsby*	Matthew J. Bruccoli, ed. F. Scott Fitzgerald, *The Great Gatsby* (Cambridge: Cambridge University Press, 1991).
Bryer, *New Approaches*	Jackson R. Bryer, ed. *The Short Stories of F. Scott Fitzgerald: New Approaches in Criticism* (Madison: University of Wisconsin Press, 1982).
Bryer, *New Essays*	Jackson R. Bryer, ed. *New Essays on F. Scott Fitzgerald's Neglected Stories* (Columbia: University of Missouri Press, 1996).
Eble	Kenneth Eble. *F. Scott Fitzgerald* (rev. ed., Boston: Twayne Publishers, 1977).
FH/A	*Fitzgerald/Hemingway Annual.*
Kuehl	John Kuehl. *F. Scott Fitzgerald: A Study of the Short Fiction* (Boston: Twayne Publishers, 1991).
Lambert	*Norma Shearer: A Life* (New York: Knopf, 1990).
Latham	Aaron Latham. *Crazy Sundays: F. Scott Fitzgerald in Hollywood* (New York: Viking Press, 1971).
Margolies	Alan Margolies, ed. *F. Scott Fitzgerald's St. Paul Plays 1911–1914.* (Princeton: Princeton University Library, 1978).
Matterson	Stephen Matterson. *The Great Gatsby* (London: Macmillan, 1990).
Roulston	Robert Roulston and Helen H. Roulston. *The Winding Road to West Egg: The Artistic Development of F. Scott Fitzgerald* (Lewisburg, Pa.: Bucknell University Press, 1995).

A

ABBOT, HAMILTON ("HAM"). In "The Love Boat," he is a Harvard friend of Bill Frothington. He boards the love boat with Bill and Ellsworth Ames.

ABBOT, THE. In "In the Darkest Hour," he is the leading churchman of the Loire Valley region to which Count Philippe of Villefranche returns. He opposes Philippe's plans to rid the area of Viking invaders.

ABBOTT, CHARLEY. In "Diamond Dick and the First Law of Woman," he was a combat pilot from Boston during World War I. He married Diana Dickey in France, was shot down, and suffered amnesia. His memory is jogged by Diana in New York five years later, when he is twenty-nine.

ABBY. In "The Intimate Strangers," she is Marquise Sara de la Guillet de la Guimpé's friend. She has a home on Long Island and is married to a diplomat.

ABDUL. In "Indecision," he is the worker who handles the lighting for a dance in Tommy McLane's Swiss hotel.

ABERCROMBIE. In *The Beautiful and Damned*, this is the name of a Kansas City family with whom Maury Noble had tea in New York.

ABERCROMBIE. In "The Dance," he is a congressman and the father of Bill Abercrombie, the sheriff of Davis.

ABERCROMBIE. In "Two for a Cent," he is a New Yorker, about forty-five, who returns to the Alabama town of his youth to see the house he lived in. He meets Henry W. Hemmick, and the two reminisce. Abercrombie never wished to leave home but got into a high school scrape. He found a penny needed to complete the sum necessary to buy a train ticket to an Atlanta army recruiting office, joined up for three years, and rose to prominence in shipping and finance. Hemmick lost the penny Abercrombie found.

ABERCROMBIE, BILL. In "The Dance," he is the sheriff of Davis, which the narrator visits. He hangs his holster and revolver on a wall during the country-club dance. The weapon figures in the killing of Marie Bannerman.

ABRAMS, MRS. In *Tender Is the Night*, she is a sycophantic American tourist on the Riviera.

ABRAMS, STONEWALL JACKSON. In *The Great Gatsby*, Nick Carraway lists him on a timetable as among Jay Gatsby's summer guests. The Abramses are from Georgia.

ABRISINI, PRINCE. In "A Penny Spent," Corcoran buys Prince Abrisini's presence to entertain Jessie Pepper Bushmill and her daughter, Hallie Bushmill, in Brussels.

" 'LES ABSENTS ONT TOUJOURS TORT' " (1981). Poem. A parody of a nursery rhyme.

"ABSOLUTION" (1924). Short story. (Characters: Jeanne Brady, Carl Miller, Mrs. Carl Miller, Rudolph Miller, Romberg, Father Adolphus Schwartz.) Rudolph Miller, eleven, confesses to Father Adolphus Schwartz in the Catholic church of Ludwig, a Dakota town with wheat fields all about, that he sinned with his friends—by yelling at an old woman, believing he was not his parents' son (he had even invented Blatchford Sarnemington, an alter ego), being disobedient, smoking, and thinking dirty thoughts. Then he lies to the priest, when asked, by saying that he never lies. Hoping to avoid having to take communion on Sunday morning while in a state of sin, he starts to drink forbidden water but is stopped by his father, who strikes him and orders him to go to church. He reluctantly accepts communion and feels damned. Three days later, he talks with Father Schwartz, who is vaguely but strongly attracted to the boy and who rambles on about the attractions of glistening amusement parks—as long as you do not get too close. Rudolph proudly feels his independent beliefs somehow validated. The priest collapses on the floor. In the wheat fields beyond, Swedish girls and young farmhands will be lying together under the moon.

Fitzgerald once lied in the confessional but returned and asked for absolution. Rudolph is confused by conflicting signals from his two father figures. Fitzgerald once considered making this plot part of *The Great Gatsby* to illustrate an event in Jay Gatsby's boyhood.

Bibliography: Allen; Keith Cushman, "Scott Fitzgerald's Scrupulous Meanness: 'Absolution' and [James Joyce's] 'The Sisters,' " *FH/A 1979*, 115–21; E. R. Hagemann, "Should Scott Fitzgerald Be Absolved for the Sins of 'Absolution'?," *Journal of Modern Literature* 12 (March 1985): 169–74); Kuehl.

ACOMBA. In "The Cameo Frame," he is a page who dresses the hair of the cameo-like lady and kisses her by moonlight, but must lose her.

"THE ADJUSTER" (1925). Short story. (Characters: Mrs. Danski, Charles Hemple, Chuck Hemple, Luella Hemple, Alphonse Karr, Ede Karr, Dr. Moon.) In 1920 Luella Hemple, twenty-three, has been married for three years to Charles Hemple, a successful New York businessman in his mid-thirties. Their son Chuck is two. While having tea at the Ritz with Ede Karr, Luella complains she is so bored that she is half-planning to quit her marriage. She wants fun regardless of cost. That evening her tired husband comes home with a guest for dinner. He is Dr. Moon, who presents himself to his inhospitable hostess as a seedy, unwelcome marriage counselor. He says he can promise nothing. Charles Hemple suffers a sudden nervous collapse. As the unwelcome Dr. Moon comes and goes, Luella ministers to Charles as well as she can but manages the servants so badly that they do not remain long. One evening in 1921 Chuck is ill; while Luella enlists his nurse to help her in the kitchen, the child dies. At first Luella remains egocentric and even packs a trunk to leave, but the shadowy Moon persuades her not only that Charles is getting better but that she cannot hope to leave her mistakes behind by running away. Luella gradually learns to consider others, and Charles grows well again. Moon, saying she no longer requires him, defines himself as five years and leaves. The Hemples now have two children and a harmonious life. Toward the close of the story, Moon tells Luella that when we wrongly have children sit in the audience and not participate in the play we later must work hard to enable them to enjoy life's "light and glitter." Fitzgerald surely wanted Zelda to take a lesson from "The Adjuster" (*see* Fitzgerald, Zelda Sayre).

"THE ADOLESCENT MARRIAGE" (1926). Short story. (Characters: Carson, Jesse Clark, Llewellyn Clark, Lucy Wharton Clark, Chauncey Garnett, George Hemmick, Linquist, Elsie Wharton, George Wharton.) In summer 1925 Chauncey Garnett, an experienced Philadelphia architect, is requested by his friends George and Elsie Wharton to try to salvage the marriage of their daughter Lucy, sixteen, to Garnett's talented assistant, Llewellyn Clark, twenty-three. The adolescents eloped to Connecticut, argued, and want to split up. Garnett gets nowhere talking with them separately, so he visits Connecticut and returns with the information that an annulment has been managed. During the next months, Llewellyn broods, sees Lucy by chance, and learns she plans to marry George Hemmick, her father's business associate in Chicago, and live there. Garnett encourages Llewellyn to design a cottage in a contest; he does so, wins a prize, and one evening wanders into the finished structure imagining himself happy there. Garnett appears at the door, thinks of his first house with his wife, tells Llewellyn that Lucy is on the porch and is expecting a baby, mentions that he never arranged any annulment, leaves the couple together, and wonders guiltily whether he meddled too much.

"AFTERNOON OF AN AUTHOR" (1936). Short story. The wobbly author gets up one April morning in Maryland, notes that his daughter is out, has his breakfast prepared by his maid, rests, and when his secretary phones says he has written nothing. He rides the bus to his hotel barbershop and thinks about a barber story he wrote ["A Change of Class"]. He looks at dancers in the cocktail room, catches another bus, sees a happy young couple, and returns home. Maybe an idea will come to him before dinner.

AGGIE, PRINCE. In *The Last Tycoon*, he is a visitor Monroe Stahr shows around the studio and adjacent property. His character is based on Prince Agge of Denmark (d. 1940).

Bibliography: Gabrielle Winkel, "Fitzgerald's Agge of Denmark," *FH/A 1975*, 131–32.

AHEARN, CLARENCE. In "The Cut-Glass Bowl," he is a businessman who plans to merge with Harold Piper until he is insulted at Evylyn Piper's birthday party. Harold gets drunk and tells him why Ahearn is having difficulty gaining membership in an exclusive country club.

AHEARN, MRS. CLARENCE. In "The Cut-Glass Bowl," she is Clarence Ahearn's wife, whom Evylyn instantly dislikes at the birthday party.

"AH MAY, SHALL I SPLATTER MY THOUGHTS IN THE AIR" (1981). Poem. The poet feels that May gives him no chance, wonders what sort of man she does like, and tries to define her.

ALBRUCKSBURGER. In *The Great Gatsby*, Nick Carraway lists his name on a timetable as one of Jay Gatsby's summer guests. He came with his fiancée Miss Haag.

"AN ALCOHOLIC CASE" (1937). Short story. (Characters: Dr. Carter, Hattie, Gretta Hawks, Mrs. Hixson, Josephine Markham, Bill Markoe, Svensen.) A nice nurse cares for a combat war veteran now an alcoholic cartoonist living at an inn. He has a photograph of a wife and two sons. Five years ago he was handsome. To keep him from drinking, the nurse takes away a bottle of gin. He grabs her wrists. The bottle drops and breaks on the bathroom tiles. After she cuts herself picking up the pieces, she returns to Mrs. Hixson's employment agency on a messy bus. When Mrs. Hixson can find no other nurse, the same nice one agrees to return for duty, although Mrs. Hixon is concerned because alcoholics become ugly. The nurse finds her patient getting dressed in dinner clothes. When he sits on the toilet seat and lets her change his mussed shirt, she notices a copper plate covering a wound in his side. Suddenly he stands up, stares past her—at death. Later the saddened nurse tells Mrs. Hixson she can do nothing for such cases. This story, long neglected, has been reprinted often. It reflects Fitzgerald's miseries in 1936. The nurse is based on Theodora Gager, Fitzgerald's private nurse at one time.

Bibliography: Arnold Waldhorn, ''The Cartoonist, the Nurse, and the Writer: 'An Alcoholic Case,' '' Bryer, *New Essays*, 244–52.

ALCOHOLISM IN FITZGERALD. Throughout adulthood, Fitzgerald had a problem with alcohol. He drank at Princeton. He and Zelda (*see* Fitzgerald, Zelda Sayre) drank and misbehaved in the United States and abroad. He tried to swear off frequently but without success, and he lied about his addiction. Alcohol contributed to his death. Critics note his repeated displays of the alcoholic's cardinal traits: denial and self-deception, a tendency toward violence when drunk, and Jekyll-and-Hyde personality changes. Some of Fitzgerald's best fiction depicts alcoholic characters revealingly if with deceptive unobtrusiveness. *See* especially ''An Alcoholic Case,'' ''Babylon Revisited,'' *The Beautiful and Damned*, ''Crazy Sunday,'' ''Family in the Wind,'' *The Great Gatsby*, ''Her Last Case,'' ''The Lost Decade,'' ''A New Leaf,'' ''One Trip Abroad,'' the Pat Hobby stories, ''Shadow Laurels,'' *Tender Is the Night*, and *This Side of Paradise*. Fitzgerald writes more directly about alcoholism in *The Crack-Up*.

Bibliography: Tony Buttitta, *After the Good Gay Times—Summer of '35: A Season with F. Scott Fitzgerald* (New York: Viking, 1974); John W. Crowley, *The White Logic: Alcoholism and Gender in American Modernist Fiction* (Amherst: University of Massachusetts Press, 1994); Tom Dardis, *The Thirsty Muse: Alcoholism and the American Writer* (New York: Ticknor and Fields, 1989); Kenneth E. Eble, ''Touches of Disaster and Mental Illness in Fitzgerald's Short Stories''; Bryer, *New Approaches*, 39–52; Thomas B. Gilmore, *Equivocal Spirits: Alcohol and Drinking in Twentieth-Century Literature* (Chapel Hill: University of North Carolina Press, 1987); Laura Guthrie Hearne, ''A Summer with F. Scott Fitzgerald,'' *Esquire*, December 1964, 160; Latham; Edwin A. Peeples, ''Twilight of a God: A Brief, Beery Encounter with F. Scott Fitzgerald,'' *Mademoiselle*, November 1973, 170; Dwight Taylor, *Joy Ride* (New York: Putnam, 1959).

"ALDOUS HUXLEY'S CROME YELLOW" (1922). Review. *See* Huxley, Aldous.

ALEXANDRE, APOSTLE. In *Tender Is the Night*, his name is read in the *New York Herald*.

ALFONSO. In ''One Interne,'' he is a character in a roast song at the medical school.

ALICE. In ''The Family Bus,'' she is a relative, friend, or servant in Jannekin Melon-Loper's home.

ALIX. In ''Babylon Revisited,'' he is a Paris bartender who gossips with Charles J. Wales about former American drinkers.

ALLEN. In ''The Trail of the Duke,'' he is Dodson Garland's patient, drink-serving butler.

ALLENBY. In *This Side of Paradise*, he is the captain of the Princeton football team during Amory Blaine's freshman year.

ALLERDYCE, MRS. THOMAS. She is a character in ''O Russet Witch!'' *See* Caroline.

ALLERDYCE, THOMAS. In ''O Russet Witch!,'' he is Caroline's wealthy husband. They married shortly after the Throckmorton divorce scandal in which she was the correspondent. The couple have a grandson.

ALLISON, PARKER. In *The Beautiful and Damned*, he is one of Anthony Patch's drinking companions in New York.

"ALL THE GIRLS AND MANS" (1973). Poem. Everyone rushes to meet ''Herbert Sherbet Gorman.''

ALL THE SAD YOUNG MEN (1926). Short story collection.

ALTWATER, PERCY, LIEUTENANT. In *Coward*, he is a British-born officer in the Confederate Army who is a friend of Lieutenant Charles Douglas. He is supercilious but impresses Virginia Taylor, the friend of Lindy Douglas, Charles's sister.

AMBLER, JOE. In ''The Cut-Glass Bowl,'' he is a bachelor friendly toward Irene, Evylyn Piper's unmarried sister. They attend Evylyn's birthday party.

AMES. In ''Two Wrongs,'' he is a show-business competitor mentioned by William McChesney in conversation with Brancusi.

AMES, ELLSWORTH ("ELLIE"). In ''The Love Boat,'' he is Bill Frothington's Harvard friend. He boards the love boat with Bill and Hamilton Abbot. Ames later marries, and he and his wife socialize with Bill and Stella Frothington.

AMES, MRS. ELLSWORTH. In ''The Love Boat,'' she is the wife of Bill Frothington's Harvard friend.

AMES, T. In *Thoughtbook*, he is a boy who likes Marie Hersey.

AMY. In ''The Hotel Child,'' she is mentioned by Mrs. Schwartz as a family friend in the United States.

AMY. In ''Zone of Accident,'' she is the girlfriend of William Tullivers. She wants a movie career, embraces her agent to get ahead, and wins a Baltimore beauty contest.

ANDERSON, SHERWOOD (1876–1941). Author. Born in Camden, Ohio, Anderson moved about with his family and attended high school in Clyde, Ohio, for nine months. He worked in Chicago, served with the National Guard in Cuba during the Spanish-American War, graduated from Wittenberg College in Springfield, Ohio, in 1900, and worked in Cleveland and Elyria, Ohio. In 1904 he married Cornelia Platt Lane; they had three children. In 1909 he started writing fiction. In 1912 he suffered a breakdown and walked out of his job. From 1913 to 1922 he did advertising work in Chicago. In 1914 he published the first of many short stories. Four days after his divorce in 1916 he married Tennessee Claflin Mitchell, a music teacher with connections to Chicago's bohemian life. Between 1916 and 1925, Anderson published four novels, three short story collections, a book of free verse, and a fictionalized autobiography. His masterpiece, *Winesburg, Ohio* (1919), contains plotless tales of frustration, grotesquerie, revolt, and love in a small town; *Poor White* (1920) narrates the ruin of community spirit when commercialism blights an Ohio town; *Many Marriages* (1923) reveals the author's discontent with America's slick business tricks and hypocrisy in matters of sex. In 1921 he met and aided Ernest Hemingway* in Chicago; and Paul Rosenfeld, a wealthy New York critic, financed Anderson's trip to England and France, where he met James Joyce and Gertrude Stein.* In 1922 Anderson left his wife, lived in New Orleans, then moved to New York. In 1924 he was divorced and married Elizabeth Prall the next day, moved to New Orleans, and then bought a farm near Marion, Virginia. From 1926 Anderson wrote less well, revisited Paris (1926–1927), edited two weekly Marion newspapers (1927–1929), divorced (1932), married Eleanor Copenhaver (1933), and traveled and did newspaper work. He died in Panama of a perforated intestine and peritonitis, caused by a swallowed toothpick. *Sherwood Anderson's Memoirs* appeared posthumously, in 1942.

Fitzgerald knew Anderson in New York by 1922. In ''Sherwood Anderson on the Marriage Question,'' a 1923 review of *Many Marriages*, Fitzgerald says that, whereas it formerly took time for literary reputations to ''solidify,'' Sherwood Anderson's fame, an exception, has been quick. Fitzgerald opines that *Many Marriages*—about the end of one marriage, an elopement and a second marriage, and the suicide of the first wife—is not concerned with justifying specific behavior but rather with the whole man-woman "relation." He calls Anderson's style "tortuous" at times. Anderson wrote to Fitzgerald (mid-March 1923) to express delight in the review and a desire to know Fitzgerald and "Mrs. Fitz" better. In a June 1925 letter sent to Max Perkins* at Scribner's, Fitzgerald opined that, although Anderson has few ideas, he is one of best writers in English now living and singled out "rythms [sic]" in *Winesburg, Ohio* for praise. In December 1925, he wrote to Perkins to ridicule Anderson's recent work and urged Perkins to accept Hemingway's *The Torrents of Spring*, which Anderson's publisher Horace Liveright rejected and which contains a cruel parody of Anderson. Perkins agreed, mainly to get Hemingway's next book, *The Sun Also Rises*. Fitzgerald was happy that Hemingway was published by Scribner's.

Bibliography: Wilford Dunaway Taylor, *Sherwood Anderson* (New York: Ungar, 1977); Kim Townsend, *Sherwood Anderson* (Boston: Houghton Mifflin, 1987).

ANDRÉ. In "Gods of Darkness," he is a lazy guard who works for Count Philippe of Villefranche.

ANDROS, EDE. In "The Baby Party," she is the daughter, aged two and a half, of Edith and John Andros. When Ede shoves Billy Markey, aged two, at his birthday party, both she and her mother laugh, triggering an argument between the mothers.

ANDROS, EDITH. In "The Baby Party," she is Ede Andros's neurotic mother. At Billy Markey's birthday party, she and Ede laugh and cause an argument. After Edith's husband, John Andros, fights Billy's father, Joe Markey, John urges Edith to apologize.

ANDROS, JOHN. In "The Baby Party," he is a businessman, thirty-eight, who commutes to work from his country home. After arriving late at the baby party, he hears abusive remarks being traded by his wife and Mrs. Joe Markey, Billy Markey's mother. John and Billy's father, Joe Markey, fight in the snowy yard, make up, and make their wives apologize.

ANDY, LIEUTENANT. In "The Last of the Belles," he is the narrator. Twenty-three years old at the beginning, he is a regularly commissioned army officer during World War I, trains at a base outside Tarleton, and becomes enamored of Ailie Calhoun, who prefers to play the field and treats him as a Northern confidant, hence unacceptable as a husband. The war ends before he can get overseas. He goes to Harvard Law School, becomes successful, and returns years later to Tarleton, only to learn Ailie is marrying a Savannah man.

ANNA. In ''John Jackson's Arcady,'' she is mentioned as Alice Harland's cook.

ANNE. In ''Babes in the Woods,'' she is a schoolmate of Elaine Terrell and Isabelle. According to Elaine, Anne told Kenneth Powers that Isabelle had been kissed.

ANNE. In ''Martin's Thoughts,'' she is one of Martin's girlfriends.

ANNE. In ''To Anne,'' she is the poet's dream girl.

ANNE. In ''What a Handsome Pair!,'' she is a golf player who defeats Helen Van Beck Oldhorne in a golf tournament.

"ANSWER TO A POEM" (1981). Poem. Burning her missive, the poet advises her to seek love from a successful old man and ignore teary competitors.

ANTIONETTE. In ''Martin's Thoughts,'' she is one of Martin's girlfriends.

"THE ANTS AT PRINCETON" (1936). Short story. (Characters: Aunty, Fritz Crisler, Big Bill Edwards, Hillebrand, Biffy Lee, Poe, Cabot Saltonville.) A Princeton bacteriology professor and a trustee enroll ants, whose ability to organize and discipline themselves to work will motivate human students. While some ants flunk out, others are admirably diligent. One, called Aunty, is so huge that Fritz Crisler, the football coach, makes him a varsity star. Soon only Harvard stands between Princeton and the Rose Bowl. But when Cabot Saltonville, Harvard's football captain, objects, Aunty is benched. When the score is 65–0 against Princeton, Saltonville agrees to let Aunty play during the final minutes. Since Aunty can run on four legs and carry the ball under any of eight arms, Harvard is defeated. Princeton ants infest enemy uniforms. To save himself, Saltonville, pursued to the press box, must voice formal praise of Aunty to sports reporters. Later, lesser ants are wiped off Princeton's campus, but Aunty now teaches insectology and coaches at Yale.

"APOLOGY TO OGDEN NASH" (1981). Poem. Each California female is shy an ovary without reading *Madame Bovary*.

APPLETON. In ''Basil and Cleopatra,'' he is a Yale freshman football quarterback.

APPLETON. In ''Strange Sanctuary,'' he is Dolly Haines's host.

APPLETON, LILA. In ''Strange Sanctuary,'' she is Dolly Haines's hostess, who does not welcome the girl nicely.

APPLETON, WARREN. In ''Myra Meets His Family,'' he is a Chinese-looking actor whom Knowleton Whitney hires to impersonate his father, to scare Myra Harper from wishing to marry him.

AQUILLA. In ''On Schedule,'' he is an African American whose sister and brother work for René du Cary.

ARCHIE. In *Fie Fie! Fie! Fi-Fi!*, he sings with Celeste.

ARMSTRONG, MARGARET. In *Thoughtbook*, she is a friend Fitzgerald is ''crazy about.'' In real life, she became Mrs. Francis Dean.

ARONSTAEL. In ''Two Wrongs,'' he is a show-business friend with whom William McChesney quarrels.

ARROT, BEN. In ''The Ice Palace,'' he is a friend of Sally Carrol Happer and her group.

ART. In *The Last Tycoon*, Monroe Stahr says Red Ridingwood should discuss a problem with him.

ASHTON, CECILIA ("CELIA"). In *Coward*, she is a neighbor of Lindy Douglas and John Ashton's sister.

ASHTON, JOHN. In *Coward*, Cecilia Ashton's brother, he was evidently killed in action.

ASSORTED SPIRITS (1978). Play. (Characters: Madame Caruse, William Chapman, Margureta Du Chene, Amelia Hendrix, Josephus Hendrix, Hulda, Clara King, Mulligan, O'Flarity, Ole, Second Story Salle, Miss Spigot, Cecile Wetherby, Peter Wetherby, Richard Wetherby). Peter Wetherby must sell his house for $10,000 or lose his business. His second cousin, Josephus Hendrix, accompanied by his wealthy ward Clara King, arrives to buy it but plans to lower the price by dressing in a devil's costume and argue that it is haunted. William Chapman leaves a costume party, dressed as a devil, to visit Miss Spigot, his aunt, but taxis to Wetherby's house by mistake. Wetherby asks Madama Zada, his sister, to exorcize all ghosts. The ''devils'' pop out of closets. Second Story Salle steals Hendrix's $10,000 which Wetherby's son, Richard (''Dickie'') is holding. The Wetherbys' maid Hulda takes it when Salle drops it as she leaves. Wetherby's daughter Cecile has liked Chapman for a long while. Salle pretends to be an actress interested in Dickie's play. Next morning Miss Spigot, who knows the Wetherbys, comes looking for her nephew. Dickie confesses losing the money to his father, who tells him to marry Clara. The devils' hiding ceases. Zada, really Josephus's abandoned wife Amelia, gets and gives him his money and they are reconciled. Chapman, a contracting engineer for a railroad needing Wetherby's property for a new line, offers $15,000 for it. Cecile and Chapman agree to wed. *Assorted Spirits* was presented in St. Paul in September 1914.

Bibliography: Margolies.

ATKINS, TOMMY. He is a character in *Fie! Fie! Fi-Fi! See* Cholmondely.

"AT YOUR AGE" (1929). Short story. (Characters: Mary Betts, D. B. Cambell, Randy Cambell, Caroline, Jansen, Leland Jaques, Lorry, Annie Lorry, Mabel Tollman Lorry, Hal Meigs, Tom Squires, Mrs. Trumble.) Tom Squires, fifty, a rich, unattached Yale man, is rejuvenated on seeing a beautiful girl clerking in a drugstore in wintry Minneapolis. This encourages him to pursue Annie Lorry, a girl he sees dancing at his club with several boyish men, including Randy Cambell. Tom takes the Lorrys to a ball, then escorts Annie to several places; once he says her mother disapproves, she grows friendly. She continues to see Randy but prefers Tom's suave attentions. Her eagerness grows offputting; so Tom decides to vacation in Mexico. Resisting a smooth woman's advances on the train to El Paso and a teenage Juarez floozy, he returns to Annie and—her mother yielding—the two announce their engagement. One May night while Tom sits with her mother on her porch, Annie is out driving with Randy and some other youngsters. She returns tousled. Tom walks away. When he learns that the drugstore girl got married, he sends her a present. He lost his fight with youth and springtime but has precious memories of Annie.

AUERBACH, HUBERT. In *The Great Gatsby*, Nick Carraway lists his name on a timetable as one of Jay Gatsby's summer guests. He came with Mrs. Chrystie.

AUGUSTINE. In *Tender Is the Night*, she is the Divers' alcoholic cook. She calls Dick Diver an alcoholic and threatens him before she is discharged.

AUGUSTUS. In " 'Why Blame It on the Poor Kiss If the Girl Veteran of Many Petting Parties Is Prone to Affairs After Marriage?'," he is a harmless oldster Harry will not let his wife Georgianna go out with.

AUNTY. In "The Ants at Princeton," he is a huge ant and formidable football player at Princeton.

"AUTHOR'S HOUSE" (1936). Short story. (Characters: Thomas Kracklin, Mrs. Kracklin Lee, Miss Palmer.) The author conducts a visitor through his house. The basement contains evidence of his infancy, childhood, destroyed love, love of self. Children playing outside the living room window remind the author that since he played football ingloriously, he could only write about it. The dining room contains too much fancy food and alcohol. In the study he once heartlessly answered a person who wrote to one of his fictional characters, thinking the character was real. The author now realizes it is typical of writers to meddle irreparably in other people's emotions. In the bedroom the author asks the visitor not to move a cloth left there by someone. The attic contains a veritable library of the author's life, full of printed memorabilia. From the watch tower the author and visitor view the river, lawns, houses, and birds and hear the wind at twilight. The author would not, could not, live up here again; this house, however, is probably like other houses. When a Mrs. Albert Kibble, Jr., wrote to Fitzgerald's character Basil Duke Lee, care of the *Saturday Evening Post*, asking whether Lee was her half brother, Fitzgerald answered (24 April 1935) as from prison awaiting execution that they probably were related and signed the letter Basil Duke.

"AN AUTHOR'S MOTHER" (1936). Short story. (Characters: Mrs. Johnston, Hamilton T. Johnston, John Johnston.) Mrs. Johnston, over eighty, frail and with cataracts, enters a bookstore to buy a birthday present for her son, Hamilton T. Johnston, a successful author whose career she regards as chancy and odd. She cannot find anything written by Alice and Phoebe Cary, who wrote lovely poetry. She grows faint, falls, cuts her forehead, is taken to the hospital, and dies thinking about those favorite poets of hers.

AVERY, HELEN TOMPKINS. In "Magnetism," she is the beautiful movie actress, eighteen and the object of the almost groundless jealousy of Kay Hannaford, the wife of actor George Hannaford.

B

"BABES IN THE WOODS" (1917; rev., 1919). Short story. (Characters: Anne, Peter Carroll, Isabelle, Kenneth Powers, Elaine Terrell, Mrs. Terrell.) Isabelle, sixteen, an attractive girl from Pittsburg[h], is her friend Elaine Terrell's guest over Christmas vacation. Isabelle wishes to meet Kenneth Powers, eighteen, a college freshman about to return to school. She is stuck with Peter Carroll but at dinner flirts with Kenneth; at the dance the two vie with each other ambiguously. They go to a den, sit on a lounge, and are about to kiss—a remembrance of their time together—when fellow dancers intervene. That night she lies to Elaine that Kenneth wanted to kiss her but she does not do that any longer. The action of "Babes in the Woods" was incorporated in *This Side of Paradise*. Fitzgerald sold "Babes in the Woods," his first story to appear in a commercial magazine, to *Smart Set* for $30.

"BABYLON REVISITED" (1931). Short story. (Characters: Alix, Campbell, Claude Fessenden, George Hardt, Paul, Elsie Peters, Lincoln Peters, Marion Peters, Richard Peters, Lorraine Quarles, Duncan Schaeffer, The Snow Bird, Charles J. Wales, Helen Wales, Honoria Wales, Webb.) In Paris about three years ago—before the Crash—Charles J. Wales, an American, frequently argued with his wife, Helen, also an American. Both were evidently from Vermont. One night when she paid attention to another man at a drunken party, he went home alone and locked her out. She caught cold in the snow and later died. Charlie, then an alcoholic, lost custody of their daughter, Honoria, to Helen's sister, Marion Peters, whose husband, Lincoln Peters, is an American banker in Paris. Charlie, now financially responsible and on the wagon for more than a year, returns from his business office in Prague to Paris to try to reclaim Honoria. He endures Marion's criticism at dinner, takes happy Honoria to the circus, buys presents for the Peter's two children, and is about to win legal control of Honoria when flirtatious Lorraine Quarles and noisy Duncan Schaeffer, two drunks from his past, burst in and outrage Marion, who retires with a headache. Charlie, who is denied custody of Honoria for at least six more months, is wretched and alone. In 1940 Lester Cowan, a Hollywood movie producer, hired Fitzgerald to write a scenario based on "Babylon Revisited" in the expectation of having it filmed by Columbia Pictures. Fitzgerald did so, but the movie was never produced. The scenario was published as *Babylon Revisited: The Screenplay*, with an introduction by Budd Schulberg* (New York: Carroll & Graf, 1993).

Bibliography: Kuehl; André Le Vot, "Fitzgerald in Paris," *FH/A 1973*, 49–68.

"THE BABY PARTY" (1925). Short story. (Characters: Ede Andros, Edith Andros, John Andros, Billy Markey, Joe Markey, Mrs. Joe Markey.) John Andros, thirty-eight, takes solace in Ede, his daughter, two and a half, when he is especially aware of his own mortality. One December day he boards the commuter train to his country home early because his wife has phoned that the three are invited to a party to celebrate the second birthday of Billy Markey, next door. When Andros arrives late, the other babies and their mothers have left, and Edith is arguing with Billy's mother. Ede fought Billy for his teddy bear, pushed him down, hurt his head, and laughed so infectiously that Edith laughed too. Billy's mother was outraged. Careless name calling followed, and John and Joe march outside to fight in the snowy yard. Hurt and abashed after twenty clumsy minutes, they shake hands. When John is home tending to his injuries, the Markeys come over to make amends. John urges Edith to do so as well; but before following her downstairs, he goes to Ede's room and embraces his sleeping child—the precious embodiment of his vanished youth. Fitzgerald wrote "The Baby Party" in one night and sold it to *Hearst's International* for $1,500.

Bibliography: Sanford Pinsker, "Fitzgerald's 'The Baby Party,' " *Explicator* 45 (Winter 1987): 52–55.

BACH. In "A Man in the Way," he is a business associate whose conference with Jack Berners cannot be interrupted by Pat Hobby.

BACH. In "Zone of Accident," he is the German-born father, living in Baltimore, of movie actress Loretta Brooke. He takes her to the hospital after she is stabbed.

BACHUS. In *Thoughtbook*, they are a family who give a school party.

BACHUS, UNA. In *Thoughtbook*, she is an unpopular girl.

BACKHYSSON. In *The Great Gatsby*, Nick Carraway lists his name on a timetable as one of Jay Gatsby's summer guests. He is from New York.

BACON, DR. In ''The Freshest Boy,'' he is a handsome Episcopalian clergyman, fifty, now the headmaster at St. Regis. He grounds Basil Duke Lee and criticizes him, but relents and lets him go to New York accompanied by Rooney. In ''The Perfect Life,'' he commends Basil for playing football well against Exeter.

BADENUFF ("BADDY"). In ''The Prince of Pests,'' he is the chancellor of a Shakespeare-Goethe league and does quick research on Daniel Webster for the Kaiser.

BAEDEKER. In *The Great Gatsby*, this is the name of girls Nick Carraway remembers as being among Jay Gatsby's summer guests. One of them gets drunk at a Gatsby party and leans on Nick.

BAER, DR. BILL. In *The Last Tycoon*, he is Monroe Stahr's physician. After examining Starr, he concludes that he will die in about six months but senses Stahr knows it.

BAILEY, BUZZ. In ''Basil and Cleopatra,'' he is one of Erminie Gilberte Labouisse Bibble's boyfriends.

BAILEY, JOHN BOYNTON. In ''A Snobbish Story,'' he is a *Chicago Tribune* reporter who meets Josephine Perry at a Lake Forest tennis tournament he is covering, lunches with her in Chicago, introduces her to his wife Evelyn, and asks her to act in his socialist play *Race Riot*. While a luncheon guest at Josephine's home, he persuades her father, Herbert T. Perry, to help finance his play, but is called away by the police after Evelyn has attempted suicide. In ''Emotional Bankruptcy,'' he is mentioned as one of Josephine's former boyfriends.

BAILEY, MISS. In ''The Curious Case of Benjamin Button,'' she is Benjamin Button's kindergarten teacher.

BAILY. In ''The Camel's Back,'' he is the friend who persuades Perry Parkhurst to come drink in the hotel with Martin Macy.

BAIRD, TUDOR. In *The Beautiful and Damned*, he was one of Gloria Gilbert Patch's former boyfriends. He was a handsome Yale man. They were once engaged. While Anthony Patch is away in the army, she sees him in New York. She is glad they kissed then, because he is soon killed in an army airplane training accident.

BAKER. In *Thoughtbook*, he is a dance teacher.

BAKER, BICKER. In ''The Rich Boy,'' he was a rowdy friend Anson Hunter reminisces about to Nick the Plaza Hotel bartender.

BAKER, EDDIE. In ''Crazy Sunday,'' he is a New Yorker whose friendship with Stella Walker Calman made her husband Miles Calman jealous.

BAKER, ELLEN. In ''A Short Trip Home,'' she is a student home from the East for Christmas vacation in St. Paul. Eddie Stinson, also home on vacation and in love with her, saves her from consorting with the evil spirit of Joe Varland on their return train trip.

BAKER, GEORGE. In ''Discard,'' he is Dolly Bordon's nephew, sixteen at the beginning of the story and two years later a Yale student. He is mainly a witness of the action.

BAKER, JORDAN. In *The Great Gatsby*, she is a golf champion and Daisy Fay Buchanan's friend. Jordan and Nick Carraway become close, but he dislikes rumors of her cheating and fibbing and her carelessness at the wheel of a car. He breaks their relationship. Her name combines the name of Jordan, the sports car, and Baker, the electric car. She is partly modeled on Edith Cummings, a national golf champion and close friend of Ginevra King,* the model for Daisy Fay Buchanan.

BAKER, MRS. In ''A Short Trip Home,'' she is Ellen Baker's naive mother. She tells Eddie Stinson that Ellen is returning early to school in the East, toward the end of Christmas vacation.

BALDWIN. In ''Family in the Wind,'' he is a neighbor of the Janneys whose house is destroyed by the first tornado.

BALES, DR. In ''Crazy Sunday,'' he is the physician Joel Coles summons when Stella Walker Calman learns of the death of her husband, Miles Calman.

''THE BALTIMORE ANTI-CHRIST'' (1921). Review. In this review of H. L. Mencken's *Prejudices, Second Series* (1921), Fitzgerald expresses the fear H. L. Mencken* ''will be exiled'' by too much praise, calls Mencken's essay on Theodore Roosevelt the best in the book, says ''The Sahara of the Bozart'' is a devastating criticism of America's South, criticizes Mencken's adverse opinion of modern dances, and comments on other items in the ''excellent book.'' He is sad the future may provide Mencken with no new idols to knock down.

BANGS, ANGELINA. In *Coward*, she is a sanctimonious, critical friend of Lindy Douglas and critical of most of those about her.

BANGS, GEORGIE. In *Coward*, he is Angelina Bangs's father.

BANIZON. In ''Pat Hobby's Secret,'' he is the movie executive who cannot remember the ending to R. Parke Woll's script. Pat Hobby offers to find out for a bribe but fails to do so.

BANKLAND. In ''How to Life on $36,000 a Year,'' he is the Fitzgeralds' neighbor who suggests that a budget might solve their fiscal woes. Since Bankland and his wife lost $2,000 a month last year, they have started to follow a budget themselves.

BANKLAND, MRS. In ''How to Live on $36,000 a Year,'' she and her husband are the Fitzgeralds' neighbors.

BANNERMAN, MARIE. In ''The Dance,'' she is a pretty resident of Davis. She is engaged to Charley Kincaid but is seen kissing Joe Cable, whom Catherine Jones loves so much that she kills Marie.

BAPTISTE. In *The Beautiful and Damned*, he is a soldier in Anthony Patch's brigade. He is ordered to work in the stables, but he knows nothing about horses and is kicked to death.

BARBAN, TOMMY. In *Tender Is the Night*, he is a tough mercenary, half-American, half-French. He is friendly with Dick and Nicole Diver on the Riviera, takes her away from Dick, and marries her.

BARBARA. In *This Side of Paradise*, she is a person whom any mother would keep from drinking early in life.

BARBER, RALPH HENRY. In ''The Bowl,'' he is a radio announcer at a Princeton-Yale game.

"THE BARBER'S TOO SLICK" (1981). Poem. The guest leaves the efficient but noisy place content but a little sad.

BARBOUR, CARL. In ''Jacob's Ladder,'' he costars with Jenny Prince in her latest movie, which is a success.

BARKIS, PRIVATE. In *Coward*, he is a Union soldier, along with Private Willings.

BARKS, MAJOR. In ''The Rubber Check,'' he is killed in an airplane crash. Val Schuyler pretends he was at Deauville with him and might have taken the same airplane.

BARLEY. In *The Beautiful and Damned*, he was a former admirer, from Georgia, of Gloria Gilbert Patch. When he learned Percy Wolcott had tried to take advantage of her, Barley fought him.

BARLOW. In "May Day," he is a man whom Edith Bradin recalls as a fellow guest at a party hosted by Howard Marshall.

BARLOW. In *This Side of Paradise*, he is the president of Bascome and Barlow's advertising agency, where Amory Blaine works briefly. When he quits, he tells Barlow he underpays his secretaries.

BARNES. In "No Harm Trying," he is a Hollywood executive whom Jeff Manfred recommends to Pat Hobby as a contact.

BARNES, ED. In "Six of One—," he is a rich, childless friend of rich Schofield, who has two sons. The men disagree about the advantages of wealth for sons. Barnes sends six boys, worthy but poor or middle class, from his Ohio hometown to college. They are Louis Ireland, James Matsko, Otto Schlach, Jack Stubbs, Gordon Vandervere, and George Winfield. His experiment generally succeeds, whereas one of Schofield's sons and their four close, spoiled friends all fail.

BARNES, RACHAEL JERRYL. In *The Beautiful and Damned*, she is a friend of Gloria Gilbert Patch, who knew Rachael before Rachael was married. When Rachael's husband, Rodman Barnes, becomes a captain and is sent overseas, Rachael double-dates with Gloria and becomes intimate with Captain Wolf.

BARNES, RODMAN. In *The Beautiful and Damned*, he marries Rachael Jerryl, a friend of Gloria Gilbert Patch, is a quartermaster captain, and goes overseas.

BARNETT, DR. In "One Interne," he is a specialist in internal medicine at the medical school.

BARNEY, CHARLES. In "On Your Own," he is the producer of Evelyn Lovejoy's London show. When she is called home and the show closes, he and his wife return to New York on the same ship.

BARNEY, MRS. CHARLES. In "On Your Own," she is the producer's wife.

BARNFIELD, TEDDY. In "The Captured Shadow," he is Basil Duke Lee's neighbor boy who has the mumps.

BARROWS, COLONEL. In "A Debt of Honor," he is a Confederate Army officer to whom Lieutenant Robert E. Lee gives permission to attack the frame house held by the enemy.

BARTHELMI. In "The Count of Darkness," he works for Count Philippe of Villefranche, who orders him to get some women from the settlement.

BARTHOLOMEW. In "May Day," he works with Henry Bradin in the newspaper office.

BARTLETT, DOLLY. In "That Kind of Party," she is a girl, ten, whose flirty ways enthrall Terrence R. Tipton. After the children's kissing party at the Shoonover home, her mother invites Terrence to supper.

BARTLETT, MRS. In "That Kind of Party," she is Dolly Bartlett's mother.

BARTNEY, WALTER HAMILTON. In "Pain and the Scientist," he is a law student who hurts himself in a fall while walking to visit Dr. Hepezia Skiggs, a Christian Scientist. Skiggs tells Bartney to tell himself that he feels no pain. When Bartney catches Skiggs trespassing, he shakes Skiggs until he says "ouch."

BARTOLLO. In "On Your Own," he is a member of Evelyn Lovejoy's cast aboard the ship returning to New York.

BARTON. In *This Side of Paradise*, he is the head of the Barton and Krogman law firm. Barton handles the diminishing finances of Amory Blaine's family.

BASCOME. In *This Side of Paradise*, he is a member of Bascome and Barton's advertising agency, for which Amory Blaine works briefly.

"BASIL AND CLEOPATRA" (1929). Short story. (Characters: Appleton, Buzz Bailey, Miss Beecher, Erminie Gilberte Labouisse Bibble, Bispam, Carson, Bessie Belle Cheever, Cullum, Danziger, Connie Davies, George Dorsey, Jobena Dorsey, William Gaspar, Jubal, Krutch, Basil Duke Lee, Littleboy Le Moyne, Waite, Brick Wales, Sam White.) Basil was so enchanted by beautiful Erminie Gilberte Labouisse Bibble, sixteen and from New Orleans, when they met in St. Paul that when she is a guest in Mobile he asks to be invited too. She toys with him at tennis and club dances and protracts his stay by the promise of a kiss, but gets intimate with Littleboy Le Moyne on the train trip back to the East. Basil returns to Yale, Le Moyne to Princeton, and Minnie to a finishing school near New Haven. Basil qualifies for the freshman football team and visits Minnie unsatisfactorily. He stars in his team's defeat of Princeton's freshman team, on which Le Moyne played hard. Le Moyne tells Basil that Minnie is currently the girlfriend of Jubal, another Yale man. At a New Haven club party, Jobena Dorsey, a former girlfriend, tells Basil not to want Minnie, who is there, but to realize it is over and show her it is. The two dance briefly. She is falsely contrite until Jubal arrives. Basil walks away and hopes for a life of effort and success.

THE BASIL DUKE LEE AND JOSEPHINE PERRY STORIES. Fitzgerald published eight Basil Duke Lee stories in the *Saturday Evening Post* between 28 April 1928 and 27 April 1929. He also wrote ''That Kind of Party,'' intending it to be another Basil story, but it was not accepted. He changed the name of the protagonist to Terrence R. Tipton, and the story was published posthumously in 1951. Fitzgerald published five Josephine Perry stories in the *Post* between 5 April 1930 and 15 August 1931.

Bibliography: Jackson R. Bryer and John Kuehl, eds., *The Basil and Josephine Stories by F. Scott Fitzgerald* (New York: Macmillan, 1973); James Nagel, ''Initiation and Intertextuality in *The Basil and Josephine Stories*,'' Bryer, *New Essays*, 265–90.

BATES. In ''The Perfect Life,'' he was a St. Regis student who, according to Basil Duke Lee, was expelled for drinking.

BATTLES, JOHANNA. In ''I Got Shoes,'' she is a society reporter, the niece of a friend of actress Nell Margery, who grants her an interview. Johanna is called ''The Lovely Thing.''

BEARD, THE. In ''Shaggy's Morning,'' he is the owner, along with the Brain, of Shaggy.

THE BEAUTIFUL AND DAMNED (1922). Novel. (Characters: Abercrombie, Parker Allison, Tudor Baird, Baptiste, Barley, Rodman Barnes, Rachael Jerryl Barnes, Bedros, Samuele Bendiri, Joseph Black, Bounds, Calvin Boyd, Brett, Eugene Bronson, Geraldine Burke, Cable, Richard Caramel, Sammy Carleton, Bill Carstairs, Cartwright-Smith, Mrs. Cartwright-Smith, Captain Collins, Kenneth Cowan, Crawford, Daly, Percy B. Debris, Mack Dodge, Sergeant Pop Donnelly, Captain Dunning, Ellinger, Larry Fenwick, Cyrus Fielding, ''Fish-eye'' Fry, Catherine Gilbert, Russel Gilbert, Alec Granby, Mrs. Alec Granby, Peter Granby, R. Gugimoniki, Gunter, Haight, Halloran, Hardy, Hiemer, Stuart Holcome, Hopkins, Howland, Joe Hull, Miss Hulme, Mrs. Hulme, Hunt, Jerry Jinks, Judy Jinks, Justine Johnson, Johnston, William Jordan, Kahler, Muriel Kane, Florence Kelley, Carter Kirby, Lieutenant Kretching, Lacy, Mrs. Lacy, Bob Lamar, Ceci Larrabee, Pete Lytell, Minnie McGlook, Miss McGovern, ''Curly'' McGregor, Charlie McIntyre, Jenny Martin, Gaston Mears, Constance Shaw Merriam, Eric Merriam, Michaud, Maury Noble, Chevalier O'Keefe, Otis, Frederick E. Paramore, Jim Parsons, Pat, Adam Patch, Adam Ulysses Patch, Alicia Withers Patch, Annie Patch, Anthony Patch, Gloria Gilbert

Patch, Henrietta Lebrune Patch, Dorothy Raycroft, Mrs. Raycroft, Eltynge Reardon, Marty Reffer, Reisenweber, Rivers, Miss Rooney, Willa Sable, Schroeder, Severance, Edward Shuttleworth, ''Gypsy'' Smith, Sohenberg, John Summer, Tanalahaka, Henry W. Terral, Thérèse, Barbara Wainwright, Percy B. Weatherbee, R. Meggs Widdlestien, Wilson, Percy Wolcott, Captain Wolf, Wrenn.)

Book One. Anthony Patch, slim, dark, and handsome, lives in Washington Square, New York City, the only child of Henrietta Lebrune Patch of Boston, who died when he was five, and of Adam Ulysses Patch, who died when Anthony was eleven. He lived with his rich grandfather, Adam Patch, in Tarrytown, New York, was tutored in Europe for two years, and at sixteen entered Harvard, where with a sizable allowance he became a romantic, scholarly recluse, graduating at twenty in 1909. After idling in Rome for three years, he returned to America. In October 1913, on an annual income of $7,500 from bonds, he has a charming apartment on Fifty-second Street and is waited on by Bounds, his British male servant, each morning. Anthony thinks about writing a book on the Renaissance popes. When he visits Adam, he is rebuked for idleness. His closest male friends, both from Harvard, are Richard (''Dick'') Caramel, a note-taking writer, and Maury Noble, indolent and catlike. Geraldine Burke visits Anthony occasionally, for kisses, cocktails, and nothing else.

In November Anthony goes with Dick to the rooms of Russel Gilbert and his wife, Catherine Gilbert, Dick's aunt, on the tenth floor of the Plaza. Their daughter, Gloria Gilbert, twenty-two, also lives there. She is out, and the young men endure dull talk with the well-to-do Gilbert, who is associated with the movies, and his browbeaten, platitudinous wife. In December Anthony visits Maury at his apartment on Forty-fourth Street. They discuss Dick, aesthetics, and literature until Maury intrigues Anthony by describing Dick's gorgeous cousin Gloria. Anthony invites Dick and Gloria to tea. She and Anthony banter about names, reforms, and her tan. Over drinks at the Plaza, she is totally self-centered, and he explains that he gracefully does nothing. One pre-Christmas afternoon, they go to a cabaret he fears she will dislike, but she says she loves the place and its colorful, lowlife crowd.

After Harvard Dick works with the poor, becomes a reporter, and works on a novel called *The Demon Lover*. He discusses Gloria with her mother; the frivolous girl is bored going to dances with numerous boyfriends. She enters with jumpy Muriel Kane and shy Rachael Jerryl. She hosts a Biltmore dinner dance; her guests are Muriel, Rachael, Anthony, Dick, Maury, and a man named Joseph Bloeckman, her father's movie-business acquaintance. She and Anthony slip away, kiss in a taxi, and return—to Bloeckman's annoyance. When she and Anthony walk together in February, she becomes aloof and rebuffs him, but when he leaves she calls him an ass for not being aggressive. In love, he considers marriage, although he dislikes the idea; hates Bloeckman's seeming success with Gloria; is happy when Dick's novel is accepted; and lets things cool. He spends a day with Gloria in March, and in April they kiss in his apartment and he tells her he loves her.

Book Two. Anthony and Gloria agree to marry in June. She does not mind events in his past but feels tainted by some in hers. They argue, like to hurt each other, enjoy bus rides up Fifth Avenue, and plan to travel and have a nice house when his grandfather dies and wills them money. The old man suggests they have the wedding at his place in Tarrytown and sends them a $5,000 check. When Dick's novel is published in April and does well, he grows conceited and boring. The wedding ceremony takes place, with Dick and Maury serving as two of the six ushers and with 250 guests. Anthony and Gloria travel to California, Chicago, and Washington, D.C. She is tense, selfish, fearless, finicky with food, careless with laundry, limited, and annoyed by criticism. He is proud and reckless but cowardly when he hears a sound at their hotel window in San Francisco. When they visit Robert E. Lee's home outside Washington, she criticizes attempts made to preserve the past instead of letting it deteriorate. They drive around looking for a place to live, and Gloria wrecks the car. They lease a gray house in Marietta, Connecticut, where Anthony will write his history and Gloria will play around and eat. Muriel and also Dick visit. The Patches attend dinner dances and meet friends. Gloria dislikes talk about other women's babies but wants one or two herself, starting in three years. Suddenly her mother dies.

Anthony and Gloria return to Marietta. They dance, swim, entertain, are entertained, and drink. They hire a Japanese servant named Tanalahaka ("Tana"). They often argue because Gloria is selfish and Anthony wants to domineer. Her verve is leaving her, and she does not give a damn. To his critical grandfather Anthony reports he has published an essay, to which the old man suggests Anthony become a war correspondent in Europe. Gloria ridicules Anthony's so-called work. Bloeckman visits and suggests that Gloria might do well in the movies. He infuriates Anthony by taking her for a drive. After a binge in New York in February 1916, Anthony slugs a taxi driver and is arrested. He realizes he is low on funds. By contrast, Dick is selling stories to the movies. Anthony tries selling bonds but soon quits. While hung over, he and Gloria sign a new lease for the house at Marietta, where they drink with friends, sometimes at a club. In July, Maury and Dick bring Joe Hull out as a guest for a wild party. Hull scares drunken Gloria late in the night, and she runs out before dawn to the railroad station. Anthony, Dick, and Maury follow. After Maury lectures the group in favor of naturalism and in opposition to the Bible and Christianity, Gloria goes alone into New York.

One August evening Frederick E. Paramore, a Harvard classmate, visits Anthony's house. Maury is there, recognizes him, and learns he works as a social worker in Stamford. Anthony, Gloria, Dick, Muriel, and Rachael and her husband, Rodman Barnes, burst in. Amid drinks Gloria warns Anthony to stop paying everyone's bills and to quit flirting with Rachael. Maury gets Paramore drunk and makes antidemocratic and anti-Christian comments. Frenzied dancing ensues. Suddenly Adam, who phoned earlier but was cut off, totters in with Edward Shuttleworth, his tough aide. Adam, a rabid prohibitionist, leaves in horror. Because Anthony and Gloria are afraid they will be cut out of Adam's will, Anthony goes to Tarrytown, but Adam will not see him. After moving to New York City, they find their marriage weakening and rely more on alcohol. They rent a cheaper place on Fifty-seventh Street and get along with one servant, an Irishwoman. Bounds has joined the British army, and Tana is gone. In November Adam dies and leaves $40 million, mostly to charities, a million to Shuttleworth, some to minor relatives, and nothing to Anthony. Gossip has it that seeing Anthony's wild party caused Adam's death. Anthony retains an attorney to contest the will. He and Gloria soothe themselves with more parties. Dick advises Anthony to write short stories, which he does but without success. Gloria's father dies, leaving her $3,000. When Bloeckman, back from England, offers Gloria some movie work, she and Anthony argue. Soon after the United States enters the war in April 1917, Anthony tries for officers' training but is rejected because of high blood pressure.

Book Three. In October Anthony is drafted into the infantry, takes a troop train to Camp Hooker, South Carolina, drills, and rests in his tent. One night he picks up Dorothy (''Dot'') Raycroft in town. He and shallow Dot, whose father is dead and whose mother is stupid, and who has earlier known three men intimately, drift into an affair. He tells her he is married, but she hopes for the best. He begins to like both the army regimen and the langorous South, and makes corporal. In July 1918 his brigade is ordered to Camp Boone, Mississippi, and he puts Dot up in a local hotel. Gloria writes to him less and less, and he wonders whether she is unfaithful. By phone Dot hints at suicide; he rushes to her, is late returning to camp, is demoted, is sentenced to three weeks in the guardhouse, and grows ill. In November his regiment is transferred to Camp Mills, Long Island. Suddenly the war is over, and Anthony rushes to his Manhattan apartment. He learns from a servant that Gloria is at an armistice dance at the Astor. He finds her there, and they embrace.

Behold Gloria when Anthony first left for the army: she is sleepless, writes him often, is bored. January 1918: she double-dates with Rachael, whose husband is a captain now overseas. After dinner one evening in Rachael's apartment, while she is busy kissing Captain Wolf, Gloria is being hugged by Captain Collins, whose advances she sarcastically repels. February: she meets Tudor Baird, a former flame training as a pilot; they go to the theater; one evening she lets him kiss her. Soon thereafter he is killed in an airplane crash. October: Anthony's letters hint she should not visit him in camp, but a month later they are reunited. In 1919 they party frequently, despite less and less income and no word Adam's will can be broken. Gloria wants but cannot afford a gray squirrel fur coat. Anthony answers Sammy Carleton's advertisement to learn how to sell shares of his ''Heart Talks'' books, attends classes, fails utterly, and gets even drunker. His annual income shrinks to $4,500. Gloria contracts influenza and pneumonia, recovers, and in February 1920 persuades Bloeckman, now calling himself Black, to arrange a screen test for her. She takes it nervously and returns home to await results. Black writes to tell her the director wants a younger woman. Gloria, twenty-nine on this day, dissolves in tears.

The Patches move to a cheaper place on 127th Street. Muriel chastises Anthony, now thirty-two, for doing nothing. Leaving Gloria in tears, he goes to a place on Forty-third Street to drink with two shallow buddies, and runs into Dick, who boasts of his publications. Learning at home that they have almost no cash, Anthony leaves to hock his watch but drinks until his pawnshop is closed, finds Black at a Biltmore party and swings at him, but is knocked down and tossed out. Three weeks later Dot suddenly appears at Anthony's door, after finding him through newspaper coverage of his ongoing lawsuit. He hurls a chair at her, and she disappears. Gloria finds him insanely playing with his old stamp albums. She tells him the appellate court has just awarded him $30 million. A few months later, he is voyaging, dotty and feisty, the subject of pointed gossip, with Gloria to Europe.

Rejected titles for *The Beautiful and Damned* were ''The Beautiful Lady without Mercy'' and ''The Flight of the Rocket.'' Fitzgerald inserted passages from Zelda's diary into the novel (*see* Fitzgerald, Zelda Sayre), which was serialized in the *Metropolitan* (September 1921–March 1922). For book publication he revised its point of view, drew the characters more skillfully, and made the ending more ironic. Cuts were made at the editorial level to avoid offending conservative readers. The book was dedicated to Shane Leslie,* George Jean Nathan,* and Max Perkins,* all of whom had helped Fitzgerald. Notable in the novel are patterns of imagery concerned with communication; dirt, disease, and decay; light and darkness; and water. *The Beautiful and Damned* was printed three times in 1922 and sold 50,000 copies. Fitzgerald disliked the movie version of the novel made by Warner Brothers in 1922.

Bibliography: Amy J. Elias, ''The Composition and Revision of *The Beautiful and Damned*,'' *Princeton University Library Chronicle* 51 (Spring 1990): 245–66; Robert Roulston, ''*The Beautiful and Damned*: The Alcoholic's Revenge,'' *Literature and Psychology* 27, no. 4 (1977): 156–63.

BEAUTY BOY. In ''Dearly Beloved,'' he is an African American railroad worker who is married to Lilymary, has a baby with her, loses a leg in an accident, and dies. He plays golf in heaven.

BEAVER, EDGAR. In *The Great Gatsby*, Nick Carraway lists his name on a timetable as one of Jay Gatsby's summer guests. His hair turned white one winter afternoon.

BEBÉ. In ''Gretchen's Forty Winks,'' she is the housework girl employed by Gretchen Halsey.

"BECAUSE" (1981). Poem. When she hints she is near and asks ''why?,'' he answers ''because.''

BECKER. In *The Great Gatsby*, he is mentioned by Meyer Wolfsheim as having been executed for Rosy Rosenthal's murder.

BECKER, CHESTER. In *The Great Gatsby*, Nick Carraway lists his name on a timetable as one of Jay Gatsby's summer guests.

BECKER, GWEN. In "Magnetism," she is a girl in San Francisco who tries unsuccessfully to blackmail George Hannaford.

BECKER, JOE. In "Last Kiss," he is a Hollywood agent who introduces Pamela Knighton, would-be actress, to Jim Leonard, a movie producer. When Leonard delays, Becker signs her up with Bernie Wise, a rival producer, who drops her because she cannot act.

BEDROS. In *The Beautiful and Damned*, he is a bootlegger who supplies Anthony Patch.

BEEBE, EVELYN. In "The Captured Shadow," she is the pretty girl, sixteen, who plays Leilia Van Baker in Basil Duke Lee's play *The Captured Shadow*. She likes Andy Lockheart and Hubert Blair but finally kisses Basil and will remain his friend.

BEEBE, HAM. In "The Captured Shadow," he is Evelyn Beebe's little brother, nine, who gets the mumps when Basil Duke Lee fails to warn him that Teddy Barnfield has the mumps.

BEEBE, MRS. In "Dalyrimple Goes Wrong," she is the owner of the boardinghouse in which Bryan Dalyrimple has a room.

BEECHER, MISS. In "Basil and Cleopatra," she is or was the founder of a school near New Haven attended by Erminie Gilberte Labouisse Bibble.

BEEF. In "Head and Shoulders," he is named as a supposed butcher.

"BEG YOU TO LISTEN" (1981). Poem. The poet types memories of visions of their being together four years ago. The poem was written to Bert Barr, born Bertha Weinberg and the wife of Louis Goldstein, a Brooklyn judge. Fitzgerald was intrigued when he met her on a transatlantic vessel in 1931 and bombarded her with letters then and later.

BEHRER, BILL. In "No Harm Trying," he is a Hollywood executive Jeff Manfred recommends to Pat Hobby as a possible contact.

BEHRER, DR. In ''Family in the Wind,'' he is a physician in Bending, Alabama. Dr. Forrest Janney dislikes him, but the two cooperate in treating the injured after the first tornado.

BELCHER, S. W. In *The Great Gatsby*, Nick Carraway lists Belcher's name on a timetable as one of Jay Gatsby's summer guests. He is from New York.

BELL. In ''Crazy Sunday,'' he is presumably a cameraman who is part of Miles Calman's moviemaking crew.

BELL, MRS. In ''The Hotel Child,'' she is mentioned by Mrs. Schwartz as a family friend in the United States.

BELLAMY. In ''The Ice Palace,'' he is Harry Bellamy's father, whom Sally Carrol Happer likes upon first meeting him. He is from Kentucky.

BELLAMY, GORDON. In ''The Ice Palace,'' he is Harry Bellamy's older brother, whom Sally Carrol Happer does not like.

BELLAMY, HARRY. In ''The Ice Palace,'' a Yale man, he met Sally Carrol Happer in Asheville, North Carolina, and became engaged to her, visits her in Tarleton, Georgia, and invites her to meet his family in the chilly North. She dislikes them and the North and returns home.

BELLAMY, MRS. In ''The Ice Palace,'' she is Harry Bellamy's dumpy, ungracious mother, whom Sally Carrol Happer dislikes, especially when the woman disapproves of Sally's smoking.

BELLAMY, MYRA. In ''The Ice Palace,'' she is Gordon Bellamy's wife, whom Sally Carrol Happer regards as spiritless and conventional.

BELLOIS, MLLE. In *Tender Is the Night*, she is the Divers' servant who supervises their luggage from Switzerland to the Riviera.

BELTZER. In ''Crazy Sunday,'' he was presumably a financier who tried to force Miles Calman to change one of his movies.

BELTZMAN. In ''The Freshest Boy,'' he is the casting director who gave Jerry the fine part in the play Basil Duke Lee attends. Jerry has promised to marry Beltzman.

BELUGA. In *The Great Gatsby*, his name is listed by Nick Carraway on a timetable as one of Jay Gatsby's summer guests. He is a tobacco importer and brings girls with him.

BEMBERG. In *The Great Gatsby*, Nick Carraway lists Bembeig's name on a timetable as one of Jay Gatsby's summer guests.

BEMENT, ED. In "First Blood," he is Josephine Perry's most reliable friend and lives in Chicago. He drives her to a rendezvous with Anthony Harker and beats up Travis de Coppet for gossiping about her. In "A Nice Quiet Place," Josephine learns that Ed visited her boyfriend, Ridgeway Saunders, in Philadelphia and saw Ridgeway with his new girlfriend, Evangeline Ticknor. Both are guests at Ed's house party in Lake Forest. After much confusion, Ed takes Josephine to the railroad station for her return trip to Island Farms. In "A Woman with a Past," he dances with Josephine at the Yale prom and tells her she has been in love too often. In "A Snobbish Story," he is mentioned as attending a Lake Forest tennis tournament. In "Emotional Bankruptcy," Ed is Josephine's friend and calls on her, with Travis de Coppet, in Chicago—to no avail, since she is currently interested in Captain Edward Dicer.

BEMENT, HOWARD. In "The Bowl," he is a Princeton football player.

BEN. In "The Jelly-Bean," he is a friend James Powell greets at Soda Sam's before the dance.

BEN. In "A Short Autobiography," he is a fellow drinker in France in 1926.

BEN. In *Tender Is the Night*, he is a sailor whom Tommy Barban and Nicole Diver see fighting on the beach, while they are in their hotel room.

BENBOWER, MISS. In "First Blood," she runs a private school in Chicago that is attended by Josephine Perry.

BENDIRI, SAMUELE ("SAMMY"). In *The Beautiful and Damned*, he owns a New York bar where Anthony Patch drinks.

"BENEDICTION" (1920). Short story. (Characters: Gerald Carter, Mrs. Comstock, Howard, Jarvis, Mrs. Jarvis, Jimmy, Freddy Kebble, Maury Kebble, Keith, Lois, Regan.) Pretty Lois, nineteen and nominally Catholic, wires Howard, her lover, from the Baltimore railroad station to meet her in Wilmington on Wednesday. She visits her brother, Keith, thirty-six and a student for the priesthood in a Jesuit seminary in Baltimore. Their mother moved with Lois to Europe when the girl was four, and she and Keith, who was wild in his youth, have been apart ever since. Though different in many ways, the two like each other at once. He tells her how when he was on a train a voice told him to become a priest. They discuss their nervous mother, and Lois, who cared for her a long time, says youth should not be sacrificed thus. Keith, whom Lois regards as evincing a properly hard sweetness, explains that the seminary regimen eliminates self-pity and pride to make one useful to others; she regards Catholicism as inconvenient. He introduces her to some friends at the seminary. Grinning amiably, one asks her to show them the shimmy, which with a laugh she declines to do. When they attend a benediction service in the hot chapel, she senses that evil in a flaming candle at the altar is extinguished by light from a stained-glass window, faints, and on recovering feels chastened. She tenderly parts from her brother, who prays for her at a pietà. She returns to the Baltimore station, discards a telegram telling Howard to leave her, and evidently will meet him in Wilmington. Fitzgerald incorporated parts from his 1915 story ''The Ordeal'' in ''Benediction.''

BENNETT, JIM. In ''Inside the House,'' he is one of the three boys Gwen Bowers has asked to help her decorate her Christmas tree. Satterly Brown and Jason Crawford, who is her favorite, are the others.

BENNY. In ''No Harm Trying,'' he is the proprietor of the bar in front of which Pat Hobby tells Eric to meet him to discuss pay for his movie idea.

BENSON, EDWARD FREDERIC. (1867–1940). English writer. He attended Marlborough College and King's College, Cambridge, did archaeological work in Athens (1892–1895), and became popular as a novelist with *Dodo* (1893). Some of his other novels take place in modern Greece. In a 1917 review, Fitzgerald praises Benson's *David Blaize* as a fine boys' book, neither cynical nor sentimental, but criticizes its disunity. By hinting at sources in fiction of a similar genre, Fitzgerald parades his reading background.

BERGSON. In *Porcelain and Pink*, he is mentioned in nonsense talk by Julie Marvis to Calkins.

BERL. In ''Reade, Substitute Right Half,'' he is the captain of the Warrentown football team.

BERME, COMTE DE. In ''Flight and Pursuit,'' he is a nobleman from Cannes of no interest to Caroline Martin Corcoran.

BERNERS, JACK. In ''A Man in the Way,'' he is a Hollywood producer. Pat Hobby tries to sell Pricilla Smith's idea to him, only to learn that she is Berners' current girlfriend. In ''Teamed with Genius,'' Berners teams Pat Hobby with René Wilcox. Pat's attempts to take credit for a script Wilcox mostly wrote backfires. In ''Pat Hobby and Orson Welles,'' Berners, being out of town, cannot help the temporarily strapped Pat Hobby. In ''Pat Hobby, Putative Father,'' he asks Pat to escort Sir Singrim Dak Raj and his nephew Prince John Brown Hobby Indore around the lot. In ''Pat Hobby Does His Bit,'' Berners and George Hilliard must hire Pat to complete a film in which he accidentally and otherwise ruinously appears. In "Pat Hobby's Preview," as a joke, he gives Pat tickets to a burlesque show, not to the movie preview Pat believes he will be taking Eleanor Carter to. In "A Patriotic Short," he orders Pat to work for a week on a script about General Fitzhugh Lee and rejects Pat's idea to include Jews in the plot. In "On the Trail of Pat Hobby," when Berners offers a $50 reward for anyone providing a title for a movie about tourists, Pat offers *Grand Motel* and wins. In "Mightier Than the Sword," Berners is mentioned as liking Dick Dale's script about Reginald De Koven which E. Brunswick Hudson wrote. In "Pat Hobby's College Days," Louie the bookie tells Pat that Berners wants a movie made about the University of the Western Coast because his son plays basketball there.

BERNICE. In "Bernice Bobs Her Hair," she is Majorie Harvey's cousin from a wealthy Eau Claire family and is visiting the Harveys one August. She is unappealing at dances until Majorie tells her to fix her eyebrows, dance less stiffly, and engage dull boys in talk so as to entice more charming ones. She even suggests that Bernice bob her hair. When Marjorie's boyfriend Warren MacIntyre pays attention to Bernice, Marjorie grows jealous and dares Bernice to have her hair bobbed as she boasted she might. She does so but looks awful and gets revenge by cutting off the sleeping Marjorie's blond braids and leaving them on Warren's porch on her way home.

"BERNICE BOBS HER HAIR" (1920). Short story. (Characters: Bernice, Martha Carey, Ethel Demorest, Draycott Deyo, Mrs. Deyo, Roberta Dillon, Dyer, Harvey, Josephine Harvey, Marjorie Harvey, Madeleine Hogue, Sarah Hopkins, Warren McIntyre, Bessie MacRae, O'Reilly, Genevieve Ormonde, Otis Ormonde, Charley Paulson, Willy Schuneman, G. Reece Stoddard, Jim Strain.) Saturday night dances during the summer feature attractive couples, pretty girls cut in on by stags, wallflowers, and disapproving matrons. Among other young men, Warren McIntyre, a Yale student, is home now and pursuing vivacious Marjorie Harvey, whose cousin Bernice is visiting from Eau Claire. Marjorie persuades Warren to dance with Bernice, who seems dull and out of it. That night Marjorie complains to her mother about Bernice's behavior. Next morning, after an argument, Bernice agrees to do everything Marjorie orders: fix her eyebrows, get her teeth straightened (later), dance in a less dignified way, and surround herself with dull boys so as to entice bright ones. When Marjorie suggests that Bernice bob her hair, the girl collapses. At the next dance, Bernice is witty and sought after, hints at bobbing her hair, and begins to respond to Warren's attentions. Feeling threatened, Marjorie after a bridge party challenges Bernice to have her hair bobbed. Dared, the poor girl must agree, does so downtown with a crowd of onlookers, but is unattractive as a result. That final night at the Harvey home, after Marjorie triumphantly braids her long blond hair and goes to sleep, Bernice packs, leaves a thank-you note, shears off the sleeping

Marjorie's heavy tresses, tosses them on Warren's porch, and sallies forth to catch her night train home.

BERNIE. In *The Last Tycoon*, he is the photographer at the Trocadero whom Monroe Stahr will not let take pictures of Cecelia Brady, of Brimmer, or of him.

BERRY. In "A Change of Class," he is a bootlegger Earl Johnson does not like to see his wife Violet manicuring. Berry works for Howard Shalder.

BERRY, RALPH ("RAFE"). In "The Hotel Child," he is a British friend of Lady Capps-Karr and Marquis Bopes Kilkallow.

BERTRAM DE VILLEFRANCHE. In "The Kingdom in the Dark," he is named by Count Philippe of Villefranche as his deceased father.

BETTS, MARY. In "At Your Age," she is a cousin of Annie Lorry's who disapproves of Annie's conduct.

BETTY. In *Safety First!*, she is one of the singers.

BETTY, RUSSELL. In *The Great Gatsby*, Nick Carraway lists his name on a timetable as one of Jay Gatsby's summer guests. He is from New York.

"BETWEEN THREE AND FOUR" (1931). Short story. (Characters: Howard Butler, Eddington, B. B. Eddington, George Eddington, Muller, Miss Rousseau, Jack Summer, John Summer, Sarah Belknap Summer, Mrs. Thomas, Miss Wiess.) Howard Butler, who works for the Eddington family's New York furniture company, fired Sarah Belknap Summer, whom he loved years earlier but who married someone else and is now a widow. She pleads to be rehired and threatens to jump out his ninth-floor office window or out another high one if she is not. He tells her to come back in a week between three and four; but when she does, he declines to see her—except through his office-door peephole. Next, a newspaper headline screams that a despondent woman leaped to her death from a ninth-floor office window somewhere. His eyes blur as he tries to read the account; but Mrs. Thomas, his cleaning lady, agrees when he asks whether the victim was identified as Mrs. Summer. Becoming demented a few days later when he spies Mrs. Summer through his peephole, he leaps to his death (unaware that Mrs. Thomas could not read). Mrs. Summer was in the outer office to answer George Eddington's invitation to be rehired. This is Fitzgerald's grimmest story evoking Depression-era misery.

BIBBLE. In ''Forging Ahead,'' she is identified as Erminie Gilberte Labouisse Bibble's younger sister. Basil Duke Lee thinks her face resembles her older sister's. The Bibble family visits William S. Kampf, the Bibble sisters' cousin.

BIBBLE. In ''He Thinks He's Wonderful,'' he is Erminie Gilberte Labouisse Bibble's father, from New Orleans. He, his wife, and their daughter are visiting George Kampf, his wife, and their son William S. Kampf near St. Paul. Basil Duke Lee meets and delights Erminie, but Bibble is offended by the boy's egotism. In ''Forging Ahead,'' the Bibble family again visits Bill Kampf and his family.

BIBBLE, ERMINIE GILBERTE LABOUISSE ("MINNIE"). In ''He Thinks He's Wonderful,'' she is a pretty, New Orleans girl, fifteen. She and her parents visit her cousin William S. Kampf and his parents near St. Paul. She meets and likes Basil Duke Lee, who is the Kampfs' house guest, hopes he can go with the Bibble family to Glacier National Park, but is disappointed when his conceit offends her father, who vetoes the idea. In ''The Perfect Life,'' Basil recalls his time with Minnie. In ''Forging Ahead,'' she is accompanied by her parents and younger sister as they visit her cousin Bill Kampf again. A sparkling beauty, Minnie, fifteen, entices Basil away from dancing with Rhoda Sinclair, and soon is engaged to him. In ''Basil and Cleopatra,'' she is the beautiful, spoiled daughter, sixteen, of New Orleans parents, who are divorcing. While attending a private school near New Haven, she flirts with many students in Eastern universities, including Buzz Bailey, Littleboy Le Moyne, and Jubal. Basil Duke Lee is smitten but outgrows her wiles.

BIBBLE, MISS. In ''Forging Ahead,'' she is Erminie Gilberte Labouisse Bible's kid sister.

BIBBLE, MRS. In ''He Thinks He's Wonderful,'' she is Erminie Gilberte Labouisse Bibble's mother. The Bibble family, from New Orleans, visits George Kampf, her uncle, his wife, and their son William S. Kampf at their home near St. Paul. In ''Forging Ahead,'' the Bibble family again visits Bill Kampf and his family.

BIBELICK. In ''The Cruise of the Rolling Junk,'' he is a Philadelphia garageman who sells F. Scott and Zelda Fitzgerald a new tire.

BICKLE. In ''Majesty,'' he is a guest at the wedding ceremony Emily Castleton calls off.

BIEMAN. In ''Design in Plaster,'' he is a movie executive Mary Harris finds boring. She declines his invitation to a preview.

"THE BIG ACADEMY DINNER" (1967). Poem. (Characters: [Gary] Cooper, [Greta] Garbo.) Fitzgerald ridicules everyone—women, writers, winners, and criminals alike—at the Academy banquet held in Hollywood and will not attend another one.

BIGELOW, ALIDA. In *Thoughtbook*, she is a very popular girl. In real life, she became Mrs. Francis Butler.

BIGELOW, DONALD ("DON"). In *Thoughtbook*, he is Fitzgerald's friend.

BIGGS. In "Jacob's Ladder," he is a member of the law firm of Read, Van Tyne, Biggs & Company, with which Jacob C. K. Booth threatens Jenny Prince's would-be blackmailer Scharnhorst. The name Biggs came from that of Fitzgerald's Princeton roommate John Biggs, Jr.*

BIGGS, JOHN, JR. (1895–1979). Lawyer and judge. He was one of Fitzgerald's Princeton roommates. The two were on the *Princeton Tiger* board and coauthored *Safety First!*, a Triangle Club presentation. At Fitzgerald's recommendation, Scribner's published Biggs's two novels, *Demigods* (1926) and *Seven Days Whipping* (1928), the latter a horror fantasy about an uneasy judge. Biggs and his wife Anna lived in Wilmington, Delaware, where Biggs practiced law early in his career. They helped the Fitzgeralds find "Ellerslie," the mansion they rented there (1927–1929). Biggs got Fitzgerald out of trouble more than once, when he was held by police for drunkenness. Biggs became a judge on the Third U.S. Circuit Court of Appeals in Philadelphia. In 1937 Fitzgerald named Biggs an executor of his will. Reading it in 1940, Biggs remarked that Fitzgerald left a millionaire's will but a pauper's estate. He appealed vainly to the bishop of Baltimore for Fitzgerald to be buried beside his parents in Baltimore, in consecrated soil. Fitzgerald's survivors fortunately did not follow Biggs's suggestion to sell most of Fitzgerald's papers for the $1,000 informally offered by Princeton. Biggs administered Fitzgerald's estate for eight years gratis. His wife was kind to Zelda Sayre Fitzgerald* in the 1940s. Biggs published *The Guilty Mind: Psychiatry and the Law of Homicide* (1955) about insanity, criminality, and jurisprudence. In 1974 the Biggses attended the premiere of the movie version of *The Great Gatsby* starring Robert Redford and Mia Farrow.

Bibliography: Seymour I. Toll. *A Judge Uncommon: A Life of John Biggs, Jr.* (Philadelphia: Legal Communications, 1993).

BIGLOW. In *Thoughtbook*, he is mentioned as Fitzgerald's friend. He may be Donald Bigelow.

BILL. In *Fie! Fie! Fi-Fi!*, he is pursued by Gwen but likes Gladys.

BILL. In ''The Freshest Boy,'' he is a boy at St. Regis who participates in the basketball scrimmage.

BILL. In ''A Luckless Santa Claus,'' he gives a dollar to Harry Talbot when Harry tries to give him two dollars.

BILL. In ''The Rubber Check,'' he is forgiven for writing rubber checks in New York because he is in college.

BILL. In *Safety First!*, he is one of the singers. He likes Cynthia.

BILL. In ''Truth and—consequences,'' he is involved in the game and is said to love Ruth.

BILL. In ''Two Wrongs,'' he is a friend William McChesney greets when he is taking Emmy Pinkard to lunch in New York.

BILLINGS, SENATOR. In ''One Interne,'' he is a politician who is brought to the hospital for diagnosis. Since he is an alcoholic suffering from a cold, he is soon discharged.

BILLY. In ''Family in the Wind,'' he is one of the people who were injured by the first tornado and is treated by Dr. Forrest Janney.

BILLY. In ''Myra Meets His Family,'' Lilah Elkins tells Myra Harper not to compare his singing with the singing of any husband Myra might choose. Choose and be satisfied.

BISBY, MRS. CAXTON. In ''The Intimate Strangers,'' she is one of Marquise Sara de la Guillet de la Guimpé's sisters. In New York, she tries to interfere in Sara's private life.

BISHOP, JOHN PEALE (1892–1944). Poet and critic. Bishop was born in Charles Town, West Virginia, attended high school in Hagerstown, Maryland, and suffered temporary blindness in 1909 and then psychosomatic illness until 1913. He attended Mercersburg, entered Princeton, published poems in and co-edited the *Nassau Literary Magazine* with Edmund Wilson,* and was close to Fitzgerald. After graduating in 1917 as class poet, Bishop served in the U.S. infantry in France (1917–1919). He married Margaret Grosvenor Hutchins in 1922. In New York, he worked for and published in *Vanity Fair* (1920–1922, 1925–1926), between which times he and his wealthy wife lived in Europe, where Bishop associated with e. e. cummings, Ernest Hemingway,* Archibald MacLeish, Ezra Pound, and Allen Tate. In 1926 the Bishops bought a château outside Paris, had three sons, and lived there until 1933. After residences in

Connecticut and New Orleans, the Bishops lived on Cape Cod from 1935. About 1939, disliking capitalism but mistrusting utopian radicals, Bishop became depressed. In 1940 he lectured at Princeton and Yale and became chief poetry reviewer for the *Nation*. His books of verse include *Green Fruits* (1917), *Now with His Love* (1933), *Minute Particulars* (1935), and *Selected Poems* (1941), which Tate persuaded Max Perkins* to publish. Bishop's fiction includes *Many Thousands Gone* (1931, Civil War stories) and *Act of Darkness* (1935, a novel). His collected poetry and collected critical essays were issued posthumously in 1948.

While at Princeton Fitzgerald admired Bishop, who was condescending. The two agreed their English professors were mostly dull, and Fitzgerald was grateful when Bishop helped him understand poetry better. Fitzgerald based the character Thomas Parke D'Invilliers in *This Side of Paradise* on Bishop, discusses him in ''Princeton,'' and called himself James Boswell to Bishop's Samuel Johnson. Their friendship sputtered because Fitzgerald—among others—disliked Bishop's wife. Fitzgerald thought Bishop was not evolving critically. Bishop deplored Fitzgerald's drinking and regarded Zelda Sayre Fitzgerald* as evil. Fitzgerald liked *Many Thousands Gone* but criticized the unbalanced structure of *Act of Darkness*. Bishop praised *Tender Is the Night*, but his ''The Missing All'' (*Virginia Quarterly* 13 [Winter 1937]: 106–21) includes adverse comments on Fitzgerald, whose death, all the same, depressed Bishop. ''The Hours,'' his elegy on Fitzgerald (*New Republic*, 3 March 1941, 312–13), combines grief, sympathy, praise, and a sense of hopelessness.

Bibliography: Robert L. White, *John Peale Bishop* (New York: Twayne, 1966).

BISPAM. In ''Basil and Cleopatra,'' he is a Yale freshman football player, who plays end.

BISPAM. In *This Side of Paradise*, he is a student at Yale, according to his mother, whom Beatrice O'Hara Blaine meets.

BISPAM, MRS. In *This Side of Paradise*, she is the mother of a Yale student. Amory Blaine's mother writes to him about the lad.

BISSEL. In ''The Captured Shadow,'' he is Imogene Bissel's father, who is concerned about the alleged attack on Hubert Blair.

BISSEL, DOROTHY. She is the addressee of Fitzgerald's ''Spring Song.''

BISSEL, IMOGENE. In ''The Scandal Detectives,'' she turns thirteen, delights Basil Duke Lee, but prefers Hubert Blair. In ''He Thinks He's Wonderful,'' she is dark, beautiful, and fond of Basil. She is Riply Buckner, Jr.'s date at Connie Davies's party, at which Basil tries but fails to woo her away. Later Basil takes her for a drive in his grandfather's electric car. In ''The Captured Shadow,'' she was to play Leilia Van Baker in Basil's play *The Captured Shadow* until she went to Rochester, Minnesota, for an appendectomy.

BISSEL, MRS. In ''He Thinks He's Wonderful,'' she is Imogene Bissel's mother. In ''The Captured Shadow,'' she is concerned about the alleged attack on Hubert Blair but dislikes his father's calling at their home about it.

BISTOLARY. In *This Side of Paradise*, he is the owner of a restaurant at Princeton frequented by Amory Blaine and his friends.

BIXBY, THE HONORABLE HOWARD. In ''The Pierian Springs and the Last Straw,'' he is the man Myra Fulham jilts the night before their wedding to elope with George Rombert.

BLACHFORD, LADY. In ''Sentiment—and the Use of Rouge,'' she is Lord Blachford's wife and the mother of Clara Syneforth, Captain Clayton Harrington Syneforth, and Lieutenant Richard Harrington Syneforth. Clayton does not object to her rouge but dislikes Clara's use of it.

BLACHFORD, LORD. In ''Sentiment—and the Use of Rouge,'' he is Lady Blachford's husband and the father of Clara Syneforth, Captain Clayton Harrington Syneforth, and Lieutenant Richard Harrington Syneforth.

BLACHT. In ''A Snobbish Story,'' he is a reporter John Boynton Bailey introduces Josephine Perry to at the theater workshop.

BLACK. In ''A Freeze-Out,'' this is the name of some of the many people who attended the Rikkers' party shortly after New Year's Day.

BLACK, JOSEPH. In *The Beautiful and Damned*, he is an executive with Films Par Excellence. Born Joseph Bloeckman, he is nicknamed ''Blockhead'' by Gloria Gilbert Patch, whose father he knows and whom he likes. He fails to get her into the movies. Anthony Patch is annoyed with Black, tries to fight him, and gets knocked down.

BLACKBUCK. In *The Great Gatsby*, this is the name of a supercilious ''clan'' Nick Carraway lists on a timetable as among Jay Gatsby's summer guests.

BLAINE, AMORY. In *This Side of Paradise*, he is the spoiled son, born in spring 1896, of Beatrice O'Hara Blaine and Stephen Blaine, who live in the Minneapolis area. After a hit-or-miss Catholic upbringing, Amory attends St. Regis, a Connecticut preparatory school, and Princeton, where he makes many friends and goes on escapades. Monsignor Thayer Darcy is his steadying influence. Amory serves in France in 1918–1919 as an infantry lieutenant. In the course of a decade, he has love affairs with Phoebe Column, Rosalind Connage, Clara Page, and Eleanor Savage. His greatest loss is Rosalind Connage, who weds someone else. He works for an advertising agency in New York, goes on binges, and then learns his family finances are reduced. At the end, remaining a romantic egotist and not knowing whether to enter the field of art or politics or religion, he decides he knows nothing but himself. Into his characterization of Amory, Fitzgerald puts some of his own less desirable qualities and some pleasant qualities of his Princeton friend Walker Ellis.

Bibliography: Susan Harris Smith, ''Some Biographical Aspects of *This Side of Paradise*,'' *FH/A 1970*, 96–101.

BLAINE, BEATRICE O'HARA. In *This Side of Paradise*, she is Amory Blaine's beautiful Irish-Catholic mother. She lived with her wealthy family at Lake Geneva, Wisconsin, studied in Rome, and associated with celebrities. She spoils Amory, worries about him, is affected, admires Monsignor Thayer Darcy, and dies in 1918 or 1919.

BLAINE, STEPHEN. In *This Side of Paradise*, he is Beatrice O'Hara Blaine's husband and Amory Blaine's father. Wealthy by inheritance, he spends much time reading and dies during Amory's junior year at Princeton.

BLAIR. In ''Majesty,'' he is the son of William Brevoort Blair and Olive Mercy Blair.

BLAIR. In ''Majesty,'' she is the daughter of William Brevoort Blair and Olive Mercy Blair.

BLAIR, GARDINER, JR. In ''Majesty,'' he is a guest at the wedding ceremony called off by Emily Castleton.

BLAIR, GARDINER, SR. In ''Majesty,'' he is a guest at the wedding ceremony called off by Emily Castleton.

BLAIR, GEORGE P. In ''The Scandal Detectives,'' he is Hubert Blair's father and is concerned about the alleged attack on his son.

BLAIR, HUBERT (''HUBE''). In ''The Scandal Detectives,'' he is the popular, athletic boy whose friendship with Imogene Bissel causes Basil Duke Lee to become jealous, especially when he hears the two kissing. In ''A Night at the Fair,'' he is the handsome, cocky lad, fifteen, who takes Riply Buckner Jr.'s girlfriend, Olive, away from him and is more attractive to Gladys Van Schellinger than Basil is. Hubert calls himself Bill Jones when he first meets

Olive. In "He Thinks He's Wonderful," Basil mentions him, with the implication that Hubert is popular. Joe Gorman drives him, and Lewis Crum as well, to Connie Davies's party. In "The Captured Shadow," he is the handsome, popular, but unreliable boy, fifteen, who rehearses indifferently as the lead in Basil's play *The Captured Shadow*; when he backs out, Evelyn Beebe, in the role of the heroine, loses interest. The model for Blair was Fitzgerald's St. Paul friend Reuben Warner.

BLAIR, MASTER GARDINER, III. In "Majesty," he is a guest at the wedding ceremony called off by Emily Castleton.

BLAIR, MISS GLORIA. In "Majesty," she is a guest at the wedding ceremony called off by Emily Castleton.

BLAIR, MRS. GEORGE P. In "The Scandal Detectives," she is Hubert Blair's mother and is concerned about the alleged attack on her son.

BLAIR, MRS. POTTER. In "Majesty," she is a guest at the wedding ceremony called off by Emily Castleton.

BLAIR, MRS. PRINCESS POTOWSKI PARR. In "Majesty," she is a guest at the wedding ceremony called off by Emily Castleton.

BLAIR, OLIVE MERCY. In "Majesty," she is Emily Castleton's cousin. When Emily declines to marry William Brevoort Blair, Olive marries him, has two children with him, and seeks to rescue Emily, but rejoices in Emily's majestic life with Prince Gabriel Petrocobesco.

BLAIR, WILLIAM BREVOORT. In "Majesty," he is a high-society man from Newport, Rhode Island, whom Emily Castleton agrees to marry. When she calls off the wedding, he marries Emily's cousin, Olive Mercy. They have two children.

BLAKE. In "A Freeze-Out," Blake is the name of some of the many people who attended the Rikkers' party shortly after New Year's Day.

BLISS, DR. In "Her Last Case," he is Ben Dragonet's physician.

BLOECKMAN, JOSEPH. In *The Beautiful and Damned. See* Black, Joseph.

BLOSSOM. In *Fie! Fie! Fi-Fi!*, she and Clover love Archie.

"A BLUES" (1981). Poem. The poet feels inexplicably driven and must be fed by someone's kindness.

BLUM, CARMEL MYERS. In ''Lines on Reading through an Autograph Album,'' she is the wife of Ralph Blum and, named simply Carmel, is with him the album owner. In ''Orange pajamas and heaven's guitars,'' it is recommended one seek a Carmel rather than candy. She was the movie actress Carmel Myers.

BLUM, RALPH. In ''Lines on Reading through an Autograph Album,'' he, named simply Ralph, owns the album with Carmel. He is the husband of Carmel Myers Blum.

BLUTCHDAK. In ''Rags Martin-Jones and the Pr-nce of W-les,'' John B. Chestnut hires and pays Blutchdak to pretend to Rags Martin-Jones in Europe that he is a warmonger.

BOARDMAN, LAURENCE. In *Thoughtbook*, he is a friend.

BOB. In ''The Love Boat,'' he is a student McVitty orders to stop fighting.

BOB. In ''One Hundred False Starts,'' he is Fitzgerald's Uncle Bob, an African American from Alabama. When Fitzgerald asks him what he does when false starts stymie him, Bob says, ''I wuks.''

BOBBÉ. In ''How to Live on Practically Nothing a Year,'' he is a French military aviator who is to be the Riviera dinner guest of F. Scott and Zelda Sayre Fitzgerald.*

BOBBY. In *This Side of Paradise*, she is a person whom any mother would keep from drinking early in life.

BOBBY. In ''Truth and—consequences,'' he is in the game.

BODMAN. In ''A Freeze-Out,'' he is the undertaker, mistakenly invited to the Rikkers' party shortly after New Year's Day, then told not to come.

BOILEAU. In *The Evil Eye*, he sings with others about William Jones and also about maidens jumping off the wall.

BOILING OIL. In *This Side of Paradise*, this is the name of a pirate lieutenant in the Princeton Triangle play *Ha-Ha Hortense!* Amory Blaine takes the part during his sophomore year.

'' 'BOIL SOME WATER—LOTS OF IT' '' (1940). Short story. (Characters: Cushman, Helen Earle, Ned Harman, Walter Herrick, Pat Hobby, Max Leam, Paterson, Miss Stacy, Big Jack Wilson.) Pat Hobby, forty, has been a screenwriter for nineteen years but is now only a minor one. He lunches with a newly hired nurse to ask her about a script he is touching up concerning doctors. He says his only original line is "Boil some water—lots of it." Executives are seated nearby when a man in a Cossack costume bothers them. Pat crowns him with a tray, then learns that he is Walter Herrick, a writer who is acting out a gag. A doctor, summoned to treat Herrick's bleeding head, shouts for someone to boil lots of water.

BOLDINI, JEFF. In "Pat Hobby and Orson Welles," he is the makeup artist who, for a joke and a $10 bribe, glues a beard on Pat Hobby to make him look like Orson Welles.

BOLOGNA, IONA. In *Safety First!*, this is the name assigned by the chorus to the faddish hula singer.

BONAPARTE, PRINCE. In "The End of Hate," he is attached to General Jubal Early's staff and is grateful for Dr. Pilgrim's treatment of him.

BONNEASSE, MME. In *Tender Is the Night*, her name is read in the *New York Herald*.

"A BOOK OF ONE'S OWN" (1937). Essay. Fitzgerald says that, in this age of condensation, an anthology of everything one could read over a weekend to make him omniscient might sell. His list of contents concerns mispronounced words, Indian sex, welding, operas, laughs from Shakespeare, Tony Adverse, *Reader's Digest* when condensed, selections from "Orphan Annie," how to write scenarios and make beer, astrology simplified, unexpurgated *Tales of the Wayside Inn*, Shirley Temple cutouts, and unsolved murders condensed. The publisher might include an O. Henry set in ten volumes to fill a purchaser's bookcase or might bind the anthology to resemble a radio.

BOONE. In "Zone of Accident," he is a medical student whose blood type does not match Loretta Brooke's.

BOONE, JOE. In " 'I Didn't Get Over,' " he is a member of the 1916 class who did get over. When he and some of his classmates reminisce at their twentieth reunion, he says that while he was in France he mainly had a good time, which included guarding prisoners at Brest.

BOONE, SERGEANT. In "A Woman with a Past," he is a friend of Book Chaffee, who gets Josephine Perry into Boone's room in the armory.

BOOPSIE DEE. In "One Hundred False Starts," she is a cute girl Fitzgerald cannot write about or even remember how she got her name.

BOOTH, JACOB ("JAKE") C. K. In "Jacob's Ladder," he is Jenny Prince's thirty-three-year-old rich benefactor. He helps launch her career as a movie star by introducing her to Billy Farrelly and proposes to her, but he loses her to her director.

BOOTH, JOHN WILKES. In "The Room with the Green Blinds," he is the man who stole Carmatle's son's clothes and escaped to the Raymond house near Macon, Georgia, only to be shot by Carmatle. The initials "J. W. B." are found on the door of the mysterious room.

BORDLEY, BOB. In "Last Kiss," he is a man Jim Leonard sees at the charity ball with a sandwich board advertising a Hollywood Bowl event.

BORDON, DOLLY. In "Discard," she is a Hollywood star, George Baker's aunt and guardian, and the wife of Count Hennen de Lanclerc, and hence Countess de Lanclerc in private life. Twenty-five at the outset of the action, she loses a part in *Sense and Sensibility* to Phyllis Burns, four years her junior. Dolly also loses her husband to Phyllis but rebounds to take a part in *Portrait of a Woman* away from Phyllis. Director James Jerome proposes to her, but she prefers to have only a professional career.

BORGÉ, ISABELLE. In *This Side of Paradise*, she is Sally Weatherby's flirtatious cousin, sixteen. When she visits Minneapolis from her home in Baltimore during Christmas vacation in his sophomore year, Amory Blaine meets her, dances with her, and would kiss her but for an interruption. After she attends the Princeton prom as his guest, he visits the Borgé summer home on Long Island. They kiss but then argue.

BORGÉ, MRS. In *This Side of Paradise*, she is Isabelle Borgé's mother, who chaperones the girl at the Princeton prom and invites Amory Blaine to their summer home.

BORGIA, JOHN ALEXANDER. "The High Cost of Macaroni," he is the chief of the secret police knocked down by the narrator during a fight over quoted taxi fares.

BORIS. In "Teamed with Genius," he is a character in a script of *Ballet Shoes*.

BOROWKI, STANISLAS KARL JOSEPH. In "The Hotel Child," he is a chaser of moneyed women. He robs Fifi Schwartz's mother, proposes to Fifi, leaves the hotel with Miss Howard, is caught and imprisoned, but is bailed out by Lady Capps-Karr.

BOUNDS. In *The Beautiful and Damned*, he is Anthony Patch's part-time servant in New York. When the war begins, he returns to England, where he was born, to enlist.

BOURNE, MARK H. In "More Than Just a House," he is the mortgage holder on the Gunther mansion who strips it for lack of payment.

BOVINE, MRS. In *Fie! Fie! Fi-Fi!*, she gossips with Sady, a manicurist. After they have a fight, they ask Del Monti to arbitrate.

BOWERS, BRYAN. In "Too Cute for Words," he is a widower who has just moved into an apartment, perhaps in or near New York, with his daughter Gwen Bowers, who is thirteen. He permits her to attend a dance in Mrs. Charles Wrotten Ray's Princeton home, to be held before the Princeton-Harvard football game. Gwen is to be with her friends Dizzy Campbell and Clara Hannaman. While he is chaperoning the prom dance held that evening, with Helen Hannaman, they see Gwen dancing with Tommy Ray, Mrs. Ray's short, shy son. In "Inside the House," he is Gwen Bowers's widowered father. He tells Gwen she cannot go with Jason Crawford to a movie starring Peppy Velance, her favorite actress. He tries to surprise Gwen by inviting Peppy to be a dinner guest at a restaurant with their friend Ed Harrison. Gwen pleads homework and sneaks out with Jason, but misses Peppy, who, however, will be a dinner guest at the Bowers' house the following night.

BOWERS, DONALD. In "Three Hours Between Planes," he is the boyfriend of Nancy Holmes Gifford, whose photograph she wrongly identifies as that of Donald Plant, to the latter's chagrin.

BOWERS, GWEN. In "Too Cute for Words," she is the daughter, thirteen, of Bryan Bowers. She talks him into permitting her to attend a dance, with her girlfriends Dizzy Campbell and Clara Hannaman, to be held in the Princeton home of Mrs. Charles Wrotten Ray. When the illness of Mrs. Ray's mother causes the dance to be cancelled, Gwen instigates plans, young though the three girls are, to crash the prom dance the evening before the Princeton-Harvard football game. In "Inside the House," at fourteen, she is popular with the boys. Against Bryan's orders, she sneaks out to a movie starring Peppy Velance, her favorite actress and ideal, and misses meeting Peppy. Her father arranges to have Peppy come to their house as a dinner guest the next night. Gwen's personality, talk, and taste are based on those of Fitzgerald's daughter Scottie (*see* Smith, Frances Scott Fitzgerald Lanahan). A third Gwen story became "Strange Sanctuary," with freshly named Dolly Haines as heroine. Fitzgerald wrote and sold a fourth Gwen story, "The Pearl and the Fur," but it was never published.

Bibliography: Jennifer McCabe Atkinson, "Lost and Unpublished Stories by F. Scott Fitzgerald," in *FH/A 1971*, 32–63.

"THE BOWL" (1928). Short story. (Characters: Ralph Henry Barber, Howard Bement, Bunker, Daisy Cary, Harold Case, Ted Coy, Tad Davis, Jeff Deering, Devereaux, Jack Devlin, Joe Dougherty, Bean Gile, Doctor Glock, Captain Gottlieb, Dolly Harlan, Mrs. Harlan, Red Hopman, Frank Kane, Keene, Ed Kimball, Josh Logan, Lillian Lorraine, Joe McDonald, Mullins, Josephine Pickman, Poore, Al Ratoni, Bill Roper, Rubber, Wash Sampson, Carl Sanderson, George Spears, Captain Tasker, Bob Tatnall, Vienna Thorne, Tony, Toole, Tunti, Jack Whitehead.) Jeff Deering, the narrator, rooms at Princeton with Dolly Harlan, a reluctant football star. Harlan enables his team to defeat Yale in the Yale Bowl. He and Deering double-date with Vienna Thorne and Josephine Pickman by driving to the Midnight Frolic in New York. Vienna, whose father is in the diplomatic service, hates football because her brother was killed playing football. Carl Sanderson approaches Vienna, argues with her, and in a suicide attempt shoots himself through the shoulder. After more than a year abroad, during which Dolly has played well but still dislikes football, Vienna attends a Princeton dance, and soon she and Dolly are engaged. She persuades him to quit football. He hurts his ankle playing tennis in the summer, tells Deering he will not play football, then breaks his ankle and does not play. Deering finds him less interesting. During her coming-out party in Washington, D.C., Vienna and Dolly argue because he intends to play football again. A movie star named Daisy Cary watches him practice. During the Princeton-Yale game, Dolly drops some punts but catches a pass to tie the game. He goes to New York where he plans to share a room with Vienna at the Madison Hotel but instead goes to the Ambassador Hotel, where Daisy is staying. He is able to press past a crowd seeking her—because of his football fame, which he briefly relishes.

BOWMAN, TOM. In "The Popular Girl," he is Yanci Bowman's father. A Yale man, he has been in Midwest real estate but has been widowed for ten years and is an alcoholic. He embarrasses Yanci at a country-club dance and penitently gives her $300 to visit New York. He dies and leaves her almost no inheritance.

BOWMAN, YANCI. In "The Popular Girl," she is the pretty, bored, quick-thinking daughter, twenty, of Tom Bowman. They live in a rented house in the Midwest. She attends a country-club dance with Jerry O'Rourke but meets rich New Yorker Scott Kimberly who is visiting there and wants him. After her father dies, she goes to New York where she pretends she is wealthy and popular. Though he discovers her ruse, Scott loves her and rescues her from embarrassment. They undoubtedly will marry.

BOXLEY, GEORGE. In *The Last Tycoon*, he is a British writer whom Monroe Stahr has hired but who feels he is too good for Hollywood. Stahr mollifies him. Boxley is partly based on Aldous Huxley,* with whom Fitzgerald worked in Hollywood (1937, 1938–1939).

BOYD, CALVIN. In *The Beautiful and Damned*, he is a Harvard alumnus who, Anthony Patch reads, discovered a treatment for typhus.

BOYD, MARGARET ("PEGGY") WOODWARD (1898–1965). An American novelist and wife of Thomas Alexander Boyd.* Fitzgerald recommended *The Love Legend*, her first novel, to Max Perkins,* who published it in 1922. In a 1922 review, ''A Rugged Novel,'' Fitzgerald calls it well written, honest, amusing, and alive, adding that its formlessness is excusable since it is Boyd's first novel. He shows how the main characters—four sisters—are all different, identifies points of excellence in the novel, and says its depiction of Chicago is the best of any novel since Theodore Dreiser's *Sister Carrie* (1900). Fitzgerald later expressed regret to Perkins for recommending Boyd.

BOYD, THOMAS ALEXANDER (1898–1935). American novelist. He was born in Defiance, Ohio, attended public and private schools, enlisted in the Marine Corps in 1917, saw action in France, and was gassed in 1918. He worked in Chicago, was a reporter for the *Minneapolis Star* and the *St. Paul Daily News*, opened a bookstore in St. Paul, and began editing a *Daily News* weekly book page. Boyd married his third cousin, Margaret Woodward Smith, in 1920 (*see* Boyd, Margaret Woodward). He met Sinclair Lewis, Grace Hodgson Flandrau,* and in 1921 Fitzgerald, who frequented his bookstore and sent him his ''Public Letter to Thomas Boyd.'' Boyd, who admired Fitzgerald, arranged for publication of the letter in the *Daily News*. Fitzgerald knew Boyd's wife, who wrote as Woodward Boyd, and recommended Thomas Boyd's first book, a war novel titled *Through the Wheat*, to Max Perkins,* who published it in 1923. It established Boyd's initially high reputation and was his best work. In a 1923 review, titled ''Under Fire,'' of *Through the Wheat*, Fitzgerald says the book concerns a charge made through a French wheat field in June 1918 by American marines ''sustained'' only by a romantic desire for adventure. He praises the work, which is not patriotic, not pacifistic, not propagandistic, for being more emotional than thoughtful. In the review Fitzgerald mentions e. e. cummings's *The Enormous Room* (1922) and *Three Soldiers* (1921) by John Dos Passos* and calls *Through the Wheat* the best combat war novel since Stephen Crane's *The Red Badge of Courage* (1895). To Perkins, Fitzgerald also recommended Boyd's second novel, *The Dark Cloud* (1924), and his collection of war stories, *Points of Honor* (1925). After Boyd and Peggy were divorced, Boyd married Ruth Fitch Bartlett in 1929. In 1933 they moved to Vermont, where he joined the Communist party and ran unsuccessfully for governor of Vermont on the Communist ticket. *In Time of Peace*, a sequel to *Through the Wheat*, was published in 1935, soon after Boyd had died of a cerebral hemorrhage. Earlier, Fitzgerald had written to Perkins (c. 1 June 1925) to express misgivings to Perkins about *Through the Wheat*, and he labeled Boyd ignorant, intolerant, and gross and called his later work hasty and concerned with topics he knew little about. Fitzgerald wrote to Perkins (21 January 1930) that director King Vidor* had filched scenes from *Through the Wheat* for *The Big Parade*, his 1925 World War I movie.

"THE BOY WHO KILLED HIS MOTHER" (1952). *See* "In a dear little vine-covered cottage."

BRADEN, CARTY. In "The Popular Girl," he is a friend of Yanci Bowman and happily obliges when she asks him to dance at the country-club party where her father is drinking too much.

BRADIN, EDITH. In "May Day," she is a beautiful, selfish girl, twenty-two, from Harrisburg. She goes with Peter Himmel to the Yale dance at Delmonico's, ignores her friend Gordon Sterrett because he is depressed and drunk, goes to her brother Henry Bradin's office, and is terrified by the mob that storms it.

BRADIN, HENRY. In "May Day," he was a Cornell economics instructor, from Harrisburg, who is an editor of a socialist newspaper. He suffers a broken leg when a mob storms his office.

BRADLEE. In "The Love Boat," he is a Harvard football player recalled by Bill Frothington.

BRADLEY. In "The Rich Boy," he is the proprietor of a gambling house in Palm Beach, Florida.

BRADY, CECELIA ("CELIA"). In *The Last Tycoon*, she is Pat Brady's daughter, nineteen, a junior at Bennington. She narrates the novel. She is in love with Monroe Stahr, regards Kathleen Moore as her rival, asks her father to help actress Martha Dodd, sees he has concealed his secretary Birdy Peters in his office closet naked, and introduces Stahr to Brimmer. At the end, Louella (Parsons*) incorrectly reports that Cecelia and Stahr are married. Fitzgerald had trouble presenting Cecelia as a convincing narrator. She is based partly on his daughter Scottie (*see* Smith, Frances Scott Fitzgerald Lanahan). Her name is spelled Cecilia in some editions.

BRADY, EARL. In *Tender Is the Night*, he is a movie director who praises Rosemary Hoyt's ability.

BRADY, ELEANOR. In *The Last Tycoon*, she is Cecelia Brady's sister, who died a few years before Cecelia's junior year at Bennington.

BRADY, JEANNE. In ''Absolution,'' she sits in church behind Rudolph Miller, who fears she will notice his family's poverty.

BRADY, MRS. PAT. In *The Last Tycoon*, she is Pat Brady's deceased wife and the mother of Eleanor Brady and Cecelia Brady. He has a chalk drawing of his wife in his office.

BRADY, PAT. In *The Last Tycoon*, he is a shrewd Irish-American producer, forty-seven, who is associated with Monroe Stahr. His daughter is Cecelia Brady who catches him fooling around with his secretary, Birdy Peters.

BRAEGDORT. In ''O Russet Witch!,'' he is the owner of a New York delicatessen patronized by Merlin Grainger.

BRAIN, THE. In ''Shaggy's Morning,'' she is the owner, along with the Beard, of Shaggy.

BRANCUSI. In ''Two Wrongs,'' he is a New York producer who is friendly with William McChesney, has worked with him, criticizes him amiably, and goes to London to try to persuade him to return to New York, but he drops him when he sees McChesney is sliding into alcoholic ineffectuality. Fitzgerald may have picked up the name Brancusi from Constantin Brancusi, a Parisian sculptor in the 1920s. In ''One Trip Abroad,'' Nelson Kelly visits Brancusi's studio in Paris.

BRAUN. In *Tender Is the Night*, he owns the clinic on the Zugersee that Dr. Franz Gregorovius persuades Dick Diver to buy.

BRAY, MRS. In ''First Blood,'' she is a friend of Josephine Perry's mother. The two discuss the puzzling girl.

BREEN, JOE. In *The Last Tycoon*, he is a person with whom Monroe Stahr says he has discussed a movie sequence in which a priest is struck. In real life, Joseph Breen (1890–1965) was a film censor in the Will Hays office, who was famous for requiring Walt Disney to erase udders from cows in his animated cartoons.

BRENT, EVELYN. In *The Last Tycoon*, she is a discarded actress whom Cecelia Brady hopes to persuade her father, Pat Brady, to help.

BRERETON, MISS. In ''A Woman with a Past,'' she is the proprietor of the Brereton School where Lillian Hammel and Josephine Perry are students. Josephine is expected to be nice to Ernest Waterbury, a Yale student who is Miss

Brereton's nephew. In ''A Snobbish Story,'' Josephine imagines Miss Brereton attending a play starring Josephine.

BRETT. In *The Beautiful and Damned*, he is Adam J. Patch's lawyer, whom Anthony Patch calls after Adam dies.

BRETT, SUKEY. In *This Side of Paradise*, Amory Blaine, after a drunken brawl, tells Thomas Parke D'Invilliers that he is dining with Brett. The statement is untrue.

BREWER. In *The Great Gatsby*, Nick Carraway remembers Brewer as being among Jay Gatsby's summer guests. His nose was shot off in the war.

BRIAN, BROTHER. In ''In the Darkest Hour,'' he is the Irish monk who helps Count Philippe of Villefranche rid their Loire Valley region of invading Vikings. In ''The Count of Darkness,'' now called Friar Brian, he continues to aid Philippe. In ''The Kingdom in the Dark,'' now called Brian, Brother Brian, and Friar Brian, he continues to aid Philippe.

BRIAN, FRIAR. In ''The Count of Darkness.'' *See* Brian, Brother.

"THE BRIDAL PARTY" (1930). Short story. (Characters: Marjorie Collins, Michael Curly, Caroline Dandy, Mrs. Dandy, Johnson, George Packman, Pat, Rutherford, Hamilton Rutherford, Mrs. Rutherford, T. G. Vance, Jebby West.) Michael Curly, down on his luck, receives a surprise invitation from Caroline Dandy, nineteen, to her June wedding ceremony in Paris to Hamilton Rutherford, a broker who has survived the Crash. Michael fell in love with Caroline in New York two years earlier and thought she still loved him. He bumps into the happy couple in front of some shops. Rutherford invites Michael to his Ritz bachelor party and to the postwedding reception and breakfast at the Hotel George-Cinq. Caroline invites him to a prewedding party and a tea. He learns he has just inherited $250,000 from his grandfather's estate. Is it too late? He attends the functions, at one of which he tells Rutherford that his domineering attitude toward women is out of fashion. Rutherford remains cocksure. At another gathering Michael learns Rutherford has lost in the market; then an intoxicated woman named Marjorie Collins appears and accuses Rutherford of abandoning her. Michael goes to Caroline at her hotel and tells her about the incident and about his inheritance. Rutherford enters, explains that the police have silenced Miss Collins, and adds that he is now almost penniless. Caroline sticks with him. The wedding, the swirl of guests, and the champagne reception afterward are beautiful. A friend tells Michael that ten minutes before the ceremony Rutherford was offered a $50,000-a-year job by T. G. Vance. Michael gazes at the joyful couple, feels cured, and tries to remember with which bridesmaid he has arranged a dinner date. The inspiration for ''The Bridal Party'' was the 1930 wedding in Paris, which Fitzgerald attended, of Powell Fowler, the brother of Ludlow Fowler. Fitzgerald's Princeton classmate, best man, and model for Anson Hunter in "The Rich Boy."

BRIDGEBANE, DR. In "Crazy Sunday," he is Miles Calman's psychiatrist.

BRIMMER. In *The Last Tycoon*, he is a Communist party member and would-be unionizer of the screenwriters. Cecelia Brady introduces him to Monroe Stahr, at Stahr's request. The two argue. When Stahr gets drunk and tries to hit Brimmer at the Bradys' home, Brimmer knocks him down and departs. Brimmer is based partly on Donald Ogden Stewart.*

BRINSON, MARJORIE SAYRE. She was one of Fitzgerald's sisters-in-law. In 1932 she accused Fitzgerald of institutionalizing Zelda Sayre Fitzgerald* to get her out of his way. He regarded Marjorie as a neurotic. In 1940 she agreed with other Sayre family members that Zelda should live back home in Montgomery, Alabama.

BROACA, JOHN. In *The Last Tycoon*, he is a movie director who works with Monroe Stahr. Twenty years earlier, he had an affair with screenwriter Rose Meloney. Broaca has a fine war record. He dislikes Joe Rienmund and feels dishonored for letting Ike Franklin slap him.

"THE BROADCAST WE ALMOST HEARD LAST SEPTEMBER" (1947). Short story. (Characters: Poke McFiddle, Ned, Prince Paul Obaloney, Tony.) While in a dugout watching military action through a periscope, Poke McFiddle presents a radio broadcast as though what he sees is a delightful show. The survivors plan a champagne dinner but are gassed. Fitzgerald evidently wrote this piece in 1935.

BROKAW, BILL. In "A Short Trip Home," he is a Yale student and Eddie Stinson's classmate. When Eddie realizes the Brokaws are not in Chicago, he rushes to save Ellen Baker from the mysterious stranger.

BRONSON. In "The Cut-Glass Bowl," he is the person to whose home Harold Piper rushes to remind his wife, Evylyn Piper, that they are invited. In doing so, he discovers her departing lover, Fred Gedney.

BRONSON, ED. In "Hot and Cold Blood," he is James Mather's friend. Bronson tells Mather he had some trouble with a girl and needs $300. Mather loans it to him, knowing he will probably never get it back. When Mather's wife, Jaqueline Mather, learns Bronson has bought a sportscar, she is upset and tells Mather so.

BRONSON, EDGAR. In ''The Family Bus,'' he is Dick Henderson's rival in high school, at youthful gatherings, and in business. He instigates the painting of graffiti on Dick's family car.

BRONSON, EUGENE. In *The Beautiful and Damned*, he is a Harvard alumnus who, Anthony Patch reads, is a respected magazine writer, of the sort Fitzgerald respected Edmund Wilson* for being.

BRONSON, WILL. In ''Pat Hobby's Christmas Wish,'' he was Harry Gooddorf's associate at First National Studios and the recipient of Harry's seemingly but not really self-incriminating letter.

BROOKE, LORETTA. In ''Zone of Accident,'' she is a movie actress who was successful as a juvenile. When she is in Baltimore visiting her father, whose name is Bach (German for ''Brook''), she is stabbed and becomes the patient of William Tullivers IV. The two fall in love, and she arranges for his girlfriend, Amy, to win a beauty contest and go to Hollywood.

BROUN, HEYWOOD (1888–1939). (Full name: Heywood Campbell Broun.) American journalist and author. He was born in Brooklyn, New York, attended the Horace Mann private school in New York, enrolled at Harvard in 1906, got a summer job in 1908 with the *New York Morning Telegraph*, and left Harvard in 1910 without a degree to work for the *Morning Telegraph*. In 1911 he moved to the *New York Tribune*, as a copyreader and then as a sports writer-editor. In 1915 he became the drama critic for the *Tribune*. In 1917 he married Ruth Hale, a vociferous feminist and press agent for a theatrical producer. Heywood Hale Broun, their only child, became a journalist. Broun's 1917–1918 stint in France as a *Tribune* war correspondent resulted in his *A.E.F.: With General Pershing and the American Forces* and *Our Army at the Front* (both 1918). After writing book reviews and personal columns for the *Tribune* until 1921, Broun moved to the *New York World* and started a column titled ''It Seems to Me.'' By this time Broun was on friendly terms with many notable writers in New York, including fellow members of the Algonquin Round Table in Manhattan. He assembled some of his columns and essays into *Seeing Things at Night* (1921) and *Pieces of Hate* (1922). Always working fast, he published three novels: *The Boy Grew Older* (1922), *The Sun Field* (1923), and *Gandle Follows His Nose* (1926). The first two are autobiographical and are about a sportswriter. *Gandle* is an allegorical fairy tale Deems Taylor converted into an opera.

In ''The Defeat of Art,'' a 1923 review of *The Boy Grew Older*, Fitzgerald agrees Broun is America's most versatile newspaperman but adds Broun's taste is often philistine and absurd, as when he recommended *Moon-Calf* (1920), Floyd Dell's inartistic novel. Broun's reading background seems largely limited to post-1900 titles. Fitzgerald surprisingly says *The Boy Grew Older* is competent and interesting. Broun handles his hero Peter Neale's love affairs unconvincingly, but he nicely presents Peter's cafe fight and the liberal New York editor for whom Peter works. Though disliking the novel's close, Fitzgerald anticipates Broun's next one eagerly. These comments were generous, given that Broun, in the *Tribune* three years earlier, had called *This Side of Paradise* callow and overwritten and its author complacent and pretentious.

In 1927 Broun coauthored a biography of Anthony Comstock, a rigid fighter against pornography. A year later Broun wrote antiestablishment columns for the *World* on the Sacco-Vanzetti case, disputed with his publisher, quit, returned, was fired for his continuing liberalism, and was hired at $30,000 a year to write for the *New York Telegram (World-Telegram* after 1931). In 1930 he ran for Congress as a Socialist but was defeated. In 1931 he coauthored *Christians Only* . . . , opposed to religious and racial prejudice. In 1931 he worked hard to find jobs for the unemployed. In November 1933 his wife obtained a divorce. (Less than a year later, after refusing medical attention, she died.) In December 1933 Broun was elected president of the American Newspaper Guild, which he had helped organize to improve reporters' salaries. In 1935 he married a widowed chorus girl named Maria Incoronata Fruscella Dooley (stage name, Connie Madison). He assembled columns and essays into *It Seems to Me: 1925–1935* (1935). In 1938 he helped found the weekly tabloid *Connecticut Nutmeg*, soon *Broun's Nutmeg*. The year 1939 was momentous. He became a Roman Catholic, was released by the *World-Telegram* for guild activity, published a column for the *New York Post*, and died a few days later.

Bibliography: Richard O'Connor, *Heywood Broun: A Biography* (New York: Putnam, 1975).

BROWN, BEN. In ''A Patriotic Short,'' he is the head of the movie shorts department and orders Pat Hobby not to introduce new angles into the script *True to Two Flags*.

BROWN, BUGS. In ''The Freshest Boy,'' he is a nervous, hysterical St. Regis pupil who refuses to go to New York with Basil Duke Lee.

BROWN, CAPTAIN. In '' 'I Didn't Get Over.' '' *See* Hibbing, Captain.

BROWN, CARTER. In ''Pilgrimage,'' he is sent the horse named Fido. In ''To Carter, a Friendly Finger,'' he has survived an automobile accident and receives Fitzgerald's humorous get-well poem. Carter Brown, who was Fitzgerald's friend from Tryon, North Carolina, had been in a car crash in 1937.

BROWN, DELIA. In ''Pat Hobby, Putative Father,'' she was Pat Hobby's wife in 1926. They divorced a year later. She and their son, John Brown Hobby, went to India, where she married Rajah Dak Raj Indore. John is now Prince John Indore.

BROWN, MARY. In *The Evil Eye*, Boileau and Harris would like to dance with her.

BROWN, MIDGET. In ''The Freshest Boy,'' he is the quarterback on the St. Regis team, or perhaps a player only in Basil Duke Lee's imagination.

BROWN, ORRISON. In ''The Lost Decade,'' he is a recent Dartmouth graduate, now a subeditor for a New York news weekly. When his boss orders him to take Louis Trimble out to lunch, Brown learns Trimble is recovering from a decade-long binge. Brown may be based in part on Budd Schulberg,* a Dartmouth graduate assigned in 1938 to write a movie script with Fitzgerald, who drank too much throughout the 1930s. Fitzgerald may have chosen the name Brown because Brown University, like Dartmouth College, is an Ivy League school.

BROWN, SATTERLY. In ''Inside the House,'' he is one of three boys Gwen Bowers has asked to help her decorate her Christmas tree. Jim Bennett and Jason Crawford, who is her favorite, are the others.

BRUNE, DR. In ''One Interne,'' he is a physician who is kidded at the medical school roast for inventing and naming diseases.

BRUNE, EDDIE. In ''Diagnosis,'' he is an acquaintance who Charlie Clayhorne suggests should not have quit working.

BUCHANAN, DAISY FAY. In *The Great Gatsby*, she is from Louisville, Kentucky, met and fell in love with Jay Gatsby in 1917, married Tom Buchanan in 1919, and is the mother of Pammy Buchanan. She is Nick Carraway's cousin. Beautiful and with an attractive voice, but disillusioned, bored, and cynical, Daisy, now twenty-three, remains the object of Jay Gatsby's undying, tragic love.

BUCHANAN, PAMMY. In *The Great Gatsby*, she is the daughter, two, of Tom Buchanan and Daisy Fay Buchanan.

BUCHANAN, TOM. In *The Great Gatsby*, a Yale man, he is the rich, hulking husband of Daisy Fay Buchanan, whom he married in 1919. They have a daughter named Pammy. Tom, now thirty, is a libertine, a prig, and a racist. He finances a New York apartment for his mistress, Myrtle Wilson. He despises Jay Gatsby, whose wealth, unlike Tom's, has been criminally obtained. Gatsby turns out not to be the threat to Buchanan's marriage that Gatsby wants to be. Tom conspires with Daisy to let Gatsby take the blame for Myrtle Wilson's death and thus causes Gatsby's death at the hands of Myrtle's husband, George B. Wilson.

BUCK. In ''Pat Hobby's Christmas Wish,'' he is a character in a horse-opera script Pat Hobby is dictating.

BUCKNER, MRS. RIPLY, SR. In ''The Scandal Detectives,'' she is Riply Buckner Jr.'s mother and serves Riply and Basil Duke Lee lemonade while they work on their scandal book. In ''A Night at the Fair,'' she is mentioned as likely to hear about her son's conduct at the state fair.

BUCKNER, RIPLY, JR. (''RIP''). In ''The Scandal Detectives,'' he is Basil Duke Lee's confederate in recording items in their scandal book and in planning the abortive attack on Hubert Blair. In ''A Night at the Fair,'' Riply is in long pants and therefore lords it over Basil, still in short pants. The two join Elwood Leaming to pick up two girls at the state fair. The next night Hubert Blair steals Olive, Riply's date. In ''He Thinks He's Wonderful,'' Riply, who sees Basil at Imogene Bissel's house, is annoyed when Basil tries unsuccessfully to steal Imogene, Riply's date, at Connie Davies's party. In ''The Captured Shadow,'' he is Basil's friend and plays the crook in Basil's play *The Captured Shadow*. In ''Forging Ahead,'' Riply and Basil are together during the summer at home before Basil's departure for Yale. The model for Riply was Fitzgerald's St. Paul friend Cecil Read.

BUCKNER, RIPLY, SR. In ''A Night at the Fair,'' he is identified as the deceased father of Riply Buckner, Jr.

BULGE, MISS. In ''The Diamond as Big as the Ritz,'' she runs a New York school Kismine Washington hopes to attend but never will.

BULHAM, P. In *Thoughtbook*, he is a member of Fitzgerald's club.

BULL, FRANCIS. In *The Great Gatsby*, Nick Carraway lists his name on a timetable as among Jay Gatsby's summer guests. He is in theater work.

BUNKER. In ''The Bowl,'' he is a player on the Princeton football team.

BUNSEN. In *The Great Gatsby*, Nick Carraway lists Bunsen's name on a timetable as one of Jay Gatsby's summer guests. Nick knew him at Yale.

BURCH, DR. EDWIN. In ''Dearly Beloved,'' he is Lilymary's obstetrician.

BURKE, GERALDINE. In *The Beautiful and Damned*, she is a theater usher and a girlfriend who visits Anthony Patch at his apartment. He is not seriously interested, and she knows it.

BURLING. In ''Two for a Cent,'' he is a slightly deaf person Henry W. Hemmick would have asked for a penny except for the appearance of Deems, Hemmick's suspicious boss.

BURNE-DENNISON, THE HON. MARTHA. In ''The Intimate Strangers,'' she is one of Marquise Sara de la Guillet de la Guimpé's sisters. She tries to interfere from London in Sara's private life.

BURNS, PHYLLIS. In ''Discard,'' she is a actress, twenty-one at the outset, who seeks to take both Dolly Bordon's movie roles and her husband, Count Hennen de Lanclerc. Phyllis wins one role and gains Hennen's affections, at least for a while.

BURT, MRS. In *The Evil Eye*, she is a person who, according to gossipy Margot, became a brunette.

BURTON. In *The Last Tycoon*, he is evidently a movie director who, according to Mort Flieshacker, wants to rearrange parts of a set.

BUSCH, ARTHUR. In ''Magnetism,'' he is a Hollywood writer turned director who loves and unsuccessfully pursues Kay Hannaford, the wife of actor George Hannaford.

BUSHMILL, HALLIE. In ''A Penny Spent,'' she is the attractive daughter of rich Julius Bushmill and Jessie Pepper Bushmill and is Claude Nosby's nominal fiancée. While the Bushmills are traveling in Europe, Julius Bushmill, who must be at times absent on business, hires Corcoran to act as the women's courier. In showing them a good time, Corcoran legitimately but extravagantly spends Bushmill's money, proves to be more exciting than Nosby, who joins them, and later marries Hallie.

BUSHMILL, JESSIE PEPPER. In ''A Penny Spent,'' she is rich Julius Bushmill's passive wife and the mother of Hallie Bushmill. She accompanies her daughter when Corcoran acts as their tour guide in France, Belgium, the Netherlands, and Italy.

BUSHMILL, JULIUS. In ''A Penny Spent,'' he is an Ohio millionaire, about fifty, who is on a business trip in Europe. He hires Corcoran to escort his wife, Jessie Pepper Bushmill, and their daughter, Hallie Bushmill, from Paris to Belgium and the Netherlands. He briefly objects when Corcoran spends Bushmill's money lavishly but agrees to let Corcoran take them, and Hallie's nominal fiancé Claude Nosby as well, to Italy, while Bushmill is on business in France. Corcoran marries Hallie and joins Bushmill in business.

BUSTANOBY. In ''A Short Autobiography,'' he is the proprietor of a place where Fitzgerald went for drinks in 1915.

BUTLER. In ''The Room with the Green Blinds,'' he is Carmatle's friend. The two accompany Robert Calvin Raymond when he returns to the house to investigate its mysterious room. Butler will not tell what then happened.

BUTLER, HOWARD. In ''Between Three and Four,'' he is employed by the Eddington family's New York furniture company. He fired the widowed Mrs. Sarah Belknap Summer largely because she had jilted him years earlier. He grows so demented when her apparent ghost haunts him that he commits suicide.

BUTLER, VERNARD. In ''The Honor of the Goon,'' he is one of the students who called Ella Lei Chamoro a goon.

BUTTERFIELD, WARREN. In ''The Camel's Back,'' he is a New York architect and a guest in Howard Tate's home. Tate asks him to seize the ''camel.''

BUTTERWORTH. In ''The Ice Palace,'' this is the name of a family who owns a mansion next to the Happers' mansion in Tarleton, Georgia.

BUTTERWORTH. In ''The Rough Crossing,'' he is the flat-nosed, alcoholic passenger who is overly attentive to Eva Smith.

BUTTON. In ''The Curious Case of Benjamin Button,'' he is Benjamin's grandson, born in 1920.

BUTTON, BENJAMIN. In ''The Curious Case of Benjamin Button,'' he is the central character, born seemingly age seventy in 1860 and growing younger. He is a baby, a schoolchild, a Harvard student, his father's business associate, a husband and father, a Spanish-American War officer, and a happy little grandfather—all in reverse order.

BUTTON, HILDEGARDE MONCRIEF. In ''The Curious Case of Benjamin Button,'' she is Benjamin Button's wife and Roscoe Button's mother. When she cannot tolerate her husband's growing ever younger, she moves to Italy.

BUTTON, MRS. ROGER. In ''The Curious Case of Benjamin Button,'' she is Benjamin Button's mother. She does not figure in the story.

BUTTON, ROGER ("CUFF"). In ''The Curious Case of Benjamin Button,'' he is Benjamin Button's father. He is in the hardware business.

BUTTON, ROSCOE. In ''The Curious Case of Benjamin Button,'' he is Benjamin Button's son.

C

CABLE. In *The Beautiful and Damned*, he is an usher at Anthony Patch's wedding.

CABLE, JOE. In ''The Dance,'' he is the handsome, dissipated son of a former governor of the state in which Davis, the Southern town, is located. Catherine Jones loves him; when she sees Marie Bannerman kissing him she becomes so angry she kills Marie.

CADMUS. In ''The Kingdom in the Dark,'' he is one of Count Philippe of Villefranche's loyal men. He saw the arsonists.

CADORNA. In ''Two Wrongs,'' he is a business associate William McChesney tells Emmy Pinkard to visit. She says she has done so to no avail.

CAHILL. In ''The Rich Boy,'' he is a Yale Club friend for news of whom lonely Anson Hunter asks the bartender, Oscar.

CAKEBOOK. In ''Ten Years in the Advertising Business,'' he was Fitzgerald's boss in the advertising office in 1919. He evidently declined Fitzgerald's request to raise his pay of $90 a month. Ten years later he is willing to pay Fitzgerald $1,500 to be a judge in a contest.

CALE. In ''Lo, the Poor Peacock!,'' he is a pawnbroker Jason Davis talks to about raising money on the family silver.

CALHOUN, AILIE. In ''The Last of the Belles,'' she is a Southern belle, living in Tarleton and nineteen at the beginning of the story. She flirts irresponsibly with Lieutenant Andy (the narrator), Lieutenant Horace Canby, Bill

Knowles, and Lieutenant Earl Schoen. Six years after World War I, Andy learns she has broken an engagement to a Cincinnati man and he visits her in Tarleton, only to learn she is marrying a Savannah man.

CALHOUN, BELLE POPE. In ''The Offshore Pirate,'' she is the African American named by ''Curtis Carlyle'' as having played the piano at parties for white children in Tennessee.

CALHOUN, C.T.J. In ''The Unspeakable Egg,'' he is a well-to-do person whose daughter ran away with a taxi driver, to her social detriment. Dr. Roswell Gallup tells Fifi about her to frighten Fifi into making a proper marriage.

CALHOUN, MRS. In ''The Last of the Belles,'' she is Ailie Calhoun's evidently permissive mother.

CALKINS. In *Porcelain and Pink*, he is a literary fellow who arrives for a date with Lois Marvis and mistakes her sister Julie Marvis for Lois.

CALLAGHAN, MORLEY (1903–1990). Fiction writer born in Toronto, Ontario, Canada. While attending the University of Toronto, he boxed, played baseball and hockey, was a reporter on the *Toronto Daily Star*, and met and was encouraged by Ernest Hemingway* (1923). After receiving his B.A. (1925), Callaghan attended classes at Osgoode Law School in Toronto. He began publishing short stories in 1926, was praised by Robert Menzies McAlmon* and Ezra Pound, and through his friendship with Fitzgerald in 1928 met Max Perkins,* who published his novel *Strange Fugitive* (1928) and his short-story collection *A Native Argosy* (1929).

Callaghan passed the bar in 1928 but never practiced law. In 1929 he married Loretto Florence Dee, and the couple spent seven months in Paris. From 1930 they lived in Toronto, and through the 1930s Callaghan published in many magazines and the following books: *It's Never Over* (1930), *No Man's Meat* (1931), *A Broken Journey* (1932), *Such Is My Beloved* (1934), *They Shall Inherit the Earth* (1935), *Now That April's Here and Other Stories* (1936), and *More Joy in Heaven* (1937). During World War II Callaghan worked for the Canadian navy and the Canadian Broadcasting Company. During the remainder of his career, he wrote prize-winning fiction, saw two of his plays into production, hosted a radio talk show, made guest appearances on television, and encouraged a host of younger writers. Continuing to be active, he published three books in the 1980s. It has been said that Callaghan's major theme is that spiritual development through altruistic love is of supreme importance.

In June 1929 Callaghan and Hemingway engaged in a little boxing match in Paris, with Fitzgerald acting as timekeeper. Fitzgerald let a three-minute round go a minute too long, probably because of nothing more than excitement. Callaghan decked Hemingway, who was probably hung over to a degree, and Hemingway never forgave either Callaghan or Fitzgerald for the minor humiliation. In *That Summer in Paris: Memories of Tangled Friendships with Hemingway, Fitzgerald and Some Others* (1963), Callaghan reminisces about his Parisian adventures, sets the record straight on the knockdown (about which Hemingway wrote inconsistently), and calls "tragic" both Hemingway's desire to "make legends out of his life" and Fitzgerald's "instinct for courting humiliation from his inferiors."

Bibliography: Brandon Conron, *Morley Callaghan* (New York: Twayne, 1966).

CALMAN, MILES. In "Crazy Sunday," he is the brilliant, unbalanced movie director who employs writer Joel Coles, is married to Stella Walker Calman, has been unfaithful to her with Eva Goebel, and dies in an airplane crash. Calman's character is based partly on Irving Thalberg,* the movie producer and the husband of actress Norma Shearer.* When Fitzgerald was in Hollywood in 1937, he wrote for Thalberg and attended a Sunday tea at his mansion. Calman's extramarital affair is not based on anything in Thalberg's life but on actress Eleanor Boardman's divorce from director King Vidor.*

Bibliography: Lambert.

CALMAN, MRS. In "Crazy Sunday," she is Miles Calman's quietly proud mother. Her character is based partly on Henrietta Heyman Thalberg, the mother of Irving Thalberg,* who was ambitious for and confident of her son.

Bibliography: Bob Thomas, *Thalberg: Life and Legend* (Garden City, N.Y.: Doubleday, 1969).

CALMAN, STELLA WALKER. In "Crazy Sunday," she is Miles Calman's wife, an actress who uses the professional name Stella Walker, who knows about his affair with Eva Goebel and who goes after Miles's writer Joel Coles immediately after learning of Miles's death in an airplane crash. The character of Stella is based partly on actress Norma Shearer,* the wife of Irving Thalberg.*

Bibliography: Lambert.

CAMBELL. In *This Side of Paradise*, a member of a firm called Cambell & Hambell, he is said to be engaged to the Popular Girl.

CAMBELL, D. B. In "At Your Age," he is evidently Randy Cambell's father.

CAMBELL, RANDY. In "At Your Age," he is Annie Lorry's boyfriend.

"THE CAMEL'S BACK" (1920). Short story. (Characters: Baily, Warren Butterfield, Marion Cloud, Jumbo, Martin Macy, Betty Medill, Cyrus Medill, Nolack, Mrs. Nolak, Perry Parkhurst, Rus, Emily Tate, Howard Tate, Millicent Tate, Mrs. Howard Tate, Townsend, Mrs. Townsend, Warburton.) During the

1919 Christmas season in Toledo, Perry Parkhurst, who has long courted Betty Medill, gets a marriage license and demands she wed him now or never. Getting a never, he drives to a hotel where his friend Baily persuades him to join Martin Macy upstairs for champagne. They decide not to attend either the circus ball at the Townsends' home or the dance party at the Tates' home. Perry, quite drunk, decides, however, to go to the circus ball after all. When his car will not start, he taxis to a costume shop, rents a camel suit, bribes the taxi driver to be the camel's back end, and goes by mistake not to the Townsends' but to the Tates', in disguise. Howard Tate, who knows Perry, gives a drink to him and a bottle to the sweaty man in the camel's back. The three proceed to the Townsend party, held at a club, where Perry, still hidden in the camel's head and front, encounters Betty, costumed as an Egyptian snake charmer and flirting with several men. She dances the cotillion with her unrecognized lover. After winning first prizes for their costumes, they are to be mock-married, with Jumbo, a black waiter, acting as minister. He produces a Bible, accepts a piece of paper from Perry as a marriage license and a ring from the taxi man still hiding in back, and performs the ceremony. To everyone's horror, Jumbo says not only that the license is legal, having the couple's names duly inscribed, but also that he is a Baptist minister. Perry, denying any untoward intent, is unmasked; he and Betty argue until he grows inspired and says the taxi driver can be her husband since her ring was his, but is delighted when Betty accepts Perry as her real husband and agrees to go West with him. "The Camel's Back" is one of Fitzgerald's few purely comic efforts.

"THE CAMEO FRAME" (1917). Poem. (Character: Acomba.) The afternoon air is golden. Acomba, a page, dresses the hair of the lady, who whispers to him even as he comments to her lord that the gold, gray, and rose colors by the marble pool create a cameo frame. She leaves, and the sun sets. At night she glides down a guarded hall to Acomba. The moon glow produces a different setting now; so his kiss presses the cameo back into its silver frame. When each day's sunset colors provide that frame of gold and rose, he, poor mortal, will think of golden hair and lips he cannot kiss.

CAMPBELL. In "Babylon Revisited," he is an American ex-drinker. Alix, a bartender in Paris, tells Charles J. Wales that Campbell is sick in Switzerland.

CAMPBELL. In "Too Cute for Words," he is Dizzy Campbell's father, who plans to drive his family to the Princeton-Harvard football game.

CAMPBELL, DIZZY. In "Too Cute for Words," she is Gwen Bowers's close friend, fourteen. The two girls and their friend Clara Hannaman visit the home of Dizzy's aunt, Mrs. Charles Wrotten Ray, primp there, and crash the Princeton prom dance.

CAMPBELL, GEORGIA BERRIMAN. In "Two Wrongs," she is a dancing instructor from whom Emmy Pinkard took lessons back home.

CAMPBELL, MRS. In "Too Cute for Words," she is Dizzy Campbell's mother. She and her family plan to attend the Princeton-Harvard football game.

CAMPION, LUIS. In *Tender Is the Night*, he is a homosexual who voyeuristically watches the duel between Tommy Barban and Albert McKisco on the Riviera golf course.

CANBY, CARLETON. In "The Cut-Glass Bowl," he is the frustrated suitor of Evylyn (*see* Piper, Evylyn), who marries Harold Piper. For a wedding present, Canby gives her the cut-glass bowl, which he says is like her—hard, beautiful, empty, and easy to see through.

CANBY, HORACE, LIEUTENANT. In "The Last of the Belles," he is an army pilot. When Ailie Calhoun encourages and then spurns him, he commits suicide by crashing his airplane.

CANISIUS, JOHN. In "The Guest in Room Nineteen," he is mentioned as Cass's partner, neither old nor young looking, but pockmarked.

CANNEL, JOHN. In "The Debutante," he is a handsome would-be suitor, twenty-two, of Helen Halycon. He is a guest at her coming-out party. She has encouraged him with kisses; but when he climbs toward her "boudoir" window to chat before the party, she rebuffs him. On the way down, he tears his suit.

CANNON. In "Financing Finnegan," he is the literary agent of the narrator and Finnegan. Cannon is modeled partly on Fitzgerald's agent Harold Ober.*

CAPPS-KARR, LADY. In "The Hotel Child," she is a British baronet's widow. She knows Ralph Berry and Marquis Bopes Kilkallow, gossips about Fifi Schwartz, and bails out Count Stanislas Karl Joseph Borowki.

"THE CAPTURED SHADOW" (1928). Short story. (Characters: Teddy Barnfield, Evelyn Beebe, Ham Beebe, Imogene Bissel, Hubert Blair, Riply Buckner, Jr., Estella Carrage, Connie Davies, Mayall De Bec, Joe Gorman, Miss Halliburton, Hilda, William S. Kampf, Basil Duke Lee, Mrs. Lee, Andy Lockheart, Mulligan, O'Hara, Professor Pumpkin, Chinaman Rudd, Miss Saunders, The Shadow, Rabbit Simmons, Washington Square, Stuyvesant, Margaret Torrence, Leilia Van Baker, Victor Van Baker, Gladys Van Schellinger, Mrs. Van Schellinger.) Basil, fifteen and a student at St. Regis in Eastchester, Connecticut, writes a three-act farce called *The Captured Shadow* and enlists his friends during summer vacation at home to act in it. Imogene Bissel is to play the female lead but has appendicitis and must go to Rochester, Minnesota, for surgery. So Basil persuades lovely Evelyn Beebe, sixteen, to take the part by getting Hubert Blair, only fifteen but popular and graceful—though cocky—to be the hero. Rehearsals start in August, but Hubert backs out with a lame excuse. Soon Evelyn must quit and accompany her family on a trip east. When Basil learns from his mother that Teddy Barnfield, a neighbor boy, has the mumps, he observes the boy playing safely alone in his yard. He does not advise Ham Beebe, Evelyn's brother, to avoid Teddy, thus allowing Ham to catch the disease, keeping the family in town, and he glories in Evelyn's performance when *The Captured Shadow*—with a leading boy imported from another school at the last minute—is put on for parents and friends. Basil and Evelyn kiss, but he is remorseful because of the mumps episode and conceals his shame from his puzzled mother.

THE CAPTURED SHADOW (1978). Play. (Characters: Charley, Beverly Connage, Dorothy Connage, Hubert Connage, Mrs. Beverly Connage, Thorton Hart Dudley, Leon Dureal, Emma Kate, James, McGinness, Helen Mayburn, Chinyman Rudd, Miss Saunders, Rabbit Simmons.) For some time Thorton Hart Dudley, known as the Shadow, has been robbing houses but then returning the loot. He sneaks into the New York home of Beverly Connage and her family, planning to do the same. When he is about to be arrested there, he shifts the blame first to the Connages' wayward son, Hubert, and then to a detective named Leon Dureal, and then he disappears. After much confusion, he returns, impresses the Connages' daughter, Dorothy, and reveals he made a bet he could outwit the New York police by committing daring robberies for a period of two weeks—now up, as the clock strikes twelve. Produced in St. Paul in August 1912, this play is noteworthy for its remarkably clever dialogue.

Bibliography: Margolies.

CARAMEL, RICHARD ("DICK"). In *The Beautiful and Damned*, he is one of Anthony Patch's closest friends and is from Kansas City. Gloria Gilbert's cousin, he introduces her to Anthony Patch. After Dick becomes a successful novelist with *The Demon Lover*, he writes short stories and more novels and sells his work to the movies. He shows off a little but genuinely tries to advise Anthony. Dick's career partly parallels that of Fitzgerald, whose portrayal of Dick's turning somewhat meretricious may be self-criticism.

CAREY, MARTHA. In "Bernice Bobs Her Hair," she is an acquaintance who Marjorie Harvey says would like to have Bernice's fine coloring. Martha Corey was hanged in 1692 for witchcraft.

CARHART, PETER. In "The Four Fists," he is a tough, successful New York businessman, built like Hercules. Through his friendship with Samuel Meredith's father, he hires Samuel. Ten years pass. When Samuel destroys a business deal in Texas, which would have deprived several ranchers of their beloved land, Carhart applauds Samuel and makes him his partner.

CARICAMENTO, JANICE. In *Tender Is the Night*, she is a woman Dick Diver, while at Innsbruck, imagines sleeping with on the Riviera.

CARL. In ''The Rich Boy,'' he is the night watchman at the Long Island lodge to which Anson Hunter takes Dolly Karger.

CARLETON, MRS. In ''A Freeze-Out,'' she was invited to the Rikkers' party after New Year's Day. She pretended deafness to avoid responding.

CARLETON, SAMMY. In *The Beautiful and Damned*, he is allegedly a supersalesman who recruits men to sell shares in his ''Heart Talks'' program. Anthony Patch tries to follow his suggestions, fails, and gets drunk.

CARLING. In ''Forging Ahead,'' he is the proprietor of a restaurant where Basil Duke Lee, when he is unhappy, thinks of going to drink with Elwood Leaming.

CARLING. In *This Side of Paradise*, he is a member of the 1915 Princeton class with whom Amory Blaine gets drunk in New York.

CARLSON, MISS. In ''Financing Finnegan,'' she is one of Cannon's secretaries.

CARLTON. In ''A Debt of Honor,'' he is a Confederate soldier too sick for sentry duty.

CARLYLE, CURTIS. In ''The Offshore Pirate,'' Toby Moreland assigns himself this name in the ruse. *See* Moreland, Toby.

CARMATLE. In ''The Room with the Green Blinds,'' he is the governor of Georgia. When Robert Calvin Raymond tells him about the mysterious room, he goes with Butler and Raymond to explore it and shoots John Wilkes Booth to death. Carmatle's name is also spelled Carmattyle.

CARMATLE. In ''The Room with the Green Blinds,'' he is the son of the man who later becomes governor of Georgia. John Wilkes Booth stole his Confederate uniform and left his own civilian clothes. Young Carmatle was later shot by Union soldiers.

CARMEL. In ''Crazy Sunday,'' she is a friend of Stella Walker Calman. Joel Coles offers to ask Carmel to comfort Stella after her husband's death. The name Carmel may have been suggested by that of Carmel Myers, a Hollywood actress whom Fitzgerald knew. In ''Lines on Reading through an Autograph Album,'' Carmel is named. *See* Blum, Carmel Myers.

CARNEY, HOWARD, DR. In ''Her Last Case,'' he is Bette Weaver's fiancé. He practices in New York, visits Bette while she is Ben Dragonet's nurse in Virginia, and trusts her too much.

CAROLINE. In ''At Your Age,'' she is Annie Lorry's aunt who disapproves of Annie's conduct.

CAROLINE. In ''O Russet Witch!,'' she is the beautiful, insolent, russet-haired New York woman who, when about nineteen, intrigues Merlin Grainger. When she dances on a table in Pulpat's restaurant, he resists her bewitching appeal and continues his engagement to Olive Masters. When Caroline stops traffic on Fifth Avenue, Olive, now his wife, drags him away. At that time Caroline was the correspondent in the Throckmorton divorce case. When she returns, white-haired, old, but still domineering, to his bookstore, it is too late. Caroline was the ex-dancer Alicia Dare and later the wealthy Mrs. Thomas Allerdyce. She has a grandson.

CAROLINE. In ''Sleeping and Waking,'' she is a girl Fitzgerald danced with in 1916, at least in a poem associated with his morning sleep.

CAROLINE. In ''A Snobbish Story,'' she is a person to whom John Boynton Bailey introduces Josephine Perry at the theater workshop.

CAROS MOROS, COUNT DE. In ''Indecision,'' he is a Spanish nobleman vacationing in Switzerland. He likes Rosemary Merriweather, who prefers Tommy McLane and accidentally breaks Caros's guitar while sleighing.

CARRAGE, ESTELLA. In ''The Captured Shadow,'' this is a character in Basil Duke Lee's play *The Captured Shadow* which was played by Margaret Torrence.

CARRAWAY. In *The Great Gatsby*, he is in the wholesale hardware business and advises his son, Nick Carraway, that if tempted to criticize others he should remember few have had his advantages.

CARRAWAY, NICK. In *The Great Gatsby*, he is the narrator. He graduated from Yale in 1915, served in the army in France during the war, and in spring 1922 begins to sell bonds in New York. Renting a house in West Egg, on Long Island, he becomes the neighbor of Jay Gatsby, whom he meets and only partly admires. He socializes with his cousin, Daisy Fay Buchanan, and her husband,

Tom Buchanan, who live in nearby East Egg. Through them Nick meets and falls in love with Jordan Baker, who tells him about Gatsby's love affair with Daisy. Nick makes arrangements for Gatsby's funeral, after which, coming to despise the fecklessness of rich Daisy and Tom, he plans to return to the Midwest. At one point, Nick laments turning thirty. The degree of Nick's trustworthiness as a narrator is the subject of critical debate.

CARROLL, PETER. In ''Babes in the Woods,'' he is a student in the sixth form at Hotchkiss. He is a guest at Elaine Terrell's party, where he meets Isabelle, but is dumped for Kenneth Powers.

CARSON. In ''The Adolescent Marriage,'' he is a person Llewellyn Clark helps design a country club.

CARSON. In ''Basil and Cleopatra,'' he is an assistant coach of the Yale freshman football team.

CARSON, MISS. In ''Lo, the Poor Peacock!,'' she is a nurse in the hospital where Annie Lee Davis is treated.

CARSTAIRS. In *This Side of Paradise*, he is a student at St. Regis whom Amory Blaine cites as a typical ''slicker.'' Unlike ''The Big Man,'' the slicker has social values, dresses well, chooses activities he can shine in, goes to college, is materialistically successful, and slicks his hair back.

CARSTAIRS, BILL. In *The Beautiful and Damned*, he is Gloria Gilbert Patch's former boyfriend.

CARTER. In ''A New Leaf,'' she is a mutual friend of Phil Hoffman and Dick Ragland. They mention his travels in Spain.

CARTER, DR. In ''An Alcoholic Case,'' he is the doctor assigned to the alcoholic cartoonist's case.

CARTER, ELEANOR. In ''Pat Hobby's Preview,'' she is a pretty blond from Boise, Idaho, in Hollywood touring the studio where Pat Hobby works. He thinks he is impressing her by taking her to ''his'' preview, but she considers him a loud-mouthed failure.

CARTER, GERALD. In ''Benediction,'' he is a novelist whom Lois knows and who, she tells Keith, laughs at the concept of immortality.

CARTON, JAMES. In ''The Rough Crossing,'' he is the steward who has appendicitis aboard ship, is operated on, dies, and is buried at sea.

CARTWRIGHT-SMITH. In *The Beautiful and Damned*, he is a man who suddenly called on Anthony Patch upon learning he was a millionaire.

CARTWRIGHT-SMITH, MRS. In *The Beautiful and Damned*, she and her husband suddenly recognized Anthony Patch socially upon learning of his wealth.

CARUSE, MADAME. In *Assorted Spirits*, she is the authoress of *Delia the Double-died*, cited by Second Story Salle.

CARUTHERS, MISS. In "Diamond Dick and the First Law of Woman," she was the Dickeys' cook when Diana Dickey was little.

CARVER. In "The Freshest Boy," he is the captain of the football team at St. Regis and is abusive to Basil Duke Lee.

CARY. In " 'The Sensible Thing,' " he is Jonquil Cary's quiet father. He likes George O'Kelly.

CARY, COLONEL. In "On Your Own," he is an aging Maryland friend of George Ives and his mother. His being a smirking guest at the Iveses' in New York embarrasses Evelyn Lovejoy, because six years earlier she had entertained him in New York as a "party girl."

CARY, DAISY. In "The Bowl," she is a movie actress, eighteen, who admires Dolly Harlan's courage and takes him away from Vienna Thorne.

CARY, EDITH. In "The Passionate Eskimo," she is the beautiful girl Pan-e-Troon regards as a goddess in Chicago. He rescues her family jewels from her butler, Christopher, and helps her become reconciled with Westgate.

CARY, ESTHER. In "A New Leaf," she is Julia Ross's former schoolmate. Julia introduces her to Dick Ragland to prove he has reformed. He soon pursues Esther.

CARY, HARRIET. In "The Jelly-Bean," she is one of the girls at the country-club dance.

CARY, JONQUIL. In " 'The Sensible Thing,' " she is the beautiful brunette in Tennessee who breaks her engagement to George O'Kelly, waits for him, and accepts him when he returns from Peru. Jonquil somewhat resembles Zelda Sayre Fitzgerald* before she married Fitzgerald.

CARY, MISS. In "One Interne," she is a nurse at the hospital. The egocentric behavior of William Tulliver IV as a patient causes her to say she will give up nursing.

CARY, MRS. In "The Scandal Detectives," she is the mother of Walter Cary and has consumption, according to the scandal book. In "That Kind of Party," she is the principal of Mrs. Cary's Academy, where Terrence R. Tipton is a sassy pupil. She threatens to tell his parents about his impertinence.

CARY, MRS. R. B. In " 'The Sensible Thing,' " she is Jonquil Cary's mother. She likes George O'Kelly.

CARY, WALTER. In "The Scandal Detectives," he is a boy expelled from school, according to the scandal book.

CASASUS. In *Tender Is the Night*, he is a Spanish bank teller in Paris with whom Dick Diver discusses their friend Featherstone.

CASE, HAROLD. In "The Bowl," he is an escort for Vienna Thorne and then Daisy Cary.

CASHMAEL, T. In "The Pusher-in-the-Face," he is the proprietor of the restaurant where Charles David Stuart is employed. When Stuart pushes the face of a customer who is then arrested for planning to rob the place, Cashmael is delighted.

CASS. In "The Guest in Room Nineteen," he is the old man, a stroke victim, who stays in a hotel and may fatally mistake a hotel worker for death personified. Or the worker may be death personified.

CASSIUS. In " 'Send Me In, Coach,' " he is a stupid boy, thirteen, who plays the part of Dr. McDougall in the play he and other lads rehearse.

CASTLE. In "Magnetism," he is the lawyer of George Hannaford, who finally does not need him to handle either his divorce or a blackmail scheme.

CASTLETON. In "Majesty," any of Theodore Castleton's children.

CASTLETON, EMILY. In "Majesty." *See* Petrocobesco, Emily Castleton.

CASTLETON, HAROLD, JR. In "Majesty," he is Emily Castleton's evidently ineffectual brother. He is a Harvard student.

CASTLETON, HAROLD, SR. In ''Majesty,'' he is Emily Castleton's wealthy father, distraught when she calls off her wedding to William Brevoort Blair. Later, when seventy-two and ill, he sends his niece, Olive Mercy Blair, who has married Blair, and Blair to Europe to try to rescue Emily from Prince Gabriel Petrocobesco.

CASTLETON, MRS. THEODORE. In ''Majesty,'' she is a guest at the wedding ceremony canceled by Emily Castleton.

CASTLETON, THEODORE. In ''Majesty,'' he is a guest at the wedding ceremony canceled by Emily Castleton.

CATES. In ''On an Ocean Wave,'' he is the shipboard swimming-pool steward, who, for a big bribe from Gaston T. Scheer, is going to throw overboard Professor Dollard, the lover of Scheer's wife, Minna Scheer.

CATHCART. In '' 'Send Me In, Coach,' '' he is a college athlete whose fringe benefits Rickey envies.

CATHCART, JIM. In ''A Short Trip Home,'' he is a friend of Eddie Stinson and Joe Jelke. Jim discovers that the mysterious stranger slugged Joe with brass knuckles.

CATHERINE. In *The Great Gatsby*, she is Myrtle Wilson's sister, about thirty. Myrtle uses the ruse of meeting Catherine in New York to rendezvous with Tom Buchanan. Catherine gossips inaccurately to Nick Carraway about the Buchanans and Jay Gatsby.

CATHERINE. In ''A Short Trip Home,'' she is one of the group at the hotel dance, including Ellen Baker, Jim Cathcart, Joe Jelke, and Eddie Stinson.

CATLIP. In *The Great Gatsby*, Nick Carraway lists his name on a timetable as among Jay Gatsby's summer guests.

CATO. In ''The Cruise of the Rolling Junk,'' this is the name Fitzgerald assigns to the haughty young man who tightens the Junk's loose wheel in Clarksville, North Carolina.

CAXTER, PETER. In ''Tarquin of Cheapside,'' he is a former Cambridge student and sailor, who is reading *The Faery Queene* when Soft Shoes (William Shakespeare) bursts into his room, demands to be hidden there from pursuers, and, when once safe, writes the beginning of ''The Rape of Lucrece.''

CECIL. In ''The Love Boat,'' he is a student McVitty orders to quit fighting.

CEDRIC. In ''Rags Martin-Jones and the Pr-nce of W-les,'' he is the elevator boy, from Wessex, whom John B. Chestnut hires to pretend to be the Prince of Wales.

CELESTE. In *Fie! Fie! Fi-Fi!*, she flirts and sings love songs with Archie, comments on various lovers, and uses makeup.

CELIE. In ''What a Handsome Pair!,'' she is Helen Van Beck Oldhorne's polo-playing friend. Joe Morgan, perhaps Celie's husband, wants her to ride sidesaddle while playing.

"CENSORSHIP OR NOT" (1923). Statement. Fitzgerald feels that a New York state bill to prohibit the sale of immoral books is itself immoral. It would allow books so dull they should be branded ''immoral'' to continue circulating but would also suppress misunderstood masterpieces by fine writers, a few of whom he specifies.

CHAFFEE, BOOK. In ''A Woman with a Past,'' he is a smooth-talking Yale student from Alabama. He lures Josephine Perry to the room in the armory of his friend Sergeant Boone. When she suspects a trap, she orders Chaffee to help her escape through a window. In ''Emotional Bankruptcy,'' he is one of several former boyfriends of Josephine Perry.

CHAMBERS. In '' 'The Sensible Thing,' '' he is George O'Kelly's boss in the New York insurance company. He fires George for demanding a second vacation too soon after the first.

CHAMBERS, MISS. In ''A Woman with a Past,'' she is a chaperone from Miss Brereton's school. She escorts Adele Craw, Lillian Hammel, and Josephine Perry when they go to the Yale prom.

CHAMORO, ELLA LEI. In ''The Honor of the Goon,'' she is a gentle college student, a Malay, who is hurt by being called a goon.

CHAMORO, LEI. In ''The Honor of the Goon,'' he is a well-to-do Malay relative of Ella Lei Chamoro. He resents her being called a goon by Bomar Winlock and Oates Mulkley and, in revenge, has Fingarson, his chauffeur, knock down both young men.

CHAMSON, ANDRÉ (1900–1983). Author, filmmaker, and museum curator. He was born into a Protestant family in Nîmes, France, was educated at Alès and Montpellier, earned a diploma as a museum director from the École des Chartes (1924) while serving in the French army (1918–1924), and moved up the ranks in this field. He married Lucie Mazauric in 1924. He wrote many books, including novels—notably *Les Hommes de la route* (1927) and antideterministic studies—converted several of his plots into movies, and lectured in Germany and Switzerland. He visited the Soviet Union in 1936 and Spain a year later, supported the Front Populaire, rejoined the French army in 1939, and fought in the resistance movement (1941–1945). Chamson was elected to the Académie Française (1956), became director of the National Archives in Paris (1960), and was then a popular cultural ambassador in Europe, Africa, and South America.

Chamson was Fitzgerald's closest French friend. They met in 1929 through their acquaintance Sylvia Beach, the Montparnasse bookstore proprietor who knew many American and French writers then in Paris. The two men proved congenial, despite language and money differences. Fitzgerald was instrumental in getting Max Perkins* to publish Chamson's *Les Hommes de la route*, as *The Road* (1929, translated by Van Wyck Brooks). Fitzgerald and Chamson planned to make a movie based on it, which King Vidor,* the American director then in Paris, agreed to make; but it proved untenable when Chamson decided not to visit Hollywood. Vidor's 1934 *Our Daily Bread* was so close to Chamson's work that he might have been sued for plagiarism. When Fitzgerald returned to Paris in 1929, he and Chamson saw each other a final time.

Bibliography: André Chamson, *La Petite Odyssée* (Paris: Gallimard, 1965), and ''Remarks by André Chamson,'' in *FH/A 1973*, 69–76; André Le Vot, *F. Scott Fitzgerald: A Biography*, trans. William Byron (Garden City, N.Y.: Doubleday, 1983).

CHANDELLE, JAQUES. In *Shadow Laurels*, he is the person, about thirty-seven, who returns to Paris to find out about his father, Jean Chandelle, who let him go as a child to America with an uncle.

CHANDELLE, JEAN. In *Shadow Laurels*, he is the deceased father of Jaques Chandelle, who let Jaques go to America with an uncle and never saw his son again. Jaques returns to Paris and learns from Jean's friends that Jean was a genius who could express their thoughts but who never wrote anything. Instead, he drank too much, fought, and died two years after being stabbed in a brawl.

CHANDLER. In ''Presumption,'' he is Cora Chandler's old father, who is dying upstairs in their Culpepper Bay home and is not to be disturbed.

CHANDLER. In ''Presumption,'' he is San Juan Chandler's father, now deceased. Wounded in the battle of San Juan Hill, he named his son in honor of the event.

CHANDLER, CORA. In ''Presumption,'' she is San Juan Chandler's mother's cousin. She is a Bostonian and has a Culpepper Bay home which San Juan visits. She demeans him as a poor relative but fortunately tells him Noel Garneau's aunt is Jo Poindexter of New York.

CHANDLER, MRS. In ''Presumption,'' she is San Juan Chandler's widowed mother, of Akron, Ohio. She is tearful when he quits college, takes his inheritance, and moves to Boston.

CHANDLER, SAN JUAN ("DON," "SANTY"). In ''Presumption,'' he is from Akron, Ohio. He was named San Juan because his father was wounded at the battle of San Juan Hill. Juan is a shy student at Henderson College, when at twenty during the summer before his senior year he visits Cora Chandler, his mother's cousin at Culpepper Bay, near Boston, to see Noel Garneau again. Juan takes her father Harold Garneau's indirect advice, quits school, gains a fortune through an investment, and successfully pursues Noel from Boston to New York.

"A CHANGE OF CLASS" (1931). Short story. (Characters: Berry, Dunois, Hertzog, Cecil Jadwin, Philip Jadwin, Earl Johnson, Violet Johnson, Dr. Jordan, Mrs. Lemmon, Shalder, Howard Shalder, Irene Shalder.) In 1926 (in Wilmington), rich Philip Jadwin, thirty-one, is asked by his barber, Earl Johnson, in the Jadwin Hotel barbershop, for a stock-market tip and brusquely gives him one. The result is quick wealth for Earl, who buys property and quits barbering. His wife, Violet, once a manicurist in the shop, puts on airs and gets too friendly with their bootlegger neighbor, Howard Shalder, even though—as Jadwin discovers while driving in Earl's neighborhood in June 1929—Shalder is married to sweet Irene, whom Jadwin was silently in love with when she was his office typist in the Hertzog Building. Then comes the Crash, and Earl returns to barbering. In April 1930 Violet takes the family savings of $2,000 and leaves with Shalder. Irene, who has a baby, laments to Jadwin. He rehires her. Earl, never at ease with his wealth and new class, happy his materialistic wife is leaving, but not knowing his money is gone, asks Jadwin to let him buy the barbershop in the Hertzog Building. Jadwin agrees, accepts his check, knowing it is worthless, and tears it up. Earl is happy in the shop. In ''Afternoon of an Author,'' Fitzgerald says that ''A Change of Class'' caused hard feelings because its origins were identifiable.

CHAPMAN, WILLIAM. In *Assorted Spirits*, he is Miss Spigot's nephew, returns to town after three years, and as a railroad contracting engineer offers Peter Wetherby $15,000 for his property. He will marry Cecile Wetherby, who has loved him a long while.

CHARLEY. In *The Captured Shadow*, he is the owner of an opium den known by Chinyman Rudd and Rabbit Simmons.

CHARLIE. In ''A Short Autobiography,'' he is a fellow drinker in France in 1916.

CHARLIE. In *Tender Is the Night*, he is a sailor Tommy Barban and Nicole Diver, while in their hotel room, see fighting on the beach.

CHASE. In ''No Flowers,'' he is a twin whose driving a taxi distresses Marjorie Clark.

CHASE, REYNOLD. In ''A Freeze-Out,'' he is named as the father of Cathy Chase Rikker.

CHÂTEAU. In *Tender Is the Night*, he is a swimmer who aids Dick Diver after he falls foolishly while trying to water ski.

CHEADLE. In *The Great Gatsby*, Nick Carraway lists his name on a timetable as one of Jay Gatsby's summer guests. He is from farther out on Long Island.

"A CHEER FOR PRINCETON" (1915). Poem. When the black-and-orange Princeton tiger growls and plays, Eli has no chance. Raise a cheer, and Nassau will make the town proud.

CHEEVER, BESSIE BELLE. In ''Basil and Cleopatra,'' she is a girlfriend who invites Erminie Gilberte Labouisse Bibble to visit her in Mobile, Alabama.

CHESTNUT, JOHN B. In ''Rags Martin-Jones and the Pr-nce of W-les,'' he is the wealthy American who stages a ruse in a New York night club to get Rags Martin-Jones to marry him.

CHEVRIL. In ''Diagnosis,'' he is a former Confederate soldier who chats with Charlie Clayhorne in Tuscarora, Alabama.

CHILICHEFF. In ''The Rich Boy,'' this is the name of the Russian family Edna Hunter and Cary Sloane tell Anson Hunter must have gossiped falsely about their affair.

CHILLICHEFF, PRINCE. In *Tender Is the Night*, he is a white Russian, about fifty, whom Tommy Barban helps escape from Communist Russia. Tommy introduces him to Dick Diver in Munich.

CHOLMONDELY. In *Fie! Fie! Fi-Fi!*, he calls himself Tommy Atkins of the Guards and hints at his ability to break hearts.

CHOYNSKI, MRS. In ''Jacob's Ladder,'' she is the sister of young Jenny Delehanty (later Jenny Prince) and is convicted in New York of murdering her sailor lover with a meat axe. Mrs. Choynski's maiden name was Delehanty.

CHRISTOPHER. In "The Passionate Eskimo," he is the butler in Edith Cary's home. He steals her jewels, but Pan-e-troon gets them back.

CHROME. In *The Great Gatsby*, his name is listed by Nick Carraway on a timetable as among Jay Gatsby's summer guests. He is from New York.

CHRYSTIE, MRS. In *The Great Gatsby*, Nick Carraway lists her name on a timetable as one of Jay Gatsby's summer guests. She came with Hubert Auerbach.

"CITY DUSK" (1918). Poem. As darkness flows past, the poet closes his book, hears street sounds, and eagerly awaits his lovely friend.

CIVET, WEBSTER, DR. In *The Great Gatsby*, Nick Carraway lists his name on a timetable as among Jay Gatsby's summer guests. He later drowned in Maine.

"THE CLAIMS OF THE *LIT*" (1920). Letter. Fitzgerald writes in the *Princeton Alumni Weekly* that the *Nassau Literary Magazine* should be endowed but that the blue-nosed Philadelphian society should not be.

CLAIR, ELENOR. In *Thoughtbook*, she is a friend.

CLAN-CARLY, LORD. In "The Rubber Check," he is a person about whose 1929 Newport coming-of-age party Val Schuyler reminisces.

CLANCY, MISS. In "Hot and Cold Blood," she is an employee of James Mather, who is so good-natured that he apologizes to her for being irritable.

CLARA. In " 'Why Blame It on the Poor Kiss if the Girl Veteran of Many Petting Parties Is Prone to Affairs After Marriage?'," she is the wife of Harry's best friend. Still, Harry's wife, Georgianna, will not let him go out with her.

CLARE. In "A Snobbish Story," this is evidently the name of the heroine in John Boynton Bailey's play *Race Riot*. Bailey wants Josephine Perry, not his wife Evelyn, to take the role.

CLARENCE. In "Imagination—and a Few Mothers," he is a person for whom Mrs. Paxton did not organize a family orchestra.

CLARIS. In *The Last Tycoon*, she is evidently a prostitute whom the unhappy, handsome actor tells Monroe Stahr he visited.

CLARK. In ''No Flowers,'' he is Amanda Rawlins Clark's husband and Marjorie Clark's father.

CLARK, AMANDA RAWLINS. In ''No Flowers,'' she is Marjorie Clark's beautiful mother. She recalls events at the university prom twenty years earlier, when she lost Carter McLane's affection. She chaperones the prom to which Marjorie is invited and wishes the young people all around her would seize happiness now.

CLARK, BOB. In *Thoughtbook*, he is a close friend.

CLARK, CAROLINE. In *Thoughtbook*, she is a tomboy friend.

CLARK, JESSE. In ''The Adolescent Marriage,'' he is mentioned as Llewellyn Clark's father.

CLARK, LLEWELLYN. In ''The Adolescent Marriage,'' he is the architect, twenty, employed by Chauncey Garnett. Llewellyn eloped with Lucy Wharton; they are reconciled after arguments and a separation.

CLARK, LUCY WHARTON. In ''The Adolescent Marriage,'' she is the spoiled, rebellious girl, sixteen, who elopes with Llewellyn Clark, thinks their marriage is annulled, plans to wed George Hemmick, but returns pregnant to Llewellyn.

CLARK, MARJORIE. In ''No Flowers,'' she is Amanda Rawlins Clark's attractive daughter, eighteen. She is happy to be attending the prom as William Delaney Johns's date, despite regarding her dull life as in a ''tin age'' compared to her mother's ''gold age.''

CLAUDE. In ''The Evil Eye,'' he and Dulcinea sing about dreams.

CLAUDE. In *Tender Is the Night*, he is a bartender at the Ritz in Paris. Abe North talks with him.

CLAVINE. In *Shadow Laurels*, he was a person with whom Jean Chandelle fought in Pitou's wineshop long ago.

CLAY, COLLINS. In *Tender Is the Night*, he is a Yale student from Georgia. He likes Rosemary Hoyt and sees her first in Paris and again later, while he is studying architecture, in Rome. He tells Dick Diver about her affair with Bill Hillis of Yale. She regards Clay as a nitwit.

"CLAY FEET" (1981). Poem. The poet sees wrecked spots once glorified by brave men and graceful women. Were they fakes? He is free, but liberty weighs him down.

CLAYHORNE. In ''Diagnosis,'' he was the father of Ben Clayhorne and Dicky Clayhorne by his third wife, Charlie Clayhorne by his second wife, and Pete Clayhorne by his first wife. He left a vindictive last will and testament.

CLAYHORNE, BEN. In ''Diagnosis,'' he is Charlie Clayhorne's younger half brother, a Princeton student.

CLAYHORNE, CHARLIE. In ''Diagnosis,'' he is a half brother of Ben Clayhorne, Dicky Clayhorne, and Pete Clayhorne. Charlie is the fiancé of Sara Etherington and an employee of her uncle, Henry Cortelyou, in New York. He goes to Tuscarora, Alabama, to rectify the consequences of having hidden his father's final will.

CLAYHORNE, DICKY. In ''Diagnosis,'' he is Charlie Clayhorne's youngest half brother, eleven.

CLAYHORNE, PETE. In ''Diagnosis,'' he is Charlie Clayhorne's older half brother and an ex-convict.

CLAYTON. In ''Hot and Cold Blood,'' he is a broker of the firm of Clayton and Drake. James Mather unsuccessfully asks Clayton's partner, Fred Drake, for a temporary loan.

CLEOPATRA. In *Safety First!*, she is a latter-day Cleopatra who deals with parlor snakes now.

CLOS D'HIRONDELLE, MARQUIS DE LA. In ''One Trip Abroad,'' he is Count Chiki Sarolai's brother-in-law, supposedly a successful Paris banker.

CLOTHILDE. In ''New Types,'' she is Emily Holliday's maid. Fitzgerald probably had fun naming this character Clothilde (and the next one listed) after his sister-in-law, Clothilde Sayre Palmer, whom he disliked.

CLOTHILDE. In *This Side of Paradise*, she is a servant in Beatrice O'Hara Blaine's home. *See* Clothilde, immediately above.

CLOUD, MARION. In ''The Camel's Back,'' she is the pretty girl at the circus ball who suggests that the marriage of Betty Medill and Perry Parkhurst can be annulled, perhaps because she likes Perry herself.

CLOVER. In *Fie! Fie! Fi-Fi!*, she is a girl with parts partly replaced by her physician father. She and Blossom love Archie. Clover criticizes Celeste for using makeup.

CODMAN, RUSSEL. In "Your Way and Mine," he is Harry McComas's business associate. Codman's successful commercial way resembles McComas's more than McComas likes; so he hopes Codman will not marry his daughter, Honoria McComas.

CODY, DAN. In *The Great Gatsby*, he was a millionaire prospector in his fifties whom Jay Gatsby met in 1907, stayed with as loyal companion and assistant for five years, and would have been willed $25,000 when Cody died in 1912 but for the machinations of Ella Kaye. Gatsby's friendship with Cody is based on the friendship of Fitzgerald's friend Robert Kerr, of Great Neck, Long Island, and a yachtsman named Major Edward (or Edwin) R. Gilman.

Bibliography: Joseph Corso, "One Not-Forgotten Summer Night: Sources for Fitzgerald's Symbols of American Character in *The Great Gatsby*," *FH/A 1976*, 8–33.

COE, JACK. In "A Woman with a Past," he is a Yale student leader whose attack of appendicitis makes it necessary for Dudley Knowleton to supervise, in his place, the Yale prom attended by Josephine Perry and others.

COHEN, CLYDE. In *The Great Gatsby*, his name is listed by Nick Carraway on a timetable as among Jay Gatsby's summer guests. He is from West Egg and is connected with the movies.

COHEN, DR. In "Family in the Wind," he is an old physician who comes from Wettala to Bending to help treat those injured in the first tornado, for as long as he is able.

COLA, CAPONE. In "Indecision," he is an American vacationing with family and friends in Switzerland. His group is called his harem.

COLA, MRS. In "Indecision," she is vacationing with her husband and family in Switzerland.

COLAHAN, MISS. In "Two Wrongs," she is William McChesney's secretary in his New York office.

COLAZZO, DR. In *Tender Is the Night*, he is a Roman physician whom Baby Warren asks an embassy official to summon to help Dick Diver.

COLBERT, CLAUDETTE (1905–1996). Movie actress. In *The Last Tycoon*, she and Ronald Colman* appear in a Monroe Stahr film.

COLBY. In ''One Trip Abroad,'' he, with his wife, is defined by Oscar Dane as a third-rate member of the Kellys' drifting, drinking crowd.

COLBY, MRS. In ''One Trip Abroad,'' she is defined by Oscar Dane as third-rate.

COLE, MISS. In ''That Kind of Party,'' she is the teacher Terrence R. Tipton corrects when she says Mexico City is the capitol of Central America.

COLEMAN, MRS. HENRY. In ''Dalyrimple Goes Wrong,'' she does not recognize Bryan Dalyrimple when he flashes his electric torch in her face during a robbery in her home.

COLES, JOEL. In ''Crazy Sunday,'' he is a screenwriter, twenty-eight, who works for Miles Calman and tries to lessen his alcohol intake. He listens to the squabbles of Miles and his wife, Stella Walker Calman, with whom Joel falls in love. When Miles is killed in an airplane crash, Joel bitterly accepts the fact that he will return (to Stella, to Hollywood?). Coles is partly an autobiographical figure but is also partly based on the screenwriter Dwight Taylor, who attended the Sunday tea party with Fitzgerald at the mansion of Irving Thalberg* and his wife, Norma Shearer.*

Bibliography: Dwight Taylor, *Joy Ride* (New York: Putnam, 1959); Lambert.

COLLINS, CAPTAIN. In *The Beautiful and Damned*, he is Captain Wolf's friend. The two double-date with Gloria Gilbert Patch and Rachel Jerryl Barnes. When Collins gets fresh, Gloria tells him off.

COLLINS, MARJORIE. In ''The Bridal Party,'' she knew Hamilton Rutherford two years earlier, tries to blackmail him in Paris, but is silenced by the police.

COLLINS, MISS. In ''In the Holidays,'' she is the pretty nurse Joe Kinney gets fresh with in the hospital he has checked himself into for an alibi.

COLMAN, RONALD (1891–1958). Movie actor, born in Richmond, Surrey, England. After service in the British army in World War I, he left the British theater for a career in Hollywood, in silent pictures at first, and then in sound movies, most successfully because of his cultivated voice. In ''The Homes of the Stars,'' Pat Hobby, pretending to be Colman's close friend, is showing Deering R. Robinson and his wife Colman's home when the actor fortuitously comes out and addresses Pat by his first name. In *The Last Tycoon*, Monroe Stahr names him, along with Margaret Sullavan, as one he would not cast in a movie under discussion; Colman and Claudette Colbert* appear in another Stahr movie. In ''Pat Hobby's Preview,'' Pat takes Eleanor Carter to Colman's rehearsal in a vain attempt to impress her. When Fitzgerald thought of making a movie out of *Tender Is the Night*, he suggested Colman for the part of Dick Diver. In other fiction, Fitzgerald occasionally mentions Colman.

Bibliography: R. Dixon Smith, *Ronald Colman, a Gentleman of the Cinema: A Biography and Filmography* (Jefferson, N.C.: McFarland, 1991).

COLMAR, MME DE. In ''Flight and Pursuit,'' she is a woman from Deauville of no interest to Caroline Martin Corcoran.

"COLORS HAS SHE IN HER SOUL" (1981). Poem. Although her inner being is colorful, rain, lights, trees, and busy people are outside.

COLUMN, PHOEBE. In *This Side of Paradise*, she is a girl whose apartment in Manhattan Amory Blaine goes to on a double date with Fred Sloane and Axia Marlowe. From there Amory follows what proves to be the ghost of Dick Humbird.

COMBRINCK, LADY SYBIL. In ''Two Wrongs,'' she is the London high-society lady with whom William McChesney was evidently intimate. When he appears uninvited at her evening party, she indicates her resentment at his gossiping about her by having him thrown out. In the original version of ''Two Wrongs,'' her name is Lady Caroline Sibley-Biers.

COMBRINCK, LORD. In ''Two Wrongs,'' he is Lady Sybil Combrinck's husband.

"COME IN! COME IN!" (1981). Poem. The poet offers a dangerous drink.

COMERFORD, R. R. In ''The Popular Girl,'' he is a Midwestern flour millionaire whose mansion Yanci Bowman shows Scott Kimberly when they are driving together after the dance.

COMPSON, DR. In '' 'Trouble,' '' he is the supervisor to whom Mrs. Johnston reports nurse Glenola McClurg's discourtesy in an unsuccessful effort to get her fired.

COMSTOCK, MRS. In ''Benediction,'' she is a friend of the mother of Keith and Lois. He tells Lois that when she was an infant, their nervous mother used to go and cry with Mrs. Comstock for comfort.

"CONFESSIONS" (1923). Open letter. *See* Conrad, Joseph.

CONK. In "Pat Hobby's Secret," he is the owner of the Los Angeles bar where Pat Hobby tricks R. Parke Woll into revealing the secret ending of his movie script.

CONKLIN, CUCKOO. In "The Perfect Life," he is a teacher of French at St. Regis.

CONNAGE, ALEC. In *This Side of Paradise*, he is a Princeton student, from Hotchkiss. Amory Blaine becomes his friend, falls in love with his sister, Rosalind Connage, and rooms with him in New York. When Alec is about to be caught in a hotel room with a woman not his wife, Amory takes the blame, which favor he predicts will alienate him from Alec.

CONNAGE, BEVERLY. In *The Captured Shadow*, he is owner of the New York home robbed by Thorton Hart Dudley, known as the Shadow. His children are Hubert Connage and Dorothy Connage.

CONNAGE, CECELIA. In *This Side of Paradise*, she is the young sister of Alec Connage and Rosalind Connage.

CONNAGE, DOROTHY. In *The Captured Shadow*, she is Beverly Connage's daughter, eighteen, and is attracted to Thorton Hart Dudley.

CONNAGE, HUBERT. In *The Captured Shadow*, he is Beverly Connage's son, twenty-two. His drunkenness makes it possible for Thorton Hart Dudley to enter the Connages' house. Hubert is to marry Helen Mayburn.

CONNAGE, LELAND R. In *This Side of Paradise*, he is the well-to-do New Yorker who, with his wife, seeks a marriage into wealth for their daughter, Rosalind Connage.

CONNAGE, MRS. BEVERLY. In *The Captured Shadow*, she is Beverly Connage's wife and the mother of Hubert Connage and Dorothy Connage.

CONNAGE, MRS. LELAND R. In *This Side of Paradise*, she is the dignified, worn-out mother of Alec Connage, Cecelia Connage, and Rosalind Connage. She likes Amory Blaine but wants Rosalind to marry money.

CONNAGE, ROSALIND. In *This Side of Paradise*, she is the beautiful, spoiled daughter of wealthy Leland R. Connage and his wife, of New York. As a debutante, nineteen, she is given a fancy dance party and loves Amory Blaine, who is twenty-three. She cannot accept the notion of a life of poverty with him, however, and will marry instead J. Dawson Ryder. She remains the main love of Amory's life. Rosalind's personality is based partly on Zelda Sayre Fitzgerald's.*

CONRAD, JOSEPH (1857–1924). Author. He was born Józef Teodor Konrad Korzeniowski in or near Berdichev, in Polish Ukraine. After his parents died, he attended school in Kraków (1869–1873), went to Marseilles (1874), and embarked on a career at sea, rising from common sailor to mate and master (1875–1894). He became a naturalized British citizen (1885) and began to write (1886). He married Jessie George (1896); they had two sons and lived in some poverty. His friends included Stephen Crane, Henry James, and H. G. Wells.* Conrad wrote out of his own experience and with painful slowness; his purpose was to make his reader see and feel what he had known. His extensive list of novels and short stories includes *Almayer's Folly* (1895), *The Nigger of the ''Narcissus''* (1898), ''Youth'' (1898), ''Heart of Darkness'' (1899), *Lord Jim* (1900), *Nostromo* (1904), *The Secret Agent* (1907), ''The Secret Sharer'' (1910), *Under Western Eyes* (1911), *Victory* (1915), and *The Rover* (1923).

Fitzgerald held Conrad in high esteem. Perhaps encouraged by H. L. Mencken,* he began to appreciate Conrad's technique in 1920 or so. In 1923, when Conrad was a guest of publisher Frank Nelson Doubleday, at Oyster Bay, Long Island, Fitzgerald and Ring Lardner* got drunk, danced on Doubleday's lawn hoping to attract Conrad, but were ejected by a caretaker for trespassing. In a 1923 open letter, Fitzgerald replied to a *Chicago Tribune* critic who had asked him what book he would most wish he had written by naming *Nostromo*. Fitzgerald says that although its hero both exists in reality and has appeared in fiction, Conrad has treated him completely. Conrad regarded *Nostromo* as his best book. Fitzgerald praised Conrad twice more in 1923: in ''10 Best Books I Have Read,'' he lists *Nostromo* and describes it as ''[t]he great novel'' of the last half century; and in a review of *Through the Wheat* by Thomas Alexander Boyd* he says Conrad's ''Youth'' gives him an almost unique thrill. The stylistic advance shown in *The Great Gatsby* is partly owing to Fitzgerald's awareness of Conrad's skill in employing the observer-narrator, notably in ''Heart of Darkness'' and *Lord Jim*. Fitzgerald wrote to Mencken (23 April 1934) and Ernest Hemingway* (1 June 1934) that the understated ending of *Tender Is the Night* was deliberate because Conrad, in his preface to *The Nigger of the ''Narcissus''*, discusses the effectiveness of planting aftereffects in a reader's imagination.

Bibliography: Adam Gillon, *Joseph Conrad* (Boston: Twayne, 1982); Frederick R. Karl, *Joseph Conrad: Three Lives, a Biography* (New York: Farrar, Straus, and Giroux, 1979).

CONSTANCE. In ''Emotional Bankruptcy,'' she is Josephine Perry's married sister and lives in Chicago.

CONSUELA. In *The Great Gatsby*, she is a person Nick Carraway vaguely remembers as among Jay Gatsby's summer guests.

"CONTEMPORARY WRITERS AND THEIR WORK, A SERIES OF AUTOBIOGRAPHICAL LETTERS—F. SCOTT FITZGERALD" (1920). Letter. Fitzgerald explains how "The Ice Palace" evolved out of conversations with three girls—first, in St. Paul, about cold climates making people chilly and hard; second, in Montgomery, about feelings in a Confederate graveyard; and third, about personalities of cats and dogs. Fitzgerald explains how he wrote the story in stages and enjoyed the process. In "The Ice Palace," which contrasts South and North, Tarleton is based on Montgomery, Zelda Sayre Fitzgerald's* hometown; the Northern city, on St. Paul. Sally Carrol Happer calls Southerners feline and Northerners canine.

CONVERSE, TED. In *This Side of Paradise*, he is a St. Regis student for whom Amory Blaine predicts school failure, business and marital success, and early death.

COOK, DR. In *Safety First!*, he is identified by Percy as a patron of Post-impressionist art.

COOLEY, JAMES ("JIM"). In "Not in the Guidebook," he is an American war veteran who stole German regimental orders from an enemy corpse near Château-Thierry and made himself a hero by lying about it. In 1922 in Brooklyn he marries Milly, spends her inheritance, and returns with her to France, where he says he has a job caring for graves of the American dead. An abusive alcoholic, he leaves the train taking them toward Paris and goes without Milly on a binge in Evreux. Authorities locate him, and he proceeds to Paris.

COOLEY, MILLY. In "Not in the Guidebook," she is a sweet Brooklyn girl of Czech-Romanian descent. In 1922, at eighteen, she marries James Cooley. When she inherits $250 from her mother, they go to France. Jim abandons her and goes on a binge in Evreux. She is befriended in Paris by William Driscoll, a veteran and now a tour guide. They soon marry.

COOLIDGE, CALVIN (1872–1933). Thirtieth president of the United States. In "Outside the Cabinet-Maker's," his collar box hides a clue in the fairy tale the man tells to his daughter.

COOPER, GARY (1901–1961). Movie actor. In *The Last Tycoon*, he dines at the Trocadero when Cecelia Brady, Monroe Stahr, and Brimmer are there. In "The Big Academy Dinner," he is mentioned as present.

COOTS, MRS. In ''Not in the Guidebook,'' she is an affluent American in Paris. She wants to hire Milly Cooley as a companion for $25 a week, but Milly prefers to remain with Mrs. Horton.

CORCORAN. In ''A Penny Spent,'' he is a American, born in Paris and penniless there. Julius Bushmill hires him to escort his wife, Jessie Pepper Bushmill, and their daughter, Hallie Bushmill, around Europe while he is off on business. Corcoran legitimately but extravagantly spends Bushmill's money showing the women a fine time, mostly in Brussels. Claude Nosby, Hallie's fiancé, joins them to go to Italy but is no match for Corcoran, who shows Hallie Capri's Blue Grotto while Nosby is seasick, foils would-be Italian robbers south of Naples, marries Hallie, and joins her father's company as head of the purchasing department.

CORCORAN, CAROLINE MARTIN. In ''Flight and Pursuit,'' she is the girl from Derby, Virginia, who when mistreated by Sidney Lahaye marries weak George Corcoran on the rebound. After living in poverty in Dayton, Ohio, with him and his domineering mother for three years, she takes her son, Dexter Corcoran, to New York. She works as a secretary, goes to Europe with Helen O'Connor, sees repentant and generous Sidney, but rebuffs him. When, while in a Swiss sanitorium recovering from tuberculosis, she hears Sidney is missing and is then rescued, she cables her love to him and asks him to come back to her.

CORCORAN, DEXTER. In ''Flight and Pursuit,'' he is the son of Caroline Martin Corcoran and George Corcoran. She takes him to New York and Europe. He attends school in France. Fitzgerald both hints and denies that Dexter is Sidney Lehaye's son.

CORCORAN, GEORGE (''GEORGIE''). In ''Flight and Pursuit,'' he is Caroline Martin Corcoran's weak husband. They live in Dayton, Ohio, until Caroline leaves with their son, Dexter. There is a hint that George is unfaithful to Caroline.

CORCORAN, MRS. In ''Flight and Pursuit,'' she is George Corcoran's domineering mother and his wife, Caroline's, meddling mother-in-law.

CORCORAN, MRS. In ''Your Way and Mine,'' she is a housekeeper in the New York home of Henry McComas and his wife Stella McComas. Her deafness prevents her from hearing businessmen at the McComas's front door.

CORKER, BILL. In ''Two Old-Timers,'' he was the director of *The Final Push*, the 1925 war movie starring Phil Macedon. Corker got a good scene out of Macedon without his knowing it was being filmed.

CORLISS, JOHN. In "No Flowers," he is a local movie usher, which distresses Marjorie Clark.

CORN, CAPTAIN. In *This Side of Paradise*, he is a British officer in New York after World War I. Amory Blaine remembers meeting him while Amory is drunk.

CORNHILL, MRS. In *The Last Tycoon*, she is one of three people eager to discuss the Russian movie Monroe Stahr wants to make. The other two are Drummon and Kirstoff.

CORRIGAN. In *The Great Gatsby*, Nick Carraway lists his name on a timetable as among Jay Gatsby's summer guests.

CORTELYOU, HENRY. In "Diagnosis," he is Charlie Clayhorne's boss and Sara Etherington's uncle.

COSTELLO. In "The Offshore Pirate," this is one of the names in one of Curtis Carlyle's songs.

COSTELLO, BILL. In "A Man in the Way," he is a business associate whose conference with Jack Berners cannot be interrupted by Pat Hobby.

"COUNTER SONG TO THE 'UNDERTAKER' " (1981). Poem. Princeton is happy only when defeating Yale.

"THE COUNT OF DARKNESS" (1935). Short story. (Characters: Barthelmi, Friar Brian, Gautier, Granny, Guescelin, Jacques, Letgarde, Count Philippe of Villefranche, Renaud.) Philippe, Count of Villefranche, now master of a domain near the Loire in Touraine, prepares to organize his fiefdom. He spies Letgarde, a comely girl of seventeen from Aquitaine, and kisses her roughly. After breakfast in camp, he gallops off with her to a hill and orders several men to build a house there. After posting sullen Letgarde to warn him of any danger, he rides off, but she deserts with a singing, blond-bearded tramp. When a caravan of traders headed for Brittany arrives, Philippe, supported by his followers, demands a tithe of their possessions as tribute before letting them cross "his" ford. The singer has led some of the traders, however, to another crossing. Philippe gathers women from the region and will soon supervise some quick marriages. Ten days pass. Gossip has it that the girl, whose features Philippe muses about, has departed. Two days later, while fishing for eels, he finds Letgarde's drowned body, is sorry for treating her roughly, orders her careful burial, and solemnly adopts a tiny girl orphaned in the recent fighting. The editors captioned "The Count of Darkness" "this majestic story of 879 A.D."

COURRU, PIERRE. In *Shadow Laurels*, he is a person Jean Chandelle long ago tried to stab in Pitou's wineshop for drinking his sherry.

COWAN, KENNETH. In *The Beautiful and Damned*, he is Gloria Gilbert Patch's former boyfriend.

COWAN, MARY. In ''A Freeze-Out,'' she is named by Pierce Winslow as a person with whom he would not socialize. She invited Cathy Chase Rikker to parties in Washington, D.C., but Mrs. Rikker never appeared—perhaps because she was embarrassed about her husband's business dealings.

COWARD (1978). Play. (Characters: Lieutenant Percy Altwater, Cecilia Ashton, John Ashton, Angelina Bangs, Georgie Bangs, Private Barkis, Judge Arthur Douglas, Charles Douglas, Clara Douglas, Lindy Douglas, Mary Douglas, Tommy Douglas, Miss Finch, Miss Grayson, Miss Hazelton, Jim Holworthy, Ned Holworthy, Jefferson, Private Johnson, Captain Ormsby, Miss Pruit, Eddie Randolph, Miss Spence, Miss Spindle, Dick Taylor, Virginia Taylor, Tompkins, Mrs. Tompkins, Wilkins, Private Willings.) The scene is a Virginia plantation in 1861. Charles Douglas is a Confederate lieutenant. Arthur Douglas and Mary Douglas, his parents, want their neighbor, Jim Holworthy, to join up. Their daughter, Lindy Douglas, refuses his proposal and calls him a coward. Charles, his unit in retreat, enters and hands Lindy $12,000 in Union money he confiscated, but he is captured when Jim reveals his hiding place. Jim joins the Confederate army, fights bravely, saves Charles after that man escapes, and becomes a captain. The two return home when peace is declared. Jefferson, a black servant of Mary Douglas, who is now a widow, finds the Union money in a chest of unused linens. Jim proposes again to Lindy, saves her from two pillaging Union soldiers, and is accepted. A subplot involves Lieutenant Percy Altwater, Charles's British-born army friend, and Virginia Taylor, Lindy's friend. The play was performed in St. Paul in August 1913 and in Dellwood, Minnesota, in September 1913.

Bibliography: Margolies.

COWLEY, MALCOLM (1898–1989). Critic and editor. He was born near Belsano, Pennsylvania, attended public school in Pittsburgh (with future critic Kenneth Burke, perhaps his closest friend), entered Harvard in 1915, drove munitions trucks for the Franco-American Military Transport Service in France during the war (1917), vacillated between Harvard and New York (1918–1920), married painter Marguerite Baird (1919), and graduated from Harvard (1920). After living on little money as a freelance writer in New York's Greenwich Village (1920–1921), he and his wife went to France, where he studied French literature at the University of Montpellier and earned a diploma there (1922). He associated with American expatriates in Paris, including Ernest Hemingway,* Ezra Pound, and Gertrude Stein,* before returning to New York in 1923. He coedited *Broom* (1923–1924), bought a farm in New York near Sherman, Connecticut (1927), published a book of poetry titled *Blue Juniata* (1929), became literary editor of the *New Republic* (1929–1940), and was divorced by his wayward wife (1931). He married fashion editor Muriel Maurer (1932); published *Exile's Return: A Narrative of Ideas* (1934), a study of the American expatriation movement in postwar France; flirted with aspects of Marxism; attended the World Congress of Writers in Madrid (1937); and edited and contributed essays to *After the Genteel Tradition* (1937). During the early years of World War II, Cowley was smeared for alleged Communist leanings but continued his career: he translated French works; edited works by Hemingway (1944), his friend William Faulkner (1946), and Nathaniel Hawthorne (1948); taught at universities (1950–1966); and, by publishing into his late eighties, made himself into a premier critic, memoirist, and cultural historian of his times.

Cowley's life rarely intersected with Fitzgerald's, although the two addressed each other in letters as Scott and Malcolm. Cowley visited the Fitzgeralds in 1933 in Baltimore, where the novelist's out-of-control condition depressed him. He wrote to Fitzgerald (22 May 1933) that Zelda Sayre Fitzgerald's* *Save Me the Waltz* moved him greatly. In his *New Republic* review of *Tender Is the Night* (6 June 1934), he stated that Fitzgerald, in many plots, was both an enraptured actor and a shutout observer. Fitzgerald called him "Malcolm Republic of the New Cowlick." Cowley edited and introduced a selection of Fitzgerald's stories (1951), edited and introduced a controversial version of *Tender Is the Night* (1951) based on a reconsideration of its manuscripts, and summed up Fitzgerald's accomplishments in *A Second Flowering: Works and Days of the Lost Generation* (1973).

Bibliography: Hans Bak, *Malcolm Cowley: The Formative Years* (Athens: University of Georgia Press, 1993).

COY, TED. In "The Bowl," he was the star of a football game played a dozen years earlier and remembered by a confused fan.

COYNE, COUNTESS. In *Fie! Fie! Fi-Fi!*, she is gossiped about as an aging actress worried about men who want to marry her daughter.

"THE CRACK-UP" (1934). Essay. Fitzgerald defines life as a series of big and little breakdowns, from outside and inside. A good mind can function while holding opposite thoughts, for example, that things are hopeless but we must strive to improve them. Fitzgerald regretted not being a hero at football or in war. He felt he could struggle against futility to age forty-nine; but when he cracked up a decade early, he got angry, wept, lamented the undone in his life, sought listless isolation, lost pride and direction and confidence, and combined fake friendliness and dislike of most types—except doctors, little children, and worn-out old men. Someone tried but failed to instill in him her vitality by telling him to regard the rest of the world as cracked, not himself.

THE CRACK-UP (1945). A book containing mostly items by Fitzgerald and assembled and edited by Edmund Wilson.* The central part is Fitzgerald's "The Crack-Up," "Pasting It Together," and "Handle with Care." It also includes his "Echoes of the Jazz Age," "My Lost City," "Ring," "Sleeping and Waking," "Early Success," notebook material, and letters to and from Fitzgerald. The central essays were in response to a suggestion from publisher Arnold Gingrich* for anything that might come into Fitzgerald's head. Gingrich published the three essays in *Esquire* in 1936. Max Perkins* regarded the book as embarrassing and declined to publish it. Wilson agreed with Perkins in 1936 but, after Fitzgerald's death, felt the main essays were truthful and sincere. Ernest Hemingway* called them cowardly. When Perkins held to his opinion, New Directions published the book.

CRADDOCK. In " 'The Sensible Thing,' " he is one of Jonquil Cary's friends who pick up George O'Kelly at the railroad station in Tennessee. The other is Jerry Holt.

CRAIG. In "Dalyrimple Goes Wrong," he is a person whose residence Bryan Dalyrimple does not rob.

CRAIG, CHARLIE. In "Strange Sanctuary," he is Dolly Haines's uncle, whose tardy appearance enables Dodo Gilbert and Birdie Lukas (also known as Willie Lukas) to occupy his house and deceive Dolly.

CRAKER, CAPTAIN. In "The Last of the Belles," he is a commanding officer over Lieutenant Andy, Lieutenant Earl Schoen, and others at an army base outside Tarleton, Georgia. He attends the party before the unit moves to Long Island.

CRAMNER, H. P. In "The Scandal Detectives," he committed a theft in the East and had to move to Basil Duke Lee's hometown, according to the scandal book.

CRAW, ADELE. In "A Woman with a Past," she is a Brereton school student whose thick ankles cause beautiful but unprincipled Josephine Perry to question the fine, decent girl's ability to attract Yale student Dudley Knowleton.

CRAWFORD. In *The Beautiful and Damned*, he telephones the apartment of Anthony Patch, who has just been discharged from the army. Crawford is clearly an acquaintance of Gloria and is never mentioned again.

CRAWFORD, JASON. In "Inside the House," he is one of the three boys Gwen Bowers has asked to help her decorate her Christmas tree. Jim Bennett and Satterly Brown are the others. Gwen likes Jason, a preschool lad, best, goes to a movie with him, and thus misses her first opportunity to meet Peppy Velance, her favorite actress.

CRAWSHAW. In "On Your Own," this is a comfortingly familiar family name in the old Maryland cemetery in which Evelyn Lovejoy attends her father's burial.

CRAWSHOW. In *Tender Is the Night*, he is "un nègre" mentioned as involved in the fracas Abe North caused in Paris.

"CRAZY SUNDAY" (1932). Short story. (Characters: Eddie Baker, Dr. Bales, Bell, Beltzer, Dr. Bridgebane, Miles Calman, Mrs. Calman, Stella Walker Calman, Carmel, Joel Coles, Eva Goebel, The Great Lover, Joan, Jack Johnson, June, Nat Keogh, Lois, Perry, Mrs. Perry, Dave Silverstein, Joe Squires.) One pre-Christmas Sunday Joel Coles, a screenwriter, goes to a party at the Beverly Hills mansion of Miles Calman, the illustrious, psychotic movie director for whom he works, and Stella Walker Miles, his gorgeous second wife. Though promising himself to abstain, Joel drinks too much, offers a silly skit, and is booed. He is buoyed up when Stella sends a complimentary telegram and invites him to her sister June's buffet supper next Sunday, where fellow-guests Miles and Stella tell him their marriage is going badly. For two years, Miles has been having an affair with Eva Goebel but remains possessive of Stella. She invites Joel to escort her to a Saturday party hosted by the Perrys without Miles, who is supposedly flying to Notre Dame to see a football game. Joel discusses everything with Miles. After the show, Joel and Stella return to the Calman mansion, where she says Miles may not be at Notre Dame at all, but where she and Joel drink and make love anyway—although Joel feels like a pawn in her game. In the morning they receive word that Miles has been killed in a plane crash on his way back to California. Joel summons a doctor to minister to Stella, who unsuccessfully beseeches him to stay. Even while lamenting Miles's death, he bitterly assures himself he will return (to Stella, to Hollywood?).

"Crazy Sunday" resulted from Fitzgerald's attending a Sunday party in 1931 at the home of movie-producer Irving Thalberg* and his actress wife Norma Shearer.* Fitzgerald drank too much, sang a silly lullaby, and was booed by actor John Gilbert,* but was quickly forgiven by Shearer. The Calmans' marital squabble is based on the trouble director King Vidor* was having with his actress wife Eleanor Boardman. Because "Crazy Sunday" satirized Hollywood types, it was rejected by the *Saturday Evening Post* and *Cosmopolitan* before it was sold for $200 to the *American Mercury*.

Bibliography: Lambert; Dwight Taylor, "Scott Fitzgerald in Hollywood," *Harper's* 218 (March 1959): 67–71.

"THE CREDO OF F. SCOTT FITZGERALD" (1921). *See* "Public Letter to Thomas Boyd."

CRESSWELL, CLARKE. In "Strange Sanctuary," he is a boy, fifteen, immediately liked by Dolly Haines. He is Grace Terhune's nephew. He likes and helps Dolly.

CRISLER, FRITZ. He was a football coach Fitzgerald knew at Princeton. Fitzgerald published an open letter to Crisler (*Princeton Athletic News*, 16 June 1934) advising him to play Princeton trustees and professors in a football game. In "The Ants at Princeton," Crisler is the football coach at Princeton, to which he came from the University of Minnesota. Fritz Crisler's name is obviously based on that of the American violinist and composer Fritz Kreisler (1875–1962).

CRITCHTICHIELLO. In "The Diamond as Big as the Ritz," he was an aviator of Italian extraction. He was shot down by Braddock Tarleton Washington, tutored Kismine, escaped, and evidently alerted reinforcements.

CROIRIER. In *The Great Gatsby*, this is the name of the store where Jay Gatsby obtained a gown to replace the one Lucille McKee tore at one of his parties.

CROIRIER. In "Image on the Heart," this is a name mentioned at the cafe where Tom, Tudy, and Riccard eat. Croirier is a friend of Riccard's.

CROMWELL, GEORGE. In "The Lees of Happiness," he is the little son of Harry and Kitty Carr Cromwell. After they are divorced, George is placed in a school.

CROMWELL, HARRY. In "The Lees of Happiness," he is Kitty Carr Cromwell's husband and George Cromwell's father. After his divorce, Harry resumes his platonic interest in Roxanne Milbank Curtain.

CROMWELL, KITTY CARR. In "The Lees of Happiness," she is the spoiled wife, from New York, of Harry Cromwell, of Chicago, and is George Cromwell's indifferent mother. After her divorce, she marries a Seattle lumber king named Horton. Her maiden name, Kitty Carr, suggests her infantile personality.

CROSBY, ESTHER. In "Six of One—," she is wealthy banker H. B. Crosby's only daughter. Ed Barnes's protégé, Gordon Vandervere, will marry her and go with her to Paris while in the diplomatic service.

CROSBY, H. B. In "Six of One—," he is a wealthy banker. His only daughter, Esther Crosby, will marry Ed Barnes's protégé, Gordon Vandervere, and serve with him in Paris while he is in the diplomatic corps.

CROSBY, MRS. WALDRON. In "The Smilers," she is the wife of the bond salesman who is about to lose his job. When he telephones home, Dr. Shipman tells him his wife is about to have a baby.

CROSBY, WALDRON. In "The Smilers," he is a bond salesman who seems happy to Sylvester Stockton and smiles at him. In reality, he is about to lose his job during his wife's pregnancy.

CROWDER. In *Tender Is the Night*, he is a movie employee in Rosemary Hoyt's studio in Paris.

"THE CRUISE OF THE ROLLING JUNK" (1924). Narrative. (Characters: Bibelick, Cato, Dr. Jones, Louie, Morgan, Schneider, Violet.) Longing for biscuits and peaches one July morning, Fitzgerald and his wife, Zelda Sayre Fitzgerald,* drive their secondhand 1918 Expenso, dubbed the Rolling Junk, out of Westport, Connecticut, to visit her Alabama homestead. They drive past ugly New Jersey towns, sleep at Princeton's Nassau Inn, and next day in Trenton buy Dr. Jones's guidebook which misguides them to Philadelphia, where they buy a new tire for the Rolling Junk. On to Delaware and lovely Maryland. A wheel comes off in Baltimore. After two locals replace it, they drive to Washington's New Willard Hotel. Next afternoon, after a Russian-looking garageman has repaired the Junk, they drive past Civil War battlefields toward Richmond. Having taken the Junk's steering wheel, Zelda bravely speeds past a highwayman in the dark. They buy gasoline from a mysterious group of "negroes" and find a hotel in Richmond. Next day they visit humid war museums while the Junk's body is rewelded. They find no peaches. They have more tire trouble on the road and rain in the dark on the way to a squalid hotel in Clarksville, Virginia. Sunday follows; they drive with engine trouble into a North Carolina town. A haughty owner of a new Expenso repairs their wheel, and they proceed to rainy Durham and on gummy roads to Greensboro. Next day they speed on nice sunny roads up to 74 mph, are stopped by a motorcycle policeman, bribe him $5 to let them go, and proceed to Charlotte. After a bad meal, they have engine trouble on the road toward South Carolina but are helped by a flirtatious passerby, after which Fitzgerald emerges from hiding. They arrive in Spartansburg, South Carolina, penniless. They wire to Greenville for $300, have the Junk overhauled, cross into familiar Georgia, sleep in Athens, and have breakfast in Atlanta. They travel into hot, nostalgic Alabama, to Montgomery. Zelda's parents' house is locked. A neighbor tells them the Sayres left Sunday for Connecticut to surprise the Fitzgeralds. Friends call on popular Zelda. They sell the Junk, redolent of youthful memories, and return home by train. In "The Cruise of the Rolling Junk,'' Fitzgerald combines a cavalier attitude toward money and a confession of mechanical ineptitude. Although he employs comic lines, his progress is from enthusiasm to disappointment.

Bibliography: Roderick S. Speer, ''*The Great Gatsby*'s 'Romance of Motoring' and 'The Cruise of the Rolling Junk,' '' *Modern Fiction Studies* 20 (Winter 1974–1975): 540–43; Robert F. Lucid, review of *The Cruise of the Rolling Junk, FH/A 1976*, 280–82; Janet Lewis, ''*The Cruise of the Rolling Junk*—The Fictionalized Joys of Motoring,'' *FH/A 1978*, 69–81.

CRUM, HECTOR. In ''Forging Ahead,'' he is Lewis Crum's young cousin. The two are guests at Benjamin Reilly's dull dinner party, which Basil Duke Lee must attend. Hector, who ''squeaks'' because his voice is changing, dances with Rhoda Sinclair at a later function.

CRUM, LEWIS. In ''The Freshest Boy,'' he comes from Basil Duke Lee's hometown, is a sophomore at St. Regis, is with Basil when he goes by train to enter school, and calls Basil fresh. In ''He Thinks He's Wonderful,'' he is driven, as is Hubert Blair, by Joe Gorman to Connie Davies's party. In ''Forging Ahead,'' he is a guest, with his cousin, Hector Crum, at Benjamin Reilly's dull party, which Basil must attend.

CRUSOE, JOE. In ''On Your Own,'' he is a soft-shoe dancer Evelyn Lovejoy rehearses with in New York.

CULLUM. In ''Basil and Cleopatra,'' he is a member of the Yale freshman football team and may be moved from quarterback to halfback.

CUNEO, FLUTE. In ''In the Holidays,'' he is one of three gunmen Joe Kinney relishes thinking about in connection with the planned murder of Griffin. The others are Oaky and Vandervere.

CUNIZZA. In *This Side of Paradise*, she is a beautiful character in an undergraduate poem written by Thomas Parke D'Invilliers.

CUOMO, VICTORIA. In ''One Hundred False Starts,'' she is a person about whom Fitzgerald cannot write. She may have been involved in a murder one cold winter.

CUPP, MISS. In ''The Rubber Check,'' she is either one of wealthy twins. Val Schuyler thinks that he could have married either one.

CUPPS, WALTER (''WALT''). In ''Family in the Wind,'' he is a neighbor of the Janneys whose house escapes damage during the first tornado. He waits on the porch armed with a shotgun to ward off possible looters.

"THE CURIOUS CASE OF BENJAMIN BUTTON" (1922). Short story. (Characters: Miss Bailey, Button, Benjamin Button, Hildegarde Moncrief Button, Mrs. Roger Button, Roger Button, Roscoe Button, Chief Justice Fossile, Hart, Dr. Keene, General Moncrief, Nana, Shevlin.) The scene is Baltimore in 1860. Roger Button and his wife have a baby. The hospital staff is nonplussed, because Benjamin is born fully grown, with beard, and seems about seventy. His embarrassed father hustles him home. He eschews rattles, prefers daddy's cigars, reads the *Encyclopædia Britannica*, likes his grandfather, goes to kindergarten at five, grows younger, tries to attend Yale College but is hooted away, and does well in his father's hardware business beginning in 1880. When he attends a dance, he meets Hildegarde Moncrief, and soon woos and marries her. They have a son named Roscoe. Benjamin's father retires in 1895. Benjamin buys and drives the first automobile in Baltimore, begins to find his wife dull, and joins the army during the Spanish-American War and is wounded, with the rank of lieutenant colonel, at San Juan Hill. As Hildegarde ages, he masters the new dances of the new century. After his son graduates from Harvard, Benjamin hands him the business, enters Harvard himself, plays football with vicious success his first year, grows less able on the gridiron, and graduates in 1914. Hildegarde now resides in Italy, and Benjamin lives with his son. He reads boys' adventure books, gets a commission as brigadier general in 1917, but despite his uniform is laughed out of camp as a youthful impostor. Roscoe snubs Benjamin, who delights in his grandson, born in 1920. Both attend kindergarten five years later. The grandson matures in school, but Benjamin loses the power to speak clearly, sleeps a lot, remembers less and less, and mainly cries for his warm milk.

Fitzgerald got the idea for this story when he read about Mark Twain's wish that God let people be born old and grow younger. Fitzgerald wrote the story at the time he and his wife, Zelda Sayre Fitzgerald,* were distressed by her second pregnancy, which she ended by having an abortion.

Bibliography: Andrew Crosland, ''Sources for Fitzgerald's 'The Curious Case of Benjamin Button,' '' *FH/A 1979*, 135–39.

CURLY, MICHAEL. In ''The Bridal Party,'' he is an impoverished American expatriate. He is in love with Carolina Dandy, is invited to her wedding in Paris to the broker Hamilton Rutherford, tries unsuccessfully to persuade her to prefer him now that he has inherited $250,000, attends the ceremony, and suddenly feels free.

CURTAIN, JEFFREY ("JEFF"). In ''The Lees of Happiness,'' he is a Chicago writer of fiction. He marries Roxanne Milbank, and they buy a house near Marlowe, outside Chicago. They have no children. In 1908 a brain clot renders him paralyzed, blind, dumb, and unconscious. Roxanna cares for him until his death eleven years later.

CURTAIN, ROXANNE MILBANK. In "The Lees of Happiness," she is a chorus girl and an actress until she marries author Jeffrey Curtain. They live outside Chicago. When he becomes paralyzed, she cares for him tenderly until his death. She has a platonic relationship with Harry Cromwell. The two have long known pity and pain. Roxanne plans to convert her home into a boarding-house.

CUSHMAN. In " 'Boil Some Water—Lots of It,' " he is the personnel man at the movie studio where Pat Hobby works.

"THE CUT-GLASS BOWL" (1920). Short story. (Characters: Clarence Ahearn, Mrs. Clarence Ahearn, Joe Ambler, Bronson, Carleton Canby, Mrs. Roger Fairboalt, Dr. Foulke, Fred Gedney, Hilda, Irene, Jessie Piper Lowrie, Tom Lowrie, Martha, Dr. Martin, Marx, Donald Piper, Evylyn Piper, Harold Piper, Julie Piper, Milton Piper, Ridgeway, Stearne.) The life of Evylyn Piper is shown over a period of almost two decades. During each set of episodes, a large cut-glass bowl is her nemesis. It was the wedding gift of a disappointed suitor, who said the bowl was like Evylyn—hard, beautiful, empty, and easy to see through. It is 1899, and Evylyn, twenty-seven, has been married for seven years to Harold Piper, thirty-six and in the hardware business in a city evidently not far from Chicago. They have a son Donald, three. Harold comes home early and discovers Evylyn's lover, Fred Gedney, whom she has promised not to see again. When Fred, who is hiding in the dining room, tries to sneak out the back door, he bumps into the cut-glass bowl which rings alarmingly. Next, Evylyn is celebrating her thirty-fifth birthday with a party. Her marriage with Harold has continued—they now have Julie, two—but it is strained. Julie cuts her thumb on the bowl, which Harold, who drinks too much, insists on filling with strong punch. Guests arrive, including Clarence Ahearn and his wife. He is about to merge his hardware concern with Harold's. But Harold and some others get drunk on the punch, and Harold insults Clarence. Julie's bandage falls off, and she contracts blood poisoning. Finally, Evylyn, forty-six, is miserable. She and Harold are quietly antagonistic. Julie, her hand amputated, is listless. Donald is in the infantry overseas. The maid confesses she has misplaced a letter, which Evylyn is certain is hiding in the damnable bowl and is a War Department report of her son's death. She seizes the bowl in a fatal embrace intending to hurl it over the stone steps out front but falls with it to her death.

CYNTHIA. In *Safety First!*, she is one of the singers. She likes Bill.

D

DA FONTANO. In *The Great Gatsby*, Nick Carraway lists his name on a timetable as one of Jay Gatsby's summer guests. A promoter, he came to gamble.

DAHLGRIM. In ''No Flowers,'' he is the Trenton jeweler Carter McLane purchased an engagement ring from for Amanda Rawlins—now Amanda Rawlins Clark.

DALE, DICK. In ''Mightier Than the Sword,'' he is a Hollywood movie director. He initially dislikes E. Brunswick Hudson's script about composer Reginald De Koven. After failing to write a better one with Pat Hobby's trivial help, he submits Hudson's to producer Jack Berners, who likes it. Dale will give a screen credit to Mabel Hatman, his script girl.

DALE, MISS. In ''The Rubber Check,'' she is a person whom Val Schuyler thinks he could have married.

DALEY, IRENE. In ''Six of One—,'' she is the beautiful follies girl with a movie contract. While visiting Beau Lebaume, Howard Kavenaugh, Wister Schofield, and George Winfield at Yale she is disfigured in an accident while Wister was driving Howard's car. She sues and accepts $40,000.

DALY. In *The Beautiful and Damned*, he is a Harvard alumnus who, Anthony Patch reads, was suspended for advocating Marxism.

DALYRIMPLE, BRYAN. In ''Dalyrimple Goes Wrong,'' he is a war hero, twenty-three, feted by his hometown. Having had only two years of college, he is able to get only a job in the stockroom of Theron G. Macy's wholesale grocery house. Ambitious and dissatisfied, he sticks up one man and robs several mansions. Staying at his menial job for four months to avoid suspicion but planning in time to leave town and perhaps the country, he is surprised when invited by Alfred J. Fraser to run for state senate. Fraser, influential in political circles, guarantees his success, if he will take advice. Dalyrimple concludes success involves cutting corners, not getting caught, and not having a conscience.

"DALYRIMPLE GOES WRONG" (1920). Short story. (Characters: Mrs. Beebe, Mrs. Henry Coleman, Craig, Bryan Dalyrimple, Demming, Dent, Donahoe, Eisenhaur, Tom Everett, Fraser, Alfred J. Fraser, Allen Gregg, G. P. Gregg, Hanson, Hawkins, Mrs. Hawkins, Hesse, Peter Jordan, Krupstadt, Theron G. Macy, Markham, Charley Moore, Sterner, Watts, Willoughby.) Bryan Dalyrimple, twenty-three, returns from the war a bemedaled hero. His hometown honors him but forgets him when he looks for work. He had two useless years at the state university before his father died, and he never held a civilian job. All he can get is a stockroom job at $40 a month in the wholesale grocery house of Theron G. Macy, who promises him a promotion but reneges. Dalyrimple masks himself one night, sticks up a frightened man, and takes his roll of bills. He regards himself as a rebel seeking the happiness money might buy. One night he slips past various homes, selects one, slits a screen, goes upstairs feeling more alone than when on combat patrol, and steals $66.62, odds and ends, and some false teeth. In remorse, he bundles the teeth up and throws them onto the lawn of the house. Breaking into more houses, he feels a combination of freedom and horror. He philosophizes that he is not a rebel but that his victims are fools. Four months pass; Dalyrimple plans to accumulate some thousands of dollars and go east or perhaps abroad. One afternoon Macy asks him to see Alfred J. Fraser at his mansion. Fraser, an important political leader who knows about him, praises his work, brains, and steadiness, and says he can put him in the state senate if Dalyrimple is willing to run. He agrees to let Fraser handle publicity and advise him. Macy enters the mansion, and the two men beam on Dalyrimple, who concludes that permanent success depends on a commonsense, hard, conscienceless cutting of corners and not getting caught.

D'AMIDO, ELIZABETH ("BETSY"). In "The Rough Crossing," she is an attractive passenger, eighteen. She flirts with Adrian Smith, plays deck tennis as his partner, but happily greets her fiancé when the ship docks in France.

DANA, LORD. In "Strange Sanctuary," this is one of the aliases of Dodo Gilbert. *See* Gilbert, Dodo.

DANA, VIOLA (1897–1987). Movie actress, born Viola Flugrath. A petite and attractive silent film star, she first appeared at age twelve in Thomas A. Edison's *A Christmas Carol* and then as Viola Dana with Metro from 1916 to 1924. She starred as Marcia Meadows in *The Chorus Girl's Romance* (1920), based on Fitzgerald's ''Head and Shoulders,'' and as Ardita Farnham in *The Offshore Pirate* (1921), based on Fitzgerald's short story of that name. She appeared in more than a hundred movies.

Bibliography: David Ragan, *Who's Who in Hollywood: The Largest Cast of International Film Personalities Ever Assembled* (New York: Facts on File, 1992).

DANBY, MADELAINE. In ''A Snobbish Story,'' she dances with Travis de Coppet in the vaudeville skit, in place of Josephine Perry.

"THE DANCE" (1926). Short story (Characters: Abercrombie, Bill Abercrombie, Marie Bannerman, Joe Cable, Katie Goldstien, Musidora Hale, Catherine Jones, Charley Kincaid, Mrs. Charley Kincaid, Moses, Thomas.) In 1921 the female narrator, who lives in New York, visits Musidora Hale, her aunt, for three weeks in May, in Davis, a Southern town. At a country-club dance the narrator resists falling in love with Charley Kincaid because he is engaged to Marie Bannerman, but the narrator and Charley glimpse Marie and Joe Cable kissing. Embarrassed, Marie asks the narrator who else might have seen them. A feature of the evening is a solo Charleston and shimmy by Catherine Jones, who is ambitious to perform professionally. A shot rings out: Marie has been killed upstairs. No weapon is found. Bill Abercrombie, the sheriff, who is attending the dance, discovers that his revolver is missing. Charley, who was alone in the locker room, is arrested. The narrator concludes that Catherine, who loves Joe, saw him kissing Marie and became jealous. Catherine killed Marie during a noisy time before Catherine's dance, and had Katie Goldstien, a black maid at the country club and formerly Catherine's nurse, fire a second, audible, shot out an upstairs window during Catherine's performance, as an alibi. The weapon was found where it had been hidden by Katie in the narrator's golf bag. Five years later, the narrator is married to Charley, and the two hope to see Catherine on the New York stage soon. Catherine claimed that Marie had threatened her with the sheriff's revolver and was shot during the ensuing struggle, and Catherine was given only a five-year sentence. Fitzgerald wrote to Harold Ober* (January 1926) that this was his first detective story and was probably valueless.

DANCIE. In *The Great Gatsby*, Nick Carraway lists his name on a timetable as among Jay Gatsby's summer guests.

DANDY, CAROLINE. In ''The Bridal Party,'' she loved Michael Curly but marries Hamilton Rutherford in Paris.

DANDY, MRS. In ''The Bridal Party,'' she is the invalid mother of Caroline Dandy and attends her daughter's wedding. She prefers kind Michael Curly.

DANE, OSCAR. In ''One Trip Abroad,'' he is Nicole Kelly's golf-playing friend in Monte Carlo. He is a self-proclaimed sponge who proudly lives off wealthy drinking travelers he despises.

DANGUE, DR. In *Tender Is the Night*, he is a physician from Geneva who tells Dick Diver that Devereux Warren's liver is failing.

DANIELS, TOM. In *Thoughtbook*, he is an admirer of Elenor Mitchell.

DANSKI, MRS. In ''The Adjuster,'' she is one of Luella Hemple's many servants who quit because of Luella's selfish demands.

DANZER, ABE, LIEUTENANT. In '' 'I Didn't Get Over,' '' he was an army officer, twenty-one, who during training in Georgia saved his men from a mortar accident and minimized drowning deaths by taking over from the inept Captain Hibbing. Later Hibbing arrested Abe in Kansas City for a prank. While serving a ten-year sentence in Leavenworth, Abe was shot to death trying to escape. He is the subject of reminiscences by members of the class of 1916 at their reunion twenty years later.

DANZIGER. In ''Basil and Cleopatra,'' he is a member of the Yale freshman football team and may make quarterback over Cullum.

DARCY, JACK. In *The Girl from Lazy J*, he is from ''Frisco'' and is visiting rancher George Kendall, his uncle. Jack plans to marry Leticia Larned. Late in his life, Fitzgerald suggested in a letter to Arnold Gingrich* (23 February 1940) that a good pseudonym might be John Darcy.

DARCY, THAYER, MONSIGNOR. In *This Side of Paradise*, he is a hedonist turned Roman Catholic priest. He knows Amory Blaine's mother, Beatrice O'Hara Blaine, lives near the Hudson River, becomes Amory's counselor, advises Amory to be a personage rather than a personality, goes to Rome, and when assigned to Boston writes to Amory he might be promoted to cardinal. Amory is grief-stricken at his sudden death. Darcy is based on Monsignor Cyril Sigourney Webster Fay,* whom Fitzgerald knew and regarded as an attractive, versatile Catholic mentor. Shane Leslie* attended Monsignor Fay's funeral in New York in 1919 and wrote to Fitzgerald to describe it. Fitzgerald incorporates part of the description in his treatment of Darcy's funeral. Fitzgerald dedicated *This Side of Paradise* to Sigourney Fay.

Bibliography: Allen.

DARE, ALICIA. In ''O Russet Witch!'' *See* Caroline.

DARROW, CLARK. In ''The Ice Palace,'' he is a graduate of Georgia Tech, has a small income, and takes Sally Carrol Happer swimming with her friends in Tarleton, Georgia. In ''The Jelly-Bean,'' he is the friend from school days who takes James Powell to the dance, loans him a bottle of corn liquor, and tells him Nancy Lamar has eloped with Ogden Merritt of Savannah.

DAVEY, GEORGE. In ''A Woman with a Past,'' he is mentioned as a Yale sophomore and a glee-club member who knows Lillian Hammel and Josephine Perry. He is presumably Lillian's escort to the Yale prom.

DAVIDSON. In ''First Blood,'' this is the name of a family at whose home Josephine Perry and Travis de Coppet danced.

DAVIES. In ''A Full Life,'' he is the father of Comptesse Gwendolyn de Frejus.

DAVIES, CONNIE. In ''The Scandal Detectives,'' she is a friend, thirteen, of Imogene Bissel and Margaret Torrence. They associate with Riply Buckner, Jr., and Basil Duke Lee. In ''He Thinks He's Wonderful,'' she invites Basil to a dance at her home where he talks too much to Imogene. In ''The Captured Shadow,'' she plays Miss Saunders in Basil's play *The Captured Shadow*. In ''Basil and Cleopatra,'' Erminie Gilberte Labouisse Bibble thinks Connie may be gossiping about her in St. Paul.

DAVIES, GWENDOLYN. In ''A Full Life.'' *See* Frejus, Comptesse Gwendolyn de.

DAVIES, MRS. In ''A Full Life,'' she is the mother of Comptesse Gwendolyn de Frejus.

DAVIS. In ''The Freshest Boy,'' he is a teacher at St. Regis.

DAVIS. In *Porcelain and Pink*, he is named by Julie Marvis in a song.

DAVIS, ANNIE LEE. In ''Lo, the Poor Peacock!,'' she is Jason Davis's wife and Josephine Davis's mother. For two years Annie has been in the hospital.

DAVIS, JASON. In ''Lo, the Poor Peacock!,'' he is a businessman, thirty-eight, in Maryland. His wife is Annie Lee Davis, and their daughter is Josephine Davis. They lived well for ten years in Paris before the Depression. Now Annie is in the hospital, commissions on textile accounts he handles are falling, sales of sausage from his wife's farm are dropping, and Josephine has been expelled from school. Suddenly, however, his fortunes improve.

DAVIS, JOSEPHINE ("JO"). In "Lo, the Poor Peacock!," she is the daughter of Jason Davis and Annie Lee Davis. Jo is sad to be withdrawn from private school, is expelled from public school, and is tutored by her father. She is reinstated at school because she did not raid the boys' locker room as first reported. She handles one of her father's potential clients so charmingly that the account is his. At the zoo, Jo tells her father troubled peacocks do not worry.

DAVIS, KATHERINE. In "Magnetism," she is the hostess of the Hollywood party where actor George Hannaford sees actress Helen Tompkins Avery and where George's wife, Kay Hannaford, gets drunk and too friendly with director Arthur Busch.

DAVIS, SAM. In "The Scandal Detectives," he is named by Hubert Blair as the only person he knows with the initials S. D.

DAVIS, TAD. In "The Bowl," he drives with Daisy Cary and others to New York after the final football game.

DAY, HELEN. In "One Interne," she is the debutante whose engagement to Dr. Howard Durfee is announced by her mother, Mrs. Truby Ponsonby Day. He offers to break the engagement to marry Thea Singelton, who declines.

DAY, MRS. TRUBY PONSONBY. In "One Interne," she is the woman who announces the engagement of her daughter, Helen Day, to Dr. Howard Durfee.

DAYFIELD, WILLIAM. In *This Side of Paradise*, he was evidently a Civil War casualty in 1864. Amory Blaine is moved by the sight of his grave at Princeton.

DEAN. In "The Offshore Pirate," this is one of the names in one of Curtis Carlyle's songs.

DEAN, ELIZABETH. In *Thoughtbook*, she is a friend.

DEAN, PHILIP ("PHIL"). In "May Day," he is the son, twenty-four, of indulgent parents, a Yale graduate, and Gordon Sterrett's former roommate at Yale. He gives Gordon $80 instead of enough to pay off Jewel Hudson. Phil attends the Yale dance at Delmonico's, drinks with Peter Himmel there and elsewhere, and plays Mr. Out to Peter's Mr. In. In the original published version of "May Day," Philip Dean was called Philip Cory.

"DEARLY BELOVED" (1969). Short story. (Characters: Beauty Boy, Dr. Edwin Burch, Lilymary.) Beauty Boy is an African American passenger car employee working out of Chicago. He and his wife, Lilymary, have a baby. In a train accident Beauty Boy loses a leg. He and his wife die of influenza and go to heaven, where he plays golf well again, for a while, until their memories grow confused.

Bibliography: James L. W. West III, "F. Scott Fitzgerald to Arnold Gingrich: A Composition Date for 'Dearly Beloved,' " *Papers of the Bibliographic Society of America* 67 (1973): 452–54.

"THE DEATH OF MY FATHER" (1951). Essay. Fitzgerald loved his unenergetic father, Edward Fitzgerald. The man was sensitive to his wife's condition after their two older daughters died, relayed comments on life from his mother and boring grandmother, taught his son outmoded courteous behavior, spanked him for running away from home at age seven, and hit him once when Fitzgerald called him a liar. His father's favorite story concerned General Jubal Anderson Early.*

DE BEC, MAYALL. In "The Captured Shadow," he is a replacement from another school for Hubert Blair as the leading male in Basil Duke Lee's play *The Captured Shadow*.

DEBRIS, PERCY B. In *The Beautiful and Damned*, he is a movie producer who gives Gloria Gilbert Patch a screen test but rejects her as too old for a certain part.

"A DEBT OF HONOR" (1910). Short story. (Characters: Colonel Barrows, Carlton, General [Thomas ("Stonewall")] Jackson, Lieutenant General Robert E. Lee, Martin, Prayle, John Sanderson.) In January 1863, John Sanderson, a Confederate private, though wounded, volunteers for sentry duty but falls asleep and is sentenced to be shot. Lieutenant General Robert E. Lee lets him off with a reprimand. Sanderson says the Confederacy will not regret his being spared. Six weeks later, near Chancellorsville, Sanderson, now a lieutenant, leads a charge on a house and flushes out the enemy by burning it, but is killed.

"THE DEBUTANTE" (1917). Play. (Characters: John Cannel, Halycon, Cecilia Halycon, Helen Halycon, Mrs. Halycon, Blaine MacDonough, Narry, Charlie Wordsworth.) Helen Halycon, eighteen, is primping in her "boudoir" before attending her coming-out party downstairs. Narry, a servant, is sewing for her. Her mother comes in to advise her daughter not to chat with anyone in a corner and not to give John Cannel, twenty-two and a suitor, more than two dances. Helen's father says he wants her to meet a certain bright man from Providence. When alone, Helen and her sister Cecilia, sixteen, argue over cigarettes and liquor; neither tattles because each knows the other kisses boyfriends. Cecilia eavesdrops when Cannel climbs up to the window, only to be rebuffed by Helen, who says that she likes to control incipient romances and hints that Charlie Wordsworth is her current favorite. Cannel disappears. Helen primps in the mirror and leaves. Cecilia emerges, has a smoke and a drink, and pretends to flirt with a middle-aged admirer. Fitzgerald reworked some of this material into *This Side of Paradise*.

DECKER, MARY. In "Family in the Wind," she was a girl whom Dr. Forrest Janney befriended in the drugstore and whom Pinky Janney evidently abused and allowed to starve to death at seventeen. She died six months before the story begins. Forrest and Rose Janney, Pinky's mother, argue about Mary.

DE COPPET, TRAVIS. In "First Blood," he is Josephine Perry's high-strung boyfriend, with whom she once tried to elope. She goes to dances with him but deserts him to pursue Anthony Harker. Ed Bement beats up Travis for gossiping about her. In "A Snobbish Story," he attends the tennis tournament and dances in the vaudeville skit but not as Josephine Perry's partner. In "Emotional Bankruptcy," he is Josephine's friend and calls on her, with Ed Bement, in Chicago—to no avail, since she is then interested in Captain Edward Dicer.

DEEMS. In "Two for a Cent," he was the vice president of the bank in the Alabama town where Henry W. Hemmick worked as a youth. After a bank robbery, Deems grew so suspicious of everyone that Hemmick became too nervous even to borrow a penny from anyone. The unusual name Deems may derive from that of musician Deems Taylor, one of the lovers of Fitzgerald's friend Dorothy Parker.*

DEERING, HUMPHREY. In "The Passionate Eskimo," he is an acquaintance of Edith Cary and Westgate and seems to have some control over the latter. Pan-e-troon is instrumental in reconciling Edith and Westgate.

DEERING, JEFF. In "The Bowl," he is the narrator. From Dayton, he rooms at Princeton with Dolly Harlan, is Josephine Pickman's date when Dolly first meets Vienna Thorne, and admires Dolly less when he briefly discontinues playing football. Dolly calls Deering an intellectual.

"THE DEFEAT OF ART" (1923). Review by Fitzgerald of *The Boy Grew Older* by Heywood Broun.*

DE FERRIAC, MRS. In "The Four Fists," she is a widow Samuel Meredith is friendly with before he meets Marjorie.

DEGLEN, JORIS. In "Design in Plaster," he is a Frenchman who is visiting an American movie studio with his wife, Marianne Deglen. Joris is interested in Mary Harris, who encourages him when her husband, Martin, becomes jealous without cause.

DEGLEN, MARIANNE. In "Design in Plaster," she is Joris Deglen's wife. When she has a sick headache, Joris goes to see Mary Harris.

DE JONG. In *The Great Gatsby*, Nick Carraway lists his name on a timetable as among Jay Gatsby's summer guests. He came to gamble.

DE KOVEN, REGINALD (1861–1920). (Full name: Henry Louis Reginald de Koven.) Musical composer, born in Middleton, Connecticut, he lived in England as a youth, received a B.A. from St. John's College, Oxford (1880), and studied music on the Continent and in England. During and after a stint in business in Chicago (1882–1890), he composed light operas, including *Don Quixote* (1889) and *Robin Hood* (1890) and ultimately about twenty more. He also composed more than 375 songs, including "O Promise Me" and "Indian Love Song," as well as ballet music and instrumental works. He was a music editor, music critic, and drama critic for Chicago and New York newspapers (1889–1911). He married Anna Farwell in Lake Forest, Illinois; she was the daughter of U.S. Senator Charles B. Farwell of Chicago. In "Mightier Than the Sword," De Koven is named as a real-life composer in a script by E. Brunswick Hudson. Dick Dale, a director, rejects Hudson's plot that De Koven stole his music from a Vermont sheepherder. Dale's script about De Koven as an alcoholic is rejected by producer Jack Berners, who accepts Hudson's script instead.

DELAUNEY, MADAME NOEL. In "One Trip Abroad," she is a beautiful young woman who is Nicole Kelly's friend in Monte Carlo but who Nicole discovers is intimate with her husband, Nelson Kelly. Nicole makes a scene.

DELEHANTY, JENNY. In "Jacob's Ladder." *See* Prince, Jenny.

DELIHANT, THOMAS (1878–1949). Jesuit priest and Fitzgerald's first cousin. He was born in Chicago and moved at thirteen to Maryland with his family, then to Georgetown, Washington, D.C. After studying for two years at Georgetown University, Delihant entered the Jesuit order at Frederick, Maryland. Following a four-year study period, he taught at Holy Cross High School, Baltimore, Maryland, and at St. Joseph's College in Philadelphia. In 1909 he undertook additional theological studies in Woodstock, Maryland, was ordained as a priest in 1912, and took final vows in 1914. He was a chaplain in the armed forces and an itinerant priest (1914–1918) and served as a parish priest in Baltimore until 1922. He served at St. Ignatius Church, in New York City, until 1943. He retired to Inisfada, Long Island, New York, where he died. Father Delihant combined spiritual decency, gentleness, nervousness, and preacherly engagement. He liked to ride horses and to sail. He was sympathetic to the Confederacy's "Lost Cause."

When Fitzgerald visited Cecilia Delihant Taylor, his favorite cousin, in Norfolk, Virginia, in 1912, he went to the Jesuit seminary at Woodstock and met

Delihant, Cecilia's brother, a novice about to take his final vows. Fitzgerald was impressed by Delihant's devotion, humaneness, and sweetness of temperament. Fitzgerald's ''The Ordeal'' (1915) and ''Benediction'' (1920) grew directly out of his admiration for Delihant, and in his ''Wait Till You Have Children of Your Own'' (1924), he implicitly places Delihant as one of his heroes.

Bibliography: Allen.

DELL, HENRY HAVEN. In ''News from Paris—Fifteen Years Ago,'' he is a Harvard man, twenty-six, in postwar Paris. He flits aimlessly from Ruth, whom he may have loved, to Bessie Leighton Wing, whom he once knew, to Hélène, whose convent education he has supported.

DEL MONTI. In *Fie! Fie! Fi-Fi!*, he is a diplomat turned gentleman bandit with his ''council.'' He arbitrates the dispute between Mrs. Bovine and Sady. He prefers night flowers to day flowers, and dreams rather than regrets.

DE MARTEL, DR. In ''The Love Boat,'' he is one of eight physicians panicky Bill Frothington thinks he might consult.

DE MILLE, CECIL B. (1881–1959). Movie director. In *The Last Tycoon*, he is mentioned as needing a set prop being used by Monroe Stahr's crew.

DEMMING. In ''Dalyrimple Goes Wrong,'' he is a worker for Theron G. Macy whose salary Bryan Dalyrimple is annoyed to see on a ledger.

DEMOREST, ETHEL. In ''Bernice Bobs Her Hair,'' she is Jim Strain's friend. They have been gloomily engaged for three years.

DEMPSEY, WILLIAM HARRISON (''JACK'') (1895–1983). American heavyweight boxing champion from 1919 to 1926. In *Tender Is the Night*, Dick Diver sees him in 1925 in a Parisian bank. In ''Two Wrongs,'' William McChesney greets him, to impress Emmy Pinkard, when he is taking her to lunch in New York.

DEMPSTER, EMILY HOPE. In ''Imagination—and a Few Mothers,'' she is an authority on mothers whose image of the ''ideal'' mother Mrs. Paxton does not emulate.

DEMPSTER, PAUL. In ''Emotional Bankruptcy,'' he is a Princeton student, nineteen, who invites Josephine Perry to a prom and is dumped.

DENBY, VAN BUREN. In *Tender Is the Night*, he is a person Albert McKisco persists in asking Dick Diver if he knows. Dick does not.

DENNICKER. In *The Great Gatsby*, Nick Carraway lists his name on a timetable as among Jay Gatsby's summer guests. He is from New York.

DENT. In ''Dalyrimple Goes Wrong,'' he is a person whose residence Bryan Dalyrimple does not rob.

DENZER, CATHERINE. In ''On an Ocean Wave,'' she is Gaston T. Scheer's mistress, whom he has placed aboard ship discreetly and plans to take with him on a business trip in Europe.

DEREHIEMER. In ''Flight and Pursuit,'' this is the name of a French family of no interest to Caroline Martin Corcoran.

DEROCCO, DR. In ''The Swimmers,'' he is the physician Choupette Marston summons when her husband, Henry Clay Marston, has a nervous breakdown following his discovery of her first adultery.

DE SADE, GILLES. In *The Beautiful and Damned. See* Patch, Anthony.

DESHHACKER, MRS. In ''Lo, the Poor Peacock!,'' she is a grocer to whom Jason Davis owes a big bill.

"DESIGN IN PLASTER" (1939). Short story. (Characters: Bieman, Joris Deglen, Marianne Deglen, Martin Harris, Mary Harris.) Martin Harris, chief electrical engineer at a movie studio, fell a few months earlier and dislocated his shoulder, and he now is recuperating in a hotel room with his arm in a plaster cast. His wife, Mary, from whom he has been separated for four months, visits him and says she loves only him, but she annoys him by saying she is going out that evening with a French group including Joris Deglen and his wife, Marianne Deglen, both of whom Martin dislikes. She says the Deglens are leaving soon. Martin imagines Mary and Joris are in love; so, when she returns to her apartment, Martin grows jealous, phones her, gets no answer, and painfully makes his way out of the hotel. Meanwhile, Joris phones Mary and says his wife is sick in bed and tells her not to come over to say farewell. Martin, making his way to her apartment, falls near her door, reinjures his shoulder, and has to go to the hospital again. Not wishing to be alone that night, she phones Joris, who comes to her—perhaps rather permanently.

DESLYS, GABY. In *Porcelain and Pink*, he or she is mentioned in nonsense talk by Julie Marvis to Calkins.

DESLYS, MISS. In *The Evil Eye*, Boileau and Harris would not like to look at her.

DESTAGE. In *Shadow Laurels*, he is Jean Chandelle's former friend and praises him to his son, Jaques.

DETINC. In "Fun in an Artist's Studio," he is Pat Hobby's boss, who lets Princess Dignanni paint a portrait of Pat.

DEVEREAUX. In "The Bowl," he is a Yale football player.

DE VINCI, LEONARD EDWARD DAVIES ("SKIDDY"). In "The Perfect Life," he is a Yale dropout, nineteen, living in New York. He and Jobena Dorsey were engaged at Bar Harbor earlier. His passion for alcohol enables Basil Duke Lee, whom he rather likes, to lure him to a bar in the Biltmore and drink so much that he misses his planned elopement with Jobena.

DE VINCI, MARK. In "One Hundred False Starts," he is a person about whom Fitzgerald cannot write. He may have been involved in a murder one cold winter.

DEVINERIES. In "May Day," this is the name of a person (or place) to whom (or which) Jewell Hudson encourages Gordon Sterrett to go with her for a drink.

DEVLIN. In "Winter Dreams," he is the Detroit businessman who tells Dexter Green about Judy Jones's unhappy marriage.

DEVLIN, ESTELLE HOBBY. In "No Harm Trying," she is Pat Hobby's ex-wife. He has not seen her for ten years. During this time she married John Devlin, had a child, lost husband and child, and returned to Los Angeles. When she attempted to commit suicide, producer Carl Le Vigne, who admired her as a fine script girl, notes she has money, visits her in the hospital, and sees through Pat's plan to exploit both her and Eric, a gifted script boy.

DEVLIN, JACK. In "The Bowl," he is a star Princeton football player.

DEWAR. In *The Great Gatsby*, Nick Carraway lists his name on a timetable as among Jay Gatsby's summer guests. He is from New York.

DE WITT, MARYLYN. In *This Side of Paradise*, she is a girl from the Twin Cities. As a teenager Amory Blaine knows her.

DEYO, DRAYCOTT. In "Bernice Bobs Her Hair," he is a young man studying for the ministry.

DEYO, MRS. In "Bernice Bobs Her Hair," she is Draycott Deyo's mother and holds dances at her home.

"DIAGNOSIS" (1931). Short story. (Characters: Eddie Brune, Chevril, Clayhorne, Ben Clayhorne, Charlie Clayhorne, Dicky Clayhorne, Pete Clayhorne, Henry Cortelyou, Sara Etherington, Julia, Jim Mason, Marston Raines, Sam, Stoneman.) Charlie Clayhorne greets his fiancée, Sara Etherington, at a New York pier. Returning from Europe early in the Depression, she notes an uneasiness in Charlie, who is back in his apartment with his younger half brothers, Ben and Dicky. She persuades her uncle, Henry Cortelyou, Charlie's boss, to give him time off and gets the listless fellow to talk with Marston Raines, a wise friend, who urges him to quit fearing whatever is crouching in his head. Charlie goes to the deserted family house in Tuscarora, Alabama, and retrieves a revised will his irate father made out that Charlie hid unopened behind a mantel. It seems the dying father had turned against Charlie, giving him reason to fear the new will, and favored Pete, the oldest of Charlie's three half brothers and at the time in prison. Charlie, Ben, and Dicky shared what seemed a small inheritance and moved to New York, where Charlie cared for the boys lovingly and got a good financial start. When Pete enters the old house and sees Charlie, he confesses that on release from prison he found $10,000 on their father's property and bought a farm. He offers to pay Charlie a share. After declining, Charlie opens the new will, in which the father says he has no loving sons and has hidden much of his cash, which belongs to whoever finds it. Well again, Charlie returns to Sara, his half brothers, and his job.

"THE DIAMOND AS BIG AS THE RITZ" (1922). Short story. (Characters: Miss Bulge, Critchtichiello, Gygsum, Gwendolyn Schnlitzer-Murphy, Vivian Schnlitzer-Murphy, Unger, John T. Unger, Mrs. Unger, Washington, Braddock Tarleton Washington, Fitz-Norman Culpepper Washington, Jasmine Washington, Kismine Washington, Mrs. Braddock Tarleton Washington, Percy Washington.) After the Civil War, Braddock Tarleton Washington's father, Fitz-Norman Culpepper Washington, took two dozen faithful blacks to Montana, where he found a solid diamond mountain, and made a billion dollars marketing gems around the world. Braddock bought radium and built a château, complete with sumptuous grounds, worked by more than two hundred black slaves and protected by antiaircraft nests. The hero, John T. Unger, of Hades along the Mississippi River, attended St. Midas School near Boston, where he met Braddock's son, Percy Washington. Percy now invites John home for the summer. The two pass through Fish, Montana, and are lifted by cable car to the château, where John cannot believe his eyes: gemmy antechambers, fountains, perfumed and flowery baths, restful music, lush viands, velvety golf course, obedient servants—and Percy's beautiful sister, Kismine, with whom he falls in love. John learns that certain downed aviators are imprisoned, visitors are used and killed, and the slaves are kept ignorant. Braddock suspects that John and Kismine plan to escape. A new aerial attack precipitates the finale. John, Kismine—who gathers up some stray jewels—and her sister, Jasmine, make their way out. John sees the entire establishment destroyed by the airplanes, some of which land.

As ground troops approach Braddock, he offers a gigantic diamond as a bribe to God, who darkens the sky in answer. Braddock blows up his entire wired mountain; he, his wife, Percy, and the remaining slaves are destroyed. John plans to go back to Hades with Jasmine and Kismine, who discovers the gems she took along are rhinestones, not diamonds. Nobody seems to mind.

Bibliography: Kuehl.

"DIAMOND DICK AND THE FIRST LAW OF WOMAN" (1924). (Characters: Charley Abbott, Miss Caruthers, Dickey, Breck Dickey, Diana Dickey, Mrs. Dickey, Elaine Russel.) Diana Dickey, nicknamed "Diamond Dick," returns to her family in Greenwich, Connecticut, from France, where she was a Red Cross worker, eighteen, during World War I and where she fell in love with Charley Abbott of Boston. He was an aviator who was shot down, grievously hurt, and seemingly now forgetful of her. One day, five years later, after many dances but no romances, she sees Charley, twenty-nine, at a New York restaurant. Broke and alcoholic, he is with a blond actress, Elaine Russel. Diamond Dick persuades the listless fellow to come to her parents' home, where her father hints he could provide him with business opportunities. Diamond Dick and Charley reminisce until he says he must return to Elaine. When Elaine telephones Diamond Dick and doubts her word that Charley has left, Diamond Dick drives into Manhattan, learns Elaine's address from a waiter, and locates Charley there with Elaine. Brandishing her father's forty-four, she slaps Elaine into silence and reminds Charley of details of their time together in France. Memories flood back, and Diamond Dick tells the outraged blond that she has been Charley's wife for five years.

DIAMOND, MARGARET. In *This Side of Paradise*, she is a drunken girl whose escort objects when she makes advances toward Amory Blaine during his New York binge.

"THE DIARY OF A SOPHOMORE" (1917). Sketch. (Characters: Doris, Heck, Peter Hype, Jim, Joe, Sinclair.) The diarist feverishly hopes that undergraduate clubs will invite him, vows to stick with his friends, but drops them as drags as soon as he signs with the Seaweed group.

DIBBY. In *This Side of Paradise*, he is a Princeton student whose election to a society gains him congratulations.

"DICE, BRASS KNUCKLES & GUITAR" (1923). Short Story. (Characters: Mrs. Clifton Garneau, Israel Glucose, Genevieve Harlan, Madison Harlan, Ronald Harlan, Hugo, Martha Katzby, Mrs. Poindexter Katzby, Rastus Muldoon, Amanthis Powell, James Powell, Martin Van Vleek.) In June, James ("Jim") Powell with income from a recent inheritance drives his jalopy from Tarleton,

Georgia, to New Jersey, accompanied by his black servant, Hugo, stops at a Victorian house, and asks a sweet girl named Amanthis Powell (no relation) for tools to repair his car. When Jim announces his intention to seek work in Southampton, she agrees to go dancing there with him. He goes to Southampton and sets up a school for people between sixteen and twenty to learn crap shooting, brass-knuckle defense punches, jazz, and dancing. He attracts many pupils, including the son and daughter of Madison Harlan and also Amanthis, whom he invites by wire and who rents a room nearby. His rules are no underage smoking, no drinking, and no crooked dice. When, in September, he orders Martin Van Vleck out for smuggling in alcohol, the cocky fellow calls Jim a servant and encourages his associates to depart. Two fashionable matrons arrive to complete the school's breakup. Barely able to pay his bills, Jim is encouraged when Amanthis stands by him, dines with him, and persuades him to attend a dance party at the Harlans' home. Jim enters and is made welcome by the host, who is Amanthis's cousin and at whose home she has really been staying. A few days later, bidding Amanthis goodbye, Jim says he will not be back next year, and he and Hugo drive away.

DICER, CAPTAIN EDWARD. In ''Emotional Bankruptcy,'' he is an American, twenty-three, reared in Europe, and a combat pilot in the French army in 1916. On leave in New York, he meets and falls in love with Josephine Perry, would like to marry her, but is rejected.

DICER, CHRISTINE. In ''Emotional Bankruptcy,'' she is Josephine Perry's friend. At the Dicer home, Josephine meets Captain Edward Dicer, Christine's cousin.

DICER, MRS. In ''Emotional Bankruptcy,'' she is Christine Dicer's mother and Captain Edward Dicer's aunt.

DICK. In *The Last Tycoon*, Cecelia Brady remembers Dick's being pleased when he saw sheep on a movie lot long ago.

DICK. In ''A Nice Quiet Place,'' he is Josephine Perry's cousin, fifteen and inexperienced. She upbraids him but, to keep him from revealing her pursuit of Sonny Dorrance, lets him kiss her.

DICKEY. In ''Diamond Dick and the First Law of Woman,'' he is Diana Dickey's father, who offers to employ Charley Abbott.

DICKEY, BRECK. In ''Diamond Dick and the First Law of Woman,'' he is Diana Dickey's young brother, eighteen and a Yale student. He admires Charley Abbott for his wartime prowess.

DICKEY, DIANA ("DIAMOND DICK"). In "Diamond Dick and the First Law of Woman," she is a Red Cross canteen veteran from the war. She married Charley Abbott in France, suffers when he has amnesia for five years, but jogs his memory in New York.

DICKEY, HARRY. In "Fate in Her Hands," he is a friend in whom Carol (later Carol Kastler) confides about the palmist's predictions.

DICKEY, MRS. In "Diamond Dick and the First Law of Woman," she is Diana Dickey's mother, distressed since hearing rumors of her daughter's broken romance with Charley Abbott.

DIFFENDORFER. In "Majesty," he is a guest at the wedding ceremony canceled by Emily Castleton.

DIGNANNI, PRINCESS. In "Fun in an Artist's Studio," she is a portrait painter from Boston. She paints Pat Hobby's portrait and prefers his "shattered face" to those of successful Hollywood workers.

DILLINGER, PROFESSOR. In "Head and Shoulders," he is a Princeton professor puzzled by Horace Tarbox's aloof conversation.

DILLON. In "Emotional Bankruptcy," he and his wife are friends of Josephine Perry's family.

DILLON, JACKSON. In "First Blood," he and Mary Jackson get married, and Josephine Perry attends the wedding.

DILLON, MRS. In "Emotional Bankruptcy," she and her husband are friends of Josephine Perry's family.

DILLON, ROBERTA. In "Bernice Bobs Her Hair," she is a regular Ivy League party guest, according to Warren MacIntyre.

D'INVILLIERS, MRS. In *This Side of Paradise*, she is Thomas Parke D'Invilliers's mother. Her illness causes him to quit rooming in New York with Amory Blaine and return home.

D'INVILLIERS, THOMAS PARKE ("TOM"). In *This Side of Paradise*, he is one of Amory Blaine's closest Princeton friends. Tom is a romantic poet, publishes in undergraduate magazines, and becomes a book reviewer in New York for the *New Democracy*. He, Amory, and Alec Connage share an apartment in New York for a time. The poem on the title page of *The Great Gatsby* is allegedly written by Thomas Parke D'Invilliers. D'Invilliers is based on John

Peale Bishop,* Fitzgerald's Princeton classmate and later the distinguished poet, whose first book was *Green Fruit* (1917).

"A DIRGE (APOLOGIES TO WORDSWORTH)" (1919). Poem. The poet remembers a lonely bar beside a way untrodden. It served tea with a wink. Oh, how different now that it is closed.

"DISCARD" (1948). Short story. (Characters: George Baker, Dolly Bordon, Phyllis Burns, Hymie Fink, Freddie, James Jerome, Count Hennen de Lanclerc, Martha, Aunt Prissy.) Dolly Bordon is George Baker's aunt and guardian, Count Hennen de Lanclerc's wife, and a Hollywood star in the running for a role in *Sense and Sensibility*. Movie director James Jerome likes Dolly and George, gives George a ride to school, and tells him Dolly is "*une grande cliente*." After a party at Dolly's beautiful home, George drives Phyllis Baker, a young actress, to her place. She pumps him about Dolly's future. A year passes, and Phyllis gets the part in *Sense and Sensibility*. The following June, Hennen and George, now at Yale, voyage to Europe—Hennen first class; George, tourist. Dolly will fly over later. One evening George wanders to first class and stumbles on Hennen and Phyllis, who took passage too, in intimate conversation. George cables Dolly, who meets all three in Paris and restrains George from beating up Hennen. In September, Dolly, without funds, puts her house up for sale, and Phyllis strolls in to report she owns the mortgage. Jerome returns from England and will direct her in *Portrait of a Woman*. George joyfully tells this to Phyllis, who is stunned because she thought she had the part. She seems to decide against taking title to Dolly's mansion after all.

DIVER. In *Tender Is the Night*, he is Dick Diver's father, a clergyman with a Virginia family background. Dick admires him, learns in Innsbruck of his death, and returns to the United States for the funeral in Buffalo and the burial in Virginia.

DIVER, DICK. (Full name: Dr. Richard Diver.) In *Tender Is the Night*, he is the well-trained physician hero, born in 1891. In 1917 he studies psychiatry in Zurich, where he meets Nicole Warren. They marry in 1919. He publishes a book on psychiatry in Zurich in 1920. He and Nicole have a son and a daughter, buy a Riviera villa in 1925, and have a luxurious, tempestuous life together. His affair with Rosemary Hoyt and hers with Tommy Barban, as well as drink which results in his loss of a partnership with Dr. Franz Gregorovius in Zurich, combine to cause their divorce.

DIVER, LANIER. In *Tender Is the Night*, he is the son of Dick and Nicole Diver, born in 1920. He likes his father, even though he feels betrayed when Dick breaks his promise not to reveal details about the allegedly contaminated bath water.

DIVER, NICOLE. In *Tender Is the Night*, she is Devereux Warren's daughter, born in 1897. She has an older sister, Beth Evan Warren. Guilty of incest with Nicole, her father places her at sixteen in a psychiatric clinic in Zurich. Dick Diver meets her there, and they marry in 1919, have two children, and live on the Riviera. She is periodically unstable, especially when she discovers his affair with Rosemary Hoyt, after which she is willingly seduced by Tommy Barban. The Divers divorce in 1929, and she marries Tommy.

Bibliography: Sarah Beebe Fryer, *Fitzgerald's New Women: Harbingers of Change* (Ann Arbor: UMI Research Press, 1988).

DIVER, TOPSY. In *Tender Is the Night*, she is the daughter of Dick and Nicole Diver, born in 1922.

DIVINE, BABE. In "The Offshore Pirate," he is an African American member of Curtis Carlyle's band which entertains Ardita Farnham.

DIVINE, RODNEY. In *Mister Icky*, he is Ulsa Icky's suitor. Called the Honourable Rodney Divine, he is evidently from London.

DIXON, LESLIE. In "New Types," he is an American, thirty-four, returning home after spending years in China. He falls in love with Paula Jorgensen, a beautiful but mysterious model he regards as a new type of American. He attends a dance given by her aunt, Emily Holliday. After confusion following the party, she sketches in her background, and he goes with Paula to her dying husband, Lord Eric Tressiger. She pays for an operation for him. When he does not survive surgery, Dixon and Paula strengthen their love for each other.

DIZZY. In "Inside the House," she is a friend who cannot go to the movies with Gwen Bowers because there is a plumbing problem in Dizzy's house.

DODD, MARTHA. In *The Last Tycoon*, she is a down-and-out movie actress Cecelia Brady tries to help. In gratitude, Martha tries, without success, to introduce Cecelia to Kathleen Moore.

DODGE, MACK. In *The Beautiful and Damned*, he is a movie actor whose photographs, stamped as though autographed, are sent to fans.

"DOES A MOMENT OF REVOLT COME SOMETIME TO EVERY MARRIED MAN?" (1924). Essay. (Characters: Mr. Egg, Mrs. Egg, Mrs. Yoke.) A husband must rebel daily or feel he is either a loser or a mere spectator. So Mr. Egg orders Mrs. Egg not to overuse makeup, avoid doing what other wives do attractively, and talk meaninglessly to safe Mrs. Yoke. One longs to evade one's heavy responsibilities and be free—that is, for a few hours.

"DOG! DOG! DOG!" (1975). Poem. Dogs are better in every way than other creatures, many of which, including humans, the poet humorously lists, from lice to elephants.

DOHMLER, DR. In *Tender Is the Night*, he is the head of the Zurichsee clinic where Dr. Franz Gregorovius works. He dies not long after Dick Diver meets him.

DOLDRUM, BOSCOE, HARTSUM, HECK, AND JEM. In ''Jemina,'' they are participants, past and present, in the Tantrum-Doldrum feud. Jem was an instigator and is now deceased.

DOLLARD, PROFESSOR. In ''On an Ocean Wave,'' he is a mathematics teacher, about forty, at Weston Technical College. He is Minna Scheer's lover. When Minna's husband, Gaston T. Scheer, sees them in an embrace aboard ship, he bribes Cates to throw Dollard overboard.

DOLLY. In ''To Dolly,'' she is the recipient of the poem.

DOLORES. In ''Magnetism,'' she is the Mexican servant who works for George Hannaford and his wife, Kay Hannaford. Dolores stands too near George when she can and likes to imagine having an affair with him.

DOMINIQUE. In ''Rags Martin-Jones and the Pr-nce of W-les,'' she is one of the three maids working for Rags Martin-Jones. The other two are Germaine and Louise.

DONAHUE. In ''Dalyrimple Goes Wrong,'' he is a worker for Theron G. Macy whose salary Bryan Dalyrimple sees on a ledger.

DONALD. In ''One Hundred False Starts,'' he is a person about whom Fitzgerald cannot write. He, his wife, Vivian, and their child were shipwrecked on a barren island.

DONALD. In ''A Snobbish Story,'' he is Jenny McRae's nephew from Minneapolis. Jenny asks reluctant Josephine Perry to be nice to him. Disappointed elsewhere, Josephine plays up to him when he is the winner at the tennis tournament.

DONCASTLE, LADY. In ''The Rubber Check,'' she is killed in an airplane crash. Val Schuyler pretends he was at Deauville with her and might have taken the same airplane.

DONILOF. In ''Two Wrongs,'' he is Emmy Pinkard McChesney's New York ballet dancing instructor who says she is ready to go on stage.

DONNELLY, POP, SERGEANT. In *The Beautiful and Damned*, he is a soldier in Anthony Patch's brigade. He has been in the service for eighteen years, gets drunk every weekend, and looks forward to retiring on a pension of $55 a month.

DONNY. In ''The Smilers,'' he is a friend Waldron Crosby, when financially ruined, successfully appeals to for a menial job.

DONOVAN. In ''Magnetism,'' he is Margaret Donovan's brother, who has recently served a six-year prison sentence. He hatches the aborted plot to blackmail George Hannaford.

DONOVAN, MARGARET. In ''Magnetism,'' she is the pretty script girl for actor George Hannaford. After seven years of adoring him unrequitedly, she agrees with her brother to blackmail Hannaford, repents, and shoots herself—but not fatally.

DONOWSKA, DR. In '' 'Trouble,' '' he is the physician Dr. Dick Wheelock referred Glenola McClurg to for the treatment of her broken ankle.

"DONT EXPECT ME . . ." (1981). Poem. The poet reports he is busy being elegant with ''fairies.'' This poem was a telegram to Fitzgerald's friend Elizabeth Beckwith MacKie.

Bibliography: Elizabeth Beckwith MacKie, ''My Friend, Scott Fitzgerald,'' *FH/A 1970*, 20–21.

"DON'T YOU WORRY I SURRENDER" (1981). Poem. The poet surrenders because life is weird, even though nighttime is sweet.

DOOFUS. In '' 'Trouble,' '' he is a dying black patient in the hospital. Dr. Dick Wheelock recognizes his bass voice in the spirituals sung by ''the dark choir'' there.

DOOLAN, CATHERINE ("KATY"). In *The Last Tycoon*, she is one of Pat Brady's secretaries. Others include Birdy Peters and Rosemary Schmiel.

DOOLAN, KIT. In ''Pat Hobby's College Days,'' he is a famous ex-tackle, now athletic superintendent at the University of the Western Coast. He owes $3,000 to Louie, the bookie at the studio where Pat Hobby works. Louie helps Pat meet Doolan, who introduces him to Samuel K. Wiskith, dean of students.

DOOLAN, MRS. KIT. In ''Pat Hobby's College Days,'' she is the athletic superintendent's wife. She is sympathetic when her husband tells her about Pat and his pillow case full of empty liquor bottles.

DOREMUS. In ''One Interne,'' he is a patient whose illness William Tulliver V correctly diagnosed. Dr. Norton criticizes Tulliver for ordering too many blood tests during his workup.

DORIS. In ''The Diary of a Sophomore,'' she is a friend the diarist wrote to about his worries.

DORIS. In *The Vegetable*, she is the sister, nineteen, of Charlotte Frost and marries Joseph Fish.

DOROTHY. In ''Martin's Thoughts,'' she is one of Martin's girlfriends.

DORR, JULIA. In *Thoughtbook*, she is a friend.

DORRANCE, CHARLES. In ''A Nice Quiet Place,'' he is the wealthy Island Farms neighbor to whom the family of Gladys, Mrs. Perry's daughter Josephine Perry's aunt, no longer speaks. He is Sonny Dorrance's uncle.

DORRANCE, SONNY. In ''A Nice Quiet Place,'' he is the incredibly handsome, rich Harvard youth. Josephine Perry is attracted to him, but he puts her off by telling her he is married to a mulatto. This is his habitual lie, to keep fortune-hunting women at a distance.

DORSEY. In ''On Your Own,'' this is a comfortingly familiar family name in the old Maryland cemetery in which Evelyn Lovejoy attends her father's burial.

DORSEY. In ''The Perfect Life,'' he is the well-to-do, hospitable host whose Manhattan home Basil Duke Lee visits over Thanksgiving vacation.

DORSEY. In *Tender Is the Night*, this name is associated with Dick Diver's father's family.

DORSEY, GEORGE. In ''The Perfect Life,'' he is a St. Regis student. He invites Basil Duke Lee to his New York home over Thanksgiving. He is puzzled by Basil's brief conversion to excessively moral behavior. In ''Basil and Cleopatra,'' he is one of Basil's Yale roommates at Yale, along with Brick Wales. George's sister is Jobena Dorsey.

DORSEY, JOBENA. In ''The Perfect Life,'' she is George Dorsey's pretty sister, eighteen. When Basil Duke Lee visits the Dorsey home in Manhattan, he is attracted to her, lectures her priggishly on becoming more moral, saves her from impetuously eloping with Leonard Edward Davies De Vinci, and is rewarded with a kiss and friendship. In ''Basil and Cleopatra,'' she is the sister of Basil's Yale roommate and acts as his sensible confidante.

DORSEY, MRS. In ''The Perfect Life,'' she visits her son, George Dorsey, at St. Regis and agrees to invite Basil Duke Lee home for Thanksgiving vacation.

DOS PASSOS, JOHN (1896–1970). American novelist who was born in Chicago, graduated from Harvard (1916), and saw action during World War I in France first in the French ambulance service and then in the U.S. medical corps. These experiences resulted in his first two novels, *One Man's Initiation—1917* (1920) and *Three Soldiers* (1921). After writing about his travels in Spain, he returned to fiction. *Manhattan Transfer* (1925) is a brilliant, sprawling novel. He collected *The 42nd Parallel* (1930), *1919* (1932), and *The Big Money* (1936) into his technically innovative trilogy, *U.S.A.* (1938). Dos Passos's *In All Countries* (1934) includes comments on the Sacco-Vanzetti case, Russian communism, and Mexican agrarian socialism. His *District of Columbia* (1952), a second trilogy, makes a unit of *Adventures of a Young Man* (1939), *Number One* (1943), and *The Grand Design* (1949) and marks the beginning of a shift from earlier radicalism to conservatism and disillusionment. His book of reminiscences is *The Best Times* (1966).

In a 1921 review titled ''*Three Soldiers*,'' Fitzgerald lauds Dos Passos's *Three Soldiers* as a uniquely fine American war novel, far better than *The Red Badge of Courage* by Stephen Crane. Calling Dos Passos the best young writer in the United States, he analyzes the three soldiers in the story, praises Dos Passos's weaving of their actions into one pattern, is critical of the portrayal of John Andrews (the most important of the three soldiers), and compares *Three Soldiers* to popular novelist Owen Johnson's ''absurd'' and ''painful'' war novel *The Wasted Generation* (also 1921). Dos Passos met Fitzgerald and Zelda Sayre Fitzgerald* in New York in 1922, visited Ring Lardner* on Long Island with them, regarded Fitzgerald as intellectually limited until he spoke well about the writing profession, and judged Zelda to be a scary combination of physical beauty and emotional instability. In 1927, when Dos Passos was the Fitzgeralds' guest in Delaware, he deplored the abundance of alcohol and the scarcity of food. The three socialized in American and European circles populated by Morley Callaghan,* Ernest Hemingway,* Gerald Murphy,* Sara Murphy,* and others. When Zelda grew worse, Dos Passos applauded her husband's ''nobility of character'' in trying to cope. Dos Passos admired *The Great Gatsby* and *Tender Is the Night*, rebuked Fitzgerald for publishing *The Crack-Up*, contributed an essay on Fitzgerald when Edmund Wilson* requested one for the *New Republic* in 1941, and saw unique greatness in *The Last Tycoon*.

Bibliography: Virginia Spencer Carr, *John Dos Passos: A Life* (Garden City, N.Y.: Doubleday, 1984).

DOUGALL, DR. In *This Side of Paradise*, he is a St. Regis teacher who tells Amory Blaine incorrectly that he could get tip-top grades.

DOUGHERTY, JOE. In "The Bowl," he is a Princeton football player who kicks a field goal.

DOUGIE. In "Pat Hobby, Putative Father," he is a bookie who humorously wires from London, when World War I begins, that England will win, France will place, and Russia will show.

DOUGLAS. In "Magnetism," he is the Hollywood producer for whom actor George Hannaford and his script girl, Margaret Donovan, work.

DOUGLAS, ARTHUR, JUDGE. In *Coward*, he is Mary Douglas's husband and the father of Charles Douglas, Clara Douglas, Lindy Douglas, and Tommy Douglas. He owns a Virginia plantation, is a feisty invalid, and dies during the Civil War.

DOUGLAS, CHARLES ("CHARLEY"). In *Coward*, he is a Confederate lieutenant. He hides $12,000 in Union money, is captured, escapes, and returns home as a captain when peace is declared.

DOUGLAS, CLARA. In *Coward*, she is the young daughter of Judge Arthur Douglas and Mary Douglas. Clara and her brother Tommy Douglas play at soldiering.

DOUGLAS, LINDY. In *Coward*, she is the daughter of Judge Arthur Douglas and Mary Douglas. She calls Jim Holworthy a coward and rejects his proposal of marriage. After her father dies, she becomes a schoolteacher. At war's end, she accepts Jim after he has proved his bravery.

DOUGLAS, MARY. In *Coward*, she is the wife, and then the widow, of Judge Arthur Douglas and the mother of Charles Douglas, Clara Douglas, Lindy Douglas, and Tommy Douglas.

DOUGLAS, TOMMY. In *Coward*, he is the young son of Judge Arthur Douglas and Mary Douglas. Tommy and Clara Douglas play at soldiering.

DOYLE, CONAN. In "The Rich Boy," this is the name of a probably phony Englishman being looked for at a Palm Beach club.

DRAGONET, AMALIE EUSTACE BEDFORD. In "Her Last Case," she is the daughter, nine, of Ben Dragonet. Bette Weaver likes her at once.

DRAGONET, BEN. In "Her Last Case," he is the owner, about thirty-five, of the beautiful old Virginia family mansion to which Bette Weaver reports to become his private nurse. Since suffering a head wound in World War I, he has been listless and alcoholic. He is the father of Amalie Eustace Bedford Dragonet, whose mother, his ex-wife, is diabolical. Ben so attracts Bette that she breaks her engagement to Dr. Howard Carney to remain with him.

DRAGONET, MRS. BEN. In "Her Last Case," she is Amalie Eustace Bedford Dragonet's mother and Ben Dragonet's vicious ex-wife.

DRAKE, FRED. In "Hot and Cold Blood," he is a broker of the firm of Clayton and Drake. About thirty, he is affable until his friend James Mather asks to borrow $50 for one day to pay a COD bill. Drake refuses.

DRAKE, JANE. In "A Freeze-Out," she is Forrest Winslow's girlfriend until her snobbish attitude toward the Rikkers causes him to drop her in preference to Alida Rikker.

DRINKWATER, MOLLIE. In "Your Way and Mine," she is Theodore Drinkwater's wife. The Drinkwaters, Henry McComas, and Stella McComas socialize but are never friendly.

DRINKWATER, THEODORE ("TED"). In "Your Way and Mine," he is Henry McComas's plodding business partner and president of the company. Drinkwater foolishly advises McComas's wife, Stella McComas, to go into debt so McComas will work harder. When McComas suffers a stroke, Drinkwater dissolves the partnership.

DRISCOLL, BOB. In *Thoughtbook*, he is an admirer of Elenor Mitchell.

DRISCOLL, D. In *Thoughtbook*, he is a male friend.

DRISCOLL, E. In *Thoughtbook*, he has a crush on Alida Bigelow.

DRISCOLL, WILLIAM ("BILL"). In "Not in the Guidebook," he is an American tour guide in and around Paris. An ex-soldier, Bill befriends and falls in love with Milly Cooley and criticizes her husband, James Cooley, who has abandoned her in France. When he innocently tells her about his combat experience five years earlier at Château-Thierry, she correctly concludes her husband lied to her and in time marries Bill.

DRUMMON. In *The Last Tycoon*, he is one of three people eager to discuss the Russian movie Monroe Stahr wants to make. The other two are Mrs. Cornhill and Kirstoff.

DU CARY, EDITH. In ''On Schedule,'' she was René du Cary's wife. After a lingering illness, she died a little more than six years earlier, leaving a will obliging René not to remarry for seven years on pain of losing a substantial inheritance.

DU CARY, NOËL. In ''On Schedule,'' she is René du Cary's peppy, pretty daughter, twelve. She misplaces her copy of the schedule, with her father's scientific notes on the back.

DU CARY, RENÉ. In ''On Schedule,'' he is the father of Noël du Cary. His wife, Edith du Cary, is deceased. Now thirty-six, he is doing scientific work for a foundation in a university town. He falls in love with Becky Snyder, who is nineteen. He makes out a schedule in three copies for Noël, Becky, and himself to follow. By violating it, Becky saves his laboratory experiment. The two announce their engagement. The name René may have been inspired by that of René Lacoste, the French tennis champion in the late 1920s and early 1930s. Fitzgerald mentions Lacoste in ''On Schedule.''

DU CHENE, MARGURETA. In *Assorted Spirits*, she is the authoress of *Innocent as a Flower*, cited by Second Story Salle.

DUCHMAN. In ''Fun in an Artist's Studio,'' he is a Hollywood sin specialist with whom DeTinc, Pat Hobby's boss, has been photographed.

DUCKNEY, ANGELA. In ''Strange Sanctuary,'' she is a debutante whom Dolly Haines knows and who invites Dodo Gilbert to a dinner party.

DUCKNEY, L. P. In ''Strange Sanctuary,'' he is Angela Duckney's father and the host of the dinner party to which she invites Dodo Gilbert.

DUCKWEED, GEORGE. In *The Great Gatsby*, Nick Carraway lists his name on a timetable as among Jay Gatsby's summer guests. He is in theater work.

DUDLEY, THORTON HART. In *The Captured Shadow*, he is the Shadow. Calling himself Johnston, he robs New York houses, returns the loot, and thus wins a bet. Dorothy Connage, whose home he robs, likes him.

DUKE. In *The Great Gatsby*, his name is listed by Nick Carraway on a timetable as among Jay Gatsby's summer guests. He is supposed to be a prince, whose real name Nick forgot or never knew.

DUKE, EUBERT M. In "The Honor of the Goon," he is one of the students who called Ella Lei Chamoro a goon.

DULANY, TIB. In "The End of Hate," he is a Confederate soldier hanged by his thumbs, which must later be amputated. He hates Dr. Pilgrim, who ordered the punishment, but loves his sister, Josie Pilgrim.

DULCETTE. In *Fie! Fie! Fi-Fi!*, she sings with Mrs. Bovine about their willingness to be unconventional at night.

DULCINEA. In "The Evil Eye," she and Claude sing about dreams and honeymoons and with others about William Jones. She also sings about the returning fishermen.

DULSCHMIT. In *Tender Is the Night*, he is a sailor whom Tommy Barban and Nicole Diver see fighting on the beach while in their hotel room.

DUMBELLA, PAOLA. In "The High Cost of Macaroni," she is named in a history book the narrator bought in Rome.

DUMBELLA, PRINCESS. In "The High Cost of Macaroni," she is a member of a wicked, ruthless, impoverished old Roman family. She commandeers the table at which the narrator and his wife are seated.

DUMPHRY, ROYAL. In *Tender Is the Night*, he is a Riviera homosexual. In some editions, his last name is given as Dumphrey.

DUNCAN, MISS. In "Magnetism," she and her sister sing at Katherine Davis's Hollywood party.

DUNN. In "The Freshest Boy," he is a St. Regis teacher. His group going to New York is allegedly too full to include the unpopular Basil Duke Lee.

DUNN, SIR HUMPHREY. In "Two Wrongs," he is a guest at Lady Sybil Combrinck's party. He convinces her footman to admit William McChesney, who is her uninvited friend, but he is soon thrown out.

DUNNING, CAPTAIN. In *The Beautiful and Damned*, he is an officer in Anthony Patch's brigade. He harangues his men verbosely. By his order, Anthony is promoted to corporal, briefly.

DUNOIS. In "A Change of Class," this is the name of a rich family (in Wilmington). The name may have been suggested by that of the fabulously wealthy Duponts of Delaware.

DUPONT, PERE. In ''Sentiment—and the Use of Rouge,'' he is a priest, perhaps imaginary, mentioned by Sergeant O'Flaherty shortly before he dies.

DUREAL, LEON. In *The Captured Shadow*, he is a French detective in New York. Thorton Hart Dudley fools him.

DURFEE, DR. HOWARD. In ''One Interne,'' he is a skillful, sure-handed, swaggering surgeon at the hospital. He makes the anaesthetist, Thea Singleton, his ''girl,'' becomes engaged to Helen Day, operates on William Tulliver V, and offers to marry Thea but is rejected.

DWAN, ALLAN. (1885–1981). (Original name: Joseph Aloysius Dwan.) Born in Toronto and with a degree from Notre Dame (1907) in electrical engineering, he was a lighting expert and worked in California for the American Film Company (1911–1913). He became a movie director of legendary fame, working for several companies, directing more than 400 films, and producing, supervising, or writing at least a hundred more. His best movie was *Sands of Two Jima* (1945). In the 1920s the Fitzgeralds met and admired Dwan. In 1922 Fitzgerald wrote the titles for the silent movie *Glimpses of the Moon*, based on the novel by Edith Wharton.* The Fitzgeralds watched Dwan film the movie in January 1924. In ''Two Old-Timers,'' Dwan is a former Hollywood personality Pat Hobby asks conceited Phil Macedon if he remembers.

Bibliography: Peter Bogdanovich, *Allan Dwan: The Last Pioneer* (New York: Praeger, 1971).

DYER. In ''Bernice Bobs Her Hair,'' he conducts a dance orchestra that plays African rhythms.

E

EARL. In "The Passionate Eskimo," he is a worker in a store visited by Pan-e-troon. Earl takes him over to the five-and-dime store.

EARL. In *Thoughtbook*, he is a friend.

EARLE, HELEN. In " 'Boil Some Water—Lots of It,' " she is the new nurse who lunches with Pat Hobby.

EARLY, JUBAL [ANDERSON], GENERAL (1816–1894). Virginia-born Confederate officer. He was a colonel at the first Battle of Bull Run, was promoted to general, and served with General Robert E. Lee's* Army of Northern Virginia. He almost captured Washington, D.C., in 1864. In "The End of Hate," Early is the commander of ragged Confederate troops who capture Dr. Pilgrim and Josie Pilgrim in Maryland.

"EARLY SUCCESS" (1937). Essay. Fitzgerald recalls steps to his first professional success: quitting work for an advertising firm, completing his first novel, changing from amateur to professional, selling stories, and receiving fan mail. Watching America's postwar boom years, he regards himself as positioned between the older generation and people younger than he; much of what he wrote then had elements of gloom. When Princetonians disliked *This Side of Paradise*, the popularity of which satisfied him, he felt hurt for years. His income in 1920 was $18,000. Early success sadly makes one value willpower more than destiny or fate but happily puts a romantic glow on life. Later, on the Riviera, Fitzgerald realized that the dream was over.

"THE EARTH CALLS" (1981). Poem. When the ground grabbed him he knew that the answer to the puzzle was "death."

EASTBY, H. P. In ''Indecision,'' he is a banker Sage orders Tommy McLane to meet in Geneva.

"EAST OF THE SUN, WEST OF THE MOON" (1981). Poem. Princeton is everywhere, including in his heart.

EBERHARDT, MRS. In *The Great Gatsby*, she is a person who Myrtle Wilson, to boast, tells Lucille McKee overcharged her for a foot examination.

"ECHOES OF THE JAZZ AGE" (1931). Essay. Fitzgerald takes a nostalgic, frightened look back to the period from 1919, marked by the May Day riots, to 1929, marked by the stock-market crash. Failed idealism led to cynicism and indifference to politics. The age featured art, excess, miracles, and satire. Automobiles changed ''petting'' and ''necking'' habits. Oldsters tried to rejuvenate themselves with alcohol. Hedonism ruled. The word ''jazz'' first connoted sex, then dancing, then music. Honest people got cheated by quacks and criminals. Even though literature, movies, Freud, Jung, and ''Negro'' music dealt more frankly with sex, morals were not injured. Travelers enjoyed Florida and the Riviera, the latter not for swimming so much as for drinking. American athletes grew soft, and crossword puzzles became faddish. Fitzgerald was appalled by news of friends' violent deaths. Flying, memorialized by one hero (Charles Lindbergh), became another mode of escape. Rich, powerful Americans in the process of wide traveling displayed their lack of refinement and good judgment. Though ending only two years ago, ''the Jazz Age'' now seems far away. Americans now no longer young feel their surroundings less intensely.

ECKHAUST. In *The Great Gatsby*, his name is listed by Nick Carraway on a timetable as among Jay Gatsby's summer guests. He is from West Egg and is connected with the movies.

ECKLEBURG, DR. T. J. In *The Great Gatsby*, he is an oculist whose enormous billboard featuring retinas three feet high dominates the ashy valley between West Egg and New York city and has an eerie symbolic effect.

Bibliography: Warren Bennett, ''Prefigurations of Gatsby, Eckleburg, Owl Eyes, and Klipspringer,'' *FH/A 1979*, 207–23.

EDDIE. In ''What Kind of Husbands Do 'Jimmies' Make?,'' he is a head waiter in a French restaurant who welcomes Jimmy Worthington, although Jimmy is drunk, so that he will spend his money there.

EDDINGTON. In ''Between Three and Four,'' he is one of the sons of B. B. Eddington, founder of the firm for which Howard Butler works.

EDDINGTON, B. B. In ''Between Three and Four,'' he is the founder of B. B. Eddington's Sons, the firm for which Howard Butler works.

EDDINGTON, GEORGE. In ''Between Three and Four,'' he is one of the sons of B. B. Eddington, works at the firm, and offers to rehire Sarah Belknap Summer.

EDGAR. In *The Great Gatsby*, he is named by Meyer Wolfshiem in his letter to Nick Carraway as a person through whom Nick can get in touch with him.

EDISON, EDGAR. In ''Jemina,'' he is an outsider who enters the region to buy gold-rich land, falls in love with Jemina Tantrum, and burns to death with her.

EDNA. In *The Last Tycoon*, she is the tourist who, with Kathleen Moore, visits Monroe Stahr's studio lot. Both young women are caught in the flood there, after the earthquake. Edna leads Stahr to Kathleen.

EDWARDS, BIG BILL. In ''The Ants at Princeton,'' he is a former Princeton football player of legendary fame.

EGAN. In ''The Mystery of the Raymond Mortgage,'' he is the inept Santuka chief of police who cannot solve the mystery, which is solved by John Syrel. Egan is the unwittingly stupid narrator of the story.

EGBERT. In *Thoughtbook*, he is a boy Alida Bigelow likes.

EGG, MR. In ''Does a Moment of Revolt Come Some Time to Every Married Man?,'' he is a typically uneasy husband who wants to revolt—briefly.

EGG, MRS. In ''Does a Moment of Revolt Come Some Time to Every Married Man?,'' she is the wife of the typical husband who wants her to be unadventuresome.

EISENHAUR. In ''Dalyrimple Goes Wrong,'' he is a person whose residence Bryan Dalyrimple does not rob.

ELENOR. In ''Martin's Thoughts,'' she is one of Martin's girlfriends.

ELKINS. In ''A Letter to Helen,'' he is a person who Ruth Sturtevant should not know has been hurt.

ELKINS, ARTHUR. In ''Myra Meets His Family,'' he is Lilah Elkins's husband.

ELKINS, ED. In *Tender Is the Night*, he is an American embassy secretary in Vienna and shares Dick Diver's apartment there.

ELKINS, LILAH. In "Myra Meets His Family," she is Myra Harper's old roommate, who advises her not to compare a husband she chooses to former boyfriends. Her husband is Arthur Elkins.

ELLEN. In *Coward*, she is Lindy Douglas's friend.

"ELLERSLIE" (1981). Poem. Some like to or must live in the United States, the best of which is Maryland. The very soul of Maryland is Ellerslie, which the Pope and even dissenters must smile on. "Ellerslie" was the house near Wilmington, Delaware, which the Fitzgeralds rented in 1927 and 1928.

ELLINGER. In *The Beautiful and Damned*, he is the first vice president of the bond company where Anthony Patch works briefly.

ELLIOT, EMILY. In "Indecision," she is a twenty-five-year-old divorced woman, with children, with whom Tommy McLane thinks he has fallen in love on his Swiss vacation. She is friendly but not encouraging.

ELSA. In "The Rubber Check," she is a person who Ellen Mortmain says was unable to find the guests Ellen wanted for Mrs. Halbird's party. This is an insult to Val Schuyler, who is to be Ellen's date.

ELSIE. In "One Hundred False Starts," she is a person about whom Fitzgerald can write no further. He used her up by assigning her mannerisms to other characters.

EM. In *The Last Tycoon*, she is a character in a movie. When John Broaca says he likes her, Monroe Stahr says he does not.

EMIL. In "The Perfect Life," he is the proprietor of a Manhattan cabaret where George Dorsey's group, including Basil Duke Lee, dance.

EMILE. In *Tender Is the Night*, he is an innkeeper who helps the Diver family after their car accident near the Zurichsee clinic.

EMMA. In "Fate in Her Hands," she is Carol Kastler's black maid, who says Carol's son, George, was bitten by a dog.

EMMA KATE. In *The Captured Shadow*, she is a gossipy servant in the Connages' home.

"EMOTIONAL BANKRUPTCY" (1931). Short story. (Characters: John Boynton Bailey, Ed Bement, Book Chaffee, Constance, Travis de Coppet, Paul Dempster, Captain Edward Dicer, Christine Dicer, Mrs. Dicer, Dillon, Mrs. Dillon, Lillian Hammel, Anthony Harker, Ikey, Joe, Martin Munn, Herbert T. Perry, Mrs. Herbert T. Perry, Josephine Perry, Ralph, Louie Randall, Ridgeway Saunders, Miss Truby, Wally.) In the fall of 1916, Josephine Perry of Chicago and Lillian Hammel are students at a New York finishing school, have Ivy League boyfriends, and go to a Princeton prom. Lillian is with Martin Munn, while Josephine, though Paul Dempster's date, dumps Paul, is pursued by Louie Randall of Yale, and teases Martin. Next evening after the football game she dumps Louie and, with Lillian, rendezvouses at the Ritz with two other young men. So it goes. Time passes, and Josephine grows unconsciously jaded, never finding her ideal. During Thanksgiving vacation at Christine Dicer's Grammercy Park home, she meets Christine's cousin, Captain Edward Dicer, twenty-three, on leave from combat service in the French army. Resplendent, he sweeps her off her feet, send flowers and takes her for drives, and follows her to Chicago at Christmas time, during which she turns eighteen. They have a climactic meeting at her parents' home. She admires his perfect appearance and behavior. He says he loves her and they kiss, but, stepping back, she says she feels nothing, and he leaves. Sensing an emptiness, she weeps. Tragically, Josephine has frittered away her emotions on casual affairs until she realizes, too late and aghast, she has no ''capital'' to invest in a true lover. ''Emotional Bankruptcy'' is a quietly terrifying little morality ''play.''

ENDIVE, CLARENCE. In *The Great Gatsby*, his name is listed by Nick Carraway on a timetable as among Jay Gatsby's summer guests. He is from East Egg and had a fight with Etty.

"THE END OF HATE" (1940). Short story. (Characters: Prince Bonaparte, Tib Dulany, General Jubal [Anderson] Early, Dr. Pilgrim, Josie Pilgrim, Captain Taswell, Wash.) Dr. Pilgrim, a dentist, and his sister Josie Pilgrim, a nurse, are captured in Maryland by ragged Confederate soldiers under the command of General Jubal Early as they travel by buggy during the Civil War from Ohio to Washington, D.C. They will be allowed to proceed unharmed if Pilgrim can treat a toothache of Prince Bonaparte, who is attached to Early's staff. He does so, but when Federal troops overrun the camp, he identifies Confederate soldier Tib Dulany as a guerrilla, and Dulany is strung up by his thumbs. Josie cuts him down and finds a doctor to amputate his destroyed thumbs. She and Tib, attracted to each other, proceed toward Georgetown but part. Eight months later, it is April 1865. Tib seeks out Pilgrim, successful owing to Bonaparte's gratitude, to kill him, but news of President Abraham Lincoln's assassination causes all parties to reconsider, and Josie proposes to Tib. This story reflects Fitzgerald's great interest in the Civil War. He suggests in ''The Death of My Father'' that his source was an anecdote told by his father, Edward Fitzgerald.* Earlier titles were ''Thumbs Up,'' ''Dentist Appointment,'' and ''When This Cruel War—.''

Bibliography: Scott Donaldson, ''Scott Fitzgerald's Romance with the South,'' *Southern Literary Journal* 5 (Spring 1963): 3–17.

ENGELS, CRENSHAW. In ''The Fiend,'' he is a Stillwater, Minnesota, resident whose wife and son, Mark, were murdered by the Fiend. Crenshaw determines on a scheme of revenge, but after visiting the Fiend in prison for decades, he laments the loss of his only friend when the Fiend dies.

ENGELS, MARK. In ''The Fiend,'' he was Crenshaw Engels's son, murdered when seven by the Fiend on 3 June 1895. Why would Fitzgerald give this boy a name suggestive of Karl Marx and Friedrich Engels?

ENGELS, MRS. CRENSHAW. In ''The Fiend,'' the wife of Crenshaw Engels, she was murdered by the Fiend on 3 June 1895 with her son, Mark Engels.

ERIC. In ''Indecision,'' he is a stable worker Tommy McLane bribes to get a sleigh to go in pursuit of Rosemary Merriweather.

ERIC. In ''No Harm Trying,'' he is a script boy whose idea for a movie Pat Hobby tries to exploit for his own gain. Producer Carl Le Vigne admires Eric and will hire him.

ESSIE. In ''Sleeping and Waking,'' she begins to handle a telephone call Fitzgerald will accept in a dream during his morning sleep.

ESSIE. In ''That Kind of Party,'' she is one of the Shoonover family's servants.

ESTE, CHARLES, LORD. In ''Rags Martin-Jones and the Pr-nce of W-les,'' this is the name a friend of John B. Chestnut takes when he pretends to be a friend of the Prince of Wales.

ESTELLE. In ''No Flowers,'' she is Stanley's date at the prom. When his tuxedo is missing, the two cannot go to the dance. William Delaney Johns, who took it, returns it, and all is well.

ESTHER. In *The Last Tycoon*, she is the former girlfriend of the handsome actor, who is now frustrated. Monroe Stahr advises him.

ESTHER. In ''Love in the Night,'' she is one of a group of Americans aware in a Cannes taxi driven by Val Rostoff that he is a Russian prince.

ETHERINGTON, SARA. In ''Diagnosis,'' she is Charlie Clayhorne's fiancée. She persuades him to consult Marston Raines, a friend. All is well when Charlie returns from Tuscarora to her in New York.

ETTY. In *The Great Gatsby*, Nick Carraway lists his name on a timetable as among Jay Gatsby's summer guests. Nick calls him a bum. Etty had a fight with Clarence Endive.

EUGÉNIE. In ''How to Live on Practically Nothing a Year,'' she is one of the Fitzgeralds' Riviera servants.

EUROPE, JIM. In ''No Flowers,'' he was a dance-band leader in 1913, when Amanda Rawlins Clark was Carter McLane's date at the prom.

EV. In ''Family in the Wind,'' she helps Dr. Forrest Janney treat the injured after the first tornado.

EVARTS, GERTRUDE. In ''Sentiment—and the Use of Rouge,'' she is Eleanor Marbrooke's friend. Eleanor shocks Captain Clayton Harrington Syneforth by telling him that when she went to Colonel Hotesane's farewell party with Gertrude they found revealing garments on his floor.

EVELYN. In ''A Snobbish Story,'' she is a newspaperwoman and John Boynton Bailey's wife, although she does not use his name. John introduces Evelyn to Josephine Perry at the theater workshop. Evelyn wants to be in his play, but he prefers to cast Josephine. As a result of subsequent neglect, Evelyn tries to commit suicide.

EVELYN. In ''Strange Sanctuary,'' she is the cook at the home of Lila Appleton, who orders her by phone to prepare supper for Dolly Haines and Clarke Cresswell.

EVERETT, TOM. In ''Dalyrimple Goes Wrong,'' he is a worker for Theron G. Macy whose salary Bryan Dalyrimple sees on a ledger. Tom has been promoted because he is Macy's nephew.

''EVERYTIME I BLOW MY NOSE I THINK OF YOU'' (1981). Poem. The sound made when he blows his nose reminds him to be loyal to ''you.''

THE EVIL EYE (1916). (Full title: *The Evil Eye: A Musical Comedy in Two Acts*). Musical comedy. (Characters: Boileau, Mary Brown, Mrs. Burt, Claude, Miss Deslys, Dulcinea, Harris, Jacques, William Jones, Craig Kennedy, Margot, Mike, Mme. Mirliflore, Esmerelda Sage, Stuyvesant.) Edmund Wilson* wrote the book, and Fitzgerald provided the lyrics. The setting is a Brittany fishing village. The plot involves a girl who suffers amnesia after a shipwreck, her captor Boileau, and her rescuer Jacques, of the supposed evil eye. ''Act I Opening Chorus'': The nightwatchman is on the lookout for scoundrels and urges sleepers to rise at daybreak. ''I've Got My Eyes on You'': The chorus warns Margot as she admits she likes to denigrate uppity beauties. ''On Dreams Alone'': Claude and Dulcinea sing to each other of their love. ''The Evil Eye'': Jacques laughs when he recalls his glance produces havoc; for example, he can cause bald men to become swine. ''What I'll Forget'': An ex-dancer has forgotten her roles and experiences and calls the sea her only friend. ''Over the Waves to Me'': Jacques, asking the sea to return his faithful love, calls the sea his only friend. ''On her Eukalali'': In Honolulu, William Jones forgot his fiancée in Bangor, Maine, and fell for a hula girl who played her ''eukalali.'' ''Jump Off the Wall'': Boileau admits he likes unspoiled Brittany girls, but Paris has called him away. The Brittany maidens may well leap from the protection of walls, drawn to Paris themselves. ''Finale Act I'': The chorus rebukes Jacques and hopes he will go to the devil. In turn he begs the sea not to take away his embraceable love. ''Act II Opening Chorus'': Dulcinea tells the fishermen a girl waits for one of them. ''Harris from Paris'': Harris the detective sings about his ability to find criminals. ''Twilight'': A gypsy urges listeners to enjoy the soft, fading glow of evening. ''The Never, Never Land'': Jacques, the girl, Claude, and Dulcinea sing of their intention to run away to love in never-never land. ''My idea of Love'': Mme. Mirliflore and Harris sing about Esmerelda Sage, who rejected Mike and married millionaire Stuyvesant, who thought his pretty blue eyes had won her. ''Other Eyes'': Jacques and others sing that the man who promises honor and obedience to a new bright-eyed girl will remember other eyes and former romances. ''The Girl of the Golden West'': Jacques sings about the West, knife-wielding girls seeking husbands, and deeds both brave and dastardly; the chorus voices its temptation to head out. ''With Me'': Harris, Boileau, Mme. Mirliflore, and the girl sing that dancing with a partner is better than dancing alone. Fitzgerald's lyrics here are best when his lines are short, and when his internal and feminine rhymes are frequent.

EWING, JOE. In ''The Ice Palace,'' he is one of Sally Carrol Happer's friends in Tarleton, Georgia. In ''The Jelly-Bean,'' he associates with Sally Carrol Hopper [*sic*] and other young people.

F

FAIRBANKS, DOUGLAS (1883–1939). Movie actor. In *The Last Tycoon*, he is a person whose telephone call Monroe Stahr should return. Stahr invites Cecelia Brady to spend the night with him at Fairbanks's ranch.

FAIRBOALT, MRS. ROGER. In ''The Cut-Glass Bowl,'' she is a woman, forty, who calls on Evylyn Piper to try to learn about Evylyn's rumored love affair with Fred Gedney.

"THE FAMILY BUS" (1933). Short story. (Characters: Alice, Edgar Bronson, Bill Flint, Ben Goven, Hart, Dick Henderson, Ralph Henderson, Mrs. T. R. Henderson, T. R. Henderson, Hoker, Howard, Capone Johnson, McCaffray, Jan Melon-Loper, Jannekin Melon-Loper, Kaethe Melon-Loper, Mrs. Melon-Loper, Meredith, Earl Sedgewick.) T. R. Henderson is a wealthy Michigan furniture manufacturer. In 1910 he buys a fancy family car. His son Dick's earliest memories of it go back to 1916. Six then, he is driven in it with Jannekin (''Janny'') Melon-Loper, the cute daughter, five, of the Hendersons' gardener, Jan Melon-Loper. By 1920 Dick and Janny are best friends, and he promises she can drive the car one day, even though his mother thinks she is beneath him. Dick's older brother, Ralph, sneaks out in the car, picks up Janny's older sister, Kaethe, and plans to elope with her to Muskegon. He crashes the car and is killed. Kaethe is not hurt, but the Melon-Lopers move across the river, where Jan works for a rival furniture company, which in time he controls and which absorbs the Henderson firm after T. R.'s death. In 1926 Dick, who loves to tinker with cars, is in a technical high school where he encounters the radiant Janny and admires her. They go to a picnic in the family car, which jealous boys cover with graffiti. Janny goes to school in Europe. In 1933 Dick is a Detroit automobile factory superintendent. Janny returns, invites Dick to a party in their old hometown, and intrigues him again. He learns an inventor improved the family car in 1914 with a unique carburetor, which could be worth millions. Dick and Janny find the engine in a scrap yard, buy it, and plan to be transported to heaven by its power. Several characters in the story may be named after the following Michigan towns: Bronson, Flint, Hart, Henderson, Howard City, and Meredith. The Henderson family car owes something to a Stutz that Fitzgerald owned in Baltimore.

"FAMILY IN THE WIND" (1932). Short story. (Characters: Baldwin, Dr. Behrer, Billy, Dr. Cohen, Walter Cupps, Mary Decker, Ev, Howden, Butch Janney, Dr. Forrest Janney, Edith Janney, Eugene Janney, Pinky Janney, Rose Janney, Jeff, Ed Jenks, Kilrain, Helen Kilrain, Necrawney, Mrs. Oakey, Peltzer, Shinkey, Mrs. Wells, Wiggins, Wooley.) In quite remote Alabama, Forrest Janney, an alcoholic ex-physician now a drugstore owner in Bending, Alabama, is driving his farmer brother, Gene Janney, to Gene's home, where his son, Pinky, is near death after an argument in Birmingham left him with a bullet in his head. When the shaky Forrest declines to operate, Gene's wife, Rose, calls him a drunk and criticizes him for befriending Mary Decker, a girl half his age. According to Forrest, however, Mary was abused by Pinky and allowed to die of starvation. Forrest drives on alone, sipping from his flask. Butch, another of Gene and Rose's sons, drives up and threatens Forrest for arguing with his mother. Suddenly a tornado strikes, which whirls Butch away, wrecks his car, destroys many farmhouses, kills forty or more people, and injures many others. Forrest, galvanized into action, drives to Bending, opens a makeshift hospital, and valiantly treats the injured. When Pinky is brought in, Forrest drinks the rest of his flask, kneels beside him, and cuts out the bullet. Two days later Forrest, driving through the devastated region, encounters Helen Kilrain, eight. Hugging her kitten, she explains that during the storm her father stood over her to protect her while she stood over the kitty. Forrest knows but does not reveal that the tornado killed Helen's father. A month passes. Butch, his car destroyed, hitches a ride with Forrest, says Pinky is dying in his own home, and tries to insult Forrest's surgery. A second tornado strikes. It destroys Gene's house but spares its occupants, because they are with Pinky. Forrest sells his damaged drugstore, bids farewell to Gene and his family, loans—or gives—Gene $100 to help him rebuild, and expresses sympathy to Rose on Pinky's death. Learning Helen is with the Red Cross in Montgomery, he buys a one-way ticket there, boards the train, pats his flask goodbye, and vows to adopt Helen. In "Family in the Wind," Fitzgerald presents Faulknerian Southern dialogue well and sketches the Alabama tornadoes of 1932 skillfully.

FARNHAM. In "The Offshore Pirate," he is Ardita Farnham's uncle. He leaves his yacht the *Narcissus* off Palm Beach to start a ruse resulting in his friend Colonel Moreland's son Toby Moreland's winning the girl.

FARNHAM, ARDITA. In ''The Offshore Pirate,'' she is Farnham's niece, nineteen. Beautiful, willful, and impetuous, she plans to marry a philanderer until Toby Moreland, pretending to be Curtis Carlyle, commandeers her uncle's yacht, kidnaps her, and persuades her to marry him. Fitzgerald took the name Ardita from that of Ardita Ford, a childhood friend in St. Paul, and the name Farnham from the Farnham in King, Farnham, and Co., the brokerage firm of Ginevra King's* father.

FARRELLY, BILLY. In ''Jacob's Ladder,'' he is a Long Island movie director whom Jacob C. K. Booth knows and who at Booth's request gives Jenny Prince her start in films.

"FATE IN HER HANDS" (1936). Short story. (Characters: Harry Dickey, Emma, Uncle Jim, Benjamin Kastler, Carol Kastler, George Kastler, Jean Kastler, Mary Kenyon, Billy Riggs, Mrs. Wheelock.) Carol, nineteen, is told in December by a palmist she will marry this year, will have fame or notoriety, and in May six years hence be threatened by danger to herself or someone near to her. Alternately fighting and aiding these prophecies, she does three things. She suddenly marries Professor Benjamin Kastler, a friend of her boyfriend, Billy Riggs, in December. To avoid being in a photograph which might be bad publicity for her husband, she briefly disappears with their daughter, only to have the escape capitalized on by unsuccessful kidnappers. Six years after their marriage, she encourages her husband—late in May—to leave a termite-riddled building on campus near some demolition blasting, just before it collapses. Were all these events engraved on her palm? Or did her fright-motivated actions cause them? The story was triggered by Fitzgerald's 1935 friendship with Laura Guthrie, a palmist in Asheville, North Carolina.

Bibliography: Laura Guthrie Hearne, ''A Summer with F. Scott Fitzgerald,'' *Esquire* 62 (December 1964): 160–65, 232–60.

FAY, CYRIL SIGOURNEY WEBSTER (1875–1919). Catholic priest. He was born in Philadelphia, graduated from the University of Pennsylvania in 1897, attended the Episcopal Divinity School in Philadelphia, and was ordained at Fond du Lac, Wisconsin, in 1903. He was a professor of dogmatic and moral theology at Nashotah House, an Episcopal seminary in Fond du Lac. Influenced by the American Oxford Movement, Fay joined the Catholic Church in 1908 and was ordained for the Baltimore Archdiocese in 1910. Father Fay was popular as a retreat master and a preacher, and in 1914 he became headmaster of the Newman School for Boys in Hackensack, New Jersey. He visited Russia in 1915. In 1917 he went to Italy as an American Red Cross deputy commissioner to encourage Pope Benedict XV in the belief that Americans favored the Allies. In 1918 Father Fay became a monsignor by papal order, returned to the United

States to prepare for a diplomatic assignment to London, but before he could sail contracted influenza and died in New York.

In 1912, during his second year at Newman School, Fitzgerald met Father Fay in Washington, D.C. Father Fay was not headmaster at Newman until after Fitzgerald's graduation in 1913. Fitzgerald made a willing surrogate father of him and discussed such authors as Robert Hugh Benson, Joris Karl Huysman, Algernon Charles Swinburne, and Oscar Wilde with the brilliant man. Father Fay strengthened Fitzgerald's respect for the Catholic faith and introduced him to Henry Adams, Margaret Chanler, and Shane Leslie,* among others. While at Princeton, Fitzgerald kept in touch with Fay. In August 1917 Father Fay formulated plans to return to Russia to lead numbers of its citizens, frightened by excesses of the first revolution, back to the Church. He wanted Fitzgerald to accompany him to Russia as his secretary, but the Bolshevik coup d'état that November put an end to the mission. Father Fay read and praised parts of ''The Romantic Egotist,'' which became *This Side of Paradise*. Fitzgerald was saddened by Fay's death, idealized him as Monsignor Thayer Darcy in *This Side of Paradise*, and dedicated the novel to him. The Monsignor X in ''A Short Autobiography'' is probably Monsignor Fay. Fitzgerald also mentions him in ''My Lost City.'' Fitzgerald's letters to him have not survived.

Bibliography: Allen; Margaret Chanler, *Autumn in the Valley* (Boston: Little Brown, 1936).

FAY, TED. In ''The Freshest Boy,'' he is the handsome captain, about twenty, of the Yale football team. Broadway actress Jerry, his girlfriend, loves him but encourages him to break up with her and return to Yale.

FAY, TEENY. In ''I Got Shoes,'' she is a friend who gossips with Johanna Battles in the lobby of the hotel where the actress Nell Margery is staying.

FEATHERSTONE. In *Tender Is the Night*, he is a man from California whom Dick Diver and Parisian banker Casasus discuss.

FENWICK, LARRY. In *The Beautiful and Damned*, he is a former boyfriend of Gloria Gilbert Patch's. She admires him for telling her that if she did not kiss him she would have to get out of his car and walk home.

FERNAND. In *Tender Is the Night*, he is an artist in Paris. Dick Diver and Nicole Diver know him. Nicole says he does not need the stimulus of alcohol.

FERRENBY. In *This Side of Paradise*, he is a wealthy businessman who gives Amory Blaine a ride in his chauffeur-driven car to Princeton. The two discuss socialism, and Ferrenby identifies himself as the father of Jesse Ferrenby, killed in the war.

FERRENBY, JESSE. In *This Side of Paradise*, he is Amory Blaine's Princeton friend. He works on the *Princetonian* and knows Phyllis Styles, who likes proms. He is killed in the war.

FERRET, JAMES B. ("ROT-GUT"). In *The Great Gatsby*, Nick Carraway lists his name on a timetable as among Jay Gatsby's summer guests. He came to gamble.

FESSENDEN, CLAUDE. In ''Babylon Revisited,'' he is a former American drinker. Alix, a bartender in Paris, tells Charlie J. Wales that Fessenden failed to pay his bills and is no longer welcome.

FIDO. In ''Pilgrimage,'' he is the talking horse.

FIE! FIE! FI-FI! (1914). Musical comedy with lyrics by Fitzgerald. (Archie, Bill, Blossom, Mrs. Bovine, Celeste, Cholmondely, Clover, Countess Coyne, Del Monti, Dulcette, Fi-Fi, Giuseppe, Gladys, Gwen, Count Von Hupp, Madame Von Hupp, Mary, Peter, Sam, Susie, Tracy, Madame Tête-à-Tête, Count de Trop, Victor, Major Voe.) In the story, an American confidence man is the prime minister of Monaco. His deserted wife is a Monte Carlo hotel manicurist. In the subplot, an Englishman falls in love with Celeste. ''Opening Chorus'': guests and Cholmondely, who calls himself Tommy Atkins, sing about being bored, coming to Monte Carlo, playing roulette, breaking hearts, and flirting. ''Gentlemen Bandits We'': Del Monti and a friend hope to steal politely in the city. ''A Slave to Modern Improvements'': Clover sings about how her physician father replaced her parts with a collection of false items including metal chest and fireproof toes. ''In Her Eyes'': To Celeste, Archie expresses fear of her haunting eyes. ''What the Manicure Lady Knows'': Sady and Mrs. Bovine gossip about various aristocrats. ''Good Night and Good Bye'': Celeste and Archie sing of their love, the morrow's sorrow, and their dreams. '' 'Round and 'Round'': Celeste, Archie, Sady, and Tracy sing about the love affairs of eight changeable people. ''Chatter Trio'': Sady and Mrs. Bovine ask Del Monti to arbitrate their argument. ''Finale Act I'': Clover and Blossom both like Archie, whom Celeste rebukes for seeming to prefer them. ''Rose of the Night'': Del Monti sings that the night rose is better than morning and afternoon blooms. ''Men'': Sady reviews male types, calling them harmless insects. ''In the Dark'': Dulcette and Giuseppe join Mrs. Bovine and Del Monti in a song about all being willing to be carefree in the dark. ''Love or Eugenics'': Muscular Clover eschews rouge and powder, which Celeste uses to touch up her considerable sexiness. ''Reminiscence'': In the evening Del Monti suggests a drink and then a dream, tearful though it be. ''Fie! Fie! Fi-Fi!'': The company bids farewell to Sady, now revealed to be the married Fi-Fi, and suggests she go west. ''The Monte Carlo Moon'': Celeste and Archie sing about their love and hope dawn never comes. ''Finale Act II'': The full chorus sings about moonlight, gaiety, and wine. These seventeen songs have lilting rhythms and catchy rhymes, often internal and feminine. Walker M. Ellis, a member of the Princeton class of 1915 and president of the Triangle Club, chose *Fie! Fie Fi-Fi!* for presentation, revised the plot, and wrongly took credit for dialogue and characters. Fitzgerald played Celeste.

FIELDING, CYRUS. In *The Beautiful and Damned*, he is Dorothy Raycroft's ex-boyfriend. After brief intimacy, he left for the army.

FIEND, THE. In ''The Fiend,'' he is the depraved murderer of Mrs. Crenshaw Engels and her son, Mark Engels, and is imprisoned for life. Crenshaw Engels, husband and father of the victims, determines on revenge but eventually misses the Fiend, now his only friend, when the Fiend dies.

"THE FIEND" (1935). Short story. (Characters: Crenshaw Engels, Mark Engels, Mrs. Crenshaw Engels, the Fiend, Radamacher.) On 3 June 1895 Mrs. Crenshaw Engels and her son, Mark, seven, are murdered outside Stillwater, Minnesota. When the Fiend who did the atrocious act is tried, Crenshaw Engels, a photographer in town, tries to choke him to death. The Fiend is sentenced to prison, and Engels is narrowly prevented from shooting him during a visit. Engels becomes an employee in Radamacher's department store, pretends to change, and says he wants to reform the Fiend by giving him books and advice. In reality, he seeks to torture the passive prisoner by describing hell and offering him frustrating books including erotica and detective stories with the conclusions torn out. One day, after thirty years, he resolves to shoot the Fiend but finds him writhing with stomach pains. He informs a guard, who takes him to the infirmary, where he dies. Exiting the prison, Crenshaw laments the loss of his only friend.

FIFI. In ''The Unspeakable Egg,'' she is the fiancée, nineteen, of George Van Tyne, scion of a wealthy, conservative New York family. Thinking him too proper and respectable, she breaks the engagement and visits her aunts in Montauk Point, Long Island. George disguises himself as a beach bum with uncouth manners. She sees through the ruse, but they have fun terrifying the two aunts by their obvious, seemingly revolting affection.

FI-FI. In *Fie! Fie! Fi-Fi!*, as Sady she is a singing manicurist, argues with Mrs. Bovine, calls men harmless insects, and is finally revealed to be the married Fi-Fi.

"FINANCING FINNEGAN" (1938). Short story. (Characters: Cannon, Miss Carlson, Finnegan, George Jaggers, Miss Mapes.) The narrator, a fiction and movie-script writer, while in New York visits Cannon, his literary agent, and George Jaggers, his editor. They tell him that Finnegan, their star writer, needs money. Finnegan wangles financing for a trip to the North Pole with three Bryn Mawr anthropologists, in search of new material. After pledging his life insurance as collateral, he is soon reported missing. Since the insurance payment is slow, Cannon hints to the narrator that Finnegan's account is an embarrassment, and the narrator loans him $200. Finnegan cables from Oslo that he is safe and needs $200. The narrator is never repaid and hopes Finnegan does well in Hollywood, now interested in him. ''Financing Finnegan'' has autobiographical touches. Fitzgerald often appealed to his agent, Harold Ober,* and his editor, Max Perkins,* for advances, and he too hoped his movie scripts would bring him wealth. Finnegan's traveling to find new material satirizes Ernest Hemingway,* who made literary capital out of his Spanish and African forays.

FINCH, MISS. In *Coward*, she is an etiquette authority cited by Angelina Bangs.

FINCH, MRS. In *Thoughtbook*, she is Violet Stockton's aunt.

FINGARSON. In ''The Honor of the Goon,'' he is the chauffeur, a Norwegian, of Lei Chamoro, who has him beat up Bomar Winlock and Oates Mulkley.

FINK, HYMIE. In ''Discard,'' he is a photographer who is busy in Dolly Bordon's mansion.

FINNEGAN. In ''Financing Finnegan,'' he is a once-great writer in need of money. He appeals to his literary agent, Cannon, and his editor, George Jaggers, for advances, goes to the North Pole to seek new material, and is erroneously reported missing. Finnegan resembles Fitzgerald, in need of money, and Ernest Hemingway,* requiring the stimulus of travel.

FINNEY, PEACHES, PEGGY, AND PETE. In ''SING HOTCH-CHA SING HEY-HI NINNY,'' they receive the telegram.

FIREBRAND. In *This Side of Paradise*, this is the name of a pirate chief in *Ha-Ha Hortense!*, the Princeton Triangle Club musical.

"FIRST A HUG AND TEASE AND A SOMETHING ON MY KNEES" (1981). Poem. After a provocative embrace comes ''everything.''

"FIRST BLOOD" (1930). Short story. (Characters: Ed Bement, Miss Benbower, Mrs. Bray, Davidson, Travis de Coppet, Jackson Dillon, Lillian Hammel, Anthony Harker, Mary Jackson, Jenny McRae, Howard Page, Perry, Constance Perry, Herbert T. Perry, Josephine Perry, Mrs. Herbert T. Perry, Warren, Marice Whaley.) It is October 1914, in Chicago. Josephine Perry, sixteen, is a problem to her mother, older sister, Constance, and herself. She wheedles her mother's permission to go to the movies with Lillian Hammel. Instead, they go driving and kissing with Travis de Coppet and Howard Page. Josephine cools toward Travis, since she wants to flirt with Constance's boyfriend, Anthony Harker, twenty-two and back after graduating from a Virginia college. Josephine lets him cut in and dance with her at a hotel tea, kisses him when he takes her home, gets the reluctant fellow to prefer her to a less opulent girlfriend named Marice Whaley, writes him mushy letters, and persuades him to fall in love—only to drop him and cause gossip that forces him out of town. Josephine's friend, Ed Bement, beats up Travis for criticizing her, even though rumor says she and Travis tried unsuccessfully to elope once.

"1ST EPISTLE OF ST. SCOTT TO THE SMITHSONIAN" (1981). Poem. Fitzgerald addresses a poem to Alida Bigelow while he is in a certain room in a certain house and wonders about the significance of the September 1919 date included. Fitzgerald's friend Alide Bigelow was then at Smith College.

FISH, JOSEPH ("JOE"). In *The Vegetable*, he is the fiancé, twenty-four, and then husband of Doris. His father is an Idaho undertaker. In the dream sequence, Joseph is a senator from Idaho who seeks Jerry Frost's impeachment.

FISHBURN, JOHN J. In "The Ice Palace," he is the Bellamys' dinner guest. Harry Bellamy tells Sally Carrol Happer that Fishburn is an influential Northwestern financier.

FISHGUARD. In *The Great Gatsby*, Nick Carraway lists his name on a timetable as among Jay Gatsby's summer guests. He is from farther out on Long Island.

FISKE, MINNIE MADDERN. In *Assorted Spirits*, this is the name of an actress Second Story Salle pretends to be while talking with Richard Wetherby.

FISKE, MRS. In "A Snobbish Story," she is an actress Evelyn mentions as perhaps to be cast for a part in her husband John Boynton Bailey's play.

FITZGERALD, ANNABEL. Fitzgerald's sister. *See* Sprague, Annabel Fitzgerald.

FITZGERALD, EDWARD (1853–1931). Fitzgerald's father. His parents were Michael Fitzgerald* and Cecilia Ashton Scott Fitzgerald of Rockville, Maryland. Edward Fitzgerald's first cousin was Mary Surratt, who was hanged for alleged conspiracy in Abraham Lincoln's assassination. Edward was raised in the Catholic faith on a farm near Rockville, enrolled at Georgetown University in 1871 but did not graduate, and went to St. Paul, Minnesota. He probably met Mary McQuillan (*see* Fitzgerald, Mary McQuillan) there. They were married in Washington, D.C., in 1890 and honeymooned in Italy and France. They had daughters (in 1893 and 1895), both of whom died in 1896, shortly before F. Scott Fitzgerald was born. By 1893 Edward was president of the American Rattan and Willow Works in St. Paul but in 1894 experienced financial problems. In 1898 the company failed and he became a soap salesman for Procter & Gamble in Buffalo, New York. In 1900 his wife gave birth to another daughter, who died in an hour. In 1901 his company transferred him to Syracuse, New York, where F. Scott Fitzgerald's sister Annabel (*see* Sprague, Annabel Fitzgerald) was born that year. In 1903 Edward was transferred to Buffalo by Procter & Gamble, which abruptly discharged him in 1908. The family returned to St. Paul, where Edward, broken in spirit, worked for in-laws and drank too much. He read poetry to his son and regaled him with pro-Confederate war stories. Edward tried to prevent his wife from spoiling Fitzgerald, who regarded his father as a model of manners, morality, and courage; however, he also thought the man possessed little physical or mental energy and may have resented his financial inability. Fitzgerald's parents did not attend his wedding ceremony and evidently met Zelda (*see* Fitzgerald, Zelda Sayre) only a year later. Zelda found her in-laws boring. Unlike Fitzgerald's mother, Edward was proud of his son's success as an author. When Edward died in Washington, Fitzgerald crossed the Atlantic to attend his funeral in Rockville, Maryland. In *Tender Is the Night*, Dick Diver also travels from Europe to Maryland to attend a similarly limned father's final rites. Fitzgerald wrote a poignant essay titled ''The Death of My Father'' (not published until 1951).

FITZGERALD, FRANCES SCOTT. Fitzgerald's daughter. *See* Smith, Frances Scott Fitzgerald Lanahan.

FITZGERALD, MARY ("MOLLIE") MCQUILLAN (1860–1936). Fitzgerald's mother. She was the daughter of Philip McQuillan and Louisa Allen McQuillan. She was educated at the Visitation Convent in St. Paul and in Manhattanville in New York and vacationed in Europe four times before her marriage to Edward Fitzgerald* in 1890. She gave birth to two daughters, both of whom died before Fitzgerald was born. She had another daughter four years later, but she too soon died. In 1901 she had another daughter, Annabel (*see* Sprague, Annabel Fitzgerald). Annabel was so much younger than Fitzgerald that the two were never close; later, however, he advised her on how to attract young fellows. Fitzgerald regarded his mother as pathologically nervous to the point of mental unbalance. A better Fitzgerald family matriarch was Mollie's unmarried sister, Annabel McQuillan, who was firm and bright. Mollie never liked her son's being an author and would have preferred his being in business or in the military. He visited his mother, whom he never especially liked, during her final illness, in Rockville, Maryland. Shortly before she died, he ridiculed her deftly in ''An Author's Mother,'' a semifictitious sketch (1936). At her death she left $42,000. Fitzgerald sought to obtain his share quickly, even though he already owed her estate $5,000 or $6,000.

FITZGERALD, MICHAEL (?–1885). Fitzgerald's paternal grandfather. He married Cecilia Ashton Scott of Rockville, Maryland. Their son was Edward Fitzgerald.*

FITZGERALD, ZELDA SAYRE (24 July 1900–10 March 1948). Fitzgerald's wife. She was born in Montgomery, Alabama, the daughter of Anthony Dickinson Sayre,* a legislator and judge, and Minnie Buckler Machen Sayre.* She had three older sisters and an older brother: Marjorie Sayre Brinson,* Rosalind Sayre Smith,* Clothilde Sayre Palmer,* and Anthony Sayre, Jr. Her mother chose the name Zelda from a novel about gypsies. Enjoying a privileged childhood, Zelda in 1918 graduated from Sidney Lanier High School in Montgomery. She met Fitzgerald at a country-club dance in 1918, when he was a second lieutenant in the U.S. Army stationed at Camp Sheridan nearby. In February 1919 the two became engaged, but Zelda broke the engagement in June. After he published *This Side of Paradise*, they became engaged again, in November. They were married at St. Patrick's Cathedral, New York City (3 April 1920), and riotously honeymooned in Manhattan hotels. Her nicknames for him were ''Goofo'' and ''Goofy''; she later called him ''Deo'' (Latin for god), ''D. O.,'' and ''Do-Do.'' They lived in Westport, Connecticut (May–September 1920), and at 38 West 59th Street, New York City (October 20–April 1921). They were in France, Italy, and England (May–July 1921). They lived in St. Paul, Minnesota (August 1921–September 1922), where their only child, Frances Scott Fitzgerald Lanahan Smith,* was born (26 October 1921). Zelda had the first of three injurious abortions in New York (March 1922). The Fitzgeralds sailed for France (April 1924) and rented a villa at St. Raphael (June) on the Riviera, where Zelda had an affair with Édouard Jozan, a French pilot (June). In a forty-two-page letter written to Fitzgerald (summer/fall 1930), she mentioned ''Josen.'' (Jozan has been wrongly identified as René Silvé, another French aviator.) The Fitzgeralds moved to Rome (winter 1924–1925) and vacationed on Capri (February), where Zelda may have first studied painting. They rented an apartment in Paris (May–December 1925), went to Antibes (August), and rented a villa in Juan-les-Pins (March–December 1926). They spent time in the United States and France (December 1926–March 1929): Hollywood (January 1927); ''Ellerslie,''* near Wilmington, Delaware (March 1927–March 1929), partly so that Zelda could take painting and dancing lessons in Philadelphia; Paris, where she studied ballet dancing (April–September 1928); and ''Ellerslie'' (September 1928–March 1929). The Fitzgeralds lived in Paris (March 1929–April 1930); Zelda studied dancing (Cannes, June; Paris, October); and they vacationed in North Africa (February 1930).

Zelda was hospitalized at Malmaison Clinic, Paris, and at Val-Mont Clinic, Glion, Switzerland (April 1930), for nervous exhaustion; and at Dr. Oscar

Forel's Les Rives de Prangins Clinic, between Geneva and Lausanne (June 1930–September 1931), for schizophrenia. Her condition was partly the result of and also the cause of an obsession to become a professional dancer. Though giving it up, she continued to write and paint. She reasoned that since Fitzgerald was a professional success, she ought to be one also. He worsened her condition by arguing that one professional in the family was enough, that since he was that professional he should have exclusive rights to their combined experiences, and that she wanted to capitalize on his reputation. They drank too much, and she accused him of physical insufficiency. The Fitzgeralds resided in Montgomery (September 1931–spring 1932), during which time her father died (November) and Fitzgerald went to Hollywood alone (November 1931–January 1932). After another breakdown, Zelda was hospitalized at the Henry Phipps Psychiatric Clinic, Johns Hopkins Hospital, Baltimore (February–June 1932). Fitzgerald rented "La Paix," a mansion at Towson, Maryland (May–November 1933), where Zelda lived (from June 1933). The two vacationed in Bermuda (November–December 1933). Fitzgerald rented a house in Baltimore (December 1933). After another breakdown (January 1934), Zelda was intermittently institutionalized, with many visits out of confinement for various lengths of time, for the remainder of her life: Sheppard and Enoch Pratt Hospital, near Baltimore (January–March 1934, May 1934–April 1936); Craig House, Beacon, New York (March–May 1934); and Highland Hospital, Asheville, North Carolina (April 1936–April 1940, August 1943–February 1944, November 1947–March 1948). To be near Zelda, Fitzgerald lived in apartments and hotel rooms in Asheville, Hendersonville, and Tryon, North Carolina, and in Baltimore (February 1935–June 1937). He maintained residence in or near Hollywood (July 1937) until his death. When Zelda was able to leave Asheville, they vacationed in South Carolina (September 1937), Virginia (March 1938), Sarasota, Florida (February 1939), and Cuba (April 1939). Zelda studied drawing and costume designing in Sarasota. After Fitzgerald's death, Zelda spent some of her remaining years with her mother in Montgomery and some in the Asheville hospital.

Zelda wrote and published extensively. She humorously reviewed Fitzgerald's *The Beautiful and Damned* (1922) and published ten articles (1922–1934), ten short stories (1925–1932), and one novel, *Save Me the Waltz* (1932). She wrote her novel in six weeks while undergoing psychiatric treatment in Baltimore; she dedicated it to Mildred Squires, one of her doctors. Irate when Scribner's accepted it for publication, Fitzgerald demanded the right to copyedit it. It is highly autobiographical. The heroine, Alabama Beggs, is the daughter of a Southern judge and is a lively Southern belle. She marries a popular, rowdy painter, David Knight, partly to escape her restrictive father. When Knight ignores her, she seeks to emulate her husband's success by becoming a dance sensation. Soon after her debut, she injures her foot, cannot dance again, and becomes a choreographer. She falls in love with but does not sleep with a French aviator named Jacques Chevre-Feuille. The style of *Save Me the Waltz* is vigorous but weird;

the structure, somewhat unbalanced. *Tender Is the Night* may be partly interpreted as Fitzgerald's response to Zelda's implicit criticism of him by way of David Knight. Her novel, though of independent value, is mainly significant for the light it sheds on Fitzgerald. Zelda's play, *Scandalabra*, was produced in Baltimore (1933, published 1980). Fitzgerald sometimes helped her with her writing; sometimes his name appeared as coauthor so that they could gain more pay; and more than once his byline appeared over her writing. *Caesar's Things*, a novel Zelda began in 1942, remained unfinished. She left eight unpublished stories. Her artwork, exhibited in Baltimore (1933), New York (1934), Asheville (1939), and Montgomery (1942), is marked by vivid imagination, daring colors, swirling forms, and occasional psychotic messages. Zelda perished in a fire in Highland Hospital, Asheville.

Zelda was the model for Gloria Gilbert Patch in *The Beautiful and Damned*, Daisy Faye Buchanan in *The Great Gatsby*, and Nicole Diver in *Tender Is the Night*. Fitzgerald used parts of Zelda's diary in *The Beautiful and Damned*.

Bibliography: Matthew J. Bruccoli and Scottie Fitzgerald Smith, eds., *Bits of Paradise: 21 Uncollected Stories by F. Scott and Zelda Fitzgerald* (New York: Scribner's, 1974); Matthew J. Bruccoli, ed., *Zelda Fitzgerald: The Collected Writings* (New York: Scribner's, 1991); Koula Svokos Hartnett, *Zelda Fitzgerald and the Failure of the American Dream for Women* (New York: Peter Lang, 1991; Eleanor Lanahan, ed., *Zelda: An Illustrated Life* (New York: Harry N. Abrams, 1996).

FITZ-HUGH, MAJOR SIR REYNOLDS. In ''A Penny Spent,'' he is a British attaché whose presence Corcoran buys to help entertain Jessie Pepper Bushmill and her daughter, Hallie Bushmill, in Brussels.

FITZPATRICK, AL. In ''The Love Boat,'' he is Mae Purley's date, twenty-two, on the love boat. He works in the Wheatly Village mill, instantly dislikes Bill Frothington, and marries Mae and prospers.

FITZPATRICK, MAE PURLEY. In ''The Love Boat,'' she is an attractive, sensual student, seventeen, from Wheatly Village and is on the love boat with her date, Al Fitzpatrick. Bill Frothington is instantly smitten by Mae, is intimate with her during the summer, but marries someone else. When they meet eleven years later, she has long been married to Fitzpatrick. She inaccurately thinks she dropped Bill.

FITZ-PETERS, ARDITA. In *The Great Gatsby*, she is a person Nick Carraway remembers as being among Jay Gatsby's summer guests.

FLANDRAU, GRACE C. HODGSON (?–1971). Woman of letters. Born Grace C. Hodgson in St. Paul, Minnesota, she attended public schools in St. Paul and a girls' school in Paris. In 1909 she married W. Blair Flandrau, son of Charles Eugene Flandrau, a Minnesota judge and historian. Her brother-in-law was Charles Macomb Flandrau, who wrote *Viva Mexico!* (1908), a superb travel book based on his visit to Blair Flandrau's coffee plantation in Mexico. Grace Flandrau's first novel was *Cousin Julia* (1917). Fitzgerald begins ''Minnesota's Capital in the Rôle of Main Street,'' a 1923 review of her second novel, *Being Respectable* (1923), by calling it superior in some ways to Sinclair Lewis's *Babbitt*. Unity is lost, however, because it skips about among too many ''dumb-bell . . .'' members of a St. Paul family and their varied associates, though well satirized with effective bitterness. Fitzgerald hopes that from the current spate of documentary fiction, exemplified by *Being Respectable*, may emerge an American Joseph Conrad,* Anatole France, or James Joyce.

Grace Flandrau accompanied her husband and her brother-in-law on a trip from the west coast of Africa to the Indian Ocean, noting pygmies, cannibals, big-game hunters, and much else on the way. Her *Then I Saw the Congo* (1929) records the trip. She wrote more novels, short stories, and historical articles concerning the Northwest. She was active in civic and cultural affairs and lived for a while in Connecticut.

FLAPPERS AND PHILOSOPHERS (1920). Short story collection.

FLESH, S. In *Tender Is the Night*, his is a name Dick Diver read in an American newspaper.

FLIESHACKER, MORT. In *The Last Tycoon*, he is Monroe Stahr's company lawyer. He parades his New York University education and is distressed when Stahr plans to make a money-losing movie.

"FLIGHT AND PURSUIT" (1932). Short story. (Characters: Comte de Berme, Mme de Colmar, Caroline Martin Corcoran, Dexter Corcoran, George Corcoran, Mrs. Corcoran, Derehiemer, Sidney Lahaye, Helen O'Connor.) Days before the 1918 Armistice, Caroline Martin of Derby, Virginia, is mistreated by Sidney Lahaye. She marries George Corcoran on the rebound and lives with the petulant man and his domineering mother in Dayton, Ohio, for three years. Hearing of her misery, Sidney telephones but is rebuffed. Caroline feels so smothered that she takes her son, Dexter, to New York, works as a secretary for two years, sees Sidney at a Long Island party, and discourages him again. Mysteriously, a Helen O'Connor invites Caroline to tour Europe with her and lets her take Dexter along. Three years of loveless dissipation pass. One evening in Italy, Caroline faints and is diagnosed as having tuberculosis. Sidney, who financed Mrs. O'Connor's venture, turns up, takes Caroline to a Swiss sanitarium for surgery, visits Dexter at school in France, and—discouraged again—departs for the Far East. While convalescing for months, Caroline is saddened by news that Sidney, a millionaire aviator, is lost over the Black Sea. When she learns he has been rescued, she cables him to return to her and pledges her eternal love.

FLINK, MAURICE A. In *The Great Gatsby*, Nick Carraway lists his name on a timetable as among Jay Gatsby's summer guests.

FLINT, BILL. In "The Family Bus," he is a worker who alerts Dick Henderson as to the value of McCaffray's carburetor.

FLORENCE. In "Love in the Night," she is one of a pair of Americans in a Cannes taxi driven by Prince Val Rostoff. She tips him a hundred francs, shakes his hand, and will boast back home that she shook the hand of a Russian prince.

FLOWING BOOTS. In "Tarquin of Cheapside," he is either of two Londoners so designated. They arm themselves and chase after Soft Shoes because he has violated a woman. She is the sister of the younger man and the wife of the older, who is about thirty. The two unsuccessfully seek their unknown quarry in Peter Caxter's rooms.

FLOYD, CHARLES ARTHUR ("PRETTY BOY") (?–1934). Criminal. Floyd was convicted and imprisoned for a 1925 St. Louis payroll robbery; was arrested four times in 1929 in Kansas for suspicion of robbery but released for lack of evidence; was convicted of participating in a 1930 bank robbery in Sylvania, Ohio, but escaped from a speeding train en route to the penitentiary; murdered two sons of a Kansas City brothel owner in 1931; murdered a policeman in Biloxi, Oklahoma, in 1932; briefly kidnapped a man in Bolivar, Missouri, for a prank, in 1933; escaped with Bonnie Parker and Clyde Barrow from a police cordon in Cookson Hills, Oklahoma, in 1934; and was killed by FBI agents outside East Liverpool, Ohio, later in 1934. In "Pretty Boy Floyd", he is mentioned as treating women disrespectfully.

FLYNN, DR. In "The Love Boat," he is one of eight physicians panicky Bill Frothington thinks he might consult.

FOLEY, ARTHUR ("ART"). In *Thoughtbook*, he is a close friend of Fitzgerald's and also of Jack Mitchell's.

FOLEY, PHIL. In *Thoughtbook*, he is a club member.

FOLEY, R. A., SERGEANT. In *The Beautiful and Damned*, this is the name by which Anthony Patch identifies himself when returning to his army camp late. When the lie is discovered, he is broken in rank and sent to the guardhouse.

"FOOTBALL" (1912). Poem. A play starts. A player is running. A halfback tackles him. He is tackled again to stop his next run. The calm fullback passes to the end, and he scores, to the honor of the Newman School in 1911. This is Fitzgerald's first published poem.

"FOR A LONG ILLNESS" (1981). Poem. Remembering their spring and summer love, he hopes they can be whole once more and rest together.

"FOR DOLLY" (1981). Poem. The poet imagines aspects of an event that did not occur: making fudge, a dog that leaves them, a picture album, a parting kiss. (Who Dolly was is not known.)

"FORGING AHEAD" (1929). Short story. (Characters: Bibble, Erminie Gilberte Labouisse Bibble, Miss Bibble, Mrs. Bibble, Riply Buckner, Jr., Carling, Hector Crum, Lewis Crum, Betty Geer, Mary Haupt, William S. Kampf, Elwood Leaming, Basil Duke Lee, Mrs. Lee, Lindsay, Andy Lockheart, Maxim, Eddie Parmelee, Benjamin Reilly, Mrs. Benjamin Reilly, Riley, Everett Reilly, Sidney Rosen, Rhoda Sinclair, Utsonomia, Elaine Washmer.) Basil, almost seventeen, learns that his mother, her father, and her brother, Everett, have lost so much money in the stock market that Basil cannot go to Yale, as promised, but must go to the state university. Hoping to save enough money and planning to work his way through Yale anyway, he gets a job on the railroad but is soon released. For safety, he registers at the state university. He gets a summer job with his aloof great-uncle, Benjamin Reilly, but learns it is conditional upon his escorting that man's dumpy step-daughter, Rhoda Sinclair, to dances. Basil is agreeable until Erminie (''Minnie'') Gilberte Labouisse Bibble, his old flame, fifteen, and her parents and her pretty little sister arrive to visit Minnie's cousin, Bill Kampf, and his family. All goes well until he has to appear at two homes—the Reillys' and the Kampfs'—Saturday evening. He gives Eddie Parmelee $10 to go to the Reillys' in his place. Eddie sends Utsonomia, a Japanese student at the state university, instead. When Uncle Ben's wife phones Basil's mother to complain, Mrs. Lee says the Lees have sold a block of property for $400,000, are solvent again, and will send Basil to Yale. Utsonomia, a student of American society, is surprised while eavesdropping to learn Basil (free of Rhoda) is engaged to Minnie.

"FOR MARY'S EIGHTH BIRTHDAY" (1981). Poem. (Character: Mary MacArthur.) The poet wonders how to guide this young combination of Eve and a saint. With books, inventions, what?

FORNEY, EDWARD. In ''The Honor of the Goon,'' he is the college dean. When Lei Chamoro complains that his relative, Ella Lei Chamoro, has been called a goon, Forney attempts unsuccessfully to bluster.

FORREST, MRS. HUGH. In ''A Freeze-Out,'' she is the great-grandmother, eighty-four, of Forrest Winslow. Her mind is mostly fixed in the past, but her invitation to his bride, Alida Rikker Winslow, breaks the ice separating the Winslows and the Rikkers.

FORRESTER, FRANK. In ''Indecision,'' he is Emily Elliot's young cousin. He asks Tommy McLane to stop a man from allegedly spying on her. The man is a harmless German businessman. The name Frank Forrester may be Fitzgerald's echoing of the names Frank Ellinger and Marian Forrester from *A Lost Lady* (1923) by Willa Cather, one of Fitzgerald's favorite authors. He wrote to Cather (April 1925) to praise her novel.

"FOR 2ND STANZA BAOTH POEM" (1951). Poem. God's wings fluttered, and the boy lay dead, his thoughts falling chaotically. This poem laments the death in 1935 of Baoth Murphy, the son of Gerald Murphy* and Sara Murphy,* the Fitzgeralds' close friends.

"FOR SONG—IDEA—HE'S JUST A FRIEND HE SAID. BUT" (1981). Poem. The poet knows enough to wish he could be simply a friend of the fellow who says he is a friend. This poem may be the beginning of ''For the time that our man spent in pressing your suit.''

"FOR THE LADS OF THE VILLAGE TRIUMPH" (1923). Poem. Since Hackensack girls ignore him, the poet returns to St. Paul, where he has been popular.

"FOR THE TIME THAT OUR MAN SPENT IN PRESSING YOUR SUIT" (1981). Poem. (Character: Porter.) The annoyed wife will not ask careless Mr. Porter to another of their weekend parties. This poem may be the conclusion of ''For Song—Idea—He's Just a Friend he said. But.'' The name Porter is possibly a jocular reference to Fitzgerald's friend Cole Porter, composer and musical-comedy lyricist.

FOSSILE, CHIEF JUSTICE. In ''The Curious Case of Benjamin Button,'' he is a judge whose decision regarding nails increases the Buttons' hardware business profits.

FOSSILE, JUDGE. In *The Vegetable*, he is a member of the Supreme Court in the dream sequence. He seeks Jerry Frost's impeachment.

FOSTER, BILLY. In *Thoughtbook*, he is a playful friend.

FOSTER, HARRIET. In *Thoughtbook*, she is a sarcastic friend.

FOSTER, ROGER. In *Thoughtbook*, he is a playful friend.

FOULKE, DR. In ''The Cut-Glass Bowl,'' he is the Piper family physician Evylyn Piper telephones in a vain attempt to get help for her daughter, Julie Piper.

FOUQUET. In *Tender Is the Night*, he is the proprietor of a bar in Paris where the Divers go before heading for the theater.

"THE FOUR FISTS" (1920). Short story. (Characters: Peter Carhart, Mrs. De Ferriac, Hamil, Gilly Hood, McIntyre, Marjorie, Meredith, Mrs. Meredith, Samuel Meredith, Taine.) Samuel Meredith, fourteen, is a Phillips Andover Academy student whose snobbishness bothers Gilly Hood, his little roommate, thirteen. Gilly hits him in the nose, which teaches Samuel to quit being snobbish. Next year Samuel is popular. In the 1890s he attends an Ivy League school and lives in New York City. One evening he offers his seat in a horse-car to a lady, upbraids a laborer for not doing the same for another young lady, and gets slugged in the jaw. This teaches him to sympathize with fatigued workers. Upon graduating, Samuel becomes a bank runner, meets a girl named Marjorie, who is neglected by her husband, and grows greedy for intimacy. However, while he is visiting in her Jersey City home, her husband enters, invites him outside, and knocks him down. This teaches Samuel not to be selfish. Samuel, at thirty-five, married and with children, has been working well for ten years for Peter Carhart, a tough man who sends him to San Antonio to consummate a deal to buy up ranchers' oil-rich land. A holdout Texan named McIntyre meets with him, agrees to sign, but in anguish slugs Samuel. This teaches Samuel to respect the little fellow, and he wires Carhart that the deal is off and gets promoted for being humane. Samuel enjoys stroking his jawbone because its lumps remind him of valuable lessons. Fitzgerald wrote to Max Perkins* (c. 1 December 1921) about being ashamed of "The Four Fists" for its nerveless didacticism.

FOWLER. In "John Jackson's Arcady," he is John Jackson's head clerk, with Jackson for twenty years. Fowler quietly admires Jackson, praises him at the town meeting, and says he and two other employees have named their sons after him.

FOWLER, JOHN JACKSON. In "John Jackson's Arcady," he is John Jackson's head clerk's son, nine, named after John Jackson.

FRAGELLE, LADY. In "One Trip Abroad," she is General Sir Evelyne Fragelle's arrogant wife.

FRAGELLE, SIR EVELYNE, GENERAL. In "One Trip Abroad," he is a fellow resident in the apartment building where Nelson Kelly and his wife, Nicole Kelly, first live in Paris. Fragelle objects to Nelson's piano playing in the salon.

"FRANCES KROLL" (1973). Poem. It is not her soul that Frances Kroll shows the man in the front row when she dances. Frances Kroll* was Fitzgerald's loyal Hollywood secretary.

Bibliography: R. L. Samwell, "Sisyphus in Hollywood," *FH/A 1973*, 102.

FRANKLIN, IKE. In *The Last Tycoon*, he is mentioned as having slapped John Broaca in the face.

FRASER. In ''Dalyrimple Goes Wrong,'' he is a congressman and Alfred J. Fraser's brother.

FRASER. In ''Majesty,'' he is Harold Castleton Sr.'s physician and is concerned about his patient's health.

FRASER, ALFRED J. In ''Dalyrimple Goes Wrong,'' he is a congressman's brother and the person supposedly with the town's most political influence. He will put Bryan Dalyrimple in the state senate.

FREDDIE. In ''Discard,'' he is an actor and may be George Baker's cousin.

FREDERICO. In ''A Penny Spent,'' he is the boatman who takes Corcoran and Hallie Bushmill into Capri's Blue Grotto.

FREEMAN. In *Tender Is the Night*, he is evidently a restaurateur in Paris who is wrongly imprisoned after the fracas caused by Abe North.

"A FREEZE-OUT" (1931). Short story. (Characters: Black, Bodman, Reynold Chase, Mary Cowan, Jane Drake, Mrs. Hugh Forrest, Helen Hannan, Walter Hannan, Hilda, Stella Horrick, Kaye, Martin, Mrs. Carleton, Norma Nash, Olsen, Alida Rikker, Cathy Chase Rikker, Chauncey Rikker, Teddy Rikker, Schwane, Dan Warner, Charlotte Winslow, Eleanor Winslow, Forrest Winslow, Pierce Winslow.) After graduating in the late 1920s from Yale, Forrest Winslow returns to his Minnesota home, works with his wealthy, snobbish, hypocritical father, Pierce Winslow, in the fur business, and suddenly sees Alida Rikker. She is the stunning daughter of Chauncey Rikker and Cathy Chase Rikker. Ten years earlier, Rikker was involved in criminal activities in the East, fled to Europe, returned to serve a prison term in America, and has returned home to live in Minnesota with his family. Pierce Winslow wants to blackball Rikker from clubs but is willing, as are his associates, to do business with him. Forrest quits being friendly with censorious Jane Drake, attends a Rikker party, and falls in love with Alida. Over his gossip-conscious parents' objections, he will marry her. His parents reluctantly attend the wedding; and his great-grandmother, Mrs. Hugh Forrest, who lives with the Winslows, guarantees his bride's social acceptance by asking her to come visit after the honeymoon.

FREJUS, COMPTE RENÉ DE. In ''A Full Life,'' he is the second husband of Comptesse Gwendolyn de Frejus.

FREJUS, COMPTESSE GWENDOLYN DE. In ''A Full Life,'' she is the former Gwendolyn Davies of Delphis, New York. She runs away from home, jumps in an inflated suit from a New York skyscraper, marries Cornelius B. Hasbrouk, is divorced, marries Compte René de Frejus, jumps from an ocean liner out of New York, becomes a human cannon ball in a Long Island circus, and blows herself up with dynamite. Dr. Harvey Wilkinson treats her, follows her career, and dies with her.

"THE FRESHEST BOY" (1928). Short story. (Characters: Dr. Bacon, Beltzman, Bill, Bugs Brown, Midget Brown, Carver, Lewis Crum, Davis, Dunn, Ted Fay, Fat Gaspar, Dan Haskins, Heatherly, Jerry, Basil Duke Lee, Mrs. Lee, Maplewood, Rooney, Treadway, Van Astor, Brick Wales, Weasel Weems.) While on his way by train east to begin studies at St. Regis in Westchester (Connecticut), Basil, fifteen, imagines he is a gentleman thief at a Broadway restaurant and also a star football player. On the train, in reality, sophomore Lewis Crum is criticizing Basil for being bossy and fresh. Things go badly during fall term: he boasts, is not daring at football, is critical of others, and parades his intelligence. When Dr. Bacon, the headmaster, tells him he can attend a Broadway matinee only if he can get two other boys to go also, he sneaks out of bounds, goes to town, and is rebuked by Bugs Brown, Fat Gasper, and his roommate Treadway, who completes the humiliation by moving out and becoming Brick Wales's roommate. Relenting, Dr. Bacon lets Basil go to New York with Rooney, a history teacher and football coach. Rooney sends Basil to the theater while he heads for the nearest saloon. Basil reads a letter from his mother, unopened until now, inviting him to quit St. Regis and accompany her father and her to Europe, where he can study and enter Yale a year late. Basil is ecstatic and in his imagination dramatizes such freedom—which would include forgetting St. Regis and everyone there. After the enjoyable matinee, he follows an actress named Jerry in it when she and her date, Ted Fay, the Yale football captain, go for tea. Eavesdropping, he hears them break off their love affair because Jerry has promised to marry her casting director and Ted must return to Yale. Basil, inspired by this incident to a renewed sense of responsibility, arouses Rooney, asleep in the saloon. Basil finds life at St. Regis better. His chums gradually stop snubbing him. One day in February, during a basketball scrimmage, Brick calls Basil by a new and welcome nickname— ''Lee-y''—not the old and hated ''Bossy.''

FROILICH. In ''A Letter to Helen,'' he is mentioned as swallowing his gum.

"FROM SCOTT FITZGERALD" (1957). Poem. Fitzgerald offers gloomy news to joyless Horace McCoy. *See* McCoy, Horace Stanley.

FROST, CHARLOTTE. In *The Vegetable*, she is Jerry Frost's wife, thirty, and Doris's sister. Charlotte and Jerry have been unhappily married for five years. She nags him until he disappears. She will welcome him back.

FROST, HORATIO ("DADA"). In *The Vegetable*, he is Jerry Frost's partly deaf, senile father, born in 1834 and therefore about eighty-eight. In the dream sequence, he is the secretary of the treasury.

FROST, JERRY. In *The Vegetable*, he is Charlotte Frost's husband, thirty-five. His real name is Jeremiah. She has nagged him for their five years of marriage. He unhappily works as a clerk for a railroad company and would prefer to be a postman or the president of the United States. He gets drunk, dreams he is president, disappears for a week, and returns as a happy postman. Charlotte will welcome him back.

FROTHINGTON. In "The Love Boat," he is the self-sacrificial great-grandfather of Bill Frothington, whom his mother urges him to emulate by dumping Mae Purley.

FROTHINGTON. In "The Love Boat," he is the proud father of Bill Frothington, whom his mother urges him to emulate.

FROTHINGTON, BILL. In "The Love Boat," he is the only son of a proud Boston family and is a recent Harvard graduate. With his friends Hamilton Abbot and Ellsworth Ames, he boards the high school love boat. Bill meets Mae Purley (*see* Fitzpatrick, Mae Purley) on the steamer, flirts and dances with her, and grows intimate with her during the summer, but he is encouraged by his class-conscious mother to drop her. Bill sees ambulance service in Europe, marries Stella in 1919, and does well as a banker in Boston. He and his wife have three children. Eleven years after first seeing Mae, he goes to her town again, and, by now, she is married. After getting drunk and making a fool of himself aboard an almost identical love boat, he realizes that pursuing his lost youth is futile.

FROTHINGTON, GEORGE. In "The Love Boat," he is an upstanding uncle of Bill Frothington, whom his mother urges him to emulate.

FROTHINGTON, MRS. In "The Love Boat," she is a class-conscious Bostonian and Bill Frothington's mother. When he seems attracted to Mae Purley (*see* Fitzpatrick, Mae Purley), Mrs. Frothington urges him to emulate his proper forebears.

FROTHINGTON, STELLA. In "The Love Boat," she is Bill Frothington's wife. The two met on the Lido and played golf and drank in speakeasies. They have three children. She socializes with some of his Harvard friends in ways that needlessly alarm Bill.

FRY, "FISH-EYE." In *The Beautiful and Damned*, he is a former boyfriend of Gloria Gilbert Patch, who liked him because he was ugly.

"F. SCOTT FITZGERALD AND THE ROARING TWENTIES! AFTER THE WHOOPEE CAME SADNESS, THEN THESE LETTERS TO AN ONLY DAUGHTER" (1963). Several 1933–1940 annotated letters are presented here from Fitzgerald to "Pie" and "Scottina," full of advice, worry, and love.

"F. SCOTT FITZGERALD IS BORED BY EFFORTS AT REALISM IN 'LIT' " (1928). Review. Fitzgerald surveys the March 1928 *Nassau Literary Magazine* and finds characters in most of the stories in it limp and passive and only a few poems in it with any imagination and strength. He labels the issue sedate, not adventurous.

FULHAM. In "The Pierian Springs and the Last Straw," he is Myra Fulham's late husband. They were married for five years. When she tells George Rombert she prevented Fulham from assaulting him, George blows up and defines Fulham as a dishonest broker.

FULHAM, MYRA. In "The Pierian Springs and the Last Straw," she is the femme fatale in novelist George Rombert's life. They met during his sophomore year at Williams and began a stormy affair. After an argument during his senior year at her New York school dance, he let her constantly demean him. She was married to Fulham for five years, became a widow, was engaged to the Honorable Howard Bixby, and stopped humiliating George when he blew up at her. They get married, and his writing and drinking stop.

"A FULL LIFE" (1988). Short story. (Characters: Davies, Mrs. Davies, Compte René de Frejus, Comptesse Gwendolyn de Frejus, Hasbrouk, Cornelius B. Hasbrouk, Dr. Harvey Wilkinson, Mrs. Harvey Wilkinson.) In 1923 Gwendolyn Davies leaves Delphis, New York. Dressed in an inflatable rubber flying suit, she jumps from a New York skyscraper but lands on a projecting roof, is treated by Dr. Harvey Wilkinson, and disappears. He follows her career: a brief marriage to Cornelius B. Hasbrouk, a divorce, marriage to Compte René de Frejus, a jump from an ocean liner, and performance as a human cannon ball in a Long Island circus. Wilkinson finds her there in 1937 and asks her to explain, but she says she is filled with dynamite and explodes, killing herself and him. Fitzgerald wrote "A Full Life" in 1937, but his agent Harold Ober* could not place it. If Fitzgerald had not lost interest, he would surely have retouched it. It was published posthumously.

Bibliography: James L. W. West III, "Fitzgerald Explodes His Heroine," *Princeton University Library Chronicle* 49 (Winter 1988): 159–72.

"FUN IN AN ARTIST'S STUDIO" (1941). Short story. (Characters: DeTinc, Princess Dignanni, Duchman, Pat Hobby, Louie.) Princess Dignanni intends to paint Pat Hobby's portrait. His boss, DeTinc, permits her to invite him to her studio, where he hints that he would like a drink and some semidressed couch time. Instead, she summons a previously alerted policeman and tells him that Pat was to pose nude but now refuses; he is forced to do so to catch his "shattered face" accurately. Pat thinks the event barely resembles a peep-show he once saw called *Fun in an Artist's Studio*.

G

GAFFNEY. MISS. In ''O Russet Witch!,'' she is an employee hired by Merlin Grainger late in his career at the bookshop.

GALLUP, DR. ROSWELL. In ''The Unspeakable Egg,'' he is a New York psychiatrist summoned to Montauk Point by Cal Marsden and Josephine Marsden to treat Fifi, their niece, when they fear she is falling for a beach derelict. Dr. Gallup and the others learn the derelict is actually Fifi's fiancé, George Van Tyne.

GALT. In ''The Third Casket,'' he is the general manager of Cyrus Girard's Wall Street firm.

GAMBLE, HOTSY. In ''No Flowers,'' he was Marjorie Clark's boyfriend when she was twelve and he fourteen. They danced cheek-to-cheek.

GARAVOCHI. In ''Gods of Darkness,'' he is the trader leading the Venetian caravan. Count Philippe of Villefranche obtains tribute from him for crossing his ford.

GARBO, GRETA (1905–1990). Movie actress. In ''The Big Academy Dinner,'' she is mentioned as present.

GARDENER. In *Thoughtbook*, this is a family with a house three miles out of town.

GARDENER, HAM. In *Thoughtbook*, he is Nancy Gardener's big brother, who is peeved when Fitzgerald toboggans with his sister, Nancy.

GARDENER, NANCY. In *Thoughtbook*, she is a friend, eight, with whom Fitzgerald toboggans.

GARDNER. In ''The Love Boat,'' he is a Harvard football player Bill Frothington recalls.

GARDNER, GEORGE. In *Thoughtbook*, he is a club friend. His name undoubtedly should be spelled Gardener. *See* Gardener.

GARLAND, DODSON "DODDY." In ''The Trail of the Duke,'' he is the New Yorker whose fiancée, Mirabel Walmsley, sends him out one night to find the Duke. He seeks the Duke of Matterlane, but the Duke she misses is her poodle.

GARNEAU, HAROLD. In ''Presumption,'' he is Noel Garneau's wealthy father, about fifty, of Boston. He dislikes San Juan Chandler's mother's cousin, Cora Chandler. On the Culpepper Bay golf course, he hints Juan should quit college, make money, and pursue his dream girl, unaware his daughter, Noel, is that girl. In Boston later, Garneau does all he can to discourage Juan, but unsuccessfully.

GARNEAU, MRS. CLIFTON. In ''Dice, Brassknuckles & Guitar,'' she is a Southamptonite who helps break up James Powell's summer school.

GARNEAU, MRS. HAROLD. In ''Presumption,'' she is Noel Garneau's beautiful mother and a friend of San Juan Chandler's mother's cousin Cora Chandler of Culpepper Bay. The Garneaus fail to keep Noel and Juan apart.

GARNEAU, NOEL. In ''Presumption,'' she is the daughter of Harold Garneau and his wife, of Boston. At seventeen Noel met San Juan Chandler on a Montana dude ranch. She meets him again at his mother's cousin Cora Chandler's Culpepper Bay home. When their romance goes badly, she returns to Boston, becomes a debutante, and is engaged to Brooks Fish Templeton. Juan, who has made a fortune, pursues her to Boston, causes her to break her engagement, and finds her at her aunt Jo Poindexter's New York home, where her parents try to hide her.

GARNETT, CHAUNCEY. In ''The Adolescent Marriage,'' he is a successful Philadelphia architect, sixty-eight years old. At her parents' request, he talks to Llewellyn Clark, his assistant, and Lucy Wharton Clark, after the two young people elope, argue, and separate. He pretends he has arranged an annulment, helps Llewellyn, and brings Lucy to him.

GARROD, H. G. In "Gretchen's Forty Winks," he is a client whose acceptance and praise of Roger Halsey's advertising work is a godsend.

GARVIN. In *This Side of Paradise*, he is the small, silent associate of Ferrenby, who gives Amory Blaine a ride to Princeton.

GASPAR, MRS. In "Two Old-Timers," she is Sergeant Gaspar's wife, who is unimpressed by his talk about combat until they see Phil Macedon's supposedly realistic action as a soldier in *The Final Push*.

GASPAR, SERGEANT. In "Two Old-Timers," he detains both Pat Hobby and Phil Macedon after their car accident. A combat veteran, he admires Macedon's acting in *The Final Push*, a war movie, until Pat Hobby explains how Macedon was tricked into realistic footage. Gaspar promptly releases Pat.

GASPAR, WILLIAM ("FAT"). In "The Freshest Boy," he is the candy-loving St. Regis pupil who refuses to go to New York with Basil Duke Lee. In "Basil and Cleopatra," he invites Basil to visit him in Mobile, Alabama, and thus see Erminie Gilberte Labouisse Bibble there.

GATSBY, JAY. In *The Great Gatsby*, born James Gatz in 1890, and called Jimmy by Henry C. Gatz of Minnesota, his father, Gatsby is a combination of idealistic, romantic, and courteous host, war hero, dishonest businessman, and ostentatious roughneck. He was wealthy prospector Dan Cody's companion (1907 to 1912) but lost out on an inheritance from him. While training in the army in Louisville (1917), Gatsby fell in love with Daisy Fay; she did not wait for him to return from the war but married rich Tom Buchanan instead. Gatsby buys a house in West Egg, on Long Island, and hosts lavish parties to lure Daisy, who is living in more fashionable East Egg, back to him. She rendezvouses with him at Nick Carraway's house and in Gatsby's mansion but is reluctant to give up Tom's way of life. She lets Gatsby take the blame when she drives his car back from New York and kills Tom's mistress, Myrtle Wilson. Myrtle's husband, George B. Wilson, shoots Gatsby to death and then kills himself.

Bibliography: Matterson.

GATZ, HENRY C. In *The Great Gatsby*, he is Jay Gatsby's father. A solemn, dismayed old man, he comes from Minnesota to attend his son's funeral. He tells Nick Carraway about Gatsby's youthful hopes.

GAUSSE. In *Tender Is the Night*, he is a hotel owner whose success is partly due to his friend Dick Diver, whom he helps get Lady Caroline Sibly-Biers and Mary North, Contessa di Minghetti, out of jail.

GAUTIER. In ''The Count of Darkness,'' he is a farmer whom Count Philippe of Villefranche orders to supervise the division of tribute taken from the traders.

GEDNEY, FRED ("FREDDY"). In ''The Cut-Glass Bowl,'' he is the lover of Evylyn Piper. She falsely promised her husband, Harold, she would not see Fred again. When Harold comes home early, Fred, hiding in the dining room, bangs into the cut-glass bowl while trying to sneak out of the house.

GEER, BETTY. In ''Forging Ahead,'' she is a guest at Benjamin Reilly's dull party, which Basil Duke Lee must attend.

GEHRBOHM. In ''Lo, the Poor Peacock!,'' he is one of Jason Davis's shrinking number of potential clients.

GEORGE. In ''The Passionate Eskimo,'' he is a worker or a customer in a Chicago store visited by Pan-e-troon.

GEORGI, DR. In ''One Interne,'' he is a stomach specialist at the hospital.

GEORGIANNA. In '' 'Why Blame It on the Poor Kiss if the Girl Veteran of Many Petting Parties Is Prone to Affairs After Marriage?',' she is Harry's happily married wife.

GEORGIE, AUNT. In ''That Kind of Party,'' she is one of Terrence R. Tipton's aunts.

GERALD. In ''O Russet Witch!,'' he is one of three rowdy men accompanying Caroline to Pulpat's restaurant.

GERMAINE. In ''Rags Martin-Jones and the Pr-nce of W-les,'' she is one of the three maids working for Rags Martin-Jones. The other two are Dominique and Louise.

GIFFORD, NANCY HOLMES. In ''Three Hours between Planes,'' she was the object of Donald Plant's affection when both were children. Having time between planes, Donald visits her and finds her unhappily married to Walter Gifford. She confuses Donald Plant with Donald Bowers, another childhood pal.

GIFFORD, WALTER. In''Three Hours between Planes,'' he is Nancy Holmes Gifford's husband, who is away in New York and is probably unfaithful to her.

GILBERT, CATHERINE. In *The Beautiful and Damned*, she is Russel Gilbert's wife and Gloria Gilbert Patch's mother. From Kansas City, she is domineered by her husband, is vapid with her daughter, and dies in the course of the novel.

GILBERT, DODO. In ''Strange Sanctuary,'' he is a thief, in cahoots with Birdie Lukas (also known as Willie Lukas). He pretends to be Major Redfern, Charlie Craig's friend, to fool Dolly Haines, Charlie's niece. He attended a party at Angela Duckney's home but was unable to rob anyone there. The authorities also know him as Lord Dana and George Whilomville.

GILBERT, GLORIA. In *The Beautiful and Damned. See* Patch, Gloria Gilbert.

GILBERT, JOHN (1895–1936). Movie actor. He was catapulted to fame in *The Big Parade* (1925), directed by King Vidor.* When Fitzgerald was making a fool of himself at the 1931 Hollywood party in the home of Irving Thalberg* and his wife Norma Shearer,* Gilbert was also a guest and booed him. Perhaps in revenge, Fitzgerald modeled Phil Macedon, the conceited, cowardly actor in ''Two Old-Timers,'' on Gilbert. In *The Last Tycoon*, Gilbert is mentioned as having been bitten by a chimpanzee the previous year.

GILBERT, RUSSEL. In *The Beautiful and Damned*, he is Catherine Gilbert's domineering, bullying, ever-optimistic husband and Gloria Gilbert Patch's father. From Kansas City originally, he was in the celluloid business and is now associated with the movie business in New York, especially with Joseph Black.

GILE, BEAN. In ''The Bowl,'' he is a Princeton football player, at tackle.

GILLESPIE, DR. In ''One Interne,'' he is a physician at the hospital. His domestic problems are aired during the roast.

GILLESPIE, HOWARD. In *This Side of Paradise*, he is Rosalind Connage's unsuccessful suitor, twenty-four, at her coming-out party in New York.

GILRAY. In ''That Kind of Party,'' this is the person at whose home the first party was held at which Terrence R. Tipton was smitten by Dolly Bartlett's charms. Terrence's father regards Gilray as an ordinary man from upstate.

GILRAY, MRS. In ''That Kind of Party,'' she is evidently the hostess at the first party.

GINEVRA. In ''A Letter to Helen.'' *See* King, Ginevra.

GINGRICH, ARNOLD. (1903–1976). Editor and writer. He was born in Grand Rapids, Michigan, graduated from the University of Michigan in 1925, and did advertising work in Chicago. In 1928 he began an association with David Archibald Smart, cofounder of the Men's Wear Service Corporation, which produced fashion and trade publications. In 1931 the two men started *Apparel Arts*, a trade paper combining business and culture. In 1933 came their *Esquire*, an instant success with sales totaling more than ten million copies by 1937, mostly to middle-class men with money and leisure despite the Depression. *Esquire* combined eye-catching cartoons, girlie illustrations, and works by fine authors. For Esquire, Inc., Gingrich edited *Coronet* (1936–1945), *Verve* (1938–1939), and *Ken* (1938–1939). From 1942 to early 1945 he and his associates fought the government over the alleged obscenity of *Esquire* contents, finally winning. Gingrich lived abroad (1945–1949), then returned to the United States to edit *Flair* (1949–1951) and help *Esquire* (1952–1973) battle new competitors. Gingrich married Helen Mary Rowe in 1924, was widowered in 1955, and married Jane Kendall later that year. His hobbies were playing the violin and flyfishing.

For the first issue of *Esquire*, Gingrich helped assemble pieces by John Dos Passos,* Ernest Hemingway,* and Gilbert Seldes.* In 1936 he published ''The Snows of Kilimanjaro,'' in which Hemingway ridicules Fitzgerald's alleged worship of the rich. In 1934 Fitzgerald turned to *Esquire* and Gingrich, who was happy to publish him for small payments (the top being $250). In 1936 Gingrich suggested Fitzgerald write what became his *Crack-Up* pieces for *Esquire*. Between 1934 and 1979 Fitzgerald appeared in *Esquire* fifty times—two pieces evidently being by Zelda. Gingrich accepted Fitzgerald's Pat Hobby stories and introduced their 1962 reissue in book form. Gingrich was one of Fitzgerald's most loyal friends. Fitzgerald's letters and telegrams to him, usually from Hollywood, are mostly about deadlines, quick money, and pleas for higher pay. Gingrich edited collections of *Esquire* pieces in book form and wrote several books.

Bibliography: George H. Douglas, *The Smart Magazines: 50 Years of Literary Revelry and High Jinks at Vanity Fair, the New Yorker, Life, Esquire, and the Smart Set* (Hamden, Conn.: Archon, 1991); Arnold Gingrich, *Nothing But People: The Early Days of Esquire, A Personal History* (New York: Crown, 1971); James L. W. West III, ''Fitzgerald and *Esquire*,'' Bryer, *New Approaches*, 149–66.

GIRARD, CYRUS. In ''The Third Casket,'' he is a successful Wall Street businessman, sixty. Lacking a son, he decides to retire and wants to give his firm to the best young man he can find. He challenges Oswald Jones, Joseph Hardwick Parrish, and George Van Buren to work hard for three months. Whoever pleases him most will have the firm and can marry his daughter, Lola Girard. Jones wins by continuing to work and thus proving Girard himself does not wish to retire.

GIRARD, LOLA. In ''The Third Casket,'' she is Cyrus Girard's pretty, ivory-and-gold daughter. Courted by Oswald Jones, Joseph Hardwick Parrish, and George Van Buren, she chooses Jones.

THE GIRL FROM LAZY J. (1978). Play. (Characters: Jack Darcy, Tony Gonzoles, Jim, José, George Kendall, Mrs. George Kendall, Leticia Larned.) Jack Darcy is to guard the money of George Kendall, his uncle, who owns the Diamond O ranch in Texas, but Jack falls asleep. Tony Gonzoles ties him up and would steal the money, but Leticia Larned, a cowgirl from the Lazy J ranch, enters and stops Tony. Jack and Leticia plan to wed. This juvenile play, Fitzgerald's first drama, was performed in St. Paul in August 1911.

Bibliography: Margolies.

"GIRLS BELIEVE IN GIRLS" (1930). Essay. The era of the flapper started in 1912 when cabarets first mixed nice girls and those less so; it ended in 1922 when young people, educated by women, accepted postwar freedoms. Fiction, war, heroine worship, and males' social irrelevance all played a part. Women seek separate distinction and care less to remain innocent after twenty. America is a matriarchy of prewar mothers and postwar sisters. Fine American girls in Europe are more confident than their immature British and stiff French counterparts.

GISLER. In *Tender Is the Night*, he is the owner of a clinic on the Interlaken. Dr. Franz Gregorovius warns Dick Diver not to accept employment there.

GIUSEPPE. In *Fie! Fie! Fi-Fi!*, he sings with Del Monti in an effort to persuade Mrs. Bovine and Dulcette to have a lark in the dark with them.

GIUSEPPI. In "Imagination—and a Few Mothers," he is a typical laborer. Do-gooders suggest he play uplifting charades at home.

GIVEN, DR. In "The Love Boat," he is one of eight physicians panicky Bill Frothington thinks he might consult. The two knew each other at Harvard.

GLADYS. In *Fie! Fie! Fi-Fi!*, she is liked by Bill but captivated by Peter.

GLADYS. In "The Hotel Child," she is mentioned by Mrs. Schwartz as a family friend in the United States.

GLADYS. In "A Nice Quiet Place," she is Josephine Perry's aunt and owns property with her husband at Farm Islands, Michigan. They do not speak to their neighbor, Charles Dorrance, because of a boundary dispute. Gladys is Dick's mother and may be Josephine's mother's sister. The Perrys visit her this summer.

GLADYS. In "That Kind of Party," she is a girl with whom Terrence R. Tipton will let Joe Shoonover play.

GLEASON, MISS. In ''In the Holidays,'' she is the night superintendent who orders nurse Miss Collins to process Griffin's body.

GLOCK, DOCTOR. In ''The Bowl,'' he is a psychoanalyst who Jeff Deering says would incorrectly blame Dolly Harlan's dislike of football on fear of crowds and railroad travel.

GLORIA. In *The Great Gatsby*, she is a person whom Nick Carraway vaguely remembers as being among Jay Gatsby's summer guests.

GLUCOSE, ISRAEL. In ''Dice, Brassknuckles & Guitar,'' he is a writer, probably imaginary, the narrator would hire to write a transition if his work were a scenario rather than fiction.

GLYNN, MADAME. In ''What Became of Our Flappers and Sheiks?,'' she is a reputed expert who says girls check their corsets at dances.

"A GOD INTOXICATED FLY" (1981). Poem. A fly in a room listens to boastful, lying men and when they leave sucks up wet imprints of their hands.

"GODS OF DARKNESS" (1941). Short story. (Characters: André, Garavochi, Countess Griselda, Jaques, Josephe, Becquette Le Poire, Duke of Maine, Count Philippe of Villefranche, Pierre.) While swimming one October day, Count Philippe of Villefranche and Countess Griselda learn that some Venetian traders under Garavochi are approaching their ford. They exact tribute and then attend a party at the nearby monastery, where the abbott warns Philippe that his trusty friend Jaques belongs to a pagan cult that ought to be exterminated. The sinister Duke of Maine and his troops enter; it takes Jaques, along with Griselda, to disarm them and capture Maine by using mysterious words influencing Philippe to believe both are cultists. That night, while Maine is their prisoner, the three enter the cult's secret cave, where Becquette Le Poire, their leader, would like to punish Philippe for killing her father in the settlement last spring. But Jaques tells her the Northmen did the deed, and Griselda neutralizes the girl by identifying herself as the chief priestess of the Touraine witches. Maine agrees to depart in peace, and Philippe vows to save his people even if it means being half Christian and half pagan. He and Griselda will wed. Although Fitzgerald hoped to continue the Philippe stories to novel length, ''Gods of Darkness'' was the fourth and final such tale.

GOEBEL, EVA. In ''Crazy Sunday,'' she has been Miles Calman's lover for two years. His wife, Stella Walker Calman, knows about the affair, which Miles is trying to break off.

GOLDBERG. In ''The Offshore Pirate,'' this is one of the names in one of Curtis Carlyle's songs.

GOLDBERG, RUBE (1883–1970). (Full name: Reuben Lucius Goldberg.) American cartoonist, writer, and sculptor. He was born in San Francisco, earned a B.S. in engineering at the University of California in Berkeley, but became a newspaper cartoonist in San Francisco in 1905 and New York beginning in 1907. In 1915 he was first widely syndicated. A year later he married Irma Seeman, and they had two sons. By 1920 Goldberg's annual income was $185,000. He and his family had a Manhattan townhouse and in 1921 rented a summer home in Great Neck, Long Island. Fitzgerald and Ring Lardner* called on them almost immediately. When Goldberg said he wanted to get a haircut and then return home to finish a cartoon, his two visitors took him out for lunch, got him drunk, and persuaded a local barber to leave his shop, let them give Goldberg his haircut, and lock up. Goldberg fell asleep in the barber's chair and awoke to find his head shaved. Between 1922 and 1930 Goldberg published nineteen short stories and articles, often in the same issue of magazines featuring stories by Fitzgerald. In the 1930s Goldberg, while engaged in other activity, drew political cartoons. During World War II he entertained troops in the United States. His 1947 cartoon ''Peace Today'' warned of the dangers of the atomic bomb and won a Pulitzer Prize. In 1964 he became a sculptor and was honored with a retrospective exhibition at the Smithsonian Institution shortly before he died.

Bibliography: Peter C. Marzio, *Rube Goldberg: His Life and Work* (New York: Harper and Row, 1973).

GOLDEN. In ''Gretchen's Forty Winks,'' he is the superintendent of the building in which Roger Halsey has an office. He reminds Roger his rent is overdue.

GOLDGREAVES. In ''In the Darkest Hour,'' he is a Viking, the son of Robert the Frog. Count Philippe of Villefranche successfully attacks the Viking encampment in the Loire Valley and reluctantly orders Goldgreaves's execution.

GOLDING, T. F. In ''One Trip Abroad,'' he is the owner of a yacht in the Monacan Bay. His party is at lunch when Nicole Kelly discovers her husband, Nelson, kissing Madame Noel Delauney. In *Tender Is the Night*, he graciously entertains the Divers when they crash his yacht party in the Nicean Bay. His guests also include Tommy Barban and Lady Caroline Sibly-Biers.

GOLDSTIEN, KATIE. In ''The Dance,'' she is a black maid at the country club. Now about fifty, she was once Catherine Jones's nurse. Catherine gets her to fire a revolver upstairs while Catherine is dancing downstairs at the club in an unsuccessful effort to throw suspicion off Catherine, who had killed Marie Bannerman a little earlier. Katie is the sister of Thomas, the band leader.

GONZOLES, TONY. In *The Girl from Lazy J*, he is the Mexican cowboy whose blackmail and robbery scheme Leticia Larned foils. He is also called Dead Shot Hoskins.

GOODDORF, HARRY. In ''Pat Hobby's Christmas Wish,'' he is Pat Hobby's producer. He went to Hollywood at sixteen, worked for Biograph until 1920, and by 1921 was associated with First National Studios. He has been married twice. When Pat and his secretary, Helen Kagle, Harry's former mistress, try to blackmail Harry, he laughs easily and adequately explains his innocence. In ''Pat Hobby's Preview,'' he is mentioned as one to whom Pat might appeal to get Eleanor Carter a screen test.

GORMAN, HERBERT SHERBET. In ''All the girls and mans,'' he is an object of attention.

GORMAN, JOE. In ''He Thinks He's Wonderful,'' he is Basil Duke Lee's hometown friend. Joe, who sings well, invites Basil to his home overnight. Once there, Basil boasts that girls think he is wonderful and tells Joe how to shape up. To retaliate, Joe puts Basil in his back seat and Lewis Crum and Hubert Blair in the front seat when he drives to Connie Davis's party, where he tells the girls Basil thinks they admire him. In ''The Captured Shadow,'' he is a boy Basil would not want to act in his play *The Captured Shadow*.

GOTROCKS. In ''A Snobbish Story,'' this is the name John Boynton Bailey calls Josephine Perry, to hint at the Perry family wealth.

GOTTLIEB, CAPTAIN. In ''The Bowl,'' he is the captain of the Yale football team.

GOULD, HARRIET. In *Thoughtbook*, she is a playful friend.

GOVAN, BEN. In ''The Family Bus,'' he is a man who owned the family car before the value of its carburetor was revealed.

GOVERNOR OF CALIFORNIA, THE. In *The Last Tycoon*, he is mentioned as bringing a group of visitors to Monroe Stahr's movie studio.

GOWN, JOHNNY. In *Thoughtbook*, he is Fitzgerald's successful rival for the affections of Kitty Williams.

GRACE. In "A Short Autobiography," she is a fellow drinker in France in 1926.

GRADY, HENRY. In " 'Send Me In, Coach,' " he is one of the boys who rehearse the play.

GRAHAM. In "Myra Meets His Family," he is the owner of the kennel where Knowleton Whitney rents dogs in his scheme to scare Myra Harper out of wishing to marry him.

GRAHAM, SHEILAH (1904?–1988). Hollywood columnist and writer. She was born Lily Sheil in London's East End, lived in an orphanage from six to fourteen, and was a factory worker, housemaid, and department-store employee. She married Major John Graham Gillam, who though not well off paid for acting lessons for her. Calling herself Sheilah Graham, she became a musical comedy chorus girl and mingled in high society. In 1933 she left her husband to go to New York, where she worked as a journalist and gossip columnist for the New York *Evening Journal*. Starting in 1935 she was a Hollywood gossip writer syndicated by the North American Newspaper Alliance. In July 1937 Sheilah, divorced earlier that year, met Fitzgerald at a party given by Robert Benchley. The occasion was Sheilah's "engagement" to the Marquess of Donegall, another Hollywood gossip writer. Fitzgerald noticed her startling resemblance to his wife, Zelda (*see* Fitzgerald, Zelda Sayre). Soon they were going places together; before long they were lovers, and she broke off her relationship with the marquess. The two might have married but for Zelda's condition. When Sheilah revealed a desire to do serious writing, Fitzgerald provided encouragement and helped her with *Dame Rumor*, a play about a Hollywood gossip columnist. He persuaded his agent, Harold Ober,* with whom he often corresponded about Sheilah, to prepare a contract for the play in February 1938; it soon came to naught. In April she persuaded Fitzgerald to move from the expensive Garden of Allah hotel to Malibu; in October he moved to Encino. By then she had written a story or sketch critical of radio; at Fitzgerald's request, Ober tried but failed to sell it. In fall 1938 Fitzgerald took Sheilah to visit Ober, Gerald Murphy,* Sara Murphy,* and Edmund Wilson,* among other friends in the East. In 1938 and 1939 Fitzgerald worked up a two-year reading list for Sheilah. Stressing literature and history but featuring art and music as well, it aimed to fill gaps in her education. He tutored her in what she called her "College of One." When she lectured about Hollywood on tour in 1939, Fitzgerald helped her with comments on the significance of movie directors. When a reporter criticized her lecture, Fitzgerald went to the man's Sunset Boulevard office to beat him up but could not find him. The result of a vacation Fitzgerald and Sheilah enjoyed in Tijuana, Mexico, early in 1940, was a rare picture of the two taken together. In May 1940 he moved to a Hollywood apartment a block from her apartment at 1443 North Hayworth Avenue. The two conducted their often tempestuous affair as discreetly as possible. They maintained separate residences. Much of the time, Sheilah, who did not drink, helped him abstain; when he was drunk, he was often vicious to her. During his disastrous trip to Dartmouth, she flew on the same airplane with him but sat some distance away, stayed in New York, and helped him get to a New York hospital afterward. After a heart attack, in November 1940, Fitzgerald moved into Sheilah's apartment and died there a month later. She did not attend his funeral. Zelda probably did not know about Sheilah's affair with Fitzgerald; however, hints in *The Last Tycoon*, in which Kathleen Moore is based on Sheilah, undoubtedly helped Zelda draw valid conclusions when she read the novel in 1941. Pamela Knighton in ''Last Kiss,'' which Zelda never read, is also closely patterned on Sheilah.

Sheilah Graham richly capitalized on her liaison with Fitzgerald in *Beloved Infidel: The Education of a Woman* (1958, with Gerold Frank), *The Rest of the Story* (1964), *College of One* (1967), *The Real Scott Fitzgerald* (1976), and several articles. Her other books are *Confessions of a Hollywood Columnist* (1969), *The Garden of Allah* (1970), *A State of Heat* (1972), and *Hollywood Revisited: A Fiftieth Anniversary Celebration* (1984), many of which contain deliberate, self-glamorizing falsehoods. The front endpapers of *Beloved Infidel* contain ''For Sheilah, a Beloved Infidel,'' Fitzgerald's poem about her flirtatiousness. In 1941 she married Trevor Westbrook, a British aviation-production man, had two children (one not Westbrook's), and obtained a divorce. In the 1950s she married W. S. Wojkiewicz, a young football coach, and grew wealthy through writing and radio and television appearances. She died in Florida.

GRAINGER, ARTHUR. In ''O Russet Witch!,'' he is the son of Merlin Grainger and Olive Masters Grainger. He sells bonds on Wall Street and treats his father abusively. The names Merlin and Arthur have ironic implications: this Arthur is not chivalric, nor does Merlin Wield any magic.

GRAINGER, MERLIN. In ''O Russet Witch!,'' he works in Moonlight Quill's bookshop, resists the bewitching Caroline, marries Olive Masters, becomes Arthur's father, and inherits the bookshop. Late in his dull life, when sixty-five, he and Caroline meet again, in his shop, but too late. The only magic in his life comes from his books.

GRAINGER, OLIVE MASTERS. In ''O Russet Witch!,'' she is an employee in Moonlight Quill's bookshop. She and Merlin Grainger get married and have a son, Arthur. She keeps Merlin from Caroline's bewitching influence and treats him abusively.

GRANBY, ALEC. In *The Beautiful and Damned*, he and his wife live in Marietta, visit Anthony Patch and Gloria Gilbert Patch when the Patches first arrive there, but ignore them thereafter.

GRANBY, JOHN. In ''The Perfect Life,'' he is a St. Regis alumnus and now a rigidly righteous Princeton student. His persuading Basil Duke Lee to be a role model by leading ''the perfect life'' is effective only temporarily.

GRANBY, MRS. ALEC. In *The Beautiful and Damned*, she and her husband are the Patches' Marietta neighbors.

GRANBY, PETER. In *The Beautiful and Damned*, he is mentioned by Maury Noble as a friend with whom he had a Turkish bath in Boston. He does not appear to be related to Alec Granby.

GRANGE, RED. In ''No Flowers,'' he is William Delaney Johns's university friend. Although his hair is black, he is nicknamed Red after Harold Edward ''Red'' Grange (1903–1991), the famous football player. Grange here is admired because, although from a wealthy family, he affects poverty by having patches sewn onto his new clothes. Johns finds Red passed out and dressed in a beautiful tuxedo, and Johns appropriates it for himself.

GRANNY ("GRANDMA"). In ''The Count of Darkness,'' she is a peasant hag, eighty, dispirited because her son died in the previous day's fight. Count Philippe of Villefranche cajols her into cooperating by flattering her.

GRANT, CARY (1904–1986). A movie actor. In *The Last Tycoon*, he is described by Monroe Stahr as not liking his lines in a movie being filmed that Stahr calls trashy.

GRANT, ULYSSES SIMPSON (1822–1885). Union army general during the Civil War and eighteenth president of the United States. In ''The True Story of Appomattox,'' General Grant offered to surrender to General Robert E. Lee until Grant broke his pencil and Lee offered his sword to sharpen it.

GRANVILLE, BONITA (1923–1988). Movie actress. She began her career playing roles as a vicious adolescent, starred in four Nancy Drew adventure movies, and appeared in mature roles in the 1940s. In ''Pat Hobby, Putative Father,'' Bonita Granville is on the stage that Pat Hobby takes Prince John Brown Hobby Indore and his uncle, Sir Singrim Dak Raj, to see.

GRAYSON, MISS. In *Coward*, she is an authority on etiquette, cited by Angelina Bangs.

THE GREAT GATSBY (1925). Novel. (Characters: Stonewall Jackson Abrams, Albrucksburger, Hubert Auerbach, Backhysson, Miss Baedeker, Jordan Baker, Edgar Beaver, Becker, Chester Becker, S. W. Belcher, Beluga, Bemberg, Russell Betty, Blackbuck, Brewer, Daisy Fay Buchanan, Pammy Buchanan,

Tom Buchanan, Francis Bull, Bunsen, Carraway, Nick Carraway, Catherine, Catlip, Cheadle, Chrome, Mrs. Chrystie, Dr. Webster Civet, Dan Cody, Clyde Cohen, Consuela, Corrigan, Croirier, Da Fontano, Dancie, De Jong, Dennicker, Dewar, George Duckweed, Duke, Mrs. Eberhardt, Eckhaust, Dr. T. J. Eckleburg, Edgar, Clarence Endive, Etty, James B. Ferret, Fishguard, Ardita Fitz-Peters, Maurice A. Flink, Jay Gatsby, Henry C. Gatz, Gloria, Gulick, Miss Haag, Hammerhead, Hersey, Claudia Hip, Hornbeam, Mrs. Sigourney Howard, Ismay, Jaqueline, P. Jewett, Jimmy, Judy, June, Katspaugh, Ella Kaye, Kelleher, Ewing Klipspringer, Leech, Ed Legros, Ernest Lilly, Arthur McCarty, Benny McClenahan, Chester McKee, Lucille McKee, Mavro Michaelis, Muldoon, G. Earl Muldoon, Mulready, Mr. Mumble, Lester Myer, Faustina O'Brien, Horace O'Donavan, Newton Orchid, Ordway, Owl-Eyes, Henry L. Palmetto, Pole, Quinn, Cecil Roebuck, Mrs. Claude Roosevelt, Rosy Rosenthal, Cecil Schoen, O.R.P. Schraeder, Schultze, Don S. Schwartze, Scully, Sloane, Smirke, Ripley Snell, Stella, Mrs. Ulysses Swett, Vladimir Tostoff, Willie Voltaire, Gus Waize, S. B. Whitebait, George B. Wilson, Myrtle Wilson, Winebrenner, Meyer Wolfsheim.)

Nick Carraway, the narrator, graduated from Yale in 1915, served in France during the war, and after returning to his wealthy Midwestern family comes to New York in spring 1922 to sell bonds. When he rents a small house in West Egg, on Long Island (based on Great Neck), he becomes Jay Gatsby's next-door neighbor. Nick's cousin, Daisy Fay Buchanan, twenty-three, and her wealthy husband, Tom Buchanan, an overbearing Yale man, thirty, live in more fashionable nearby East Egg (based on Manhasset). When Nick is invited to dine at the Buchanans' mansion one June evening, he meets and is attracted to Jordan Baker, a jaunty golfer, twenty-one. Tom receives a telephone call, and Daisy leaves the table and is heard arguing with him. Jordan informs Nick that Tom has a girlfriend in New York. Returning, Daisy suggests to Nick that she is unhappily married. Back at his house again, Nick sees Gatsby standing in his yard and gazing across the bay toward East Egg.

Tom takes Nick to meet to his girlfriend, Myrtle Wilson, in a New York apartment he has rented for their trysts. Sensual and in her mid-thirties, she lives with her husband, George B. Wilson, a mechanic about her age in a gas station between West Egg and New York near an ashen valley. She often goes to New York by saying she is meeting her sister, Catherine. One Sunday afternoon Nick accompanies Tom there and meets Catherine. Other guests are Chester McKee, a vapid photographer, and his brassy wife, Lucille. Catherine says she has partied at Gatsby's mansion, regards him as scary, and tells Nick that Tom would marry Myrtle but for Daisy's being a Catholic and opposed to divorce—all untrue. After everyone gets drunk, Tom objects to Myrtle's saying Daisy's name, shoves her, and breaks her nose.

Gatsby throws numerous summer parties, with much drink, food, and dance music. Swarms of selfish guests attend. Gatsby sends Nick an invitation to come to his next gathering, and Nick begins to hear about the man's background.

When the two meet, Nick is impressed by his formality and courtesy. Gatsby asks Jordan, also there, to meet with him privately, after which she hints to Nick that Gatsby revealed something extraordinary.

In July Gatsby visits Nick's house and drives him to New York in a flashy yellow car. He spins an account of himself combining fact and fiction: he is from a rich Midwestern family who now live in San Francisco, attended Oxford University, was a decorated war hero, traveled widely, and was unhappy once—which he says Jordan can tell him about. Nick and Gatsby have lunch in New York with Meyer Wolfsheim, a shady gambler and Gatsby's business friend. Gatsby tells Nick that Wolfsheim fixed the 1919 World Series. When Tom appears, Gatsby seems embarrassed and absents himself.

Jordan tells Nick that in October 1917 she saw Gatsby and Daisy in a car in Louisville; that winter she was restrained by her family from going to New York to see a soldier off to the war; after the armistice she had her debut; in June 1919 she reluctantly married Tom. Seemingly happy, the couple had a three-month South Seas honeymoon. Back in California, Daisy learned of an affair Tom was having with a chambermaid. The Buchanans had a daughter and spent a year in France. Six weeks ago Jordan discovered the lieutenant Daisy loved but did not wait for was Gatsby. He still worships her, bought his West Egg mansion to be near her, and wants Nick to host a tea party for him and Daisy. Nick invites the former lovers to his house, leaves them alone, and returns to find them relaxed and joyful. The three go to Gatsby's place, where he impresses Daisy with his wealth and possessions—especially his lovely shirts.

Gatsby tells Nick he was born in North Dakota as James Gatz, a poor boy full of dreams. From 1907 to 1912 he was a companion and assistant of Dan Cody, a wealthy millionaire prospector in his fifties, whose promised legacy of $25,000 Gatsby never got, because of the machinations of Ella Kaye. She was a newspaperwoman who boarded Cody's yacht and somehow inherited his wealth. Gatsby amassed his own fortune later. He wants Daisy to deny she ever really loved Tom, to leave him, and to marry Gatsby.

The four young people socialize, and Tom despises and feels threatened by Gatsby. Sensing Daisy's disapproval of his noisy lifestyle, Gatsby replaces his servants with tougher ones hired by Wolfsheim. Daisy can now rendezvous with him safely in his mansion. When tensions mount during a gathering at the Buchanans', Daisy suggests going into New York for the hot afternoon. Sensing her defection, Tom wants to drive her in Gatsby's yellow car. She counters that she will go with Gatsby in Tom's car. When Jordan, with Tom driving both her and Nick in Gatsby's car, suggests stopping at Wilson's garage for gas, Tom leads that suspicious man to believe that Gatsby's yellow car is Tom's. Wilson terrifies Tom by reporting he and Myrtle are leaving town soon. From a window, Myrtle sees the group and thinks Jordan is Daisy. The troubled fivesome rent a hotel room and drink a good deal. Tom challenges Gatsby's romanticized account of his past. Gatsby delights Nick by explaining his war record and his brief time at Oxford's war school after the armistice. Tom accuses Gatsby of threatening his marriage. Gatsby replies that Daisy loves only Gatsby. Tom admits his waywardness but forces Daisy to say she did love him once. Gatsby is aghast when she says she has loved both men. Daisy tells Tom she will leave him, whereupon Tom accuses Gatsby of bootlegging and worse criminal activity. Feeling he has regained control of Daisy, Tom permits Gatsby to drive her home in Gatsby's car. Tom, driving his own car, will follow with Nick and Jordan.

Tragedy erupts. Myrtle sees the yellow car, thinks it is Tom's, runs onto the road to hail him, and is struck and killed. The car speeds on. Tom drives up, finds his mistress dead, and blames Gatsby. Since the police can trace the hit-and-run car, Nick, sick by now of the entire shoddy group, seeks out Gatsby to warn him, but finds him waiting loyally in the dark, outside the Buchanan home, to make sure Daisy is all right. He says Daisy was driving his car but he will take responsibility. Nick peeks in on Tom and Daisy: they are whispering in the kitchen like cozy conspirators. Nick warns Gatsby, who reminisces about Daisy, the war, and her marriage, which he calls "just personal." Nick tells Gatsby he is the best of the whole group, and Gatsby smiles radiantly. By phone in his office, Nick breaks off his affair with Jordan. Wilson, certain the car that killed his wife was driven by her lover, traces it to Gatsby through Tom's connivance, shoots Gatsby to death in his swimming pool, then kills himself.

No one at the inquest implicates Daisy. Gatsby's father, Henry C. Gatz, arrives in September for his son's funeral and speaks admiringly of him. Wolfsheim, who says he "made" Gatsby, tells Nick he will not attend his funeral, which Nick arranges and which few attend. In October, before returning to the Midwest, Nick chances to see Tom on Fifth Avenue; they speak curtly. Nick finds an obscenity scrawled on Gatsby's steps, goes to the beach, and thinks of Gatsby's romantic adoration of Daisy and all it implies.

Bibliography: Ronald Berman, *The Great Gatsby and Fitzgerald's World of Ideas* (Tuscaloosa: University of Alabama Press, 1997); Matthew J. Bruccoli, ed., *New Essays on "The Great Gatsby"* (New York: Cambridge University Press, 1985); Bruccoli, *Gatsby*; A. E. Elmore, "*The Great Gatsby* as Well Wrought Urn," in *Modern American Fiction: Form and Function*, ed. Thomas Daniel Young, 57–92 (Baton Rouge: Louisiana State University Press, 1989); Richard Lehan, *The Great Gatsby: The Limits of Wonder* (Boston: Twayne, 1991); Gary J. Scrimgeour, "Against *The Great Gatsby*," *Criticism* 8 (1966): 75–86.

GREAT LOVER, THE. In "Crazy Sunday," he is the famous actor who boos Joel Coles's drunken skit at Miles Calman's Sunday party. Nat Keogh calls him a Three Piece Suit. The Great Lover is based on the volatile movie actor John Gilbert.*

GREEN. In "The Offshore Pirate," this is one of the names in one of Curtis Carlyle's songs.

GREEN. In ''Winter Dreams,'' he is Dexter Green's father, owner of the second-best Black Bear grocery store. He can afford to send his son to the state university but not to a more sophisticated Eastern one.

GREEN, DEXTER. In ''Winter Dreams,'' he is the materialistic dreamer who caddies as a boy, fourteen, for rich men at an exclusive Minnesota club. He graduates from an Eastern university and develops a successful string of laundries—all this to win the beautiful, rich Judy Jones, back home. They become intimate and talk of marriage, but she is fickle and conscienceless. He loses her, after which, in time—learning that her beauty has faded—he lacks even the power to grieve. Green partly prefigures Jay Gatsby of *The Great Gatsby*.

GREEN, DOROTHY. In *Thoughtbook*, she is a playful, tomboy friend. She calls Fitzgerald ''dippy.'' The name is sometimes spelled Greene.

GREEN, HAROLD. In *Thoughtbook*, he is a club member. The name is sometimes spelled Greene.

GREEN, MRS. In ''Winter Dreams,'' she is Dexter Green's mother. Her maiden name was Krimslich, and she retains her Bohemian accent.

GREGG, ALLEN. In ''Dalyrimple Goes Wrong,'' he got the job on the governor's staff that was half-promised to Bryan Dalyrimple. Gregg obtained preference because he G. P. Gregg's son.

GREGG, G. P. In ''Dalyrimple Goes Wrong,'' he is evidently a friend of the governor, who gave Gregg's son, Allen Gregg, a position on his staff that Bryan Dalyrimple was led to believe he might have.

GREGOROVIUS, DR. FRANZ ("DR. GREGORY"). In *Tender Is the Night*, he is the conscientious Swiss psychiatrist at the Zurichsee clinic. Well-trained under Dr. Dohlmer, he develops a fine clinic with Dick Diver until the latter became irresponsible. He is forty in 1925. In some editions his name is spelled Gregorovious.

GREGOROVIUS, KAETHE. In *Tender Is the Night*, she is Dr. Franz Gregorovius's plain but canny wife. She tells her husband that the alcoholic Dick Diver is no longer a serious physician.

GREGORY, DR. In ''Gretchen's Forty Winks,'' he is a neighborhood physician who, when summoned by Roger Halsey, prescribes forty winks for Gretchen Halsey, reports George Tompkins has had a breakdown, and pronounces Roger in great shape.

GREGORY, WALTER. In ''Myra Meets His Family,'' he is Myra Harper's cousin, who lives in New York. She telephones him to pretend he is a minister and to ''marry'' her and Knowleton Whitney in a fake ceremony.

GREGSON. In ''The Mystery of the Raymond Mortgage,'' he is a detective who tries to help Egan, the Santuka chief of police.

GRESHAM, JOHN. In ''One Interne,'' he was a revered researcher who died of radium poisoning. Thea Singleton was in love with him. His encouraging her to get tough may have caused her reluctance to love again.

"GRETCHEN'S FORTY WINKS" (1924). Short story. (Characters: Bebé, H. G. Garrod, Golden, Dr. Gregory, Gretchen Halsey, Maxy Halsey, Roger Halsey, Kingsley, George Tompkins.) One wintry night Roger Halsey, an independent New York advertising agent, returns to his suburban home laden with paperwork. He tells his selfish, lazy wife, Gretchen, that he must toil day and night for six weeks to land some make-or-break accounts. Smoking away, she says right now they must go dine with George Tompkins, a successful New York interior decorator. Since the Halseys have no car, Tompkins will pick them up and drive them to his nice house, in his better neighborhood, as soon as Gretchen has a bath and gets ready. Roger kisses their baby, Maxy, and resigns himself to a dull evening. At dinner Tompkins criticizes him for overworking and recommends his own helpful work-and-exercise regimen. He suggests that wives suffer when husbands are workaholics. Back home Roger suggests that while he slaves for the next forty days Gretchen should sleep forty winks and awaken to their success. While he toils on, she lounges with a book and goes horseback riding and skiing and to the theater with Tompkins. One January evening she invites Tompkins over for dinner, and they have fun while Roger works upstairs. Soon the two men argue, Roger orders Tompkins out, and Gretchen stomps off to bed. Roger continues to work, grows hysterical, and falls asleep on the couch. In the morning he buys some sleeping powder and mixes it in coffee, which he takes up to sullen Gretchen. He steals all her shoes, cuts the telephone line, tells the nurse to take Maxy out all day, and goes to New York for some final desperate work. Next morning he receives word that his fine layout has pleased his biggest client and a $40,000 account is his. Roger returns home, wakes up Gretchen, explains with difficulty that she lost a whole day while he landed a fine account, and summons Dr. Gregory when Gretchen complains of near collapse. The doctor recommends forty winks for her, says Tompkins just had a breakdown because of overexercise and is moving west, and tells Roger that he has never looked better.

GRIEBEL, LOUIE. In ''Pat Hobby and Orson Welles,'' he is a Hollywood executive Pat Hobby names as a friend in an unsuccessful effort to get past the guard at the front gate.

GRIFFIN. In ''In the Holidays,'' he is the witness in a New York case who tries unsuccessfully to avoid being murdered by checking himself into the hospital. Joe Kinney does the same, having hired Flute Cuneo, Oaky, and Vandervere to shoot Griffin, which they do.

GRIFFIN, BOB. In ''Last Kiss,'' he is a Hollywood director whose success is owing to his even temper. Despite Jim Leonard's efforts, Pamela Knighton argues disastrously with him.

GRIGGS, BEN. In *Thoughtbook*, he is a boy who likes Marie Hersey.

GRISELDA, COUNTESS. In ''The Kingdom in the Dark,'' she is a beauty, about twenty, and French but with Northern coloration. She escapes the clutches of King Louis the Stammerer, is befriended by Count Philippe of Villefranche, and persuades him to remain loyal to their king, loathsome though he is. In ''Gods of Darkness,'' she is called Countess Griselda and is revealed to be a cultist and the head priestess of the Touraine witches. Her knowledge of pagan worship enables her, with the help of Jaques, to save Philippe. She and Philippe plan to wed.

GROSS, DR. In ''The Love Boat,'' he is one of eight physicians panicky Bill Frothington thinks he might consult.

GUESCELIN. In ''The Count of Darkness,'' he is a worker for Count Philippe of Villefranche, who orders him to get some women from the settlement.

GUESCULIN. In ''The Kingdom in the Dark,'' he is a squire in King Louis the Stammerer's retinue. Count Philippe of Villefranche ties him up to prevent his reporting the location of Griselda's horse.

"THE GUEST IN ROOM NINETEEN" (1937). Short story. (Characters: John Canisius, Cass.) Mr. Cass, suffering from the effects of a stroke, stays in Room 18 in a hotel. One night he seems to be flying out of himself but in reality has only fainted. Another evening he queries the night watchman about a stranger in Room 19, but there is no such room. Spring comes, and the watchman is no longer needed. One cool night after Easter, Cass asks a stranger with a face pockmarked like his partner John Canisius's to help him carry in a log and dies. This stranger was the manager's brother, kept from the guests because he was rough. Did Cass mistake him for death personified? Or was he death? The manager's brother says he saw two old guys, both resembling death.

GUGIMONIKI, R. In *The Beautiful and Damned*, he is the head of an employment agency through which Anthony Patch obtained Tanalahaka, his Japanese servant in Marietta.

GUILLET DE LA GUIMPÉ, COMTE PAUL DE LA. In "The Intimate Strangers," he is Marquise Sara de la Guillet de la Guimpé's brother-in-law.

GUILLET DE LA GUIMPÉ, MARQUIS EDUARD DE LA. In "The Intimate Strangers," he is Marquise Sara de la Guillet de la Guimpé's husband. In 1914 he is forty-one, twenty years her senior. He is wounded in World War I, is confined to a wheelchair, and dies in 1925. She never loved him, although they have a daughter, Miette de la Guillet de la Guimpé, and a son, Marquis Henri de la Guillet de la Guimpé.

GUILLET DE LA GUIMPÉ, MARQUIS HENRI DE LA. In "The Intimate Strangers," he is the son of Marquis Eduard de la Guillet de la Guimpé and the Marquise Sara de la Guillet de la Guimpé. Henri is twelve in the summer of 1926.

GUILLET DE LA GUIMPÉ, MARQUISE SARA DE LA. In "The Intimate Strangers," she at seventeen married Marquis Eduard de la Guillet de la Guimpé and had two children, Miette de la Guillet de la Guimpé and Marquis Henri de la Guillet de la Guimpé. Sara's sisters are Mrs. Caxton Bisby and the Hon. Martha Burne-Dennison, both of whom meddle in her affairs. Twenty-one in 1914, Sara meets Cedric Killian on Long Island, and the two share two weeks in North Carolina. During the war she nurses wounded soldiers in Paris. She has a one-night stand with an American officer there in 1918. Her husband dies of a war wound in 1925. A year later she meets Killian, they marry, and she becomes Sara Killian.

GUILLET DE LA GUIMPÉ, MIETTE DE LA. In "The Intimate Strangers," she is the daughter of Marquis Eduard de la Guillet de la Guimpé and Marquise Sara de la Guillet de la Guimpé. Miette is fourteen in the summer of 1926.

GUILLET DE LA GUIMPÉ, NOEL DE LA. In "The Intimate Strangers," she is the sister of Marquis Eduard de la Guillet de la Guimpé. She may be married, but if so her married name is not given.

GUISE, THE HON. ELINOR. In "The Rubber Check," she is a person Val Schuyler recalls dancing with at Lord Clan-Carly's 1929 coming-of-age party at Newport.

GULICK. In *The Great Gatsby*, Nick Carraway lists his name on a timetable as one of Jay Gatsby's summer guests. He comes from West Egg and is a state senator.

GUNTER. In *The Beautiful and Damned*, he is named as the manufacturer of a brand of whiskey.

GUNTHER. In ''More Than Just a House,'' he is the father of Amanda, Bess, and Jean. With his wife and daughters, he lives in a ramshackle mansion outside Baltimore. He appreciates Lew Lowrie's rescue of Amanda and Jean in 1925 and invites Lew to visit. In 1932 Gunther, by then widowered and senile, dies.

GUNTHER, AMANDA. In ''More Than Just a House,'' she is twenty, beautiful, and blond, when in 1925 Lew Lowrie rescued her and her sister Jean Gunther from an oncoming train. Lew attends a dance held at the Gunther mansion and falls in love with Amanda, only to learn that she is to marry George Horton and move to New York. Amanda has some babies and then in 1929 dies giving birth to yet another.

GUNTHER, BESS. In ''More Than Just a House,'' she is the youngest daughter of Gunther and his wife. In 1925 she is sixteen and wears braces on her teeth. Her sisters are Amanda Gunther and Jean Gunther. She tells Lew Lowrie she will prove to be the Cinderella of the family. After their mother dies, she cares for their father. In 1933 Lew returns to the mortgaged and stripped mansion, which Bess, now exquisite and strong, has through pride just pretended is full of guests at her imminent wedding. Not so. She and Lew will get married.

GUNTHER, JEAN. In ''More Than Just a House,'' she is the middle daughter, dark and beautiful, of the Gunthers. After their mother dies, she becomes selfish and alcoholic and lets Bess care for their father. Between 1929 and 1933, Jean marries a Chinese man and goes to China with him.

GUNTHER, MRS. In ''More Than Just a House,'' she is Gunther's wife and the mother of Amanda, Bess, and Jean. She dies between 1925 and 1929.

GUSON, ALFRED. In *Thoughtbook*, he helped Fitzgerald found a club.

GUYENNE, DUKE OF. In ''The Kingdom in the Dark,'' he is a grizzled warrior in King Louis the Stammerer's retinue. He admires Count Philippe of Villefranche's spunk but dares not oppose the king openly.

GWEN. In *Fie! Fie! Fi-Fi!*, she is to marry Peter but prefers Bill.

GYGSUM. In ''The Diamond as Big as the Ritz,'' he is the black servant assigned to wait on John T. Unger.

GYP THE BLOOD. In ''The Rough Crossing,'' he is mentioned as a broker who attends the fancy dinner aboard ship.

H

HAAG, MISS. In *The Great Gatsby*, Nick Carraway remembers her as among Jay Gatsby's summer guests. She is Albrucksburger's fiancée.

HAEDGE. In "The Popular Girl," he is a friend of Tom Bowman, after whose death he handles Bowman's will.

HAGERTY, PAULA LEGENDRE THAYER. In "The Rich Boy," she is the independently wealthy California brunette who loves and would marry reluctant Anson Hunter. Later she has three children in a loveless marriage with Lowell Thayer, divorces him, marries Peter Hagerty and is happy, but dies in childbirth.

HAGERTY, PETER ("PETE"). In "The Rich Boy," he is Paula Legendre Thayer's second husband. While in New York, he and Paula bump into Anson Hunter and invite him to their Rye residence. Because Hagerty is secure in his marriage, he tolerates Anson's overnight visit.

HAGGIN. In "New Types," he, along with his wife, is a guest at Emily Holliday's party for Paula Jorgensen.

HAGGIN, MRS. In "New Types," she is a guest at Emily Holliday's party. Paula Jorgensen smoothly explains that Emily is indisposed.

HAIGHT. In *The Beautiful and Damned*, he is a lawyer engaged for a $15,000 retainer to try to break Adam Patch's will disinheriting Anthony Patch. He eventually succeeds.

HAIGHT, GOUVERNEER. In ''Two Wrongs,'' he is a fashionable Long Islander whose name William McChesney drops to impress Emmy Pinkard when the two are having lunch in New York.

HAIGHT, MARJORIE. In ''The Jelly-Bean,'' she was a school acquaintance whose gossip about James Powell made him feel unwanted.

HAINES, DOLLY. In ''Strange Sanctuary,'' she is a student in Baltimore, thirteen, whose father, Morton Haines, shuffles her from home to home. She meets and likes Clarke Cresswell, is fooled by Dodo Gilbert, and is happy to meet her uncle, Charlie Craig, and see her father again.

HAINES, MORTON. In ''Strange Sanctuary,'' he is the widowered father of Dolly Haines. Long sick in New Mexico, he suddenly returns to Baltimore and to his daughter.

HALBIRD, JUNE. In ''The Rubber Check,'' she is Ellen Mortmain's friend who gives her permission to invite a date to a weekend party at the Halbirds' Long Island house. Ellen invites Val Schuyler.

HALBIRD, MRS. In ''The Rubber Check,'' she is June Halbird's mother and the hostess at the weekend party at her Long Island house. She deftly insults Val Schuyler, one of her guests, by reminding him of his station in life.

HALE, MUSIDORA. In ''The Dance,'' she is the aunt of the narrator, who visits her for three weeks in the Southern town of Davis.

"HALF-AND-HALF GIRL" (1981). Poem. The poet defines a girl by citing contradictory aspects of her behavior. She is, for example, alternately polite and rude and does only half her school work. Then he identifies her as his daughter.

HALKLITE. In ''Lo, the Poor Peacock!,'' he is the efficient, kind vice president of Pan-American Textile. He calls on Jason Davis at home to discuss Davis's handling of his account, but Davis is exhausted and asleep upstairs. His daughter, Josephine Davis, so charms Halklite that he gives the account to Davis.

HALLAM. In ''Majesty,'' he is Harold Castleton's European agent, who reports to Castleton that Emily Castleton is consorting with a disreputable man named Prince Gabriel Petrocobesco.

HALLIBURTON, MISS. In ''The Captured Shadow,'' she is the prissy teacher Basil Duke Lee reluctantly agrees should coach his play *The Captured Shadow*.

HALLORAN. In *The Beautiful and Damned*, he is the bank manager who closes Anthony Patch's account for writing bad checks and having no funds.

HALOGEN. In *Precaution Primarily*, this is the family name of Bromine, Chlorine, Corinne, Fluorine, and Iodine Halogen. They sing in the play.

HALSEY, GRETCHEN. In "Gretchen's Forty Winks," she is Roger Halsey's lazy, vivid-looking wife, from the South, and Maxy Halsey's mother. They live just outside New York City. Her housework is alleviated by a nurse and a general servant. Gretchen enjoys going out with George Tompkins, their successful neighbor, while Roger works too hard. To silence her gripes, Roger laces her coffee with sleeping powder one morning so she can enjoy forty winks while he completes his work.

HALSEY, MAXY. In "Gretchen's Forty Winks," he is the infant son of Roger Halsey and Gretchen Halsey. The nurse conveniently takes Maxy away for one important day.

HALSEY, ROGER. In "Gretchen's Forty Winks," he is the overworked New York advertising agent whose wife, Gretchen Halsey, gripes too much. He drugs her with sleeping powder to complete his work successfully for H. G. Garrod, his most important client.

HALYCON. In "The Debutante," he is the father of Helen Halycon and Cecilia Halycon. He wants Helen to meet a bright, older man from Providence.

HALYCON. In "The Debutante," he is the son of Halcyon and his wife, who does not worry about his extravagant ways.

HALYCON, CECILIA. In "The Debutante," she is the sister, sixteen, of Helen Halycon, who is about to come out as a debutante. Cecilia cannot tattle on Helen's behavior with boyfriends because Helen saw her kiss Blaine MacDonough. Alone in Helen's room, Cecilia smokes, drinks, and pretends in the mirror to flirt with an imaginary middle-aged man.

HALYCON, HELEN. In "The Debutante," she is the debutante about to be entertained at a downstairs party. She primps at her mirror, is lectured by her parents, rejects John Cannel and tells him what kissing means to her, and is prepared to encourage Charlie Wordsworth.

HALYCON, MRS. In "The Debutante," she is the bejeweled, rouged mother of Helen Halycon and Cecilia Halycon. She asks Helen not to dance more than twice with John Cannel, who has been invited to attend Helen's coming-out party. Mrs. Halycon does not worry about Helen's slang or the bills her son is accumulating.

HAMBELL. In *This Side of Paradise*, he is a member of a firm called Cambell & Hambell. The Popular Daughter becomes temporarily engaged to Cambell.

HAMIL. In "The Four Fists," he is Peter Carhart's Texas business associate. Samuel Meredith goes to San Antonio, where he meets Hamil, but then destroys a business opportunity for Carhart. Hamil calls Samuel a fool, checks with Carhart, and severs ties with him.

HAMILTON. In "Majesty," he is William Brevoort Blair's uncle, a Virginian. He warns newspaper editors not to play up Emily Castleton's calling off of her wedding ceremony to William.

HAMILTON, JOHN. In "Strange Sanctuary," he is a friend of Dolly Haines and a fellow guest with her at the Halloween party.

HAMMEL, LILLIAN ("LIL"). In "First Blood," she is Josephine Perry's friend. They deceive their parents, go on drives with their boyfriends—Howard Page is Lillian's friend—and attend dances. In "A Nice Quiet Place," Lillian ("Lil") writes to Josephine that Josephine's boyfriend, Ridgeway Saunders, is seeing Evangeline Ticknor. In "A Woman with a Past," Lillian goes with Josephine and others to the Yale prom. Lillian is presumably escorted by sophomore George Davey. In "A Snobbish Story," she is mentioned as attending the Lake Forest tennis tournament. In "Emotional Bankruptcy," Lillian is Josephine's friend and confidante, and the two tease several young Ivy League men.

HAMMERHEAD. In *The Great Gatsby*, Nick Carraway lists his name on a timetable as one of Jay Gatsby's summer guests.

HAMMERTON, ELSIE. In "A Snobbish Story," she is a trousered author whose play is rejected by the group at the theater workshop.

HAMMOND, MRS. RICHARD BARTON. In *The Vegetable*, she is a person Doris saw walking a pink dog.

HAMN. In "Majesty," he is a guest at the wedding ceremony canceled by Emily Castleton.

HANCOCK, THORNTON. In *This Side of Paradise*, he is a Catholic in occasional need of comfort from Monsignor Thayer Darcy. Hancock, an ex-diplomat and a historian, attends Darcy's funeral.

"HANDLE WITH CARE" (1936). Essay. Fitzgerald resembles a cracked plate, to be preserved but not used again. It does no good to remind him others are worse off, especially when he wakes up at 3:00 A.M., with his personality gone. He first went quiet when illness prevented his becoming important at Princeton. After the war he turned quiet again, when he lost his loved one through lack of money, then made money on a novel, won the girl, but thereafter hated men who had money all along. Now, sixteen years later, his values are gone again. Good novels have become outmoded. He has thought too little, let others set his intellectual, artistic, and social standards for him, ignored politics, and now hardly exists. But wait, someone—neither Lenin nor God—is asleep who might have helped him. By error, the titles for ''Handle with Care'' and ''Pasting It Together'' were transposed when the two essays were republished in *The Crack-Up*.

HANNAFORD, GEORGE. In ''Magnetism,'' he is a successful Hollywood actor, thirty. His charm gets him in trouble with young actress Helen Tompkins Avery and script girl Margaret Donovan. His Mexican servant Dolores would like to have an affair with him. Gwen Becker tries to blackmail him. George and his needlessly jealous wife, Kay Hannaford, whom he met when he was acting at Yale and with whom he has a baby boy, reconcile their differences.

HANNAFORD, KAY. In ''Magnetism,'' she is a Western senator's daughter, a former actress, and George Hannaford's needlessly jealous wife. She almost gets a divorce to marry Arthur Busch.

HANNAMAN, CLARA. In ''Too Cute for Words,'' she is Gwen Bowers's close friend, fourteen. The two and their friend Dizzy Campbell visit Mrs. Charles Wrotten Ray's home, primp there, and then crash the Princeton prom dance.

HANNAMAN, HELEN. In ''Too Cute for Words,'' she is Clara Hannaman's mother and the friend of Bryan Bowers, Clara's friend Gwen Bowers's father. Helen likes Bryan, compliments Gwen, and with him chaperones the Princeton's prom dance the evening before the Princeton-Harvard football game.

HANNAN, CARLY. In *Tender Is the Night*, he and McKibben are friends of Tommy Barban and listen in Munich as he tells Dick Diver how he got Prince Chillicheff out of Russia.

HANNAN, HELEN. In ''A Freeze-Out,'' she is the hostess who invites Alida Rikker to play golf. Forrest Winslow eavesdrops on them.

HANNAN, WALTER. In ''A Freeze-Out,'' he is Pierce Winslow's friend who unsuccessfully appeals to Pierce to sponsor Chauncey Rikker for membership in a club. Walter is probably Helen Hannan's father.

HANSON. In ''Dalyrimple Goes Wrong,'' he is an employee of Theron G. Macy, who tells Bryan Dalyrimple to report to Hanson to be told about stock-room work.

HANSON. In *The Last Tycoon*, he is a person in New York with whom Monroe Stahr talks on the telephone.

HANSON, CLAUD. In ''On an Ocean Wave,'' he is one of Gaston T. Scheer's secretaries. The more important secretary is O'Kane.

HAPPER, SALLY CARROL. In ''The Ice Palace,'' she is an attractive, languid girl, nineteen, from Tarleton, Georgia. When she finds her local friends slow, she accepts the invitation of her fiancé, Harry Bellamy, to meet his family (in Minnesota). It does not take her long to dislike the chilly North, symbolized by an ice palace in which she gets lost, to break her engagement with Harry, and to return home. In ''The Last of the Belles,'' she is Ailie Calhoun's friend. The two, with Nancy Lamar, go on dates with army officers from the base outside Tarleton during World War I. Sally Carrol Happer is partly based on Zelda Sayre Fitzgerald.* *See also* Hopper, Sally Carrol.

HARDT, GEORGE. In ''Babylon Revisited,'' he is a former American drinker. Alix, a bartender in Paris, tells Charlie J. Wales that Hardt has returned to America to work.

HARDY. In *The Beautiful and Damned*, he is a member of the bond firm of Wilson, Hiemer and Hardy, which Anthony Patch works for briefly.

HAREBELL. In *This Side of Paradise*, he is the flour producer for whose company Amory Blaine tells Barlow, his advertising-agency boss, he is tired of writing ads.

HARKER, ANTHONY ("TONY"). In ''First Blood,'' he is a recent graduate, twenty-two, of a Virginia college. In Chicago in 1914, he is the object of Josephine Perry's dishonestly motivated infatuation. Gossip about his relationship with her forces him out of Chicago. In ''Emotional Bankruptcy,'' he is mentioned as one of Josephine's former boyfriends.

HARKLESS, LUKE. In '' 'Trouble,' '' he is the man after whom the Luke Harkless Hospital was named. Glenola McClurg and Dr. Dick Wheelock, among others, work there.

HARLAN. In ''Two for a Cent,'' he was the man whose $300.86 Alabama bank debt Henry W. Hemmick collected in cash.

HARLAN, DOLLY. In ''The Bowl,'' he is the star of the Princeton football team. He punts and is a receiver, but he also often drops punts. He dislikes playing in the Yale Bowl, but does well, is persuaded by his fiancée, Vienna Thorne, to quit playing, breaks his ankle, quits, then plays again, and prefers the movie actress Daisy Cary—and brief fame—to Vienna.

HARLAN, GENEVIEVE. In ''Dice, Brassknuckles & Guitar,'' she is a student at James Powell's school, as is her brother Ronald Harlan.

HARLAN, MADISON. In ''Dice, Brassknuckles & Guitar,'' he is the owner of a Southampton home where Amanthis Powell, his cousin, stays a while. He invites James Powell to a dance in his home.

HARLAN, MRS. In ''The Bowl,'' she is Dolly Harlan's mother. At her Long Island vacation home, Dolly breaks his ankle.

HARLAN, RONALD. In ''Dice, Brassknuckles & Guitar,'' he is a student, fifteen, at James Powell's school, as is his sister Genevieve Harlan.

HARLAND, ALICE. In ''John Jackson's Arcady,'' she is John Jackson's childhood sweetheart. They meet again twenty years later. She agrees to leave her husband, George, and their three children and run away with Jackson but soon sanely reneges.

HARLAND, GEORGE. In ''John Jackson's Arcady,'' he is a garageman, fifty, in the town where John Jackson grew up. George has married Jackson's childhood sweetheart, Alice Harland, and they have three children. George feels secure enough in his marriage to tolerate Jackson's coming to dinner at his home.

HARLEY. In *The Last Tycoon*, he is a movie director who Monroe Stahr tells Red Ridingwood is going to be his replacement. Ridingwood, though agreeable, is crushed.

HARLEY, ELLEN. In ''The Popular Girl,'' she is Yanci Bowman's friend who suddenly appears at the railroad station in New York. Yanci lied to Scott Kimberly, who takes her to the station, that she was going to the Princeton prom. Since Ellen is really going, Yanci must also board the train.

HARLOW, JEAN (1911–1937). Movie actress. In *The Last Tycoon*, she is a person whose telephone call Monroe Stahr should return.

HARMAN, NED. In " 'Boil Some Water—Lots of It,' " he is the production manager at the movie studio where Pat Hobby works.

HARMON, DOROTHY. In "A Luckless Santa Claus," she is Harry Talbot's fiancée. Her plan to have Harry give money away on Christmas Eve instead of wasting it backfires when he celebrates with two men who beat him up when he tries to give them money.

HARPER, BILLY. In "Presumption," he is Holly Morgan's date at the party which Noel Garneau gives at Culpepper Bay and which she also invites San Juan Chandler to attend.

HARPER, MYRA. In "Myra Meets His Family," she is the husband-seeking heroine, twenty-one, living in New York. She and wealthy Knowleton Whitney of Westchester County fall in love, and she thinks he will do. Fearing his parents' disapproval, however, he concocts a scheme to scare her away by hiring actors to impersonate his repulsive parents. When Myra discovers the ruse, he apologizes and professes his love. In revenge, Myra has her cousin, Walter Gregory, conduct a fake wedding ceremony and then deserts Knowleton on their honeymoon train.

HARRINGTON, BOB. In *Thoughtbook*, he is an admirer of Elenor Mitchell.

HARRIS. In *The Evil Eye*, he is a Broadway detective who in Paris boasts of his ability.

HARRIS. In "Two Wrongs," he is a show-business competitor mentioned by William McChesney in conversation with Brancusi.

HARRIS, ELLEN. In "New Types," she is Leslie Dixon's cousin. She introduces Dixon to Paula Jorgensen.

HARRIS, GEORGE. In "Magnetism," his initials Margaret Donovan says resemble those of her boss, George Hannaford.

HARRIS, MARTIN. In "Design in Plaster," he is the chief electrical engineer of a movie studio. He dislocated his shoulder two months earlier and is recuperating in a hotel room with his arm in a plaster cast. Irrationally thinking that his estranged wife, Mary Harris, is in love with Joris Deglen, he painfully makes his way to her apartment but falls, reinjures his arm, and is taken to the hospital.

HARRIS, MARY. In "Design in Plaster," she is the estranged wife of Martin Harris, who is recuperating with his arm in a cast in a hotel room. She visits Martin and tells him she loves him; but when he accuses her of caring for Joris

Deglen and makes his way to her apartment to check on them, she determines to seek her freedom—perhaps with Joris.

HARRIS, MIKE. In "Last Kiss," he is the studio head under whom Jim Leonard is a producer. Harris tells Leonard he is reluctant to sign Pamela Knighton because Bernie Wise told him she cannot act.

HARRISON, DR. In "Her Last Case," he is the Baltimore physician who recommends Bette Weaver to be Ben Dragonet's nurse.

HARRISON, ED. In "Inside the House," he is Bryan Bowers's friend, gassed in World War I and now about forty. Harrison does business with theatrical people and therefore can introduce the actress Peppy Velance to Gwen Bowers, Bryan's star-struck daughter.

HARRY. In "Too Cute for Words," he is Marion Lamb's date. When Gwen Bowers, Dizzy Campbell, and Clara Hannaman catch the couple embracing in a car, the girls blackmail him into helping them crash the prom dance held the evening before the Princeton-Harvard football game.

HARRY. In " 'Why Blame It on the Poor Kiss if the Girl Veteran of Many Petting Parties Is Prone to Affairs After Marriage?' ", he is Georgianna's happily married husband.

HART. In "The Curious Case of Benjamin Button," he is the Yale registrar who expels Benjamin.

HART. In "The Family Bus," he is the coach on the high school football team on which Dick Henderson plays.

HART. In "Winter Dreams," he is a member of the exclusive golf club, gives Dexter Green a guest card, and plays in a foursome with him.

HART, CHARLEY. In "One of My Oldest Friends," he is the artist friend of Michael, who is Marion's husband. Despite learning that Charley asked Marion to run away with him, Michael, in the nick of time, saves Charley's life and offers to give him $2,000 to prevent his being arrested for embezzling funds from an artists' benefit.

HARVEY. In "Bernice Bobs Her Hair," he is Marjorie's father.

HARVEY, JOSEPHINE. In "Bernice Bobs Her Hair," she is Marjorie Harvey's mother and Bernice's aunt.

HARVEY, MARJORIE. In ''Bernice Bobs Her Hair,'' she is Bernice's cousin, eighteen. She lectures Bernice on improving her popularity at dances, grows jealous of Bernice's success with Marjorie's boyfriend, Warren MacIntyre, and goads her into bobbing her hair. Bernice gets even by cutting off Marjorie's blond braids while the girl is asleep.

HASBROUK. In ''A Full Life,'' he was a munitions manufacturer and willed $20 million to his son, Cornelius B. Hasbrouk.

HASBROUK, CORNELIUS B. In ''A Full Life,'' he was a Harvard junior, age twenty, when he inherited $20 million from his munitions-making father and married Gwendolyn Davies. They were quickly divorced.

HASBROUK, GWENDOLYN. In ''A Full Life.'' *See* Frejus, Comptesse Gwendolyn de.

HASKINS, DAN. In ''The Freshest Boy,'' he is a bullying football player at St. Regis.

HASYLTON, MORRIS. In ''Love in the Night,'' he is the father of Prince Val Rostoff's mother. He evidently began his successful career as a Chicago butcher and in 1892 helped finance the Chicago Fair.

HAT. In ''Head and Shoulders,'' he is named as a supposed haberdasher.

HATMAN, MABEL. In ''Mightier Than the Sword,'' she is Hollywood director Dick Dale's faithful script girl. When E. Brunswick Hudson wants to have nothing to do with Dale's script concerning composer Reginald De Koven, Dale promises to give a screen credit to Mabel.

HATTIE. In ''An Alcoholic Case,'' she is a person with whom Mrs. Hixson discusses problems involving personnel.

HAUGHTON, AD. In ''The Love Boat,'' he is a Harvard football player Bill Frothington recalls while aboard the love boat. Ad socializes with Bill and his wife, Stella Frothington, later. He visits Bill just before Bill reads the letter from Stella which he mistakenly fears will end or at least jeopardize their marriage.

HAUPT, MARY. In ''He Thinks He's Wonderful,'' she is named, during a children's gathering on Imogene Bissel's veranda, as a repulsive girl. In ''Forging Ahead,'' she is a guest at Benjamin Reilly's dull party, which Basil Duke Lee must attend.

HAWKINS. In ''Dalyrimple Goes Wrong,'' he is the town mayor and invites Bryan Dalyrimple, upon his heroic return from the war, to stay with him for a while.

HAWKINS, MRS. In ''Dalyrimple Goes Wrong,'' she is the mayor's wife. After Bryan Dalyrimple has been their house guest for a month, she wants him to leave, and he does.

HAWKS, GRETTA. In ''An Alcoholic Case,'' she is a nurse whose assignments Mrs. Hixson handles.

HAZELDAWN. In ''Strange Sanctuary,'' she is a black servant who takes Dolly Haines to Lila Appleton's home and returns to Mrs. Martin, her employer.

HAZELTON, MISS. In *Coward*, she is Lindy Douglas's friend.

"HEAD AND SHOULDERS" (1920). Short story. (Characters: Beef, Professor Dillinger, Hat, Jessie, Jordan, Anton Laurier, Charlie Moon, Charlie Paulson, Peat, Sandra Pepys, Skipper, Tarbox, Horace Tarbox, Marcia Tarbox, Peter Boyce Wendell.) In 1915 Horace Tarbox, raised to be a great prodigy, is thirteen, passes the entrance examination at Princeton, studies philosophy there, and enrolls for the master's program at Yale in 1919. His cousin, Charlie Moon, takes pity on the withdrawn scholar and gets Marcia Meadow, nineteen and a shoulder-shaking chorus girl, to go see him. Despite their differences, they fall in love and marry. When Marcia gets pregnant, Horace, who has taken a job as a clerk, finds that his talent as a mathematically precise trapeze artist with muscular shoulders can earn him great money. Meanwhile, he tells Marcia, though nearly illiterate, to read Samuel Pepys's diary. Inspired by it, she puts together a youthfully styled autobiographical novel, which becomes a best-seller. Marcia and Horace are beatifically happy and will call their daughter Marcia Hume. Anton Laurier, Horace's favorite philosopher, calls on the pair—to praise Marcia's writing.

This story was the first Fitzgerald sold, for $400, to the *Saturday Evening Post*. For $2,500 he sold film rights to ''Head and Shoulders,'' which Metro made into *The Chorus Girl's Romance*, 1920, starring Viola Dana* as Marcia Meadow.

HEALY. In *This Side of Paradise*, he is the owner of a New York place for food or entertainment. Amory Blaine and those on a date with him leave it to go by taxi elsewhere.

HEARST. In ''Reade, Substitute Right Half,'' he is the injured right tackle of the Warrentown team.

HEATHERLY. In ''The Freshest Boy,'' he is a foreign secret agent in the episode during which Basil Duke Lee imagines himself to be a gentleman thief at a Broadway restaurant.

HECK. In ''The Diary of a Sophomore,'' he is the diarist's friend.

HECKSHER. In ''Jacob's Ladder,'' he is evidently Jenny Prince's Hollywood agent.

HEDRICK, T. A. In ''Winter Dreams,'' he is a member of an exclusive golf club. Dexter Green plays in a foursome with him. Judy Jones hits him in the stomach with a carelessly driven ball, after which he criticizes her spoiled nature.

HELEN. In ''A Letter to Helen,'' she is the respected addressee.

HELEN. In ''Martin's Thoughts,'' she is one of Martin's girlfriends.

HELEN. In *Tender Is the Night*, she is an American girl, fifteen and one of Dick Diver's patients at the Zurichsee clinic.

HELEN. In ''That Kind of Party,'' she is the Tipton family cook. Terrence R. Tipton promises not to quit calling her a Kitchen Mechanic if she will participate in his scheme to have supper at the Bartletts'.

HELENA. In ''Thousand-and-First Ship,'' she promised to take the persona away to a pleasant land but married another.

HELENA SOMETHING-OR-OTHER, LADY. In ''Myra Meets His Family,'' she is a titled woman Knowleton Whitney's mother was supposedly bringing home for him to consider marrying.

HÉLÈNE. In ''News from Paris—Fifteen Years Ago,'' she is a French orphan whose convent education Henry Haven Dell has supported for three years after World War I. He is sad to see her drinking with two Americans.

HEMINGWAY, ERNEST (1899–1961). American writer. He was born in Oak Park, Illinois, graduated from high school there, and worked as a reporter for the *Kansas City Star* in 1917 and 1918. He was an ambulance driver for the Red Cross in Italy, where he was wounded in 1918. From 1920 to 1924 he was a reporter for the *Toronto Star* and *Star Weekly*. He published *Three Stories and Ten Poems* in Paris in 1923, was friendly with American expatriates including Ezra Pound and Gertrude Stein,* covered the Graeco-Turkish War in 1922, and published *in our time* (Paris, 1924; as *In Our Time*, New York, 1925). Scribner's became his almost exclusive publisher in 1928 when it issued *The Torrents of*

Spring and *The Sun Also Rises* that year. For the next several years, Hemingway combined writing, traveling, and strenuous vacationing: *Men Without Women* (1927), while living in Florida and fishing in the Gulf Stream; *A Farewell to Arms* (1929), after suffering a car accident in Montana (1930); *Death in the Afternoon* (1932); *Winner Take Nothing* (1933), while enjoying an African safari and seeing France and Spain again along with other American expatriates; and *Green Hills of Africa* (1935). Beginning in 1937 he reported events in the Spanish Civil War for the North American Newspaper Alliance and then published *To Have and Have Not* (1937), *The Fifth Column and the First Forty-Nine Stories* (1938), and *For Whom the Bell Tolls* (1940). From 1942 to 1945 he was a war correspondent and an unofficial, in fact, illegal, combatant in World War II. He published *Across the River and into the Trees* (1950) and *The Old Man and the Sea* (1952), was in two airplane crashes in Africa (1953), and was awarded the Nobel Prize for Literature (1954). Alcoholism, nervous disorders, and personal and professional depression finally drove him to suicide in Idaho. *A Moveable Feast*, in which Hemingway reminisces—at times inaccurately—about Fitzgerald, appeared posthumously (1964). Hemingway was married four times: Hadley Richardson (1921, divorced 1927), Pauline Pfeiffer (1927, divorced 1940), Martha Gelhorn (1940, divorced 1944), and Mary Welsh (1944).

In 1924 Fitzgerald recommended Hemingway's writing to Max Perkins* and in 1925 met Hemingway at a bar in Paris. Fitzgerald's 1926 "How to Waste Material—A Note on My Generation" includes praise of *In Our Time*. Also in 1926 Fitzgerald, Zelda Sayre Fitzgerald, and Hemingway vacationed with Gerald Murphy* and his wife, Sara Murphy,* on the Riviera. From almost the start of his association with the Fitzgeralds, Hemingway regarded Zelda, beautiful though she was, as a deadly menace to her husband's professional career. In 1928 Fitzgerald, Hemingway, and their wives attended the Princeton-Yale football game at Princeton, after which the Hemingways were the Fitzgeralds' guests at "Ellerslie."* In 1929 Fitzgerald and Hemingway were in Paris together, during which time Hemingway ingloriously boxed Canadian novelist Morley Callaghan,* with Fitzgerald keeping time—not accurately, according to Hemingway. In his 1929 "A Short Autobiography," Fitzgerald mentions Hemingway as a fellow drinker in France in 1925. In the 1930s the two men met occasionally—in 1931, probably in New York; in 1933 and 1937, certainly in New York; and finally, in 1937, in Hollywood.

The Fitzgerald-Hemingway relationship is complex. In 1924 Fitzgerald was popular and successful, whereas Hemingway was only on the verge of fame. Yet Fitzgerald was awed by Hemingway's artistic potential, as well as by his combat experience and athletic prowess. By the late 1920s Fitzgerald, somewhat quiescent after *The Great Gatsby*, felt eclipsed by Hemingway, whom he inaccurately regarded as a superb, well-balanced artist intolerant of wives and critics alike and immune to the deleterious effects of alcohol. Hemingway regarded as intolerable not only Fitzgerald's embarrassing binges but also his confessions of shortcomings including sexual, his destructive behavior, and his disrespect for his talent; moreover, Hemingway resented Fitzgerald's wise criticism of Hemingway's own work, including detailed suggestions to improve *The Sun Also Rises*, which he had read in draft form. Hemingway made use of several suggestions but later denied having done so. He rebuked Fitzgerald for whining in *The Crack-Up* and derided him in *A Moveable Feast*. The most famous anecdote concerning the two men has to do with "the rich." In 1936 Hemingway was in Bimini with Perkins and critic Mary Colum and said he was getting to know the rich, to which Colum replied that the only difference between the rich and others was that the rich have more money. In "The Snows of Kilimanjaro" Hemingway alludes to "The Rich Boy," says that "poor Scott Fitzgerald" was ruined by romanticizing the wealthy, quotes inaccurately from the story to the effect that the rich are different from the rest of us, and adds Fitzgerald was squelched by the rejoinder that, yes, the rich have more money. Thus Hemingway fobbed off on Fitzgerald the embarrassment he had felt because of Colum's remark. Fitzgerald wrote Hemingway to praise "The Snows of Kilimanjaro"—spoiled though it was, he added, by the dig. Perkins demanded "poor Scott Fitzgerald" be changed to "poor Julian" when the story was reprinted. Fitzgerald continued to admire Hemingway's work, but their friendship cooled. Ultimately, Fitzgerald proved more courageous than Hemingway in confronting agonies: Fitzgerald died while supporting his family and trying to finish *The Last Tycoon*; Hemingway blew his head off.

Bibliography: Carlos Baker, *Ernest Hemingway: A Life Story* (New York: Scribner's, 1969); Matthew J. Bruccoli, *Scott and Ernest: The Authority of Failure and the Authority of Success* (New York: Random House, 1978); Matthew J. Bruccoli, *Fitzgerald and Hemingway: A Dangerous Friendship* (New York: Carroll and Graf, 1994); Leonard J. Leff, *Hemingway and His Conspirators: Hollywood, Scribners, and the Making of American Celebrity Culture* (Lanham, Md.: Rowan and Littlefield, 1997); Michael Reynolds, *Hemingway: The Paris Years* (New York: Oxford University Press, 1997).

HEMMICK, GEORGE. In "The Adolescent Marriage," he is a Chicago associate of George Wharton, a Philadelphia businessman. When Lucy Wharton Clark, Wharton's daughter, thinks her marriage to Llewellyn Clark has been annulled, she briefly plans to marry Hemmick.

HEMMICK, HENRY W. In "Two for a Cent," he is the stolid, rather unthinking resident, forty-six, of the Alabama town to which Abercrombie returns. The two men reminisce. Years ago, Hemmick would have left town to work in Cincinnati except he was disgraced by losing one penny of a bank payment which, as a runner, he was responsible for depositing. He remained to clear his name, which took years; he married, had a family, and never left. Abercrombie, from the same town, found the penny that Hemmick had lost.

HEMMICK, NELL. In "Two for a Cent," she is Henry W. Hemmick's wife. They have four children.

HEMPLE, CHARLES. In "The Adjuster," he is an overworked New York businessman, in his mid-thirties. He is Luella Hemple's husband and Chuck Hemple's father. His nervous collapse, followed by Chuck's death, causes Luella to become less bored and selfish.

HEMPLE, CHUCK. In "The Adjuster," he is the son of Charles Hemple and Luella Hemple. Chuck's death at the age of two, following the nervous collapse of his father, causes Luella to rethink her way of life.

HEMPLE, LUELLA. In "The Adjuster," she is Charles Hemple's spoiled wife, twenty-three, and Chuck Hemple's mother. Charles's bringing his friend Dr. Moon home for dinner signals her five-year evolution from being a bored, selfish wife into a woman who thinks about others more than about herself.

HENDERSON, DICK. In "The Family Bus," he is the boy and then young man who adores the family car, laments his brother Ralph Henderson's death, becomes a fine Detroit auto mechanic, and loves Jannekin Melon-Loper.

HENDERSON, MRS. T. R. In "The Family Bus," she is T. R. Henderson's wishy-washy wife and the mother of Ralph and Dick Henderson.

HENDERSON, RALPH. In "The Family Bus," he is Dick Henderson's older brother. He drinks too much, tries to elope in the family car with Kaethe Melon-Roper, but dies when he crashes it.

HENDERSON, T. R. In "The Family Bus," he is the ineffectual father of Ralph and Dick Henderson. He owns a furniture store in Michigan. When he dies, the family loses its money.

HENDRIX, AMELIA. In *Assorted Spirits*, she is Josephus Hendrix's estranged wife. Peter Wetherby hires Amelia, who works as Madame Zada the fortune-teller and medium, to rid his house of ghosts. She and Josephus are reconciled at the end.

HENDRIX, JOSEPHUS ("JOSEPH"). In *Assorted Spirits*, he is Amelia Hendrix's estranged husband, Peter Wetherby's second cousin, and Clara King's guardian. Joseph dresses in a devil's costume to lower the price of Wetherby's house, which he wants, by making it seem haunted. He and Amelia are reconciled at the end.

HENGEST, MAJOR. In *Tender Is the Night*, this is the name Abe North uses to introduce one Englishman when Abe is drunk in Rome. Another Englishman he introduces as Mr. Horsa.

HENRIETTE. In ''The Intimate Strangers,'' she is Marquise Sara de la Guillet de la Guimpé's maid in Paris. In 1926 she packs for Sara's getaway with Cedric Killian.

HENRY. In *Safety First!*, he is mentioned as an author whose stories might well be read to prisoners. The allusion may be to Henry James (1843–1916), whose fiction Fitzgerald greatly admired.

HERBRUGGE. In *Tender Is the Night*, he is a physician Dick Diver asks Dr. Dangue to bring from Geneva to examine Devereux Warren.

"HER LAST CASE" (1934). Short story. (Characters: Dr. Bliss, Dr. Howard Carney, Amalie Eustace Bedford Dragonet, Ben Dragonet, Mrs. Ben Dragonet, Dr. Harrison, Jean Keith, Bette Weaver, Whisper.) Arriving on a sultry July day at Ben Dragonet's mansion in Warrenburg, Virginia, Bette Weaver, a Baltimore nurse, begins her last case. She is to marry Dr. Howard Carney of New York and quit nursing. But Ben, her attractive, courteous patient, intrigues her. Suffering from a head wound suffered in World War I, he is alternately listless, in need of alcohol, and profoundly charming. While ministering to him professionally, Bette swims and goes horseback riding with him, and the two fall in love. One stormy night, Ben's ex-wife and Amalie Eustace Bedford Dragonet, their sweet daughter, nine, arrive, and the two parents soon argue. Jean Keith, the housekeeper, begs Bette to do something to rid Ben of this woman she defines as a witch and a harmful influence on him. The ex-wife impulsively departs, leaving Amalie with Ben. Dr. Carney, who has telephoned, arrives. After dining with Ben, Bette, and Amalie, he tells Bette to complete this last case of hers; then he returns to New York. Ben and Amalie gloomily say nice people regularly leave them; but Bette, writing Dr. Carney an explanatory letter, concludes her last case will last a lifetime.

Fitzgerald patterns the handsome Southern mansion of the Dragonets after Welbourne, a mansion in Middleburg, Virginia, which was owned by relatives of his editor, Max Perkins,* and which the two visited in July 1934. ''Her Last Case'' is the most charming of Fitzgerald's several doctor-nurse stories.

HERRICK, WALTER. In '' 'Boil Some Water—Lots of It,' '' he is an important writer at the movie studio where Pat Hobby works. Pat hits him in an ill-advised effort to protect some important executives.

HERSEY. In *The Great Gatsby*, this is the name of a family Nick Carraway used to remember hoping to see in Chicago during Christmas vacations from prep school and college.

HERSEY, MARIE. In *Thoughtbook*, she is one of Fitzgerald's best friends. She writes him to express her regard. In real life, she became Mrs. William Hamm.

HERTZOG. In "A Change of Class," this is the name of a rich family (in Wilmington). The Jadwin and the Hertzog families have formed the Hert-win financial combine.

HESSE. In "Dalyrimple Goes Wrong," he is Theron G. Macy's bookkeeper, whose ledger Bryan Dalyrimple steals a look at to learn about the salaries of fellow employees.

"HE THINKS HE'S WONDERFUL" (1928). Short story. (Characters: Bibble, Ermine Gilberte Labouisse Bibble, Mrs. Bibble, Imogene Bissel, Mrs. Bissel, Hubert Blair, Riply Buckner Jr., Lewis Crum, Connie Davies, Joe Gorman, Hilda, Passion Johnson, George Kampf, Mrs. George Kampf, William S. Kampf, Thurston Kohler, Lambert, Elwood Leaming, Alice Riley Lee, Basil Duke Lee, Reilly, Smith, Margaret Torrence, Mrs. Torrence, Gladys Van Schellinger.) Basil, fifteen, returns to St. Paul for the summer, before a final year at St. Regis in the East, in preparation for Yale. He has learned other boys have strong wills too, and more power. He and some friends gather on Imogene Bissel's veranda and talk about kissing. Basil, popular at first, annoys Joe Gorman by boasting that the girls all think he is wonderful and by advising Joe how to shape up. Connie Davies gives a party, during which Basil talks too much about himself to Imogene, who voices her preference for Joe. Margaret Torrence, a friend Basil neglected, criticizes him for thinking he's wonderful. Basil visits for a week at the lakeside home near Black Bear of the parents of William S. Kampf, whose cousin Ermine ("Minnie") Gilberte Labouisse Bibble is visiting with her parents from New Orleans. Basil impresses the Bibbles by his manners and intelligence, and he and Minnie fall in love. She asks her parents to invite him to accompany them to Glacier National Park; but when Bibble drives him to the railroad station, Basil falls into his habit of boasting—about his reading, grades, and ability to please girls. Minnie phones Basil to say he will not be asked. He is abashed, knows he talks too much, but rebounds, gets permission to drive his grandfather Reilly's electric car, calls on Imogene, and they go for a lemonade.

HIBBING ("HIB"), CAPTAIN. In " 'I Didn't Get Over,' " he is a member of the class of 1916. When survivors of the war have a class reunion twenty years later, Hib, apologetic for not having gotten over, tells about Lieutenant Abe Danzer. Hib ineptly took over from Abe during a training maneuver crossing a Georgia river, causing the death of twenty-two men. Later he arrested Abe for impersonating a "tart" in a Kansas City hotel. Abe, imprisoned at Leavenworth, was shot trying to escape. In telling the story, Hib says that the inept officer at the river was Captain Brown but later confesses to the narrator that Hib was the guilty one. Hib rationalizes that Abe snobbishly did not acknowledge before the tragic incident that the two were classmates. The name Hibbing may be a deliberate variation on that of John Grier Hibben, president of Princeton University when Fitzgerald was there.

HICKS. In ''The Perfect Life,'' he is the St. Regis housemaster who congratulates Basil Duke Lee for playing football well against Exeter.

HIEMER. In *The Beautiful and Damned*, he is a member of the bond firm of Wilson, Hiemer and Hardy, where Anthony Patch works briefly.

HIGGINS, SYBIL. In ''Last Kiss.'' This is the real name of Pamela Knighton. *See* Knighton, Pamela.

"THE HIGH COST OF MACARONI" (1954). Sketch. (Characters: John Alexander Borgia, Paola Dumbella, Princess Dumbella.) The narrator and his wife drive from France to Rome. They encounter exorbitant prices for their hotel rooms, a dining room made out of a coat room, and too much macaroni. They are ordered away from their table in a better hotel when Princess Dumbella wants it. To strengthen his argument, the narrator pretends he is a politically influential banker named Claude Lightfoot. He fights with taxi drivers who want to charge him too much, decks a secret policeman named John Alexander Borgia in the melee, and escapes to Capri. Fitzgerald put part of this unfinished sketch, considerably revised, in *Tender Is the Night*.

HILDA. In ''The Cut-Glass Bowl,'' she is the Swedish maid who tells Evylyn Piper her daughter, Julie Piper, cut her thumb on the bowl.

HILDA. In ''A Freeze-Out,'' she is the Winslows' maid.

HILDA. In ''A Night at the Fair,'' ''The Captured Shadow,'' and ''He Thinks He's Wonderful,'' she is the Lees' maid.

HILDA. In ''The Scandal Detectives,'' she is the Blairs' cook. She almost catches Riply Buckner, Jr., or Basil Duke Lee when one or both of them deliver warnings signed S. D.

HILDA. In ''Winter Dreams,'' she is Judy Jones's nanny when the girl is eleven. Judy is tempted to hit her with a golf club after an argument.

HILLEBRAND. In ''The Ants at Princeton,'' he is a former Princeton football player of legendary fame.

HILLIARD, GEORGE. In ''Pat Hobby Does His Bit,'' he is a Hollywood director. He and producer Jack Berners must hire Pat to complete a movie after he accidentally and otherwise ruinously appears in it.

HILLIS, BILL. In *Tender Is the Night*, he is a Yale man and was briefly Rosemary Hoyt's lover—or so Collis Clay tells Dick Diver, who immediately becomes jealous.

HILMA. In ''The Popular Girl,'' she is the maid in the rented home in which Tom Bowman and his daughter, Yanci Bowman, live.

HIMMEL, PETER. In ''May Day,'' he is the Yale man who escorts Edith Bradin to the dance at Delmonico's only to be snubbed for trying to kiss her. He gets drunk there with Private Carrol Key and Private Gus Rose and drinks some more with Philip Dean there and elsewhere. He plays Mr. In to Philip's Mr. Out.

HIP, CLAUDIA. In *The Great Gatsby*, Nick Carraway remembers her as being among Jay Gatsby's summer guests. She came with a man who was supposedly her chauffeur.

HIRST. In ''The Hotel Child,'' this is the name of a family mentioned by Mrs. Schwartz as friendly with them in the United States.

HIXSON, MRS. In ''An Alcoholic Case,'' she is an ex-nurse who runs an agency that dispatches nurses to various cases. She reluctantly lets the unnamed nurse return to the alcoholic case.

HOBBY, ESTELLE. In ''No Harm Trying.'' *See* Devlin, Mrs. Estelle Hobby.

HOBBY, JOHN BROWN. In ''Pat Hobby, Putative Father.'' *See* Indore, Prince John.

HOBBY, PAT. He is an alcoholic, dishonest, reminiscing, would-be womanizing Hollywood has-been writer, forty-nine. Fitzgerald once described him as a rat but not a sinister one. In ''Pat Hobby's Christmas Wish,'' on Christmas Eve 1939, he is ordered by producer Harry Gooddorf to complete work on a horse opera. Pat and his secretary, Helen Kagle, try but fail to blackmail Gooddorf into improving their status. In ''A Man in the Way,'' he tries to steal writer Pricilla Smith's idea for a script, which he presents to his boss, Jack Berners; his plan will backfire because Pricilla is Berners's girlfriend. In '' 'Boil Some Water—Lots of It,' '' he misunderstands a gag, hits Walter Herrick to protect important executives, and is laughed at. In ''Teamed with Genius,'' he is paired with British writer René Wilcox and tries to steal his supposed script by modifying it and showing it to Berners, only to be told the script was an old discarded one. In ''Pat Hobby and Orson Welles,'' Jeff Boldini makes Pat up with a beard to look like Orson Welles, only to have Hollywood financier Marcus think he actually is Orson Welles and suffer a heart attack. In ''Pat Hobby's Secret,'' Pat offers, for a bribe from executive Banizon, to get the secret ending to R. Parke Woll's script, does so, but forgets it during a bar fight when everything gets blurry. In ''Pat Hobby, Putative Father,'' he escorts Prince John Brown Hobby Indore and his uncle, Sir Singrim Dak Raj, to a stage to see Bonita Granville. In ''The Homes of the Stars,'' he substitutes himself for Hollywood guide Gus Venske and shows Deering R. Robinson and his wife from Kansas City the home of Ronald Colman and a mansion he says belongs to Shirley Temple. The Robinsons go upstairs. When producer Marcus drives up, Pat escapes out back. In ''Pat Hobby Does His Bit,'' Pat spoils a scene being filmed, must be hired to act in a necessarily revised script, and passes out drunk in an iron corselet. In ''Pat Hobby's Preview,'' Pat asks Berners for tickets to a preview of a movie the script of which he coauthored with Ward Wainwright. Pat takes Eleanor Carter to the show to impress her, but Berners had his secretary put tickets to a Los Angeles burlesque in the envelope instead. Wainwright leaves the preview early and gives Pat his ticket stubs. In go Pat and Eleanor, who is still disillusioned with him. In ''No Harm Trying,'' Pat learns his ex-wife, Estelle Hobby Devlin, is in the hospital; he gets her to work with Eric, a script boy with a movie idea. When Pat presents the script Estelle has typed to producer Carl Le Vigne as mostly his own, Le Vigne sees through the plan, praises Eric, will pay him well, and warns Pat he will expose him unless he tells the truth for a change. In ''A Patriotic Short,'' Berners orders Pat to work on *True to Two Flags*, a short about ex-Confederate General Fitzhugh Lee and the Spanish-American War. Pat contrasts his happy past, when he owned a swimming pool and lunched with the visiting president of the United States, with his present wretched position. He defiantly writes a cynical line into the script. In ''On the Trail of Pat Hobby,'' he has escaped hatless ahead of a police raid at a tourist-cabin complex where he was a night clerk (calling himself Don Smith). He learns Jack Berners needs a title for Bee McIlvaine's script about tourists, steals a hat (belonging to Marcus) from the studio commissary, snitches brandy from Berners's office, and boozily suggests the title *Grand Motel*. Berners will pay Pat $50 when he recovers from his binge. In ''Fun in an Artist's Studio,'' Pat agrees to pose for portrait-painter Princess Dignanni in Hollywood. He hopes to have drinks and other fun with her but is tricked into having to pose nude, so she can catch his expression of failure. In ''Two Old-Timers,'' Pat and retired actor Phil Macedon, while driving, collide. Police Sergeant Gaspar sides with Macedon, who snubs Pat and whose 1925 war movie *The Final Push* Gaspar relished. When Pat explains Macedon was tricked into some combat footage, Gaspar has Macedon detained and drives Pat to freedom. In ''Mightier Than the Sword,'' Pat is hired by Dick Dale, a director who does not know him well, to polish a script about composer Reginald De Koven.* By mainly listening for four weeks, he earns $350 a week, most of which he loses betting at the Santa Anita race track. He tells E. Brunswick Hudson, whose original script Dale finally uses, that Hollywood wants writers like Pat, not authors like Hudson. In ''Pat Hobby's College Days,'' Pat is finishing a four-week writing assignment, puts empty liquor bottles in a pillow case, and asks his secretary, Evylyn Lascalles, to dump them. Unable to do so, she returns them to Pat while he is trying to sketch the plot of a campus movie to personnel at the University of the Western Coast.

Bibliography: Thomas E. Daniels, ''Pat Hobby: Anti-Hero,'' *FH/A 1973*, 131–39.

HODGE, KATHERINE. In ''Teamed with Genius,'' she was Pat Hobby's secretary in Hollywood three years earlier and is now assigned to him to work with René Wilcox on the *Ballet Shoes* script. She likes Wilcox and is in on his scheme to discomfit Pat.

HOFFMAN, PHIL. In ''A New Leaf,'' he is a New York lawyer and later an assistant district attorney there. He is in love with Julia Ross. Her trouble begins when he introduces her in Paris to Dick Ragland, a hopeless alcoholic. Phil warns her against Dick, but not until he commits suicide at sea is Phil able to propose marriage to her successfully. He still conceals from her the degree of Dick's malady.

HOFTZER. In ''A Snobbish Story,'' he is the proprietor of the Chicago rathskeller where John Boynton Bailey decides he and Josephine Perry should not have lunch.

HOGUE, MADELEINE. In ''Bernice Bobs Her Hair,'' she is a newcomer at the young people's dances.

HOKER. In ''The Family Bus,'' he is the owner of a garage and often needs Dick Henderson's expertise with cars.

HOLCOME, STUART. In *The Beautiful and Damned*, he is a former boyfriend, from Pasadena, of Gloria Gilbert Patch. He tried to force her into marriage by driving away with her.

HOLIDAY, BURNE. In *This Side of Paradise*, he is a member of Amory Blaine's Princeton class. They become close friends. He reads liberal books, takes pity on Phyllis Styles and invites her to the prom, becomes a pacifist and a socialist during World War I, sells his possessions, and disappears. His brother, Kerry Holiday, also at Princeton, is a year older. Burne may be based in part on Fitzgerald's Princeton friend Henry Hyacinth Strater, discussed in ''Princeton.''

HOLIDAY, KERRY. In *This Side of Paradise*, he is the older brother of Burne Holiday, one of Amory Blaine's friends at Princeton, which Kerry also attends. Kerry went to prep school at Andover.

HOLLIDAY, EMILY. In "New Types," she is Paula Jorgensen's father's sister and hence Paula's aunt, who lives on Long Island. She was too stingy to help the Jorgensen family when her brother died. While upbraiding the family, she gives a party for Paula, apparently dies in her room just before the party, but revives and is told she slept through it all.

HOLLIDAY, ESTELLE. In "The Unspeakable Egg," she ran away with one of her father's servants who became an alcoholic and was abusive to her. Dr. Roswell Gallup tells Fifi about her, in an effort to persuade her not to marry beneath her class.

HOLLISTER, DEAN. In *This Side of Paradise*, he is a Princeton administrative official. When he says a certain taxi fare is so high he might as well buy the taxi, students disassemble a taxi overnight and place it in his office for a prank.

HOLMES. In *Tender Is the Night*, he is Dick Diver's father's curate and the ex-facto rector of his Buffalo church. Holmes cables Dick of his father's death.

HOLMES, HARMON, JUDGE. In "Three Hours between Planes," he is Nancy Holmes Gifford's father. To get in touch with her, Donald Plant phones Judge Holmes's residence, learns Nancy's married name, and is able to phone her.

HOLT, JERRY. In " 'The Sensible Thing,' " he is one of Jonquil Cary's friends who pick up George O'Kelly at the Tennessee railroad station. The other is Craddock.

HOLWORTHY, JIM. In *Coward*, he is Lindy Douglas's admirer. Calling him a coward for not enlisting in the Confederate Army in 1861, she declines his proposal. He enlists, saves her brother, Lieutenant Charles Douglas, is promoted to captain, and returns home when peace is declared. He proves his bravery by offering to play a kind of Russian roulette with Private Willings, a Union pillager, whereupon Lindy accepts him.

HOLWORTHY, NED. In *Coward*, he is mentioned as Jim Holworthy's father by Arthur Douglas, Ned's friend.

HOLYOKE. In "Presumption," he and his wife are guests at Cora Chandler's Culpepper Bay party, which is attended by San Juan Chandler.

HOLYOKE, MISS. In "Presumption," she is the ugly, bespectacled daughter of Holyoke and his wife. San Juan Chandler has met her at Culpepper Bay and is not attracted to her.

HOLYOKE, MRS. In "Presumption," she is the ugly Miss Holyoke's mother.

"HOMAGE TO THE VICTORIANS" (1922). Review of *The Oppidan* by Shane Leslie.*

"THE HOMES OF THE STARS" (1940). Short story. (Characters: Ronald Colman, Pat Hobby, Mrs. Horace J. Ives, Jr., Harold Marcus, Deering R. Robinson, Mrs. Deering R. Robinson, Gus Venske.) Pat Hobby stops his overheated car at the stand of Gus Venske, who advertises himself here in Hollywood as a guide able to show visitors the stars' homes. When Gus goes to lunch, Pat, short of money, persuades Mr. and Mrs. Deering R. Robinson of Kansas City, when their chauffeur stops at the stand, that he can be their guide—for $5 down. He gets into their car, suggests homes they can visit, and stops near the home of Ronald Colman. Colman comes out and greets Pat by his first name. His customers want to see Shirley Temple's home; so Pat, after exchanging part of his $5 for some gin at a drugstore, takes them to an unoccupied mansion chosen at random. They enter, and the Robinsons rush upstairs to look around. Pat sees Marcus, a producer for whom he was press agent twenty years earlier, and escapes out the back, hoping Colman did not remember his last name.

"THE HONOR OF THE GOON" (1937). Short story. (Characters: Vernard Butler, Ella Lei Chamoro, Lei Chamoro, Eubert M. Duke, Fingarson, Edward Forney, Bug Face Lovett, Gloria Matezka, Oates Mulkley, Claude Negrotto, Porter S. Spaulding, Maurice de Ware, Waveline Wilson, Bomar Winlock.) In a military academy, Bomar Winlock perfects the art of falling down stairs, to friends' delight and casual observers' alarm. He does the same in college. When he falls dramatically one day, Ella Lei Chamoro, a sweet Malay student, rushes to his aid. Her solicitation bothers him, and thereafter he and his friends call her a goon and shun her. By her junior year her face displays suspicion and hurt. One February day Lei Chamoro, her impeccably dressed relative, complains to Dean Edward Forney, who is so evasive that Chamoro demands the names of students who have called Ella a goon, obtains Bomar's address, and goes to his room. Bomar and his roommate, Oates Mulkley, who are preparing for the midwinter dance, open their door to Chamoro. When they lie about calling Ella a goon, Chamoro signals to Fingarson, his Norwegian chauffeur, who knocks both lads down. Then Chamoro spits on their girlfriends' photographs and on one of Bomar's deceased mother, and leaves with Fingarson. Oates says Bomar can tell their dates the bruises on his face were caused by a fall.

HOOD, GILLY. In ''The Four Fists,'' he is the roommate, thirteen, of Samuel Meredith at Phillips Andover. He slugs the snobbish Samuel.

"HOORAY" (1981). Poem. The poet gives a ''Hooray'' for lads who shout ''Hurray.''

HOPKINS. In *The Beautiful and Damned*, he is an officer in Anthony Patch's brigade. He was a sergeant in the regular army and takes himself seriously.

HOPKINS. In ''Two Wrongs,'' he is a show-business competitor mentioned by William McChesney in conversation with Brancusi.

HOPKINS, SARAH. In ''Bernice Bobs Her Hair,'' she is a European-educated girl critical of Marjorie Harvey and her crowd.

HOPMAN, RED. In ''The Bowl,'' he is a Princeton football player.

HOPP. In ''The Love Boat,'' he is a member of the Boston banking house of Read, Hopp and Company, which Bill Frothington will presumably settle into.

HOPPER, JOE. In ''Pat Hobby's Christmas Wish,'' he is Pat Hobby's writing associate. He knows Pat will not have his contract extended but does not tell him.

HOPPER, SALLY CARROL. In ''The Jelly-Bean,'' she is Nancy Lamar's flirtatious friend, based in part on Zelda Sayre Fitzgerald.* *See also* Happer, Sally Carrol.

HORATIO. In *Safety First!*, he is named as a detective.

HORNBEAM. In *The Great Gatsby*, his name is listed by Nick Carraway on a timetable as one of Jay Gatsby's summer guests.

HORRICK, STELLA. In ''A Freeze-Out,'' she is identified as a splendid golf player at an exclusive club.

HORSA, MR. In *Tender Is the Night*, this is the name Abe North uses to introduce one Englishman when Abe is drunk in Rome. Another Englishman he introduces as Major Hengest.

HORSEPROTECTION, GEORGE T. In *Tender Is the Night*, he is an oil-rich American Indian seen in Paris during Abe North's supposedly last night there.

HORTENSE. In "Hortense—To a Cast-Off Lover," she rejects the man who loves her because he grovels and lacks self-esteem.

HORTENSE. In *This Side of Paradise*, she is the leading character in *Ha-Ha Hortense!*, the Princeton Triangle musical in which Amory Blaine appears on tour.

"HORTENSE—TO A CAST-OFF LOVER" (1981). Poem. (Character: Hortense.) Tired of pretense, the persona rejects her lover because of his groveling lack of self-esteem and despite his deep love for her.

HORTON. In "The Lees of Happiness," he is the Seattle lumber king Kitty Cromwell marries after her divorce from Harry Cromwell.

HORTON, GEORGE. In "More Than Just a House," he is the New Yorker Amanda Gunther marries mainly to get away from the old Gunther house. She moves to Long Island with him, has some babies, and dies giving birth to another baby in 1929. She calls Horton "Bubbles."

HORTON, MRS. In "Not in the Guidebook," she is a kind American widow, now a landlady in Paris. William Driscoll rents accommodations at her pension, and she befriends Milly Cooley.

HOSKINS, DEAD SHOT. In *The Girl from Lazy J. See* Gonzoles, Tony.

"HOT AND COLD BLOOD" (1923). Short story. (Characters: Ed Bronson, Miss Clancy, Clayton, Fred Drake, Edward Lacy, Miss Lacy, James Mather, Jacqueline Mather.) James and Jaqueline Mather have been married about a year. His hardware brokerage business would support them better if he were not so generous in loaning others money he does not expect to get back. One day in February Jacqueline catches him "loaning" Ed Bronson $300. Bronson said he was in trouble with a girl. Since they have not saved enough for a new automobile, the Mathers go home by streetcar, and Jacqueline rebukes Jim for being an easy mark and even for giving his seat to a discourteous fat woman. In April she happens to see Bronson with a new sportscar and confronts Jim with this news. When he tries to borrow $50 from his friend, Fred Drake, for a day, to pay for a COD delivery, he is refused. Jim decides to reform. He grows hard, stops doing favors, and one August day even refuses his deceased father's generous friend, Edward Lacy, a loan of $450 to save his borrowed-on life insurance policy, as security for his unmarried daughter. Jim says he has special need of his money now because his wife is expecting. While he sits on the home-bound trolley buried in his newspaper, a woman standing above him moves away from him and suddenly faints. She is his wife. He carries her safely home and that evening telephones Lacy and promises to loan him the sum he needs.

"THE HOTEL CHILD" (1931). Short story. (Characters: Amy, Mrs. Bell, Ralph Berry, Count Stanislas Karl Joseph Borowki, Lady Capps-Karr, Gladys, Hirst, Miss Howard, Marquis Bopes Kilkallow, Marjorie, Schenzi, Fifi Schwartz, John Schwartz, Mrs. Schwartz, Taylor, Mrs. Taylor, Weicker.) Mrs. Schwartz, an American Jewish widow, her alcoholic son, John, nineteen, and her beautiful daughter, Fifi, are staying at an elite hotel but have been hurt by the Crash in America. They have traveled for three years and are now homeward bound. Nicely dressed Fifi is having a party to celebrate her eighteenth birthday and attracts lots of boys. Older guests watch her like Furies, and many make snide comments. Miss Howard is traveling with the Taylors, fellow Americans. Lady Capps-Karr is with fellow Britishers Ralph Berry and Marquis Bopes Kilkallow. Count Stanislas Karl Joseph Borowki, behind in his hotel bill, has his eye on Fifi and Miss Howard. Bopes drives Fifi to a bar to seek her brother, gets fresh, and soon sports a scratched face. Weicker, assistant manager of the hotel, surveys everyone with suspicion. In the morning, Mrs. Schwartz reports a theft of $200 in American bills from their rooms. Several days later, Borowki gives Fifi an expensive cigarette case, tells her about his family, and proposes an over-the-border elopement. She is tempted, fears her mother's anguish, and will let him know that evening. She and her mother dispute about their uncertain future. Fifi sends the count a note. Late at night Weicker sees Borowki at his car. A fire erupts in the hotel. Weicker alerts everybody. Officials rush in. Borowki is arrested with a young woman—Miss Howard. It seems that Borowki had robbed Mrs. Schwartz and that when Fifi overheard him ridiculing her mother to Lady Capps-Karr, who incidentally caused the fire by heating potato chips over alcohol, she grew suspicious and ascertained that he had bought her gift with a $100 bill. Lady Capps-Karr bailed Borowki out of jail. Will Fifi, who went to the police, yet escape the Furies?

In a deleted passage Fitzgerald describes how Marquis Bopes Kilkallow feeds hasheesh to Lady Capps-Karr's Pekingese and calls Fifi Schwartz a beautiful "sheeny." "The Hotel Child" echoes elements in Henry James's "Daisy Miller: A Study." Fifi, like Daisy, is a fine American girl gossiped about by her inferiors while abroad with her wealthy, dense mother and her awkward brother. The name of their Hotel des Trois Mondes, probably in Switzerland, may owe something to the Trois Couronnes, named in the first paragraph of James's story, which begins in Switzerland.

HOTESANE, COLONEL. In "Sentiment—and the Use of Rouge," he is Eleanor Marbrooke's friend. She shocks Captain Clayton Harrington Syneforth by telling him that when she and Gertrude Evarts went to Hotesane's farewell party they found revealing garments on his floor.

HOWARD. In "Benediction," he is the bright Harvard graduate who is Lois's lover. He is to meet her in Wilmington after she visits her brother Keith at his Baltimore seminary.

HOWARD. In "The Family Bus," he is the Hendersons' chauffeur.

HOWARD. In "No Flowers," he was Carter McLane's roommate who, during prom weekend in 1913, briefly met Marjorie Rawlins (later Marjorie Clark) and got her to discard Carter's corsage for his.

HOWARD. In *Safety First!*, he sings with Percy in ridicule of cubism.

HOWARD, LADY MARY BOWES (NÉE INCHBIT). In "Majesty," she is a guest at the wedding ceremony called off by Emily Castleton.

HOWARD, MISS. In "The Hotel Child," she is an American who is traveling in Europe with the Taylors. When Count Stanislas Karl Joseph Borowki cannot elope with Fifi Schwartz, he tries to elope with Miss Howard. When he is arrested, she is disgraced.

HOWARD, MRS. SIGOURNEY. In *The Great Gatsby*, she is Jordan Baker's New York aunt, with whom Jordan stays. Nick Carraway tries to ingratiate himself with the old woman.

HOWARD, SIDNEY (1891–1939). A playwright and screenwriter. In *The Last Tycoon*, Monroe Stahr orders a staff member to consult with Howard about an unsatisfactory script.

HOWDEN. In "Family in the Wind," any of the three members of the Howden family killed in the first tornado.

"HOW I WOULD SELL MY BOOK IF I WERE A BOOKSELLER" (1923). Essay. After facetiously suggesting odd window displays of books, Fitzgerald says if he were a bookseller he would push trashy popular books but also take orders for new good ones praised by reviewers. He calls reviewers powerfully influential. He would suggest books by Fitzgerald, who, according to reviewers, has made flappers voguish.

HOWLAND. In *The Beautiful and Damned*, he is Anthony Patch's broker. Anthony periodically asks him to sell one of his bonds for ready cash.

"HOW THE UPPER CLASS IS BEING SAVED BY 'MEN LIKE MENCKEN' " (1921). *See* "Public Letter to Thomas Boyd."

"HOW TO LIVE ON PRACTICALLY NOTHING A YEAR" (1924). Essay. (Characters: Bobbé, Eugénie, Jeanne, W. F. King, Marthe, René, Serpolette.) Fitzgerald, his wife, Zelda Sayre Fitzgerald,* and their daughter, Frances Scott Fitzgerald,* with $7,000 in savings, move to France to economize. In Paris they hire an English nurse for $26 a month, go by train in May to the Riviera, and check into a hotel in Hyères. They buy a wretched car for $750 and drive around looking for a villa to rent. After five weeks they find one, not in expensive Cannes but near Fréjus. W. F. King, a British real estate agent, helped them find the villa, which costs $79 a month. Their first servants are Jeanne (*femme de chambre*, $13 a month) and Marthe (for marketing, $16 plus 45 percent in kited prices). The Fitzgeralds now have $3,500 left. By September they are tan and happy, eat food expensively imported from Illinois and Ohio, but save by buying French perfume in France. In October their money is gone, partly because their new servants, Eugénie and Serpolette, sisters of the former pair, had to be expensively insured. French food is awful. Grocery bills are dishonest. On the other hand, the twilight is enchanting, and two French aviators, René and Bobbé, are coming to dinner. Besides, the perfume is cheap here. They'll stay another year.

"HOW TO LIVE ON $36,000 A YEAR" (1924). Essay. (Characters: Bankland, Mrs. Bankland.) Fitzgerald is persuaded to buy a $1,000 bond for long-term security. After he and his wife have been married a while and can neither pay their hotel bill nor cash the bond to do so, they plan to keep track of their expenses in a book. Food is costly, especially in the East and when charged at the grocer's. Fitzgerald's play (*The Vegetable*) seems great during rehearsal in New York but quickly closes in Atlantic City. Having nothing left of their $36,000, they try to trace their losses by listing household expenses, which come to $1,600 a month, and their pleasure expenses, which come to $400. This means $1,200 a year still missing. Their neighbors, the Banklands, visit and offer a solution: a budget. They started one yesterday. When Fitzgerald's wife says they can recoup their losses if he writes "How to Live on $36,000 a Year," he pooh-poohs the suggestion.

"HOW TO WASTE MATERIAL—A NOTE ON MY GENERATION" (1926). Essay. Fitzgerald ridicules American writers for being too "literary"—writing about American life prettily, romantically, without living and imagining it honestly. They loot material. H. L. Mencken* aided good writers immensely, but his concern was moral not artistic; and Sherwood Anderson* was incorrectly praised for his ideas, which are thin, rather than for his excellent style. After praising *The Enormous Room* by e. e. cummings, Fitzgerald turns to *In Our Time* by Ernest Hemingway* and defines the best elements in its crisp stories and vignettes.

HOYT. In "May Day," this is the name of the family Edith Bradin stays with at the Biltmore.

HOYT. In ''Two for a Cent,'' he was the cashier who stole $30,000 from the bank in the Alabama town. The theft causes Deems, vice president of the bank, to become unnaturally suspicious.

HOYT, ROSEMARY. In *Tender Is the Night*, she is Elsie Speers's daughter. The two are close. Rosemary is a hard-working American movie actress whose role in *Daddy's Girl* made her a success. She turns eighteen in Paris in 1925, admires Dick Diver, regards her follower, Collis Clay, as a nitwit, and willingly consummates her love with Dick in Rome in 1928. Nicole Diver ultimately rebukes her. Rosemary is based in part on Lois Moran,* an actress Fitzgerald met in Hollywood in 1927.

HUBBARD, SPUD. In ''The Ice Palace,'' he is identified by Harry Bellamy at his family's party for Sally Carrol Happer as tackle on last year's Princeton team.

HUBBEL. In ''Two Wrongs,'' he is a friend of Brancusi. In London, the two discuss William McChesney's professional decline.

HUBBEL, WILLARD. In ''Zone of Accident,'' Amy says he is willing to aid her in the beauty contest.

HUDSON, E. BRUNSWICK. In ''Mightier Than the Sword,'' he is a conceited New England author in and out of Hollywood. He is so offended when director Dick Dale initially rejects his script about a composer named Reginald De Koven,* who steals his music from a Vermont sheepherder, that when the script is finally approved for production, he will not accept a screen credit.

HUDSON, JEWEL. In ''May Day,'' she is the young woman with whom Gordon Sterrett had a quick affair and who demands $300 for her silence. She finds him drunk at the Yale dance at Delmonico's and without the money, gets him more drunk, and marries him. When he wakes up in the morning, he commits suicide. In the original published version of ''May Day,'' Jewel Hudson was called Gloria Hudson.

HUGHES, EASTON. In ''Two Wrongs,'' he is Emmy Pinkark's friend from Delaney, South Carolina. He is studying dentistry at Columbia.

HUGHES, LEONORA. In ''Not in the Guidebook,'' she is a dancer in Paris the narrator reads about in the *Franco-American Star*.

HUGO. In ''Dice, Brassknuckles & Guitar,'' he is James Powell's loyal black servant who accompanies Powell from Tarleton, Georgia, to New Jersey and Southampton.

HULDA. In *Assorted Spirits*, she is Peter Wetherby's maid from Sweden. Her boyfriend is Ole. She is friendly with Second Story Salle.

HULL, JOE. In *The Beautiful and Damned*, he is a friend Maury Noble brings to the Marietta home of Anthony Patch and Gloria Gilbert Patch. Hull, about thirty, is a drunk and terrifies Gloria by trying to take advantage of her.

HULL, PERRY. In "The Rich Boy," he is a Chicagoan. Dolly Karger tells Anson Hunter that Hull wants to marry her. Anson scoffs at the ploy, takes Dolly to Long Island, mistreats her, then dumps her.

HULME, MISS. In *The Beautiful and Damned*, she is a person who snubs Anthony Patch and Gloria Gilbert Patch after they are impoverished.

HULME, MRS. In *The Beautiful and Damned*, she is a person, perhaps Miss Hulme's mother, who snubs Anthony Patch and Gloria Gilbert Patch.

HUMBIRD, DICK. In *This Side of Paradise*, he is the aristocratic-looking son of a man who made a fortune in real estate in Tacoma and moved to New York. Dick, a graduate of St. Paul's prep school, is one of Amory Blaine's Princeton classmates. On his way back from New York to Princeton, having had too much to drink, Dick dies in a car accident. Amory later sees Dick's ghost.

HUME, CHARLES. In "On Schedule," he is René du Cary's chief assistant in the laboratory.

HUME, DELORES. In "On Schedule," she is the wife of Charles Hume, the assistant of René du Cary, with whom she was "a little in love" before her marriage. She worries more than her husband does about the impropriety of René's relationship with Becky Snyder. Eventually Delores believes his regard for Becky is touching.

HUNT. In *The Beautiful and Damned*, he is a member of the firm of Wrenn and Hunt. Adam Patch boasts of having sent three members of the firm to the poorhouse.

HUNTER. In "The Rich Boy," he is Anson Hunter's wealthy father. His six children will ultimately divide a fortune of $15 million. When he dies, Anson becomes more influential in the family.

HUNTER. In *Tender Is the Night*, this is a name associated with Dick Diver's father's family.

HUNTER, ANSON. In ''The Rich Boy,'' he is ''the rich boy.'' Born in 1895 into New York wealth, he is always accustomed to it, attends Yale, graduates in 1917, becomes a naval pilot, and after World War I develops into a well-paid Wall Street broker. He has love affairs with Paula Legendre and Dolly Karger; however, because he is domineering, proud, and alcoholic, he declines to commit himself fully. He breaks up the affair of his uncle Robert Hunter's wife, Edna Hunter, with Cary Sloane, who then commits suicide. Anson's circle of Yale friends drifts away, and he grows lonely. He bumps into Paula, who is now married to Peter Hagerty, and visits them at Rye. Before sailing for a vacation in Europe, he learns that Paula died in childbirth. Aboard ship, he goes after yet another pretty girl. He always wants someone to love him, help him understand himself, and promise him something—to reinforce his sense of superiority. A partial model for Anson Hunter was Ludlow Fowler, one of Fitzgerald's Princeton classmates; Fowler was a rich, hard-drinking young man.

HUNTER, EDNA. In ''The Rich Boy,'' she is the wife of Anson Hunter's uncle, Robert Hunter, married eighteen years and nearly forty years old. Anson breaks up the neglected woman's affair with Cary Sloane.

HUNTER, MISS. In ''In the Holidays,'' she is the nurse whose patient is Joe Kinney. Scheming to have Griffin murdered, Kinney is caught when he leaves fingerprints on a letter she wrote to her fiancé, a police officer, and asks him to mail.

HUNTER, MRS. In ''The Rich Boy,'' she is Anson Hunter's rather unimportant mother, an Episcopalian. When she dies, Anson becomes head of the family.

HUNTER, ROBERT. In ''The Rich Boy,'' he is Anson Hunter's uncle, described as married to Edna Hunter and horsey. The two men get along until Anson neglects his uncle's club, declines to enter his uncle's brokerage house, and breaks up Edna's affair with Cary Sloane.

[HUNTER?], SCHUYLER. In ''The Rich Boy,'' he is mentioned as missing a party through being drunk. Is he Robert Hunter's son?

[HUNTER?], TOM. In ''The Rich Boy,'' he is mentioned as having loaned a limousine to the Chilicheffs. Is he Robert Hunter's son?

HUPP, VON, COUNT. In *Fie! Fie! Fi-Fi!*, he has had a fit because Madame Von Hupp is too fond of clothes.

HUPP, VON, MADAME. In *Fie! Fie! Fi-Fi!*, she has distressed Count Von Hupp because of her fondness for clothes.

HUSTON-CARMELITE, MRS. In *This Side of Paradise*, she is a typical Victorian mother who incorrectly doubts her daughter engages in preengagement kissing.

HUXLEY, ALDOUS (1894–1963). English novelist and essayist. After being educated at Eton and Balliol College, Oxford, he quit medical studies, became a journalist, and then a novelist. His novels include *Crome Yellow* (1921), *Antic Hay* (1923), *Point Counter Point* (1926), *Brave New World* (1932), *Eyeless in Gaza* (1936), *The Devils of Loudon* (1952), and *Island* (1962). *On the Margin* (1923), *Jesting Pilate* (1926), and *Brave New World Revisited* (1958) are books of essays. In a 1922 review, ''Aldous Huxley's *Crome Yellow*,'' Fitzgerald says *Chrome Yellow* satirizes guests at an English country house and in a pale way mocks mockery. He says there is too much irony in the novel for it to be called satire and too much scorn to be called ironic. He calls Huxley and Max Beerbohm the two wittiest writers in the English language. In 1937 Fitzgerald occasionally had lunch at the MGM commissary with Huxley, then in Hollywood. In 1938 and 1939 Fitzgerald was assigned to write a script for *Madame Curie*, which Huxley, also working on *Pride and Prejudice*, had outlined; the two, however, did not collaborate. On occasion Fitzgerald saw Huxley at Hollywood parties. Huxley was not well regarded as a scriptwriter. In *The Last Tycoon*, George Boxley is based partly on Huxley.

HYPE, PETER. In ''The Diary of a Sophomore,'' he is the diarist's friend.

I

"THE ICE PALACE" (1920). Short story. (Characters: Ben Arrot, Bellamy, Gordon Bellamy, Harry Bellamy, Mrs. Bellamy, Myra Bellamy, Butterworth, Clark Darrow, Joe Ewing, John J. Fishburn, Sally Carrol Happer, Spud Hubbard, Larkin, Margery Lee, Junie Morton, Roger Patton, Marylyn Wade, Wally.) Sally Carrol Happer, nineteen, is discontent with her stay-at-home friends in Tarleton, Georgia. She is happy to have her fiancé, Harry Bellamy, a Yale student from the North she met the previous summer in Asheville, North Carolina, visit her in November. In his presence, she sentimentalizes in a Southern cemetery, which includes many Confederate dead. In January she goes by cold Pullman car to meet his family (in Minnesota). She soon dislikes his father, mother, older brother, Gordon Bellamy, and Gordon's wife, Myra Bellamy, and their offputting manners. Nor does she like snowy horse-and-buggy rides. She does admire fellow dinner guest Roger Patton, a professor of French the local university attracted from Harvard. She agrees when he comments that Scandinavians hereabouts remind him of cheerless Ibsen characters. Harry's admiration of everything Northern bothers Sally Carrol, as does his criticism of Southern lassitude. One evening she is stirred when they go to a vaudeville show and the orchestra plays "Dixie." Harry takes her to a three-story palace of ice. She gets lost in its dark labyrinth, grows terrified, must be rescued, and is happy to return to her warm, easygoing Tarleton friends. *See also* "Contemporary Writers and Their Work, a Series of Autobiographical Letters—F. Scott Fitzgerald."

Bibliography: Barbara Drushell, "Fitzgerald's 'The Ice Palace,' " *Explicator* 51 (Summer 1993): 237–38; Kuehl.

ICKY. In *Mister Icky*, he is an old man whose children, including Charles Icky and Ulsa Icky, plan to leave him.

ICKY, CHARLES. In *Mister Icky*, he is Icky's son, who plans to go to sea.

ICKY, ULSA. In *Mister Icky*, she is Icky's daughter, who plans to marry Rodney Divine.

" 'I DIDN'T GET OVER' " (1936). Short story. (Characters: Joe Boone, Lieutenant Abe Danzer, Captain Hibbing, Pop McGowan, Pete, Tomlinson.) A group of 1916 graduates reminisce about World War I during their twentieth reunion. Joe Boone, Tomlinson, and the narrator, who got over to France, recall that Abe Danzer and Pop McGowan are dead. Hibbing tells his story. He apologizes for not getting over. While in officer training in Georgia, he saw Abe save some men from a mortar accident, take over from inept Captain Brown, and minimize loss of life in a clumsy river maneuver. The captain wrongly blamed Abe. Later, as a military police captain, Hibbing arrested Abe for dressing like a tart in a Kansas City hotel. Sentenced to ten years in Leavenworth, he was shot during an attempt to escape. Hibbing confesses to the narrator that in reality he was Captain Brown. The river tragedy was based on an incident involving Fitzgerald while he was in infantry training at the Tallapoosa River near Montgomery, Alabama. In " 'I Didn't Get Over,' " Fitzgerald skillfully uses a double first-person narrator.

"I DON'T NEED A BIT OF ASSISTANCE" (1981). Poem. The poet needs no help. The noise is only distant music.

["IF HOOVER CAME OUT FOR THE N.R.A"] (1981). Poem. The poet complains that if anything really untoward occurred his daughter would label it silly, stupid, or something like that.

"IF YOU HAVE A LITTLE JEW" (1981). Poem. The persona suggests hitting a Jew should he sneeze.

"I GOT SHOES" (1933). Short story. (Characters: Johanna Battles, Teeny Fay, Jaccy, Warren Livingstone, Nell Margery.) Johanna Battles, a reporter, interviews successful actress Nell Margery in her hotel room, to which Warren Livingstone, a well-to-do, high-society explorer, has just arrived to renew his proposal and be spurned again. Johanna asks Nell about the rumor that she saves trunks of shoes. Initially resentful, Nell says when her widowed mother was a struggling actress she had to put cardboard in Nell's shoes to cover holes in the soles, and her feet got bloody once. This is responsible for her obsessive habit. When her French maid, Jaccy, says she tried on her discarded shoes, Nell is annoyed; later, she gets a phone call from Warren downstairs, accepts him, and gives Jaccy the shoes.

"I HATE THEIR GUTS" (1981). Poem. The poet despises ugly dogs.

IKE. In "Pat Hobby and Orson Welles," he is a former guard Pat Hobby names in an unsuccessful effort to get past a new guard at the studio side entrance.

IKEY. In "Emotional Bankruptcy," any one of several former neighbor boys Josephine Perry remembers fondly.

"IMAGE ON THE HEART" (1936). Short story. (Characters: Croirier, Riccard, Silvé, Tom, Tudy.) Tudy, nineteen, meets Tom's train at Avignon, where she has been studying. A year earlier, her husband drowned off Rehoboth Beach, Delaware, during their honeymoon. Tom, then thirty and staying at their hotel, took charge during the calamity, fell in love with Tudy, and financed a year of study for her in France to get over her loss. By correspondence, they agreed to marry. At Avignon, however, Tudy seems interested in Riccard, a French aviator from Toulon. Tom, after amusing them at dinner with a tube-inflatable bulb to make Riccard's plate wiggle, gives the device to Riccard. Gradually he comes to feel that Tudy loves Riccard; she insists otherwise, however, goes shopping in Paris for a few days, returns by train, and marries Tom. When the train conductor seeks Tom out and gives him Tudy's cloak and also the inflatable bulb, both left on the train, Tudy admits Riccard flew to Paris, accompanied her back by train, and chanced to leave the bulb. Tudy says there was nothing between them. Tom wonders. They agree never to indulge in reproaches. "Image on the Heart" was sadly inspired by the 1924 love affair of his wife, Zelda Sayre Fitzgerald,* in St. Raphael with French aviator Édouard Jozan. Unlike Tom, with respect to Tudy, however, Fitzgerald was left in no doubt concerning Zelda's infidelity.

"IMAGINATION—AND A FEW MOTHERS" (1923). Essay. (Characters: Clarence, Emily Hope Dempster, Giuseppi, Judkins, Anita Judkins, Clifford Judkins, Mrs. Judkins, Maisie, Paxton, Paxton, Harry Paxton, Mrs. Paxton, Prudence Paxton, Viscountess Salisbury, Vivian.) Most homes are dull places, with husbands off at clubs, mothers at the movies, and children on moonlit drives. Daughters often marry only to leave such homes and then wish they could return. Using one's imagination can improve the home. Dull Mrs. Judkins, however, queries her daughter, pampers her son, and leads a self-sacrificial life too depressing to discuss. Such mothers, having given too much to their children, are subsequently regarded as objects of sentiment or are ignored. By contrast, Mrs. Paxton, knowing nothing about her husband's business or her three children's activities, lets them evolve independently and enjoy natural friendships, and has a life of her own, which she, with her congenial husband, continues after the children's inevitable, proper drifting off into personal maturity, privacy, and freedom.

"IN A DEAR LITTLE VINE-COVERED COTTAGE" (1952). Poem. (Character: Gus Schnlitski.) Gus Schnlitski, sixteen, laments his approaching electrocution merely for shooting his mother (with a stolen gun). After all, she taunted him. He had, to be sure, been expelled earlier from school for rape. Still, the present event should be regarded as a family concern, since morphine contributed to his becoming an orphan. This poem was published without proper authorization as ''The Boy Who Killed His Mother'' in *Neurotica*.

INCOME FOR FITZGERALD. Fitzgerald, who was foolish with money to the point of idiocy, kept a ledger of his income from 1919 through 1936. His annual rounded income was as follows: 1919, $880; 1920, $18,850; 1921, $19,070; 1922, $25,140; 1923, $28,760; 1924, $20,310; 1925, $18,330; 1926, $25,980; 1927, $29,740; 1928, $25,730; 1929, $30,020; 1930; $29,340; 1931, $37,600; 1932, $15,820; 1933, $16,330; 1934, $20,030; 1935, $16,850; 1936, $10,180. These sums total $388,960, or an average of $21,610 per year. Magazine publication paid him the best; for example, *Saturday Evening Post* editors gave him $3,600 for each of eight stories in 1931, though less both earlier and later. Hollywood was also a source of good, if irregular, money; for example, he was paid $5,400, also in 1931, for working on *Red-Headed Woman*, a script that quickly came to naught.

Fitzgerald's income from publishing in 1937 declined; for example, he sold five pieces to *Esquire* but for only $250 each. So he hired on with MGM in Hollywood in July for $1,000 a week for six months, by which time he was perhaps $40,000 in debt—to his agent, Harold Ober,* his editor, Max Perkins,* his publisher, Scribner's, and Zelda Sayre Fitzgerald's* hospital. Through 1938 MGM paid him $1,250 a week but did not renew his contract. Thus, MGM paid him $85,000—virtually his only income during that period—but little was left after medical expenses, other costs (including bills for Scottie [*see* Fitzgerald, Francis Scott*] and his own life with Sheilah Graham*), taxes, and debt reduction. In 1939 United Artists paid him $1,250 to work on *Winter Carnival*, but Walter Wanger fired him in mid-February for drunkenness. In 1940 Twentieth Century-Fox paid him $1,000 a week for seven weeks to write a script, then rejected it. Ironically, it was based on *The Light of Heart*, the 1940 London play by George Emlyn Williams (1905–1987) about an alcoholic, has-been actor. In 1939 and 1940 Fitzgerald published sixteen magazine items, a dozen of which were Pat Hobby stories in *Esquire* (for $250 each). In addition, he had been working on *The Last Tycoon*, left incomplete at his death. The last royalty statement Fitzgerald ever received from Scribner's (1 August 1940) was for $13.13, for sales of forty copies of his books. In 1940 his income was $14,570. His estate, once debts were paid and apart from personal possessions (including manuscripts), amounted to about $34,000. Since Fitzgerald's death, however, publishers, scholars, critics, collectors, and writers adapting his plots for movies, radio, and television and the actors performing in them have made millions from his artistic creativity.

''INDECISION'' (1931). Short story. (Characters: Abdul, Count de Caros Moros, Capone Cola, Mrs. Cola, H. P. Eastby, Emily Elliot, Eric, Frank Forrester,

Tommy McLane, Rosemary Merriweather, Sage, Harry Whitby.) During the 1930 Christmas holidays in the Swiss Alps, Tommy McLane, manager of a New York bank in Paris, enjoys skiing with fellow hotel guests, taking tea, flirting, dancing, and sleighing into nearby Doldorp. Twenty-seven and on the rise professionally, he is regarded by many, including himself, as a catch. He alternately pursues Emily Elliot, twenty-five, divorced and charming, and Rosemary Merriweather, eighteen and gorgeous. When he is with Rosemary at his hotel, he thinks of Emily, at another hotel next door. Tommy is jealous when a young Spanish nobleman named Count de Caros Moros, about whom he makes racist comments, and an American family named Cola give Rosemary a sleigh ride. At a ball Tommy plays Emily and Rosemary against each other by avoiding both. His tardy pursuit of Rosemary is interrupted when Emily's cousin, Frank Forrester, asks his help to keep an alleged spy, hired by her ex-husband, from bothering her. The suspect turns out to be a harmless German businessman. Tommy's boss orders him by telegram to attend a meeting in Geneva. Next morning, on the train he encounters a tearful Rosemary, thinks of Emily while approaching Rosemary, but blurts out a proposal to Rosemary anyway.

In some ways, "Indecision" rehearses aspects of *Tender Is the Night*, with Tommy leading to Dick Diver and Rosemary Merriweather to Rosemary Hoyt. Tommy, however, is ignorant of his personality flaws.

INDORE, PRINCE JOHN BROWN HOBBY. In "Pat Hobby, Putative Father," he is the "putative" son, born John Brown Hobby in 1926, of Pat Hobby and Delia Brown, now his ex-wife. When Delia went to India and married Raj Dak Raj Indore, John became Prince John Hobby Brown Indore. Visiting in Hollywood, he wants to see Bonita Granville.* Pat takes him, along with the lad's uncle, Sir Singrim Dak Raj, to a stage where she is acting. Although they wreck the set when seen and filmed from its rear, John is thrilled.

INDORE, RAJAH DAK RAJ. In "Pat Hobby, Putative Father," he is the legal father of Prince John Hobby Brown Indore, Pat Hobby's son by Delia Brown.

"INFIDELITY" (1973). A screenplay Fitzgerald began in 1938 and never finished. The plot concerns a rich couple much in love until the wife visits Europe, returns unexpectedly, and discovers her husband's infidelity. They live on together, and the wife rejects a former suitor and becomes friendly with a physician.

INGERSOLL. In "A Short Trip Home," any girl named Ingersoll that Ellen Baker fibs to her mother she is going to Chicago with, to see the Brokaws.

INGLES, MISS. In "The Pusher-in-the-Face," she is a companion of Mrs. George D. Robinson, when the latter is so rude to Charles David Stuart that he pushes her in the face. Miss Ingles attends the hearing at which the judge dismisses charges against Stuart.

"IN LITERARY NEW YORK" (1923). Open letter. Fitzgerald replies to a *St. Paul Daily News* editor asking about news from literary New York. After commenting on several writers who seem not very interesting, he says the real news will be the appearance next January of the *American Mercury*, established by H. L. Mencken* and George Jean Nathan.* He adds his own foundering play, *The Vegetable*, is being repaired.

"INSIDE THE HOUSE" (1936). Short story. (Characters: Jim Bennett, Bryan Bowers, Gwen Bowers, Satterly Brown, Jason Crawford, Dizzy, Ed Harrison, Peppy Velance.) It is winter near Chesapeake Bay. Gwen Bowers, fourteen, daughter of Bryan Bowers and his wife, now deceased, is decorating their Christmas tree with the help of Jason Crawford and two other boys. Bryan tells her she cannot go with Jason to a movie starring Peppy Velance, Gwen's ideal. Bryan's friend Ed Harrison, a New York businessman who associates with theatrical people, is the Bowerses' dinner guest, tells Gwen about his friend Peppy, but becomes ill—he was gassed in World War I—and stays under nurses' care at the Bowers home. Several days later Gwen goes to see Peppy in a neighborhood movie house against her father's orders, because he wanted her to join him for dinner out with some special people. The roof of the theater collapses under a weight of snow, and Gwen returns home. When her father tells her that the surprise dinner guest was Peppy, Gwen is crushed. Bryan leaves her a note: Peppy and Harrison are coming to dinner at their house next evening. When Harrison tells Gwen that Peppy is stupid, that beauty and intelligence are seldom in one person, and that neither ingredient can help the other, is Fitzgerald warning his daughter Scottie (*see* Fitzgerald, Frances Scott)? She was fourteen when this story was published. *See also* "Too Cute for Words."

"AN INTERVIEW WITH F. SCOTT FITZGERALD" (1920, 1960). Essay. Fitzgerald composes an interview of himself. The reporter finds the author in a messy hotel room, notes he looks "Nordic," and hears him tell how he laboriously lived events in *This Side of Paradise* but composed it in three months. He does not feel consumed by "big" ideas. He hopes to write for the young of his generation, critics of the next, and teachers after that. He theorizes any given literary tradition is killed by the next. He hopes to develop a colorful style and names several authors whose styles he admires.

"IN THE DARKEST HOUR" (1934). Short story. (Characters: the Abbot, Brother Brian, Goldgreaves, Jacques, Le Poire, Count Philippe of Villefranche, Robert the Frog.) In May 872, Philippe, a stalwart Frenchman formerly a prisoner in Moorish Spain, rides into the Loire Valley, calls himself the Count of Villefranche, and intends to reclaim his land and rescue his race from Viking bondage. Gathering a squad of churchmen and peasants, he destroys a Viking encampment nearby, kills several Vikings and demands loyalty of others, and plans for his people's future. Philippe speaks in a hard-boiled way, and the peasants sound like southern American tenant farmers; one even says "right smart."

"IN THE HOLIDAYS" (1937). Short story. (Characters: Miss Collins, Flute Cuneo, Miss Gleason, Griffin, Miss Hunter, Dr. Kamp, Joe Kinney, Oaky, Vandervere.) A patient calling himself McKenna is in the hospital on New Year's Eve. The only interesting test, according to Dr. Kamp, was an x-ray revealing bullets in McKenna's buttocks. McKenna prefers pretty nurse Miss Collins to plain nurse Miss Hunter. He and Miss Hunter discuss another patient, named Griffin, who also has nothing wrong with him. Miss Hunter lets McKenna take a walk and asks him to mail a letter for her. He leaves, tears the letter into four pieces and drops it in a mailbox, buys some wine, returns to his bed, and rings for Miss Collins. Amid the noise of midnight revelry he thinks he hears gunfire. He gets fresh with Miss Collins, soon ordered to care for Griffin, who has been shot. Next day the recipient of Miss Hunter's letter, who is her fiancé and a policeman, enters posing as a resident, matches McKenna's x-ray with those of a wounded suspect named Joe Kinney, and tells McKenna that a postman retrieved the letter and gave it to him and that Kinney's fingerprints are on it.

"THE INTIMATE STRANGERS" (1935). Short story. (Characters: Abby, Mrs. Caxton Bisby, the Hon. Martha Burne-Dennison, Marquis Eduard de la Guillet de la Guimpé, Marquis Henri de la Guillet de la Guimpé, Marquise Sara de la Guillet de la Guimpé, Miette de la Guillet de la Guimpé, Henriette, Cedric Killian, Dorothy Killian, Noel, Margot Pechard, Paul Pechard, Mrs. Selby, Madame Villegris, Virginie.) In 1914, Marquise Sara de la Guillet de la Guimpé, twenty-one, has for four years been the wife of Marquis Eduard de la Guillet de la Guimpé, forty-one; she is also the mother of Miette de la Guillet de la Guimpé, two, and Henri de la Guillet de la Guimpé, newly born. Sara, who is vacationing on Long Island with her friend, Abby, has never loved her old husband and dislikes his letter from the French embassy in Washington that says they must soon go to France. When Cedric Killian, Abby's handsome friend, comes in, he and Sara become intimate almost instantly. They spend two weeks together, on a whirlwind musical tour in North Carolina—she plays the ukelele; he, the guitar—and for a hundred torrid hours in a cabin near Asheville. Adoring Killian's memory, Sara returns with her husband and children to France as World War I begins. Eduard joins his regiment and is wounded in the spine. Sara nurses wounded soldiers in Paris. Toward war's end she meets a handsome American army officer at the Ritz in Paris, and they spend a night together. Sara tends to Eduard, who is bound to a wheelchair, until he dies in 1925. After a year of mourning, she attends a ball, where her former servant tells her Killian is in Paris. He telephones her at the Guillet de la Guimpé family residence, and she rushes to meet him at his hotel—despite objections from her in-laws. Killian was married, is widowered, and drinks a lot. He and Sara elope to Algiers. In 1928, while visiting Abby on Long Island, the couple seem distant—until Killian rides off to a private grave. Sara follows by car. He explains that he did not marry Dorothy on the rebound but because he loved her, and that he did not love Sara earlier but does so now, profoundly. Although this makes her love for him deeper, she realizes she and Killian are partly strangers to each other. But they will also be really intimate now. Charles East may have taken from this story part of the title of his *Distant Friends and Intimate Strangers: Stories* (1996).

"INTRODUCTION" (1934). Essay. In his Introduction to the Modern Library reprint of *The Great Gatsby*, Fitzgerald praises H. L. Mencken* for improving American literary criticism, attacks cowardly reviewers for not guiding the public to worthy young writers, and urges authors to be proud of their work. While writing *The Great Gatsby* he kept his professional conscience clean, sounded his imagination deeply, wrote honestly rather than sentimentally, and endured loneliness.

IRELAND, LOUIS. In "Six of One—," he is a talented but undisciplined Ohio lad Ed Barnes sees artistic talent in and sends to Harvard. Louis regards his time there as wasted. He thinks of entering a monastery, marches in support of Sacco and Vanzetti, runs off with a professor's wife, and goes to Paris, where he succeeds as a sculptor. Louis sends Barnes a scathing letter criticizing his benefactor's commercialism.

IRENE. In "The Cut-Glass Bowl," she is Evylyn Piper's unmarried sister. She and her friend Joe Ambler attend Evylyn's birthday party. During a bridge game eleven years later, Irene tactlessly tells Evylyn it is dangerous to be in the infantry, as her son Donald Piper is.

IRMA. In "That Kind of Party," she is one of the Shoonover family servants.

IRVING, GLADYS. In "Six of One—," she is a married woman, two years older than Charley Schofield. He falls in love with her, but she urges him to go to college. Later, widowed, she marries him.

ISABELLE. In "Babes in the Woods," she is a flirtatious girl from Pittsburg[h], sixteen. She is her schoolmate Elaine Terrell's guest during Christmas vacation and eyes fellow-guest Kenneth Powers, with whom she dances and would let kiss her but for their being interrupted. She relishes her reputation as a "speed." Isabelle is Fitzgerald's first flapper and appears in this very early story. His later flappers, less sweet and less fresh, shake the grip of family and become prom trotters.

ISMAY. In *The Great Gatsby*, Nick Carraway lists his name on a timetable as one of Jay Gatsby's summer guests. He is from East Egg.

IVES, GEORGE. In "On Your Own," he is a wealthy, idle lawyer from Maryland, thirty. On his way around the world, he stopped in London and saw Evelyn Lovejoy starring in a stage show. He bumps into her aboard a ship taking both to New York. He attends her father's funeral in Maryland, drives her to Washington, D.C., sees her again in New York, half proposes to her, and takes her with his mother to dinner in New York. Her behavior at dinner offends him, and he wishes to end their friendship. At the end, however, they are embracing.

IVES, MRS. In "On Your Own," she is George Ives's mother. At a New York dinner for four, she does not patronize Evelyn Lovejoy and seems to mind less than her son does when Evelyn reveals she was a "party girl" at a New York gathering six years earlier attended by Colonel Cary, who is Mrs. Ives's dinner companion.

IVES, MRS. HORACE J., JR. In "The Homes of the Stars," she is named by Mrs. Deering R. Robinson as a neighbor who once had her picture taken with actor George Brent.

J

JACCY. In ''I Got Shoes,'' she is actress Nell Margery's French maid, who confesses she tried on Nell's discarded shoes.

JACK. In ''A Penny Spent,'' he is the bartender at the Brix Grill in Paris. Corcoran knows but does not patronize him.

JACK. In ''My Old New England Homestead on the Erie,'' he is the purchaser of an old house he and his wife happily de-renovate into a stagnant pile full of moldy antiques. They have a baby.

JACKSON. In ''Rags Martin-Jones and the Pr-nce of W-les,'' he is an employee of John B. Chestnut, who orders Jackson to immobilize the actors, in an effort to impress Rags Martin-Jones.

JACKSON, ELLERY HAMIL. In ''John Jackson's Arcady,'' he is John Jackson's son and is being expelled from Yale for misconduct. His father wires him not to come home and to expect $50 a month for life unless he is jailed. Father welcomes son home, however, in the end.

JACKSON, JOHN. In ''John Jackson's Arcady,'' he is a successful, generous businessman, forty-five, who becomes cynical. His wife—the mother of their wayward son, Ellery Hamil Jackson—left him ten years ago for another man. Jackson has given his city much, feels unappreciated, returns to his hometown, chances to see his childhood sweetheart Alice MacDowell, and asks her to abandon her husband and children and run away with him. She agrees but next day declines. After returning to his own city, he is praised at a town meeting for his philanthropic acts.

JACKSON, MARY. In ''First Blood,'' she is an evidently decent girl who marries Jackson Dillon. Josephine Perry attends their wedding.

JACKSON, MRS. In ''Love in the Night,'' she invites the Rostoffs to a party aboard her yacht, the *Minnehaha*, in the harbor at Cannes.

JACKSON, [THOMAS "STONEWALL"], GENERAL (1824–1863). He was a courageous Confederate officer. In ''A Debt of Honor,'' he permits Colonel Barrows to attack the frame house held by the enemy.

"JACOB'S LADDER" (1927). Short story. (Characters: Carl Barbour, Biggs, Jacob C. K. Booth, Mrs. Choynski, Billy Farrelly, Hecksher, Lorenzo, Jenny Prince, Raffino, Read, Scharnhorst, Van Tyne.) Jacob C. K. Booth, having made $800,000 on a 1924 Florida land deal, becomes quite independent. Later, thirty-three and single, he watches the trial in New York of Mrs. Choynski, who murdered her lover and is soon convicted. Her sister, Jenny Delehanty, who as a baby was separated from the older woman and is now sixteen, attends the trial, is bothered by reporters, and is whisked off to a Long Island dinner by Jacob. He is enthralled by her beauty though aware of her cultural limitations. Through a friend, he gets her a bit part in a movie being filmed on Long Island. Jacob gives her the stage name of Jenny Prince and encourages her to accept a Hollywood contract. Some months later he follows her to Hollywood, and they attend many alcoholic ''teas,'' where he suspects handsome actor Raffino is in love with her. When Jacob proposes marriage, she is agreeable but says he does not thrill her. He hopes thrills will come later. A would-be blackmailer threatens to expose her relationship with her jailed sister, but Jacob returns to the East and saves her. After starring in another movie, she comes to New York to Jacob, who renews his proposal. She says she has fallen in love with her director. Jacob goes to see her new movie and, with the rest of the audience, is thrilled to be a brief part of her enchanting image, which he helped create. Aspects of ''Jacob's Ladder'' found their way into *Tender Is the Night*.

JACOBY. In ''Zone of Accident,'' he is a medical student whose blood type does not match that of Loretta Brooke.

JACQUES. In *The Evil Eye*, he sings to the sea about his lost, desired love. Later, he and Claude sing with a girl and Dulcinea about honeymoons.

JACQUES. In ''In the Darkest Hour,'' he is a Loire Valley farmer. When Count Philippe of Villefranche recruits him, he fights well against the Viking invaders. In ''The Count of Darkness,'' he continues to serve Philippe loyally. In ''The Kingdom in the Dark'' (in which his name is spelled Jaques and Philippe calls him Sir Jaques), he rides with Philippe to survey his property and helps him conceal Griselda. In ''Gods of Darkness'' (in which Philippe again calls him

Sir Jaques), he is revealed to be a pagan cultist, along with Griselda. His mysterious words help save Philippe from the Duke of Maine's men, one of whom, however, wounds him with an arrow in his calf. It is revealed that Pierre, a man also loyal to Philippe, is Jaques's son. It is said that Jaques will become the forebear of French kings.

JADWIN, CECIL. In "A Change of Class," he is Philip Jadwin's rich father.

JADWIN, PHILIP. In "A Change of Class," he is the well-to-do, handsome, shy customer of barber Earl Johnson. In 1926 Philip is thirty-one. His reluctantly given tip concerning the Hert-win commercial interests results in Earl's gaining wealth. Philip is secretly in love with Irene, a typist in his office who later marries a bootlegger, Howard Shalder. A few months after the Crash, Philip aids Earl again and offers comfort to Irene, when her husband runs off with Earl's wife, Violet Johnson. The name Jadwin may derive from that of Curtis Jadwin, the heroic speculator in *The Pit: A Story of Chicago* (1903), by Frank Norris.

JAGGERS, GEORGE. In "Financing Finnegan," he is the narrator's and Finnegan's editor. Jaggers is modeled partly on Fitzgerald's generous editor Max Perkins.*

JAMES. In *The Captured Shadow*, he is a Connage family servant.

JAMES. In "The Mystery of the Raymond Mortgage," he is an assistant in Egan's office and shows John Syrel out when Egan orders him to do so.

JAMES, CONSTANCE. In *Thoughtbook*, she is a new girl at the dance school.

JAMES, ENKY. In *Thoughtbook*, he is one of Fitzgerald's best friends.

JAMES, TRUDY. In "Three Hours between Planes," she was a childhood friend of Donald Plant and Nancy Holmes Gifford and evidently gave a picnic both attended.

JANICE. In "The Woman from Twenty-one," she is a person whose photograph Elizabeth Torrence admires. Janice may be the daughter of Elizabeth Torrence and Raymond Torrence.

JANIERKA. In "Majesty," he is evidently a servant of Prince Gabriel Petrocobesco.

JANNEY, BUTCH. In "Family in the Wind," he is the son, nineteen, of Gene Janney and Rose Janney. Butch threatens his uncle, Dr. Forrest Janney, when he will not treat his brother, Pinky Janney. Butch is separated from his car during the first tornado. He criticizes Forrest after he operates on Pinky, who he reports is dying.

JANNEY, DR. FORREST. In ''Family in the Wind,'' he is Gene Janney's alcoholic brother, forty-seven (he calls himself forty-five). When he got the shakes, he gave up practicing in Montgomery, Alabama, and became part-owner of a drugstore in Bending. His befriending of Mary Decker causes family gossip. Transformed by the first tornado, Forrest treats the injured and reluctantly removes a bullet from the head of his nephew, Pinky Janney. Forrest plans to return to medicine in Montgomery and adopt Helen Kilrain.

JANNEY, EDITH. In ''Family in the Wind,'' she is the young daughter of Gene Janney and Rose Janney.

JANNEY, EUGENE. In ''Family in the Wind,'' he is Rose Janney's husband, in his mid-forties, and the father of Pinky, Butch, Edith, and Eugene Janney. Gene is Dr. Forrest Janney's brother. He asks Forrest to operate on Pinky, who has been shot in the head.

JANNEY, PINKY. In ''Family in the Wind,'' he is the oldest child, nineteen, of Gene Janney and Rose Janney. He evidently abused Mary Decker and allowed her to die of starvation six months before the story begins. He was later shot in the head in a brawl in Birmingham, Alabama, and was moved to his parents' home in Bending. Dr. Behrer, the local doctor, will not operate to remove the bullet. Dr. Forrest Janney, Pinky's uncle, declines at first also but later removes the bullet. Pinky dies anyway.

JANNEY, ROSE. In ''Family in the Wind,'' she is Gene Janney's wife and the mother of Pinky, Butch, Edith, and Eugene Janney. She rebukes her brother-in-law, Dr. Forrest Janney, for his alleged mistreatment of Mary Decker. Evidently the root of her dislike of Forrest was his being better educated than Gene.

JANSEN. In ''At Your Age,'' he was the owner of Minneapolis livery stables in the 1890s.

JAQUELINE. In *The Great Gatsby*, she is a person Nick Carraway vaguely remembers as being among Jay Gatsby's summer guests.

JAQUES. In ''The Kingdom in the Dark'' and ''Gods of Darkness.'' *See* Jacques.

JAQUES, LELAND. In ''At Your Age,'' he is a fatuous lad who chats with Tom Squires at the College Club.

JARVIS. In ''Benediction,'' he is a young seminarian. He idolizes Keith, who tells Lois that Jarvis would be a good man to have on one's side in a fight.

JARVIS, MRS. In ''Benediction,'' she is Jarvis's grandmother, whom Lois remembers from some time ago.

JEANNE. In ''How to Live on Practically Nothing a Year,'' she is one of the Fitzgeralds' Riviera servants.

JEFF. In ''Family in the Wind,'' he is a neighbor of the Janneys whom Dr. Forrest Janney treats after he is injured in the first tornado.

JEFFERSON (''JEFF''). In *Coward*, he is Judge Arthur Douglas's loyal black servant. After the judge's death, he remains with his widow, Mary Douglas.

JELKE, JOE. In ''A Short Trip Home,'' he is a St. Paul friend of Eddie Stinson and is a Yale senior. When Joe goes outside the hotel where the dance is being held to dispute with the stranger, he is knocked out with brass knuckles.

JELLY-BEAN. In ''The Jelly-Bean.'' *See* Powell, James.

''THE JELLY-BEAN'' (1920). Short story. (Characters: Ben, Harriet Cary, Clark Darrow, Joe Ewing, Marjorie Haight, Sally Carrol Hopper, Dr. Lamar, Nancy Lamar, Aunt Mamie, Ogden Merritt, Alice Powell, James Powell, Soda Sam, Taylor, Tilly, Marylyn Wade.) Jim Powell is a Jelly-bean, an example of harmless, pleasant Southern lassitude. He went to high school in a Georgia town (Tarleton), was afraid of girls, became an expert auto mechanic, served in the navy in Charleston and Brooklyn, and in 1918, at war's end, has come home again—age twenty-one and an expert cheater at craps. As his friend Clark Darrow's reluctant guest at a local country club, Jim sees lovely, socially ambitious Nancy Lamar, a former school friend he has not spoken to in fifteen years. To tease her rich beau, Ogden Merritt of Savannah, Nancy accepts some corn liquor from Jim, who also taps the fuel tank of a nearby car, owned by an older man named Taylor, for gasoline to remove chewing gum from her shoe. They drink some more; when Nancy loses at dice to Taylor, who is annoyed that someone emptied his gas tank, she gives him worthless personal checks to cover her losses. Jim steps in, defeats Taylor at dice with canny tosses, retrieves the girl's checks, and destroys them. In gratitude Nancy gives him a wild, drunken kiss. Feeling guilty but in love, he is restless until next afternoon, when Clark informs him that Nancy, Merritt, and some others continued to drink, and that Nancy and Merritt eloped. Jim, stunned, wanders into a local poolhall.

''JEMINA'' (1916). (Full title: ''Jemina: A Story of the Blue Ridge Mountains by John Phlox, Jr.'') Short story. (Characters: Boscoe Doldrum, Hartsum Doldrum, Heck Doldrum, Jem Doldrum, Edgar Edison, Miss Lafarge, Gore Tantrum, Ham Tantrum, Japhet Tantrum, Jem Tantrum, Jemina Tantrum, Mappy Tantrum, Pappy Tantrum.) Edgar Edison enters the mountainous region of Kentucky when gold is discovered on land owned by the moonshiner Tantrum family. He wants to buy the land cheap, but the feud resumes between the Tantrums and their hated moonshiner neighbors, the Doldrums. When the Doldrums set fire to the Tantrum house, Jemina Tantrum, sixteen, and Edison, who are attracted to one another, burn to death, melt together, and are cast into the river as one. This story was reprinted as ''Jemina, the Mountain Girl (One of Those Family Feud Stories of the Blue Ridge Mountains with Apologies to Stephen Leacock)'' in 1921.

JENKINS. In '' 'Send Me In, Coach,' '' he is the baseball coach in the play rehearsed by the boys.

JENKS, ED. In ''Family in the Wind,'' he is a resident of Bending, Alabama, and helps Dr. Forrest Janney after the first tornado injures a number of people.

JENNINGS, HUGHIE. In *Precaution Primarily*, he is named in a song.

JEROME, JAMES ("JIM"). In ''Discard,'' he is a distinguished movie director, loves actress Dolly Bordon, and casts her in *Portrait of a Woman*. He proposes to her, but she prefers a professional career.

JERRY. In ''The Freshest Boy,'' she is a beautiful Broadway actress, nineteen. She is in love with Ted Fay, captain of the Yale football team. Since she has promised to marry her casting director, Beltzman, she urges Ted simply to return to Yale.

JERRY. In ''The Smilers,'' he is a room waiter at the hotel where Sylvester Stockton lives. Jerry seems happy to Sylvester and smiles at him. In reality Jerry is about to lose his girlfriend, whose willingness to marry him has come to an end because he lacks money.

JERRYL, RACHAEL. In *The Beautiful and Damned. See* Barnes, Rachael Jerryl.

JESSIE. In ''Head and Shoulders,'' she is Marcia Meadow's friend who, according to Marcia, called herself ''only sixteen'' when ''only'' is unnecessary when one tells one's age.

JEWETT, DR. In ''The Lees of Happiness,'' he is the New York specialist who examines Jeffrey Curtain at his home outside Chicago and pronounces his paralysis hopeless.

JEWETT, P. In *The Great Gatsby*, he is a person Nick Carraway remembers as being among Jay Gatsby's summer guests.

JIDGE. In "The Woman from Twenty-one," he is the escort of the loud woman called Mrs. Richbitch. Hat Milbank calls her by this name at the theater.

JIGGS, MRS. In "The Woman from Twenty-one," she is a person Raymond Torrence associates with the selfish Mrs. Richbitch.

JIM. In "The Diary of a Sophomore," he is the diarist's friend.

JIM. In *The Girl from Lazy J*, he is a cowboy employed by George Kendall.

JIM. In "A Luckless Santa Claus," he is one of the two men who beat up Harry Talbot for offering them money. He later celebrates Christmas Eve with them.

JIM. In "May Day," this is a generic name for any of several dates Edith Bradin recalls.

JIM, UNCLE. In "Fate in Her Hands," he is a minister and the uncle of Carol (later Carol Kastler). He reluctantly and hastily marries her to Benjamin Kastler instead of to Billy Riggs.

JIMMY. In "Benediction," he is a seminarian who with a grin asks Lois to show fellow seminarians the shimmy. Laughing, she declines.

JIMMY. In "Two Wrongs," he is a friend William McChesney greets when he is taking Emmy Pinkard to lunch in New York.

JIMMY. In "What Kind of Husbands Do 'Jimmies' Make?," he is a typical son of wealthy parents. *See* Worthington, Jimmy, more specifically discussed.

JIMMY, MRS. In "What Kind of Husbands Do 'Jimmies' Make?," she is the typical Jimmy's typical wife. She will suffer if not agreeable.

JINKS, JERRY. In *The Beautiful and Damned*, she is a twin of Judy Jinks. Gloria Gilbert Patch likes them only because of their alliterative names.

JINKS, JUDY. In *The Beautiful and Damned*, she and Jerry Jinks are twins Gloria Patch likes.

JINNIE, AUNT. In "Lo, the Poor Peacock!," she is a worker on the sausage farm of Annie Lee Davis and Jason Davis.

JO. In ''The Rich Boy,'' she is Paula Legendre's cousin, twenty-five, who told Mrs. Legendre that Anson Hunter was drunk at the Hempstead party.

JOAN. In ''Crazy Sunday,'' she is Stella Walker Calman's friend. Joel Coles offers to ask Joan to comfort Stella after her husband's death. Fitzgerald knew movie actresses Joan Crawford and Joan Blondell and may for that reason have used the name Joan here.

JOE. In ''The Diary of a Sophomore,'' he is the diarist's friend.

JOE. In ''Emotional Bankruptcy,'' he is a friend Josephine Perry and Lillian Hammel plan to meet, along with Wallie, at the Ritz.

JOE. In ''Pat Hobby and Orson Welles,'' he is the Hollywood studio barber who notes Pat Hobby's resemblance to Orson Welles.

JOE. In *This Side of Paradise*, he is the owner of a Princeton establishment where Amory Blaine eats as a freshman.

JOE. In ''Two Wrongs,'' he is a casting agent William McChesney orders to give Emmy Pinkard a part in a New York play.

"JOHN JACKSON'S ARCADY" (1924). Short story. (Characters: Anna, Fowler, John Jackson Fowler, Alice Harland, George Harland, Ellery Hamil Jackson, John Jackson, Thomas J. MacDowell, Mrs. Ralston, Anthony Roreback, Austin Schemmerhorn, George Stirling.) John Jackson, a successful, generous businessman, forty-five, receives two letters in his office, one about his promise to speak to a civic group on what he has gotten out of life, the other from the Yale College dean informing him his son, Ellery Hamil Jackson, is being expelled for misconduct. Jackson muses about his marriage—his wife left him for another man ten years ago—and on his unappreciated gifts to the city. When Thomas J. MacDowell, a crass politician, enters and asks him to donate a block of land Jackson owns, which can be converted into a new railroad station, he sends the man away. Jackson tells Fowler, his chief clerk, he is leaving for an indeterminate time and asks him to cancel his appointments, pay his servants, and close his house. He wires his son not to come home, since there will be no home, but to expect $50 a month for life through a New York trust company. Jackson takes a train to Florence, his hometown seventy miles away, engages a hotel room, and wanders to the closed-up house in which he grew up happily but which he has not visited in twenty years. He encounters Alice there, and they kiss. She was his childhood sweetheart but married George Harland, a garageman, and has three children. She invites him to dinner. George lets the two reminisce on the porch, and Jackson persuades Alice to run away with him, since they agree they have always loved one another. At lunch next day she declines, and Jackson returns to his city. That afternoon he takes a shadowy back seat in the civic hall, where to his surprise speaker after speaker—including MacDowell—commend the supposedly absent Jackson for philanthropy. Discovered, he is carried to the platform where he tells the cheering audience of five hundred that what he got out of life was everything. When he returns home, his prodigal son is there and is made genuinely welcome.

JOHNS, WILLIAM ("BILLY") DELANEY. In "No Flowers," he is Marjorie Clark's escort to the prom. He writes to her that a student committee has decided on a "no-flower" policy. Lacking funds to get a tuxedo, he takes one from the students' pressing service but gives it back and takes another one from a student, who is drunk and asleep. Marjorie is shocked when he tells her he is working his way through school to prove his mettle to a rich Midwestern uncle, who will provide him with a secure position after graduation.

JOHNSON. In "The Bridal Party," he is a practical joker who hires a girl to pretend Hamilton Rutherford has abandoned her and their child.

JOHNSON, CAPONE. In "The Family Bus," he is the football team captain at Dick Henderson's high school. He probably participates in painting graffiti on Dick's family car.

JOHNSON, EARL. In "A Change of Class," he is the good-looking, decent barber, twenty-six in 1926, who gains wealth when Philip Jadwin gives him a stock-market tip. He grows uneasy in his new economic class and is relieved when, after the Crash, his wife, Violet Johnson, leaves him. He happily returns to barbering when Jadwin makes it financially possible for him to do so.

JOHNSON, JACK. In "Crazy Sunday," he is the owner of a nightclub to which Joel Coles and Stella Walker Calman do not go after the Perrys' theater party.

JOHNSON, JUSTINE. In *The Beautiful and Damned*, she is the owner of a club frequented by Gloria Gilbert Patch when she first came to New York.

JOHNSON, MISS. In "Your Way and Mine," she is a member of the office staff of Henry McComas and his partner, Theodore Drinkwater.

JOHNSON, PASSION. In "He Thinks He's Wonderful," she is a girl named by Imogene Bissel as her favorite friend.

JOHNSON, PRIVATE. In *Coward*, he is evidently a Union soldier under Captain Ormsby.

JOHNSON, VIOLET ("Vi"). In "A Change of Class," she is a manicurist in the barber shop where her husband, Earl Johnson, works. She glories in their wealth, turns against him after the Crash, and runs off with Howard Shalder.

JOHNSTON. In *The Beautiful and Damned*, he is the owner of a dance hall frequented by Anthony Patch while in the army in the South.

JOHNSTON. In *The Captured Shadow*, this is an alias of Thorton Hart Dudley. *See* Dudley, Thorton Hart.

JOHNSTON, HAMILTON T. In "An Author's Mother," he is the author whose mother is proud of him without understanding his books.

JOHNSTON, JOHN. In "An Author's Mother," he is Mrs. Johnston's other son, a businessman in the West.

JOHNSTON, MRS. In "An Author's Mother," she is the mother of Hamilton T. Johnston, John Johnston, and a deceased daughter. She is proud of Hamilton but thinks his profession odd. On her way out of a bookstore, where she has gone to buy him a birthday present, she sustains a fatal fall.

JOHNSTON, MRS. In " 'Trouble,' " she is the nurses' superintendent in the hospital where Glenola McClurg works. She tries to get Glenola fired, but Dr. Dick Wheelock reverses the decision.

JONES. In "The Rubber Check," he is Val Schuyler's deceased father.

JONES. In *The Vegetable*, he is the man in the dream sequence who tells Jerry Frost he has been nominated for the presidency. When Jerry is president, Jones is his secretary.

JONES, BILL. In "A Night at the Fair." *See* Blair, Hubert.

JONES, CATHERINE. In "The Dance," she is a dancer in Davis, a Southern town. When she sees Marie Bannerman kissing Joe Cable, whom Catherine loves, she grows so jealous that she shoots Marie. Her alibi is so clever that she nearly gets away with murder. When she is caught, her excuse is self-defense, and she receives only a five-year sentence.

JONES, DR. In "The Cruise of the Rolling Junk," he reputedly wrote the misleading guidebook for motorists bought by the Fitzgeralds in Trenton.

JONES, HIRAM. In " 'Send Me In, Coach,' " he is the president of the rival school, St. Berries College, in the play rehearsed by the boys.

JONES, JUDY. In ''Winter Dreams,'' she is the beautiful, spoiled, conscienceless daughter of wealthy Mr. and Mrs. Mortimer Jones of Sherry Island, on Bear Lake, Minnesota. At eleven, she wants Dexter Green, fourteen, to caddy for her. After he returns from the East with a university degree and has begun to make good money, she invites him to dinner, becomes intimate, drops him, proposes to him, dumps him, interferes with his later engagement to Irene Scheerer, and leaves. Years later, Dexter, now in New York, learns she is unhappily married to and has children by Lud Simms. Judy Jones is modeled on Fitzgerald's early love, Ginevra King,* of Lake Forest, Illinois.

JONES, MORTIMER. In ''Winter Dreams,'' he is the wealthy, indulgent father of Judy Jones. They have a mansion in Sherry Lake, Minnesota.

JONES, MRS. MORTIMER. In ''Winter Dreams,'' she is Judy Jones's mother.

JONES, OSWALD ("RIP"). In ''The Third Casket,'' he is the black-eyed, black-haired Southern youth, about thirty, in the contest to take over the successful Wall Street firm of Cyrus Girard, who is ostensibly retiring. When Rip uses his supposed leisure time to do more work for the firm, he unexpectedly wins both a partnership with Girard and his lovely daughter, Lola Girard.

JONES, SAM. In ''Pat Hobby and Orson Welles,'' he is the set director who Jeff Boldini tells Pat Hobby needs bearded extras.

JONES, WILLIAM. In *The Evil Eye*, he left his fiancée in Bangor, Maine, and fell in love with a hula in Honolulu.

JORDAN. In ''Head and Shoulders,'' he is pretty Marcia Tarbox's delighted publisher. He brings Anton Laurier to meet Marcia.

JORDAN, DR. In ''A Change of Class,'' he is a person whose paper profits Earl Johnson mentions to Philip Jadwin just before the Crash.

JORDAN, PETER. In ''Dalyrimple Goes Wrong,'' he is a person who mentioned a vacancy in his store to Bryan Dalyrimple. On learning the job was that of a floorwalker, he declined.

JORDAN, WILLIAM. In *The Beautiful and Damned*, he is a writer whose exclusive credit for the scenario based on Richard Caramel's novel *The Demon Lover* distresses the novelist.

JORGENSEN, PAULA. In ''New Types,'' she is a beautiful model. When her father died leaving a widow and five children, Paula's aunt, Emily Holliday, refused to help. Paula, when seventeen, married Lord Eric Tressiger, who became a burden to the hard-working girl. Now, twenty-four, she is invited to a party by Emily, living on Long Island. She meets Leslie Dixon on the beach. He finds her a new type of American girl. She invites him to the party, and they fall in love. When Emily apparently dies, Paula goes ahead with the party anyway, because she is to be professionally photographed there for $500. She tells Dixon the money is needed for surgery for her husband Eric. Soon after the operation, he dies, and Paula and Dixon strengthen their love for one another.

JOSÉ. In *The Girl from Lazy J*, he is a cowboy employed by George Kendall.

JOSEPHE. In ''Gods of Darkness,'' he is a blacksmith working for Count Philippe of Villefranche.

JUBAL. In ''Basil and Cleopatra,'' he is a Yale man and Erminie Gilberte Labouisse Bibble's latest conquest.

JUDKINS. In ''Imagination—and a Few Mothers,'' he is the unhappy husband of Mrs. Judkins.

JUDKINS, ANITA. In ''Imagination—and a Few Mothers,'' she is the pretty daughter, seventeen, about whose fun her mother worries.

JUDKINS, CLIFFORD. In ''Imagination—and a Few Mothers,'' he is the son, twelve, whom his mother, Mrs. Judkins, foolishly pampers.

JUDKINS, MRS. In ''Imagination—and a Few Mothers,'' she is the foolishly self-sacrificial, meddling mother of Anita Judkins and Clifford Judkins.

JUDY. In *The Great Gatsby*, she is a person Nick Carraway vaguely remembers as being among Jay Gatsby's summer guests.

JULIA. In ''Diagnosis,'' she was a quiet servant in Charlie Clayhorne's father's home in Tuscarora, Alabama.

JUMBO. In ''The Camel's Back,'' he is the black waiter at the circus ball. He is also a Baptist minister and marries Perry Parkhurst and Betty Medill.

JUNE. In ''Crazy Sunday,'' she is Stella Walker Calman's sister, at whose Sunday buffet supper Joel Coles is a guest.

JUNE. In *The Great Gatsby*, she is a person Nick Carraway vaguely remembers as being among Jay Gatsby's summer guests.

K

KAGLE, HELEN. In "Pat Hobby's Christmas Wish," she is the secretary and mistress, twice married and now about thirty-six, of Hollywood producer Harry Gooddorf. When he dumps her and assigns her to Pat Hobby, they try unsuccessfully to blackmail Harry with a letter he wrote eighteen years earlier.

KAHLER. In *The Beautiful and Damned*, he is an employee for the Wilson, Hiemer, and Hardy bond firm who tells Anthony Patch how one gets ahead in the business.

KAISER. In "The Prince of Pests," he is the ruler of Germany who in Berlin in 1914 fusses with subordinates and is being prepared to have his photograph taken. He is William (Wilhelm) II, Friedrich Wilhelm Viktor Albert (1859–1941).

DE KALB, MARQUIS. In "One Trip Abroad," he is defined by Oscar Dane as a peculiar member of the Kellys' drifting, drinking crowd.

DE KALB, MARQUISE. In "One Trip Abroad," she is defined by Oscar Dane as a drug-addicted member of the Kellys' crowd.

KALUKA. In *This Side of Paradise*, she is a homely girl Kerry Holiday picks up and pays excessive—but cruelly brief—attention to when he, Amory Blaine, and others from Princeton go to Asbury Park.

KALY. In "A Short Autobiography," he is a bartender at a place in St. Paul where Fitzgerald drank in 1922.

KAMP, DR. In ''In the Holidays,'' he can find nothing wrong with the patient calling himself McKenna.

KAMPF, GEORGE. In ''He Thinks He's Wonderful,'' he is Basil Duke Lee's close friend William Kampf's father and also Erminie Gilberte Labouisse Bibble's uncle. In ''The Perfect Life,'' the Kampf family is mentioned.

KAMPF, MRS. GEORGE. In ''He Thinks He's Wonderful,'' she is William S. Kampf's mother. When Basil Duke Lee is the Kampf family guest, he impresses her by his courtesy. In ''The Perfect Life,'' the Kampf family is mentioned.

KAMPF, WILLIAM S. (''BILL''). In ''The Scandal Detectives,'' Basil Duke Lee and his friend Riply Buckner, Jr., draft Bill Kampf to help attack Hubert Blair. In ''He Thinks He's Wonderful,'' he is Basil's friend who invites Basil for a week to his parents' home at Bear Lake, near St. Paul. Once there, Basil meets Erminie Gilberte Labouisse Bibble, Bill's cousin. In ''The Captured Shadow,'' he is Basil's friend who plays a crook in Basil's play *The Captured Shadow*. In ''The Perfect Life,'' the Kampf family is mentioned. In ''Forging Ahead,'' he tells Basil the Bibble family is visiting the Kampf family again. Bill Kampf is partly modeled on Fitzgerald's St. Paul friend Paul Ballion.

KANE, FRANK. In ''The Bowl,'' he is a knowledgeable sporting goods salesman on Nassau Street in Princeton.

KANE, GARLAND. In ''Majesty,'' he is evidently Emily Castleton's former lover.

KANE, MURIEL. In *The Beautiful and Damned*, she is one of Gloria Gilbert Patch's closest friends. Gloria and Anthony Patch tolerate with limited amusement Muriel's brash ways as she self-deceptively flirts with men and ineffectually advises Anthony.

KAPPER. In *The Last Tycoon*, he is an art director Monroe Stahr criticizes for something wrong with a movie set.

KARGER. In ''The Rich Boy,'' he is Dolly Karger's father and a publicist of ill repute. He married into a better social position.

KARGER, DOLLY. In ''The Rich Boy,'' she is an attractive young woman, dark and lovely, but also wild and indiscreet. She meets Anson Hunter when he is on the rebound from Paula Legendre and falls for him but is abused by him.

KARGER, MRS. In "The Rich Boy," she is Dolly Karger's mother, well placed in society. Misjudging Anson Hunter as reliable, she tolerates his taking Dolly places without proper supervision.

KARR, ALPHONSE. In "The Adjuster," he is Luella Hemple's friend and Ede Karr's husband.

KARR, EDE. In "The Adjuster," she is Luella Hemple's close friend, twenty-three and married five years to Alphonse. Luella tells Ede she can hardly endure marriage and motherhood. Five years later, Luella, having evolved into a considerate woman, will welcome the Kerrs to the home she and her husband share.

KASPER. In "Pat Hobby and Orson Welles," he is a Hollywood studio executive who, a guard tells Pat Hobby, is tightening security following an accident. A visitor from Chicago fell into the wind machine.

KASTLER, BENJAMIN ("BEN"). In "Fate in Her Hands," he is an economics professor, then a dean, and finally a university president. His wife is Carol Kastler.

KASTLER, CAROL. In "Fate in Her Hands," she is the person to whom a palmist makes predictions Carol helps both to make true and to circumvent. She marries Benjamin Kastler instead of Billy Riggs, has two children, avoids notoriety by hiding, and saves Ben's life.

KASTLER, GEORGE. In "Fate in Her Hands," he is the son of Carol Kastler and Benjamin Kastler. George is two at the end of the story.

KASTLER, JEAN. In "Fate in Her Hands," she is the daughter of Carol Kastler and Benjamin Kastler, five at the end of the story.

KATE, EMMA. In *The Captured Shadow*, she is the gossipy maid in the home of Beverly Connage and his family.

KATIE. In *The Last Tycoon*, she is the assistant of Catherine Doolan, who is Monroe Stahr's secretary.

KATSPAUGH. In *The Great Gatsby*, he is evidently a criminal associate mentioned by Meyer Wolfsheim in conversation with Jay Gatsby.

KATZBY, MARTHA. In "Dice, Brassknuckles & Guitar," she is a student, sixteen, at James Powell's school. Martin Van Vleek tries to impress her.

KATZBY, MRS. POINDEXTER. In ''Dice, Brassknuckles & Guitar,'' she is a flustered Southampton matron who is Martha Katzby's mother and helps break up James Powell's school.

KAVENAUGH. In ''Six of One—,'' he is the stocky, athletic younger brother of Howard Kavenaugh. Their rich family is in the flour business in Minneapolis. He never can get into college, marries a manicurist, and lives with her quietly in Minneapolis.

KAVENAUGH, HOWARD. In ''Six of One—,'' he is the brother of young Kavenaugh, nineteen at the beginning of the story, and plays hockey well. He is expelled from Yale when he, Beau Lebaume, Wister Schofield, and George Winfield are in an accident. Wister was driving Howard's car, and Irene Daley was disfigured. Howard marries a woman from the East, and they run with a drinking crowd and will be getting divorced in 1930 or so.

KAYE. In ''A Freeze-Out,'' this is the name of some of the many people who attended the Rikkers' party shortly after New Year's Day.

KAYE, ELLA. In *The Great Gatsby*, she is a newspaperwoman who boarded rich Dan Cody's yacht shortly before he died and left her his millions. Fitzgerald's friend, Robert Kerr, of Great Neck, Long Island, told him about a yachtsman named Edward Gilman whose covetous mistress was Nellie Bly, the sensational journalist.

Bibliography: Joseph Corso, ''One Not-Forgotten Summer Night: Sources for Fitzgerald's Symbols of American Character in *The Great Gatsby*,'' FH/A 1976, 8–33.

KAYE, MARTY. In *This Side of Paradise*, he is evidently a Princeton student whom Amory Blaine, in conversation with Thomas Parke D'Invilliers, regards as stupid.

KEARNS, DR. In ''Two Wrongs,'' he is the New York physician who tells William McChesney he has a disease-destroyed lung and must go to Denver to rest.

KEATTS, LILY. In ''Pat Hobby Does His Bit,'' she is an English actress. Too quickly after Pat spoils the filming of her final scene she disappears for England. He must be hired to act in a newly written scene introducing him.

KEBBLE, FREDDY. In ''Benediction,'' he is a man Lois tells her brother Keith she talked with about sweetness in people. Whereas he thought sweetness was soppy, she thought it could be properly hard.

KEBBLE, MAURY. In ''Benediction,'' he is Freddy Kebble's brother. Lois is surprised her brother Keith knew Maury.

KEENE. In ''The Bowl,'' he is the coach of the Princeton football team.

KEENE, DR. In ''The Curious Case of Benjamin Button,'' he delivers Benjamin in the Baltimore hospital and is terrified at what he sees.

"KEEP THE WATCH!". (1981). Poem. Until we thousands return to Princeton, guard the place well.

KEITH. In ''Benediction,'' he is nineteen-year-old Lois's brother, age thirty-six and a Jesuit seminary student in Baltimore. He led a wild youth but will become a priest. The two meet at the seminary after fourteen years apart. They like each other at once. They discuss their nervous mother and, more important, Catholicism. She leaves after they attend benediction, and he prays for her for hours at a pietà. The characterization of Keith owes something to Thomas Delihant,* whom Fitzgerald met in 1912 when Delihant was a Jesuit seminary novice and whom he remembered and admired. In some editions, the name Keith is spelled ''Kieth.''

Bibliography: Allen.

KEITH, JEAN. In ''Her Last Case,'' she is Ben Dragonet's sturdy Scottish housekeeper. She urges Bette Weaver to get rid of Ben's ex-wife, whom she calls a devil and a witch.

KELLEHER. In *The Great Gatsby*, Nick Carraway lists his name on a timetable as one of Jay Gatsby's summer guests. He is from New York.

KELLERMAN, ANNETTE. In *This Side of Paradise*, she is a girl whose dive from the roof of a Westchester County summer house impresses Rosalind Connage, who does the same and dares Howard Gillespie to do it, too.

KELLEY, FLORENCE. In *The Beautiful and Damned*, she is an actress whose photographs, stamped as though autographed, are sent to fans.

KELLY. In ''Myra Meets His Family,'' he is an actor Knowleton Whitney hires to impersonate his low-voiced mother.

KELLY. In ''A Snobbish Story,'' he is the policeman who comes to Herbert T. Perry's home to tell John Boynton Bailey his wife has attempted to commit suicide and is in the hospital.

KELLY, BRIDGET. In *Safety First!*, she is a girl Ralph loved but lost when she began to smoke with Tony.

KELLY, DR. In "Three Acts of Music," he is a physician the unnamed nurse in the story saw from a distance but never met.

KELLY, NELSON. In "One Trip Abroad," he inherits $500,000, quits work in the Alaskan fur business, and is ambitious to paint. He and his wife, Nicole Kelly, take an extended trip. They go, increasingly aloof toward each other, to Algeria, Sorrento, Paris, Monte Carlo, and Paris again. He drinks too much, evidently has an affair with Madame Noel Delauney, and is cheated and robbed by Count Chiki Sarolai. He goes to Geneva to be treated for jaundice. He and Nicole are dogged everywhere by their doubles, who degenerate like themselves. At the end, Nelson is twenty-nine.

KELLY, NICOLE. In "One Trip Abroad," she is Nelson Kelly's wife. Earlier, she was often alone with her asthmatic father. Nicole, who wants to become a singer, and Nelson travel in North Africa and Europe. She plays golf with parasitic Oscar Dane in Monte Carlo, has a baby in Paris, and requires surgery in Geneva. She and Nelson are followed by a couple she defines as their double. In some ways, Nicole Kelly prefigures Nicole Diver in *Tender Is the Night*.

KELLY, SONNY. In "One Trip Abroad," he is the son of Nelson Kelly and Nicole Kelly, born in Paris.

KENDALL, GEORGE. In *The Girl from Lazy J*, he is the owner of the Texas ranch called the Diamond O. He is Jack Darcy's uncle. Tony Gonzoles tries to rob Kendall but is foiled.

KENDALL, MRS. GEORGE. In *The Girl from Lazy J*, she is Jack Darcy's aunt.

KENNEDY, BILL. In "Two for a Cent," he was a person from whom Henry W. Hemmick could not borrow a penny because Bill was driving his one-horse surrey away too fast to be hailed.

KENNEDY, CRAIG. In *The Evil Eye*, Harris mentions that he is the king.

KENNEDY, DR. JOHN. In *The Last Tycoon*, he is Monroe Stahr's oculist, to whom Stahr generously sends Pete Zavras.

KENYON, MARY. In "Fate in Her Hands," she is a friend to whose cabin Carol Kastler escapes to try to avoid tabloid notoriety.

KEOGH, NAT. In ''Crazy Sunday,'' he is one of Miles Calman's screenwriters and offers comforting advice to fellow-writer Joel Coles.

KERR, ELSIE. In ''A Snobbish Story,'' she is mentioned as attending the Lake Forest tennis tournament.

KEY, CARROL, PRIVATE. In ''May Day,'' he is a tall, degenerate soldier who associates with Private Gus Rose and is tossed out of Henry Bradin's office window to his death during a mob's attack.

KEY, FRANCIS SCOTT (1779–1843). American lawyer and writer of ''The Star-Spangled Banner.'' Fitzgerald was named after him because they were distantly related. Francis Key (1731–1770), Francis Scott Key's grandfather, and John Key (1730–1755), Fitzgerald's great-great-great-grandfather, were sons of Philip Key (1697–1764). Hence Fitzgerald and Francis Scott Key were second cousins thrice removed.

KEY, GEORGE. In ''May Day,'' he is Private Carrol Key's older brother. He is a waiter at Delmonico's and gives Carrol and Private Gus Rose some liquor.

KEYES, DR. In ''The Love Boat,'' he is one of eight physicians panicky Bill Frothington thinks he might consult.

KEYSTER, DR. In ''Lo, the Poor Peacock!,'' he is the physician who tells Jason Davis his wife Annie Lee's case is hopeless.

KILKALLOW, BOPES, MARQUIS. In ''The Hotel Child,'' he is a Britisher flitting around Europe. He is a friend of Ralph Berry and Lady Capps-Karr. When he gets fresh with Fifi Schwartz, she scratches his face.

KILLIAN, CEDRIC. In ''The Intimate Strangers,'' he is Marquise Sara de la Guillet de la Guimpé's main lover. They meet on Long Island. He is a Harvard dropout, almost plays ball for the Red Sox, strums the guitar, and spends two torrid weeks in North Carolina with Sara. Later, Dorothy Killian becomes his wife. After Dorothy's death and the death of Sara's husband, Marquis Eduard de la Guillet de la Guimpé, the two reunite in Paris, marry in Algiers, and return to the United States.

KILLIAN, DOROTHY. In ''The Intimate Strangers,'' she is the wife of Cedric Killian. Although after her death Cedric marries Marquise Sara de la Guillet de la Guimpé, he remembers Dorothy tenderly. Fitzgerald may have associated the name Dorothy Killian with that of Dorothy Kilgallen (1913–1965), the journalist who by the early 1930s was well known for her sensational news reports.

KILLIAN, SARA. In "The Intimate Strangers." *See* Guillet de la Guimpé, Marquise Sara de la.

KILRAIN. In "Family in the Wind," he is Helen Kilrain's father. He dies protecting Helen during the first tornado.

KILRAIN, HELEN. In "Family in the Wind," she is the girl, eight, Dr. Forrest Janney sees with her kitten. During the first tornado, she and her kitty survive, but her father does not. Forrest will adopt her.

KIMBALL, ED. In "The Bowl," he is a Princeton football player and once almost substituted for Dolly Harlan.

KIMBERLY, SCOTT. In "The Popular Girl," he is a rich, single New Yorker and a Yale graduate, now twenty-five. While visiting his cousin, Orrin Rogers, in a Midwestern city, he meets Yanci Bowman at a dance. They fall half in love. After her impoverished father's death, Yanci, whom Scott wants to marry, goes to New York, pretends she is rich and sought after, and keeps Scott dangling. He sees through her ruse, loves her anyway, and rescues her from financial embarrassment at her hotel. They will get married.

KINCAID, CHARLEY. In "The Dance," he is Marie Bannerman's good-looking, well-educated fiancé. The narrator is drawn to him while attending a dance in the Southern town of Davis. When Catherine Jones kills Marie out of jealousy, the narrator solves the murder and later marries Charley.

KINCAID, MRS. CHARLEY. In "The Dance," she is the initially unnamed narrator. She goes from New York in 1921 to visit her aunt, Musidora Hale, in the town of Davis. She is present at a dance there when Catherine Jones kills Marie Bannerman, at the time Charley's fiancée. The narrator solves the murder and is free to marry Charley. In 1926 they hope to see Catherine on stage in New York, since she was sentenced to serve only a five-year term in prison.

KING, CLARA. In *Assorted Spirits*, she is Josephus Hendrix's wealthy ward, seventeen, from St. Joseph, Missouri. She accompanies Hendrix to Peter Wetherby's home. She boasts to Peter's son, Richard Wetherby, that she smokes and has been thrice engaged. Peter tells Richard to propose to her if he needs money.

KING, GEORGE. In "The Long Way Out," he is a well-to-do Philadelphian. His wife is hospitalized for schizophrenia. He is about to take her out of the hospital for five days in Virginia Beach when he is killed in a car crash.

KING, GINEVRA. A beautiful woman from a wealthy, socially prominent family in Lake Forest, Illinois. She was a student at Westover, a girls' school in

Connecticut, when at sixteen she visited her roommate Marie Hersey at her home in St. Paul, Minnesota, over Christmas vacation in 1914. Fitzgerald met and dated her and fell in love. Back at Princeton in January 1915, he wrote her long letters and visited her at her school. In June she was his guest at the Princeton prom and for dinner and the theater in New York. He visited her at Lake Forest on his way to St. Paul. In October he dined with her at Waterbury, Connecticut, and thereafter continued writing to her. In January 1917 the two broke up. She was both narcissistic and eager to surround herself with well-to-do young men. Fitzgerald kept her letters, carefully bound; she destroyed his in 1917. She boasted that during World War I she was engaged to two men in case she lost one. In 1918 she married a naval officer but in 1936 divorced him. While visiting California in 1937, she got in touch with Fitzgerald, and they saw each once more, for the first time in nineteen years. At that juncture, he was involved with Sheilah Graham.* Ginevra later married a Chicago department-store heir named Pirie. A person named simply Ginevra is mentioned in ''A Letter to Helen.'' Ginevra King is the model for several selfish girls from rich families in Fitzgerald's fiction, including Isabelle Borgé in *This Side of Paradise*, Judy Jones in ''Winter Dreams,'' Daisy Fay Buchanan in *The Great Gatsby* (in which he calls Daisy ''the king's daughter''), and Josephine Perry in five stories. Fellow debutantes of Ginevra King's year included her friends Peggy Carry, Edith Cummings, and Courtney Letts, whose personalities are reflected in several of Josephine Perry's friends.

Bibliography: Finis Farr, *Chicago: A Personal History of America's Most American City* (New Rochelle, N.Y.: Arlington House, 1973).

KING, MRS. GEORGE. In ''The Long Way Out,'' she is a girlishly appealing young woman who was courted in Mexico, married, had two children, and was hospitalized at twenty-one for schizophrenia near Philadelphia. She is about to be taken by her husband for five days in Virginia Beach when he is killed in a car crash. Hospital personnel equivocate a while, and when they finally tell her the truth, she refuses to believe it. She is allowed to continue dressing neatly each day and wait for George to pick her up.

KING, W. F. In ''How to Live on Practically Nothing a Year,'' he is a British real estate agent who finds the Fitzgeralds a Riviera villa to rent.

"THE KINGDOM IN THE DARK" (1935). Short story. (Characters: Bertram de Villefranche, Brother Brian, Cadmus, Countess Griselda, Guesculin, Duke of Guyenne, Jaques, King Louis the Stammerer, Duke of Maine, Marius, Count Philippe of Villefranche, Pierre, Count of Poitiers, Rolf.) In the fall, Count Philippe of Villefranche rides with Brian and Jaques to survey the boundary of his fiefdom ten miles beyond his wooden fort. An old woman tells them that a girl recently rode up in the gray palfrey they see and is now asleep. When they wake her up, beautiful Griselda tells them she has just escaped the would-be embraces of King Louis the Stammerer, who is even now approaching on his way to Nantes. Soon after Philippe takes her to his home, King Louis and his elaborate retinue ride in. Philippe hides Griselda, kneels before Louis, disputes with his abbott, who wants Philippe's property, but impresses the Duke of Guyenne when he reports the possible approach of Northmen. Unconcerned, Louis begins to lead his group on, but when his men see Griselda's horse he asks Philippe about the girl. Philippe falsely swears he knows nothing about her. In revenge anyway, Louis later sends three arsonists back to destroy Philippe's buildings. Philippe kills the successful trio, is tempted to join the Northmen against France, but is persuaded by Griselda to rebuild and remain loyal to Louis, who dies three days later.

KINGSLEY. In "Gretchen's Forty Winks," he is the druggist from whom Roger Halsey buys the sleeping powder to give his wife, Gretchen Halsey, forty winks.

KINNEY, JOE. In "In the Holidays," calling himself McKenna, he is the front man, from Jersey City, for the murder of Griffin in a New York hospital. For an alibi, he also checks himself into the hospital. He makes the mistake of leaving his fingerprints on Miss Hunter's letter when he drops it in a mailbox for her.

KIPPERY, LADY. In "The Rubber Check," she was killed in an airplane crash. Val Schuyler pretends he was at Deauville with her and might have taken the same airplane.

KIRBY, CARTER. In *The Beautiful and Damned*, he was a former Kansas City boyfriend of Gloria Gilbert Patch's. When rebuffed, he sailed immediately for Europe.

KIRSTOFF. In *The Last Tycoon*, he is one of three people eager to discuss the Russian movie Monroe Stahr wants to make. The other two are Mrs. Cornhill and Drummon.

KITTY. in "Martin's Thoughts," she is one of Martin's girlfriends.

KITTY. In "A New Leaf," she is a friend of Phil Hoffman and Dick Ragland, who mention her having been traveling in Spain.

KITTY. In "That Kind of Party," she is a girl with whom Terrence R. Tipton will let Joe Shoonover play.

KITTY. In "Three Hours between Planes," she was Nancy Holmes Gifford's childhood friend. She took a photograph of Nancy and Donald Bowers, whom Nancy misidentifies in the picture as Donald Plant.

KLIPSPRINGER, EWING. In *The Great Gatsby*, Nick Carraway lists his name on a timetable as one of Jay Gatsby's summer guests. He is there so much he is called "the boarder." At one point Gatsby orders the reluctant, selfish sponge to play the piano. Nick hangs up on him when he appears unwilling to attend Gatsby's funeral but wants his tennis shoes sent on to him.

KNIGHTON, PAMELA ("PAM"). In "Last Kiss," she is a would-be actress, twenty, who financed her escape from England to Hollywood by selling jewelry given to her by old men. Pam is innocent, rapacious, and stupidly inflexible. She muffs her chance for stardom given to her by Jim Leonard, a producer wistfully half in love with her. She lets him kiss her because, as she says, doing so helps her sleep. Soon after being ruinously advised by Chauncey Ward, a foolish old British actor in Hollywood, to fight beastly Hollywood men, she dies of pneumonia. Her real name was Sybil Higgins. She is based partly on Fitzgerald's lover Sheilah Graham.*

KNOWLES, BILL, LIEUTENANT. In "The Last of the Belles," he is Lieutenant Andy's army friend. The two are Harvard men. Knowles loves Ailie Calhoun but is rejected.

KNOWLES, GLADYS. In "On Your Own," she is an actress mentioned by Evelyn Lovejoy as more welcome socially in Europe than in condescending parts of the United States.

KNOWLETON, DUDLEY ("DUD"). In "A Woman with a Past," he is a popular Yale student from Cincinnati, captain of the baseball team, and a member of Skull and Bones. He likes and respects Adele Craw, a student at Miss Brereton's school. The two, who grew up as friends, are partly in charge of the prom attended by Lillian Hammel and Josephine Perry. Josephine makes a play for him that fails dismally.

KNOX, DOROTHY. In *Thoughtbook*, she is a friend of Kitty Williams.

KNOX, EMIL. In *Thoughtbook*, he is a friend Fitzgerald dares to tell Kitty Williams that Emil loves her. Emil declines.

KOHL, EMILY. In "A Snobbish Story," she is Evelyn's friend and lives in Lake Forest. Evelyn asks Josephine Perry if she knows her. Josephine pleasantly replies she does not.

KOHLER, THURSTON. In ''He Thinks He's Wonderful,'' he is named by Gladys Van Schellinger as her favorite friend. She adds that he is in the East.

KOHLSATT. In ''The Love Boat,'' he is Al Fitzpatrick's mill boss. Fitzgerald might have derived the unusual name Kohlsatt from that of Herman Henry Kohlsaat (1853–1924), a Chicago entrepreneur, newspaperman in Chicago and New York, and adviser of presidents. Early in his life, Kohlsaat was a cashier for Carson, Pirie, Scott, and Company, a Chicago drygoods concern. He and his wife, the former Mabel E. Blake, had two daughters, Pauline, who married Potter Palmer, Jr., of Chicago, and Katherine, who married Roger B. Shepard of St. Paul, Minnesota. *See* King, Ginevra; Perry, Josephine; and Pirie.

KRACKLIN, THOMAS. In ''Author's House,'' he is a character in one of the author's stories. When Mrs. Kracklin Lee wrote to the character, care of the *Saturday Evening Post*, the author heartlessly replied he was her brother, was in a Baltimore prison, and if released would like to come and stay with her. *See* Lee, Mrs. Kracklin, for details in Fitzgerald's life on which this incident was based.

KRESGE, JIM. In ''Pat Hobby's College Days,'' he frequents the sport shop at the University of the Western Coast. Louie, the studio bookie, tells Pat Hobby to get Kresge to introduce Pat to Kit Doolan, the athletic superintendent.

KRETCHING, LIEUTENANT. In *The Beautiful and Damned*, he is in charge of calisthenics and drill instruction at Anthony Patch's first army base.

KRIMSLICH. In ''Winter Dreams,'' this is the maiden name of Dexter Green's mother. *See* Green, Mrs.

KROGMAN. In *This Side of Paradise*, he is a member of law firm of Barton and Krogman, handling the finances of Beatrice O'Hara Blaine.

KROLL, FRANCES (b. 1919). Fitzgerald's trustworthy, intelligent secretary in Hollywood beginning in November 1938. He affectionately called her Françoise. She aided him when Scottie (*see* Fitzgerald, Frances Scott) visited, found him an apartment, packed items for him, was discreet regarding his relationship with Sheilah Graham,* helped arrange for his funeral, and flew to New York to give the manuscript of *The Last Tycoon* to John Biggs, Jr.* Kroll is a background character in several of the Pat Hobby stories.

Bibliography: Frances Kroll Ring, *Against the Current: As I Remember F. Scott Fitzgerald* (San Francisco: Donald S. Ellis, 1985).

KRUPSTADT. In ''Dalyrimple Goes Wrong,'' he is a person whose residence Bryan Dalyrimple does not rob.

KRUTCH. In ''Basil and Cleopatra,'' he is a Yale freshman football team player, at end.

KURMAN. In ''No Flowers,'' he is the proprietor of a tailor shop, from which William Delaney Johns lacks funds to redeem his tuxedo.

KWAIN, MISS. In ''A Woman with a Past,'' she is a member of the staff at Miss Brereton's school. She puts Josephine Perry and three other girls on probation.

L

LA BORWITZ, JAQUES. In *The Last Tycoon*, he is an assistant movie producer who associates with Pat Brady and Monroe Stahr.

LACY. In *The Beautiful and Damned*, he is a New Yorker. Anthony Patch and Gloria Gilbert Patch call on Lacy and his wife after a drunken party and collapse outside their door.

LACY, EDWARD. In ''Hot and Cold Blood,'' he is a broken old man who asks James Mather, son of a deceased man he once loaned money to, for a loan of $450 to keep his life insurance policy from lapsing. Mather refuses, later repents, and agrees to provide the sum.

LACY, MISS. In ''Hot and Cold Blood,'' she is the unmarried woman who lives with her father, Edward Lacy. He needs a loan to keep his life insurance policy valid for her later benefit.

LACY, MRS. In *The Beautiful and Damned*, she is a New Yorker. When Anthony Patch and Gloria Gilbert Patch appear in a drunken stupor at her door, she and her husband offer to call them a taxi.

LADISLAU, DR. In *Tender Is the Night*, he is the dour Slavic physician in the Zurichsee clinic owned and run by Dick Diver and Dr. Franz Gregorovius.

LAFARGE, MISS. In ''Jemina,'' she was Jemina Tantrum's schoolteacher until she died from drinking too much Tantrum moonshine when Jemina was six.

LAFOUQUET. In *Shadow Laurels*, he was a fellow drinker with Jean Chandelle in Pitou's wineshop, stabbed Jean in the lung, and was killed later by François Meridien for doing so.

LAHAYE, SIDNEY. In "Flight and Pursuit," he is a lover who mistreated Caroline Martin. She then unhappily married George Corcoran. Sidney pursues her to Dayton, Ohio; Long Island; Italy; and Switzerland—always rebuffed. Only when Sidney, now a millionaire aviator, is reported missing and then is rescued, does Caroline cable her love to him and request his return to her.

LALLETTE. In "Six of One—," she is the actress whose bust Louis Ireland creates and sells in Paris.

LAMAR, BOB. In *The Beautiful and Damned*, he is, according to her 1907 diary entry, the first boy Gloria Gilbert Patch kissed.

LAMAR, DR. In "The Jelly-Bean," he is Nancy Lamar's father, who fusses but capitulates when she elopes with Ogden Merritt. The name Lamar derives from that of Lucius Quintus Cincinnatus Lamar (1825–1893), distinguished Mississippi jurist and statesman.

LAMAR, NANCY. In "The Jelly-Bean," she is the wild flirt who encourages James Powell, who has not spoken to her since school fifteen years before, by letting him clean gum from her shoe and rescue her from a potentially disastrous dice game. She rewards him with a wild kiss but then elopes with rich Ogden Merritt of Savannah, Georgia. In "The Last of the Belles," she attends a farewell party at the army base and later tells Lieutenant Andy in New York that Ailie Calhoun was engaged to a Cincinnati man, visited his family, and broke off the engagement.

LAMARQUE. In *Shadow Laurels*, he is Jean Chandelle's former friend who praises Jean to Jean's son, Jaques.

LA MARR. In "Last Kiss." *See* La Marr, Barbara.

LA MARR, BARBARA (1896–1926). (Reatha Watson) Movie actress, called "too beautiful for her own good." She was arrested at fourteen for dancing in a burlesque show. She married at sixteen. Widowed, she married a bigamist, who died. She entered Los Angeles show business in 1914. She married a vaudeville comic in 1918. By 1920 she was active in Hollywood both as a writer and as an actress. Douglas Fairbanks* cast her in movies in 1920 and 1921. She married in 1923 but without a divorce from the comic, who sued her. In 1923 she sprained her ankle while acting, was given morphine to continue working though in pain, and became addicted to drugs. She was indiscreet, suffered a nervous breakdown, returned to her parents' home in Altadena, California, and died. La Marr was the sort of ravishing beauty whose tempestuous career attracted Fitzgerald. LaMarr, in ''Last Kiss,'' is a Hollywood actress mentioned by Joe Becker as having seen Pamela Knighton at Twenty-One. Barbara LaMarr is mentioned in ''No Harm Trying'' as a deceased movie star whose signed photograph Pat Hobby regards as of little value. Her last name appears both as ''La Marr'' and as ''LaMarr.''

Bibliography: James Robert Parish, *The Hollywood Celebrity Death Book* (Las Vegas: Pioneer Books, 1993).

LAMB, MARION. In ''Too Cute for Words,'' she is a debutante, twenty, invited to the Princeton prom the evening before the Princeton-Harvard football game. Boasting of being engaged often, she tries to upstage Gwen Bowers, Dizzy Campbell, and Clara Hannaman, her younger schoolmates, until they catch her embracing Harry in a car near the gymnasium where the prom is being held. The girls blackmail the couple into helping them crash the dance.

LAMB, NANCY. In ''The Rubber Check,'' she is the New York debutante at whose dance Val Schuyler, then twenty-two, first gets snubbed.

LAMBERT. In ''He Thinks He's Wonderful,'' he is the proprietor of the drugstore where Basil Duke Lee and Joe Gorman go for a soda.

"LAMP IN A WINDOW" (1935). Poem. The poet recalls their trivial quarrels—swimming naked, space in hotel bureaus, roadmaps. Now desolate, he grieves that June has become December.

LANAHAN, FRANCES SCOTT FITZGERALD. Fitzgerald's daughter. *See* Smith, Frances Scott Fitzgerald Lanahan.

LANCLERC, COUNT HENNEN DE. In ''Discard,'' he is actress Dolly Bordon's philandering husband. He sails off with Phyllis Burns, a younger actress, and tries to lie about it.

LANCLERC, COUNTESS DE. In ''Discard.'' *See* Bordon, Dolly.

LANDIG. In *Thoughtbook*, he is a newcomer at the dance school.

LANE, DR. In ''One Interne,'' he is the hospital's brain surgeon.

LANGUEDUC, SLIM. In *This Side of Paradise*, he is discussed by Amory Blaine and his friends as an illiterate star on the Princeton football team.

LAPHAM, CHARLOTTE. In ''That Kind of Party,'' she is the sister in Lockport to whom Mrs. Tipton rushes, thinking she is ill, when she receives the forged telegram Terrence R. Tipton mistakenly sent to her.

LARDNER, ELLIS ABBOTT. She was the wife of Ring Lardner.* In ''To the Ring Lardners,'' she is humorously addressed.

LARDNER, RING (1885–1933). (Full name: Ringgold Wilmer Lardner). Journalist, fiction writer, and humorist. Lardner was born in Niles, Michigan, was taught for a while at home by his mother and a tutor, became interested in baseball, music, and theatrical events in childhood, and graduated from high school in 1901. He flunked out of Armour Institute in Chicago after one term (1902). He worked for the Niles Gas Company (1903–1905) and wrote for and performed in a Niles minstrel group, creating part of a musical comedy titled *Zanzibar* (1905). He worked as a journalist (1905–1919) as a reporter, general sports writer, baseball reporter, managing editor, feature writer, sports editor, copyreader, and variety columnist—in South Bend, Indiana; Chicago; St. Louis; Boston; and Chicago again. He married Ellis Abbott in 1911; they had four sons. Lardner coauthored a booklet on the Chicago White Sox and the New York Giants (1914), published stories in the *Saturday Evening Post* (1914–1915) and *Redbook* (1915–1916), and was a *Collier's* war correspondent in France (1917). By 1919 Lardner had published books about baseball players (*You Know Me Al*, 1916; *Treat 'Em Rough*, 1918; *The Real Dope*, 1919), ''wise boob'' travelers (*Gullible's Travels*, 1917), the war (*My Four Weeks in France*, 1918), and a detective (*Own Your Own Home*, 1919). In 1919 the Lardners moved to Greenwich, Connecticut, and later to Long Island (Great Neck, 1921; East Hampton, 1928). For the Bell Syndicate he wrote weekly columns (1919–1927) and 3,744 panels for a ''You Know Me Al'' comic strip (1922–1925). At his peak, ending about 1928, he made almost $100,000 a year, including up to $4,500 per short story. He published in many periodicals. His story collections include *The Big Town* (1921), *How to Write Short Stories* (1924), *The Love Nest and Other Stories* (1926), and *The Round Up* (1929). With George S. Kaufman he coauthored *June Moon*, a successful play. In 1926 Lardner learned he had tuberculosis. He wrote autobiographical sketches for the *Saturday Evening Post* (1931), more baseball stories (*Lose with a Smile*, 1933), and a radio column for the *New Yorker* (1932–1933) to crusade against pornography.

Fitzgerald and Zelda Sayre Fitzgerald,* who were the Lardners' neighbors in Great Neck, Long Island, drank, talked, and horsed around with them riotously from 1922 to 1924. Lardner once called Fitzgerald a novelist and Zelda a novelty. In 1923 Fitzgerald and Lardner got drunk and sought to meet Joseph Conrad* when he was a guest at publisher Frank Nelson Doubleday's home at Oyster Bay but were thrown out for trespassing. Fitzgerald persuaded Lardner to collect his short stories for book publication and recommended Lardner to the attention of Max Perkins,* who published *How to Write Short Stories*; Fitzgerald even suggested its foolish title. Scribner's remained Lardner's fortunate publisher. When Fitzgerald and Perkins urged Lardner to switch from his habitual first-person to third-person narrative point of view, the results were not usually more effective. The Lardners visited the Fitzgeralds in France in the fall of 1924. Jay Gatsby's house in *The Great Gatsby* owes something to the Lardners' Great Neck residence and those of richer neighbors. Without a doubt Fitzgerald pumped Lardner about the Black Sox scandal in connection with the 1919 World Series, reflected in the characterization of Gatsby's friend Meyer Wolfsheim. Fitzgerald dedicated *All the Sad Young Men* to Lardner and his wife. Fitzgerald was happy when in 1928 Lardner met Ernest Hemingway,* whose early work may be slightly indebted to Lardner. Hemingway turned against Lardner—as he did against Fitzgerald—and ridiculed Lardner's objections to sleaze.

In "A Short Autobiography," Fitzgerald mentions Lardner as a fellow drinker in Great Neck in 1923. When Perkins asked Fitzgerald to prepare a posthumous miscellany of Lardner's nonfiction, he declined and persuaded Perkins to ask Gilbert Seldes* to do it instead; the result was *First and Last* (1934). Fitzgerald's "Ring" is an analytic but also gentle tribute to his friend. Abe North in *Tender Is the Night* is partly based on Lardner. Lardner is now regarded as a complex author whose best satirical work, always humorous but often also savage, appeals to popular audiences and discerning critics alike. Fitzgerald addressed "To the Ring Lardners" to Lardner and his wife.

Bibliography: Douglas Robinson, *Ring Lardner and the Other* (New York: Oxford University Press, 1992); Jonathan Yardley, *Ring: A Biography of Ring Lardner* (New York: Random House, 1977).

LARKIN. In "The Ice Palace," this is the name of a family that owns a mansion next to the Happer mansion in Tarleton, Georgia.

LARNED, LETICIA. In *The Girl from Lazy J*, she is a cowgirl from the Lazy J ranch who prevents Tony Gonzoles from robbing rancher George Kendall. She will marry Jack Darcy, Kendall's nephew.

LARRABEE, CECI. In *The Beautiful and Damned*, she is the Philadelphia heiress a tabloid says Maury Noble is going to marry.

LASCALLES, EVYLYN. In "Pat Hobby's College Days," she is Pat Hobby's secretary, from Brooklyn. Pat asks her to dispose of his empty liquor bottles out of town. Instead, she takes them to him while he is at the University of the Western Coast trying to arrange for a movie about campus life. Evylyn may be based in part on Frances Kroll,* Fitzgerald's secretary in Hollywood.

"LAST KISS" (1940). Short story. (Characters: Joe Becker, Bob Bordley, Bob Griffin, Mike Harris, Pamela Knighton, LaMarr, Jim Leonard, Elsa Maxwell,

Simone, Chauncey Ward, Bernie Wise.) At a charity-ball dance, Hollywood movie producer Jim Leonard meets Pamela (''Pam'') Knighton, a would-be actress—real name, Sybil Higgins—who coolly says she financed her departure from England by being a gold digger with rich old Britishers. During an evening drive, Jim is smitten by her fragile beauty but put off by her innocence, stupidity, and predatory selfishness. They kiss tenderly; she says doing so helps her sleep. Delaying to sign her and distressed by a note full of lies from her, he loses her to rival producer Mike Harris, who, however, drops her because she cannot act. Jim signs her for a minor part, which she loses when she argues with the director. Jim goes to her rented bungalow to advise her but finds her with aged British actor Chauncey Ward, who persuades her to stand firm and not compromise with ruthless Hollywood producers. Time passes, and Jim learns that Pam has died, at twenty-one, of pneumonia. After going to her gravesite, feeling wistful, he screens a few film clips in which she appeared.

A working title for ''Last Kiss'' was ''Pink and Silver Frost,'' by which metaphor Fitzgerald images Pam early in the story. She was based on Sheilah Graham,* Fitzgerald's lover, as was Kathleen Moore of *The Last Tycoon*, whom Pam resembles in some ways. An early version of ''Last Kiss'' was published by *Collier's*, which gave Fitzgerald's estate a $1,000 bonus as the best story of its 16 April 1949 issue.

"THE LAST OF THE BELLES" (1929). Short Story. (Characters: Lieutenant Andy, Ailie Calhoun, Mrs. Calhoun, Lieutenant Horace Canby, Captain Craker, Sally Carrol Happer, Bill Knowles, Nancy Lamar, Oliver, Kitty Preston, Rich, Lieutenant Earl Schoen, Lieutenant Warren.) Andy, the narrator, twenty-three, is a lieutenant from the North in training at an army base near Tarleton, Georgia, during World War I. He is enamored of Ailie Calhoun—or perhaps only her legendary Southern charm. Ailie, nineteen, is promiscuous at country-club and camp dances. She flirts first with Lieutenant Horace Canby, a pilot who when she spurns him kills himself by crashing his airplane, and then with handsome but rustic Lieutenant Earl Schoen, whom she dislikes for his casual ways. Their unit heads north and spends a month at a Long Island camp preparatory to going to France, when the war suddenly ends. Andy returns to Tarleton in January, is delayed in being demobilized until December, and observes Ailie is waiting for Schoen. When that cocky man calls, his appearance out of uniform displeases her, and he and Andy return north. Six years later, Andy, a successful Harvard Law School graduate, hears in New York that Ailie has been disappointed in love, and he returns to Tarleton. The two attend a party and a dance, but she says he is only a Northern confidant and she is going to marry a man from Savannah. She and Andy taxi out to where his camp was, but he cannot recover remnants of his lost past.

Tarleton and its army base activities are modeled after Montgomery, Alabama, and Fitzgerald's military experience nearby. There was a 1974 ABC-TV teleplay showing the relationship between this story and Fitzgerald's personal life.

Bibliography: Heidi Kunz Bullock, ''The Southern and the Satirical in ''The Last of the Belles,' '' Bryer, *New Essays*, 130–37.

THE LAST OF THE TYCOONS. A title, in manuscript, of *The Last Tycoon*

THE LAST TYCOON. Unfinished novel (1941, 1993). (Characters: Prince Aggie, Art, Dr. Bill Baer, Bernie, George Boxley, Cecelia Brady, Eleanor Brady, Mrs. Pat Brady, Pat Brady, Joe Breen, Evelyn Brent, Brimmer, John Broaca, Burton, Claris, Claudette Colbert, Ronald Colman, Gary Cooper, Mrs. Cornhill, Cecil B. De Mille, Dick, Martha Dodd, Catherine Doolan, Drummon, Edna, Em, Esther, Douglas Fairbanks, Mort Flieshacker, Ike Franklin, John Gilbert, the Governor of California, Cary Grant, Hanson, Harley, Jean Harlow, Sidney Howard, Kapper, Katie, Dr. John Kennedy, Kirstoff, Jaques La Borwitz, Leanbaum, Lew, Carole Lombard, Malone, Marcus, Marquand, Mrs. Marquand, Maude, Rose Meloney, Glen Miller, Kathleen Moore, Morgan, O'Brien, O'Ney, Louella Oettinger Parsons, Birdy Peters, Joe Popolous, Ransome, Reina, Red Ridingwood, Joe Rienmund, Robby Robinson, Rosemary Schmiel, Mannie Schwartze, Spyros Panagiotes Skouras, Ned Sollinger, Minna Davis Stahr, Monroe Stahr, Johnny Swanson, Tim, Spencer Tracy, Rudolph Valentino, Mike Van Dyke, Wylie White, Ken Willard, Joe Wyman, Mrs. Pete Zavras, Pete Zavras.)

During a delay in Nashville, Tennessee, on a flight to California, the narrator, Cecelia Brady, who is the daughter of Hollywood producer Pat Brady and who is a junior at Bennington, is taken by Wylie White, a Hollywood writer, to Andrew Jackson's Hermitage. Mannie Schwartze, a Hollywood executive spurned by Monroe Stahr, who is ''the last tycoon'' and a passenger, also goes to the Hermitage but remains behind and commits suicide. Cecelia is hopelessly in love with Stahr.

One July night, while Cecelia is watching her shrewd father and Stahr confer, an earthquake hits. Robby Robinson, a studio technician, helps two female tourists caught in the ensuing flood. One of them reminds Stahr of his deceased wife, Minna. Next morning Pete Zavras, a camera man said to be going blind, jumps off a nearby building to commit suicide but only breaks an arm. While busy meeting people, Stahr asks Robby to find the attractive young tourist.

A hectic day follows. Stahr mollifies George Boxley, a miffed British writer, and a handsome star having trouble with his girlfriend. At noon Stahr holds a conference about a picture with which he is dissatisfied. Present are experienced director John Broaca, supervisor Joe Rienmund, writers White and Rose Meloney, and Stahr's secretary, Catherine Doolan. After saying he is going to scrap their movie, he orders specific changes instead. At the private dining room of the commissary, Stahr impresses Prince Aggie of Denmark, a happy visitor, when he convinces some financial backers, including Marcus, Leanbaum, and Joe Popolous, that he will produce a money-losing but good quality movie about South America. Stahr tells Red Ridingwood, a director, that Harley is replacing him because Red has let a bitchy, borrowed star dictate to Red. Stahr judges some rushes in the projection room—a Canadian river scene with Claudette Colbert and Ronald Colman, a fight scene with Spencer Tracy, and a boy in a tree dropping an apple core on a girl's head. Stahr wants his new film about Manon Lescaut to remain tragic, discusses an earthquake benefit, and persuades Marquand and his wife to continue writing. When the tourist is found and telephones him, he persuades her to meet him. He worries about his big movie about Russia. Zavras is grateful Stahr had his oculist examine him. After dinner, he drives his little-used roadster, picks up Edna, the tourist who looks nothing like Minna, and takes her to her friend Kathleen Moore's home. Kathleen, who is Irish, has lived in London, and is single, looks much like Minna, and Stahr falls in love with her.

A week later Cecelia gets White, who likes her, to drive her to Stahr's office. She kisses him but is told he is too old for her. That night the screenwriters host a ball at the Ambassador Hotel in Los Angeles. Stahr finds Kathleen there. They dance, and she agrees to meet him the next day, which is Sunday. That afternoon they drive out past Malibu, where his new house is under construction. While they are looking through it, an agent named Lew telephones Stahr to report he has a talking orangutan for a movie. Stahr declines. When he drives Kathleen home, she will not let him come in; when they kiss, however, they decide to drive some more. They go back to his unfinished house, make love, speak tenderly and mysteriously, and watch the grunion wash onto the beach. While Stahr is driving Kathleen home, she looks for but cannot find an envelope. When he gets to his Bel-Air place, he finds the envelope, which contains a letter to him telling him she is to be married.

Wanting to learn Kathleen's identity, Cecelia takes Martha Dodd, a down-and-out actress who was with Kathleen at the dance, to her father's offices to ask him to give Martha a job. In return, Martha will aid Cecelia. Barging into the inner office alone, she finds her father sweaty and his secretary, Birdy, naked in a stuffy closet. Cecelia and Martha, who do not know about Birdy, proceed to Kathleen's house; she is gone. Stahr is examined in his office by Dr. Bill Baer, who senses his patient is aware he is dying. Kathleen phones, and the two take a limousine drive. She explains she was a king's mistress and was rescued by an American now coming to California to marry her. Stahr is tempted to propose marriage himself but instead suggests they go into the mountains for the weekend. She seems to want him to propose. The following day she wires him to tell him she got married that noon.

A week later, in mid-August, Stahr asks Cecelia to introduce him to a Communist party member. She finds Brimmer for him, and they meet at her glum father's home. Stahr, Brimmer, and Cecelia dine at the Trocadero. The two men amiably argue about screenwriters' rights, but back at the Brady home Stahr, miserable and drunk, lurches at Brimmer, who knocks him out and leaves. Stahr invites Cecelia to Doug Fairbanks's ranch. Soon a columnist reports the pair are married.

The titling of this novel has been troublesome. Edmund Wilson,* who edited it for its first publication, in 1941, called it *The Last Tycoon: An Unfinished Novel*. Fitzgerald called it *The Last of the Tycoons, The Love of the Last Tycoon: A Western*, and *Stahr: A Romance*. Wilson put its separate episodes into chapters unlike what Fitzgerald would have done. Matthew J. Bruccoli's 1993 edition rightly emphasizes its unfinished state by leaving it as chapters and episodes, and correcting only unfunctional errors and misspellings. Fitzgerald would have improved the point of view, which is partly that of Cecelia Brady, often not privy to the action. Fitzgerald also had trouble with the time line. He wanted the action to occur in 1935. However, a real California earthquake occurred in March 1933; moreover, new songs mentioned place the action between 1933 and 1938. The novel has several characters based partly on Hollywood personalities. Stahr combines aspects of Irving Thalberg* and Fitzgerald. Kathleen Moore resembles Sheilah Graham.* Wylie White, whose alcoholism echoes Fitzgerald's, owes something to screenwriters Maurice Rapf and Budd Schulberg.* Cecelia Brady resembles Scottie* to a degree. Pat Brady is based on Louis B. Mayer, Thalberg's MGM rival. For his ending, Fitzgerald considered having Brady hire a gunman to kill Stahr so as to take over the movie company, having Stahr think of hiring someone to kill Brady but change his mind during a flight east, and having Stahr die in a plane crash.

Bibliography: Matthew J. Bruccoli, ed., F. Scott Fitzgerald, *The Love of the Last Tycoon: A Western* (New York: Simon and Schuster, 1993).

LAURA. In *Tender Is the Night*, she is the sister, married to a Frenchman, of Maria Wallis, who shoots a man to death in a Paris railroad station.

LAURIE. In *Thoughtbook*, she is a member of a children's club competing with one of Fitzgerald's clubs.

LAURIER, ANTON. In "Head and Shoulders," he is Horace Tarbox's revered philosopher. When Horace's pretty wife, Marcia Tarbox, becomes a famous writer, Laurier wants to meet her, not Horace.

LAWRENCE, MISS. In "One of My Oldest Friends," she is the girl Michael learns Charley Hart is to marry. Evidently he never does so.

LAWRENCE, MRS. In *This Side of Paradise*, she is Monsignor Thayer Darcy's Catholic-convert friend. She has lived in Italy and Spain, graciously welcomes Amory Blaine to her New York home, and attends Darcy's funeral. Mrs. Lawrence is based on Margaret Terry Chanler (1862–1952), who was born in Rome, was popular novelist Francis Marion Crawford's half sister, married diplomat Winthrop Chanler in 1886, and traveled extensively with him. She wrote two books of reminiscence: *Roman Spring: Memoirs* (1934) and *Autumn* *in the Valley* (1936); in the latter she discusses her friendship with Cyril Sigourney Webster Fay,* the model for Monsignor Thayer Darcy.

LAWSON. In " 'Send Me In, Coach,' " he is a college athlete whose fringe benefits Rickey envies.

LEAM, MAX. In " 'Boil Some Water—Lots of It,' " he is a movie producer who offers Pat Hobby writing assignments but does not want to have lunch with him.

LEAMING, ELWOOD ("EL"). In "The Scandal Detectives," he is a boy Riply Buckner, Jr., and Basil Duke Lee record in their scandal book as having been to three or four burlesque shows. In "A Night at the Fair," he is fifteen and dominates Basil and Riply when the three pick up two girls at the fair the first night. He tricks Basil into dating an ugly girl the second night. Elwood is said to smoke too much. In "He Thinks He's Wonderful," someone says Elwood is home. In "Forging Ahead," he is the friend Basil, when unhappy, thinks of drinking with.

LEANBAUM. In *The Last Tycoon*, he is one of Monroe Stahr's financial backers. He bought stock in the movie company at an advantageous time.

LEBAUME, BEAU. In "Six of One—," he is the handsome friend of Schofield's sons and their other friends. He is expelled from Yale when he is involved in the accident during which Wister Schofield was driving Howard Kavenaugh's car and which resulted in Irene Daley's disfigurement. He becomes an alcoholic and is disinherited by his wealthy family.

LEE. In "A Night at the Fair," he is Basil Duke Lee's father, mentioned as deceased.

LEE, ALICE RILEY (REILLY). In "A Night at the Fair," she is Basil Duke Lee's mother. He pressures her into letting him buy long pants to wear to the state fair. Basil is identified there by Mrs. Van Schellinger as Alice Riley's son. In "The Freshest Boy," she invites Basil to quit St. Regis and accompany her and her father to Europe. He declines. In "He Thinks He's Wonderful," she lets him drive his grandfather's car. In "The Captured Shadow," she is overly protective. When he declines to tell her he let Ham Beebe get the mumps, she feels shut out from his emotional life. In "Forging Ahead," she tells him that the Lee family fortune is too depleted for him to go to Yale. The family later recoups by selling some property. (Her maiden name Riley is Reilly in this story.)

LEE, BASIL DUKE ("BOSSY," "LEE-Y"). In "The Scandal Detectives," he is, at fourteen, an instigator with Riply Buckner, Jr., of the scandal book. Both still wear short pants. Smitten with Imogene Bissel, Basil retrieves his class ring from Margaret Torrence and gives it to Imogene, only to have her prefer Hubert Blair. Basil and Rip plan an attack on Hubert, but it fails. In "A Night at the Fair," though fifteen, Basil is still in short pants. He is embarrassed at the fair the first night when Rip chides him for wearing short pants and again when he is ignored by two girls. He persuades his mother to get him long pants, goes to the fair, is humiliated when the blind date provided for him by Elwood Leaming is ugly, kisses her courteously anyway, sits with Gladys Van Schellinger for the fireworks display, but is deflated again when she asks him to bring Hubert along to visit her next day. In "The Freshest Boy," Basil, fifteen, becomes a student at St. Regis. He makes himself unpopular by boasting and being critical. His hated nickname is "Bossy." When his chums Bugs Brown, William Gaspar, and Treadway refuse to go to a New York matinee with him, he is escorted there by Rooney, the history teacher and football coach. When he overhears Jerry, an actress, break off her love affair with Yale football hero Ted Fay because she has promised to marry her casting director, Basil gains a sense of responsibility. He could quit school and go to Europe with his mother, who has just invited him to do so. But he returns to school and in time is accepted there. In "He Thinks He's Wonderful," he returns home in June, flatters then ignores Margaret, visits Imogene, stays overnight with Joe Gorman but offends him, and attends Connie Davies's dance party only to offend Imogene and her date Rip. While a guest at his friend William S. Kampf's parents' home near Bear Lake, he meets Bill's cousin, Erminie ("Minnie") Gilberte LaBouisse Bibble, and falls in love with her. But he so annoys Minnie's father by his boasting that he is not invited to accompany the Bibble family to Glacier National Park. Back home, saddened and only a little wiser, he drives Imogene in his grandfather's electric car downtown for a lemonade. In "The Captured Shadow," he is the author, fifteen, of the play *The Captured Shadow*. He selects the cast and gets Evelyn Beebe to take the female lead by persuading Hubert to play opposite. Hubert argues with Basil, calls him by his school nickname "Bossy," and backs out. Basil avoids telling Evelyn's brother Ham that Teddy Barnfield has the mumps; thus, when Ham plays with Teddy and contracts the disease, Evelyn's family cannot go on vacation and Evelyn remains in the cast. She and Basil kiss and will remain friends, but Basil is ashamed of being responsible for Ham's becoming ill. In "The Perfect Life," Basil, sixteen, plays quarterback well on the St. Regis team against victorious Exeter. He is invited by George Dorsey home to Manhattan for the Thanksgiving vacation. Persuaded by Princetonian John Granby to lead and exemplify "the perfect life," Basil makes a prig of himself at dances and elsewhere with George's attractive sister, Jobena Dorsey, but then gets her temporary fiancé, Yale dropout Leonard Edward Davies De Vinci, so drunk he forgets to elope with Jobena—to her relief. Basil and Jobena kiss. In "Forging Ahead," Basil learns the Lee family has lost so much money he cannot go to Yale in the fall. After working briefly for the railroad company, he gets a better job through Benjamin Reilly, his great-uncle, but only on condition that he escort Reilly's stepdaughter, Rhoda Sinclair, to dances. He attends Reilly's dinner party and takes Rhoda to dances until enchanting Minnie shows up on another visit to the Kampfs. He tentatively registers at the state university. He bribes Eddie Parmelee to be Rhoda's substitute escort so he can be with Minnie. He learns the Lees have recouped their financial losses by selling some property. In "Basil and Cleopatra," he plays football on the Yale freshman team. He falls temporarily for flirtatious but shallow Minnie, argues briefly with Littleboy Le Moyne about her, and is sensibly advised by Jobena.

The name Basil Duke Lee derives from that of Basil W. Duke, a Confederate cavalry general and the first cousin of Musidora Morgan, Zelda Sayre Fitzgerald's* grandmother. St. Regis School is based on the Newman School in Hackensack, New Jersey, which Fitzgerald attended from 1911 to 1913.

LEE, BIFFY. In "The Ants at Princeton," he is a former Princeton football player of legendary fame.

LEE, FITZHUGH, GENERAL. In "A Patriotic Short," he is the fictitious character in *True to Two Flags*, a movie short, the script of which Jack Berners orders Pat Hobby to work on for a week. This Lee is the nephew of Robert E. Lee.*

LEE, MARGERY. In "The Ice Palace," she is the Southern girl at whose grave Sally Carrol Happer communes tenderly.

LEE, MRS. KRACKLIN. In "Author's House," she is a person in Michigan who wrote to the author's character, Thomas Kracklin, care of the *Saturday Evening Post*, to ask whether they were siblings. The author got hold of the letter and heartlessly wrote that they were. Fitzgerald used the name Lee here because, in real life, a woman wrote to Fitzgerald's character Basil Lee asking whether Lee was her half brother, and Fitzgerald led her on for a time.

LEE, ROBERT E(DWARD) (1807–1870). Confederate officer. Lee was born in Stratford, Virginia, graduated from West Point (1829), declined President Abraham Lincoln's invitation to command Union troops, advised Confederate president Jefferson Davis (1861), and soon was in charge of the Confederate Army (1862). Lee was victorious at the Second Battle of Bull Run, lost at Antietam, won at Chancellorsville (1862), lost at Gettysburg (1863), and surrendered to General Ulysses S. Grant* at Appomattox (1865). In "A Debt of Honor," Lieutenant General Robert E. Lee orders the execution of John Sanderson, for sleeping while on sentry duty, but later reprimands him and spares his life. In "The True Story of Appomattox," Grant offered to surrender to General Lee until Grant broke his pencil and Lee offered his sword to sharpen it.

LEECH. In *The Great Gatsby*, Nick Carraway lists his name on a timetable as one of Jay Gatsby's summer guests. He is from East Egg.

"THE LEES OF HAPPINESS" (1920). Short story. (Characters: George Cromwell, Harry Cromwell, Kitty Carr Cromwell, Jeffrey Curtain, Roxanne Milbank Curtain, Horton, Dr. Jewett.) Jeffrey Curtain, a fiction writer until about 1908, marries pretty Roxanne Milbank. They buy a house near Marlowe, half an hour outside Chicago. Jeff's best friend, Harry Cromwell, is married to Kitty. Harry visits the Curtains while his wife, having given birth six months earlier to a son named George, is recuperating in New York with her mother. Harry compares Roxanne and Kitty Cromwell to the latter's disadvantage. Jeff collapses with a brain clot, and Roxanne cares for him tenderly for the next six months. Once, when she takes time to visit Kitty, now back in Chicago, she is aghast: Kitty, in a dirty pink kimono, is pretty but shallow and egocentric, indifferent to little George's soiled rompers, and proud of her closet of expensive lingerie. Harry calls on Jeff and is telling Roxanne that Kitty has decamped with George for New York and mamma when a specialist arrives. The nurse informs Harry that Jeff will live on as a blind, dumb, unconscious paralytic. Roxanne is lauded as his loving nurse, until after eleven years he dies one May night. Roxanne, thirty-six, is strong and free but has little money. Harry, divorced eight years, saw her often until he was transferred to the East soon after Jeff's funeral. He comes out to have dinner with her one beautiful evening that fall. She says she is planning to convert her place into a boardinghouse. The two, who have known mainly pity and pain, reminisce and look kindly into one another's eyes.

LEGENDRE, MRS. In "The Rich Boy," she is Paula Legendre's mother. The family is from California. She is suspicious of Anson Hunter and tries to warn her daughter about his drinking, but he is overpowering.

LEGENDRE, PAULA. In "The Rich Boy." *See* Hagerty, Paula Legendre Thayer.

LEGOUPY. In "Salesmanship in the Champs-Elysées," he is a car salesman next door to the indifferent car salesman. Legoupy also declines to sell a car to the author.

LEGROS. In *The Great Gatsby*, Nick Carraway lists his name on a timetable as one of Jay Gatsby's summer guests. He came to gamble.

LEIGH, BARTON. In ''A Night at the Fair,'' he is the owner of the store where Basil Duke Lee buys his first suits with long pants.

LEMMON, MRS. In ''A Change of Class,'' Violet Johnson drops this name to impress Philip Jadwin. She says her friend Mrs. Lemmon knows Philip's sister.

LE MOYNE, LITTLEBOY. In ''Basil and Cleopatra,'' he is Basil Duke Lee's rival for the attentions of flirtatious Erminie Gilberte Labouisse Bibble and evidently became intimate with her on the train from Mobile to New England. He plays on the Princeton freshman football team against Basil. The two lads, both unsuccessful with Erminie, become friends.

LEONARD, JIM. In ''Last Kiss,'' he is a successful, respected Hollywood movie producer, always cool and tactful. Thirty-five and single, he is smitten by beautiful Pamela Knighton, would-be actress from England, but is put off by her egocentric inflexibility. He tries to bring her to stardom, fails, and is saddened by her premature death.

LE POIRE. In ''In the Darkest Hour,'' he is the uncooperative head man, forty, of the Loire Valley community into which Count Philippe of Villefranche gallops to rid it of the Viking invaders. In ''Gods of Darkness,'' he is mentioned as the deceased father of Becquette Le Poire.

LE POIRE, BECQUETTE. In ''Gods of Darkness,'' she is a pagan witch who wants to kill Count Philippe of Villefranche for allegedly killing her father, until Jacques tells her Northmen did the deed.

LESLIE, SHANE (1885–1971). (Full name: Sir Shane Leslie.) Anglo-Irish writer. He was born John Randolph Leslie at Leslie Castle, County Monaghan, Ireland. His mother was American. He was Sir Winston Churchill's first cousin. Educated at Eton and King's College, Cambridge, Leslie graduated in 1907. A man of wealth, dash, and influence, he visited Russia in 1907, met Leo Tolstoy, and regarded him as the greatest influence on his life. He converted to Catholicism in 1908, took the name Shane, an Irish version of John, grew interested in the Irish revival movement, espoused Irish nationalism and Home Rule, and in 1911 toured the United States seeking pro-nationalist funds. In 1912 he married Marjorie Ide of Vermont; her father was U.S. ambassador to Spain. The couple had three children. Leslie edited the *Dublin Review*, beginning in 1916. He served in the American Ambulance Corps in France during World War I. He became an associate member of the Irish Academy of Letters in 1933. Pope

Pius XI made him a Privy Chamberlain. In 1944 he succeeded his father as third baronet. In 1944 he gave the University of Notre Dame, where he had been a bibliographer, a ninth-century manuscript of the calendar of Aengus the Culdee, which had long been a Leslie family treasure. From 1908 to 1966 he wrote and published more than forty books of poetry, novels, short stories, a play, and nonfiction. His *Oppidan* (1922) is a novel based on his schooling at Eton. *Doomsland* (1923) is an autobiographical *Bildungsroman*. His cousin Clare Sheridan unfairly depicted him as a religious fanatic in her novel *Make Believe* (1926). Leslie withdrew his novel *Cantab* (1926) when it proved offensive to a Catholic bishop. His autobiographies are *The End of a Chapter* (1917), *The Passing Chapter* (1934), *The Film of Memory* (1938), and *Long Shadows* (1966). He died at Hove, Sussex.

Fitzgerald met Leslie through Cyril Sigourney Webster Fay* in Washington, D.C., in 1912. In a 1917 review, ''Homage to the Victorians,'' Fitzgerald says Leslie in *The Celt and the World* traces the history of Celts, stresses their mysticism, and contrasts them favorably to Teutons. He says the book makes one desire to see Ireland free and notes Leslie predicts a war between the United States and Japan. In a second 1917 review, that of Leslie's *Verses in Peace and War*, Fitzgerald notes his combination of light touch and ''rare and haunting depth'' and quotes tellingly. In an aside Fitzgerald glibly judges Edgar Lee Master's poems to be idiotic. In 1918 Leslie, by then a Scribner's author, recommended to Max Perkins* what became *This Side of Paradise* and made suggestions for improving it. He later exaggerated the importance of his help. In 1919 Leslie attended Monsignor Fay's funeral and wrote to Fitzgerald about it. In 1921 Fitzgerald and Zelda Sayre Fitzgerald* met Leslie in England, and he showed them around the docks of London, near Wapping, where he had done social work. In 1922 Fitzgerald dedicated *The Beautiful and Damned* to Leslie (and to George Jean Nathan* and Perkins as well). Also in 1922 he reviewed Leslie's *Oppidan*, lauding it for accurately depicting Victorian-age manners through the eyes of an ''oppidan,'' or a person connected with Eton; he calls Leslie the most romantic figure he has ever known. On 31 October and 21 November 1958 the (London) *Times Literary Supplement* published Leslie's ''Some Memories of Scott Fitzgerald''; in these pieces and later in *Long Shadows*, Leslie writes disparagingly about both Fitzgerald and Zelda.

"LEST WE FORGET (FRANCE BY BIG SHOTS)" (1981). Poem. To help Sheilah Graham* learn about France, Fitzgerald composed this rollicking poem, which he divided into seven historical periods from Gallo-Roman times to the nineteenth century. He ridicules most historical figures; Saint Louis, for example, is labeled ''a pious blade.'' Deliberately gauche rhymes abound, among them '' 'Merde!' on/Verdun,'' ''ass/mass,'' and ''Fat Cats hate/Forty-eight.''

LETGARDE. In ''The Count of Darkness,'' she is a girl, about seventeen, from Aquitaine, in civilized Roman Gaul. Count Philippe of Villefranche finds her, desires her, gallops roughly with her to a hill, and orders her to stand guard there. She deserts him for a wandering singer and drowns while trying to cross a dangerous part of the Loire River. Philippe is sorry for his conduct toward her.

"A LETTER TO HELEN" (1981). Poem. (Characters: Elkins, Froilich, Helen, Ginevra King, Stuart, Ruth Sturtevant.) Fitzgerald apologizes to Helen for saying something rude, comments on her intriguing eyes, and says he can be trusted. Who Helen was is unknown.

LE VIGNE, CARL. In "No Harm Trying," he is a movie executive who provides money for Pat Hobby's hospitalized ex-wife, sees through Pat's plan to capitalize on script boy Eric's fine movie idea, praises Eric, and will tolerate Pat only if he tells the truth for a change.

LEW. In *The Last Tycoon*, he is an agent who telephones Monroe Stahr at his unfinished house to report he has a talking orangutan.

LIBBY, MALCOLM. In "A Nice Quiet Place," he is the husband-to-be of Constance Perry, Josephine Perry's sister. Josephine almost wrecks the marriage ceremony by luring Malcolm into an embrace in a garden.

"LIFE'S TOO SHORT TO" (1981). Poem. The persona says life is too short for her either to wait for him to come to a decision or to fool around with anyone else but him.

LIGHTFOOT, CLAUDE. In "The High Cost of Macaroni," this is the made-up name the narrator once calls himself.

LILLY, ERNEST. In *The Great Gatsby*, Nick Carraway lists his name on a timetable as one of Jay Gatsby's summer guests. He came to gamble.

LILYMARY. In "Dearly Beloved," she is Beauty Boy's wife, has his baby, dies later, and goes to heaven with him.

LINCOLN, SOL. In "Two Wrongs," he is William McChesney's New York business associate. When Lincoln cannot have lunch with him, McChesney takes Emmy Pinkard to lunch.

LINDSAY. In "Forging Ahead," this is the name of Basil Duke Lee's neighbors.

"LINES ON READING THROUGH AN AUTOGRAPH ALBUM" (1951). Poem. (Characters: Carmel Myers Blum, Ralph Blum.) Fitzgerald says most of the people who wrote flattering statements in the hospitable Blums' album were probably drunk or hypocritical. He professes his sincerity and asks for another drink.

LINQUIST. In ''The Adolescent Marriage,'' he is or was architect Chauncey Garnett's partner.

"LISTEN TO THE HOOP LA" (1981). Poem. The cheering is for Betty Boop.

"LITTLE BY LITTLE" (1981). Poem. One can whittle one's troubles away by doing things a little at a time.

LIVINGSTONE, PETE. In *Tender Is the Night*, he was a Yale student whose hiding on Tap Day enabled Dick Diver to be tapped.

LIVINGSTONE, WARREN. In ''I Got Shoes,'' he is the well-to-do, high-society explorer who repeatedly proposed marriage to actress Nell Margery. She finally accepts him.

LLEWELLEN, FRANK. In ''Two Wrongs,'' he is the handsome actor who plays opposite Irene Rikker in William McChesney's production. Because McChesney is jealous of Llewellen's attentions to Irene, the two men argue in Atlantic City and Llewellen knocks McChesney down.

LOCKHEART, ANDY. In ''The Captured Shadow,'' he is a Yale man, eighteen, who visits Evelyn Beebe. In ''Forging Ahead,'' he is mentioned as having brought a popular dance step from Yale to St. Paul.

LOEY. In ''Martin's Thoughts,'' she is one of Martin's girlfriends.

LOGAN, JOSH. In ''The Bowl,'' he is a Yale football quarterback.

LOIS. In ''Benediction,'' she is the sister, nineteen, of Keith, whom she visits at the Baltimore seminary, where he, thirty-six, is studying for the priesthood. They have not seen each other for fourteen years, since she has been in Europe with her nervous mother and in Catholic convent schools. They like each other at once, discuss their mother, now worse, and Catholicism. They attend benediction together, where she feels spiritually bared and faints. She returns to the Baltimore railroad station and prepares to go to Wilmington to meet Howard, her lover.

LOIS. In ''Crazy Sunday,'' she is Stella Walker Calman's friend. Joel Coles offers to ask Lois to comfort Stella after her husband's death. In naming Lois, Fitzgerald probably had in mind the actress Lois Moran,* whom he met in Hollywood in 1927 and on whom he also modeled Rosemary Hoyt in *Tender Is the Night.*

LOMBARD, CAROLE (1908–1942). A movie actress. In *The Last Tycoon*, Cecelia Brady, Brimmer, and Monroe Stahr see her when they dine at the Trocadero.

LONG, JIMMY. In ''The Popular Girl,'' he is a young man Yanci Bowman knew when they were children. He is now working in New York. She phones him to set up a date and thus make Scott Kimberly think she is more popular than she really is.

LONGSTREET. In *Tender Is the Night*, he is a patient at the clinic run by Dick Diver and Dr. Franz Gregorovius. He provides music for fellow patients.

"THE LONG WAY OUT" (1937). Short story. (Characters: George King, Mrs. George King, Dr. Pirie.) A group touring France and discussing tortures in the time of Louis XVI thinks it will be a relief for a doctor in the group to tell a story. It seems that Mrs. King, twenty-one and girlishly appealing, developed schizophrenia after the birth of her second child and was hospitalized. When she was better, she dressed meticulously in anticipation of being picked up by her husband for an outing at Virginia Beach. He was in a car crash, however, and her attendants, reluctant to tell her he was hanging between life and death, told her she had to wait a day. When he died, they continued to equivocate but finally told her the truth. She refused to believe them and to this day dresses daily to meet her husband. The tourists in France are happy to return to the subject of oubliettes. The story gains both distance and focus by Fitzgerald's having a narrative within a narrative. Much might be made of Fitzgerald's naming the beautiful but mentally disturbed heroine of this 1937 story King and her doctor Pirie. Fitzgerald's early love, Ginevra King,* married a man named Pirie in 1937.

LOOS, ANITA (1893–1981). Novelist and screenwriter. Born in Sissons (now Mount Shasta), California, she began her theatrical career as a child actress in San Francisco, Los Angeles, and San Diego and also appeared in silent films. Her scenario, *The New York Hat*, was produced in 1912 by D. W. Griffith and starred Lionel Barrymore, Dorothy Gish, Lillian Gish, and Mary Pickford. Loos was a success as a screenwriter by twenty, scripted popular silents in the early 1920s, including movies with Douglas Fairbanks* and Constance Talmadge,* and ultimately wrote or coauthored more than sixty silents. She also wrote title cards for Griffith's *Intolerance* (1916). Fame came with her novel *''Gentlemen Prefer Blondes'': The Illuminating Diary of a Professional Lady* (1925), inspired by the alleged delight of her friend H. L. Mencken* in ''dumb blondes.'' Loos's main character is Lorelei Lee, sex siren and jazz-age flapper who cultivates rich men for the diamonds they scatter around. Loos's *''But Gentlemen Marry Brunettes''* (1928) was an anticlimactic sequel. *''Gentlemen Prefer Blondes''* was converted into a play, two musical comedies, and two movies, and by 1980 had been translated into fourteen languages and had enjoyed more than eighty editions. Loos wrote successfully for talking movies produced by Irving Thalberg,* beginning in 1931. He paid her $3,500 a week. Her most notable screen credits in the 1930s were *San Francisco* (1936), Thalberg's most profitable film, and *The Women* (1939), starring Thalberg's wife Norma Shearer* and Joan Crawford. Loos was married twice, first to Frank Palma, Jr., in 1915; but she deserted after one night to return to work, and the marriage was annulled. In 1919 she married John Emerson, an actor turned director, twenty years her senior, with whom she coauthored *How to Write Photoplays* in 1920. Emerson became unstable and unfaithful and also betrayed her professionally and financially. She supported him even after he became psychotic and was institutionalized. In later life, Loos wrote much more, including successful plays, novels, and memoirs of her colorful life. Fitzgerald was one of her many friends, who also included Sherwood Anderson,* Aldous Huxley,* Leopold Stokowski, and Wilson Mizner, the Barbary Coast rogue. In ''This book tells that Anita Loos,'' she is the owner of the guestbook in which Fitzgerald wrote the poem.

Bibliography: Anita Loos, *A Girl Like I* (New York: Viking, 1966); *Kiss Hollywood Good-By* (New York: Viking, 1974); *Cast of Thousands* (New York: Grosset and Dunlap, 1977); and *The Talmadge Girls: A Memoir* (New York: Viking, 1978).

LORENZO. In ''Jacob's Ladder,'' he is a New York waiter. Jacob C. K. Booth asks him to treat Jenny Prince with great respect always.

LORRAINE, LILLIAN. In ''The Bowl,'' she is an entertainer at the Midnight Frolic in New York.

LORRY. In ''At Your Age,'' he is Annie Lorry's indifferent father.

LORRY, ANNIE. In ''At Your Age,'' she is the beautiful, passionate, fickle girl who falls in and out of love with Tom Squires and finally prefers Randy Cambell.

LORRY, MABEL TOLLMAN. In ''At Your Age,'' she is Annie Lorry's mother, who disapproves of Tom Squires, agrees to their marrying, and bides her time until Annie drops him.

"THE LOST DECADE" (1939). Short story. (Characters: Orrison Brown, Louis Trimble.) Orrison Brown is a recent Dartmouth graduate who is now working as a subeditor for a New York news weekly. His boss tells him to take Louis Trimble, a handsome visitor to the office, to lunch. As the two walk up Fifth Avenue, Trimble responds with quiet delight to everything about him, says he was once a distinguished architect, and confesses to be recovering from a decade-long bout with alcoholism beginning in 1928. This story is partly autobiographical. Fitzgerald wasted much of his talent by excessive drinking in the 1930s. Brown is partly patterned on Budd Schulberg,* a Dartmouth graduate who, when he learned that he was to work with Fitzgerald in 1938 on a movie, said he thought Fitzgerald was dead.

Bibliography: Alice Hall Petry, ''Recovering 'The Lost Decade,' '' Bryer, *New Essays*, 253–262.

"LO, THE POOR PEACOCK!" (1971). Short story. (Characters: Cale, Miss Carson, Annie Lee Davis, Jason Davis, Josephine Davis, Mrs. Deshhacker, Gehrbohm, Halklite, Aunt Jinnie, Dr. Keyster, Miss McCrary, McCutcheon, Aunt Rose, Young Seneca.) Times are bad in Maryland for Jason Davis, thirty-eight. Commissions are down on textile accounts he sells. His wife, Annie Lee Davis, has been hospitalized for two years and seems incurable. He must release his secretary, Miss McCrary, and withdraw his daughter, Josephine (''Jo''), from private school. Times were not always bad. The Davises lived well in Paris for ten years. Annie Lee inherited a farm now reduced to sausage production. Davis and Jo visit the place and learn customers are complaining that the quality of their sausage has slipped, as have sales. At home, bills pile up to such an extent Davis thinks of killing himself with his service revolver. But Jo needs him, as is evident when she is expelled from public school. Declining to inquire into charges, he tutors her at home. Times suddenly improve. Annie Lee explains tenderloin and hickory ash are essential ingredients in their sausages. Jo's principal reinstates the girl, now deemed innocent of invading the boys' locker room. Halklite, a rich client, comes to visit Davis, who, however, exhausted from overwork, has fainted and is resting upstairs. Jo handles Halklite with such charm, even popping a little French into her talk, that he tells her to inform her father the account is his. When Davis takes Jo to the zoo and they see peacocks, she says they should be like peacocks, which though sometimes sad don't worry. Fitzgerald wrote this story in 1935, when Zelda Sayre Fitzgerald* was in a hospital outside Baltimore, and his finances were so low he pawned some family silver. Rejected by the *Saturday Evening Post* and *Ladies' Home Journal*, ''Lo, the Poor Peacock!'' appeared posthumously in *Esquire*.

LOUIE. In ''The Cruise of the Rolling Junk,'' he is the bartender at the Nassau Inn in Princeton.

LOUIE (ALSO LOU). In ''A Man in the Way,'' he is Pat Hobby's Hollywood studio bookie, who places bets at the Santa Anita racetrack. In ''Pat Hobby and Orson Welles,'' he is the bookie with whom Pat Hobby discusses Orson Welles's undeserved fame and pay. In ''Pat Hobby's Secret,'' he listens while Banizon tells Pat Hobby he cannot recall the surprise ending of R. Parke Woll's movie script. In "Pat Hobby Does His Bit," his name crosses Pat's mind when Pat is seeking a loan to make a car payment. In "Pat Hobby's Preview," Pat thinks of having a drink with Louie. In "No Harm Trying," Pat chats with Louie at one point. In "On the Trail of Pat Hobby," Pat visits Louie. In "Fun in an Artist's Studio," Louie is the bookie to whom Pat chronically owes money. In "Pat Hobby's College Days," Louie tells Pat producer Jack Berners wants a movie about campus life and advises Pat to get Jim Kresge, often on campus, to take him to Kit Doolan, the athletic superintendent, for ideas. Louie adds that Doolan owes him $3,000.

LOUIS THE STAMMERER, KING (846–879). King of France (877–879). In "The Kingdom in the Dark," he is the ineffectual king who wants countess Griselda for his "harem." She escapes and is befriended by Count Philippe of Villefranche. In annoyance, Louis orders Philippe's wooden fort and houses burned. Louis dies three days later.

LOUISE. In "Rags Martin-Jones and the Pr-nce of W-les," she is one of the three maids working for Rags Martin-Jones. The other two are Dominique and Germaine.

LOUISE. In "The Swimmers," she is Choupette Marston's maid in Paris. With Choupette's family thirty years, Louise is aghast when Choupette's husband, Henry Clay Marston, comes home early, because Choupette is entertaining a male visitor.

"THE LOVE BOAT" (1927). Short story. (Characters: Hamilton Abbot, Ellsworth Ames, Mrs. Ellsworth Ames, Bob, Bradlee, Cecil, Dr. de Martel, Al Fitzpatrick, Mae Purley Fitzpatrick, Dr. Flynn, Frothington, Frothington, Bill Frothington, George Frothington, Mrs. Frothington, Stella Frothington, Gardner, Dr. Given, Dr. Gross, Ad Haughton, Hopp, Dr. Keyes, Kohlsatt, McVitty, Mahan, Dr. Ogden, Purley, Purley, Mrs. Purley, Dr. Ramsay, Read, Red, George Roberg, May Schaffer, Dr. Studeford.) Bostonians Bill Frothington, Hamilton Abbot, and Ellsworth Ames, three recent Harvard graduates, moor their crew launch on a river near a steamer full of high school couples from Wheatly Village near Truro. The three friends are permitted to board the steamer. McVitty, the school principal, tries to supervise. But Bill flirts and dances with pretty Mae Purley, seventeen, whose escort, Al Fitzpatrick, grows annoyed. When the other Harvard men get rude, a fight ensues, and they are put ashore, but not until Bill has arranged to pick up Mae next Sunday at her parents' apartment. They grow intimate despite his superior social position. His mother effectively disapproves of her only son's conduct. After Bill drives an ambulance during the war, he returns and in 1919 marries Stella. He succeeds in his job in a Boston bank, they have three children, and eight years pass; however, something seems missing. One weekend Bill tells Stella, who seems ill at ease, that he is going to New York for a school-board meeting but instead stops at Wheatly Village, inquires about Mae, and taxis to her address. She is now married to Fitzpatrick, who has a mill job and is briefly away in Boston. She says she dated Ham Abbot after Bill and before she got married. After sampling Fitzpatrick's applejack, Bill goes to a wharf where the taxi driver gets him more applejack. Couples come by to take the same steamer, for the same sort of outing, with McVitty still in charge. Bill sneaks aboard, tells McVitty he is a widower, dances with another pretty girl, drinks from his hip pint, and misbehaves again. This time, however, he is ridiculed as "old daddy," punched, and thrown overboard. Next afternoon he gets home, only to find a note from Stella. Fearing she too is wayward, he has a bath and a drink, then reads her note: she has gone to New York to a dentist. Shaking his head, he looks up at the moon, symbolic of "uncapturable" youth.

"LOVE IN THE NIGHT" (1925). Short story. (Characters: Esther, Florence, Morris Hasylton, Mrs. Jackson, Count Mendicant, Prince Paul Serge Boris Rostoff, Prince Val Rostoff, Prince Vladimir Rostoff, Princess Rostoff.) It is April 1914 in Cannes. Prince Val Rostoff, half Russian, half American, and seventeen, yearns for romance at Cannes, where he and his rich family are vacationing. His father, Prince Paul, is a grand duke's grandson and the czar's third cousin once removed. His mother comes from a quarrelsome Chicago family. One moonlit night he follows his parents by hired boat toward the *Minnehaha* and the *Privateer*, a pair of American yachts. On one is a dinner party. He passes the silent *Privateer* and heads toward the noisy *Minnehaha* until a girl's voice asks him to board her *Privateer*. Romantic talk follows. The two do not exchange names, but each admits to being seventeen. They sit on deck, kiss, embrace, and fall in love. She tells him she is married. When her husband, white haired, weary, and sixty, returns from the *Minnehaha*, she tells him that Val was headed for the party but visited with her instead. World War I erupts, and Val serves on the Imperial Russian army's Eastern front. The Russian revolution ruins his family, and his parents die. Val returns to Cannes, where he drives a taxi and works for an English bank. April 1922 arrives. A boatman tells Val that the *Privateer* has docked here each April for three years. Checking on the yacht with the American consul, Val learns she is indeed in the harbor. He finds his love from that moonlit night now widowed and seeking him. The international marriage that follows is an unusual success. Val runs a fleet of New York taxis, but the couple vacation in Cannes each April. "Love in the Night," Fitzgerald's first fiction with a Riviera setting, helped lead him to *Tender Is the Night*.

LOVEJOY. In "On Your Own," he is Evelyn Lovejoy's brother. He picks her up in a neighbor's car when she returns home to Maryland to attend their father's funeral.

LOVEJOY, DR. In ''On Your Own,'' he was a country physician, practicing in Maryland, and was the proud father of Evelyn Lovejoy, a stage dancer. When he dies, she returns from London to attend his funeral and is comforted to see him laid to rest among family friends.

LOVEJOY, EVELYN. In ''On Your Own,'' she is an attractive singer and dancer, twenty-six, from Rocktown, Maryland. She has performed for five years in London, where she is more popular than she was in the United States. Called home by her father's death, she meets George Ives, a rich young Maryland lawyer, aboard ship. When she attends her father's funeral, she encounters Ives again. They develop a relationship, although she initially objects to his forward ''American'' ways. At a small New York dinner with his mother and her Maryland friend, Colonel Cary, Evelyn candidly reveals she was a New York ''party girl'' six years ago and had thus met old Cary. Ives has tentatively proposed but wishes to end their friendship. She is so disconsolate, however, that he embraces her encouragingly. Evelyn Lovejoy is based on Bert Barr (Bertha [Mrs. Sidney] Weinberg). When Fitzgerald was crossing the Atlantic in 1931 to attend his father's funeral in Maryland, he met the dark, vivacious Bert. While aboard ship, she half-persuaded him she was a professional gambler. He later sent her funny letters.

LOVELY THING, THE. In ''I Got Shoes.'' *See* Battles, Johanna.

LOVETT, BUG FACE. In ''The Honor of the Goon,'' he is one of the students who called Ella Lei Chamoro a goon.

LOWRIE, JESSIE PIPER. In ''The Cut-Glass Bowl,'' she is Harold Piper's cousin. As Jessie Piper, she tells Harold about the affair of his wife, Evylyn Piper, with Fred Gedney. Later, having married Tom Lowrie, she and Tom attend Evylyn Piper's birthday party.

LOWRIE, LEW. In ''More Than Just a House,'' he is a Baltimore businessman, twenty-six in 1925. His father was a gardener. Lew, having rescued Amanda Gunther and Jean Gunther from an oncoming train, is invited by the grateful Gunthers to visit their ramshackle mansion outside Baltimore. Attending a dance at the mansion later, he falls in love with Amanda, only to learn she is getting married. In 1929 Lew, now a business success in New York, revisits the mansion, learns that Mrs. Gunther has died, Gunther is senile, Bess Gunther is caring for him, and Jean is an alcoholic. When he returns in 1933, Bess tells him that her father has died and Jean has married and moved to China. He proposes to Bess.

LOWRIE, TOM. In ''The Cut-Glass Bowl,'' he and his wife, Jessie Piper Lowrie, who is Harold Piper's cousin, attend Evylyn Piper's birthday party. Tom gets drunk.

"A LUCKLESS SANTA CLAUS" (1912). Short story. (Characters: Billy, Dorothy Harmon, Jim, Harry Talbot.) One Christmas Eve Dorothy Harmon challenges her wealthy fiancé, Harry Talbot, to avoid wasting money and instead give away $25, $2 at a time, in an hour and a half. He trudges through snowy streets, arouses the suspicions of many he tries to give the money to, is beaten up, but at last returns to her having succeeded. She is pleased—until he leaves to celebrate with the two men who had beaten him.

LUCY. In ''No Flowers,'' she is the girl in Marjorie Clark's dream who breaks her engagement when her boyfriend, Phil Savage, reveals his expulsion from the university for cheating on an examination. She tells herself she could marry a cheat but not a fool.

LUKAS, BIRDIE (ALSO WILLIE). In ''Strange Sanctuary,'' she is a thief, in cahoots with Dodo Gilbert. She steals jewelry while in disguise at the Halloween party attended by Dolly Haines, among others. She calls herself Willie Sugrue and pretends to be Dolly's uncle Charlie Craig's nurse.

LUPIN, ARSÈNE. In ''The Scandal Detectives,'' he is a fictitious French detective after whose career Basil Duke Lee at one point wishes to pattern his own.

LUTHER. In ''No Flowers,'' he is the hall boy at the club, in which the Engagement Room is located, in Marjorie Clark's dream about Phil Savage and Lucy. He is the club manager when Marjorie and William Delaney Johns are sitting in the same room later. Luther and Johns put drunk Red Grange to bed upstairs.

LYTELL, PETE. In *The Beautiful and Damned*, he is one of Anthony Patch's drinking companions in New York.

M

MCALMON, ROBERT MENZIES (1896–1956). Author and publisher. He was born in Clifton, Kansas, moved about with his family, graduated from high school in Minneapolis, and attended the University of Minnesota in 1916. While taking classes at the University of Southern California (1917–1920), he trained as a U.S. Army pilot, edited an aviation magazine, and published six poems about flying in *Poetry: A Magazine of Verse* (1919). In 1920 he worked as a nude model in New York City, where he met William Carlos Williams and other poets. McAlmon and Williams founded *Contact* to publish emerging American poets and critics (1920–1921, 1923). In 1920 McAlmon, an alcoholic homosexual, married Annie Winifred Ellerman, a British lesbian (pen name: Bryher), probably because of her family money and to conceal their lifestyles. In 1921 McAlmon joined American and British expatriates and French artists in Paris, where James Joyce encouraged him to publish, at his own expense, a collection of his racy stories called *A Hasty Bunch*. In 1923 his father-in-law, Sir John Reeves Ellerman, gave him $70,000 (added to later), which enabled him to establish his Contact Publishing Company, issue his own writing, and publish—and often subsidize—writers more talented than he, for example, Djuna Barnes and Nathanael West.* McAlmon's own fiction mirrors the chaos and decadence of his times, but often crudely and cynically. *Contact Collection of Contemporary Writers* (1925) is his fine anthology of pieces by Bryher, Ernest Hemingway,* Ezra Pound, Gertrude Stein,* Williams, and others. McAlmon's peak years were 1921–1925, after which he drank and danced too much, got divorced (1927), visited but disliked the New Mexico literary colony (1929), quarreled in New York and Paris with colleagues, and closed his Contact company (1929) with three books (including a long poem of his own). Finding Mexico not to his liking (1930), he returned to Paris (1932). In 1938 he issued his memoirs, *Being Geniuses Together* (revised in 1968 by Kay Boyle, his most loyal friend), which contains sketches, often unfair, of many contemporaries.

Impoverished through generosity to others and ignored, McAlmon died in Desert Hot Springs, California—his eleven books mostly forgotten.

Fitzgerald met McAlmon in Paris in 1925, probably through Hemingway or Stein, saw him there later, and detested him. In a letter to Max Perkins* (c. 15 November 1929), he defined McAlmon as ''a bitter rat'' and a failed author playing up to Joyce and Stein and gossiping that Fitzgerald and Hemingway were homosexuals. Such talk resulted in Perkins's refusal to have Scribner's publish McAlmon and in Hemingway's slugging him.

Bibliography: Paul Mariani, *William Carlos Williams: A New World Naked* (New York: McGraw-Hall, 1981); Sanford J. Smoller, *Adrift Among Geniuses: Robert McAlmon, Writer and Publisher of the Twenties* (University Park: Pennsylvania State University Press, 1975).

MACARTHUR, MARY. In ''For Mary's Eighth Birthday,'' she is the subject of the birthday poem and is named only Mary. In ''Oh papa—'' she is the girl, not named, who calls the poet ''papa.''

MCBETH. In *Tender Is the Night*, he is the manager-owner of the hotel in Paris in which Jules Peterson is murdered. Dick Diver persuades McBeth to deposit the corpse elsewhere.

MCCAFFRAY. In ''The Family Bus,'' he was the inventor of an advanced carburetor. Only one is left, and that is in the Henderson family car.

MCCARTHY, GYP. In ''Pat Hobby Does His Bit,'' he is a Hollywood stunt man who reluctantly agrees to loan Pat money for a car payment.

MCCARTY, ARTHUR. In *The Great Gatsby*, Nick Carraway lists his name on a timetable as one of Jay Gatsby's summer guests. From West Egg, he is connected with the movies.

MCCHESNEY, BILLY. In ''Two Wrongs,'' he is the young son of William McChesney and Emmy Pinkard McChesney.

MCCHESNEY, EMMY PINKARD. In ''Two Wrongs,'' she is a would-be dancer from Delaney, South Carolina. Eighteen at the beginning of the story, she is a beautiful redhead possessed of character. New York producer William McChesney takes her to lunch and gets her a part in a play which proves successful. After marrying, the two go to London where he philanders. Her second child is stillborn partly owing to his neglect. When they return to New York, Emmy, twenty-six, trains under Donilof to be a ballet dancer, has a chance to perform with Paul Makova at the Metropolitan, and separates from her husband to do so.

MCCHESNEY, WILLIAM ("BILL," "THE FRESH BOY," "MAC"). In "Two Wrongs," he is a Harvard graduate and by twenty-six, at the beginning of the story, an egocentric, successful New York play producer. He gives would-be dancer Emmy Pinkard a professional break, marries her, has a son with her, and takes her to London so he can produce a few former American successes there. He declines professionally and socially because of argumentativeness, alcoholism, and philandering. Back in New York, he continues to slide while Emmy is about to succeed as a ballet dancer. He develops severe lung disease and leaves for Denver to try to recuperate. Throughout, McChesney is depicted as having a split personality—alternately brash and sensitive.

MCCLENAHAN, BENNY. In *The Great Gatsby*, Nick Carraway lists his name on a timetable as one of Jay Gatsby's summer guests. Nick remembers his always coming with four girls.

MCCLURG, GLENOLA ("TROUBLE"). In " 'Trouble,' " she is a dedicated nurse in the Luke Harkless Hospital, aware of the effect her beauty has on interns. "Trouble" falls for Dr. Dick Wheelock, is fired when she sasses her superintendent, Mrs. Johnston, and agrees to marry a patient named Frederic Winslow. When Fred breaks his promise, resumes drinking, and tries to fight Dr. Wheelock, Trouble cancels her wedding plans and is happy to return to the hospital—and to Dr. Wheelock, who has arranged for her dismissal to be reversed. She probably loves hospital work, however, more than she will any man.

MCCOMAS. In "Your Way and Mine," he is the son of Henry McComas and Stella McComas. He disappears from the story.

MCCOMAS, HENRY ("MAC"). In "Your Way and Mine," he is a farmboy from Elmira, New York. In 1900, at twenty-one, he fails to obtain work under Woodley in his Broadway office but soon succeeds because of intuitive commercial savvy in a partnership with Theodore Drinkwater—so long as Mac keeps his own leisure hours. His wife, Stella McComas, is persuaded by Drinkwater to go into debt so Mac will have to work harder. As a result, Mac suffers a stroke in 1916. After Drinkwater dissolves the partnership, Mac recovers, starts his own firm, and is a millionaire by 1926. He has a daughter, Honoria McComas, and a son.

MCCOMAS, HONORIA. In "Your Way and Mine," she is the daughter of Henry McComas and Stella McComas. At nineteen, she thinks she loves Russel Codman more than she does Max Van Camp, who are McComas's business associates, but she is likely to marry Max, whose way is different from her father's.

MCCOMAS, STELLA. In "Your Way and Mine," she is a physical culture teacher in Utica, New York, who has married Henry McComas. In New York City they have a daughter, Honoria McComas, and a son. Stella tries to regulate her husband's diet, is advised by his partner, Theodore Drinkwater, to run their family into debt so McComas will have to work harder, and does so by making a $9,000 down payment on a Long Island summer home. She and the children are there when McComas suffers a stroke in town. She disappears from the story.

MCCOY, HORACE STANLEY (1897–1955). Journalist, author, and Hollywood scriptwriter. He was born in Pegrim, Tennessee, dropped out of high school, moved to Dallas, Texas, in 1915, joined the Texas National Guard in 1917, and served in France as a bombardier and aerial photographer in 1918. He worked in Dallas as a reporter until 1929 and as an actor until 1931. He published hard-boiled fiction beginning in 1927, then went to Hollywood in 1931 to act. Failing at that, he launched a screenwriting career in 1932 and for two decades wrote for RKO, Paramount, and Warner Brothers. He also wrote five novels, the most famous of which was *They Shoot Horses, Don't They?* (1935), about Hollywood extras in a dance marathon. McCoy's novels were especially popular in France, which he visited in 1951. *Scalpel* (1952), his last novel, was a best-seller. McCoy was married three times: to Loline Scherer (1921, one child), to a Dallas socialite (annulled), and to Helen Vinmont (1933, two children). Fitzgerald knew McCoy slightly. *See* "From Scott Fitzgerald."

Bibliography: Robert Polito, ed., *American Noir of the 1930s and 40s* (New York: Library of America, 1997).

MCCRACKEN, MISS. In "O Russet Witch!," she is the faithful accountant for Moonlight Quill in his bookshop. After Merlin Grainger inherits the shop, she tells him the truth about Caroline.

MCCRARY, MISS. In "Lo, the Poor Peacock!," she is the office secretary whom Jason Davis must dismiss because business is bad.

MCCUTCHEON. In "Lo, the Poor Peacock!," he is the principal of the school attended by Josephine Davis. He telephones her father, Jason Davis, to tell him she is being expelled, later phones to apologize for an inaccurate report, and reinstates her.

MCDONALD, JOE. In "The Bowl," he is a Princeton football team player and an all-American tackle.

MACDONOUGH, BLAINE. In "The Debutante," he is a young man Helen Halycon saw kiss her young sister, Cecilia Halycon, in the family "electric."

MCDOUGALL, DR. In ''Send Me In, Coach,'' he is, in the play the boys rehearse, the school president who cannot allow Dick Playfair to participate in the football game because he played baseball professionally. Cassius plays Dr. McDougall in the play.

MCDOWELL. In *This Side of Paradise*, he is a Princeton student who feels honored to be tutored with popular athletes. He is a sophomore when Amory Blaine, also a tutee, is a junior.

MACDOWELL, THOMAS J. ("TOM"). In ''John Jackson's Arcady,'' he is a crass city politician who asks John Jackson to donate property for a railroad station. Jackson declines and sends him away. Next day at a town meeting, MacDowell praises Jackson for his honesty and philanthropy.

MACEDON, PHIL. In ''Two Old-Timers,'' he is a pretentious 1920s Hollywood actor, still handsome but arrogant. When he and Pat Hobby are in a car accident, he pretends in front of the police not to remember fellow has-been Pat, who therefore exposes him as having been a cowardly actor in the 1925 combat movie *The Final Push*. Macedon is partly modeled on actor John Gilbert.*

MCFARLAND, PACKY. In *The Beautiful and Damned*, he is a boxer whom Anthony Patch pretends to be when he offers to fight a taxi driver.

MCFIDDLE, POKE. In ''The Broadcast We Almost Heard Last September,'' he is the radio announcer who reports a military charge as though it is a pleasant entertainment. In the evening he is gassed.

MCGINNESS. In *The Captured Shadow*, he is an inept New York detective fooled by Thorton Hart Dudley.

MCGLOOK, MINNIE. In *The Beautiful and Damned*, she is a Sauk Center fan, perhaps imaginary, to whom a studio worker sends the photograph, stamped as though autographed, of a popular movie star.

MCGOVERN, MISS. In *The Beautiful and Damned*, she is the nurse who tends Gloria Gilbert Patch when she has influenza and pneumonia.

MCGOWAN, POP. In '' 'I Didn't Get Over,' '' he is mentioned as a member of the class of 1916 killed in the war.

MCGREGOR. In ''Majesty,'' he is a servant whom Harold Castleton Sr. orders to get his masseur.

MCGREGOR, "CURLY." In *The Beautiful and Damned*, he is a former boyfriend of Gloria Gilbert Patch's.

MCILVAINE, BEE. In "On the Trail of Pat Hobby," she has a movie script about tourists that needs a title. Pat Hobby boozily suggests *Grand Motel*, which Jack Berners happily buys for $50.

MCINTOSH, DEAN. In "On Schedule," he is the dean of the faculty at the university where René du Cary has his laboratory.

MCINTOSH, MRS. In "On Schedule," she is the wife of the dean. René du Cary does not wish to explain to her why Becky Snyder was taking a bath in his house.

MCINTYRE. In "The Four Fists," he is a Texas rancher whose oil-rich land Peter Carhart dispatches Samuel Meredith to buy. McIntyre is reconciled to selling but before signing the contract slugs Samuel. This teaches Samuel a lesson, and he cancels the contract.

MCINTYRE, CHARLIE. In *The Beautiful and Damned*, he is a man at whose wedding Otis, an usher at Anthony Patch's wedding, says he was an usher.

MACINTYRE, WARREN. In "Bernice Bobs Her Hair," he is a Yale man, nineteen, who boasts of girlfriends elsewhere and likes Marjorie Harvey until he seems to prefer Bernice.

MCKEE, CHESTER. In *The Great Gatsby*, he is the affected photographer Nick Carraway meets at the New York apartment Tom Buchanan shares with Myrtle Wilson. His wife is Lucille McKee. McKee would like a chance to do more work on Long Island.

MCKEE, LUCILLE. In *The Great Gatsby*, she is Chester McKee's gossipy wife. Nick Carraway meets her at the apartment shared by Tom Buchanan and Myrtle Wilson.

MCKENNA. In "In the Holidays." *See* Kinney, Joe.

MCKENNA. In "Winter Dreams," he is the caddy master at the exclusive golf club. When he orders Dexter Green to caddy for Judy Jones, Dexter quits.

MCKIBBEN ("MAC"). In *Tender Is the Night*, he and Carly Hannan are friends of Tommy Barban and listen in Munich as Tommy tells Dick Diver how he got Prince Chillicheff out of Russia. McKibben and his family are on their way to Innsbruck.

MCKINLEY, WILLIAM (1843–1901). The twenty-fifth president of the United States. In ''A Patriotic Short,'' an actor portrays him in *True to Two Flags*, the movie short which Pat Hobby works on and in which the president offers General Fitzhugh Lee a commission during the Spanish-American War.

MCKISCO, ALBERT. In *Tender Is the Night*, he is the husband of Violet McKisco and is a novelist, thirty in 1925. The Divers meet them on the Riviera. He and Tommy Barban fight a duel. By the time Dick sees him aboard ship following Dick's father's funeral, the man has become popular by patterning his fiction on the formulas of better writers. Albert McKisco is partly based on Robert Menzies McAlmon.*

MCKISCO, VIOLET ("VI"). In *Tender Is the Night*, she is Albert McKisco's wife, from Boise, Idaho. Her gossip, after she sees Nicole Diver hysterical in her bathroom, causes her husband and Tommy Barban to fight a duel.

MACKS. In ''Three Hours between Planes,'' this is the name of the family to whose party Donald Plant recalls not being able to go because he had the mumps. He heard that the children played post office there.

MCLANE, CARTER. In ''No Flowers,'' he was the escort of Amanda Rawlins, later Amanda Rawlins Clark, to the university prom in 1913. He delayed proposing. Amanda was infatuated by Howard, his roommate. When Howard got her to discard Carter's corsage in favor of his, the engagement ring was missing that McLane had concealed in his corsage as a surprise. In annoyance, McLane stormed out. Amanda evidently regrets these events, not least when she learned that five years later he was in the army in Texas.

MCLANE, TOMMY. In ''Indecision,'' he is American banker in Paris, twenty-seven, vacationing in Switzerland during the 1930 Christmas season. While there he indecisively considers proposing to Emily Elliot and Rosemary Merriweather—all the while ignorant of his own amusingly egocentric conceit. Ordered by his boss to go to Geneva, he impulsively proposes on the train to Rosemary.

MCPHEE, HANK. In ''Our American Poets,'' he shoots his ''pa'' in Fitzgerald's Robert Service burlesque.

MCQUILLAN, LOUISA ALLEN. Fitzgerald's maternal grandmother. She married Philip T. McQuillan in 1820 and had five surviving children. The eldest was Mary McQuillan Fitzgerald,* Fitzgerald's mother.

MCQUILLAN, PHILIP T. (1834–1877). Fitzgerald's maternal grandfather. He was born in County Fermanagh, Ireland. In 1857 he moved from Illinois to St.

Paul, Minnesota, where he became a bookkeeper and then an independent businessman. In 1860 he married Louisa Allen. During the Civil War he was a grocery wholesaler. He later prospered, lived well, and was a benefactor of the Catholic Church. He died of Bright's disease and tuberculosis, leaving a wife and five children, the eldest of whom was Mary McQuillan Fitzgerald,* Fitzgerald's mother. According to his obituary, McQuillan left assets amounting to $844,000.

MACRAE, BESSIE. In ''Bernice Bobs Her Hair,'' she is described as having been popular at parties for too many years.

MCRAE, BRUCE. In *Safety First!*, he is identified as a typically handsome, well-spoken fellow.

MCRAE, JENNY. In ''First Blood,'' she runs or supervises a dancing class and was reluctant to invite Josephine Perry to attend. In ''A Snobbish Story,'' she is identified as Jim McRae's wife. She hints to Josephine Perry she will schedule her in a vaudeville skit only if the girl is nice to Mrs. McRae's Minneapolis nephew, Donald.

MCRAE, JIM. In ''A Snobbish Story,'' he is socially influential Jenny McRae's businessman husband. Herbert T. Perry hints to his daughter, Josephine Perry, that Jim will suffer if his wife demeans Josephine in any way.

MCTEAGUE. In ''Your Way and Mine,'' he is the commercial threat in Indiana and Ohio to the expanding chain of hardware stores Henry McComas wants to develop. McComas sends his associates Max Van Camp to Indiana and Russel Codman to Ohio to try to outwit McTeague.

MCVITTY. In ''The Love Boat,'' he is a Harvard graduate, class of 1907. As high school principal, he supervises the river steamer aboard which young students go dancing. He dislikes Bill Frothington's boarding the boat the first time and dislikes it more eight years later.

MACY, MARTIN. In ''The Camel's Back,'' he is the friend of Baily, who persuades Perry Parkhurst to come to Macy's hotel room and drink champagne with the two of them.

MACY, THERON G. In ''Dalyrimple Goes Wrong,'' he is the owner of the largest wholesale grocery establishment in town. He hires Bryan Dalyrimple to do storeroom work, promises but denies him a promotion, and does not raise his salary. When Dalyrimple robs some houses and stays on with Macy for four months to avoid suspicion, Macy recommends him to Alfred J. Fraser as reliable, whereupon Fraser persuades Dalyrimple to enter politics. Macy rapidly promoted his nephew, Tom Everett.

"MAGNETISM" (1928). Short story. (Characters: Helen Tompkins Avery, Gwen Becker, Arthur Busch, Castle, Katherine Davis, Dolores, Donovan, Margaret Donovan, Douglas, Miss Duncan, George Hannaford, Kay Hannaford, Harris, Jules Rennard, Pete Schroeder, Zeller.) George Hannaford, thirty, is a successful Hollywood movie actor. He is married to Kay Hannaford, and they have a baby two months old who is cared for by an English nurse. Kay is distressed by George's excessive friendliness toward everyone. After breakfast, he is chauffeured to the studio, confers with an executive, initials changes on some papers his smiling script girl Margaret Donovan hands him, and proceeds to a stage where Helen Avery is pouting. She is a gorgeous actress, eighteen, with whom George could get involved if they are ever cast together. Home again, George's intimacy with Kay is interrupted by the arrival of Arthur Busch, a writer turned director who is pursuing her. The three go to a party, where Helen is selfishly happy upon learning she has just been cast in a major part. She and George retreat from emotional attachment. Then George sees Kay mildly drunk and standing outside almost embracing Busch. Back home, George, alone downstairs, is approached by Margaret Donovan's brother, who demands $50,000 for his sister for the return of love letters he says George wrote to Margaret. It seems George initialed not script changes but letters she had typed. In the morning Helen phones George to apologize for her coolness at the party just as Kay enters to demand a divorce in order to marry Busch. George phones Castle, his lawyer, who arrives with Busch. George explains about Margaret, leaves the three to take whatever actions they wish, and is chauffeured aimlessly until he finds himself at Margaret's apartment at twilight. She confesses she has loved him silently for seven years, attracted to his magnetic charm; the blackmail scheme was hatched by her ex-convict brother. She tears up the letters and says he can stay or leave, as he wishes. Rushing out, he is driven home and explains Margaret's scheme to Kay. She says she has dumped Busch and hopes Margaret will be fired. Saying she must not be fired and suddenly concerned about her, he phones her apartment only to learn she has shot herself—though not seriously. George and Kay express their love for each other, and he prepares to go to the hospital and comfort Margaret.

MAHAN. In "The Love Boat," he is a Harvard football player Bill Frothington recalls.

MAINE, DUKE OF. In "The Kingdom in the Dark," he is mentioned by the Duke of Guyenne as holding land north of Count Philippe of Villefranche's. In "Gods of Darkness," he enters Philippe's fiefdom with an army. Countess Griselda and Jacques are able to disarm and capture Maine and his men by the use of mysterious pagan cultist words, after which he departs in peace.

MAIS, MARIA AMALIA ROTO. In *Tender Is the Night*, hers is a name read in the *New York Herald*.

MAISIE. In ''Imagination—and a Few Mothers,'' she is a person for whom Mrs. Paxton did not organize a family orchestra.

"MAJESTY" (1929). Short story. (Characters: Bickle, Blair, Blair, Gardiner Blair Jr., Gardiner Blair Sr., Master Gardiner Blair III, Miss Gloria Blair, Olive Mercy Blair, Mrs. Princess Potowski Parr Blair, Mrs. Potter Blair, William Brevoort Blair, Castleton, Emily Castleton, Harold Castleton Jr., Harold Castleton Sr., Theodore Castleton, Mrs. Theodore Castleton, Diffendorfer, Fraser, Hallam, Hamilton, Hamn, Lady Mary Bowes Howard, Janierka, Garland Kane, McGregor, Captain Marchbanks, Carl Mercy, O'Keefe, Prince Gabriel Petrocobesco, Smythe, Wakeman.) Emily Castleton, Harold Castleton Sr.'s spoiled, romantically inclined daughter, returns from having fun in Europe and decides at twenty-four to marry William Brevoort Blair of Newport. Expressing doubts to her cousin, Olive Mercy, she calls off the wedding ceremony after the guests are assembled in a New York City church. Fearing snickers, Blair proposes to Olive, is accepted, and marries her that evening. They live in New York and have a baby a year later. In Paris, Castleton, who likes Olive, sees Emily, who is traveling in Europe, but gets nowhere with her. A year later, through a European agent, he learns that the spendthrift Emily is consorting with the disreputable Prince Gabriel Petrocobesco. Castleton, ill, dispatches the Blairs to Europe. They trace Emily and her lover past Hungary to Czjeck-Hansa, a two-town, magnesium-rich county of which he is a prince, then the new king. Emily marries him, and she becomes a queen. Two years after that, the Blairs, with two children now, visit London to see Emily, the successful romantic, in a coach-crowded royal procession with the queen of England. Part of the plot echoes *The Ambassadors* by Henry James, in which ''ambassadors'' are dispatched to Europe to rescue a supposedly wayward American but fail.

MAKOVA, PAUL. In ''Two Wrongs,'' he is a successful ballet dancer with whom Emmy Pinkard McChesney, according to her instructor Donilof, is ready to perform at the Metropolitan.

MALONE. In *The Last Tycoon*, he is the studio security guard who put Edna and Kathleen Moore off the lot after the flood. Monroe Stahr orders him to identify the two young women.

MAMIE, AUNT. In ''The Jelly-Bean,'' she is the woman from Macon, Georgia, who ran the home of the fallen Powell family as a boardinghouse. James Powell sold the house and uses the interest on the proceeds to pay for Mamie's care at a sanitarium.

MANFRED, JEFF. In ''No Harm Trying,'' he is an associate producer in Hollywood. He participates in Pat Hobby's scheme to exploit script boy Eric's movie idea. Carl Le Vigne sees through the plot but tolerates Manfred because he is Le Vigne's friend Bill Behrer's wife's cousin.

''A MAN IN THE WAY'' (1940). Short story. (Characters: Bach, Jack Berners, Bill Costello, Pat Hobby, Louie, Pricilla Smith.) Pat Hobby, a has-been Hollywood writer, trying to peddle a script idea to his boss, Jack Berners, bumps into a writer named Pricilla Smith. After a brief talk with her he steals her idea of having a has-been artist see his own paintings being packed to be shipped for safety out of a war-torn city and unsuccessfully trying, his identity unknown, to get a job helping to pack them. Pat's attempt to sell this idea will fail because Pricilla is Berners's current girlfriend.

MANLY, ESTHER. In ''The Rubber Check,'' she is a person Val Schuyler thinks he could have married.

MANY MARRIAGES. Novel by Sherwood Anderson.*

MAPLES, MISS. In ''Financing Finnegan,'' she is one of Cannon's secretaries.

MAPLEWOOD. In ''The Freshest Boy,'' he is a student at St. Regis. Basil Duke Lee becomes friendly with him after Christmas, but they soon quarrel.

MARANDA. In ''A Patriotic Short,'' he was a movie executive who lived near Pat Hobby in the 1920s and invited him to replace the unavailable Douglas Fairbanks* and have lunch with the president of the United States. In a revision of this story, Maranda is named Moskin.

MARBOTSON, FINDLE. In *This Side of Paradise*, he is a Yale student seen in New York when Amory Blaine goes out with Alec Connage, Phoebe Column, and Axia Marlowe. Findle tries unsuccessfully at Bistolary's to get Axia to come over to his table.

MARBROOKE, ELEANOR. In ''Sentiment—and the Use of Rouge,'' she is the ex-fiancée of Lieutenant Richard Harrington Syneforth, who was killed in World War I. In 1917, she shocks his idealistic brother, Captain Clayton Harrington Syneforth, by her war-altered attitude toward morals and manners. She seduces him, then explains the difference between love and Love. Soon after she rejects his proposal, he is killed in action in France.

MARBROOKE, KATHERINE (''KITTY''). In ''Sentiment—and the Use of Rouge,'' she was Eleanor Marbrooke's little sister, killed in 1915 during a Zeppelin raid over London.

MARCHBANKS, CAPTAIN. In ''Majesty,'' he is a married pilot who flew Emily Castleman over the Channel and who was evidently her lover.

MARCHBANKS, TED, BARON. In ''Rags Martin-Jones and the Pr-nce of W-les,'' this is the name a friend of John B. Chestnut takes when he pretends to be a friend of the Prince of Wales.

''MARCHING STREETS'' (1919). Poem. When darkness increases and everyone is asleep, various streets—torchlit, old, of several shades, and flowery—march along, meet, and sense death at the outskirts.

MARCUS. In *The Last Tycoon*, he is a canny old member of the inner circle of moviemakers including Mort Flieshacker, Leanbaum, Joe Popolous, and Monroe Stahr.

MARCUS, HAROLD. In ''The Homes of the Stars,'' Marcus, whose first name is not given here, drives up to the mansion Pat Hobby has dishonestly called Shirley Temple's to fool Deering R. Robinson and his wife. Recognizing Marcus as the producer he was press agent for twenty years earlier, Pat escapes out the back gate. In ''Pat Hobby and Orson Welles,'' he is an important Hollywood studio finance man, now old and tired. He gives Pat Hobby a pass to enter and says he is lunching with Orson Welles. When Marcus sees Jeff Boldini's car, in which Pat is riding and which is labeled ''Orson Welles,'' he waves and has a heart attack on the sidewalk. In ''On the Trial of Pat Hobby,'' Pat steals Marcus's Homberg from the commissary and feels better, while drunk, when Bee McIlvaine locates it.

MARGERY, NELL. In ''I Got Shoes,'' she is a successful, independent-minded actress. She gets over her obsession of saving old shoes, caused by a foot injury when she was little, after she reveals it to reporter Johanna Battles. Nell can then accept the proposal of the explorer Warren Livingstone.

''MARGEY WINS THE GAME'' (1922). Review of *Margey Wins the Game* by John V. A. Weaver.*

MARGHERITA, QUEEN. In *This Side of Paradise*, she is a personage known in Rome by Amory Blaine's mother before her marriage.

MARGOT. In ''The Evil Eye,'' she confesses in a song she likes to gossip.

MARIE. In ''Martin's Thoughts,'' she is one of Martin's girlfriends.

MARIE. In ''My Very Very Dear Marie,'' she is the debonair, unfair letter writer the sad poet answers.

MARIO. In ''Pat Hobby and Orson Welles,'' he is evidently the owner of the bar Pat Hobby frequents across the street from the studio.

MARION. In ''One of My Oldest Friends,'' she is Michael's wife. When he wants to have a party for his old friend Charley Hart, she reveals Charley wanted her at one point to leave Michael for him.

MARIUS. In ''The Kingdom in the Dark,'' he is a man loyal to Count Philippe of Villefranche.

MARIUS. In *Tender Is the Night*, he is a servant who works for the Divers in their home at Tarmes, on the Riviera.

MARJORIE. In ''The Four Fists,'' she is a married woman who lives in Jersey City and who leads Samuel Meredith on, only to be caught by her husband, who slugs Samuel.

MARJORIE. In ''What Became of Our Flappers and Sheiks?,'' she is a girl-friend of Tommy, who when fifteen drives her around, perhaps harmlessly.

MARKEY, BILLY. In ''The Baby Party,'' he is the son of Joe Markey and his wife. At the party given for his second birthday, Ede Andros, a guest from next door, shoves Billy in a fight over his teddy bear. Ede's mother, Edith Andros, and Billy's mother argue so vehemently that the two fathers have a fight, make up, and make their wives apologize.

MARKEY, JOE. In ''The Baby Party,'' he is the father, thirty-five, of Billy Markey. He defends his wife, after her dispute with Edith Andros, by fighting with Edith's husband, John Andros, in the snow. Then they shake hands and tell their wives to make up.

MARKEY, MRS. JOE. In ''The Baby Party,'' she is the mother of Billy Markey, at whose birthday party Ede Andros shoves him and laughs when he bumps his head. Ede's mother also laughs, which triggers a verbal exchange resulting in their husbands' having a fight. Later, the Markeys call on the Androses to apologize.

MARKHAM. In ''Dalyrimple Goes Wrong,'' he is a person whose residence Bryan Dalyrimple does not rob.

MARKHAM, JOSEPHINE ("JOE"). In ''An Alcoholic Case,'' she is a nurse Mrs. Hixson tries but fails to send to the alcoholic case.

MARKOE, BILL. In "An Alcoholic Case," he is a man the nice young nurse did not marry. She does not tell the alcoholic case about him.

MARLOWE, AXIA. In *This Side of Paradise*, she is the girlfriend of Alec Connage when he, Amory Blaine, and Phoebe Column double-date in New York.

MARMORA. In *Tender Is the Night*, he is a banker from Milan and has something to do with Devereux Warren's investments. Marmora, his wife, and their son, Conte Tino de Marmora, are vacationing in Caux, Switzerland.

MARMORA, CONTE TINO DE. In *Tender Is the Night*, he is Nicole Warren's escort in Caux, Switzerland, when Dick Diver encounters them.

MARMORA, SEÑORA. In *Tender Is the Night*, she is vacationing in Caux, Switzerland, with her husband and their son, Conte Tino de Marmora, when Dick Diver meets them.

MARQUAND. In *The Last Tycoon*, he and his wife are a screenwriting couple. Monroe Stahr transfers them to another picture.

MARQUAND, MRS. In *The Last Tycoon*, she and her husband are a screenwriting couple. Monroe Stahr compliments her insincerely.

MARSDEN, CAL. In "The Unspeakable Egg," she is Fifi's older aunt. She and her sister, spinsters, live on Montauk Point, Long Island. They are happy when Fifi visits them, until they learn she may run off with a hairy, rude beach derelict. They summon Dr. Roswell Gallup, a psychiatrist, to treat her. All is well, however, when the derelict is revealed to be rich, handsome George Van Tyne, Fifi's fiancé, whose ability to be unconventional she is testing.

MARSDEN, JOSEPHINE ("JO"). In "The Unspeakable Egg," she is Cal Marsden's younger sister and Fifi's aunt. The two unmarried ladies worry about Fifi until her fiancé, George Van Tyne, reveals his true identity.

MARSHALL. In "The Offshore Pirate," this is one of the names in one of Curtis Carlyle's songs.

MARSHALL, HOWARD. In "May Day," he is a man who gave a house party Edith Bradin recalls.

MARSTON. In "The Swimmers," either of the two young sons of Henry Clay Marston and Choupette Marston. The unnamed swimmer at St. Jean de Luz teaches both boys how to swim.

MARSTON, CHOUPETTE. In ''The Swimmers,'' she is the unfaithful wife, from Provence, of Henry Clay Marston and the mother of his two sons. Caught in Paris with another man, she moves with her husband and children to Richmond, is adulterous with Charles Wiese, and is forced to relinquish custody of her children to Marston.

MARSTON, HENRY CLAY. In ''The Swimmers,'' he is an employee, born in Virginia, of an American promissory trust company branch located in Paris. He met Choupette in Provence in 1918, and they married. Eight years later, with two sons, he discovers her in an adulterous situation, has a nervous breakdown, recovers in a month, and forgives her. While vacationing at St. Jean de Luz, he tries to rescue a beautiful American girl from drowning but cannot swim. Both are rescued, and out of gratitude she teaches him how to swim. He returns to Richmond with his family, works for a tobacco company, and invests well. He discovers Choupette with rich Charles Wiese and demands a divorce and custody of his sons. While returning to Europe with them, he meets the unnamed swimmer aboard ship.

MARTHA. In ''The Cut-Glass Bowl,'' she is the servant of Evylyn Piper. She misplaces a letter sent to Evylyn, which that distraught woman intuits is in the cut-glass bowl and is a War Department letter informing her of the death of her son, Donald Piper.

MARTHA. In ''Discard,'' she is a casual girlfriend of George Baker aboard ship to Europe. The two stumble on Count Hennen de Lanclerc and Phyllis Burns on a first-class deck.

MARTHA. In ''Winter Dreams,'' she is one of the servants of Mortimer Jones, his wife, and their daughter, Judy Jones.

MARTHE. In ''How to Live on Practically Nothing a Year,'' she is one of the Fitzgeralds' Riviera servants. She cheats them on the grocery bills.

MARTIN. In ''A Debt of Honor,'' he is a Confederate Army soldier absent when the roll is called for soldiers available for sentry duty.

MARTIN. In ''A Freeze-Out,'' this is the name of some of the many people who attended the Rikkers' party shortly after New Year's Day.

MARTIN. In ''Martin's Thoughts,'' he names his various girlfriends.

MARTIN, ALEC. In *The Vegetable*, he is one of bootlegger Snooks's customers.

MARTIN, CONSUELA. In ''Teamed with Genius,'' this is the name of the author of an unacceptable script of the Russian ballet story. After retouching it, Pat Hobby claims it is his and René Wilcox's work.

MARTIN, DR. In ''The Cut-Glass Bowl,'' he is a physician who lives across the street from Evylyn Piper. She tries to telephone him when her daughter, Julie Piper, cut her thumb, but he was not home.

MARTIN, JENNY. In *The Beautiful and Damned*, she is a palmist consulted by Catherine Gilbert about her nephew, Richard Caramel.

MARTIN, MRS. In ''Strange Sanctuary,'' she is the former hostess of Dolly Haines and the employer of Hazeldawn.

MARTIN-JONES, RAGS. In ''Rags Martin-Jones and the Pr-nce of W-les,'' she is the American who inherits $75 million, half promises to marry John B. Chestnut of New York, goes to Europe, becomes spoiled, and returns bored to America. To win her hand, Chestnut stages an elaborate ruse involving a bogus Prince of Wales and a shooting in the nightclub. Thrilled, she accepts Chestnut.

"MARTIN'S THOUGHTS" (1961). Poem. (Characters: Anne, Antionette, Babette, Dorothy, Elenor, Helen, Kitty, Loey, Marie, Martin.) Martin names his girlfriends but does not know whom he loves the most. Martin Amorous was one of Fitzgerald's Newman School friends.

MARVIS, JULIE. In *Porcelain and Pink*, she bathes and sings in the tub, will not let her sister, Lois Marvis, bathe, and pretends to Calkins she is Lois. Julie is about twenty.

MARVIS, LOIS. In *Porcelain and Pink*, she wants to bathe before her date with Calkins, but her sister, Julie Marvis, will not relinquish the tub. Lois is a year older than Julie.

MARX. In ''The Cut-Glass Bowl,'' he is Harold Piper's hardware-business rival. When Harold's projected merger with Clarence Ahearn collapses, Ahearn presumably goes with Marx.

MARY. In *Fie! Fie! Fi-Fi!*, she is liked by Sam but yearns for Victor, even though he spurns her.

MARY. In ''For Mary's Eighth Birthday.'' *See* MacArthur, Mary.

MASON, JIM. In ''Diagnosis,'' he was a Confederate soldier about whom Chevril reminisces.

MASTERS, MRS. In ''O Russet Witch!,'' she is the mother of Olive Masters Grainger, who shared an apartment in New York City with her and married Merlin Grainger there.

MASTERS, OLIVE. In ''O Russet Witch!'' *See* Grainger, Olive Masters.

MATEZKA, GLORIA. In ''The Honor of the Goon,'' she is one of the students who called Ella Lei Chamoro a goon.

MATHER, JAMES (''JIM''). In ''Hot and Cold Blood,'' he is the husband of Jaqueline Mather and is a hardware broker. His generosity to Ed Bronson, among others, jeopardizes their financial security. She urges him to quit being an easy mark. His selfishly not giving his seat to a lady on the streetcar causes that lady to faint, and he discovers that she was his pregnant wife. This causes him to become generous again, to the point of loaning Edward Lacy a needed sum of money. In the first published version of ''Hot and Cold Blood,'' the Mathers are named Coatesworth.

MATHER, JAQUELINE (''JACK''). In ''Hot and Cold Blood,'' she is the wife of James Mather. She urges him to be less generous to his friends. When, expecting their first child, she faints on the streetcar, it is because Mather, hiding behind his newspaper in embarrassment, followed her advice and did not give a standing woman his seat. She was that woman.

MATSKO, JAMES. In ''Six of One—,'' he is a hardworking son of an alcoholic in Ed Barnes's Ohio hometown. At seventeen he is persuaded, with difficulty, by Barnes to go to Columbia and study money and banking, at his expense. In 1930, he becomes a partner in a Wall Street brokerage. Barnes thinks Matsko would have succeeded anywhere and without his aid.

MATTERLANE, DUKE OF. In ''The Trail of the Duke,'' he is the person Mirabel Walmsley and her father have come to New York City to receive. She sends her fiancé, Dodson Garland, out to find the Duke, meaning—although he does not understand—her poodle Duke. The human duke is expected next day.

MAUDE. In *The Last Tycoon*, she is one of Pat Brady's three secretaries. The other two are Birdy Peters and Rosemary Schmiel.

MAXIM. In ''Forging Ahead,'' this is the name of a place to which Basil Duke Lee, when unhappy, thinks briefly of going.

MAXWELL, ELSA (1883–1963). Hostess and writer. She was born in Keokuk, Iowa, was raised in San Francisco, and had little formal education. In 1906 she went to New York City with a Shakespeare company, played the piano in a nickelodeon, wrote songs, and was the accompanist of a vaudeville singer who took her to South Africa. Maxwell began giving big parties abroad. In 1915 she returned to New York, became a delightful hostess, and was a fund-raiser. After World War I she became known as the inventor of elements in parties catering to celebrities. In 1938 she moved Hollywood, was featured in several movies, was a film consultant, and wrote a syndicated gossip column. Remaining single, Maxwell never owned a home but held her own parties in friends' residences. Her several books include *I Live by My Wits* (1936), *R.S.V.P.—Elsa Maxwell's Own Story* (1957), and *The Celebrity Circus* (1963, containing anecdotes about the famous). In ''Last Kiss,'' Elsa Maxwell is mentioned by Joe Becker as having seen Pamela Knighton at Twenty-One.

MAYBURN, HELEN. In *The Captured Shadow*, she is a friend of Dorothy Connage and will marry Dorothy's brother, Hubert Connage.

"MAY DAY" (1920). Short story. (Characters: Barlow, Bartholomew, Edith Bradin, Henry Bradin, Philip Dean, Devineries, Harlan, Peter Himmel, Jewel Hudson, Jim, George Key, Private Carrol Key, Howard Marshall, Private Gus Rose, Gordon Sterrett.) It is New York City in May 1919. The war is over, and hordes of people are in Manhattan. Gordon Sterrett, back from France since February, is a sick, unemployed artist. He goes to the Biltmore Hotel to find Philip Dean, his class of 1916 Yale roommate, explains to Dean that blowsy Jewel Hudson is blackmailing him, and asks for a loan of $300 to pay her off. Phil manages a gift of $80. Privates Carrol Key and Gus Rose watch a crowd beat up an anticapitalistic May Day orator, go to Delmonico's, hide near a banquet room, and obtain liquor from Carrol's brother, George, a waiter. Edith Bradin, a beautiful, selfish flapper, is escorted to a Yale fraternity dance at Delmonico's by Peter Himmel, who displeases her by trying to kiss her. She sees Gordon there; a former flame, he dances with her, but she dumps him because of his depressing talk and drunkenness. Peter, feeling snubbed, spies Carrol and Gus, drinks with them, and returns to Edith, who declines his apology and goes off with a fat stranger to the nearby office of her brother, Henry Bradin, editor of a socialist newspaper. Jewel enters Delmonico's, browbeats George into locating Gordon, and insists he leave with her. Edith chats with Henry until a mob, including Carrol and Gus, storms his office, breaks Henry's leg, and tosses Carrol out a window to his death. The Yale crowd breakfasts near Columbus Circle as a magical dawn breaks. Peter and Phil taxi drunkenly to Delmonico's to retrieve Peter's coat. When they cannot find it, they wear the coatroom ''In'' and ''Out'' signs over their vests, go to the Commodore for champagne, and proceed to the Biltmore—shadowed by Gus. There they confront Edith, who snubs them and tells authorities Gus broke her brother's leg. Gordon wakes up in a hotel, notes Jewel in bed beside him, realizes he has married her, buys a revolver, goes to his room on Twenty-Seventh Street, and commits suicide over his drawing materials.

When editors at the *Saturday Evening Post* found the cynical, pessimistic naturalism of this novella unacceptable, Fitzgerald sold it to the *Smart Set* for $200. It revised the story considerably before republishing it in *Tales of the Jazz Age*. He has several autobiographical touches. Fitzgerald even gave Carrol Key part of his own name, "Key," and said the character had good but quite diluted blood.

Bibliography: Colin S. Cass, "Fitzgerald's Second Thoughts about 'May Day': A Collation and Study," *FH/A 1970*, 69–95; Kuehl; Roulston.

MEADOW, MARCIA. In "Head and Shoulders." Her real name was Veronica Meadow. *See* Tarbox, Marcia.

MEADOW, VERONICA. In "Head and Shoulders." *See* Tarbox, Marcia.

MEARS, GASTON. In *The Beautiful and Damned*, he is an actor playing opposite Willa Sable in a movie for a part in which Gloria Gilbert Patch takes an unsuccessful screen test.

MEDILL, BETTY. In "The Camel's Back," she is the beautiful, spoiled daughter of Cyrus Medill and the object of Perry Parkhurst's affections. She declines his peremptory marriage proposal. When he dresses as a camel's front end, she is unwittingly married to him but is finally pleased.

MEDILL, CYRUS. In "The Camel's Back," he is the indulgent father of Betty Medill and a man made wealthy in the aluminum business in Toledo. He is only briefly upset when Betty is unwittingly married to Perry Parkhurst at the circus ball.

MEDONCA, CORINNA. In *Tender Is the Night*, hers is a name read in the *New York Herald.*

MEIGS, HAL. In "At Your Age," he is Tom Squires's old Yale classmate, now in Houston. He tries to fix Tom up with a woman on the train.

MELONEY, ROSE. In *The Last Tycoon*, she is a dependable screenwriter who makes about $50,000 a year. Twenty years ago she had a brief affair with director John Broaca. She has been married three times, and her husbands have all beaten her. She is partly, and loosely, based on Dorothy Parker.*

MELON-LOPER, JAN. In "The Family Bus," he is the father of Kaethe Melon-Loper and Jannekin Melon-Loper. At first, he is the Henderson family gardener. After he and his family move across the river, he becomes a successful businessman, buys out the rival Henderson furniture factory, and prospers. At the end, he is in a nursing home. The name Melon-Loper derives from the name Melyn-Loper, one of Zelda Sayre Fitzgerald's* ancestors.

MELON-LOPER, JANNEKIN ("JANNY"). In "The Family Bus," she is the younger daughter of Jan Melon-Loper and his wife. Janny, who has a beautiful Dutch face, is a year younger than Dick Henderson, and they grow up partly together, partly separated. When she returns from European schooling, the two resume their tender relationship.

MELON-LOPER, KAETHE. In "The Family Bus," she is the older daughter of Jan Melon-Loper and his wife. When she tries to elope with Ralph Henderson in his family car and he is killed in a crash, the scandal causes the Melon-Loper family to move across the river.

MELON-LOPER, MRS. In "The Family Bus," she is Jan Melon-Loper's sturdy wife and the mother of Kaethe Melon-Loper and Jannekin Melon-Loper.

MENAFEE, DR. In "Three Acts of Music," he is a physician the unnamed nurse in the story assists.

MENCKEN, H. L. (1880–1956). (Full name: Henry Louis Mencken.) Journalist, critic, and essayist. He was born in Baltimore, Maryland, was educated at the Baltimore Polytechnic Institute, and beginning in 1899 worked for the *Baltimore Morning Herald*, becoming its city editor in 1903 and then its managing editor (1905–1906). He worked for the Baltimore *Sunpapers* (1906–1917, 1920–1938, 1948). He became literary editor of the *Smart Set* in 1908 and coeditor with George Jean Nathan* from 1914 to 1923. From 1911 to 1915 Mencken wrote a daily *Evening Sun* "Free Lance" column. In 1912 he first visited Europe; in 1916 and 1917 he was a war correspondent in Germany for the *Sunpapers*. In 1924 he and Nathan founded the *American Mercury*, which Mencken edited until 1934. In 1930 he married Sara Powell Haardt, who was from Montgomery, Alabama, as was Zelda Sayre Fitzgerald.* Sara died in 1935, childless. Mencken suffered a career-ending stroke in 1948. He was savagely critical of American "booboisie" democracy—especially its blundering and corrupt leaders—America's philistine "culture," and European superciliousness especially after World War I. He encouraged forward-looking American writers, notably Sherwood Anderson,* Willa Cather, Theodore Dreiser, Sinclair Lewis, Ring Lardner,* Edmund Wilson,* and Fitzgerald. Mencken's books include studies of George Bernard Shaw (1905) and Friedrich Nietzsche (1908), two plays with Nathan (1912, 1920), and a massive linguistic study titled *The American Language* (1919, with revisions and supplements [1921–1948]). He is most famous for his caustic *Prejudices* in six "series" (1919–1927). His autobiographical volumes are *Happy Days* (1940), *Newspaper Days 1899–1906* (1941), *Heathen Days* (1943), and the posthumous *My Life as Author and Editor* (1993).

Fitzgerald first met Mencken probably in summer 1919 in Nathan's New York apartment. They met there again in 1919 and 1920. Mencken and Nathan accepted several short stories written by Fitzgerald for publication in the *Smart Set*, beginning with ''Babes in the Woods'' in 1919. After Fitzgerald married Zelda, the couple and Mencken occasionally met in New York City. Mencken reviewed *This Side of Paradise* favorably and called it an exceptional first novel. He liked *The Beautiful and Damned* less, preferring Lewis's *Babbitt* the year both novels were published. Mencken accepted ''Absolution'' for the *American Mercury* in 1924. When Mencken suggested Fitzgerald read the work of Joseph Conrad,* the result was that *The Great Gatsby* represented an advance over Fitzgerald's previous work in style and form. Mencken regarded Fitzgerald as handsome enough to be called beautiful and was intrigued by Zelda; however, he soon deemed her to be money-mad and unbalanced, Fitzgerald preoccupied with royalties, both too fond of liquor, and their lifestyle foolish and irresponsible. In 1932 Fitzgerald asked Mencken to recommend a Johns Hopkins psychiatrist for Zelda. In 1933, when the Menckens were entertained by the Fitzgeralds at their home in Baltimore, Mencken noted in his diary that the evening was weird, Zelda was irrational, and her paintings were grotesque. The Menckens refused to ride along when Fitzgerald offered to drive and were annoyed when he dropped by uninvited and drunk. Mencken thought Fitzgerald made a shambles of his life during the 1930s and pretty much gave up on him, feeling that fame, Hollywood glitter, and easy-come money had ruined Fitzgerald.

On the other hand, Fitzgerald revered Mencken. In ''Public Letter to Thomas Boyd,'' reprinted as ''The Credo of F. Scott Fitzgerald'' and ''How the Upper Class Is Being Saved by 'Men Like Mencken' '' (all 1921), Fitzgerald places Mencken ''at the head of American letters.'' In ''The Baltimore Anti-Christ'' (1921), a review of Mencken's *Prejudices, Second Series*, he says Mencken ''has done more for the national letters than any [other] man alive.'' Fitzgerald included Mencken's *The Philosophy of Friedrich Nietzsche* in his ''10 Best Books I Have Read'' (1923), praising his intelligence as ''keen, hard.'' When Mencken lauded *The Great Gatsby* only somewhat, Fitzgerald wrote ''Dear Menk'' (4 May 1925) that he would rather have his praise than that of any other American.

Bibliography: George H. Douglas, *The Smart Magazines: 50 Years of Literary Revelry and High Jinks at Vanity Fair, the New Yorker, Life, Esquire, and the Smart Set* (Hamden, Conn.: Archon, 1991); Fred Hobson, *Mencken: A Life* (New York: Random House, 1994).

MENDICANT, COUNT. In ''Love in the Night,'' he is a person said in a fictitious headline to abuse his American wife.

MERCER. In *Tender Is the Night*, he was a Yale student Dick Diver recalls in connection with Tap Day.

MERCY, CARL. In "Majesty," he is a guest from Harrisburg at the wedding ceremony called off by Emily Castleton. He is evidently Olive Mercy Blair's father.

MERCY, LIVE. In "Majesty." *See* Blair, Olive Mercy.

MEREDITH. In "The Family Bus," he is a businessman and a guest at Jannekin Melon-Loper's dinner party attended by Dick Henderson.

MEREDITH. In "The Four Fists," he is Samuel Meredith's father, in the sugar business. The business does badly at about the time Samuel graduates from college and becomes a bank runner. He gets a job with Pete Carhart, a business friend of his father's.

MEREDITH, MRS. In "The Four Fists," she is Samuel Meredith's mother, who indulged him too much in Europe when he was a child.

MEREDITH, SAMUEL. In "The Four Fists," he is a young man improved by being hit in the face four separate times. Thus Gilly Hood teaches him to quit being a snob; a laborer, to respect fatigued workers; Marjorie's husband, to ward off his interest in Marjorie; and McIntyre, to realize that Texans love their ranches. Samuel ages from fourteen to thirty-five and is married with children. In his fifties, he has a face too fragile to be "hitable."

MERIDIEN, FRANÇOIS. In *Shadow Laurels*, he is a former friend of Jean Chandelle and praises him to Jean's son, Jaques Chandelle. Meridien boasts to Jaques that he killed Lafouquet for stabbing Jean.

MERRIAM, CONSTANCE SHAW. In *The Beautiful and Damned*, she is a stately neighbor of Anthony Patch and Gloria Gilbert Patch at Marietta. She comes over to visit. Later, when he asks Gloria about Constance, Gloria says she died a year ago.

MERRIAM, ERIC. In *The Beautiful and Damned*, he is a Marietta neighbor of Anthony Patch. The two drink at a nearby club while their wives swim.

MERRIL, MIMI. In "The Offshore Pirate," she is the person to whom Ardita Farnham's attractively philandering fiancé has given a Russian bracelet. Farnham, Ardita's uncle, had a detective retrieve it for Toby Moreland to give to Ardita.

MERRITT, OGDEN. In "The Jelly-Bean," he is Nancy Lamar's escort to the country-club dance. His wealth comes from his father's safety-razor business in Savannah, Georgia. Nancy and Merritt elope.

MERRIWEATHER, ROSEMARY. In "Indecision," she is a beautiful Southern girl, eighteen, vacationing in Switzerland and alternately pursued and ignored by Tommy McLane. She is in tears on the departing train until he proposes.

MERRY, OSBORNE. In *Safety First!*, he is mentioned as a sporty prisoner.

MEYERS, GUS. In "What a Handsome Pair!," he is a wealthy man who hires Stuart Oldhorne to manage his racing stables. Stuart is annoyed that Meyers feels superior because of his money.

MICHAEL. In "One Interne," a hospital ward is named for him.

MICHAEL. In "One of My Oldest Friends," he is a successful New York businessman, thirty, and for five years Marion's husband. They have children. He learns that his old friend Charley Hart is getting married and plans with Marion to throw a party for him. When Charley begs off with a lie, circumstances require Marion to confess that Charley wanted her to leave Michael for him. Later, Charley asks Michael for money, and Michael feels merciful and saves Charley's life.

MICHAELIS, MAVRO. In *The Great Gatsby*, he is a Greek friend of George B. Wilson and offers him comfort after his wife, Myrtle Wilson, was killed. The name Michaelis may come from Joseph Conrad's *The Secret Agent*. Fitzgerald touches on Conrad's handling of Michaelis in "Sherwood Anderson on the Marriage Question," his 1923 review of *Many Marriages* by Sherwood Anderson.*

Bibliography: Andrew Crosland, "*The Great Gatsby* and *The Secret Agent*," *FH/A* 1975, 75–81.

MICHAUD. In *The Beautiful and Damned*, he is a former boyfriend of Gloria Gilbert Patch's.

MICHELLE. In *Tender Is the Night*, she is a servant of the Divers in their home at Tarmes, on the Riviera.

MIEGER. In "Two for a Cent," he is undoubtedly the citizen in the Alabama town for whom the new hospital has been named.

"MIGHTIER THAN THE SWORD" (1941). Short story. (Characters: Jack Berners, Dick Dale, Reginald de Koven, Mabel Hatman, Pat Hobby, E. Brunswick Hudson.) Pat Hobby, an unemployed Hollywood screenwriter, overhears Dick Dale, a director, telling E. Brunswick Hudson, a conceited New England author, that his material is useless. Boasting to Dale about his screen credits, Pat is hired to work on a story about Reginald de Koven, a colorless composer. For four weeks Pat listens while Dale tosses out ideas concerning De Koven's alcoholism. Dale's script girl, Mabel Hatman, writes up everything. Next day Dale, gloomy because the script has been rejected, asks Hudson for permission to use his old idea of having De Koven steal his music from a Vermont sheep-herder. Hudson proudly declines to cooperate, but Dale finds Hudson's De Koven script to be company property. When producer Jack Berners likes it, Dale promises to give Mabel a screen credit. Pat tells Hudson that Hollywood wants writers like Pat, not authors like Hudson.

MIKE. In *The Evil Eye*, he is mentioned as a clerk from Yonkers who loved Esmerelda Sage but lost her to rich Stuyvesant.

MILBANK, HAT. In ''The Woman from Twenty-one,'' he is a friend of Raymond Torrence's from their college and war days. Torrence and his wife lunch with him at the Stork Club. Torrence is disappointed when Hat is not as disgusted as Torrence is at Mrs. Richbitch's spoiling of the play they attend by her noisy whispering.

MILES, CARDINE. In ''One Trip Abroad,'' she and her husband, Liddell Miles, are traveling companions of Nelson Kelly and Nicole Kelly in Africa. The Mileses have lived in Paris for fifteen years, have traveled widely, and think they can advise young expatriates. Later the Mileses are with the Kellys at the Monte Carlo lunch marred by Nicole's argument with Nelson over his affair with Madame Noel Delauney.

MILES, LIDDELL. In ''One Trip Abroad,'' he and his wife, Cardine Miles, are experienced travelers who meet Nelson Kelly and Nicole Kelly aboard ship on the way to Gibraltar. The two couples are together in Algeria and Monte Carlo.

MILLER. In ''Outside the Cabinet-Maker's,'' he is a jeweler whose clerk walks past the man in the car with his daughter. The man puts the clerk into the fairy tale he is telling her.

MILLER, CARL. In ''Absolution,'' he is Rudolph Miller's father, a freight agent in Ludwig. He beats his son for almost drinking water before communion. He is inwardly sorry.

MILLER, GLEN (1904–1944). The leader of a popular orchestra. In *The Last Tycoon*, he performs at the screenwriters' dance held at the Ambassador Hotel in Los Angeles.

MILLER, MRS. CARL. In ''Absolution,'' she is Rudolph Miller's wrinkled, ineffectual mother.

MILLER, RUDOLPH. In ''Absolution,'' he is an eleven-year-old boy, with beautiful eyes. He lies to Father Adolphus Schwartz that he never lies, takes communion in what he fears is a state of sin, and goes to the priest again, only to hear him ramble about glittering amusement parks. Then Rudolph experiences a feeling of independence.

MINERLINO, RODERIGO. In ''Rags Martin-Jones and the Pr-nce of W-les,'' he is a movie star John B. Chestnut points out to Rags Martin-Jones in the night club.

MINGHETTI. In *Tender Is the Night*, she is one of Conte Hosain di Minghetti's sisters.

MINGHETTI, CONTE HOSAIN DI. In *Tender Is the Night*, he is the rich papal count who marries Mary North after Abe North is murdered. Hosain travels with Mary, his two sisters, and his son, Tony di Minghetti, by a previous marriage. His name is spelled Hossain in some editions.

MINGHETTI, LUCIENNE. In *Tender Is the Night*, she is Conte Hosain di Minghetti's sister and travels with the Minghetti party.

MINGHETTI, MARY NORTH, CONTESSA DI. In *Tender Is the Night*, she is Abe North's patient, sweet wife and a descendant of President John Tyler. The Norths met Dick Diver and Nicole Diver on the beach in 1925. After Abe is murdered, she marries Conte Hosain di Minghetti. She argues with Dick Diver and then snubs him. When she and Lady Caroline Sibly-Biers are arrested in Antibes for displaying lesbian tendencies, Dick and Gausse get them released. Mary is based partly on Ellis Abbott Lardner, the wife of Ring Lardner.*

MINGHETTI, TONY DI. In *Tender Is the Night*, he is the son of Conte Hosain di Minghetti. An argument between Dick Diver and Mary North, now Contessa di Minghetti, results when Lanier Diver bathes in water bathed in by Tony, who is ill.

"MINNESOTA'S CAPITAL IN THE RÔLE OF MAIN STREET" (1923). Review of *Being Respectable* by Grace Flandrau.*

MINNIE THE MOOCHER. In ''Zone of Accident,'' she is an African American girl who periodically reports to the emergency room of the Baltimore hospital for treatment after being cut.

MINSKA. In "Zone of Accident," he is the Hollywood producer who grows suspicious when Dr. William Tullivers IV makes excuses for the prolonged stay of the actress Loretta Brooke in the Baltimore hospital.

MIRLIFLORE, MME. In *The Evil Eye*, she and Harris sing about Mike, Esmerelda Sage, and Stuyvesant.

MISSELDINE. In "Oh Misseldine's, dear Misseldine's," he is the proprietor of an ice-cream parlor. In "Spring Song," Misseldine fined the poet for being too quiet.

"MR. BERLIN WROTE A SONG ABOUT FORGETTING TO REMEMBER" (1981). Poem. Recalling Irving Berlin's song about forgetting to remember, the poet wonders if he can remember to forget "her" little mannerisms.

MISTER ICKY (1920). Play. (Full title: *Mister Icky the Quintessence of Quaintness in One Act.*) (Characters: Rodney Divine, Icky, Charles Icky, Ulsa Icky, Peter.) Mr. Icky and sweet little Peter are talking on Icky's lawn in Suffolkshire. Icky says he is a hundred years old, was imprisoned at fifty in America for burglary, and had the glands of a young, vicious criminal, about to be executed, transplanted into him. Rodney Divine enters, in pursuit from London of Icky's daughter, Ulsa Icky. They want to get married. Icky queries Divine, called the Honourable. Icky's son, Charles Icky, enters and announces his plan to leave this dreary place and go to sea. Dozens more of Icky's children troop in and say they are also leaving. When most depart, Icky is surrounded by moths until Peter puts a mothball on him. Odd stage directions and mangled discussion of literature add to the play's alleged humor.

MISTINGUETT, JEANNE-MARIE FLORENTINE BOURGEOIS (1875–1956). Fabulous, bizarre French-Belgian music-hall star and movie actress. In *Tender Is the Night*, it is said that Mistinguet[t] visited the Riviera in 1925. She bought a villa in Antibes and a club in Juan-les-Pins in 1932 and visited Hollywood in 1937.

Bibliography: David Bret, *The Mistinguett Legend* (London: Robson, 1990).

MITCHELL, ELENOR. In *Thoughtbook*, she is a playful friend.

MITCHELL, JACK. In *Thoughtbook*, he is a neighbor of Violet Stockton, whom he teases.

MOLLAT. In "A Short Autobiography," he is the proprietor of a place where Fitzgerald drank in 1920.

"MOMISHNESS" (1981). Poem. Why does Andrew Turnbull* use the word "dumb" so often when he really has an extensive vocabulary?

MOMUS, GENEVEVA DE. In *Tender Is the Night*, hers is a name read in the *New York Herald*.

MONCRIEF, GENERAL. In "The Curious Case of Benjamin Button," he is Hildegarde's father, objects to her marrying Benjamin, but is mollified when Benjamin finances the publication of his massive history of the Civil War.

MONROE. In "Myra Meets His Family," he is supposedly a servant whom Knowleton Whitney's supposed father says he ordered to gather neighbors for an informal show in the Whitney mansion.

MONTE. In "Rags Martin-Jones and the Pr-nce of W-les," he is a friend of John B. Chestnut, who in the ruse warns Chestnut that the authorities are after him.

MOODY. In "Two for a Cent," he was the owner of a "soda place" in the small Alabama town. He is mentioned by Henry W. Hemmick while reminiscing with Abercrombie.

MOON, CHARLIE. In "Head and Shoulders," he is a cousin of Horace Tarbox and is responsible for Horace's meeting Marcia Meadow, who becomes Horace's wife.

MOON, DR. In "The Adjuster," he is the shadowy general practitioner Charles Hemple brings home to offer his wife, Luella Hemple, advice. For five years, he is her often unwelcome counselor. At the end he says she cannot leave her mistakes behind by running away. Once she begins to understand, he leaves her, defining himself simply as five years.

MOON, MISS. In "The Rubber Check," she works in Percy Wrackham's office. After Val Schuyler has been snubbed at dances, she no longer reads about him in the society columns.

MOORE, ALBERT. In "That Kind of Party," he is the bespectacled boy whose nose Terrence R. Tipton bloodies in a fight.

MOORE, CARPENTER. In "That Kind of Party," he is Albert Moore's older brother, who has been confined to a wheelchair for five years. Terrence R. Tipton so irritates him at the Shoonover party that he jumps at him and thus can walk again.

MOORE, CHARLEY. In "Dalyrimple Goes Wrong," he is one of Theron G. Macy's stockroom employees. Charley, twenty-six, complains about the work to Bryan Dalyrimple, boasts of doing better soon, but has been with Macy four years and is a loser, as Dalyrimple rightly concludes.

MOORE, DR. In "Zone of Accident," he is the intern at the Baltimore hospital who sutures Loretta Brooke's back wound.

MOORE, KATHLEEN. In *The Last Tycoon*, she is the young Irish-born woman, twenty-five, who lived in London, was the mistress of an unidentified king, and is now an unnamed American's fiancée. She comes to Hollywood, visits Monroe Stahr's studio, and would marry him but for his reticence. After a brief affair with him, she wires to tell him she has just gotten married. She is partly based on Sheilah Graham.*

MOORE, MRS. In "That Kind of Party," she is Albert Moore's and Carpenter Moore's mother and Terrence R. Tipton's mother's best friend.

MORAN, LOIS (1908–1990). Actress. Born in Pittsburgh, she lived as a child with her widowed mother in Paris. She became a ballerina with the Paris Opera Corps de Ballet, appeared in a French movie, and moved with her mother to Hollywood. She was startling as Laurel, the daughter of Ronald Colman,* in *Stella Dallas*, 1925. Never central in any of her twenty-four subsequent movies, she moved to New York and appeared in several Broadway musicals, including George S. Kaufman's 1931 *Of Thee I Sing* and, with John Gilbert,* *West of Broadway*, 1932. Retiring in 1935, she married Clarence M. Young, later assistant secretary of commerce and a vice president of Pan American Airlines. The couple had a son. She costarred with Preston Foster in the television series *Waterfront*, 1953–1956. She made her last home in Sedona, Arizona. In January 1927 Fitzgerald met and fell in love with Moran in Hollywood. Although she perhaps never loved him in return, she did want him to star in her next picture, but he failed the screen test. Moran caused violent arguments between Fitzgerald and Zelda Sayre Fitzgerald.* Fitzgerald used her as the model of Helen Avery in "Magnetism," Jenny Prince in "Jacob's Ladder," and Rosemary Hoyt in *Tender Is the Night*.

MORELAND, COLONEL. In "The Offshore Pirate," he is Toby Moreland's father. Toby, his father, and Farnham, the colonel's close friend and Ardita Farnham's uncle, concoct the ruse resulting in Toby's impressing and persuading the girl to marry him.

MORELAND, TOBY. In "The Offshore Pirate," he is the handsome, dashing man, twenty-seven, who pretends to be Curtis Carlyle. As such, he and six African American musician cronies board the *Narcissus*, the yacht on which

Ardita Farnham is lolling alone, rename it the *Hula Hula*, and spirit her away to a Caribbean islet. He intrigues her with a fictitious story of his musical, military, and criminal background. When she agrees to marry him, he allows the ruse to terminate. She will still marry him.

"MORE THAN JUST A HOUSE" (1933). Short story. (Characters: Mark H. Bourne, Gunther, Amanda Gunther, Bess Gunther, Jean Gunther, Mrs. Gunther, George Horton, Lew Lowrie, Allen Parks, William.) In 1925, having rescued Amanda, twenty, and her younger sister, Jean Gunther, from an oncoming train, Lew Lowrie, twenty-six and rising in the Baltimore business world, is asked by the girls' grateful parents to visit the family's ramshackle mansion. Doing so shyly, he is told by Bess, the youngest sister, sixteen and with braces on her teeth, that she will be the Cinderella of the trio. He attends a dance there and falls in love with Amanda, who explains that she is going to marry George Horton in order to leave this house in the sticks for New York. In 1929, doing well in business in New York, Lew encounters Jean, learns her mother has died and Amanda has had some babies, dates Jean a few times, visits the old house, kisses her, and learns her senile father is cared for by Bess. During an electric storm, someone phones to say Amanda has died in childbirth. In 1933, on a business trip to Baltimore, Lew drives toward the house, intending to visit. But Bess, outside and on horseback, tells him her father has died, she is soon to wed, and her wedding-party visitors are at the house. Lew drives sadly away, buys cigarettes at a country store, and learns there that Bess, never engaged at all, is alone in the house, now stripped by creditors. Lew returns, and they plan to get married and do something with the house.

MORGAN. In "The Cruise of the Rolling Junk," he is a witness with his friend Violet when the Junk's wheel rolls loose down a Baltimore street.

MORGAN. In *The Last Tycoon*, he is the actor whose open fly in a movie-shooting scene two tourists reported seeing. Monroe Stahr orders the film reviewed carefully.

MORGAN, HOLLY. In "Presumption," she is a friend of Noel Garneau at Culpepper Bay. Noel invites her, Billy Harper, and San Juan Chandler to a dinner party. Juan plays up to Holly, causing Noel to snub Juan later at the beach near the Morgan home.

MORGAN, JOE. In "What a Handsome Pair!," he is Stuart Oldhorne's polo-playing friend who wants Celie to ride sidesaddle while playing polo. Profeminist Helen Van Beck Oldhorne is disgusted at the idea.

MORRIS. In *Tender Is the Night*, he and his wife are Australians. When they learn Dick Diver is treating their son, Von Cohn Morris, for alcoholism but drinks himself, they withdraw the lad from the clinic.

MORRIS, MRS. In *Tender Is the Night*, she agrees with her husband and removes their son, Von Cohn Morris, from Dick Diver's care.

MORRIS, VON COHN. In *Tender Is the Night*, he is a patient from Australia being treated by Dick Diver for alcoholism until his parents learn Dick also drinks heavily.

MORRISON, HEP J. In ''Strange Sanctuary,'' he is a rival thief whose presence at Angela Duckney's party causes Dodo Gilbert to leave.

MORTMAIN. In ''The Rubber Check,'' he or she is one of Ellen Mortmain's twin siblings.

MORTMAIN, ELLEN. In ''The Rubber Check,'' she is the beautiful daughter, eighteen, of seemingly wealthy Mrs. Mortmain. They live in a lavish mansion outside New York City. Ellen adores Val Schuyler at first, plans to elope with him, but when he stands her up begins a residence in London with her family. When twenty-two, she returns to Long Island and invites him to a party, only to stand him up cruelly. When twenty-six, Val visits her in London and learns her family is bankrupt and she plans to marry a British army man and move to India.

MORTMAIN, MRS. In ''The Rubber Check,'' she is Ellen Mortmain's seemingly wealthy mother in New York. She admires Val Schuyler because of his courtesy. She and her family move to London, where they become bankrupt.

MORTON, JUNIE. In ''The Ice Palace,'' he was a member of Harry Bellamy's Yale class, the captain of the hockey team, and a dinner guest at the Bellamys' home when Sally Carrol Happer visits.

MOSE, TROMBONE. In ''The Offshore Pirate,'' he is an African American member of Curtis Carlyle's band which entertains Ardita Farnham. Mose is assigned the task of painting out the name of the *Narcissus*, the yacht Curtis has ''captured.'' Mose's doing so may be Fitzgerald's supposedly humorous and very indirect allusion to *The Nigger of the ''Narcissus''* by Joseph Conrad,* one of his favorite authors.

MOSES. In ''The Dance,'' he is a black servant at the country club in the little Southern town of Davis. When Marie Bannerman is murdered during a country-club dance, the white guests want all black employees at the club grilled, even old Moses.

MOSKIN. In "A Patriotic Short." *See* Maranda.

"THE MOST DISGRACEFUL THING I EVER DID: 2. THE INVASION OF THE SANCTUARY" (1923). Essay. One Christmas Eve Fitzgerald entered a fashionable church (in St. Paul) in noisy overshoes, walked in front of the rector, told him to go right on with the sermon, then walked out.

"MOTHER TAUGHT ME TO—LOVE THINGS" (1981). Poem. Whereas the poet's mother wanted him to love, his addressee suggests hate and doubt.

MOVIE WORK BY FITZGERALD. Fitzgerald enjoyed going to the movies, has many fictional characters attend movies and other shows, advances his plots by cinematic descriptions and dialogue, often wrote between 1923 and 1940 in and out of Hollywood for movie producers, and died in Hollywood. He wrote dialogue titles for a silent movie adapted from *Glimpses of the Moon* by Edith Wharton*; it was released by Famous Players (later Paramount, 1923). In 1924 he wrote a screenplay about a dead gangster's son who aids authorities and wins the girl. Fitzgerald's work was augmented by another writer, and the movie became *Grit* (Film Guild, 1924). In 1927 United Artists hired Fitzgerald to go to Hollywood and write the scenario for a movie to star Constance Talmadge* and to be called *Lipstick*. Fitzgerald, suffering from conceit, worked carelessly and when the producer read his writing he cancelled the project. In November–December 1931 Irving Thalberg,* head of MGM, engaged Fitzgerald to revamp the script for *Red-Headed Woman*, forced him to work with a has-been writer named Marcel de Sano, and tactfully rejected Fitzgerald's part before completing the movie. Returning to Hollywood, in July 1937 Fitzgerald touched up the script for MGM's *A Yank at Oxford*, which was produced without giving Fitzgerald screen credit. Fitzgerald toiled from August 1937 to February 1938 on *Three Comrades*, an adaptation of Erich Maria Remarque's novel. Fitzgerald reluctantly worked with coauthor Edward E. "Ted" Paramore,* whom he had satirized as Frederick E. Paramore in *The Beautiful and Damned*, and with producer Joseph L. Mankiewicz, with whom he disagreed on professional matters—sometimes successfully. The only screen credit he ever received for his work was on *Three Comrades*. He worked February to May 1938 for MGM on *Infidelity*, based on Ursula Parrott's short story; the censors applied the Motion Picture Code to his adaptation, and the movie was never made. He worked on MGM's *Marie Antoinette* in May 1938 and on *Madame Curie*—partly with Aldous Huxley*—from November 1938 to January 1939. With Donald Ogden Stewart,* May to October 1938, Fitzgerald cowrote *The Women*, MGM's successful movie based on Clare Booth Luce's Broadway hit. In January 1939 David Selznick assigned Fitzgerald to suggest changes in the script of *Gone* *with the Wind* and to rewrite and shorten parts of it. Selznick commended Fitzgerald to his face but fired him behind his back later the same day. George Cukor, who directed *The Women* and part of *Gone with the Wind*, had admired Fitzgerald ever since Cukor's successful direction of the 1926 Broadway version of *The Great Gatsby* written by Owen Davis. Walter Wanger, producer of *Winter Carnival*, hired Fitzgerald in February 1939 to start a story line at Dartmouth College, scene of the annual carnival, with the aid of Budd Schulberg*; Fitzgerald, however, got so drunk Wanger fired him. In September 1939 Fitzgerald was hired to touch up the script of *Raffles* (Goldwyn, 1939); he did so, effectively, and the movie, starring David Niven, was a success. Independent producer Lester Cowan employed Fitzgerald March to August 1940 to turn ''Babylon Revisited'' into a movie script, which was never used. Fitzgerald was hired in October 1940 to adapt Emlyn Williams's play *The Light of Heart* for a movie, but his writing was rejected. By the time the play was made into the movie *Life Begins at 8:30* (1942), Fitzgerald was dead.

Bibliography: Tom Dardis, *Some Time in the Sun* (New York: Scribner, 1976); Wheeler Winston Dixon, *The Cinematic Vision of F. Scott Fitzgerald* (Ann Arbor: UMI Research Press, 1986); Patrick McGilligan, *George Cukor, a Double Life: A Biography of the Gentleman Director* (New York: St. Martin's Press, 1991); *Memo from David O. Selznick*, selected and ed. by Rudy Behlmer (New York: Viking, 1972); Latham; David Niven, *Bring on the Empty Horses* (New York: Putnam, 1976); Budd Schulberg, *The Disenchanted* (New York: Random House, 1950); David Thomson, *Showman: The Life of David O. Selznick* (New York: Knopf, 1992).

MRIDLE. In ''Reade, Substitute Right Half,'' he is the quarterback on the Warrentown football team.

MUCHHAUSE. In *Tender Is the Night*, he is a teller in Dick Diver's bank in Paris. Dick avoids him because he always asks whether Dick wishes to draw money from his wife Nicole Diver's account or from his own.

MUDGE, ARCHIE. In *Thoughtbook*, he is a playful friend.

MUDGE, BETTY. In *Thoughtbook*, she is a playful friend.

MULDOON. In *The Great Gatsby*, he strangled his wife and is the brother of G. Earl Muldoon.

MULDOON, ED. In ''A Short Autobiography,'' he was a frequenter of Tate's place in Seattle in 1915.

MULDOON, G. EARL. In *The Great Gatsby*, Nick Carraway lists his name on a timetable as one of Jay Gatsby's summer guests. He is from West Egg.

MULDOON, RASTUS. In ''Dice, Brassknuckles & Guitar,'' he is a musician from Savannah, Georgia, whom James Powell admires and whose band plays at the party held by Harlan, in Southampton, for a group of young people.

MULKLEY, OATES. In ''The Honor of the Goon,'' he is the college roommate of Bomar Winlock. To avenge their calling Ella Lei Chamoro a goon, her relative Lei Chamoro has Fingarson, his chauffeur, knock them down.

MULLER. In ''Between Three and Four,'' he is the person Howard Butler hired instead of hiring Sarah Belknap Summer. Butler released Muller later.

MULLIGAN. In *Assorted Spirits*, he is a policeman, called with O'Flarity to investigate the disappearance of Josephus Hendrix's $10,000. They do nothing.

MULLIGAN. In ''The Captured Shadow,'' he is a policeman in Basil Duke Lee's play *The Captured Shadow*.

MULLINS. In ''The Bowl,'' he was a prep-school football player with Jeff Deering.

MULREADY. In *The Great Gatsby*, his name is listed by Nick Carraway on a timetable as one of Jay Gatsby's summer guests. He is from West Egg.

MUMBLE, MR. In *The Great Gatsby*, this is the name Nick Carraway assigns to any of the three men escorting two noisy girls to one of Jay Gatsby's parties.

MUNN, MARTIN. In ''Emotional Bankruptcy,'' he is a Princeton student who is Lillian Hammel's prom date. Josephine Perry excites him to no avail.

MURDOCK, EVELYN. In ''Flight and Pursuit,'' she is a friend from the South who invites Caroline Martin Corcoran to a Long Island dinner party, where a fellow guest is Sidney Lahaye.

MURPHY. In ''Outside the Cabinet-Maker's,'' he or, more likely, she is a person mentioned by the man in telling his wife to order a sizable doll house. Fitzgerald is alluding to Honoria Murphy, the daughter of Gerald Murphy* and Sara Murphy,* with whom Fitzgerald, Zelda Sayre Fitzgerald,* and their daughter, Scottie,* associated on the Riviera in 1924 and later elsewhere. In her biography of her parents, Honoria describes a game with toy soldiers that Fitzgerald played with her and his daughter; the plot of the game somewhat parallels that of the fairy tale the man in ''Outside the Cabinet-Maker's'' tells his daughter.

Bibliography: Honoria Murphy Donnelly with Richard N. Billings, *Sara & Gerald: Villa America and After* (New York: New York Times Books, 1982).

MURPHY, GERALD (1888–1964). (Full name: Gerald Clery Murphy.) He was a businessman, painter, and art patron. He was born in Boston, the son of the owner of the Mark Cross Company, a leather-goods and import store. He graduated from Yale in 1912 and worked for five years in the family business. In 1915 he married Sara Sherman Wiborg, who was the daughter of an ink manufacturer in Cincinnati and who had traveled extensively in Europe. After training as a U.S. Army pilot (1918), Murphy studied landscape architecture at Harvard (1918–1920). In 1921 he, Sara, and their three children, with considerable Murphy and Wiborg family money, went briefly to England, where Murphy studied formal gardens, and then to France. Modern painting in Paris inspired him to become a painter. He and Sara painted sets for a Russian ballet by Serge Diaghilev. In 1923 Murphy and composer-lyricist Cole Porter collaborated on a ballet titled *Within the Quota*, successfully performed in Paris and on tour in the United States; Murphy's backdrops were sensational. In 1923 the Murphys bought and renovated a villa at Cap d'Antibes, on the French Riviera. They called it Villa America and entertained there extravagantly. In 1924 the Salon des Indépendants in Paris exhibited four of Murphy's paintings. The most famous was *Razor* (1923), an early example of pop art. The Murphys lived in Beverly Hills, California (1928–1929), where Murphy worked as a Hollywood consultant. His knowledge of spirituals enabled him to advise director King Vidor* in his production of the all-black *Hallelujah.* Fitzgerald had introduced Vidor to Murphy in 1928. Until 1929 Murphy continued to exhibit and brought his total number of paintings to nine. Critics praised them for the precision of their attractive combination of the abstract, the realistic, and the huge. In 1929 the Murphy's younger son contracted tuberculosis, and Murphy discontinued his painting to nurse him. During the Depression the Cross Company nearly went bankrupt, and in 1934 Murphy returned to the United States from France and rescued it. In 1935 their younger son died, and two years later their older son died of spinal meningitis. Thereafter the Murphys lived mostly in New York City (1939–1949). Murphy continued with the family company, by the 1950s a complete success again, until his retirement in 1956. Some of his paintings were included in the 1960 exhibition at the Dallas Museum for Contemporary Arts. A decade after his death in East Hampton, New York, the Museum of Modern Art in New York City mounted a one-man show, displaying his six surviving works. By then, critics were defining Murphy as an original 1920s artist. Sara Murphy lived in New York City until shortly before her death in McLean, Virginia.

The Murphys were highly respected by Americans visiting or living aboard, including Robert Benchley, Philip Barry, John Dos Passos,* Ernest Hemingway,* Lillian Hellman, Archibald MacLeish, Dorothy Parker,* Gilbert Seldes,* Donald Ogden Stewart,* and especially the Fitzgeralds, who first met them in

1924. A game the Murphy children played with Fitzgerald's daughter Scottie* is reflected in ''Outside the Cabinet-Maker's.'' In ''A Short Autobiography,'' Fitzgerald praises the Murphys' home in France in 1926 as perfect. Fitzgerald named the hero's daughter in ''Babylon Revisited'' Honoria after the Murphys' daughter. He dedicated *Tender Is the Night* to the Murphys. Several features of Dick Diver and Nicole Warren Diver reflect Fitzgerald's observation of Gerald and Sara Murphy; she resented his exploiting them thus. The Murphys deplored his egotism and rude behavior, especially when he was drunk, but remained his most steadfast friends.

Bibliography: Honoria Murphy Donnelly with Richard N. Billings, *Sara & Gerald: Villa America and After* (New York: New York Times Books, 1982); Linda Paterson Miller, '' 'As a Friend You Have Never Failed Me': The Fitzgerald-Murphy Correspondence,'' *Journal of Modern Literature* 5 (September 1976): 357–82; Calvin Tomkins, *Living Well Is the Best Revenge* (New York: Viking, 1962).

MURPHY, SARA (1883–1975). (Full name: Sara Sherman Wiborg Murphy.) She was the wife of Gerald Murphy.*

MYER, LESTER. In *The Great Gatsby*, Nick Carraway lists his name on a timetable as one of Jay Gatsby's summer guests. He is in theater work.

MYERS, CARMEL (1899–1980). Actress. Born in San Francisco, she had a bit part in D. W. Griffith's movie *Intolerance* (1916), played opposite Douglas Fairbanks,* among other actors, had a minor role in the 1926 *Ben-Hur*, and retired from the screen in the mid-1930s. When she married Ralph Blum she became Carmel Myers Blum. In ''Orange pajamas and heaven's guitars,'' she is the real-life movie actress mentioned only as Carmel.

"MY FIRST LOVE" (1919). Poem. The light she wove about him was like the lambent air above pearlfishers' seas. When they kissed, she was young but old. He saw changing colors only after she left him.

"MY GENERATION" (1968). Essay. The post–American Revolution generation seemed insignificant to the world but included explorers, hard-boiled politicians, a few fine writers, and some legends. After the Spanish-American War, the United States reluctantly gained considerable global grandeur. Fitzgerald's generation was born into cocky patriotism and power, but it faded between 1910 and 1920. World War I did not destroy his generation, which inherited a combination of hope and disillusion. His generation was wrongly accused of inventing illegal liquor and heavy petting. He lists accomplished musicians, writers, critics, movie producers, sports figures, and Princetonians of his era. This rambling essay was Fitzgerald's angry reply to ''A Short Retort,'' an essay by his daughter Scottie* (*Mademoiselle*, July 1939) that he interpreted as critical of his lack of responsibility.

"MY LOST CITY" (1945). Essay. Fitzgerald relates three symbols to New York City: a ferry boat (for triumph), actresses (romance), and Bunny [Edmund Wilson*] (city spirit). He recalls seeing New York as a dissipating undergraduate with a Midwestern girlfriend (since lost to him), visiting Bunny's culture-rich Manhattan apartment, working sorrowfully for a New York advertising firm in 1919, having a drab Bronx apartment, drinking in town too much with the "younger generation," and being involved in antics. After his baby was born in St. Paul, he and his family moved to Long Island; Fitzgerald wrote a play after his first books proved popular, but it failed in Atlantic City in 1923. Three years later, they found New York noisy, wealthy, and hysterical. Hangovers were as standard as siestas in Spain. They lived in Delaware, and he was part of "the literary racket." By 1929 New York was full of speakeasies, circuses, and easy money. They heard of the Crash while in North Africa. Two years later they returned to discover from the top of the Empire State Building that the canyoned city had geographical limits, endless greens, and blues beyond. Fitzgerald imagines that in 1945 he might be shot in New York for feathering too many love nests. As for now, his "mirage" is lost.

"MY MIND IS ALL A-TUMBLE" (1981). Poem. Since his mind is tumbling and his pen is stumbling, the poet will sign off humbly.

"MY OLD NEW ENGLAND HOMESTEAD ON THE ERIE" (1925). Short story. (Character: Jack.) The narrator, Jack, is persuaded by his wife to buy a rundown Colonial house they have dreamed about. Its shrewd New England owner releases it for 75¢ and some minor items. The couple happily de-renovate the house by replacing its modern interior and exterior, and even its subsoil, with anything and everything available that is old and moldy. They even replace the road in front with cobblestones that distress passing motorists and sell an eight-pound gong to neighbors willing to bribe their new antique-seeking neighbors for peace and quiet. This foolish piece is obviously a parody.

"MYRA MEETS HIS FAMILY" (1920). Short story. (Characters: Warren Appleton, Billy, Arthur Elkins, Lilah Elkins, Graham, Walter Gregory, Myra Harper, Lady Helena Something-or-Other, Kelly, Monroe, Knowleton Whitney, Ludlow Whitney, Mrs. Ludlow Whitney.) Myra Harper of Cleveland went to a Connecticut prep school, became a prom trotter, might have married well, but is now twenty-one and single in New York. She admits to her old roommate, Lilah Elkins, now married, that she is husband-hunting and handsome Knowleton Whitney might do. He invites her for a week to his Westchester County family mansion to meet his rich parents. When she arrives, Knowleton introduces his father, Ludlow Whitney of Wall Street, a yellow-complexioned fellow who seems vaguely familiar to her, and to his mother, a fat, low-voiced creature surrounded by poodles. That night Myra hears an infant crying in a bedroom nearby. Next evening Ludlow invites neighbors in for an amateur show and drags Myra forward to sing—which she does bravely. In a back room, Knowleton shows her several ancestors' portraits, one being of a Chinese woman, who, Knowleton explains, is his great-grandmother, whom his tea-importing great-grandfather met in Hong Kong. Myra faints, comes to at two in the morning in her bedroom, and imagines the crying child is Chinese by some family genetic reversion. She seeks Knowleton's room but on the way hears conspiratorial voices: Knowleton's "parents" are in reality actors, the dogs and the portraits are all rented, and the entire sham has been designed to discourage Myra, an obvious fortune hunter. After crying, then recovering at dawn, Myra finds Knowleton in the garden; when he starts to explain, she says she recognized his "father" as an actor she once saw. Shamed, Knowleton says his real mother wanted a titled daughter-in-law, apologizes, and vows he truly loves Myra. She says they can be married that very day by her minister cousin, Walter Gregory, whom she phones in town. After a stop at city hall and at a jewelry shop, they are pronounced husband and wife by Walter. Knowleton wires his real father the news at the railroad station. Interrupting a planned honeymoon in Chicago, Myra tells Knowleton she must pop out to telephone Walter to send on a bag she forgot and will be back in a moment. Instead, she remains in the station as the train pulls out and confers with Walter, who is not a minister at all. As for the rings, they will be her souvenirs. For $1,000 Fitzgerald sold the film rights to "Myra Meets His Family," which Fox made into *The Husband Hunter*, 1920.

"THE MYSTERY OF THE RAYMOND MORTGAGE" (1909). Short story. (Characters: Egan, Gregson, James, Raymond, Agnes Raymond, Mrs. Raymond, Smidy, John Standish, John Syrel.) In his home in Santuka Lake, near the New York City suburb of Santuka, Raymond finds his daughter, Agnes Raymond, and John Standish, a family servant, shot dead and his wife, Mrs. Raymond, and a mortgage missing. Egan, the local chief of police, and a detective named Gregson fail to solve the mystery. John Syrel, a New York reporter, analyzes the evidence, including bullets and footprints, and takes Egan by train to nearby Indianous, where he locates a young man who loved Agnes and explains everything. When Agnes repulsed Standish, he shot her; her mother then shot him and escaped. After showing Egan the body of Mrs. Raymond, who poisoned herself, the young man disappears. "The Mystery of the Raymond Mortgage" is perhaps a spoof: the mortgage is missing and remains so. Syrel is allowed to see Agnes's body, retains possession of one bullet, and must advise Egan to arm himself before they go to Indianous.

"MY TEN FAVORITE PLAYS" (1934). In a humorous letter to the *New York Sun*, 10 September 1934, Fitzgerald lists memorable performances by Charlie

Chaplin, George M. Cohan, Joan Crawford, Greta Garbo, and other performers less well known, and even himself at age nine in a magic show.

"MY VERY VERY DEAR MARIE" (1981). Poem. The poet laments that not even Lent will make the debonair Marie repent.

N

NANA. In ''The Curious Case of Benjamin Button,'' she is Benjamin's considerate nurse toward the end of his life.

NARRY. In ''The Debutante,'' she is the loyal servant of the Halycon family. Shc sews for Helen Halycon on the night of the girl's coming-out party.

NASH, NORMA. In ''A Freeze-Out,'' she is a person Alida Rikker invited to a party, although Alida had been snubbed earlier.

NATHAN, GEORGE JEAN (1882–1958). American drama critic and editor. He was born in Fort Wayne, Indiana. His father's wealth enabled him to have a fine education, including tutors, theater-going, and study abroad. He graduated from Cornell in 1904 and became a reporter for the *New York Herald* in 1905. In 1908 the owners of *Smart Set: A Magazine of Cleverness* hired Nathan as drama editor and H. L. Mencken* as literary editor. The two wrote iconoclastic columns under the pseudonym Owen Hatteras. They resigned in 1923 when Eltinge F. Warner, managing editor, forced them to withdraw their sarcastic essay on President Warren G. Harding's funeral. They cofounded the *American Mercury* in 1924, with the backing of publisher Alfred A. Knopf; Nathan coedited it until 1930, then was a contributor. In 1932 he cofounded the *American Spectator* with Ernest Boyd, James Branch Cabell, Theodore Dreiser, and Eugene O'Neill. Nathan was also associated with other periodicals and syndicated a King Features column from 1943 to 1956. He helped publicize innovative playwrights such as Sean O'Casey and Eugene O'Neill. From its inception in 1935 Nathan was a member of the Drama Critics Circle, its president from 1937 to 1939. Reviewing some six thousand plays, he was a powerful literary arbiter. He developed the pose of sophisticated, eclectic cynic. His book publications include *The Autobiography of an Attitude* (1925), *The Intimate Notebooks of*

George Jean Nathan (1932), *Encyclopedia of the Theatre* (1940), and *Theatre Book of the Year* (1943–1951). He was friendly with actress Lillian Gish, who declined his proposal of marriage and wrote that marrying him would have ruined his life. He married actress Julie Haydon in 1955. He was given the last rites of the Catholic church the day before he died.

In 1919 Edmund Wilson* introduced Fitzgerald to Nathan, who published his ''Babes in the Woods'' in *Smart Set*; it was followed there by other Fitzgerald items. Ladies' man Nathan flirted with the very willing Zelda Sayre Fitzgerald* until Fitzgerald made them stop. Fitzgerald dedicated *The Beautiful and Damned* to Nathan, and to Shane Leslie* and Max Perkins* as well. Nathan circulated the silly gossip that Tana, the Fitzgeralds' Japanese servant, was a German spy named Tannenbaum. Tana appears in *The Beautiful and Damned* and Zelda's *Save Me the Waltz*. Nathan's *American Mercury* published Fitzgerald's ''Absolution'' in 1924. To Mencken (c. 6 August 1935), Fitzgerald wrote lamenting the absence of recent communication between himself and Nathan.

Bibliography: Constance Frick, *The Dramatic Criticism of George Jean Nathan* (Port Washington, N.Y.: Kennikat Press, 1943).

NECRAWNEY. In ''Family in the Wind,'' he is a neighbor of the Janneys whose house is destroyed by the first tornado.

NED. In ''The Broadcast We Almost Heard Last September,'' he is a radio announcer. He interviews a wounded soldier who can manage only a goodbye to his mother.

NEGROTTO, CLAUDE. In ''The Honor of the Goon,'' he is one of the students who called Ella Lei Chamoro a goon.

NELL. In ''The Night of Chancellorsville,'' she is the friend of Nora, the narrator. Both are aboard the train to Chancellorsville.

NELLIE. In *Tender Is the Night*, she is any child watched over on the beach by nannies whose conduct Nicole Diver disapproves of.

"A NEW LEAF" (1931). Short story. (Characters: Carter, Esther Cary, Phil Hoffman, Kitty, Dick Ragland, Julia Ross.) Phil Hoffman, an American lawyer, has followed vacationing Julia Ross to Paris. He loves her but is not encouraged. About to return home, he introduces her to handsome, smooth Dick Ragland—reluctantly, because Dick is an alcoholic. Dick is contrite and tells Julia he plans to swear off liquor on 5 June, aboard the same ship that by coincidence will carry her to New York. Once there, however, he turns up drunk at the home of her aunt, where she is staying. He says he is working steadily for his uncle, she forgives him, and they become engaged. She introduces him to Esther Cary, a schoolmate who has gossiped about him, for her to see he has reformed. Julia cuts short a visit to her family in California because Dick's letters betray loneliness and depression. Together again, they grow impatient for their wedding date to arrive. Phil, now an assistant district attorney, warns Julia about Dick. Remaining loyal, she is surprised when Dick visits her three days later and tells her Phil ordered him to reveal something—or he would—which is that Dick was so lonely when Julia was in California that he sought brief comfort with Esther. When Julia demands a separation, Dick says he will do some business in London for his uncle, and she sees him off at the pier. Days later Phil, concealing newspaper coverage of the event, informs Julia that Dick disappeared at sea. A year later, before they marry, he continues to let Julia think the best of Dick, who, Phil knows, had returned to drinking for months before his final voyage.

"NEWS OF PARIS—FIFTEEN YEARS AGO" (1947). Short story. (Characters: Henry Haven Dell, Hélène, Ruth, Mary Tolliver, Bessie Leighton Wing, Hershell Wing.) Henry Haven Dell, former art editor of the *Harvard Lampoon*, is in Paris in April (c. 1923). He and Ruth decide to enter a certain church separately. They attend a wedding, after which the bride reminds Henry she almost married him. Planning to lunch with Ruth at the Café Dauphine, he chances to share a taxi with a woman he recognizes as Bessie Leighton Wing, who tells him she is breaking her engagement at the same cafe this noon. They agree to rendezvous if she signals him by wiggling a spoon. Henry meets Ruth and tells her he is leaving Paris at once. He and Bessie, now free, taxi to her apartment. Phoning, he learns he need not hurry to his boat train since his ship has been delayed; they go with rich Mary Tolliver, her friend, to an art show. Bidding them goodbye, Henry taxis to the Left Bank to check on an orphan, Hélène, whose postwar convent education he has supported for three years. He is discomfited to find her drinking beer with two Americans. This story was left in fragmentary form at Fitzgerald's death.

"NEW TYPES" (1934). Short story. (Characters: Clothilde, Leslie Dixon, Haggin, Mrs. Haggin, Ellen Harris, Emily Holliday, Paula Jorgensen, Lord Eric Tressiger.) After some years in China, Leslie Dixon returns to New York. On a Long Island beach with his cousin Ellen Harris, he is introduced to a beautiful model, Paula Jorgensen. She invites him to a dance which Emily Holliday, her aunt, is giving for her. Dixon hears her making a deal about money with a gross little man on the beach. After a boxing match they attend on the day of the party, she tells him that her father, Emily's brother, died leaving little to a widow and five children, and that her aunt could have helped financially but remained critical of her family to everyone who would listen. Emily even bullies Paula this afternoon. Before the dance begins Paula goes to Emily's room but finds her lifeless. She vents her grief at the unmoving woman, decides she must go on with the party, locks her aunt's room, hides the key, and tells the guests the hostess is indisposed. Paula is secretly paid $500 for being photographed in several poses. Dixon, fascinated but unable to categorize this new type of American girl, draws her into a lovely, dark embrace, exchanges words of love with her—she says she would like to trust him—and stays until the other guests have left. She calls him into her aunt's room. He pronounces her dead and is aghast that Paula would go on with the party. Before she can explain, the aunt wakes up and, though puzzled, accepts Paula's explanation she slept through the party. Dixon summons a physician for her, and he and Paula go to Manhattan together. On the way, she stops for medicine, needed, she explains, for her husband, Lord Eric Tressiger, who was shot in the war, worked as a New York banker, and now is alcoholic, paralyzed, and near death. The extra money is to pay for dangerous surgery for him. Dixon, faithful at the hospital, is there when Eric, who rallied after the operation, dies. When Paula tells Dixon she can go home now, he says he is her home. She agrees.

"A NICE QUIET PLACE" (1930). Short story. (Characters: Ed Bement, Dick, Charles Dorrance, Sonny Dorrance, Gladys, Lillian Hammel, Malcolm Libby, Constance Perry, Herbert T. Perry, Josephine Perry, Mrs. Herbert T. Perry, Ridgeway Saunders, Evangeline Ticknor.) Josephine, sixteen, dislikes her mother's plans to go north with her away from Lake Forest, near Chicago, for a nice quiet summer at Aunt Gladys's place at Island Farms, Michigan. Through June and July, Josephine, wanting to love and be loved, is bored, writes letters, and hassles Dick, her cousin, fifteen. She is distressed on learning Ridgeway Saunders, her boyfriend at Yale, is coming to Lake Forest with Evangeline Ticknor, a "speedy" Philadelphia girl. Josephine sees a neighbor youth, Sonny Dorrance, so handsome that she arranges to bump into him on a pathway. Challenged by his aloofness, she pursues him until he tells her he is married to a "colored" woman. Allowed to return home to Lake Forest to shop for her older sister Constance Perry's wedding to Malcolm Libby, Josephine attends a dance, attracts Ridgeway again, is seen kissing him, and causes Evangeline to return east. At the luncheon before her Constance's wedding, Josephine learns from a drunken usher that Sonny, handsome and rich, is sought out by so many women that he tells them he is married to a mulatto. Josephine turns diabolical, lures Malcolm into a secluded spot and a comforting embrace, and almost wrecks the wedding ceremony. Later that evening she drives to the railroad station with a friend and takes a train to Island Farms—and Sonny?

NICK. In "No Harm Trying," he is Pat Hobby's landlord, works in a delicatessen store below Pat's apartment, and delivers Carl Le Vigne's message to Pat.

NICK. In "The Rich Boy," he is the Plaza Hotel bartender. He laughs accommodatingly when lonely Anson Hunter reminisces.

NICOTERA. In *Tender Is the Night*, he is a handsome Italian movie actor who works in Rome with Rosemary Hoyt and admires her.

"A NIGHT AT THE FAIR" (1928). Short story. (Characters: Hubert Blair, Mrs. Riply Buckner, Sr., Riply Buckner, Jr., Riply Buckner, Sr., Hilda, Elwood Leaming, Lee, Basil Duke Lee, Mrs. Lee, Barton Leigh, Olive, Speed Paxton, Schwartze, Van Schellinger, Gladys Van Schellinger, Mrs. Van Schellinger, Wharton.) The state fair is held where St. Paul and Minneapolis meet. To go to it this September, Riply Buckner, Jr., wears long pants and lords it over Basil Duke Lee, still in short pants. The boys encounter Elwood Leaming, who picks up two girls with them. The five ride the Old Mill, with Basil taking a back seat. Home again, he persuades his mother to let him buy long pants, agrees to double-date with Riply—who promises him a pretty girl—that evening at the fair, and so must decline sweet Gladys Van Schellinger's sudden and tempting offer to join her and her wealthy family in their box for the fireworks. Clad in long pants, he goes with Riply, but the girl for him is ugly. Handsome, cavorting Hubert Blair blandishes away Riply's girl Olive. Riply is left with the ugly girl, whom he courteously but reluctantly kisses during a ferris wheel ride. Basil reports after all to the Van Schellingers' box for the fireworks. Hubert and Olive walk past, and Gladys sees them. Basil enjoys his time with Gladys and is ecstatic when she invites him to visit her at her home tomorrow—until she asks him to bring Hubert too.

"THE NIGHT OF CHANCELLORSVILLE" (1935). Short story. (Characters: Nell, Nora, Steve.) Nora, the narrator, from York, Pennsylvania, tells a male friend about taking a train with her friend Nell, forty or so fancy girls, and rich, uppity women. They proceed from Philadelphia to Virginia, where the Union Army expects to be fighting all summer or until the Confederates surrender. Some drunken officers move through the cars. They are awakened predawn by cannon fire and are ordered to make room for the wounded. When the girls are left alone again, two rebel soldiers enter, talk "funny," call them a contingent for General Joseph Hooker's staff, and leave. After the wounded are placed in front cars, the train returns to Washington. Nora finds it odd that the newspapers never mention that attack on a train full of girls.

NOBLE, MAURY. In *The Beautiful and Damned*, he is one of Anthony Patch's closest friends. He is a Harvard classmate. His mother and a married brother live in Philadelphia. Maury, Anthony, and Richard Caramel drink and argue together in New York. Maury marries Philadelphia heiress Ceci Larrabee. Many aspects of Maury are based on Fitzgerald's observation of his friend George Jean Nathan.*

NOEL. In "The Intimate Strangers," she is Marquis Eduard de la Guillet de la Guimpé's sister. *See also* Guillet de la Guimpé, Noel de la.

"NO FLOWERS" (1934). Short story. (Characters: Chase, Amanda Rawlins Clark, Marjorie Clark, John Corliss, Dahlgrim, Estelle, Jim Europe, Hotsy Gamble, Red Grange, Howard, William Delaney Johns, Kurman, Lucy, Luther, Carter McLane, Payson, Phil Savage, Stanley.) Marjorie Clark, twelve, persuades her mother to repeat her nice story about going to a university prom with Carter McLane back in 1913. Time advances to the depression year of 1933. Marjorie, now eighteen, is going to a prom at the same school, as the guest of William ("Billy") Delaney Johns, a student working himself through school. Amanda is a chaperone, and she and her daughter will sleep at the club. Marjorie gripes that whereas her mother lived in the "golden age," she lives in a "tin age" and notes that the girls are not supposed to have corsages now. At the pre-prom dance, Amanda retires early, and Marjorie and Billy kiss in the so-called Engagement Room of the club, unchanged since Amanda's time there twenty years earlier. While Billy gets Marjorie some water, she dreams she hears a student named Phil Savage confess in this very room to Lucy, his fiancée, that he is being expelled for cheating on an examination. Lucy flings her corsage toward the fireplace. The engagement is off. In the morning Amanda, sitting in the Engagement Room, recalls how McLane escorted her to the prom, but she fell in love with Howard, his roommate. When he persuaded her to substitute his corsage for McLane's, she thus lost an engagement ring McLane had concealed in his corsage for her as a surprise. No engagement follows. Amanda goes home in the afternoon, philosophizing that young people should seize the moment. In the evening, when Billy discovers that he lacks cash to rent a tuxedo, he sneaks into the students' pressing bureau and borrows one labeled as a freshman's. It is all right, he tells Marjorie, because freshmen are technically barred from the prom. On their way to the dance, Marjorie, waiting outside Billy's dormitory room, overhears a freshman nearby lamenting to his date about his missing tux. Marjorie gets Billy to deliver it to him. Unable to attend the prom, she and Billy return to the Engagement Room. He explains that his rich uncle will provide him with a secure job once he has proved himself by working his way through school. His current show of poverty distresses her. They see a student drunk and lying on the lounge. Billy takes his tux and puts him to bed. Marjorie and Billy embrace and head for the dance at midnight. (Who is the man named Clark, whom Amanda married? Could his first name be Howard?)

"NO HARM TRYING" (1940). Short story. (Characters: Barnes, Bill Behrer, Benny, Estelle Hobby Devlin, Eric, Pat Hobby, Barbara LaMarr, Carl Le Vigne, Louie, Jeff Manfred, Nick, Mabel Normand, Harmon Shaver, Lizzette Starheim, Dutch Waggoner.) Pat Hobby, a down-and-out Hollywood writer, forty-nine, learns from Carl Le Vigne, a powerful producer, that Pat's ex-wife, Estelle, remarried and out of his life for ten years, is in the hospital recovering from a suicide attempt. Le Vigne puts Pat on salary for three weeks, on condition that most of the pay will go quietly for Estelle's care. Le Vigne remembers Estelle as a fine script girl. Pat persuades Lizzette Starheim, a foreign actress kept idle by Le Vigne, to join three uneasy men—director Dutch Waggoner, associate producer Jeff Manfred, and money-man Harmon Shaver—in a project. Eric, a talented script boy, has confided in Pat his plot for a movie and Pat has gone to Estelle, in the hospital, to persuade her to work with Eric, to provide continuity for his script, and type it up. Shaver goes with Pat and Lizzette to Le Vigne for a showdown and gets Manfred to read Eric's prepared script. Le Vigne surprises everyone by revealing that when he visited Estelle in the hospital he found her working with Eric on the script. Adding that Lizzette cannot speak credible English yet, Le Vigne puts Waggoner on hold for a year since he is still addicted to drugs, and he ignores Shaver. He praises and buys Eric's story and agrees to tolerate Pat only if he tells the whole truth for once.

NOLAK. In "The Camel's Back," he is the owner, with his wife, of a New York costume shop. They are of European background.

NOLAK, MRS. In "The Camel's Back," she is the owner, with her husband, of the costume shop. Of European background, she rents Perry Parkhurst a camel costume but declines to go to the circus ball as its rear end.

NORA. In "The Night of Chancellorsville," she is the narrator aboard the train out of Philadelphia carrying fancy ladies to Virginia and General Joseph Hooker's army before the battle of Chancellorsville.

NORMAND, MABEL (1894–1930). Movie actress. Good-looking, charming, but untalented, she began her career as a model, acted for D. W. Griffith beginning in 1911, worked for Mack Sennett (1912–1917), and appeared in more than a hundred shorts, including some with Fatty Arbuckle and Charlie Chaplin. She was a minor director in 1914. She appeared in full-length movies (1918–1921). In 1922, by then a drug addict, she was implicated in the murder of director William Desmond Taylor. Sennett rehired her in 1923. She appeared in Hal Roach shorts in 1926. In "No Harm Trying," she is mentioned as a deceased movie star whose signed photograph Pat regards as of little value.

NORRIS, CHARLES GILMAN (1881–1945). American novelist. He was born in Chicago, raised in San Francisco, earned a B.L. from the School of Social Science at Berkeley, and became art editor of the *American Magazine* in New York. He married Kathleen Thompson there in 1909. Publishing as Kathleen Norris, she became a popular novelist beginning with *Mother* in 1911. Although Charles Norris published eleven novels of his own, beginning with *The Amateur* in 1916, he was never as successful with the public or the critics as was his wife or his older brother, novelist Frank Norris (1870–1902), author of *McTeague* (1899), *The Octopus* (1901), and other works. Charles Norris served in the U.S. Army as a major in New Jersey (1917–1918). His most significant titles include *Salt, or the Education of Griffith Adams* (1918); *Brass, a Novel of Mar-*

riage (1921), a best-seller, made into a Warner Brothers movie in 1923; *Bread* (1923); *Pig Iron* (1925); *Zelda Marsh* 1927); *Seed* (1930), another best-seller, about birth control; *Bricks without Straw* (1938); and *Flint* (1944). Norris dealt with such serious topics as the influence of heredity and environment, education, commercial ethics, and women in business.

In 1920 Norris wired Fitzgerald advising him to demand no less than $5,000 for the film rights to *This Side of Paradise*. The naturalism of *Salt* impressed Fitzgerald. After beginning a 1921 review of *Brass*, titled ''Poor Old Marriage,'' with praise, he criticizes it for clumsily detailing parallel marriages, for having neither passion nor pain, and for lacking Frank Norris's finer touch. Fitzgerald liked a few specified scenes in *Brass* but felt it displayed no freshness, no depth, no talent—which all great novels have. In 1921 or so, Norris wrote to Fitzgerald to warn him not to write trivial *Saturday Evening Post* stories but to aim higher.

Bibliography: Richard Allan Davison, *Charles Norris* (Boston: Twayne, 1983); Kathleen Norris, *A Family Gathering* (Garden City, N.Y.: Doubleday, 1959).

NORTH, ABE. In *Tender Is the Night*, he is the husband of Mary North and is a talented musical composer ruined by drink. He is partly responsible for the death of Jules Peterson in Paris and is beaten to death in a New York speakeasy. He is a close friend of Dick Diver and Nicole Diver. North reflects aspects of Fitzgerald's friend Ring Lardner.* Circumstances of North's death may have been suggested to Fitzgerald by news of the fatal fight Cornelius R. Winant, Princeton class of 1918, had in a New York speakeasy in 1928.

Bibliography: Matthew J. Bruccoli, ''Bennett Cerf's Fan Letter on *Tender Is the Night*: A Source for Abe North's Death,'' *FH/A 1979*, 229–30.

NORTH, MARY. In *Tender Is the Night*. *See* Minghetti, Mary North.

NORTON, DR. In ''One Interne,'' he is a popular diagnostician at the hospital. His well-to-do patients not needing treatment remain under his care so that their payments will subsidize sick patients in the free wards. He encourages William Tulliver V, praises George Schoatze, and persuades Tulliver to have an operation for volvulus.

NOSBY, CLAUDE. In ''A Penny Spent,'' he is a stiff, penny-pinching Ohio business associate, almost forty, of Julius Bushmill and is engaged to his daughter, Hallie Bushmill. Nosby and Bushmill meet Hallie and her mother, Jessie Pepper Bushmill, in Amsterdam, after Corcoran has escorted the two women around Belgium and the Netherlands. Nosby accompanies Jessie, Hallie, and Corcoran to Italy and loses out to Corcoran, who marries Hallie.

''NOT IN THE GUIDEBOOK'' (1925). Short story. (Characters: James Cooley, Milly Cooley, Mrs. Coots, William Driscoll, Mrs. Horton, Leonora Hughes,

Claude Peebles, Mrs. Claude Peebles.) James Cooley is called an American war hero, having, as he boasts, obtained helpful German regimental orders from an enemy officer's corpse at Château-Thierry. Back in Brooklyn, he shows his medals, drinks, and in 1922 marries Milly. She is a sweet girl, eighteen, of Czech-Romanian descent. When her mother dies the following spring and leaves her $250, Jim, who is abusive, takes it and Milly to France, where, he says, he has secured a job caring for American soldiers' graves. While they are on the Cherbourg-Paris train, he hops off at Evreux. Penniless, she continues on to Paris, where William Driscoll, an American veteran and now a tour guide, rescues her from a pair of street ruffians. They go to his left-bank pension, managed by Mrs. Horton, a decent American widow. The story of Milly's abandonment by Jim makes the papers. She happily accompanies Bill on his rubberneck bus tours, tells him about Jim, but defends Jim when Bill is critical. Meanwhile, the American Aid Society locates Jim, who has spent his money on cognac in Evreux, pawned a watch he told Milly he took from the same enemy corpse, and been jailed for street fighting, but is now on his way to Milly. Reconciled to his return, she accompanies Bill on a final tour—to Château-Thierry. After a spiel to the tourists about how he was scared during the attack there, he admits to Milly he was not at the attack proper because he had been wounded the night before. He adds that he had taken regimental orders and a watch from a dead German but that someone pinched them and probably got credit for the enemy documents. On their honeymoon the following spring, Bill and Milly visit tourist spots and a few not in the guidebook. Fitzgerald begins "Not in the Guidebook" by having the narrator, an American in Paris, read in the *Franco-American Star* about Milly's being abandoned.

"NOW IS THE TIME FOR ALL GOOD MEN TO COME TO THE AID OF THE PARTY" (1981). Poem. The poet says he and the Jews will not aid the party because he belongs to a liberal group and Jews are so wise that they are going to be slaughtered.

"NOW YOUR HEART IS COME SO NEAR" (1981). Poem. The poet says her decision has brought her close to him.

O

OAKEY, MRS. In "Family in the Wind," she is one of the persons injured by the first tornado and treated by Dr. Forrest Janney.

OAKY. In "In the Holidays," he is one of three gunmen Joe Kinney relishes thinking about in connection with the planned murder of Griffin. The others are Flute Cuneo and Vandervere.

OBALONEY, PRINCE PAUL. In "The Broadcast We Almost Heard Last September," he is a dance instructor from the Dance Hall Society. His work is interrupted when champagne party guests are gassed.

OBER, HAROLD (1881–1959). Literary agent. He was born near Lake Winnepesaukee, New Hampshire, graduated from Harvard in 1905, went to Europe for two years, and began agency work with the firm of Paul R. Reynolds and Son in 1907. He served in France during World War I with the American Red Cross (1917–1918). He became a partner with Reynolds in 1919. In 1929 Ober started his own agency, Harold Ober Associates, 40 East Forty-ninth Street, New York City; it represented such well-known authors as Faith Baldwin, Catherine Drinker Bowen, Pearl Buck, William Faulkner, Corey Ford, John Gunther, J. D. Salinger, Adlai E. Stevenson, and Philip Wylie, in addition to Fitzgerald. Ober enjoyed music, played tennis and skiied, and he was an expert carpenter, gardener, and photographer. He bred dogs, was president of the Airdale Club of America and also the Biard Club of America, was a member of the American Kennel Club, and served as a dog show judge. He was survived by his widow, Anne Reid Ober, and their two sons.

Fitzgerald worked with Ober from 1919 and soon got into the habit of asking to be paid for work when it was submitted but before it was sold. By 1928 Ober, a kind of banker for Fitzgerald, was sometimes paying him for work not yet written. When Ober severed his association with Reynolds, Fitzgerald went with him. In 1935 Fitzgerald dedicated *Taps at Reveille* to him. Ober and his wife acted as substitute parents for Fitzgerald's daughter, Scottie,* whom they welcomed into their home in Scarsdale, New York, beginning in 1935. In 1937 Fitzgerald named Ober and John Biggs, Jr.,* coexecutors of his will. Two years later he dropped Ober in favor of Max Perkins* because Ober had finally refused Fitzgerald's demands for advances. When Fitzgerald died in Hollywood, Sheilah Graham* phoned Ober, who phoned Zelda Sayre Fitzgerald* in Montgomery, to break the news. Ober and his wife attended Fitzgerald's funeral. Perkins declined to serve as coexecutor, but both he and Ober aided Biggs. Ober loaned Scottie money to help her continue at Vassar until she graduated in 1942. Cannon, Finnegan's literary agent in "Financing Finnegan," is based partly on Ober.

Bibliography: Matthew J. Bruccoli, ed., *As Ever, Scott Fitz—: Letters between F. Scott Fitzgerald and His Literary Agent Harold Ober 1919–1940* (Philadelphia: J. B. Lippincott, 1972); Eleanor Lanahan, *Scottie: The Daughter of . . . The Life of Frances Scott Fitzgerald Lanahan Smith* (New York: HarperCollins, 1995).

OBERWALTER. In "A Snobbish Story," he is a tennis player at the tournament Josephine Perry watches.

"OBIT ON PARNASSUS" (1937). Poem. Fitzgerald rhymes names of various writers who died in their thirties, forties, fifties, sixties, seventies, and eighties. He says with candor he would not like to achieve ninety, like (Walter Savage) Landor.

O'BRIEN. In *The Last Tycoon*, he is a cousin of Pat Brady, on the payroll though not as a screenwriter, as Brimmer thinks. Ransome is another such cousin about whom Brimmer is also mistaken.

O'BRIEN, FATHER. In "Sentiment—and the Use of Rouge," he is a priest mentioned by Sergeant O'Flaherty before he dies.

O'BRIEN, FAUSTINA. In *The Great Gatsby*, he is a person Nick Carraway remembers as being among Jay Gatsby's summer guests.

O'CONNOR, HELEN. In "Flight and Pursuit," she is the person whose trip to Europe with Caroline Martin Corcoran is financed by Sidney Lahaye.

O'DAY, HENRY ("HARRY"). In *Precaution Primarily*, he is named in a song.

O'DONAHUE, STEPHEN. In *This Side of Paradise*, he is a person who, according to Monsignor Thayer Darcy, may have been a common ancestor of the Blaine and Darcy families. He says the Donahues certainly were.

O'DONAVAN, HORACE. In *The Great Gatsby*, Nick Carraway lists his name on a timetable as one of Jay Gatsby's summer guests. He is in theater work.

"THE OFFSHORE PIRATE" (1920). Short story. (Characters: Belle Pope Calhoun, Costello, Dean, Babe Divine, Farnham, Ardita Farnham, Goldberg, Green, Marshall, Mimi Merril, Colonel Moreland, Toby Moreland, Trombone Mose.) On his yacht the *Narcissus* off Palm Beach, beautiful, insolent, willful Ardita Moreland, nineteen, tells her uncle, Mr. Farnham, she will not go ashore and meet Toby Moreland, his friend Colonel Moreland's son from New York. The uncle disembarks in a huff. A handsome young adventurer boards with six African American singing jazz musicians and mysterious bags. Introducing himself as Curtis Carlyle, he invites her to leave or be captured and spirits the willing girl away. He tells her about his colorful past—poor Tennessee childhood, Nashville and then New York ragtime gigs, stock-market losses, military service, and a million-dollar criminal coup. They sail to a Caribbean islet and relish three days and nights of beach activities under moon and sun—food and drink, cigarettes, swimming and diving, music and dancing, and predawn kisses. Ardita tells Curtis she is supposed to wed an attractively scandal-trailed fellow. But she and Curtis fall in love, and she agrees to escape with him, marry in Callao, go to India, and surface a decade later in England as wealthy aristocrats. An armed revenue boat appears, and all surrender to the police—and to Farnham and old Moreland, also aboard. Carlyle and Moreland explain the romantic ruse: Carlyle is really Toby, Moreland's son, who staged everything to check out Ardita, determine her love-worthiness, and show an obligatory wild streak to her. Marriage will follow.

A nice touch in "The Offshore Pirate" is Ardita's boasting that men never lie to her and being fooled by Toby Moreland, the biggest liar she will ever know. Fitzgerald originally planned to end the story by explaining the action as a dream. Metro made *The Offshore Pirate*, a 1921 movie starring Viola Dana* as Ardita Farnham.

Bibliography: Roulston.

O'FLAHERTY, SERGEANT. In "Sentiment—and the Use of Rouge," he is a combat soldier with Captain Clayton Harrington Syneforth. When both are dying of wounds in 1917, they discuss religion. As he dies, O'Flaherty begins to say his "Hail Mary."

O'FLARITY. In *Assorted Spirits*, he is a policeman, called with Mulligan to investigate the disappearance of Josephus Hendrix's $10,000. They do nothing.

"OF WONDERS IS SILAS M. HANSON THE CHAMP" (1981). Poem. (Character: Silas M. Hanson.) Silas M. Hanson asked for the poet's autograph and sent a stamp, but forgot to include his address.

OGDEN, DR. In "The Love Boat," he is one of eight physicians panicky Bill Frothington thinks he might consult. He recalls that old Ogden delivered him into the world.

O'HARA. In "The Captured Shadow," he is a character in Basil Duke Lee's incomplete play *Hic! Hic! Hic!*

"OH MISSELDINE'S, DEAR MISSELDINE'S" (1981). Poem. (Character: Misseldine.) The poet remembers the banana splits and fudge at Misseldine's "dive."

"OH PAPA—" (1965). Poem. The little girl called the poet "papa." The child was Mary MacArthur. *See* MacArthur, Mary.

Bibliography: Helen Hayes and Lewis Funke, *A Gift of Joy* (New York: M. Evans, 1965).

"OH, SISTER, CAN YOU SPARE YOUR HEART" (1971). Poem. The poet begs her to forget cars, gold, and coats and take her chances with him.

"OH WHERE ARE THE BOYS OF THE BOOM-BOOM-BOOM" (1981). Poem. The poet wonders where the boom-time boys are now.

O'KANE. In "On an Ocean Wave," he is Gaston T. Scheer's more important secretary. The other is Claud Hanson. Scheer orders O'Kane to bring Professor Dollard to his room aboard the ship so Cates can murder him.

O'KEEFE. In "Majesty," either of two old aunts invited to the wedding ceremony called off by Emily Castleton.

O'KEEFE, CHEVALIER. In *The Beautiful and Damned*, he is the main character in a parable Anthony Patch tells Gloria Gilbert. The chevalier, a lover manqué, retires to a monastery, from a window sees a peasant girl adjust her stocking, leans too far out to gawk, and falls to his death.

O'KELLY, GEORGE. In " 'The Sensible Thing,' " he is a graduate of the Massachusetts Institute of Technology who while an engineer in Tennessee became engaged to Jonquil Cary. For steady money he took a job with a New York insurance company. When Jonquil writes to break their engagement, he goes to Tennessee but fails to win her back. He makes a fortune as an engineer in Peru, returns to her in triumph only seemingly to be rejected again, and is about to lose her again until she kisses him as a rebuke for his being too interested in money. They will wed. In the magazine publication of this story, George O'Kelly is named George Rollins.

OLDHORNE. In ''What a Handsome Pair!,'' either or any of the children, one a boy, of Stuart Oldhorne and Helen Van Beck Oldhorne.

OLDHORNE, HELEN VAN BECK. In ''What a Handsome Pair!'' she is the well-to-do New York cousin of Teddy Van Beck. He continues to love her after she breaks their engagement in 1902 and marries Stuart Oldhorne a year later. The Oldhornes have two or more children. Helen plays golf, tennis, and polo, and feels competitive with and in some ways superior to Stuart. She wins amateur golf tournaments. She joins the Red Cross and goes to France in 1915. She is a protofeminist.

OLDHORNE, STUART. In ''What a Handsome Pair!,'' he is a former Yale athlete and was a Rough Rider in Cuba. From Southampton, he plays golf, tennis, and polo. He and Helen Van Beck get married in 1903. When his patrimony is lost in the 1907 panic, he becomes the manager of Gus Meyer's racing stable and by 1914 is a golf club professional. An eye injury prevents his joining the Canadian air force in 1915. He is killed in combat, presumably with American forces, in France in 1918.

OLD MAN, THE. In '' 'Send Me In, Coach,' '' he is an ex-athlete, about sixty. He manages the summer camp and coaches football at State, is married to a young woman, and warns Rickey to keep away from her. Rickey criticizes him for not obtaining fringe benefits for him as a football player.

OLE. In *Assorted Spirits*, he is Hulda's boyfriend.

OLIVE. In ''A Night at the Fair,'' she is Riply Buckner, Jr.'s date, goes to the state fair with him, but leaves Riply to go on with Hubert Blair.

OLIVER. In ''The Last of the Belles,'' he is the Calhoun family's African American servant. He likes and trusts Andy.

OLSEN. In ''A Freeze-Out,'' he is one of the Winslow family's several servants.

OLSON. In *This Side of Paradise*, he is an Atlantic City hotel guard who, with O'May, supposedly catches Amory Blaine with an unmarried woman. Amory is taking the blame to save Alec Connage.

OMAR. In "Head and Shoulders," this is the nickname Marcia Meadow gives Horace Tarbox because he reminds her of a smoked cigarette.

O'MAY. In *This Side of Paradise*, he is an Atlantic City hotel guard who, with Olson, supposedly catches Amory Blaine with an unmarried woman. Amory is taking the blame to save Alex Connage.

"ON AN OCEAN WAVE" (1941). Short story, published posthumously as by Paul Elgin. (Characters: Cates, Catherine Denzer, Professor Dollard, Claud Hanson, O'Kane, Scheer, Gaston T. Scheer, Minna Scheer.) Gaston T. Scheer is a tough, rich little businessman. Accompanied by two loyal male secretaries, he is crossing the ocean with his wife, Minna, and their children and has secreted his mistress, Catherine Denzer, aboard. He plans to park his family in France and cavort with Catherine on business trips. When he sees his wife embracing a certain Professor Dollard in a corridor, he bribes Cates, the swimming steward, to toss the interloper overboard. Meanwhile, Minna awaits her lover expectantly on the promenade deck—in vain. Fitzgerald wanted Arnold Gingrich* to publish some of his stories under pseudonyms to see if the public would like a work not knowing he was the author.

"ON A PLAY TWICE SEEN" (1917). Short story. (Characters: What's-Her-Name, Mr. X.) As the poet watches a play alone and bored, he recalls seeing it with a happy girl a year earlier. She cried at a scene during which Mr. X's defense of divorce causes What's-Her-Name to faint in his arms. (Was she happy or sad?)

"ONE HUNDRED FALSE STARTS" (1933). Essay. (Characters: Bob, Boopsie Dee, Victoria Cuomo, Mark de Vinci, Donald, Elsie, Stark, Swankins, Jason Tenweather, Trimble, Mrs. Trimble, Vivian.) Fitzgerald compares much of his effort at writing to jumping the gun in a race and having to return to the starting line. His notebook contains items about one girl and then another, a shipwrecked little family, a murder one cold winter, a couple content with second best, a newsboy and a stray dog, and an adventurer. But ideas behind all of these items have vanished like opium smoke. He can find innumerable plots in books on criminal law and by eavesdropping; but he must feel the emotions of the people involved, or their actions are of no use to him. It is good to know when to quit, but it is better to keep working—in the hope of making readers hear, feel, and see.

O'NEILL, CARDINAL. In *This Side of Paradise*, he is a guest of Monsignor Thayer Darcy in Boston and later sings at Darcy's funeral.

"ONE INTERNE" (1932). Short story. (Characters: Alfonso, Dr. Barnett, Senator Billings, Dr. Brune, Miss Cary, Helen Day, Mrs. Truby Ponsonby Day,

Doremus, Dr. Howard Durfee, Dr. Georgi, Dr. Gillespie, John Gresham, Dr. Lane, Michael, Dr. Norton, Robinson, Dr. Ruff, George Schoatze, Dr. Schwartze, Thea Singleton, William Tulliver V, Paul B. Van Schaik, Ward, Dr. Zigler.) William Tulliver V, the fifth Bill Tulliver to graduate from the Maryland hospital, participates in a ceremonial spring roast of established physicians. His hope is to catch gentle Dr. Norton in an error and be correct himself. Later that evening Bill sees a student stagger near a pretty woman, whom he helps move away. Dr. Howard Durfee, a brilliant surgeon, drives up and hops out. He and the woman recognize each other and drive away together. Bill's work as an intern starts in July. Dr. Norton orders him and his classmate, Dr. George Schoatze, to diagnose some easy cases for practice. Bill and George watch Dr. Durfee do a skillful appendectomy, with the pretty girl Bill met earlier serving as anaesthetist. Her name is Thea Singleton. A few weeks later Bill asks her for a date. They go swimming in a quarry. She says she is Dr. Durfee's "girl" but does not love him. By August Dr. Norton is commending Bill for accurate diagnoses. Bill reads that debutante Helen Day is engaged to Dr. Durfee. He rushes to Thea, who reveals her one love was the late John Gresham, a distinguished medical researcher. Next day, while examining alcoholic Senator Billings, Bill faints with intestinal pains. He becomes George's frightened, domineering patient. George and Dr. Norton say he has a twisted intestine in danger of perforating. Only Thea can persuade him to have a life-saving operation, performed by Dr. Durfee. Thea tells Bill that Dr. Durfee offered to break his engagement and marry her, but she declined. She kisses Bill, promises to swim with him in September, and keeps certain mysterious thoughts to herself.

"ONE OF MY OLDEST FRIENDS" (1925). Short story. (Characters: Charley Hart, Miss Lawrence, Marion, Michael, Willoughby, Mrs. Willoughby.) Michael, a businessman, and Marion, wed for five years, live in New York with their children. One day he tells her Charley Hart is getting married. Charley, an artist, is one of Michael's oldest friends though negligent of late. Michael suggests they have a party for him. Marion reluctantly agrees. They invite several guests for dinner and cards, only to have Charley telephone them at the last minute to beg off because of illness. They cancel the party. On their way to the theater next evening, they pop in on their sick friend to cheer him up, find a gathering in full swing, and rush away embarrassed. Marion confesses Charley wanted her to leave Michael for him a year or so ago, and she rebuffed him. While Michael and Marion are vacationing in the country the following summer, Charley dashes up by train and begs for $2,000 to avoid being arrested for embezzlement. Michael refuses, and Charley leaves—threatening suicide. Michael feels obliged to be merciful, follows Charley, and spots him under a telephone pole with an indescribable crossbar waiting on the railroad tracks to be crushed. The train approaches. Michael thrusts him aside, promises him the funds, and explains he easily saw him under that crossbar. The two look up. There is no crossbar.

"ONE SOUTHERN GIRL" (1981). Poem. The poet hopes a rose has survived their love- and beauty-filled summer to lisp their story.

"ONE TRIP ABROAD" (1930). Short story. (Characters: Marquis de la Clos d'Hirondelle, Colby, Mrs. Colby, Oscar Dane, Madame Noel Delauney, General Sir Evelyne Fragelle, Lady Fragelle, T. F. Golding, Marquis de Kalb, Marquise de Kalb, Nelson Kelly, Nicole Kelly, Sonny Kelly, Cardine Miles, Liddell Miles, Count Chiki Sarolai, Esther Sherman.) Nelson Kelly, who has inherited half a million dollars and has quit the fur business in Alaska, wants to be a painter. He is on a trip abroad with his wife, Nicole Kelly, who wants to be a singer. They proceed by Italian liner to Gibraltar and are now in Algeria, where they suffer through a storm of locusts resembling black snow. Travel companions include heavy-drinking Cardine Miles and Liddell Miles. Whether to stay at a cafe to watch a belly dance causes the Kellys to quarrel. They go to Sorrento, where Nicole takes singing lessons and Nelson tries to paint bay scenes. Feeling out of place, they move to Paris and rent an apartment, where Nelson's piano-playing in the salon bothers uppity fellow-residents General Sir Evelyne Fragelle and Lady Fragelle. The Kellys live for two years in Monte Carlo. They think having a baby might settle them down. One morning Nicole is on the golf course with a self-proclaimed deadbeat named Oscar Dane. He grows critical of the Kellys' drifting, drinking companions, off whom he sponges proudly. During the luncheon hour, Nicole catches Nelson kissing her friend, Madame Noel Delauney; in the ensuing scuffle, he accidentally gives Nicole a black eye. Back in Paris, Nelson rents a studio to paint in, and he and Nicole try to be more circumspect in choosing and entertaining friends. Count Chiki Sarolai, well connected but another sponge, appears. They like him enough to give him a room in their apartment during Nicole's confinement. Chiki arranges for his brother-in-law, a banker in Paris, to throw a canal-boat party on the Seine. Nicole gives birth to a baby boy, has complications and is ordered not to attend the party, but goes anyway and becomes ill. She and Nelson return home to discover not only that Chiki and his valet have stolen their jewelry and decamped but also that Chiki told the party caterers to send bills totaling $12,000 to Nelson. The Kellys move to Geneva, where Nicole requires surgery and Nelson is treated for jaundice. Punctuating their travels is the repeated appearance of an unnamed, silent young couple—at an Algiers camel market, at the belly dance, at a Monte Carlo florist's after Nicole's golf game, at a cafe after Nelson hurt Nicole's eye, aboard the boat on the Seine, and finally, after a violent thunderstorm, at the Swiss hospital. Nicole, who longs for peace, love, and health, tells her husband the other two, decaying in appearance and perhaps in spirit, like themselves, are doubles of themselves.

"One Trip Abroad," which Fitzgerald wrote while his wife was in a Swiss hospital and he was also ill, has autobiographical overtones.

Bibliography: John Kuehl, ''Flakes of Black Snow: 'One Trip Abroad' Reconsidered,'' Bryer, *New Essays*, 175–88; Brian Way, *F. Scott Fitzgerald and the Art of Social Fiction* (New York: St. Martin's Press, 1980).

O'NEY. In *The Last Tycoon*, he is a priest Cecelia Brady remembers as embarrassed when he went to the ballet in New York with her and her father, Pat Brady.

"ON SCHEDULE" (1933). Short story. (Characters: Aquilla, Edith du Cary, Noël du Cary, René du Cary, Charles Hume, Delores Hume, Dean McIntosh, Mrs. McIntosh, Mlle. Ségur, Sheridan, Mrs. Sheridan, Slocum, Mrs. Slocum, Becky Snyder.) René du Cary, a widower born in Normandy and now thirty-four, has for three years been a researcher at an American foundation in a university town. His object is to decompose water electrolytically. According to the will of his wife, who died in Switzerland, he will lose substantially if he marries within seven years of her death. For six and a half years, these terms kept fortune-hunters away. But he has now fallen in love with beautiful Becky Snyder, nineteen and a college student; waiting is hard for both. They met in June, it is now September, but they cannot wed until December and still enjoy the full inheritance. The lives of René, his daughter Noël, twelve, and Becky become entwined. To manage their routines—driving the car, laboratory work, classes, meeting tutors, practicing the piano and tennis, shopping—René composes a tight schedule in three copies—one for each. Associates are beginning to talk, especially when Becky, who lives nearby with Slocum and his wife, has been seen taking a bath in René's home. What would the dean's wife say? Even René's lab assistant, Charles Hume, and his wife, Delores Hume, become worried. One cold day René, Noël, and Becky are in the lab when the experiment begins to succeed. René scribbles some notes, kisses the girls, and waves them away. He opens a window to vent foul odors, then discovers he wrote his notes on Noël's schedule. After phoning the girls and searching everywhere for his notes, René returns in disarray to the lab—to find it freezing, the basement furnace cold, and jars of his water containing platinum electrodes freezing and popping. Becky saves the day by finding Noël's schedule in the car and by using her unneeded copy as kindling to fire up the furnace. René and Becky unmethodically announce their engagement. Fitzgerald here spoofs his own habit of making schedules.

"ON THE TRAIL OF PAT HOBBY" (1941). Short story. (Characters: Jack Berners, Pat Hobby, Louie, Bee McIlvaine, Harold Marcus.) Pat Hobby rushes around the Hollywood studio where he is unemployed, hatless, and in need of a mirror so he can comb his gray hair. Bee McIlvaine, a movie writer, lets him use her compact mirror. When she says there is a $50 reward for a title for her scenario about tourists, Pat, who has just stolen a hat at the commissary, recalls he clerked at a tourist cabin this morning and left hatless ahead of a police raid.

Producer Jack Berners tells Pat that production is being held up because mogul Marcus has lost his favorite Homberg. Pat meets with Bee. Berners comes in. Pat, drunk on brandy snitched from Berners's office, suggests the title *Grand Motel*, which Berners enthusiastically accepts. Bee hands Pat his hat as he escapes to the lavatory, promising to return for the reward.

"ON WATCHING THE CANDIDATES IN THE NEWSREELS" (1981). Poem. Fitzgerald raucously advises ugly political candidates to avoid being seen on the screen.

"ON YOUR OWN" (1979). Short story. (Characters: Charles Barney, Mrs. Charles Barney, Bartollo, Colonel Cary, Crawshaw, Joe Crusoe, Dorsey, George Ives, Mrs. Ives, Gladys Knowles, Lovejoy, Dr. Lovejoy, Evelyn Lovejoy, Eddie O'Sullivan, Jubal Early Robbins, Vionnet, Joseph Widdle, Mrs. Joseph Widdle.) An American musical is closed when a singer-dancer in it named Evelyn Lovejoy, twenty-six, is called home in February to attend her father's funeral in Maryland. For five years she was in England. Part of the gossipy cast is returning home too. Aboard ship Evelyn bumps into George Ives, an eligible, wealthy Maryland lawyer, who is thirty. He saw her show in London and is just completing a voyage around the world. He appears at the funeral, after which she accepts his offer to drive her to Washington, D.C., to catch her train back to New York. In his car, she is offended by his desire to kiss her, calls him too American, and asks if he will call her "baby" next. Throughout March, she rehearses new routines and considers an offer in a Gershwin show in London. Ives and his mother visit New York, where he finds Evelyn, expresses an interest in marrying her, and invites her to dine at the Plaza. Other guests are his mother and Colonel Cary, who's also from Maryland. Six years earlier, before getting a start on stage in New York, she was a paid "party girl" and in that function met old Cary. Fearing he will gossip later, Evelyn blurts out the truth and offends Ives. He takes her away by taxi, says they see things differently, wants to end their relationship, and drops her near a theater where she has a late date. Suddenly she sees Ives as resembling her dead father, feels like a "waif," calls after him, and is happy when he holds her in his arms. He calls her "poor baby."

Evelyn's farewell to her father at the Maryland family graveside and an identically described scene in *Tender Is the Night*, when Dick Diver attends his father's burial in Maryland, both relate to Fitzgerald's memory of his father's burial there. "On Your Own," which Fitzgerald wrote in 1931 but could never sell, was published posthumously.

Bibliography: Jennifer McCable Atkinson, "The Lost and Unpublished Stories of F. Scott Fitzgerald," *FH/A 1971*, 32–63.

ORAL, MRS. In "The Popular Girl," she is a neighbor who efficiently, if peremptorily, helps Yanci Bowman in the first few days after Yanci's father Tom Bowman's sudden death.

"ORANGE PAJAMAS AND HEAVEN'S GUITARS" (1981). Poem. No matter that pajamas and guitars will not meet. Find a Carmel not a sweet. Fitzgerald wrote this poem for Carmel Myers,* the movie actress.

ORCHID, NEWTON. In *The Great Gatsby*, Nick Carraway lists his name on a timetable as one of Jay Gatsby's summer guests. He is from West Egg and controls Films Par Excellence.

"THE ORDEAL" (1915). Short story. An unnamed novice, no more than twenty, is at a monastery in Maryland. About to take his vows on a hot summer day to become a Jesuit priest, he will enter a life of study and service. He recalls his schooling and travel, other possible careers, and his parents' disapproval. He is distracted by thoughts of art and love, past troubles in the Catholic Church, and scepticism of certain modern writers. He recalls a young temptress, who seems, however, to signal cold earthiness. Called to the chapel and kneeling, he sees another novice whose eyes direct him to the altar candle. It seems the embodiment of evil, but a trace of warm red light streams through a stained-glass window portrait of St. Francis Xavier and overmatches the candle. The Eucharist seems sweet and mystical, and the young novice moves up to take his vows.

Fitzgerald was inspired to write this story by a visit in 1912 to the Jesuit seminary at Woodstock, Maryland, where he met his cousin Thomas Delihant,* a priest whom he was long to admire. Out of "The Ordeal" evolved Fitzgerald's longer 1920 story "Benediction."

Bibliography: Allen.

ORDWAY. In *The Great Gatsby*, this is the name of a family Nick Carraway used to remember hoping to see in Chicago during Christmas vacations from prep school and college.

O'REILLY. In "Bernice Bobs Her Hair," he is an Irish customer at the barbershop where Bernice's hair gets bobbed.

ORMONDE, GENEVIEVE. In "Bernice Bobs Her Hair," she is a regular Ivy League party guest, according to Warren MacIntyre.

ORMONDE, OTIS. In "Bernice Bobs Her Hair," he is a shy dance guest, sixteen.

ORMSBY, CAPTAIN. In *Coward*, he is an officer in the Union Army who pursues and captures Charles Douglas, a lieutenant, but does not find the $12,000 Douglas has in Union currency.

O'ROURKE, JERRY. In "The Popular Girl," he is a young bond salesman and is Yanci Bowman's date at the country-club dance during which she meets Scott Kimberly. She lets Jerry take her home in his noisy car but that's all.

ORSINI, PRINCESS. In *Tender Is the Night*, she is the person for whom a table in a Roman hotel restaurant is supposedly reserved. Dick Diver refuses to give up his seat there.

"O RUSSET WITCH!" (1921). Short story originally titled "His Russet Witch," reprinted as "O Russet Witch!" in 1922 and "O Russet Witch" later. (Characters: Thomas Allerdyce, Braegdort, Caroline, Miss Gaffney, Gerald, Arthur Grainger, Merlin Grainger, Olive Masters Grainger, Miss McCracken, Mrs. Masters, Pulpat, Moonlight Quill, Mrs. Moonlight Quill, Miss Sutton, Throckmorton.) When Merlin Grainger is twenty-five, he has worked for six years, now at $30 a week, for Moonlight Quill in his New York City bookshop. Merlin eats supper off the dresser in his room so as to gaze at russet-haired Caroline in her apartment across the way. Men often visit her. One day she enters the shop and comments on Merlin's eating habits. He is dazzled by her radiance. When she begins to hurl books around, he joins her; they damage much of the stock. Quill hovers over his accounts but pays no attention, nor do his two assistants, Miss McCracken and $20-a-week Olive Masters. Caroline leaves, and Merlin soon cleans up the mess. Quill comments but seems unworried. Merlin takes Olive to dinner at Pulpat's French restaurant. Quill converts his shop to sell used books; the place, along with everything in it except Olive, turns seedy within a year or so. Caroline has left her apartment. Just after Merlin has proposed to Olive at Pulpat's, Caroline enters with three men and some liquor, gets noisy, and dances on a table. Disgusted, Olive drags Merlin outside. After a month they get married; four dreary years later they have a son, Arthur. Quill retires and leaves Merlin in charge at $50 a week. Merlin is happy enough until, when he is thirty-five, he sees Caroline on Easter Sunday, in an open car on Fifth Avenue. She is beautiful, with a steely smile and surrounded by eager men. Olive drags Merlin and Arthur home. Merlin ages tediously, until when fifty he inherits the store upon Quill's demise. At sixty-five Merlin is still working, though dodderingly. Arthur sells bonds in Wall Street. One day a youth asks Merlin for a copy of *The Crime of Sylvester Bonnard* for his grandmother, who is outside in a limousine. While the two haggle over the price, the old woman bursts into the shop. She is white-haired Caroline, self-assured and insolent. She cows her grandson, and she and Merlin burst into laughter. She is his symbol of radiant beauty and power. He realizes he should have responded to her deliberate appeals to him—in the store, at the restaurant, in traffic. Too late now. She departs, uneasily, forever. Miss McCracken, still the bookstore accountant, enlightens Merlin: Caroline is really ex-dancer Alicia Dare—traffic-stopping correspondent in the Throckmorton divorce scandal, hopeless object of married Quill's gaze, and for thirty years the wealthy Mrs. Thomas Allerdyce.

Merlin now feels old. He resisted temptation too often. Oh, well, he lamely concludes, in heaven he will meet others who also wasted their time on earth.

Bibliography: Leland S. Person, Jr., ''Fitzgerald's 'O Russet Witch!': Dangerous Women, Dangerous Art,'' *Studies in Short Fiction* 23 (Fall 1986): 443–48.

OSCAR. In ''The Rich Boy,'' he is the Yale Club bartender and tells Anson Hunter how busy several of lonely Anson's friends are.

O'SULLIVAN, EDDIE. In ''On Your Own,'' he is a member of Evelyn Lovejoy's cast aboard the ship returning to New York. He becomes friendly with George Ives.

OSWALD. In *Safety First!*, he is mentioned as a henpecked husband.

OTIS. In *The Beautiful and Damned*, he is an usher at Anthony Patch's wedding.

"OUR AMERICAN POETS" (1917). Poem. (Character: Hank McPhee.) This work burlesques Robert Service's violence and Robert Frost's rugged rusticity.

"OUR APRIL LETTER" (1981). Poem. The poet does not respond much to an adverse medical report delivered by telephone, nor to memories of other telephone messages, since writing his 120 stories has taken a terrible toll on his feelings.

"OUTSIDE THE CABINET-MAKER'S" (1928). Short story. (Characters: President Calvin Coolidge, Miller, Murphy, Miss Television.) While a woman goes into a cabinet-maker's shop to order a custom-made doll house for their daughter, six, her husband waits in the car with her. To amuse her, he spins a story about a fairy princess trapped in a house across the street. The little girl embroiders on the tale. The mother comes out, satisfied with the arrangement she has made with the cabinet-maker. The little girl provides an ending to the tale to her satisfaction, which distresses her father. Meanwhile, the mother sadly recalls she had no doll house when she was little. This spare story is a superb parable about the uniqueness and fragility of most constructs of the imagination.

OVERTON. In *This Side of Paradise*, he is a student who is congratulated for receiving a Princeton society invitation.

OWL-EYES. In *The Great Gatsby*, Nick Carraway finds Owl-Eyes examining the fine books in Jay Gatsby's library. He drinks too much but impresses Nick by loyally attending Gatsby's funeral.

OYSTER, EVELYN. In *Tender Is the Night*, hers is a name Nicole Diver read in an American newspaper.

P

PACKMAN, GEORGE. In "The Bridal Party," he is a fat friend of Hamilton Rutherford and gives a prewedding party at which Michael Curly meets Rutherford's fiancée Caroline Dandy's father.

PAGE. In *This Side of Paradise*, this is either of Clara Page's two little children.

PAGE, CLARA. In *This Side of Paradise*, she is Amory Blaine's charming, beautiful third cousin. She is a widow living in Philadelphia on limited means with two little children. Amory falls in love with her for a while.

PAGE, HOWARD. In "First Blood," he is Lillian Hammel's date when the two, as well as Josephine Perry and Travis de Coppet, go on a drive. In "A Snobbish Story," he is a Yale junior, is a luncheon guest at the Perry home, talks about attending the literature course of William Lyon Phelps (1865–1943), and attends the tennis finals.

"PAIN AND THE SCIENTIST" (1913). Short story. (Characters: Walter Hamilton Bartney, Dr. Hepezia Skiggs.) Walter Hamilton Bartney wants to study law quietly; he chooses a house in a Middleton suburb. One evening he walks over to visits his neighbor, Dr. Hepezia Skiggs, a Christian Scientist, out of curiosity. On the way he falls and hurts himself. Skiggs yells out a window there is no such thing as pain and lets the night watchman rescue Bartney. Later Bartney finds Skiggs picking the pansies Bartney had planted. He grabs the trespasser and shakes him until he says that he feels no pain and then says "ouch."

PALEY, LORD. In *Tender Is the Night*, he is a person Dick Diver reminds his sister-in-law, Beth Evan Warren, she was engaged to.

PALMER. In "That Kind of Party," he is the janitor of the block where the Shoonover and Tipton families live.

PALMER. In "That Kind of Party," she is any one of Fats Palmer's little sisters. By mistake, she delivers the fake telegram to Terrence R. Tipton's mother rather than Joe Shoonover's mother.

PALMER, CLOTHILDE ("TILDE") SAYRE. Fitzgerald's sister-in-law. She and her husband, John Palmer, attended Fitzgerald's wedding in 1920 to her sister Zelda Sayre Fitzgerald.* Fitzgerald regarded Clothilde as neurotic. In April 1939 John Palmer helped Fitzgerald to get to a New York hospital after an alcoholic binge. In 1940 Clothilde agreed with other Sayre family members that Zelda should live back in Montgomery, Alabama.

PALMER, FATS. In "That Kind of Party," he is the son of the janitor. A delivery boy, he gives Terrence R. Tipton and his friend, Joe Shoonover, a telegram blank on which they write the forged telegram.

PALMER, MISS. In "Author's House," she is the author's secretary. He asks her to send Mrs. Kracklin Lee $5 and say her supposed brother is out of prison and has gone to China.

PALMETTO, HENRY L. In *The Great Gatsby*, Nick Carraway lists his name on a timetable as one of Jay Gatsby's summer guests. He is from New York and committed suicide by leaping in front of a subway train in Times Square.

PAN-E-TROON. In "The Passionate Eskimo," he is a stalwart Eskimo who meets Edith Cary in Chicago, regards her as a goddess, retrieves her family jewels, enables her to reconcile with Westgate, and returns to Lapland full of stories about the trading posts in the big city. Edith calls him Mr. Troon.

PAPA JACK. In "Rags Martin-Jones and the Pr-nce of W-les," he is a character in the song sung by the black girl at the nightclub in which John B. Chestnut stages his ruse.

PARAGORIS, MME. In *Tender Is the Night*, hers is a name read in the *New York Herald*.

PARAMORE, FREDERICK E. In *The Beautiful and Damned*, he is one of Anthony Patch's Harvard classmates and later a social worker in Stamford, Connecticut. He crashes one of Anthony's wild parties at nearby Marietta. While there he mishandles the phone call from Edward Shuttleworth, indirectly causing Anthony to be disinherited. Paramore is a satirical portrait of Edward E. "Ted" Paramore (1896–1956), a friend of Edmund Wilson* and a Yale graduate. When

Fitzgerald worked in Hollywood on the screen play for *Three Comrades*, he was ordered by Joseph L. Mankiewicz to work with Paramore and did so, argued with him, and regarded him as a hack.

PARKE. In *The Great Gatsby*, he is a criminal whom fellow criminal Slagle mentions in a telephone call Nick Carraway takes in Jay Gatsby's home after Gatsby's murder.

PARKER. In *Porcelain and Pink*, he is named by Julie Marvis in a song.

PARKER, DR. In ''Too Cute for Words,'' he is a person Gwen Bowers talked to about Caesar, one of the subjects she has studied. She called Caesar ''cute.''

PARKER, DOROTHY (1893–1967). Author. She was born Dorothy Rothschild in West End, New Jersey, attended a Catholic academy in New York City (c. 1900–1907) and then a boarding school in Morristown, New Jersey, for a year or so. She was taking classes at the Art Student's League by 1912. In 1913 or 1914 she began writing verse, stories, essays, sketches, squibs, captions, and drama and book reviews for several periodicals, starting with *Vogue* and including *Vanity Fair* (1915–1934), *Ainslee's Magazine* (1920–1923), *Ladies Home Journal* (1920), *Saturday Evening Post* (1920–1923), *New York Life* (1920–1930), *Smart Set* (1922), *New Yorker* (1925–1944), *McCalls* (1928), and *Esquire* (1957–1962). She contributed pieces for ''The Conning Tower'' (1923–1931), Franklin Pierce Adams's column in the *New York World* and the *New York Herald Tribune* (1931–1933). In 1920, along with Adams, she founded the Algonquin Round Table, a Manhattan lunch club including Robert Benchley, Heywood Broun,* Marc Connelly, George S. Kaufman, Harold Ross, Robert Sherwood, and Alexander Woollcott. Through the 1920s, the membership grew, with additions including Charles MacArthur, Donald Ogden Stewart,* and Deems Taylor. Dorothy married Edwin Pond Parker II in 1917. By 1922 Dorothy Parker was an alcoholic like her husband, who was also a morphine addict. In 1922 she had an abortion and the following year attempted suicide; in 1926 (and 1932) she tried again. In 1927 she joined Boston marchers to protest the Sacco-Vanzetti case. In 1928 she and Edwin Parker were divorced. (He died in 1933 of an overdose of sleeping powder.) Beginning in 1930 Dorothy Parker demonstrated her skill as a screenwriter. In 1932 or 1933 she married Alan Campbell, an alcoholic actor and writer. In 1934 they moved to Hollywood where they worked as highly paid screenwriters; she helped organize the Screen Writers Guild that year and two years later the Anti-Nazi League. In 1937 she and her husband went briefly to Spain, from which she sent pro-Loyalist dispatches to the *New Masses*. In 1947 she and Campbell were divorced but remarried each other three years later. (He died in 1963, probably by suicide.) In 1949 Parker was blacklisted in Hollywood and a year later was labeled a ''concealed Communist'' by the FBI. In 1964 she returned to New York, where she died alone in a hotel room.

She was the wittiest epigrammist America has ever produced and perhaps its most sardonic light-verse writer. She sought to hide her chronic melancholy by pixy charm but also by backbiting, and had a host of lovers, including MacArthur and Taylor. Parker's many books, notable for acerbic, flippant, mocking wit, include verse, *Men I'm Not Married To* (1922), *Enough Rope* (1926), *Sunset Gun* (1928), *Lament for the Living* (1930), *Death and Taxes* (1931), and *Not So Deep as a Well* (1936), and short stories *After Such Pleasures* (1933) and *Collected Stories* (1942). She worked on thirty-nine screenplays (1919–1961), notably *A Star Is Born* (United Artists, 1937) and *The Little Foxes* (Warner Brothers, 1941).

Fitzgerald and Parker occasionally met in the 1920s. In 1922 they, along with Zelda Sayre Fitzgerald,* Benchley, and Sherwood, met in a Manhattan speakeasy to celebrate the defeat of Georges Carpentier by William Harrison Dempsey.* In 1926 she and the Fitzgeralds were convivial with Ernest Hemingway* in Paris and also socialized with Gerald Murphy* and Sara Murphy* on the Riviera. In New York in 1934 Parker bought a portrait of Fitzgerald painted by Zelda and now lost. Fitzgerald's and Parker's mutual friends included Ring Lardner,* Sidney J. Perelman, Stewart, and Edmund Wilson.* In 1937 Fitzgerald and Parker were both in Hollywood. He attended the opening of *A Star Is Born*. He based Rose Meloney, the Hollywood writer in *The Last Tycoon*, partly on Parker. Fitzgerald and Parker never liked each other much, probably because each saw talent in the other damaged by alcohol and unhappy marriage. When she saw his body at the Los Angeles funeral parlor, she quoted Owl-eyes's ''poor son-of-a-bitch'' comment before Jay Gatsby's corpse. In 1945 she edited Viking's *Portable Fitzgerald*.

Bibliography: Randall Calhoun, *Dorothy Parker: A Bio-Bibliography* (Westport, Conn.: Greenwood Press, 1993); Marion Meade, *Dorothy Parker: What Fresh Hell Is This?* (New York: Villard Books, 1988).

PARKER, FROG. In *This Side of Paradise*, he is a Minnesota friend of Amory Blaine when they are very young. When Amory goes to Princeton, Frog, also called Froggy, goes to Harvard. Isabelle Borgé manipulates both lads to her advantage.

PARKHURST, PERRY. In ''The Camel's Back,'' he is a Harvard graduate, twenty-eight, and a lawyer in Toledo. He is in love with Betty Medill, who likes him but keeps him dangling. When she declines his now-or-never proposal of marriage, he gets drunk with Baily and Martin Macy, goes in a camel costume to the circus ball, and is married by Jumbo to Betty in what she thinks is a mock ceremony. Ultimately she is agreeable, even to his idea of going West.

PARKS, ALLEN. In ''More Than Just a House,'' he is a casual friend of Jean Gunther. She tells him she is not in the mood for necking and calls him ''Jake.''

PARMELEE, EDDIE. In ''Forging Ahead,'' he is a friend of Basil Duke Lee. He worked during vacations on the railroad to earn money to attend the state university. He gets Basil a job, which he soon loses. Eddie introduces Basil to Utsonomia, a Japanese student at the university. Basil bribes Eddie $10 to escort Rhoda Sinclair to a function, but Eddie sends Utsonomia instead.

PARR, EMILY. In ''The Rubber Check,'' she is a person Val Schuyler thinks he could have married.

PARRISH, JOSEPH HARDWICK. In ''The Third Casket,'' he is a tall young man, about thirty, who fails to take over Cyrus Girard's Wall Street firm and marry his daughter, Lola Girard. His plan for leisure is to establish an endowment center for archaeologists and historians.

PARSONS, JIM. In *The Beautiful and Damned*, he is a former boyfriend of Gloria Gilbert Patch.

PARSONS, LOUELLA OETTINGER (1881–1972). Gossip columnist and Hollywood celebrity. In *The Last Tycoon*, Louella incorrectly reports the marriage of Cecelia Brady to Monroe Stahr.

PASCHE, MME. In *Tender Is the Night*, hers is a name read in the *New York Herald.*

PASKERT. In *This Side of Paradise*, he is a fellow student at St. Regis with whom Amory Blaine goes to a show in New York.

"THE PASSIONATE ESKIMO" (1935). Short story. (Characters: Edith Cary, Christopher, Humphrey Deering, Earl, George, Pan-e-troon, Richards, Westgate.) Pan-e-troon, an Eskimo, has visited the Chicago fair and wants one more look around the city before returning to Lapland. He shops a little and takes bus rides. He also encounters beautiful Edith Cary in a car with Westgate, her friend currently out of favor. She invites Pan-e-troon home with her; Humphrey Deering, another friend, goes along and disputes with Westgate. That evening she displays a tiara of gold, diamonds, and rubies, which Westgate places in his coattail. Suspecting Humphrey Deering of wrongdoing, Pan-e-troon invokes the power of wind and causes Humphrey's bedroom door to slam shut and lock him in and another room door to close and imprison Edith and Westgate. Westgate explains that he took the blame when his father was sued for breach of promise and had to work hard to pay the resulting debts. The two young people are reconciled. Meanwhile, Pan-e-troon rescues the missing jewels from Christopher, the Cary family butler, gives them to Edith, and returns home—to tell often his story of the great trading posts in faraway Chicago. ''The Passionate Eskimo'' is one of Fitzgerald's few purely comic efforts.

"PASTING IT TOGETHER" (1936). Essay. After his crack-up Fitzgerald feels he had no head to boast was ''bloody but unbowed'' but did still feel. He wonders how he lost his enthusiasm. He recalls pondering his sadness, melancholy, and tragedy and concluding he injuriously identified with objects of fear and sympathy. To survive, one must cleanly break off from life. So he determined to be only a writer and no longer a person. He developed a smile and a voice to repulse human appeals. Now if he saw someone dying outside, he would merely write about the incident; otherwise, as a feeling adult he would be unhappy. Our national depression followed an unnatural boom. Just so disillusion follows joy, which is also unnatural. Still, throw him a meaty bone and he may lick your fingers. By error, the titles for ''Pasting It Together'' and ''Handle with Care'' were transposed when the two essays were republished in *The Crack-Up*.

PAT. In *The Beautiful and Damned*, he is the owner of a gin mill in Hoboken formerly frequented by Edward Shuttleworth.

PAT. In ''The Bridal Party,'' he or she is mentioned as having hosted a party where Michael Curly and Hamilton Rutherford first met.

PATCH, ADAM. (Full name: Adam J. [''Cross Patch''] Patch.) In *The Beautiful and Damned*, he is Anthony Patch's grandfather. He was a major in a New York regiment in the Civil War, married Alicia Withers Patch, whose wealth provided his financial start, made $25 million in Wall Street, became a social reformer, and lives at his Tarrytown estate. His son was Adam Ulysses Patch, whose son, Anthony Patch, therefore was the old man's grandson. Old Adam is protected by Edward Shuttleworth. Anthony Patch periodically annoys and blandishes Adam, who goes to a party at Anthony's Marietta home and, being a prohibitionist, disinherits him because of drunkenness seen there. Years after Adam's death, Anthony breaks the will.

PATCH, ADAM ULYSSES. In *The Beautiful and Damned*, he was the son of Adam Patch and Alicia Withers Patch. At twenty-two he married Henrietta Lebrune. They lived in Washington Square, New York City. Their only child was Anthony Patch. After his wife's death, he and Anthony lived in Tarrytown with Adam Patch. Ulysses's memoirs, ''New York Society as I Have Seen It,'' were too dull ever to be published. He died in Switzerland when Anthony, abroad with him, was eleven. Some of Adam Ulysses Patch's stuffiness was inspired by Fitzgerald's dislike of Ward McAllister and his *Society As I Have Found It* (1890).

Bibliography: Wayne W. Westbrook, "Portrait of a Dandy in *The Beautiful and Damned*," *FH/A 1979*, 147–49.

PATCH, ALICIA WITHERS. In *The Beautiful and Damned*, she was the wife of Adam Patch, whom she married when she was thirty. She was the mother of Adam Ulysses Patch.

PATCH, ANNIE. In *The Beautiful and Damned*, she was Adam Patch's little sister, about whom he reminisces almost sixty-five years later.

PATCH, ANTHONY. In *The Beautiful and Damned*, he is the hero, born Anthony Comstock Patch, the only child of Adam Ulysses Patch and Henrietta Lebrune Patch, and the grandson of Adam Patch. After his parents' death, he lived with his grandfather, was tutored abroad for two years, and graduated at twenty from Harvard in 1909. He rents a nice apartment in New York City, drinks and converses with fellow Harvard alumni Richard Caramel and Maury Noble, dates Geraldine Burke, and marries Gloria Gilbert. The two irresponsibly spend his inheritance from his mother. They lease a gray little house in Marietta, Connecticut. He serves briefly in the army in the South, dallies with Dorothy Raycroft while there, and after the armistice returns to Manhattan. He spirals into acute alcoholism, is cut out of his dying grandfather's will, sues, succeeds in breaking the will, and is awarded $30 million. But it is too late. He has become partly insane. Gloria sticks with him. Anthony at different times calls himself Gilles de Sade, Sergeant R. A. Foley, and Packy McFarland. Although Fitzgerald makes the professional career of Richard Caramel parallel his own, the physical attributes of Anthony Patch resemble Fitzgerald's. The first name of Fitzgerald's father-in-law and brother-in-law was Anthony.

PATCH, GLORIA GILBERT. In *The Beautiful and Damned*, she is the beautiful, self-centered daughter of Russel Gilbert and Catherine Gilbert of Kansas City but lives in New York, at first with them. She is the cousin of Richard Caramel, who introduces her to his friend Anthony Patch, who is three years older than she. The two marry and share a stormy life. Her closest friends are Rachael Jerryl Barnes and Murial Kane. Gloria encourages movie executive Joseph Black and through him is given an unsuccessful screen test. She sticks with Anthony, who finally inherits $30 million. Zelda Sayre Fitzgerald* resented Fitzgerald's modeling Gloria partly on her.

PATCH, HENRIETTA LEBRUNE. In *The Beautiful and Damned*, she was the wife of Adam Ulysses Patch and the mother of Anthony Patch. She was from Boston and sang contralto. She died when Anthony was five.

PATERSON. In " 'Boil Some Water—Lots of It,' " he is a movie producer with whom Max Leam has lunch.

"PAT HOBBY AND ORSON WELLES" (1940). Short story. (Characters: Jack Berners, Jeff Boldini, Louie Griebel, Pat Hobby, Ike, Joe, Sam Jones, Kasper, Louie, Harold Marcus, Mario.) Pat, an unemployed scriptwriter, and the Hollywood studio bookie, Louie, agree that Orson Welles* does not deserve the deference and pay accorded him. Pat, barred from entering the lot without a card, hitches a ride with Harold Marcus, an important financier, who is on his way to meet Welles and tolerantly gives Pat a pass to the lot. Joe, the studio barber, tells Pat he looks like Welles but lacks only a beard. Jeff Boldini, a makeup man, bribes Pat $10 to let him glue on a beard and thus help Pat secure a job as one of several extras required to be bearded. Jeff drives Pat to the set but first secretly puts a card in the windshield with "Orson Welles" lettered on it. Crowds follow the car. Marcus sees it wheeling past, throws up his hands, and has a heart attack on the sidewalk. Someone asks "Mr. Welles" for the use of his car to take Marcus to the infirmary. Pat exits to Mario's bar and treats all the bearded actors with his $10.

"PAT HOBBY DOES HIS BIT" (1940). Short story. (Characters: Jack Berners, George Hilliard, Pat Hobby, Lily Keatts, Louie, Gyp McCarthy.) Hobby asks Hollywood stunt man Gyp McCarthy to loan him money for a car payment and waits on the set for Gyp to bring it. By mistake a trolleyed camera films Pat and leading lady Lily Keatts as she leaps out a set window. Since she immediately departs for England, producer Jack Berners and director George Hilliard must hire Pat to appear in a newly scripted scene to introduce him. To fortify Pat for the scene, in which he is to be run over by a car, Hilliard puts him in an iron corselet and gives him a drink. Lying in a ditch for the scene, Pat passes out and wakes up later to learn the car in question overturned short of the ditch. Pat is proud he held up filming twice.

"PAT HOBBY, PUTATIVE FATHER" (1940). Short story. (Characters: Jack Berners, Delia Brown, Dougie, Bonita Granville, Pat Hobby, Prince John Brown Hobby Indore, Raj Dak Raj Indore, Sir Singrim Dak Raj, Miss Raudenbush.) Early in September (1939), Jack Berners, a Hollywood executive, asks Pat Hobby, a collaborator on more than two dozen scripts (mostly before 1929), to show wealthy Sir Singrim Dak Raj and his nephew, Prince John Indore, visitors from India, around the lot. John explains he is Pat's "putative" son by Pat's wife, Delia Brown, to whom he was married (in 1926). She divorced him a year later, went to India, and married Raj Dak Raj Indore, now John's legal father. Pat does not fathom what a "potato" father is; however, smelling money, he sneaks young John into the rear of a stage where Bonita Granville, whom he especially wants to see, is acting. John is thrilled even though they wreck the scene by being visible. In gratitude Sir Singrim promises Pat $250 a month for life unless war comes and the British Empire claims his revenues. Pat is thrilled until he reads next morning, 3 September 1939, that war has erupted in Europe. A weakness here is that no ex-wife of Pat could ever attract an Indian prince.

"PAT HOBBY'S CHRISTMAS WISH" (1940). Short story. (Characters: Will Bronson, Buck, Harry Gooddorf, Pat Hobby, Joe Hopper, Helen Kagle, Pedro, William Desmond Taylor.) On Christmas Eve 1939 in Hollywood, Pat Hobby, forty-nine, is ordered by producer Harry Gooddorf to complete quickly the work on a horse-opera script. Pat's new secretary, Helen Kagle, reveals she has a letter dated 1 February 1921 and written by Gooddorf, her former lover, proving he killed William Desmond Taylor, a director. The two confront Gooddorf with the letter, hoping to improve their jobs; laughing, Gooddorf explains the letter meant simply that he and an associate let Taylor wreck himself financially. Adding someone else shot him, he tells Pat his Christmas gift will be not to be exposed.

"PAT HOBBY'S COLLEGE DAYS" (1941). Short story. (Characters: Jack Berners, Kit Doolan, Mrs. Kit Doolan, Pat Hobby, Jim Kresge, Evylyn Lascalles, Louie, Samuel K. Wiskith.) Pat Hobby, after finishing a four-week writing assignment in Hollywood, empties the contents of his desk into a pillowcase and asks his secretary, Evylyn Lascalles, to drive out of town and dump it all. She cannot find a deserted spot by the road. Meanwhile studio bookie Louie tells Pat he should go see Jim Kresge, who frequents the University of the Western Coast campus, and through him meet Louie's friend Kit Doolan, the athletic superintendent, because producer Jack Berners wants a script about campus life there and Doolan might give him an idea. Pat does so, learns from Doolan that there have been thefts on campus, is introduced to Samuel K. Wiskith, dean of students, and is summarizing his idea for a story about thefts and college football players when Evylyn bursts in with a campus guard. She wants to return his pillowcase, which contains empty liquor bottles. (Evylyn—or Pat—might easily have downloaded the bottles into a studio dumpster.)

"PAT HOBBY'S PREVIEW" (1940). Short story. (Characters: Jack Berners, Eleanor Carter, Ronald Colman, Harry Gooddorf, Pat Hobby, Louie, Ward Wainwright.) Producer Jack Berners reluctantly promises Pat Hobby tickets to the preview of a movie Pat says he wrote with Ward Wainwright. Pat picks up Eleanor Carter, a pretty blond from Boise touring the studio, boasts about his writing, and offers to take her to the preview. He picks up an envelope with tickets from Berners's secretary, thinks about borrowing an apartment and enticing Eleanor there tomorrow, and escorts her to the preview. They are denied admittance, however, because Berners deliberately gave them tickets to a Los Angeles burlesque show. Wainwright walks out of the show in disgust and gives them his ticket stubs, which they use to enter. Pat is happier than he should be because Eleanor is already distancing herself from him mentally. (Betraying carelessness here, Fitzgerald says Pat has only $12 to his name but buys a shirt, a hat, six drinks, and dinner for two.)

"PAT HOBBY'S SECRET" (1940). Short story. (Characters: Banizon, Conk, Pat Hobby, Louie, Smith, Mrs. Smith, Tarzan White, R. Parke Woll.) Executive Banizon tells Pat Hobby that playwright R. Parke Woll told him how the artillery shell got in the heroine's trunk in his play, but Banizon has forgotten and now is threatened with having to continue Parke's high salary. Pat says he will find out, for a bribe. He locates the drunken Woll at Conk's bar in Los Angeles, lies that Banizon's secretary remembers the ending but that Banizon has a better ending in mind, and induces Woll to reveal *his* ending. Realizing Pat's trick too late, Woll aims a blow at him, hits the bouncer instead, is hurled to the floor, and dies. At the inquest, Pat says he cannot describe the fight because everything went white. Banizon asks Pat what the script climax was, but Pat says everything did go blank.

THE PAT HOBBY STORIES. While Fitzgerald was working in Hollywood for Universal Studios, he wrote seventeen stories in 1939 and 1940 featuring Pat Hobby, a has-been screenwriter attempting to make a comeback in show business. The stories were all accepted by Arnold Gingrich* and published in *Esquire*. Hollywood actor Edward Everett Horton, Fitzgerald's Encinco landlord, expressed an abortive desire in February 1940 to turn the Pat Hobby stories into a movie or play for him.

Bibliography: Arnold Gingrich, Introduction to F. Scott Fitzgerald, *The Pat Hobby Stories* (New York: Simon and Schuster, 1995); Milton R. Stern, ''Will the Real Pat Hobby Please Stand Up?,'' Bryer, *New Essays*, 305–38; Elizabeth M. Varet-Ali, ''The Unfortunate Fate of Seventeen Fitzgerald 'Originals': Toward a Reading of *The Pat Hobby Stories* 'On Their Own Merit Completely,' '' *Journal of the Short Story in English* 14 (Spring 1990): 87–110.

"A PATRIOTIC SHORT" (1940). Short story. (Characters: Jack Berners, Ben Brown, Pat Hobby, General Fitzhugh Lee, [President] William McKinley, Maranda.) Pat Hobby is ordered by producer Jack Berners to work for a week, at $250, on the script of *True to Two Flags*, a movie short. It is about Fitzhugh Lee, former Confederate general, being invited by President William McKinley to serve during the Spanish-American War. Berners rejects Pat's idea of a Jewish angle in the story. Pat contrasts his glory days in the 1920s, when he had a swimming pool and lunched with the president of the United States, while the president was visiting the studio, with his present flunkie position, which is made clear when a new actress and some executives walk straight past him at the water cooler. In the script Pat has Lee reject McKinley's proffered commission. ''A Patriotic Short'' is generally regarded as the best Pat Hobby story.

PATT, LARRY. In ''Six of One—,'' he is one of the friends of Schofield's sons. Eighteen at the beginning of the story, he is described as a golf champion trying to get into Princeton.

PATTON, ROGER. In ''The Ice Palace,'' he is a professor of French, trained at Harvard and teaching at the university near the Bellamy family (in Minnesota). Sally Carrol Happer meets Patton at a Bellamy family dinner party and likes him better than the other guests.

PAUL. In ''Babylon Revisited,'' he is the head barman at a bar where Charlie Wales goes for gossip. Alix, a bartender, tells Charlie Wales that Paul is absent at his country house.

PAUL. In *Tender Is the Night*, he is the wealthy concessionaire at the bar in the Ritz in Paris. He likes hard-drinking Abe North.

PAUL. In *Thoughtbook*, he is a strong, athletic friend. He is based partly on Fitzgerald's St. Paul friend Paul Ballion.

PAULSON, CHARLEY. In ''Bernice Bobs Her Hair,'' he is a fellow whose dullness causes Bernice to converse daringly with him.

PAULSON, CHARLIE. In ''Head and Shoulders,'' he is a theater agent recommended as someone Horace Tarbox should see to have his trapeze performance booked.

PAXTON. In ''Imagination—and a Few Mothers,'' he is the happy husband of sensible Mrs. Paxton. He is in the stationery business, about which she knows nothing.

PAXTON. In ''Imagination—and a Few Mothers,'' he is a son of Paxton and his wife.

PAXTON, HARRY. In ''Imagination—and a Few Mothers,'' he is the dumb but happy and successful son of Paxton and his wife.

PAXTON, MRS. In ''Imagination—and a Few Mothers,'' she is the sensible wife of Paxton and the mother of their two sons, one named Harry, and one daughter, named Prudence. Mrs. Paxton's recipe for a joyful family is to leave its members pretty much alone and to lead her own happy life.

PAXTON, PRUDENCE. In ''Imagination—and a Few Mothers,'' she is the happy daughter of Paxton and his wife.

PAXTON, SPEED. In ''A Night at the Fair,'' he is the wild son of a local brewer, is with a blond girlfriend at the state fair, and drives a Blatz Wildcat.

PAYSON. In "No Flowers," he is evidently an official in charge of having Phil Savage expelled from the university, in Marjorie Clark's dream.

PEARSON, SLIM. In *Tender Is the Night*, he is someone Ritz concessionaire Paul tells Abe North is leaving France by ship next day.

PEAT. In "Head and Shoulders," he and his brothers are publishers of a new edition of Spinoza that Horace Tarbox would like to consult.

PECHARD, MARGOT. In "The Intimate Strangers," she is the servant, single at first, of Marquise Sara de la Guillet de la Guimpé on Long Island and elsewhere. Later, while working in Paris, Margot marries Paul Pechard. In 1926 she tells Sara that Cedric Killian is back in Paris.

PECHARD, PAUL. In "The Intimate Strangers," he is a footman at the Parisian mansion to which Marquise Sara de la Guillet de la Guimpé is invited. His wife, Margot Pechard, tells Sara about Cedric Killian.

PEDRO. In "Pat Hobby's Christmas Wish," he is a character in a horse-opera script Pat Hobby is dictating.

PEEBLES, CLAUDE. In "Not in the Guidebook," he is an American movie director. William Driscoll shows Peebles and his wife some "apache dens" in Paris.

PEEBLES, MRS. CLAUDE. In "Not in the Guidebook," she goes with her husband, a movie director, to Parisian night spots.

PELTZER. In "Family in the Wind," he is a neighbor of the Janneys. His house is destroyed by the first tornado.

"A PENNY SPENT" (1925). Short story. (Characters: Prince Abrisini, Hallie Bushmill, Jessie Pepper Bushmill, Julius Bushmill, Corcoran, Major Sir Reynolds Fitz-Hugh, Frederico, Jack, Claude Nosby, Countess Perimont.) Julius Bushmill, a millionaire businessman from Ohio, enters the Brix Grill bar in Paris one July evening and on an impulse hires Corcoran, a formerly rich, decent young American, born in Paris and knowledgeable about Europe, to escort his wife, Jessie Pepper Bushmill, and their daughter, Hallie Bushmill, who is to meet Claude Nosby, her fiancé and Bushmill's business associate, in Amsterdam a month hence. Corcoran and the Bushmill women are to visit tourist spots in Belgium and the Netherlands while Bushmill is busy in England. Corcoran is to account for money spent. The trio have limited fun until Hallie tells Corcoran to break loose and live it up with her. The resourceful man spends $12,000 drafting consulate friends in Brussels and bribing titled personages for a glittering whirl. In due time, the Americans meet Bushmill and also Nosby. When Bushmill reckons accounts, he professes to be unhappy but, with Hallie's encouragement, retains Corcoran to escort Jessie, Hallie, and Nosby to Naples. Nosby's seasickness prevents his going to nearby Capri's Blue Grotto, but the others enjoy it. When they are being driven south toward Sicily at night, Corcoran senses they have been followed ever since Nosby withdrew $10,000 from a Neapolitan bank for a business deal in Sicily. Corcoran foils an attempted robbery. Corcoran becomes Bushmill's son-in-law and is adept at making money for the firm by his daring purchases.

PEPIN, GEORGE. In "The Rubber Check," he is Val Schuyler's mother's fourth husband. When Val is nineteen, his mother and Pepin marry and go to Europe.

PEPIN, MRS. GEORGE. In "The Rubber Check," she is Val Schuyler's mother. Her first husband was a man named Jones, Val's father now deceased. Her third husband was a man named Schuyler. When Val is nineteen, she marries George Pepin, gives Val an allowance of $25 a month, tardily covers his bounced check, goes to Europe with Pepin, and dies, leaving Val $20,000 when he is about twenty-three.

PEPYS, SANDRA. In "Head and Shoulders," she is the heroine of *Sandra Pepys, Syncopated*, Marcia Tarbox's autobiographical novel.

PERCY. In *Safety First!*, he ridicules Postimpressionist cubism and modern art and is called a parlor snake by the chorus. He would like a girlfriend who resembles snappy movie actresses.

PERCY. In "The Unspeakable Egg," he is the folksy yardman of Cal Marsden and Josephine Marsden of Montauk Point. He and Dr. Roswell Gallup arm themselves when George Van Tyne makes a commotion on the beach.

"THE PERFECT LIFE" (1929). Short story. (Characters: Dr. Bacon, Bates, Erminie Gilberte Labouisse Bibble, Imogene Bissel, Cuckoo Conklin, Leonard Edward Davies De Vinci, Dorsey, George Dorsey, Jobena Dorsey, Mrs. Dorsey, Emil, John Granby, Hicks, George Kampf, Mrs. George Kampf, William S. Kampf, Basil Duke Lee, Sam.) Basil earns praise for playing quarterback well on the St. Regis school team against the winning Exeter team. John Granby, a St. Regis graduate and now an upright Princeton student, attends the game, commends Basil, walks with him, and persuades him to become a moral role model at school—no smoking, drinking, swearing, kissing girls, raiding the icebox, and so on. Basil is so impressed by the idea of leading the perfect life that when he is a guest during Thanksgiving vacation at the well-appointed Manhattan home of fellow student George Dorsey he behaves with great reserve. He accompanies George and some of his other friends to an afternoon dance. He is attracted to George's pretty sister, Jobena Dorsey, eighteen, but dislikes not only her mode of dancing but also Leonard Edward Davies De Vinci, nicknamed Skiddy, who is a Yale dropout, drinks too much, and is a clear danger to Jobena. She finds Basil alluring but when he feels she is too flirtatious in a hansom cab on the way to the theater, he lectures her on purity and is nonplussed by her chilly response. That night, back at the Dorsey home, he overhears Jobena and Skiddy talking. She calls Basil nasty and priggish and agrees to elope with Skiddy next day. After Thanksgiving Day dinner, Basil tries to inform Mr. Dorsey but is tongue-tied and instead takes a taxi to Skiddy's residence, where he finds the fellow packing and drinking. Basil lures him into having cocktails at the Biltmore. He laments the death of his dog and misses his rendezvous with Jobena. Basil returns to her—waiting at home with suitcase at the door—and tells her Skiddy has gone to visit his dog's tomb. She seems relieved, sniffs liquor on his breath, chides him for joking in the cab about the perfect life, and kisses him in the dark. On the way back to school, Basil tells George he had some drinks on Thanksgiving Day but has promised Jobena to lay off until he is twenty-one.

PERIMONT, COUNTESS. In ''A Penny Spent,'' she is a person whose appearance Corcoran buys to help entertain Jessie Pepper Bushmill and her daughter, Hallie Bushmill, in Brussels.

PERKINS, MAX (1884–1947). (Full name: Maxwell Evarts Perkins.) Editor. He was born in New York City and graduated from Harvard in 1907 with a major in economics. After some years as a reporter for the *New York Times* (1907–1910), he joined Charles Scribner's Sons, publishers. A close friend from boyhood on was critic Van Wyck Brooks. In 1910 Perkins married Louise Saunders; the couple had five daughters. In 1916 he saw military service on the Mexican border. Through brilliance and hard work, Perkins rose from being a member of Scribner's editorial staff (1914) to vice president (1932). Though competent as a writer, he realized his genius lay in helping better authors. In 1918 Fitzgerald, while in the army, gave Shane Leslie,* an Irish journalist published by Scribner's, the manuscript of ''The Romantic Egotist'' which Leslie showed to Perkins. He returned it to Fitzgerald with suggestions and encouragement. Perkins showed the revision to Charles Scribner III, the director's son; although Perkins and young Scribner liked the manuscript, it was rejected. After the war ended, Fitzgerald reworked the novel and titled it *This Side of Paradise*, which Scribner's published (March 1920) and which, partly because of Perkins's helpful suggestions, was an instant best-seller. By this time Fitzgerald had published several short pieces, many of which he sent to Perkins, who chose the stories included in *Flappers and Philosophers* (September 1920). Fitzgerald was Perkins's first major literary discovery, and Perkins remained his superb editor; thus they helped each other in their respective fields. Perkins's early suggestion that Fitzgerald could ask for advances on future royalties helped him establish a habit of spending beyond his means. Perkins saw to the publication of *The Beautiful and Damned* (March 1922). In advance of its success, Fitzgerald and Zelda Sayre Fitzgerald* went abroad in 1921 armed with a letter of introduction from Perkins to John Galsworthy. Fitzgerald dedicated *The Beautiful and Damned* to Perkins, Leslie, and also George Jean Nathan* (whose *Smart Set*, copublished with H. L. Mencken,* had accepted a few of Fitzgerald's early stories). Perkins wanted a second collection of stories to follow the second novel, bridled at Fitzgerald's title, *Tales of the Jazz Age* (September 1922), but agreed. Although Perkins wanted another novel next, Fitzgerald sent him a play tentatively titled ''Gabriel's Trombone,'' which Perkins tactfully criticized. He was right; retitled *The Vegetable*, it was a failure on stage and when published (April 1923). Also in 1923 Fitzgerald recommended Ring Lardner* to Perkins, who published Lardner's *How to Write Short Stories (with Samples)* (1924). In 1924 Fitzgerald was the first to call Perkins's attention to Ernest Hemingway,* which resulted in Hemingway's association with Perkins and Scribner's. Also in 1924 Fitzgerald sent Perkins the manuscript of ''Trimalchio in West Egg,'' retitled *The Great Gatsby* (April 1925). Perkins read the manuscript at one sitting, praised Fitzgerald, and made suggestions which Fitzgerald gratefully followed; they included hinting here and there about Gatsby's background and source of wealth, mentioning Oxford a few more times, and having Gatsby repeat ''old sport.'' Perkins dissuaded Fitzgerald from retitling the novel ''Gold-Hatted Gatsby'' or ''Under the Red White and Blue'' and was happy to publish *All the Sad Young Men* (February 1926), the next story collection; Perkins preferred its title to ''Dear Money,'' Fitzgerald's earlier idea.

Fitzgerald distanced himself from Perkins because of Zelda's illness and his going to Hollywood. Meanwhile, Perkins saw to the publication of Hemingway's *The Sun Also Rises* (1926) and *A Farewell to Arms* (1929), Lardner's *The Love Nest and Other Stories* (1926) and *The Round Up* (1929), and Thomas Wolfe's *Look Homeward, Angel: A Story of the Buried Life* (1929), and works by other first-rate authors as well. In 1932 Zelda secretly sent Perkins a chaotic draft of her novel, *Save Me the Waltz*. When Fitzgerald learned about it, he was angry, read it, and demanded certain changes. Perkins worked tactfully to get it into print. After advising Fitzgerald, he accepted the manuscript of *Tender Is the Night*, which he serialized in *Scribner's Magazine* (January-April 1934) and published in rewritten book form (April). By 1935 Fitzgerald had assembled enough previously published stories to make up *Taps at Reveille*, which Perkins persuaded Scribner's to publish (March). More than a year later, however, Fitzgerald still owed the firm just over $6,000, as well as unpaid sums Perkins had loaned him—all this because of his demands for advances, his lifestyle, and his wife's illness. Perkins did Fitzgerald two favors in 1936. First, when Hemingway wrote in ''The Snows of Kilimanjaro'' (1936) that someone had to explain to Fitzgerald that, yes, the rich are different from others because they have more money, Fitzgerald was hurt and Perkins got Hemingway to stop denigrating him.

Second, Perkins persuaded Marjorie Kinnan Rawlings, whose *The Yearling* (1938) he was editing, to visit Fitzgerald, abed with arthritis; their meeting was salubrious. In 1938 Fitzgerald capitalized humorously on his professional relationship with Perkins. George Jaggers, Finnegan's editor in Fitzgerald's short story "Financing Finnegan," advances the author-hero funds exactly as Perkins, Fitzgerald's editor, did. In 1939 Fitzgerald while in Hollywood got Perkins to try to serialize what became *The Last Tycoon*; he failed with *Collier's* and the *Saturday Evening Post*, but after reading the first part he encouraged Fitzgerald to continue writing it. When Fitzgerald died, Perkins attended the funeral, learned he had been named, with John Biggs, Jr.,* coexecutor of Fitzgerald's will, declined to serve officially, but with Harold Ober,* Fitzgerald's former literary agent, advised Biggs in careful detail. Perkins arranged for Biggs, Ober, and Gerald Murphy,* one of Fitzgerald's friends during their expatriation in France in the 1920s, to loan Fitzgerald's daughter Scottie* money to continue at Vassar College to graduation. Sheilah Graham,* who was Fitzgerald's lover in Hollywood and to whom Fitzgerald had introduced Perkins in New York in 1938, sent Perkins a typed copy of *The Last Tycoon*. He persuaded Edmund Wilson* to edit the unfinished novel as part of a 1941 book reprinting *The Great Gatsby* and five short stories. Perkins tried without success first to get personnel at Princeton to issue a volume of Fitzgerald's writings and second to encourage Matthew Josephson to prepare a biography of Fitzgerald. Before Arthur Mizener published his premier Fitzgerald biography in 1951, Perkins had died. Eerily, a year after Perkins died, Zelda burned to death, and seventeen years after that, Perkins's widow burned to death.

Bibliography: A. Scott Berg, *Max Perkins: Editor of Genius* (New York: Dutton, 1978); John Kuehl and Jackson R. Bryer, eds., *Dear Scott/Dear Max: The Fitzgerald-Perkins Correspondence* (New York: Scribner's, 1971).

PERRIN. In *Tender Is the Night*, he is a suave American now working in a bank frequented by Dick Diver.

PERRY. In "Crazy Sunday," he and his wife host a theater party Joel Coles attends with Stella Walker Calman.

PERRY. In "First Blood," he is Josephine Perry's little brother.

PERRY, CONSTANCE ("CONNIE"). In "First Blood," she is Josephine Perry's older sister. Her interest in Anthony Harker causes Josephine to want to gain his affections temporarily. In "A Nice Quiet Place," Josephine almost wrecks Constance's wedding to Malcolm Libby by luring him into an embrace in a garden before the ceremony.

PERRY, HERBERT T. In "First Blood," he is Josephine Perry's father, habitually busy at work. Revealed here is the fact that the Perry family wealth was from railroad investments. In "A Nice Quiet Place," he is mad when Josephine almost wrecks her sister Constance Perry's wedding. In "A Woman with a Past," he learns while on business in New York of Josephine's expulsion from Miss Brereton's school, provides moral support, and takes her to Hot Springs for a vacation. Perry is identified here as a Yale man. In "A Snobbish Story," Josephine sees him with a floozy, hints at what she knows while getting him to back John Boynton Bailey's play financially, and is later embarrassed to learn Perry and his wife have been paying off the floozy to leave Mrs. Perry's brother, Will, alone. In "Emotional Bankruptcy," he is Josephine's unseen father, who wants her to come home for Christmas.

PERRY, JOSEPHINE ("JO"). In "First Blood," she lives with her parents in Chicago and is sixteen in 1914. She tries to elope with Travis de Coppet and necks in cars with him, but when she sees her older sister Constance Perry's handsome boyfriend, Anthony Harker, she goes after him only to cause trouble. Her most reliable friend is Ed Bement. In "A Nice Quiet Place," her mother gets Josephine, sixteen and attractive, away to Farm Islands, a nice quiet Michigan resort area. Once there Josephine fails to get Sonny Dorrance's interest. Back in Lake Forest, outside Chicago, she attends Ed's house party, causes her ex-boyfriend's girlfriend, Evangeline Ticknor, to leave suddenly, disrupts Constance's marriage ceremony by luring Constance's groom-to-be into an embrace, and persuades Ed to help her get back to Sonny. In "A Woman with a Past," Josephine is escorted to the Yale prom by Ridgeway Saunders, dances with Ed, and tries to take her Brereton school friend Adele Craw's Yale boyfriend, Dudley Knowleton, away from her. Josephine skirts embarrassment in a locked room with Book Chaffee during the dance and is expelled from school when she innocently falls and slips into the arms of Ernest Waterbury. At Hot Springs on vacation with her father, she gets nowhere again with Dudley, recognizes she ought not to jeopardize long-range friendships by rushing into brief affairs, but strolls into the moonlight with a Princeton dropout. In "A Snobbish Story," Josephine is bored at the Lake Forest tennis tournament, has lunch with John Boynton Bailey, and sees her father with a floozy at lunch. She attends a theater workshop and is thrilled when Bailey wants to cast her rather than his wife, Evelyn, in his play. Josephine's father agrees to be a financial backer of the play until everyone learns that Bailey's wife has tried to commit suicide. Josephine learns her parents are paying off the floozy to keep her away from Mrs. Perry's brother, Will. Josephine decides to associate hereafter with the rich and powerful. Bailey sarcastically calls Josephine Miss Gotrocks and Miss Potterfield-Swiftcormick. In "Emotional Bankruptcy," Josephine is a student, seventeen, in fall 1916, at Miss Truby's New York school. Her closest friend is Lillian Hammel. Josephine dates Ivy League lads callously, becomes enamored of Captain Edward Dicer, but rejects him after they kiss. She discovers she cannot both spend and have her emotional capital. Josephine Perry is based on

Ginevra King,* a Chicago debutante whose family position and wealth made her untouchable by Fitzgerald, who was enamored of her briefly.

PERRY, MRS. In "Crazy Sunday," she and her husband host a theater party Joel Coles attends with Stella Walker Calman.

PERRY, MRS. HERBERT T. In "First Blood," she is the ineffectual mother of Constance Perry and Josephine Perry. In "A Nice Quiet Place," she requires Josephine to leave both Chicago and adjacent Lake Forest and accompany her to Farm Islands, a nice quiet place in Michigan. Back home, she is distressed when Josephine briefly disrupts Constance's wedding to Malcolm Libby. In "A Snobbish Story," it is her brother Will's disreputable girlfriend or wife that Mr. Perry is paying to stay away. In "Emotional Bankruptcy," she wants Josephine to come home for Christmas vacation and lectures her vacuously about love and marriage.

PERSIA, SHAH OF. In *Tender Is the Night*, he is the owner of a fabulously appointed automobile somehow commandeered by Dick Diver for a drunken drive through Paris.

PETE. In " 'I Didn't Get Over,' " he is the owner of a bar in the back room of which several members of the class of 1916 reminisce twenty years later. He tells Joe Boone and Tomlinson that their wives have telephoned from the inn: if left alone ten more minutes they will drive to Philadelphia.

PETER. In *Mister Icky*, he is a sweet little boy who converses courteously but often inanely with Icky.

PETER ("PETE"). In *Fie! Fie! Fi-Fi!*, he is the man Gwen is supposed to marry. She prefers Bill. Peter bides his time because Bill is after Gladys.

PETERS, BIRDY. In *The Last Tycoon*, she is one of Pat Brady's three secretaries. The others are Maude and Rosemary Schmiel. Cecelia Brady finds Birdy hiding naked in the closet of her sweaty father Pat's office, much to his embarrassment.

PETERS, ELSIE. In "Babylon Revisited," she is the daughter of Marion Peters and Lincoln Peters and therefore is Charles J. Wales's niece.

PETERS, LINCOLN. In "Babylon Revisited," he is an American banker in Paris. He is the husband of Marion Peters, Charles J. Wales's sister-in-law, and the father of Richard Peters and Elsie Peters. Lincoln defers to his wife. He is partly modeled on Newman Smith, the husband of Fitzgerald's sister-in-law Rosalind Sayre Smith,* both of whom Fitzgerald disliked.

PETERS, MARION. In ''Babylon Revisited,'' she is the sister of the deceased Helen Wales and hence Charles J. Wales's sister-in-law. She is Lincoln Peters' querulous wife and the mother of Richard Peters and Elsie Peters. She blames Charlie for Helen's death, hates him, and is jealous of his money. She has custody of his daughter, Honoria Wales. Marion is based on Rosalind Sayre Smith,* Zelda Sayre Fitzgerald's sister. Rosalind detested Fitzgerald and blamed him for Zelda's 1930 breakdown; at that time, Rosalind and her husband, Newman Smith, were in Brussels, Belgium, where he was working for the Guaranty Trust Company and where they were said to be living dull lives.

PETERS, RICHARD. In ''Babylon Revisited,'' he is the son of Marion Peters and Lincoln Peters and therefore is Charles J. Wales's nephew.

PETERSON, JULES. In *Tender Is the Night*, he is supposedly an Afro-Scandinavian shoe-polish inventor who is murdered in Rosemary Hoyt's hotel room in Paris as a result of the fracas caused in part by Abe North. Dick Diver persuades the hotel owner and manager to dispose of the body elsewhere.

PETROCOBESCO, EMILY CASTLETON. In ''Majesty,'' she is the daughter of rich Harold Castleton. She calls off her wedding to William Brevoort Blair of Newport, Rhode Island, at the last minute. She wanders in Europe, picks up with Prince Gabriel Petrocobesco, marries him, and becomes queen of Czjeck-Hansa when he becomes king.

PETROCOBESCO, PRINCE GABRIEL (''TUTU''). In ''Majesty,'' he is the prince of Czjeck-Hansa. He is reportedly an unwanted ne'er-do-well who loves and is loved by Emily Castleton. William Brevoort Blair and Olive Mercy Blair go east of Hungary to try to rescue her from the fat little man; when he becomes king of the magnesium-rich little country, they marry and she becomes queen.

PHILIPPE, COUNT OF VILLEFRANCHE. In ''In the Darkest Hour,'' he is the sturdy Frenchman, twenty in the year 872, who returns from Moorish Spain to inspire a group of churchmen and peasants in his native Loire Valley to destroy an encampment of Viking invaders. In ''The Count of Darkness,'' he orders his followers to build houses and a camp. He demands tribute from a caravan of traders for crossing ''his'' ford. He fancies Letgarde, a girl from Aquitaine; when he treats her roughly, she deserts him and drowns trying to cross the Loire. In ''The Kingdom in the Dark,'' while surveying his property, Philippe finds beautiful Griselda, who is escaping lewd King Louis the Stammerer. He conceals her when King Louis approaches, even swearing a false oath to do so. Moving on, Louis orders three of his men to burn Philippe's property. With difficulty, Griselda persuades Philippe to remain loyal to Louis. In ''Gods of Darkness,'' he is threatened first by the Duke of Maine and his army and then by pagan cultist Becquette Le Poire. Griselda, now called Countess Griselda, and Jacques save him because they too are potent cultists. Philippe vows to guard his people by a combination of Christian and pagan strength. He and Griselda will wed. Fitzgerald regarded Philippe's personality as resembling that of Ernest Hemingway,* whom Fitzgerald regarded as combining physical toughness and sensitivity. He planned to expand Philippe's adventures to novel length. "Gods of Darkness," however, was the last episode. In some of the stories, the hero is called Count Phillipe de Villefranche.

THE PHILIPPE STORIES. After the popular failure of *Tender Is the Night*, Fitzgerald hoped to win back his public with a novel to be titled "The Count of Darkness" and cast in ninth- and tenth-century France. Out of this project grew four stories. Fitzgerald wrote to Max Perkins* (3 January 1939) that he would like to continue Phillippe's adventure to 950 A.D., by which time the feudal system would be consolidated, but nothing came of the plan, probably because Fitzgerald realized his historical fiction was giving way to melodrama.

Bibliography: Peter L. Hays, "Philippe, 'Count of Darkness,' and F. Scott Fitzgerald, Feminist?," Bryer, *New Essays*, 291–304; Janet Lewis, "Fitzgerald's 'Philippe, Count of Darkness,' " *FH/A 1975*, 7–32.

PHILLIPS. In " 'Trouble,' " he is the Winslow family butler, whom Frederic Winslow curtly orders to bring him a bottle of beer for breakfast.

PICASSO, PABLO (1881–1973). Spanish painter. In *Tender Is the Night*, he was on the Riviera in 1925 near where Dick Diver and Nicole Diver live.

PICKERING, THOMAS. In "Too Cute for Words," he is a person, class of 1896, to whom a lunch basket is to be delivered. Bryan Bowers hears about the matter at his undergraduate club before the Princeton-Harvard football game.

PICKMAN, JOSEPHINE. In "The Bowl," she is Jeff Deering's date when Dolly Harlan first meets Vienna Thorne. Josephine's family has a chauffeur-driven car.

PIERCE. In *Tender Is the Night*, he is a young teller at a bank in Paris frequented by Dick Diver.

"THE PIERIAN SPRINGS AND THE LAST STRAW" (1917). Short story. (Characters: The Honorable Howard Bixby, Fulham, Myra Fulham, Rombert, George Rombert, Miss Rombert, Mrs. Thomas Rombert, Thomas Rombert, Sedgewick.) The observer-narrator is the son of Thomas Rombert, an eastern lawyer with roots in the West. When eleven, the boy hears his parents discuss George Rombert, his father's brother, an unmarried novelist notorious for scrapes with women. In the next several years, the narrator learns that the heroines of Uncle George's well-written, witty, cynical novels disturb conservative readers but impress critics with their promise. At twenty, the narrator takes a trip to the West, dines with his father's unmarried sister, with whom George lives, and goes to George's club, where the man is drinking heavily and chatting brilliantly with friends. He tells his intrigued nephew about himself. As a Williams sophomore he began a stormy affair with Myra, a fascinating femme fatale. After a quarrel during his senior year, he made the mistake of groveling and her negative response crushed him. He says his life stopped at twenty-one, and he has been writing ever since. Myra, now the widow Mrs. Fulham, is playing bridge upstairs in the club. When George introduces her, his nephew observes a magnetic creature, just under thirty, with an expressive mouth. She gives George a tongue lashing, as though he is a naughty dog, and boasts to the nephew she has been doing so for ten years. George, at first subservient, suddenly snaps. He calls her dead husband a crook, threatens to flog her next husband, and wrenches her wedding ring from her finger, breaking it in the process. Guests scream, and the two men leave. A month later, George and Myra elope just before her planned marriage to the Honorable Howard Bixby. George never drank or wrote again but took up golf. The observer-narrator's function here is similar to that of Nick Carraway, the observer-narrator in *The Great Gatsby*.

PIERRE. In "The Kingdom in the Dark," he is a man loyal to Count Philippe of Villefranche. In "Gods of Darkness," it is revealed that he is Jacques's son.

PILGRIM, DR. In "The End of Hate," he is an Ohio dentist captured with his sister, Josie Pilgrim, by Confederate troops in Maryland. He extracts Prince Bonaparte's infected tooth, orders the torture of Tib Dulany by Union troops, proceeds to Georgetown, near Washington, D.C., practices there, and in April 1865 is about to go to France when Tib tracks him down. News of the assassination of President Abraham Lincoln causes all to end well.

PILGRIM, JOSIE. In "The End of Hate," she is Dr. Pilgrim's sister and is traveling with him to be a nurse in Georgetown when the two are captured by Confederate troops. She falls in love with Tib Dulany, seeks medical aid for him, later rejects Captain Taswell, and proposes to Tib.

"PILGRIMAGE" (1981). Poem. (Characters: Carter Brown, Fido.) A horse wearing glasses comes into town, reports to Carter Brown, and says he was named Fido because people thought he would be a dog. The joke is inspired by Brown's having been told so many lies about horses that no fact about horses would surprise him.

PINKARD, EMMY. In "Two Wrongs." *See* McChesney, Emmy Pinkard.

PIPER, DONALD. In "The Cut-Glass Bowl," he is the son of Evylyn Piper and Harold Piper. In the course of the story, he is six years old, doted on by his mother; fourteen, and away at school; and twenty-five, in the infantry and presumably killed in action.

PIPER, EVYLYN ("EVIE"). In "The Cut-Glass Bowl," she is the wife of Harold Piper and the mother of Donald Piper, born in 1893, and Julie Piper, born in 1905. Evylyn rejected the marriage proposal of Carleton Canby, who for her wedding in 1892 sent her a cut-glass bowl as a symbolic present. He said it was like her—hard, beautiful, empty, and easy to see through. She is beautiful but then less so during the course of the story. At twenty-seven, she splits up with her lover, Fred Gedney, and in the process wrenches her marriage. At thirty-five, she witnesses dreadful drunks at her birthday party and the horror of her daughter's cut thumb. At forty-six, she gets a message from the War Department reporting the death of Donald in World War I and dies trying to destroy the bowl—which betrayed Fred's hiding place, cut Julie, served the alcohol, and held Donald's death notification.

PIPER, HAROLD. In "The Cut-Glass Bowl," he is the husband of Evylyn Piper, who is nine years his junior. He has a hardware business with his younger brother, Milton Piper. Harold drinks too much. In the course of the story, he learns Evylyn has been having an affair with Fred Gedney, hosts the drunken party honoring his wife's thirty-fifth birthday, loses the opportunity to merge the Piper Brothers firm with Clarence Ahearn, and undoubtedly is sorrow-stricken first when his daughter, Julie Piper, loses a hand and later when his son, Donald Piper, dies in the war.

PIPER, JESSIE. In "The Cut-Glass Bowl." *See* Lowrie, Jessie Piper.

PIPER, JULIE. In "The Cut-Glass Bowl," she is daughter of Evylyn Piper and Harold Piper. In the course of the story, she is two years old, cuts her thumb on the cut-glass bowl, and suffers blood poisoning; and thirteen, long despondent after the amputation of her hand.

PIPER, MILTON. In "The Cut-Glass Bowl," he is the passive younger brother of Harold Piper and is in the hardware business with him.

PIRIE, DR. In "The Long Way Out," he is Mrs. George King's physician and delays telling the young woman, hospitalized for schizophrenia, of her husband's being killed in a car accident.

PISTACHIO. In "The Prince of Pests," he wonders about American neutrality.

PITOU. In *Shadow Laurels*, he is the owner of a Parisian wineshop. When Jaques Chandelle returns from America to Paris seeking information about his father Jean Chandelle, Pitou says he knew Jean and serves wine to Jaques and to Destage, Lamarque, and François Meridien, Jean's three old friends who enter the shop.

PLANT, DONALD. In "Three Hours between Planes," he is a widower, thirty-two. During a break in his air flight he phones Nancy Holmes Gifford, a former girlfriend he has not seen for twenty years. He happily visits her, only to be shocked when she mistakes him for another Donald, namely Donald Bowers.

PLAYFAIR, DICK. In " 'Send Me In, Coach,' " he is, in the play the boys rehearse, barred from college football because he played professional baseball while at Crescent Range. Bill Watchman is Dick Playfair in the play.

POE. In "The Ants at Princeton," he is one of two or more former Princeton football players named Poe and of legendary fame.

POINDEXTER, JO. In "Presumption," she is Noel Garneau's New York aunt, about thirty-five. When San Juan Chandler goes to her home, she thinks he is Brooks Fish Templeton and tells him Noel wants him to leave. When he says his name is Chandler, all is well.

POINDEXTER, MORTON. In "Presumption," he is Jo Poindexter's husband. They are rich.

POITIERS, COUNT OF. In "The Kingdom in the Dark," he is a nobleman whose costly guardsmen King Louis the Stammerer will not hire.

POLE. In *The Great Gatsby*, Nick Carraway lists Pole's name on a timetable as one of Jay Gatsby's summer guests. He is from West Egg.

POMPIA. In *This Side of Paradise*, she is a person named in a freshman poem by Thomas Parke D'Invilliers. She is also called Pia.

POOLE, E. P. In "Zone of Accident," he is a wealthy chain-store magnate who is to be a judge of the Baltimore beauty contest. When he becomes ill, actress Loretta Brooke is chosen to replace him.

POORE. In "The Bowl," he is a Princeton football team player, at end.

"POOR OLD MARRIAGE" (1921). Review of *Brass, a Novel of Marriage* by Charles Gilman Norris.*

"THE POPE AT CONFESSION" (1919). Poem. This sonnet describes the pope, on his knees and with anguish in his face, making his humble confession to a ragged friar in the sumptuous Vatican.

POPOLOUS, JOE. In *The Last Tycoon*, he is a wealthy theater owner and one of Monroe Stahr's financial backers. Popolous fought in the Foreign Legion and is anti-Semitic.

POPULAR DAUGHTER. In *This Side of Paradise*, she is the generic type of flirtatious teenager whose parents incorrectly think she declines to kiss before getting engaged. She is also called "P.D."

"THE POPULAR GIRL" (1922). Short story. (Characters: Tom Bowman, Yanci Bowman, Carty Braden, R. R. Comerford, Haedge, Ellen Harley, Hilma, Scott Kimberly, Jimmy Long, Mrs. Oral, Jerry O'Rourke, Elsie Prendergast, Mrs. Orrin Rogers, Orrin Rogers, Pete Rogers, Semple.) Yanci Bowman, pretty, bored, and twenty, resolves to marry soon and well. While dancing at their country club in the Midwest one cool November evening, she hopes her widowered father, Tom Bowman, who is with her, will stay fairly sober for a change. Mrs. Orrin Rogers, their neighbor, introduces her to a family relative named Scott Kimberly, rich and twenty-five, visiting from New York. Yanci and Scott dance and spar a little, and he helps get drunken Tom to the rented house where he and Yanci live. She and Scott then enjoy a drive, kiss, and return. Yanci rebukes her sleepy father, who apologizes, contritely gives her a check for $300 for a half-promised trip to New York, then suddenly dies. After four days, Scott calls on Yanci in awkward sympathy and as a convenience gives her $300 for her check. She risks her entire small inheritance on a wild plan and writes to Scott that she will visit New York in February and will be in the Ritz Carlton for ten days. On a Monday he phones and comes to have tea and dance. She puts him off with lies about how busy her calendar is. On Wednesday, she has lunch with him, after which she pretends to take a train to the Princeton prom, to which she is not invited. On Friday, Scott phones, but she puts him off. On Monday, her first week's hotel bill leaves her with little money. After lunch with Scott on Wednesday, she meets a friend she phoned for a date to deceive Scott. On Thursday, she is robbed of her last fifty dollars by a store clerk. After paying her hotel bill, on Friday, she spends her last dime on a bun and grows faint. On Saturday, she tells Scott she is going to visit her aunt in Florida; he follows her taxi, which she cannot pay for, rescues her, and reveals that her father's $300 check bounced and that he followed her to Princeton as a surprise, has figured out everything, but still loves her.

"POPULAR PARODIES—NO. 1" (1917). Poem. The student-poet asks the professor whether he will be failed now or later.

PORCELAIN AND PINK (1920). Full title: *Porcelain and Pink (A One-Act Play)*. Play. (Characters: Bergson, Calkins, Davis, Gaby Deslys, Julie Marvis, Lois Marvis, Parker.) All prettily pink, Julie Marvis, almost twenty, is bathing and singing in a blue porcelain tub in a room in a summer cottage. Her sister, Lois, a year older, enters. She wants to bathe before keeping her date with Calkins, but Julie will not get out of the tub. Lois leaves her, without a towel. Calkins appears at a high window, unable to see down at the tub, and mistakes Julie's voice for Lois's. They discuss literature, and Julie reveals her ignorance. Lois walks in with a towel, sees and is seen by Calkins, and faints. When Calkins offers to enter, Julie plans to leave.

PORTER. In "For the time that our man spent in pressing your suit," he is the addressee of the poem, criticized for his rudeness.

PORTERFIELD, JIM. In *Thoughtbook*, he likes Marie Hersey. Fitzgerald resents Jim's affection for Margaret Armstrong.

POTTER. In "The Smilers," he is a plump broker who tells Waldron Crosby that Crosby has been wiped out in the stock market.

POTTERFIELD-SWIFTCORMICK, MISS. In "A Snobbish Story," this is a name socialist John Boynton Bailey sarcastically calls Josephine Perry of Chicago. It is a combination of several powerful Chicago names—Potter Palmer, Marshall Field, Gustavus Franklin Swift, and Joseph Medill McCormick.

POWELL, ALICE. In "The Jelly-Bean," she is one of James Powell's ancestors. Her name, with the date 1812, is in an old Church of England prayer book.

POWELL, AMANTHIS. In "Dice, Brassknuckles & Guitar," she is the New Jersey girl, eighteen, that James Powell (no relation) invites to dance after he gets his summer school established in Southampton. Her father is a judge. She stands by Jim when others try to embarrass him.

POWELL, JAMES ("JELLY-BEAN," "JIM"). In "The Jelly-Bean," he is the jelly-bean: a typically listless Southerner. His family has fallen on hard times. He was shy in school, became an expert auto mechanic and dice manipulator, served in the U.S. Navy in 1917–1918, and at twenty-one returned to his home town (Tarleton) in Georgia. He goes to a country-club dance and sees Nancy Lamar again after a silence of fifteen years. He befriends her by cleaning gum off her shoe and also saving her from a craps-game debt, is wildly kissed for his kindness, falls in love almost at once, and is stunned when she elopes with rich Ogden Merritt. In "Dice, Brassknuckles & Guitar," he is from Tarleton, Georgia. At twenty-four, he establishes a summer school in Southampton to teach crap shooting, jazz, and self-defense. He is mistreated by many Northerners.

POWERS, KENNETH. In "Babes in the Woods," he is a college freshman, eighteen, who delays returning to school in order to meet Isabelle at her schoolmate Elaine Terrell's party during Christmas vacation. He and Isabelle dance, flirt, and would kiss but for being interrupted.

PRAYLE. In "A Debt of Honor," he is a Confederate Army soldier who answers "present" when the roll is called for those available for sentry duty.

PRECAUTION PRIMARILY (1917). Play. (Characters: Bromine Halogen, Chlorine Halogen, Corinne Halogen, Fluorine Halogen, Iodine Halogen, Hughie Jennings, Henry O'Day.) The scene is a paint box with various colors. The audience is in black and white. After a chorus of gibberish, the football team and the prom committee enter in disguise. Two authors and five Halogens discuss the performance. After the Halogens sing about the ballet, a preceptor and a student conclude that people are hard to please.

PRENDERGAST, ELSIE. In "The Popular Girl," she writes society news for a paper in the Midwestern city in which Yanci Bowman lives. After Yanci's father, Tom Bowman, dies, his friend Haedge suggests Yanci might seek employment as Elsie did. Yanci declines.

PRESTON, KITTY. In "The Last of the Belles," she is a Tarleton girl who offends Ailie Calhoun by presuming to show responsive interest in Lieutenant Earl Schoen.

"PRESUMPTION" (1926). Short story. (Characters: Chandler, Chandler, Cora Chandler, San Juan Chandler, Harold Garneau, Mrs. Harold Garneau, Noel Garneau, Billy Harper, Holyoke, Miss Holyoke, Mrs. Holyoke, Holly Morgan, Jo Poindexter, Morton Poindexter, Brooks Fish Templeton.) While an impoverished student at Henderson College, San Juan Chandler, shy and pimply at twenty, worked one summer at a Montana dude ranch, where he met Noel Garneau; liking each other, they kissed. Noel, seventeen and wild, is from a wealthy Boston family with a summer home at nearby Culpepper Bay. San Juan's uppity Boston cousin, Cora Chandler, vacations there; so Juan wrote to Noel asking to see her there and is now visiting Cora before returning to school. Once Noel arrives from the Adirondacks, things go badly. She drives him to her club to watch a tennis tournament and invites him to a small dinner party including another young couple, but she repulses his clumsy embrace and is attentive to a suave fellow at the beach next day. At Cora's suggestion, Juan tries some golf at the club, where he teams up with a man about fifty who reveals he once knew Cora but quarreled with her when she thought his wife, a friend of Cora's from Boston, was too good for him, since he was from the Midwest. Encouraged, Juan blurts out his own tale of woe: poor boy still in college loves rich girl, who may not wait and is pursued by Eastern fellow. The older man tells Juan to go after the girl and if, to do so, he leaves college to get in touch with him. He gives Juan his card and departs; the name on the card is that of Harold Garneau. Juan quits school before his senior year, takes his inheritance of $1,500 and goes to Boston, and—as in a fairy tale—makes a sizable fortune by investing in a venture to keep seafood cold. Although a couple of years have passed, Juan, well dressed and confident, calls on Noel, who according to the *Boston Transcript* has now "come out." She welcomes him gaily, but their twilight chat is interrupted when Brooks Fish Templeton pops in for a visit. She encourages Juan to come again, but two days later he reads in the paper her parents' announcement of her engagement to Templeton, Harvard class of 1912. Juan goes to the Garneau residence, begs distraught Noel to marry him, is interrupted by Brooks, and waits in another room until Noel's father orders him away and spirits her out of town. Juan seeks her by phoning around. No luck. In desperation he visits Cora, who tells him Jo Poindexter, Noel's aunt in New York, may be harboring her. Rushing to the Poindexter mansion, he is courteously greeted by Aunt Jo, who shows him a letter Noel wrote to her telling her to dismiss that "intolerable bore" if he has the presumption to call. Juan blindly turns to leave, until Aunt Jo addresses him as Mr. Templeton in a sincerely sad farewell. When he dully says his name is Chandler, she ecstatically summons Noel in bell-like tones.

"PRETTY BOY FLOYD" (1981). Poem. (Characters: Pretty Boy Floyd, Schoolboy Rowe.) The persona advises Pretty Boy Floyd (*see* Floyd, Charles Arthur) and Schoolboy Rowe (*see* Rowe, Lynwood Thomas) to do as they please with girls and women.

PRINCE, JENNY. In "Jacob's Ladder," she is a beauty, sixteen and uncultured. Jacob C. K. Booth befriends her after the murder trial of her sister, Mrs. Choynski. He introduces her to filmmaker Billy Farrelly, suggests her name be changed from Jenny Delehanty, and admires her emergence as a fine actress. She goes to Hollywood, does well, and would marry Jacob—out of admiration and gratitude—even though he does not thrill her, but falls in love with her director. Jenny is based partly on the actress Lois Moran.*

"THE PRINCE OF PESTS" (1917). (Full title: "The Prince of Pests: A Story of The War.") (Characters: Badenuff, Kaiser [William II], Pistachio, Von Boodlewaden, Von Munchennoodle, Von Nicklebottom.) It is Berlin in July 1914. Associates of the Kaiser encourage him to believe Daniel Webster was a German because he once stopped at the Sauerkraut Inn in Pennsylvania. The implication seems to be that another German American might be found to kill President Woodrow Wilson. The Kaiser then has himself primped for a photograph.

"PRINCETON" (1927). Essay. Fitzgerald once lamented going to Princeton instead of Yale. Harvard, too Bostonian, was not in the running. Though surrounded by ugliness, Princeton's architecture is lovely old Gothic. He discusses football, sources of students (rich families, good prep schools, high schools), methods required after 1921 to limit enrollment, and the different quality of several departments under John Grier Hibben's progressive administration as university president. Fitzgerald describes the *Nassau Literary Magazine*, the Triangle Club, Princeton's honors system, and social clubs. He closes by reminiscing about on- and off-campus effects of the war and wondering whether the ideal of a gracious and fair university can continue. Aspects of "Princeton" relate to *This Side of Paradise*.

"PRINCETON—THE LAST DAY" (1917). Poem. The ghosts of former evenings sing along the trees. It would be fine to preserve this hour like the essence of a pressed flower. Years lie ahead and will bring changes. Oh, if this midnight the poet could only see the world's glory and sorrow.

PRISSY, AUNT. In "Discard," she is evidently George Baker's aunt and may be Freddie's mother.

"THE PRIZEFIGHTER'S WIFE" (1981). Poem. She conceals her feelings when she sees her pug knocked down and will rush to his side.

PRUIT, MISS. In *Coward*, she is the governess of the young children of Judge Arthur Douglas and his wife, Mary Douglas. Miss Pruit is from Boston.

PRUNIER. In "A Short Autobiography," he was the proprietor of a drinking place in France Fitzgerald visited when he was sad in 1928.

"PUBLIC LETTER TO THOMAS BOYD" (1921). Essay. Fitzgerald dislikes novels detailing adventures of young men, praises writers opposed to stupidity and intolerance, and delights when brilliant intellectual leaders such as H. L. Mencken* persuade even dumb readers to appreciate what they are told to appreciate. Fitzgerald reprinted these comments later in 1921 as "The Credo of F. Scott Fitzgerald" and "How the Upper Class Is Being Saved by 'Men Like Mencken.' " *See also* Boyd, Thomas Alexander.

PULPAT. In "O Russet Witch!," he is the owner of a French restaurant in New York City. Merlin Grainger takes Olive Masters there. Caroline disrupts things when she enters with three rowdy men and dances on a table.

PUMPKIN, PROFESSOR. In "The Captured Shadow," he is a character in Basil Duke Lee's incomplete play *Hic! Hic! Hic!*

PURLEY. In "The Love Boat," he is Mae Purley's father. He is a timekeeper at the textile mill near their Wheatly Village apartment.

PURLEY. In "The Love Boat," he is either of Mae Purley's two mill-worker older brothers.

PURLEY, MAE. In "The Love Boat." *See* Fitzpatrick, Mae Purley.

PURLEY, MRS. In "The Love Boat," she is Mae Purley's mother. When Bill Forthington jokes about running away with Mae, her mother says he won't.

"THE PUSHER-IN-THE-FACE" (1925). Short story. (Characters: T. Cashmael, Miss Ingles, Mrs. George D. Robinson, Edna Schaeffer, Charles David Stuart.) In court, Charles David Stuart, an unmanly little night cashier, thirty-five, at T. Cashmael's all-night restaurant, pleads guilty to pushing Mrs. George D. Robinson. As he explains to the judge, he goes to matinees, had one show ruined for him when Mrs. George D. Robinson, who sat behind him in the theater, insisted not only on rocking the back of his seat with her knees but also talking about her stomach ailments to her companions. Stuart turned around, pushed her in the face, and was arrested and jailed overnight. When the judge dismisses the case, Stuart returns to the restaurant, only to be told by Cashmael this is his last night because he missed work. Stuart is boasting of his face-pushing to Edna Schaeffer, a sweet waitress at the restaurant, when two thugs enter and are rude to her. Stuart pushes one in the face; he drops a revolver, other customers grab both men, and Stuart becomes a rehired hero. He invites Edna to a matinee, and if she will not accept, he might—. "The Pusher-in-the-Face" was made into a two-reel talking movie by Paramount (1929).

PUSHING. In *The Vegetable*, he is Jerry Frost's boss. In the dream sequence he is Major-General Pushing, who wants to declare war. His name is a satirical change on that of General John Joseph Pershing.

Q

QUARLES, LORRAINE. In ''Babylon Revisited,'' she, now thirty, is a former drinking friend of Charlie J. Wales during his irresponsible days in Paris. She and Duncan Schaeffer embarrass him by bursting into the home of Lincoln Peters and Marion Peters, his in-laws in Paris.

QUARRELS, MADELINE. In ''The Rubber Check,'' she is a person Val Schuyler thinks he could have married.

QUARTERLY. In *Tender Is the Night*, he is a heavy drinker at the Ritz bar in Paris.

QUILL, MOONLIGHT. In ''O Russet Witch!,'' he is the owner of a New York City bookshop bearing his name. He employs Merlin Grainger, Miss McCracken, and Olive Masters (later Merlin's wife). When Caroline tears up his shop, he says nothing for fear she will tell his wife how ''daffy'' he is about her. After his wife's death, Quill leaves the shop to Merlin and dies soon thereafter.

QUILL, MRS. MOONLIGHT. In ''O Russet Witch!,'' she is the wife of Moonlight Quill, a bookshop owner. She predeceases him.

QUINN. In *The Great Gatsby*, Nick Carraway lists the names of Quinn and his wife on a timetable as among Jay Gatsby's summer guests. They later divorced.

R

RADAMACHER. In "The Fiend," he is the owner of a department store in Stillwater, Minnesota. When Crenshaw Engels sells his photography business, Radamacher gives him a job.

RAFFINO. In "Jacob's Ladder," he is the handsome Hollywood actor with whom Jacob C. K. Booth mistakenly thinks Jenny Prince has fallen in love.

RAGLAND, DICK. In "A New Leaf," he is the handsome, alcoholic friend of Phil Hoffman, who reluctantly introduces him to Julia Ross in Paris. Dick, who promises to swear off liquor, intrigues Julia; back home in New York, where his uncle gives him a job, they become engaged. He secretly backslides, misses many days of work, and while Julia is away pursues her friend Esther Cary. When discovered, Dick agrees to proceed to London on business for a cooling-off period, but he drinks aboard ship and throws himself into the ocean. Fitzgerald twists aspects of his own youth to make them partly parallel aspects of Dick's early career.

"RAGS MARTIN-JONES AND THE PR-NCE OF W-LES" (1924). Short story. (Characters: Blutchdak, Cedric, John B. Chestnut, Dominique, Lord Charles Este, Germaine, Jackson, Louise, Baron Ted Marchbanks, Rags Martin-Jones, Roderigo Minerlino, Monte, Papa Jack, St. Raphael, Sheik B. Smith, Gloria Swanson, Sir Howard George Witchcraft.) Rags Martin-Jones, who inherited $70 million when her parents went down on the *Titanic*, is returning to New York ten or so years after that tragedy. She is spoiled by five years abroad. John B. Chestnut, seemingly engaged to her during those years, meets her at the dock, finds her affected and bored with the prospect of America, but hopes to win her. He persuades her to go out with him to a nightclub where the Prince of Wales is to be—down incognito from Canada. Rags is thrilled. She is taken to the quiet prince's shadowy table. After bits of entertainment, a friend warns Chestnut about something. Chestnut confesses to Rags he is suddenly wanted for murder. She begs the prince to spirit them away to Canada so she and Chestnut can escape and get married. The police break in, shots on both sides are fired, and Chestnut surrenders. He announces to one and all everything has been an elaborate joke. Soon thereafter, Rags is in Chestnut's office in a skyscraper. He explains on their way to City Hall, to get married, that the prince was really Cedric, the elevator boy. Ecstatic, she agrees her love for Chestnut is the sort of beautiful bargain she wants out of life. The ruse in this story slightly resembles that in ''The Offshore Pirate,'' published four years earlier.

RAHILL. In *This Side of Paradise*, he is a student at St. Regis with whom Amory Blaine smokes and analyzes fellow classmates.

"RAIN BEFORE DAWN" (1917). Poem. The faint sound of rain awakens the tired sleeper. He looks at his wet pillow. Dawn stares at him across the lawn. Death is in the house.

RAINES, MARSTON. In ''Diagnosis,'' he is a wise old friend of Sara Etherington. He advises Charlie Clayhorne to rid his mind of worry.

RAINY. In *Tender Is the Night*, he is evidently a movie agent who, according to Elsie Speers, had her daughter, Rosemary Hoyt, do difficult publicity stunts.

RAJ, SIR SINGRIM DAK. In ''Pat Hobby, Putative Father,'' he is Prince John Brown Hobby Indore's wealthy uncle. Pat Hobby escorts the two around the studio lot.

RALPH. In ''Emotional Bankruptcy,'' he is one of several former boyfriends of Josephine Perry.

RALPH. In *Safety First!*, he loved Bridget Kelly, lost her to slimy Tony, and warns women to play it safe.

RALSTON, MRS. In ''John Jackson's Arcady,'' she is a woman in town whom John Jackson has known for twenty years. She barred his wild son, Ellery Hamil Jackson, then sixteen, from her home. Jackson feels she might have befriended the boy. Still, Jackson has faithfully given money to charities she organized. Later, she tearfully praises the supposedly absent Jackson at the town meeting.

RAMSAY, DR. In ''The Love Boat,'' he is one of eight physicians panicky Bill Frothington thinks he might consult.

RANDALL, LOUIE. In "Emotional Bankruptcy," he is a Yale student. Josephine Perry encourages him to pursue her to Princeton and break up her date with Paul Demster, only to be rebuffed himself.

RANDOLPH, EDDIE. In *Coward*, he is a Southerner who writes to his mother to tell her that the Confederate Army has surrendered.

RANSOME. In *The Last Tycoon*, he is a cousin of Pat Brady, on the payroll but not as a screenwriter, as Brimmer thinks. O'Brien is another such cousin about whom Brimmer is also mistaken.

RATONI, AL. In "The Bowl," he is a composer. He is at the Midnight Frolic in New York. Vienna Thorne met him at the Madrid embassy.

RAUDENBUCH, MISS. In "Pat Hobby, Putative Father," she is Pat Hobby's secretary, idle because he dictates nothing all morning.

RAY, ESTHER. In "Too Cute for Words," she is the daughter, twenty, of Mrs. Charles Wrotten Ray, to whose home in Princeton Gwen Bowers, Dizzy Campbell, and Clara Hannaman are invited to a small dance. When Mrs. Ray is called to Albany, Esther, who has been invited to the Princeton prom, abandons the three young guests.

RAY, MRS. CHARLES WROTTEN. In "Too Cute for Words," she is the mother of Esther Ray and Tommy Ray and the aunt of Dizzy Campbell. She invites Dizzy, Gwen Bowers, and Clara Hannaman to her Princeton home to a small dance, but her mother's illness causes her to leave her guests and go to Albany.

RAY, TOMMY ("SHORTY"). In "Too Cute for Words," he is the small, shy son, sixteen, of Mrs. Charles Wrotten Ray. He is left alone with Gwen Bowers, Dizzy Campbell, and Clara Hannaman when his mother is called out of town. Later, he is home alone when a telegram arrives addressed to his sister, Esther Ray. His attempt to deliver it to her at the Princeton prom dance results in his dancing with Gwen, who suddenly notices he is handsome.

RAYCROFT, DOROTHY ("DOT"). In *The Beautiful and Damned*, she is a South Carolinian Anthony Patch meets and irresponsibly dallies with while in the army in the South. She follows him to Mississippi, where he discards her. She confronts him in his New York apartment; he throws a chair at her, and she disappears.

RAYCROFT, MRS. In *The Beautiful and Damned*, she is Dorothy Raycroft's vapid mother, recently widowed.

RAYMOND. In "The Mystery of the Raymond Mortgage," he is the owner of the home at Santuka Lake where his daughter, Agnes Raymond, and his servant, John Standish, are shot to death, after which his wife is reported missing.

RAYMOND, AGNES. In "The Mystery of the Raymond Mortgage," she is one victim of a double shooting at the Raymond home at Santuka Lake.

RAYMOND, MRS. In "The Mystery of the Raymond Mortgage," she is the mother of Agnes Raymond. When John Standish shoots Agnes to death, Mrs. Raymond shoots him, escapes briefly, and commits suicide by taking poison.

RAYMOND, ROBERT CALVIN. In "The Room with the Green Blinds," he is the man who inherits his grandfather's house near Macon, Georgia. With the help of Carmatle, the governor of Georgia, he discovers the old place houses John Wilkes Booth. Raymond is the narrator, but not the hero, of the story.

READ. In "Jacob's Ladder," he is a member of the law firm of Read, Van Tyne, Biggs & Company, with which Jacob C. K. Booth threatens Jenny Prince's would-be blackmailer Scharnhorst.

READ. In "The Love Boat," he is a member of the Boston banking house of Read, Hopp and Company into which Bill Frothington will presumably settle.

READ, CECIL. In *Thoughtbook*, he is a friend.

READE. In "Reade, Substitute Right Half," he is the lithe, fair-haired substitute on the Warrentown football team who wins the game.

"READE, SUBSTITUTE RIGHT HALF" (1910). Short story. (Characters: Berl, Hearst, Mridle, Reade.) When the right tackle for the Warrentown football team is injured by a member of the opposing Hilton team, the Warrentown coach reluctantly sends in slim Reade, who makes several key tackles, intercepts a pass, and scores a touchdown. This is a wish-fulfillment yarn: Fitzgerald longed to be the sort of gridiron hero he makes out of Reade.

REAL, FRANCISCO PARDO Y CUIDAD. In *Tender Is the Night*, he is the handsome Chilean, about twenty, whose father brings him to Lausanne to be treated by Dick Diver for alcoholism and homosexuality. Dick irresponsibly says he can do little for him.

REAL, PARDO Y CUIDAD. In *Tender Is the Night*, he is a Chilean and the father of Francisco Pardo y Cuidad Real. He brings his son to Lausanne to be treated by Dick Diver.

REARDON. In *This Side of Paradise*, he teaches French in Minneapolis. To show off, Amory Blaine ridicules the man's accent.

REARDON, ELTYNGE. In *The Beautiful and Damned*, he is a former boyfriend of Gloria Gilbert Patch. His unusual first name may derive from that of Eltinge F. Warner, managing editor of the *Smart Set*, in which Fitzgerald published several short stories.

RED. In ''The Love Boat,'' he is May Schaffer's date on the second love boat Bill Frothington boards. When Bill cuts in, Red is annoyed.

REDFERN, MAJOR. In ''Strange Sanctuary,'' this is one of the aliases of Dodo Gilbert. *See* Gilbert, Dodo.

REECE, LADY. In ''The Rubber Check,'' she is the London woman whose ball Val Schuyler has ''come over'' to attend—or so he tells an American friend he happens to meet on the street.

REED, CARL. In *Thoughtbook*, he is a friend who likes Marie Hersey. Fitzgerald also spells his name Read.

REFFER, MARTY. In *The Beautiful and Damned*, he is a former boyfriend of Gloria Gilbert Patch.

"REFRAIN FOR A POEM. HOW TO GET TO SO AND SO" (1981). Poem. Directions are to go and turn and go on for miles.

REGAN. In ''Benediction,'' he is a young friend of Keith, who tells Lois that Regan led a wild life before becoming a fellow seminarian. Lois notices that the stalwart young man idolizes Keith.

REILLY. In ''He Thinks He's Wonderful,'' he is Basil Duke Lee's mother Alice Riley (Reilly) Lee's father, unnamed here. Basil borrows his electric car to drive Imogene Bissel downtown for a lemonade. In ''Forging Ahead,'' when Reilly, his daughter, and his son, Everett Reilly, lose a lot of money, Basil is told he probably cannot go to Yale. They later recoup financially by selling some property.

REILLY, BENJAMIN ("BEN"). In ''Forging Ahead,'' he is Basil Duke Lee's grandfather's brother and Basil's great-uncle. The two brothers do not get along. ''Uncle Ben'' and his family have moved from Sioux City to St. Paul. Basil gets a job through him. In return, Basil must escort Rhoda Sinclair, Ben's stepdaughter, to social functions.

REILLY, EVERETT. In "Forging Ahead," he is Basil Duke Lee's mother Alice Riley (Reilly) Lee's brother. He, his sister, and their father lose a lot of money but soon recoup.

REILLY, MRS. BENJAMIN. In "Forging Ahead," she is Basil Duke Lee's great-uncle's forty-year-old wife, of six months, and Rhoda Sinclair's mother. She persuades her husband to give Basil a job so he can escort Rhoda to social functions. At the end, Basil's mother proudly tells Mrs. Reilly her son is going to Yale.

REINA. In *The Last Tycoon*, she is a girl Cecelia Brady recalls as having won the affections of Cecelia's boyfriend in New England a year or so earlier.

REISENWEBER. In *The Beautiful and Damned*, he is the owner of the New York establishment where Anthony Patch passes bad checks made good the following day.

"REMINICENSES [*SIC*] OF DONALD STEWART BY F. SCOTT FITZGERALD (IN THE MANNER OF . . . .)." *See* Stewart, Donald Ogden.

RENAUD. In "The Count of Darkness," he is a worker for Count Philippe of Villefranche, who orders him to get some women from the settlement.

RENÉ. In "How to Live on Practically Nothing a Year," he is a French military aviator and is to be the Fitzgeralds' Riviera dinner guest. Zelda Sayre Fitzgerald* was said to have had an affair with French aviator René Silvé in the summer of 1924. Her lover, however, was Édouard Jozan.

RENNARD, JULES. In "Magnetism," he is a French-Canadian now a mogul in Hollywood. He is actor George Hannaford's closest friend. Rennard paid $100,000 in a divorce settlement, after which his ex-wife smashed his hand with a telephone. The two men's plan to fish off the coast of Lower California comes to naught.

RENWICK. In *This Side of Paradise*, he is the owner of an establishment in Princeton where Amory Blaine and his friends meet.

REUBEN ("RUBE"). In *Thoughtbook*, he is a friend. Fitzgerald resents Margaret Armstrong's crush on Rube.

RICCARD. In "Image on the Heart," he is a French aviator from Toulon. He cares for Tudy, who likes him but goes through with her marriage to the less romantic Tom. Riccard is based on Édouard Jozan, a French aviator with whom Zelda Sayre Fitzgerald* had a love affair in 1924.

RICE, SUSAN. In *Thoughtbook*, she is a friend who eavesdrops on Fitzgerald's conversation at one point.

RICH. In ''The Last of the Belles,'' Mr. Rich is the owner or an employee of a drugstore in Tarleton. He lets Ailie Calhoun go out the back way to avoid seeing Lieutenant Earl Schoen.

RICHARD. In *This Side of Paradise*, he is the St. Claire family chauffeur in Minneapolis. He drives Myra St. Claire, thirteen, and Amory Blaine where she orders him to go.

RICHARDS. In ''The Passionate Eskimo,'' he is the manager of a Chicago store visited by Pan-e-Troon.

RICHBITCH, MRS. In ''The Woman from Twenty-one,'' she is an arrogant woman who spoils the play Raymond Torrence and his wife, Elizabeth Torrence, are attending in New York by her repeated noisy whispering that she wants her group to go back to the Twenty-one Club. Torrence knew her twenty years earlier in Pittsburgh.

"THE RICH BOY" (1926). Short story. (Characters: Bicker Baker, Bradley, Cahill, Carl, Chilicheff, Conan Doyle, Paula Legendre Thayer Hagerty, Peter Hagerty, Perry Hull, Hunter, Anson Hunter, Edna Hunter, Mrs. Hunter, Robert Hunter, Schuyler [Hunter?], Tom [Hunter?], Karger, Dolly Karger, Mrs. Karger, Mrs. Legendre, Nick, Oscar, Ed Saunders, Cary Sloane, Moses Sloane, Lowell Thayer, Trenholm, Teak Warden, Mrs. Teak Warden.) Anson Hunter, born in 1895, is the oldest of six children in the wealthy, old New York Hunter family, with homes in Manhattan and Connecticut. He enjoys possessions, grows tall and handsome, is sure of a fine future, goes to Yale, graduates in 1917, and becomes a naval pilot. While training in Pensacola, Florida, he meets Paula Legendre, becomes engaged, and is then told she too is rich. One night Anson gets drunk at a party in Hempstead, distresses Paula's mother, apologizes while remaining domineering, and sees Paula in Florida again. Once overseas, he crashes his airplane in the North Sea and is shipped home to recuperate. More partying ruins the proud young man's engagement. He becomes a successful Wall Street broker. When he learns Paula is engaged to Lowell Thayer of Boston, Anson goes to Palm Beach, lets slip a chance to propose to the eager girl, and returns to New York. In 1922, his father now dead, Anson becomes a Hunter family leader. He begins to see Dolly Karger, who is pretty but indiscreet. Impatient at his indecision, she writes to him that a Chicago suitor wants her. Anson domineers her, takes her to a cousin's Post Washington lodge, but at the last minute rejects her desire for a commitment. She marries someone else. Paula later divorces and marries another Bostonian. Anson learns that his uncle Robert Hunter's wife Edna is having an affair with Cary Sloane, a rich Alabaman's son, and puts a stop to it. The immediate result is Sloane's suicide, and Anson is no longer welcome in Robert's home. The death of Anson's mother puts him at the head of the family; his sisters scatter, and he sells the Connecticut home. At thirty and portly, he has fewer friends and often feels lonely and sorry for himself. Drifting out of the Plaza one day, he bumps into Paula, pregnant by Peter Hagerty, her stalwart husband. With pathetic eagerness, he accepts their invitation to visit overnight in their temporary home in Rye. His firm insists that he rest a while in Europe—his first real vacation in seven years. Just before sailing, he learns that Paula has died in childbirth. On the ship he eyes a vivacious girl, finds out she is unaccompanied, and launches a campaign by beginning to dine with her.

"The Rich Boy" is a spin-off from *The Great Gatsby*, and their narrators may be contrasted. Much is known about Nick Carraway, whereas little is revealed about the anonymous raconteur of Anson's story beyond his being an Ivy League man, a naval officer briefly, and Anson's confidant who never learns much because he is envious and hence uncritical. Opinion is divided as to each narrator's reliability. "The Rich Boy" begins with Fitzgerald's generalization about the rich differing from others: their early possessions and enjoyments make them soft where others are hard, and cynical where others are trustful. Fitzgerald here reveals envy, criticism, and admiration of the rich. When the *Saturday Evening Post* rejected "The Rich Boy," *Redbook* bought it for $3,500 and published it.

Bibliography: James L. W. West III and J. Barclay Inge, "F. Scott Fitzgerald's Revision of 'The Rich Boy,' " *Proof* 5 (1977): 127–46.

RICHEPIN, MADAME DE. In "The Swimmers," she is an American Henry Clay Marston knows. Her behavior, Choupette Marston says, differs from hers because of class and family distinctions.

RICKEY. In " 'Send Me In, Coach,' " he is the handsome counselor at the summer camp. Rickey, twenty, likes the young wife of the Old Man, who warns him to stay away from her. Rickey criticizes him for not getting him fringe benefits other college football players enjoy.

RIDGEWAY. In "The Cut-Glass Bowl," he is the owner of a house Harold Piper, when drunk, tells Clarence Ahearn he ought to consider buying. Another suitable house, he says, belongs to Stearnes.

RIDINGWOOD, RED. In *The Last Tycoon*, he is a director Monroe Stahr removes from one movie but promises another one later. Red knows this loss of status will probably prevent his marrying a third time.

RIENMUND, JOE (''RIENY''). In *The Last Tycoon*, he is a handsome Jewish movie supervisor, thirty, whose attentions to Monroe Stahr blunt Stahr's habitual acuteness.

RIGGS, BILLY. In ''Fate in Her Hands,'' he is the boyfriend of Carol (later Carol Kastler), discarded in favor of Benjamin Kastler so as to make the palmist's first prediction come true.

RIKKER, ALIDA. In ''A Freeze-Out,'' she is the beautiful blond daughter, eighteen or nineteen, of Chauncey Rikker and Cathy Chase Rikker. She was educated partly in Europe, returns with her family to Minnesota, finds it hard to make her way socially because of her father's criminal past, but does so and marries Forrest Winslow.

RIKKER, CATHY CHASE. In ''A Freeze-Out,'' she is the wife of Chauncey Rikker and the mother of Alida Rikker and Teddy Rikker. Forrest Winslow's snobbish mother knew Cathy years ago and now gossips about her.

RIKKER, CHAUNCEY. In ''A Freeze-Out,'' he is the husband of Cathy Chase Rikker and the father of Alida Rikker and Teddy Rikker. Years earlier, Chauncey Rikker went bankrupt and left Minnesota, got into shady business deals in Washington, D.C., and New York, escaped to Europe, returned to America, and served time for contempt of court. The Rikker family has now returned to Minnesota and seeks acceptance from the generally snobbish and hypocritical society and business leaders there.

RIKKER, IRENE. In ''Two Wrongs,'' she is a successful actress. She and producer William McChesney are half-heartedly engaged. They split up when McChesney and Frank Llewellen, her handsome leading man, have an argument.

RIKKER, TEDDY. In ''A Freeze-Out,'' he is the son, seventeen, of Chauncey Rikker and Cathy Chase Rikker, and the brother of Alida Rikker. He invites all sorts of people to the Rikker family's party shortly after New Year's Day.

''RING'' (1933). Essay. Fitzgerald recalls his association with Ring Lardner* from 1921 to 1931. Toward the end, Ring lost his old vitality. He was interested in everything until despair stalked him. He worried about others and helped them, and he regarded his writings as directionless. He once wanted to be a musician and write shows. His failure to achieve his potential was caused partly by his not allowing his style to evolve sufficiently beyond that of his early stories about baseball (that ''boys' game''), but his talent with words remained. He continued observing but failed to record. His ruined idealism prevented his following Fitzgerald's encouragement to write something significant. Fitzgerald admires only Lardner's *You Know Me Al* (1916) and a dozen or so stories, including pieces laboriously collected as *How to Write Short Stories* (1924); his minor pieces should not be reissued. He did what he wanted and was noble, dignified, and often melancholy. He wrote Fitzgerald some fine letters. The two drank too much. Since there was a quality in Lardner into which one could not penetrate, one wishes he had revealed it in more writing. What did he think life was, should be, should give? Still, Ring was a delight.

RITA. In ''Teamed with Genius,'' she is a character in an old script of *Ballet Shoes*.

RIVERS. In *The Beautiful and Damned*, he is a person to whom Anthony Patch, according to his memo, owes money.

ROBBIE, MARTHA. In ''That Kind of Party,'' she is a guest at the Shoonover party. Since she is a tomboy, Terrence R. Tipton plans not to kiss her.

ROBBIE, MRS. In ''That Kind of Party,'' she is Martha Robbie's mother who, with other outraged mothers, converges on the party at the Shoonovers featuring the game of post office.

ROBBINS, JUBAL EARLY. In ''On Your Own,'' he is mentioned as a passenger, with his valet, aboard the ship taking Evelyn Lovejoy and others to New York.

ROBERG, GEORGE. In ''The Love Boat,'' he is a student aboard the love boat. McVitty orders him to quit fighting.

ROBERT THE FROG. In ''In the Darkest Hour,'' he is the leader of the Viking invaders of the Loire Valley region. Count Philippe of Villefranche's forces kill him, after which Philippe orders the execution of Robert's son, Goldgreaves. Philippe then permits Robert's French girlfriend to join him.

ROBIN. In *Thoughtbook*, she is a friend who gives a party.

ROBINSON. In ''One Interne,'' he is or was evidently a teacher at the hospital. George Schoatze and William Tulliver V studied under him.

ROBINSON, DEERING R. In ''The Homes of the Stars,'' he is the Kansas City food products executive who is visiting Hollywood with his wife. Pat Hobby guides them to the home of Ronald Colman* and then to an unoccupied mansion he says belongs to Shirley Temple.

ROBINSON, MRS. DEERING R. In "The Homes of the Stars," she and her husband are duped by Pat Hobby into thinking he is guiding them to the homes of some Hollywood stars.

ROBINSON, MRS. GEORGE D. In "The Pusher-in-the-Face," she is the theatergoer, about fifty, who sat behind Charles David Stuart and whose face he pushed when she rocked the back of his seat with her knees and whispered about her stomach problems to her companions.

ROBINSON, ROBBY. In *The Last Tycoon*, he is Monroe Stahr's reliable handyman from Minnesota. He is based on an overeager Hollywood technician Fitzgerald and Budd Schulberg* encountered on location at Dartmouth College during production of *Winter Carnival*. In *The Disenchanted*, Schulberg called the technician Hutchinson.

Bibliography: Robert Westbrook, *Intimate Lies: F. Scott Fitzgerald and Sheilah Graham, Her Son's Story* (New York: HarperCollins, 1995).

ROEBUCK, CECIL. In *The Great Gatsby*, Nick Carraway lists Roebuck's name on a timetable as one of Jay Gatsby's summer guests. He is from West Egg.

ROGERS, ALAN. In "Two Wrongs," he is a playwright whose letter about her Emmy Pinkard delivers to William McChensey.

ROGERS, MRS. ORRIN. In "The Popular Girl," she is a matron living next door to Tom Bowman and his daughter, Yanci Bowman. Scott Kimberley, who according to Mrs. Rogers is her husband's cousin, visits their Midwestern city and is introduced to Yanci by Mrs. Rogers.

ROGERS, ORRIN. In "The Popular Girl," he is a neighbor of Tom Bowman and his daughter, Yanci Bowman. His wife identifies Scott Kimberley as his cousin. *See* Rogers, Pete.

ROGERS, PETE. In "The Popular Girl," he may be the son of Orrin Rogers and his wife. Scott Kimberley mentions Pete Rogers as his cousin. Pete may be Orrin Rogers' nickname.

ROLF. In "The Kingdom in the Dark," he is one of Count Philippe of Villefranche's loyal men.

ROLLINS, GEORGE. In " 'The Sensible Thing.' " *See* O'Kelly, George.

ROMBERG. In "Absolution," he owns a drugstore in Ludwig near where Rudolph Miller lives.

ROMBERT. In "The Pierian Springs and the Last Straw," he is the unnamed observer-narrator who, at eleven, first hears about George Rombert, his novel-writing-uncle. When twenty, he visits George in the West, meets Myra Fulham, the femme fatale of his uncle's life, and sees him finally snap emotionally and criticize her.

ROMBERT, GEORGE. In "The Pierian Springs and the Last Straw," he is the novelist uncle of the observer-narrator. He attended Andover and Williams and was popular. During his sophomore year, he met Myra. They argued during his senior year, and he wrongly groveled before her. Since then he has been able to write effective, controversial novels, usually about women, because of his continued and pathetic relationship with Myra Fulham. Once the alcoholic man snaps, after ten years of abuse from her—and many flings—and tells her off, they get married. His drinking and writing then cease.

ROMBERT, MISS. In "The Pierian Springs and the Last Straw," she is the unmarried sister of George Rombert and Thomas Rombert and the observer-narrator's aunt. George lives with her in the West. She keeps a scrapbook of George's life, including favorable reviews of his books, all of which she proudly shows to her nephew.

ROMBERT, MRS. GEORGE. In "The Pierian Springs and the Last Straw." *See* Fulham, Myra.

ROMBERT, MRS. THOMAS. In "The Pierian Springs and the Last Straw," she is the wife of Thomas Rombert, the mother of the observer-narrator, and the sister-in-law of controversial novelist George Rombert, whom she criticizes.

ROMBERT, THOMAS ("TOM"). In "The Pierian Springs and the Last Straw," he is the father of the observer-narrator. He is a lawyer who practices in the East but has family roots in the West. At first he shields his son from stories about George Rombert, his brother, the novelist.

"THE ROOM WITH THE GREEN BLINDS" (1911). Short story. (Characters: John Wilkes Booth, Butler, Carmatle, Carmatle, Robert Calvin Raymond.) When he turns twenty-one, narrator Robert Calvin Raymond inherits his grandfather's house near Macon, Georgia, on condition he not open a certain room in it "until Carmatle falls." Raymond, who also inherits $25,000, takes a train south and enters the house. He finds the mysterious room barred and marked "J.W.B.," naps, and then momentarily sees a blood-stained figure clad in a Confederate Army uniform who evidently has access to the room. In the morning Raymond goes outside and sees the three windows of the room are barred and have green blinds. He suddenly recalls the governor of Georgia is named Carmatle. He visits the man, tells him everything, and watches Carmatle turn pale at the mention of ''J.W.B.'' Carmatle and a friend named Butler go to the house with Raymond, who chances to lean on a ledge by the room. Pressure causes a wall to swing open. Carmatle enters the room, is shot at by the stranger, and shoots back and kills him. Carmatle explains: he and his son were in the Confederate Army, did not hear of the surrender, and were accosted by a stranger who in the night stole Carmatle's son's uniform and horse, and escaped to this pro-Confederate house in Georgia. Carmatle's son, who donned the stranger's clothes, left his father to visit an aunt in Maryland, was cornered by Union soldiers in a barn, and was shot and identified as John Wilkes Booth. For four years Carmatle has sought Booth in vain. Raymond, Carmatle, and Butler agree to say nothing.

ROONEY. In ''The Freshest Boy,'' he is a history teacher and the football coach at St. Regis. He escorts Basil Duke Lee to the Broadway matinee, is critical of him, and lets him attend the show alone while he gets drunk. Basil proves the more responsible of the two when he wakes Rooney up and presumably gets him back on the train.

ROONEY. In *This Side of Paradise*, he is a tutor at Princeton who tries to improve the comprehension in mathematics of Amory Blaine, Slim Langueduc, McDowell, Fred Sloane, and others.

ROONEY, MISS. In *The Beautiful and Damned*, she is a stenographer in a short story written by Anthony Patch. In it she discovers the recording of a song.

ROOSEVELT, MRS. CLAUDE. In *The Great Gatsby*, she is the person Owl-Eyes says brought him to Jay Gatsby's party.

ROPER, BILL. In ''The Bowl,'' he is the Princeton football team's coach.

ROREBACK, ANTHONY. In ''John Jackson's Arcady,'' he is the secretary of the Civil Welfare League. He writes to John Jackson to remind him of his promise to speak at its annual meeting on what he has gotten out of life.

ROSE. In ''Your Way and Mine,'' she is evidently a servant in the New York home of Henry McComas and Stella McComas.

ROSE, AUNT. In ''Lo, the Poor Peacock!,'' she is a worker on the sausage farm of Annie Lee Davis and Jason Davis.

ROSE, GUS, PRIVATE. In ''May Day,'' he is a degenerate soldier who consorts with Private Carrol Key, drinks with him, and is said by Edith Bradin to be the one who broke her brother Henry Bradin's leg when a mob stormed Henry's editorial office.

ROSEN, SIDNEY. In ''Forging Ahead,'' he is a guest at Benjamin Reilly's dull dinner party, which Basil Duke Lee must attend.

ROSENTHAL, ROSY. In *The Great Gatsby*, he is a person whose murder Meyer Wolfsheim casually describes to Nick Carraway while both men are lunching with Jay Gatsby. Herman Rosenthal, the real-life racketeer, was murdered in 1912 at the corner of Broadway and Forty-third Street, near where Gatsby, Nick, and Wolfsheim have lunch.

Bibliography: Bruccoli, *Gatsby*.

ROSS, JULIA. In ''A New Leaf,'' she is a New Yorker who, on vacation in Paris at twenty-one, is introduced to Dick Ragland by their mutual friend, Phil Hoffman. She falls in love with Dick and becomes engaged to him despite Phil's repeated warnings of his hopeless alcoholism. She believes he can reform. In the end, Phil conceals the details of Dick's suicide at sea and marries Julia.

ROSS, WALTER. In ''The Swimmers,'' he is a Paris representative of the tobacco company for which Henry Clay Marston also works. Marston asks Judge Waterbury to let the two exchange positions despite a loss in salary for Marston.

ROSTOFF, PRINCE PAUL SERGE BORIS. In ''Love in the Night,'' he is Prince Val Rostoff's gruff, philandering father. He dies impoverished shortly after the Russian revolution.

ROSTOFF, PRINCESS. In ''Love in the Night,'' she is the daughter of Morris Hasylton, a wealthy Chicagoan, and is Prince Val Rostoff's mother. She dies after the Russian revolution.

ROSTOFF, PRINCE VAL. In ''Love in the Night,'' he is the son of Prince Paul Serge Boris Rostoff and his American wife. Age seventeen in Cannes in April 1914, he seeks romantic adventure, happens to be called aboard the *Privateer* in the harbor, and falls in love on deck with the seventeen-year-old wife of the old man who owns the yacht. Eight years later—after Val has been a Russian soldier, an impoverished taxi driver in Cannes, and a banker there—they meet again, in Cannes, and happily marry. Val then runs a string of New York taxis. Prince Val Rostoff is modeled partly on Prince Vladimir (''Val'') N. Engalitcheff, a Russian-American whom Fitzgerald and Zelda Sayre Fitzgerald* knew, and who committed suicide in 1923.

ROSTOFF, PRINCE VLADIMIR. In ''Love in the Night,'' he is named as Prince Val Rostoff's grandfather, whose father was a grand duke.

"THE ROUGH CROSSING" (1929). Short story. (Characters: Butterworth, James Carton, Elizabeth D'Amido, Gyp the Blood, Adrian Smith, Estelle Smith, Eva Smith, Stacomb, Mrs. Worden.) Playwright Adrian Smith, Eva Smith, and their children board a liner to leave New York City and their problems behind. They have agreed to quit drinking and arguing, and plan to enjoy a simple family life for a while in Brittany. A pretty brunette named Elizabeth (''Betsy'') D'Amido and a drunk named Butterworth rush aboard. Meanwhile, a hurricane is moving south toward the ship's latitude. A man named Stacomb (''Stac'') praises Adrian's plays; and Stac, Betsy, Butterworth, and a few other passengers join the Smiths at their table. Adrian is flattered by Betsy's hovering attention. After chatting with Butterworth a while, Eva leaves, only to find James Carton, a steward, sick in her cabin. She gets him out and falls ill herself. Adrian enters and reports he and Betsy have signed up to play doubles tennis on deck. Eva, annoyed, rests while Adrian dresses for dinner and goes for drinks with his new friends. Next morning she angrily watches the tennis tournament. Since Adrian and lithe Betsy win, they must buy drinks all around. Meanwhile, Eva sits seasick alone on the rolling deck. In the afternoon Butterworth at the bar with Eva bores her with stories about himself and praise of her beauty. Betsy, busy hugging Adrian on the rainy deck, tearfully tells him she has been in love with him ever since seeing him at a play rehearsal. While dressing for the fancy dinner and ball, Adrian argues with Eva, leaves ahead of her, and sneaks another thoughtless kiss at Betsy's cabin door. The gale is growing stronger, and dinner is sparsely attended. After a little dancing, Eva hysterically notes that Adrian and Betsy are absent, feels she is being punished somehow, staggers on deck, and hurls her pearls, Adrian's gift, into the dark and roiling waters to propitiate the storm. Next morning she is so sick that Adrian summons the doctor, who says she was wandering on deck last night so irresponsibly that she will be served no more drinks, orders a bromide, and reports that Carton died following emergency surgery for appendicitis. After lunch, Adrian and Eva go on deck. Amid the worsening hurricane, Carton is ceremonially buried at sea. Sneaking drinks, Eva plays up to Butterworth, perhaps in revenge for Adrian's toying with Betsy. Dismissing Butterworth in sudden anger, Eva demands a divorce from Adrian, who calls the idea silly. She makes her way to the wireless room to alert a Parisian lawyer. As Adrian follows, they are swamped by a huge wave and tumbled into unconsciousness on the drenched planks. Two days later everyone disembarks. Adrian cashed a probably worthless check for Butterworth. Betsy met her fiancé ashore. The Smiths, seemingly happy and proceeding through the French countryside, agree the rough crossing was only a bad dream. Adrian will buy Eva some better pearls.

ROUSSEAU, MISS. In ''Between Three and Four,'' she is one of Howard Butler's office workers.

ROWE, LYNWOOD THOMAS ("SCHOOLBOY") (1910–1961). Baseball pitcher. He pitched for the Detroit Tigers (1933–1942), the Brooklyn Dodgers (1942), and the Philadelphia Phillies (1943–1949). In "Pretty Boy Floyd," he is mentioned as treating women disrespectfully.

ROXANNA. In *The Vegetable*, she is the woman named by Horatio Frost as his second wife and the mother of his son, Jerry Frost.

RUBBER. In "The Bowl," he is evidently a Princeton football team trainer. He may be Tony.

"THE RUBBER CHECK" (1932). Short story. (Characters: Major Barks, Bill, Lord Clan-Carly, Miss Cupp, Miss Dale, Lady Doncastle, Elsa, Hon. Elinor Guise, June Halbird, Mrs. Halbird, Jones, Lady Kippery, Nancy Lamb, Esther Manly, Miss Moon, Mortmain, Ellen Mortmain, Mrs. Mortmain, Emily Parr, George Pepin, Mrs. George Pepin, Madeline Quarrels, Lady Reece, Schuyler, Mrs. Martin Schuyler, Val Schuyler, Charles Martin Templeton, Mercia Templeton, V. Templeton, Mrs. Weeks-Tenliffe, Miss Whaley, Percy Wrackham.) Fatherless, impecunious Val Schuyler, eighteen, wanders uninvited into the beautiful garden of the Mortmains' estate outside New York City, where Val works at a brokerage office. His polished manners and smooth ability on the dance floor gradually make him accepted in the Mortmains' social circle. Pretty Ellen Mortmain, also eighteen, adores him. Her cousin, Mercia Templeton of Philadelphia, could love Val also, but she is not very attractive. Val solidifies his reputation. When Ellen takes Val—both now twenty-one—as her escort to Mercia's lavish Philadelphia home to a party, he plays up to Mercia briefly, even as he and Ellen plan to elope to Elkton, Maryland. Mercia sees them kissing in the cloakroom. Ellen persuades Mercia to have a group of nine lunch at a Philadelphia hotel. The waiter hands Val the $80 bill. Having too little cash, he pays by writing a check for $100 on his mother's bank, naming Mercia's father, Charles Martin Templeton, and his wife as references. To cover the check he wires his mother, who is sailing that day from New York with George Pepin, her fourth husband. When she declines by return wire, he cannot pick up Ellen at the Templetons' home as planned, rushes instead to New York to appeal to his mother—but too late. Ellen and her family go to England. By letter Mrs. Templeton rebukes Val for asking her to vouch for his rubber check. At twenty-two, he is invited to a New York debutante's ball, but girl after girl there, as he tries to cut in, rebuffs him. When he ascertains that Mercia's mother, who is present, has been telling various matrons about Val's "thousand-dollar" rubber check, he tells the woman off: he was not the host at the lunch and furthermore college boys get away with it when their checks bounce. One day Ellen writes to him from England to tell him she is visiting home again and invites him to be her date at a weekend party at the Halbirds' Long Island home. Highly hopeful, he goes; after a nice dinner, however, Ellen tells Mrs. Halbird she must dash and misses the dance. On the way there in her limousine, Mrs. Halbird grills Val and tells him he should associate only with his own kind. While at her home overnight again later, he overhears young couples chatting about his rubber check, snubs them, and leaves before dawn. Next year, Val is fired from his job, inherits $20,000 when his mother dies, and starts an ill-conceived art-dealing partnership. Behold Val in 1930, swaggering in London. His purpose is to call on Ellen, whom he finds in the confusion of family bankruptcy. Though incapable of deep love, he proposes; however, she not only reminds him of the rubber check but also says she is engaged to an army man. Reading in an American paper of the collapse of his partnership, he sneaks out of his hotel and heads for home. A year later, Val, twenty-seven, goes to Mercia's father, gripes about the consequence of his wife's gossip about the rubber check, and demands not money but a job. He ends up planting cabbages in the Templeton garden. One day Mercia rides by on her horse and proposes to him. His arrogance sends her away, but he is confident of her return.

RUDD, CHINAMAN. In "The Captured Shadow," he is a character in Basil Duke Lee's play *The Captured Shadow*.

RUDD, CHINYMAN ("CHING"). In *The Captured Shadow*, he is a would-be robber. When he and his friend, Rabbit Simmons, follow Hubert Connage into the Connage home, Thorton Hart Dudley is able to dart in after them.

RUFF, DR. In "One Interne," he is an ophthalmologist at the hospital.

"A RUGGED NOVEL" (1922). Review of *The Love Legend* by Woodward Boyd. *See* Boyd, Peggy Woodward.

RUS. In "The Camel's Back," he is one of Betty Medill's dance partners at the circus ball. She drops him to dance with the camel.

RUSSEL, ELAINE. In "Diamond Dick and the First Law of Woman," she is Charley Abbott's companion, an actress, in New York until Diana ("Diamond Dick") Dickey reveals she is amnesiac Charley's wife.

RUTH. In "News from Paris—Fifteen Years Ago," she is a woman with whom Henry Haven Dell attends a wedding in Paris, after which he dumps her at lunch for Bessie Leighton Wing.

RUTH. In "Ruth." *See* Sturtevant, Ruth.

RUTH. In "A Short Autobiography," she is a fellow drinker in France in 1926.

RUTH. In ''There was a young lady named Ruth,'' she telephones Yale and tells everything except the truth.

RUTH. In ''Truth and—consequences,'' she is said to be loved by Bill.

"RUTH" (1979). Poem. (Character: Ruth [Sturtevant].) Fitzgerald says a lady who said he would not tell the truth was wrong, or was she?

RUTHERFORD. In ''The Bridal Party,'' he is Hamilton Rutherford's father, divorced from Hamilton's mother ten years earlier and since then remarried. He attends the wedding in Paris of his son and Caroline Dandy.

RUTHERFORD, HAMILTON ("HAM"). In ''The Bridal Party,'' he is the rich, domineering fiancé of Caroline Dandy. Michael Curly loves and loses her when she and Hamilton get married in Paris. Hamilton lost money in the market but is offered a job by T. G. Vance at $50,000 a year.

RUTHERFORD, MRS. In ''The Bridal Party,'' she is Hamilton Rutherford's mother, divorced from Hamilton's father ten years earlier and since then remarried and divorced. She attends the wedding in Paris of her son and Caroline Dandy.

RUTHVEN, MRS. CASSIUS. In ''What a Handsome Pair!,'' she is a censorious Long Island matron. She disapproves not only of Helen Van Beck's (later Oldhorne) bicycling with Stuart Oldhorne before they are married but also of women polo players wearing breeches. At a party given by Teddy Van Beck, Stuart tells Mrs. Ruthven cooperative marriages often end up being competitive.

RYDER, J. DAWSON. In *This Side of Paradise*, he is a suitor for Rosalind Connage's hand during her coming-out party in New York. At twenty-six and from a wealthy Hartford family, he is successful.

S

SABLE, WILLA. In *The Beautiful and Damned*, she is an actress playing opposite Gaston Mears in a movie for a part in which Gloria Gilbert Patch takes an unsuccessful screen test.

SACHS. In *Tender Is the Night*, she is a patient in the clinic run by Dick Diver and Dr. Franz Gregorovius. She provides music for fellow patients.

"SAD CATASTROPHE" (1981). Poem. The poet is sorry he kept telling nice visitors he was busy, because now only tiresome ones come and insist on staying.

SADY. In *Fie! Fie! Fi-Fi!*. *See* Fi-Fi.

SAFETY FIRST! (1916). (Full title: *Safety First!: A Musical Comedy in Two Acts*.) Musical comedy. (Characters: Betty, Bill, Iona Bologna, Cleopatra, Dr. Cook, Cynthia, Henry, Horatio, Howard, Bridget Kelly, Bruce McRae, Osborne Merry, Oswald, Percy, Ralph, Sal, Shermy, Lord Temptation, Miss Temptation, Tom, Tony.) John Biggs, Jr.,* coauthored the book, and Fitzgerald wrote the lyrics. ''(A) Prologue'': The spirit of the future hails youth and intends to satirize the notion that safety is either fortunate or possible. ''(B) Garden of Arden'': As the spirit of the future, Ralph, Bill, Betty, and Cynthia suggest, this garden promises an escape to love and art. ''Act I Opening Chorus'': Howard, Percy, and the chorus regard Postimpressionist, cubist paintings as laughable. ''Send Him to Tom'': Convicts recommend prison for various sick losers. ''One-Lump Percy'': While Percy says he likes sentiment and gossip, the chorus labels him a ''parlor snake.'' ''Where Did Bridget Kelly Get Her Persian Temperament?'': Ralph is sorry Bridget Kelly has begun to smoke with Tony. ''It Is Art'': Percy sings about the success of ludicrous cubist art and regards the reputations of old paintings as unsafe. ''Safety First'': Ralph, Bill, Betty, and Cynthia advise playing it safe: for example, don't hit a policeman and do marry for money. ''Charlotte Corday'': Ralph, Cynthia, and the chorus tell how Charlotte Corday, not liking a gift from Marat, stabbed him. The chorus adds girls nowadays stab with their eyes. ''Underneath the April Rain'': Bill, Cynthia, and the chorus sing about finding love under an umbrella. ''Finale Act I Dance, Lady, Dance'': Ralph and the chorus sing that the lady should dance before the night and youth are gone. ''Act II (A) Safety First'': The chorus advises playing it safe and saving money for a taxi home. ''(B) Hello Temptation'': Ralph and the chorus warn about fickle Lord Temptation and nice Miss Temptation. ''When that Beautiful Chord Came True'': The pianist, with the chorus, says he once played so well that the keys streamed out like dancing girls. ''Rag-Time Melodrama'': Disguised convicts try to evade detectives. ''Scene II'': The spirit of the future calls for quiet, not commotion, in the art colony. ''Take Those Hawaiian Songs Away'': Bill, Cynthia, and the chorus argue that Hawaiian music should be ended. ''The Vampires Won't Vampire for Me'': Percy and Sal lament real-life girls' not resembling movie actresses. ''Down in Front'': Ralph, Bill, Percy, Howard, and others all sing: While ''I'' was performing in a Triangle show I saw a girl, met her, and unfortunately married the demanding creature. ''Finale'': The cast sings farewell. For safety's sake the dancers must unhook their corsets. They have outwitted Temptation and bid him goodbye. Fitzgerald's snappy lines, with crisp rhythms and catchy rhymes—including internal and feminine ones—are often clever.

SAGE. In ''Indecision,'' he is Tommy McLane's boss and orders Tommy to Geneva at once to meet H. P. Eastby.

SAGE, ESMERALDA. In *The Evil Eye*, she is loved by Mike of Yonkers but prefers rich Stuyvesant.

ST. CLAIRE, MRS. In *This Side of Paradise*, she is the affected mother of Myra St. Claire. They live in Minneapolis.

ST. CLAIRE, MYRA. In *This Side of Paradise*, she is the spoiled daughter, thirteen, of Mrs. St. Claire of Minneapolis. She likes Amory Blaine when he, fifteen, attends her bobbing party.

THE ST. PAUL DAILY DIRGE (1922). Spoof broadside. Fitzgerald wrote, privately printed, and distributed the sheet. It has headlines, illustrations, and humorous reports—about chilly weather in Chile, absence of stills in Stillwater, a furrier who will not die, and college activities.

ST. RAPHAEL. In ''Rags Martin-Jones and the Pr-nce of W-les,'' he is evidently a servant who works for Rags Martin-Jones.

SAL. In *Safety First!*, Sal mainly listens while Percy sings about types of girls he would like.

"SALESMANSHIP IN THE CHAMPS-ÉLYSÉES" (1930). Sketch. (Character: Legoupy.) The narrator is an unconsciously haughty car salesman who indifferently tells a potential American customer he lacks a six-cylinder touring car the fellow wants and may not be able to get one for days or perhaps a month. The American, called "the impolite," goes to an establishment next door and is treated with equal hauteur by Lygoupy. The humor here lies in Fitzgerald's offering his sketch as a literal, unidiomatic translation from the original French.

SALISBURY, VISCOUNTESS. In "Imagination—and a Few Mothers," this is a name silly Mrs. Judkins suggests the laborer Giuseppi use in charades he might upliftingly play at home.

SALTONVILLE, CABOT. In "The Ants of Princeton," he is the captain of the Harvard football team. He loses to Aunty and must commend Aunty to keep from being attacked.

SAM. In "Diagnosis," he was a quiet servant in the home of Charlie Clayhorne's father in Tuscarora, Alabama.

SAM. In *Fie! Fie! Fi-Fi*, he is liked by Susie but prefers Mary, who yearns for Victor.

SAM. In "The Perfect Life," he is a worker at St. Regis and evidently lets Basil Duke Lee help himself to food late at night.

SAMPSON, WASH. In "The Bowl," he is a Princeton football team player.

SANDERSON, CARL. In "The Bowl," he is a former suitor of Vienna Thorne. When she spurns him at the Midnight Frolic in New York, he tries to commit suicide but only shoots himself through the shoulder.

SANDERSON, JOHN ("JACK"). In "A Debt of Honor," he is a Confederate Army private who, in January 1863, volunteers for sentry duty, falls asleep, and is sentenced to execution, but is spared by Lieutenant General Robert E. Lee. Sanderson becomes a lieutenant, leads a charge on a frame house, and routs the enemy, but is killed.

SANDWOOD. In "Winter Dreams," he is one of the members of the exclusive golf club. Dexter Green plays in a foursome with him.

SARAH. In "She lay supine among her Pekinese," she used to be a popular hostess who talked about religion but now has changed.

SARAH. In *This Side of Paradise*, she is an innocent character in a dialogue Amory Blaine has with himself when he is feeling corrupt and is soon to leave New York at last.

SARNEMINGTON, BLATCHFORD. In "Absolution." *See* Miller, Rudolph.

SAROLAI, COUNT CHIKI. In "One Trip Abroad," he is an impoverished former Austrian courtier, who lives parasitically in Paris. His sister is married to the Marquis de la Clos d'Hirondelle, a banker there. Chiki ingratiates himself with Nelson Kelly and lives briefly with Kelly and his wife, Nicole Kelly. He plans a canal-boat party on the Seine, ostensibly hosted by his brother-in-law, invites the Kellys, but then tells the caterers to send their bills to Kelly, steals Nicole's jewelry, and decamps with his valet.

SAUNDERS, ED. In "The Rich Boy," he is a friend to whom Peter Hagerty goes to have a drink in order to leave his wife, Paula Legendre Thayer Hagerty, alone to chat with Anson Hunter.

SAUNDERS, MISS. In "The Captured Shadow," she is an old maid, about forty, in Basil Duke Lee's play *The Captured Shadow*. The part is taken by Connie Davies.

SAUNDERS, MISS. In *The Captured Shadow*, she is the housekeeper in the home of Beverly Connage and his family. She rebukes Emma Kate for gossiping but then asks her to continue.

SAUNDERS, RIDGEWAY ("RIDGE"). In "A Nice Quiet Place," he is a boyfriend of Josephine Perry. When her friend Lillian Hammel writes that Ridge is dating Evangeline Ticknor in Philadelphia, Josephine determines to end the little affair. At Ed Bement's house party in Lake Forest, Josephine necks with Ridge and Evangeline leaves early. In "A Woman with a Past," Ridge is a Yale sophomore and escorts Josephine to the prom. While there, she ignores him for Dudley Knowleton and, briefly, Book Chaffee. In "Emotional Bankruptcy," Ridge is one of Josephine's several former boyfriends.

SAVAGE, ELEANOR. In *This Side of Paradise*, she, eighteen or nineteen, is beautiful but witchlike. Amory Blaine chances to meet her during a rainstorm in Maryland. She lived in France with her mother, upon whose death she moved to an uncle in Baltimore, where her promiscuous conduct from age seventeen proved offensive. She was then cared for by Ramilly Savage, her grandfather in rural Maryland and a neighbor of Amory's aunt. Eleanor's liberal thinking intrigues Amory, and the two fall half in love for three weeks.

SAVAGE, PHIL. In "No Flowers," he is Lucy's fiancé in Marjorie Clark's dream. When, in it, he tells Lucy about his expulsion from the university for cheating, their engagement is broken.

SAVAGE, RAMILLY. In *This Side of Paradise*, he is Eleanor Savage's indulgent grandfather, who cares for her in rural Maryland.

SAYRE, ANTHONY DICKINSON (1858–1931). Husband of Minnie Buckner Machen Sayre* and father of Zelda Sayre Fitzgerald.* The Sayres, who were Episcopalians, had three daughters and one son older than Zelda: Marjorie Sayre Brinson,* Rosalind Sayre Smith,* Clothilde Sayre Palmer,* and Anthony Sayre, Jr. Anthony Sayre, Sr.'s father was a newspaper editor and a Masonic politician in Montgomery, Alabama. His mother was a sister of an Alabama senator. Sayre, an idealistic Jeffersonian democrat, was a member of the Alabama state legislature and a city judge in Montgomery. About 1902 he wrote "The Sayre Election Law" which deprived African Americans and poor whites in Alabama of the right to vote. From 1909 until his death Sayre was a judge on the Alabama Supreme Court. His salary of $6,000 was never sufficient, since he was generous to relatives. Zelda admired his moral stance while rebelling against it and baited him. At first Sayre disapproved of Fitzgerald as Zelda's suitor because of his instability. Neither he nor Minnie attended Zelda's wedding in 1920. At one point Sayre suffered a nervous breakdown. The Fitzgeralds visited the Sayres in Washington, D.C., in December 1926. When the Fitzgeralds learned in 1931 of Sayre's precarious health, they rented a house in Montgomery to be nearby. Two months after his death, Zelda suffered her second nervous breakdown. In her 1932 novel *Save Me the Waltz*, her autobiographical heroine, Alabama Beggs, is the daughter of a Southern judge. The 1933 suicide of Zelda's brother, Anthony, was proof enough for Fitzgerald that the Sayre family was unstable.

SAYRE, MINNIE BUCKNER MACHEN (c. 1861–?). Wife of Anthony Dickinson Sayre* and mother of Zelda Sayre Fitzgerald.* Minnie Sayre's father was a Kentucky senator. Her mother committed suicide. Minnie, known as "The Wild Lily of the Cumberland," had musical talent, wanted to study opera, published poems in the local newspaper, and was a devoted if indulgent mother. She condoned Zelda's wild behavior, despite Zelda's father's moral rectitude. Both mother and daughter called the judge "Old Dick." At first Minnie regarded Fitzgerald and Zelda as too immature and irresponsible to make a success of marriage. Fitzgerald blamed Zelda's breakdowns on her having been coddled, waited on, and excused by her mother. After his death, Minnie welcomed Zelda into her home in Montgomery, Alabama, when Zelda's occasionally improved health permitted. Minnie, though unable to attend Zelda's funeral, lived many more years. In 1956 Fitzgerald's daughter, Scottie (*see* Smith, Frances Fitzgerald Lanahan) visited her in Montgomery, at which time she was a reputed ninety-five.

"THE SCANDAL DETECTIVES" (1928). Short story. (Characters: Bissel, Imogene Bissel, Mrs. Bissel, George P. Blair, Hubert Blair, Mrs. George P. Blair, Mrs. Riply Buckner, Sr., Riply Buckner, Jr., Mrs. R. B. Cary, Walter Cary, H. P. Cramner, Connie Davies, Sam Davis, Hilda, William S. Kampf, Elwood Leaming, Basil Duke Lee, Arsène Lupin, Torrence, Margaret Torrence, Mrs. Torrence, Wharton.) This is the first Basil Duke Lee story. Basil, fourteen, and Riply Buckner, Jr., record in invisible ink some ''sins'' of people they know, mostly boys and girls their age. (The omniscient narrator adds they never use the book.) One May evening several youngsters gather and Basil gives his school ring to lovely Imogene Bissel, thirteen. He hopes for a kiss in return. Her sudden preference for athletic Hubert Blair causes Basil to seek revenge; he and Riply deliver warning messages signed S.D. to the Blairs and also, with a drafted confederate, William S. (''Bill'') Kampf, plan to disguise themselves, waylay Hubert at night, and stuff him in a garbage can. The plan miscarries when they do not attack Hubert in a bunch. In the aftermath Hubert and his father go to the Bissel home to voice concern. Basil, Riply, and Bill show up, pretending a party is being held there. Hubert boasts he fought off unknown, large, and armed assailants. Basil snickers but is saddened when he hears Hubert kissing Imogene, impressed by his fibs, in the Bissel kitchen. Basil feels abashed but looks forward to a lovely summer. ''That Kind of Party'' was to have been the first Basil Duke Lee story, in chronological order. When it was rejected, Fitzgerald changed its hero's name to Terrence R. Tipton.

SCHAEFFER. In *Tender Is the Night*, he is a heavy drinker in the Ritz bar in Paris. He may be Duncan Schaeffer. *See* Schaeffer, Duncan.

SCHAEFFER, DUNCAN ("DUNC"). In ''Babylon Revisited,'' he is a former drinking friend of Charles J. Wales during his irresponsible days in Paris. He and Lorraine Quarles embarrass him by bursting into the home of Lincoln Peters and Marion Peters, his in-laws. Schaeffer knew The Snow Bird in Paris a while back.

SCHAEFFER, EDNA. In ''The Pusher-in-the-Face,'' she is a mild, sweet waitress, twenty-three, at T. Cashmael's restaurant where Charles David Stuart works. She is so impressed by his face-pushing she will undoubtedly attend a matinee with him.

SCHAFFER, MAY. In ''The Love Boat,'' she is the pretty girl with whom Bill Frothington dances on the second love boat. He is struck by the coincidence that the girl he danced with on the first love boat was Mae Purley.

SCHARNHORST. In ''Jacob's Ladder,'' he is the New York lawyer who unsuccessfully defends Mrs. Choynski, Jenny Prince's sister, on a murder charge, after which he tries to blackmail Jenny. When Jacob C. K. Booth threatens to have Scharnhorst disbarred, he desists.

SCHEER. In ''On an Ocean Wave,'' any of the children of Gaston T. Scheer and his wife, Minna Scheer. The family is sailing to France.

SCHEER, GASTON T. In ''On an Ocean Wave,'' he is an unprincipled businessman who is sailing to France with his wife, Minna Scheer, and their children. He has arranged for his mistress, Catherine Denzer, to come along secretly, to have fun alone with her in Europe once he has parked his family in France. When he sees Minna embracing Professor Dollard in a corridor, he gives Cates, the swimming-pool steward, two hundred pounds to throw Dollard overboard.

SCHEER, MINNA. In ''On an Ocean Wave,'' she is the wife of Gaston T. Scheer. When he sees her embracing Professor Dollard, evidently her lover, on the ship carrying the Scheer family to France, he arranges to have Dollard thrown overboard.

SCHEERER. In ''Winter Dreams,'' he is Irene Scheerer's father. He likes Dexter Green.

SCHEERER, IRENE. In ''Winter Dreams,'' she is the sweet, plump woman Dexter Green gets engaged to after Judy Jones drops him a final time and leaves. Whether they marry is uncertain.

SCHEERER, MRS. In ''Winter Dreams,'' she is Irene Scheerer's mother. At one point she tells Dexter Green that Irene has a sick headache.

SCHEMMERHORN, AUSTIN. In ''John Jackson's Arcady,'' he is the dean of Yale College. He writes to inform John Jackson that his son, Ellery Hamil Jackson, is being expelled for misconduct.

SCHENZI. In ''The Hotel Child,'' he is named by Lady Capps-Karr as a friend, from Vienna, of Count Stanislas Karl Joseph Borowki.

SCHLACH, OTTO. In ''Six of One—,'' he is a poor farmer's son in Barnes's Ohio hometown. Barnes sends him to the Massachusetts Institute of Technology, and he becomes a successful consulting engineer.

SCHMIEL, ROSEMARY. In *The Last Tycoon*, she is one of Pat Brady's three secretaries. The other two are Maude and Birdy Peters. Rosemary tries unsuccessfully to prevent Cecelia Brady from barging in on Pat and Birdy in his inner office.

SCHNEIDER. In ''The Cruise of the Rolling Junk,'' he is the owner of a milk wagon in Westport, Connecticut. A heckler offers to race the Fitzgeralds to Alabama in the wagon.

SCHNLITSKI, GUS. In ''In a dear little vine-covered cottage,'' he shot his mother to death when he was sixteen and is now whining on death row in Sing-Sing.

SCHNLITZER-MURPHY, GWENDOLYN. In ''The Diamond as Big as the Ritz,'' she is said to have married into a wealthy West Virginia family.

SCHNLITZER-MURPHY, VIVIAN. In ''The Diamond as Big as the Ritz,'' she is the gem-collecting younger sister of Gwendolyn Schnlitzer-Murphy.

SCHOATZE, GEORGE. In ''One Interne,'' he is a classmate of William Tulliver V at the hospital. Tulliver helped him with a toxicology book. He correctly diagnoses Tulliver as having a dangerous volvulus. In ''Zone of Accident,'' he is a friend of William Tullivers IV in the Baltimore hospital.

SCHOEN, CECIL. In *The Great Gatsby*, Nick Carraway lists Schoen's name on a timetable as one of Jay Gatsby's summer guests. He is from West Egg.

SCHOEN, EARL, LIEUTENANT. In ''The Last of the Belles,'' he is the brash, good-looking officer training at the base outside Tarleton, Georgia. He interests then displeases Ailie Calhoun, who after the war rejects him as rustic when she sees him in civvies.

SCHOFIELD. In ''Six of One—,'' he is a wealthy Minneapolis businessman and a friend of Ed Barnes. Schofield and his wife have two sons, Wister Schofield and Charley Schofield. Schofield and Barnes disagree about the advantage of wealth in families rearing sons. Ultimately, Schofield is proud of Charley.

SCHOFIELD, CHARLEY. In ''Six of One—,'' he is the younger son, sixteen at the beginning of the story, of Schofield and his wife. He fails at Hotchkiss school, falls in love at eighteen with a married woman named Gladys Irving, graduates from Yale, and travels with friends. He returns to his family, marries Gladys when she is widowed, and successfully runs the family business with George Winfield.

SCHOFIELD, IRENE. In ''Six of One—.'' *See* Irving, Irene.

SCHOFIELD, MRS. In "Six of One—," she is wealthy Schofield's wife and the mother of Wister Schofield and Charley Schofield. She is happy when Charley rejoins his family and marries Gladys Irving.

SCHOFIELD, WISTER. In "Six of One—," he is the older son, nineteen at the beginning of the story, of wealthy Schofield and his wife. He goes to Yale but is soon expelled. While drunk, he drives his friend Howard Kavenaugh's car, is involved in an accident, and causes the disfigurement of a passenger named Irene Daley. She sues and receives $40,000 in damages. Barnes and his friend Schofield do not discuss Wister's later activities, evidently of no account.

SCHRAEDER, O.R.P. In *The Great Gatsby*, Nick Carraway lists Schraeder's name on a timetable as one of Jay Gatsby's summer guests. He is from farther out on Long Island.

SCHROEDER. In *The Beautiful and Damned*, he is a former boyfriend, reputedly worth millions, of Gloria Gilbert Patch.

SCHROEDER, PETE. In "Magnetism," he is a movie executive who listens with amusement while his friend actor George Hannaford gets rid of Gwen Becker, who phones him in a blackmail attempt.

SCHULBERG, BUDD (b. 1914). (Full name: Budd Wilson Schulberg). Novelist, screenwriter, and playwright. He was born in New York City but moved at five to Hollywood, where his father, B. P. Schulberg, was head of production at Paramount Famous-Lasky Studios. Schulberg graduated from Dartmouth College in 1936 and was a screenwriter for Samuel Goldwyn, David O. Selznick, and Walter Wanger from 1936 to 1939. During these years Schulberg was affiliated with the Communist party, which he later repudiated. In 1939 Wanger hired him to work with Fitzgerald on the movie *Winter Carnival* (1940). When Fitzgerald got drunk, Wanger fired him but retained Schulberg. After Fitzgerald died, Max Perkins,* editor at Scribner's, asked Schulberg to finish *The Last Tycoon*, but Schulberg declined.

Schulberg enjoyed a fine career. His first novel, *What Makes Sammy Run?* (1941), concerns life in Hollywood. For its dust jacket, Fitzgerald wrote an open letter to Bennett Cerf of Random House, Schulberg's publisher; in it, he praises the novel as grand, fearless, beautiful, rightly satirical, vivid, and full of fine vignettes. Schulberg served in the U.S. Navy (1942–1946) and took photographs of war crimes of use in the Nuremberg trials (1945–1946). He wrote *The Harder They Fall* (1947), a novel based on boxer Primo Carnera; *The Disenchanted* (1950); and the screenplay *On the Waterfront* (1954). *The Disenchanted* is a novel based on Fitzgerald's life even though Schulberg tried to deny the obvious. Ernest Hemingway* despised *The Disenchanted* and Schulberg for writing it. In 1965 Schulberg became president and producer of Schulberg Productions, and he continued to write. *The Four Seasons of Success* (1972) partly concerns the problems Fitzgerald faced as an artist in a commercial world. *Loser and Still Champion: Muhammad Ali* (1972) is a loving tribute. *Everything That Moves* (1980) is a documentary novel based on the life of Jimmy Hoffa. Schulberg presents his memoirs in *Moving Pictures: Memories of a Hollywood Prince* (1981). In 1993 he provided an introduction for Fitzgerald's *Babylon Revisited: The Screenplay*. Schulberg married Virginia Ray (1936, divorced 1942), Victoria Anderson (1943, divorced 1964), and Geraldine Brooks (1964).

SCHULTZE. In *The Great Gatsby*, this is the name of a family Nick Carraway used to remember hoping to see in Chicago during Christmas vacations from prep school and college.

SCHULTZE, KITTY. In *Thoughtbook*, she is a good-looking friend.

SCHUNEMAN, WILLY. In ''Bernice Bobs Her Hair,'' he is a little boy who is getting his monthly haircut when Bernice enters the barbershop to have her hair bobbed.

SCHUYLER. In ''The Rich Boy.'' *See* [Hunter], Schuyler.

SCHUYLER. In ''The Rubber Check,'' he was Val Schuyler's mother Mrs. George Pepin's third husband, now deceased. Val, born Val Jones, takes this man's name at eighteen.

SCHUYLER, MRS. MARTIN. In ''The Rubber Check,'' she is a Schuyler to whom Mrs. Halbird, with malicious intent, asks Val Schuyler if he is related.

SCHUYLER, VAL. In ''The Rubber Check,'' he is the son, born Val Jones, of New Yorker Mrs. George Pepin, in 1904. At eighteen he takes the name Schuyler from that of her third husband and admires the garden of wealthy Charles Martin Templeton and his family. At twenty-one, he is working in a New York brokerage firm. His writing a rubber check to cover the cost of a Philadelphia luncheon for nine makes it impossible for him to elope with Ellen Mortmain and causes his reputation to be damaged by gossip. When he inherits $20,000 upon his mother's death, he becomes a partner in an art dealership, goes at twenty-six to London in 1930, is wiped out soon after the Crash, and becomes a gardener for Templeton, whose daughter Mercia Templeton, Ellen's cousin, pursues him—no doubt successfully.

SCHWANE. In ''A Freeze-Out,'' this is the name of some of the many people who attend the Rikkers' party shortly after New Year's Eve.

SCHWARTZ, ADOLPHUS, FATHER. In ''Absolution,'' he is the Catholic priest in Ludwig. Attracted to handsome Rudolph Miller, he listens to the boy's confession; later in the rectory, he rambles to him about glistening amusement parks and collapses.

SCHWARTZ, FIFI. In ''The Hotel Child,'' she is a beautiful, vividly dressed Jewish girl who is traveling with her mother, Mrs. Schwartz, and her brother, John Schwartz, around Europe. She has a birthday party in a hotel when she turns eighteen and is gossiped about by snide observers. She attracts Count Stanislas Karl Joseph Borowki but turns him into the police when he robs her mother and proposes to elope with Fifi.

SCHWARTZ, JOHN. In ''The Hotel Child,'' he is the alcoholic brother, nineteen, of Fifi Schwartz, who rescues him from would-be victimizers.

SCHWARTZ, MRS. In ''The Hotel Child,'' she is the widowed mother of Fifi Schwartz and John Schwartz. She ineffectually traveled in Europe with them for three years before the story starts.

SCHWARTZE. In ''Inside the House,'' this is the real name of Peppy Velance. *See* Velance, Peppy.

SCHWARTZE. In ''A Night at the Fair,'' he is named as a customer of Barton Leigh, a clothing store owner.

SCHWARTZE, DON S. In *The Great Gatsby*, Nick Carraway lists Schwartze's name on a timetable as one of Jay Gatsby's summer guests. He is connected with the movies.

SCHWARTZE, DR. In ''One Interne,'' he is a physician at the hospital. His idiosyncrasies are spoofed during the roast.

SCHWARTZE, MANNIE. In *The Last Tycoon*, he is a Jewish Hollywood executive who has so displeased Monroe Stahr that he commits suicide in Nashville. In a note he warns Stahr to beware.

"SCOTT FITZGERALD SO THEY SAY" (1981). Poem. People say he is constantly courting.

SCOTTIE. Fitzgerald's daughter. *See* Smith, Frances Scott Fitzgerald Lanahan.

SCULLY. In *The Great Gatsby*, Nick Carraway lists Scully's name on a timetable as one of Jay Gatsby's summer guests. He is from New York.

SECOND STORY SALLE. In *Assorted Spirits*, she is a would-be thief whose friend Hulda lets her into the home of Peter Wetherby and his family. When Josephus Hendrix entrusts Richard Wetherby with $10,000, she pretends to be actress Minnie Maddern Fiske, discusses his play with him, and steals the money, but then drops it.

SEDGEWICK. In "The Pierian Springs and the Last Straw," he is a friend of Mrs. Thomas Rombert, the observer-narrator's mother. Sedgewick is critical of her brother-in-law George Rombert's novels.

SEDGEWICK, EARL. In "The Family Bus," he is a high school student at whose home the students gather before going to the harvest picnic.

SÉGUR, MLLE. In "On Schedule," she is Noël du Cary's French tutor.

SELASSIE, HAILE. In " 'Trouble,' " he is a member of the staff at the hospital and plays in a jazz band for the annual turtle race there.

SELBY, MRS. In "The Intimate Strangers," she is a friend of Marquise Sara de la Guillet de la Guimpé in Paris.

SELDES, GILBERT (1893–1970). Journalist and author. He was born in Alliance, New Jersey, attended Harvard, published in the *Harvard Monthly*, and graduated in 1914. Seldes began his career as a newspaperman in 1914—as a reporter in Pittsburgh, a music critic and editorial writer in Philadelphia, and a freelance war correspondent in England (1916–1918). He served briefly in the U.S. Army (1918). He married Alice ("Amanda") Wadhams Hall in 1923. They visited Europe in 1923, 1924, and 1926, during which times and later Seldes formed negative opinions of several American expatriates there, especially Ernest Hemingway,* whose anti-Semitism caused him to reciprocate against Seldes. From 1918 until 1937 he made New York City his base as an editor (*Dial*, 1920–1923), music critic, and columnist. He tried writing in Hollywood for quick money (1936). He directed television programs for the Columbia Broadcasting Company (1937–1945) and taught communications at the University of Pennsylvania (1959–1963) while reviewing plays, movies, and radio and television programs. Seldes published several books concerning popular culture. They include *The 7 Lively Arts* (1924), arguing that popular songs, vaudeville, movies, and comic strips are not hostile to "major" arts; *An Hour with the Movies and the Talkies* (1929), defining moviegoing as a unique and healthy sociocultural activity; *The Future of Drinking* (1930), concerning the stupidity of Prohibition; *The Movies Come from America* (1937), criticizing Hollywood's treatment of sex, children, and youths; *The Great Audience* (1950), discussing movie, radio, and television fans; *The Public Arts* (1956), reasoning that the media insufficiently satisfy ordinary people's cultural needs; and *The New Mass*

Media: Challenge to a Free Society (1962), arguing that the media can enhance cultural democracy. Seldes also wrote about revolution and war, nineteenth-century American culture, and the Depression; wrote detective stories and a novel; and adapted Aristophanes's *Lysistrata*. His unpublished autobiographical memoir is ''As in My Time.''

In 1922 Seldes met Fitzgerald and Zelda Sayre Fitzgerald* in New York through Seldes's friendship with Townsend Martin, who had known Fitzgerald at Princeton. In 1923 Seldes and his wife honeymooned at the Fitzgeralds' home on the Riviera and shared Christmas dinner with Edmund Wilson* and John Dos Passos* at the Fitzgeralds' home at Great Neck, Long Island. In 1925 Seldes published two rave reviews of *The Great Gatsby*. Hemingway and Malcolm Cowley* both felt Fitzgerald was unfortunately pushed by Seldes's compliments to strive too hard in subsequent writing. In 1928 the Seldeses, Wilson, and others drank to excess with the Fitzgeralds at ''Ellersie,'' their home near Wilmington. In his 1929 ''A Short Autobiography,'' Fitzgerald mentions the honeymooning Seldeses as drinkers with him in France in 1926. When the son of Ring Lardner* asked Fitzgerald to prepare a selection of his father's autobiographical pieces, he suggested Seldes instead then disliked the result—Lardner's *First and Last* (1934). (Seldes also edited *The Portable Ring Lardner* a dozen years later.) Seldes, in a review of *Tender Is the Night*, defined Fitzgerald as the leading American writer of their time. After Fitzgerald's death, Zelda asked Max Perkins* to have Seldes complete *The Last Tycoon*, but Perkins chose Wilson to edit it in unfinished form instead.

Bibliography: Michael Kammen, *The Lively Arts: Gilbert Seldes and the Transformation of Cultural Criticism in the United States* (New York: Oxford University Press, 1996).

SEMPLE. In ''The Popular Girl,'' she is a girl in the Midwestern city where Yanci Bowman lives. After Yanci's father, Tom Bowman, dies, his friend Haedge suggests that Yanci work in the same way as the Semple girl. Yanci declines.

'' 'SEND ME IN, COACH' '' (1936). Short story. (Characters: Cassius, Cathcart, Henry Grady, Jenkins, Hiram Jones, Lawson, Dr. McDougall, the Old Man, Dick Playfair, Rickey, Bugs Trevellion, Bill Watchman, Cyrus K. Watchman.) In a cottage in a summer camp four boys, Bugs, Cassius, Henry Grady, and Bill Watchman, rehearse a play. Cassius mixes his lines with parts of a letter reporting Bill's father Cyrus K. Watchman's acquittal in a court case. Rickey, a handsome counselor, enters with the Old Man, the camp boss, an ex-athlete about sixty. He postpones the rehearsal. When the boys leave, Rickey gripes that he makes no money playing football while the Old Man gains by coaching at State. He tells Rickey to stay away from his young, ignorant wife. The two exit. The boys resume rehearsing the play, which concerns Dick Playfair's ineligibility in an upcoming football game because he played professional baseball earlier. Playfair says he earned money to help build a rural schoolhouse. The Old Man enters, sends everyone but Bill out, and tells him his father has committed suicide. Saying he knew it last night, Bill expresses a desire to remain at camp, to become like Rickey, who dives well, and also like the Old Man, and—for now—to continue rehearsing the play. Agreeing, the Old Man calls the others in, and the rehearsal proceeds while Bill quietly weeps.

SENECA, OLD. In "Lo, the Poor Peacock!," he was an older worker, now probably deceased, on the sausage farm of Annie Lee Davis and Jason Davis. Old Seneca was evidently Young Seneca's father.

SENECA, YOUNG. In "Lo, the Poor Peacock!," he is a worker on the sausage farm of Annie Lee Davis and Jason Davis and also does truck farming.

" 'THE SENSIBLE THING' " (1924). Short story. (Characters: Cary, Jonquil Cary, Mrs. Cary, Chambers, Craddock, Jerry Holt, George O'Kelly.) George O'Kelly, a graduate of the Massachusetts Institute of Technology, worked in Tennessee and became engaged to Jonquil Cary, but two years after graduation he took a job in an insurance company in New York City for little, but sure, money. When Jonquil writes to him to end their relationship, he quits his job and rushes to see her. When she says it does not seem sensible to wed, he makes false accusations. He gets a job in Jersey City and then in Peru, where through work and luck he amasses a fortune. After a year and a half he writes to Jonquil and then calls on her. She has remained single, but at first he is struck only by her undiminished beauty and seeming coldness. They almost say goodbye, but she interrupts, with a kiss, his boast of wasting no time in seizing his opportunity in Peru. They have plenty of time now and will marry, but the magic of their vernal moments together is lost. The story has slight autobiographical touches. In settling for a diminished, more realistic love, George differs from Jay Gatsby, who tragically expects too much from Daisy Fay Buchanan.

Bibliography: Roulston.

"SENTIMENT—AND THE USE OF ROUGE" (1917). Short story. (Characters: Lady Blachford, Lord Blachford, Pere Dupont, Gertrude Evarts, Colonel Hotesane, Eleanor Marbrooke, Katherine Marbrooke, Father O'Brien, Sergeant O'Flaherty, Mrs. Severance, Captain Clayton Harrington Syneforth, Clara Syneforth, Lieutenant Richard Harrington Syneforth, Updike.) Captain Clayton ("Clay") Harrington Syneforth, twenty-two, is home in London on leave from the war in spring 1917. Clay, an idealist, is bothered by a change in morals and manners in the two years since he was home last. He is distressed to see his sister, Clara Blachford, eighteen, wearing too much "paint" before they go to a dance at Mrs. Severance's. Once there, he talks with Eleanor Marbrooke, former fiancée of his brother, Lieutenant Richard Harrington Syneforth, who was killed in France. She shocks Clay by her disillusioned comments on sex and marriage, politics, and religion and then by ordering her chauffeur to take them to Clay's bachelor flat, where she hypnotically talks the conservative but aroused young man into making love. Next afternoon, while accompanying him by train partway to Dover, she says the war has changed everything, including the fact that "love" is not "Love." Still, from Paris he writes to propose marriage, which she quickly declines. In March Clay and Sergeant O'Flaherty are gravely wounded. During their dying moments, they discuss patriotism, religion, and death. Clay's conclusion: everything is now a muddled game with all the players offside and no referee, but every player insisting that a referee, if present, would be on his side.

SERPOLETTE. In "How to Live on Practically Nothing a Year," she is one of the Fitzgeralds' Riviera servants.

SEVERANCE. In *The Beautiful and Damned*, he is a Harvard alumnus who joined the Foreign Legion and died in the war.

SEVERANCE, MRS. In "Sentiment—and the Use of Rouge," she is the London hostess of a dance in her home at which Captain Clayton Harrington Syneforth again meets his dead brother Lieutenant Richard Harrington Syneforth's former fiancée, Eleanor Marbrooke.

SEYMOUR. In *Thoughtbook*, he is a club friend.

SHADOW, THE. In "The Captured Shadow," he is the leading character in Basil Duke Lee's play *The Captured Shadow*. When Hubert Blair backs out, the part is taken by Mayall De Bec.

SHADOW, THE. In *The Captured Shadow*. *See* Dudley, Thorton Hart.

SHADOW LAURELS (1915). Play. (Characters: Jaques Chandelle, Jean Chandelle, Clavine, Pierre Courru, Destage, Lafouquet, Lamarque, François Meridien, Pitou.) Jaques Chandelle, about thirty-seven, comes from the United States to Paris and to Pitou's wineshop to seek information about his father, Jean Chandelle, who years earlier let his boy go to America with an uncle. Pitou says Jean drank in this shop, fought a lot, was wrongly accused of cheating, was seriously stabbed, and died two years later. He adds three other men knew him well—Lamarque, Destage, and Meridien—all of whom now enter. Over wine they reminisce about Jean, who they say worked hard but was always drunk. He was a genius—an attractive, clever, wonderful talker who recited poetry, elucidated and expressed these friends' thoughts, but wrote nothing. The three and Jaques drink a toast to Jean, a poet who wore only a wreath of shadows.

SHAGGY. In ''Shaggy's Morning,'' he is the canine narrator, owned by the Beard and the Brain and friendly with doggy neighbors.

"SHAGGY'S MORNING" (1935). Short story. (Characters: the Beard, the Brain, Shaggy.) The narrator is Shaggy, a big, hairy dog. He lives with the Brain, who feeds him before she drives out in her ''moving room,'' and with the Beard, whom he lets poke him playfully with a pole. Shaggy runs around with canine pals, buries bones uselessly—because he cannot find them later—and is sad when a friend is killed by another ''moving room'' and its owner, a little girl, cries in her swing.

SHAKESPEARE, WILLIAM (1564–1616). British playwright and poet. Soft Shoes in ''Tarquin of Cheapside'' is in reality Shakespeare, who, after he evades pursuers following his violation of a woman, writes the beginning of ''The Rape of Lucrece.'' His pursuers know his crime but not his identity.

SHALDER. In ''A Change of Class,'' he or she is the baby of Irene Shalder and Howard Shalder.

SHALDER, HOWARD. In ''A Change of Class,'' he is Irene Shalder's bootlegger husband who runs off to Chicago, presumably with Earl Johnson's wife, Violet, a step ahead of the Philadelphia mob. Shalder is Berry's boss.

SHALDER, IRENE. In ''A Change of Class,'' she is bootlegger Howard Shalder's lovely wife. Before marriage, she was a typist in Philip Jadwin's office and the object of his secret adoration. When abandoned by her husband, she is comforted by Philip, who is still in love with her.

SHANLY. In *This Side of Paradise*, he is the owner of an establishment where Amory Blaine eats with Carling during their New York binge.

SHAVER, HARMON. In ''No Harm Trying,'' he is an inept money man in Hollywood who is lured into participating in Pat Hobby's scheme to exploit script boy Eric's fine movie idea. When it is presented to producer canny Carl Le Vigne, he sees through the deception but retains Shaver.

SHEARER, NORMA (1902–1983). Movie actress. She began her career in the 1920s, was signed by producer Irving Thalberg* in 1923, and married him four years later, after which she received preferential treatment. She had roles in *The Divorcee* (1930), *The Barretts of Wimpole Street* (1934), *Romeo and Juliet* (1936), *Marie Antoinette* (1938), and *The Women* (1939). Widowed in 1936, she married Martin Jacques Arrougé in 1942. In later years, Shearer grew depressed and suicidal, and like her sister, Athole Shearer Ward Hawks, went blind. Fitzgerald, who knew Shearer and Thalberg and wrote for Thalberg, was invited to a party at the Thalbergs' beach-front home, where he got drunk, sang a foolish song, and was embarrassed. Shearer sent him a complimentary telegram to smooth things over, but he was fired a week later by Thalberg. When Fitzgerald went back to Hollywood in 1937, Shearer invited him to dinner and was sympathetic with him because her sister Athole had mental problems similar to Zelda Sayre Fitzgerald's.* Shearer read *The Last Tycoon*, the hero of which is patterned after Thalberg, took an option for movie rights in 1946, but had casting problems, and never exercised the option. She is partly the model for Stella Walker Calman in Fitzgerald's "Crazy Sunday."

Bibliography: Lambert.

SHEILAH. In "Some Interrupted Lines to Sheilah." *See* Graham, Sheilah.

"SHE LAY SUPINE AMONG HER PEKINESE" (1981). Poem. (Character: Sarah.) The poet pities and praises Sarah, who her guests hoped would never change. Her former ramblings made them feel secure.

SHELENTON, HONEY. In *Thoughtbook*, she is a neighbor.

SHEPLY. In *Thoughtbook*, he is a club member.

SHERIDAN. In "On Schedule," he and his wife are friends of René du Cary and Noël du Cary.

SHERIDAN, MRS. In "On Schedule," she and her husband are friends of the du Carys.

SHERMAN, ESTHER. In "One Trip Abroad," she is a person who Nicole Kelly tells her physician traveled soon after having a baby. But the physician says every case is unique.

SHERMY. In *Safety First!*, he is an unpleasant convict who, according to his son, has been released from prison.

"SHERWOOD ANDERSON ON THE MARRIAGE QUESTION" (1923). Review of *Many Marriages* by Sherwood Anderson.*

SHEVLIN. In "The Curious Case of Benjamin Button," this is the name of the family at whose country house Benjamin meets and dances with Hildegarde Moncrief, whom he marries.

SHINKEY. In "Family in the Wind," he is a resident of Bending whom Dr. Forrest Janney asks to guard the door of the makeshift hospital while he treats persons injured by the first tornado.

SHIPMAN, DR. In "The Smilers," he is the physician who informs Waldron Crosby, when he phones home, that his wife is about to have a baby.

SHOONOVER, JOE. In "That Kind of Party," he is Terrence R. Tipton's closest friend. The two want to have another kissing party. They plot to send Joe's mother a telegram, but it is delivered to Terrence's mother instead.

SHOONOVER, MRS. In That Kind of Party," she is Joe Shoonover's mother who tolerantly hosts the children's party. They play post office, which she accompanies on the piano.

"A SHORT AUTOBIOGRAPHY (WITH ACKNOWLEDGMENTS TO [JEAN GEORGE] NATHAN[*])" (1929). Short story. (Characters: Ben, Bustanoby, Charlie, Grace, Ernest Hemingway, Kaly, Ring Lardner, Mollat, Muldoon, Gerald Murphy, Prunier, Ruth, Gilbert Seldes, Tate, Tom, Monsignor X.) Fitzgerald presents his life story by listing year by year, from 1913 through 1929, places where and persons with whom he had a variety of drinks. In light of what happened to Fitzgerald, this piece is the reverse of amusing.

"A SHORT TRIP HOME" (1927). Short story. (Characters: Ellen Baker, Mrs. Baker, Bill Brokaw, Jim Cathcart, Catherine, Ingersoll, Joe Jelke, Shorty, Eddie Stinson, Joe Varland.) The narrator, Eddie Stinson, a Yale sophomore, is home in St. Paul for Christmas vacation. He and some friends, including Joe Jelke and Jim Cathcart, are going to a hotel dance when Eddie's adorable friend Ellen Baker, eighteen, also home on vacation from the East, is curiously overpowered by a strange, sneering man exuding a sense of evil. Joe, protesting, goes outside alone with him but is knocked unconscious. Ellen tells Eddie she met the man on the train and warns Eddie not to interfere. Next morning Eddie walks into a confusing part of town, sees the stranger, and follows him into a pool parlor, but loses him. When Eddie calls on Ellen's mother, he is relieved to learn the gentle girl is returning to school by train a day early to visit her friends the Brokaws in Chicago. Relaxing at his family home, Eddie recalls the Brokaws are vacationing in Palm Beach, determines to save Ellen, catches up with her in Chicago, and insists on traveling with her as far as New York. Her face expresses fear, cunning, and resistance—until he says he knows who the stranger is. Eddie and Ellen spend the day together in Chicago, during which he senses they are followed by contagious evil. They board the train, and when he tells her he loves her, she sneers. He suspects not only that the stranger boarded her homebound train but that he is outside her compartment now. He leaves her and confronts the stranger, who threatens him with a gun—to no avail. Eddie, seeing a small hole in the man's forehead, tells him he is ''dead'' and has failed, at which the stranger simply wilts in a blast of dark, corrupt cold. Recovering consciousness, Eddie returns to Ellen's compartment and finds her peacefully asleep. During Easter vacation he learns at the pool parlor that the stranger, Joe Varland, habitually picked up girls on trains and preyed on them for money, until he was shot to death by a Pittsburgh policeman some time ago. Summer comes, and Eddie and Ellen feel close. In a letter (October 1927) to his literary agent Harold Ober,* Fitzgerald called ''A Short Trip Home'' his first ''ghost story.''

Bibliography: Eble.

SHORTY. In ''A Short Trip Home,'' he is a jockey-like fellow in the pool parlor who for $10 tells Eddie Stinson the stranger who harassed Ellen Baker was Joe Varland, killed earlier by a Pittsburgh policeman.

SHUGRUE, MISS WILLIE. In ''Strange Sanctuary,'' this is an alias of Birdie Lukas, also known as Willie Lukas. *See* Lukas, Birdie.

SHULLY, ADOLPH. In *Thoughtbook*, he is a friend.

SHULLY, KITTY. In *Thoughtbook*, she is a playful friend.

SHURMER, BOB ("BOBBY"). In *Thoughtbook*, he is a club member.

SHUTTLEWORTH, EDWARD. In *The Beautiful and Damned*, he is a former gambler and a saloon keeper for Pat in Hoboken. Shuttleworth reformed and became the pious secretary and guardian of Adam Patch. He leaves Shuttleworth $1,000,000. After Anthony breaks Adam's will, Shuttleworth commits suicide.

SIBLEY-BIERS, LADY CAROLINE. In ''Two Wrongs,'' this was the name of Lady Sybil Combrinck in the original publication of the story. *See* Combrinck, Lady Sybil. In *Tender Is the Night*, Lady Sibley-Biers, whose name is spelled Sibly-Biers in some editions, is a snooty guest aboard T. F. Golding's yacht in the Nicean Bay. She and Dick Diver argue. She and Mary North di Minghetti evidently have lesbian tendencies, which cause their arrest in Antibes. Dick and Gausse rescue them. She is reluctant to reimburse the two for the bribes they paid to the authorities.

SIDNEY. In ''Strange Sanctuary,'' this is the name of people to whom Dolly Haines thinks she should have reported instead of to the home of Lila Appleton.

SILVÉ. In ''Image on the Heart,'' this is a name mentioned at the cafe where Tom, Tudy, and Riccard eat. Silvé is Riccard's friend.

SILVERSTEIN, DAVE. In "Crazy Sunday," he is an independent movie producer Joel Coles mimics in his unsuccessful skit at the Calmans' Sunday party.

SIMMONS, RABBIT. In "The Captured Shadow," he is a character in Basil Duke Lee's play *The Captured Shadow*.

SIMMONS, RABBIT. In *The Captured Shadow*, he is a would-be robber. When he and his friend Chinyman Rudd follow Hubert Connage into the Connage home, Thorton Hart Dudley is able to sneak in after them.

SIMMS, LUD. In "Winter Dreams," he is the man who, according to Devlin, married Judy Jones, had children with her, drinks too much, and treats her badly. Knowledge of this destroys Dexter Green's ability to grieve. Lud, an unusual name, derives from the identical nickname of Ludlow Fowler, Fitzgerald's hard-drinking Princeton friend and best man at his wedding.

SIMONE. In "Last Kiss," she is an actress mentioned by Mike Harris in conversation with Jim Leonard. Mike implies she and Pamela Knighton are troublemakers.

SINCLAIR. In "The Diary of a Sophomore," he is a businessman to whom the diarist owes money.

SINCLAIR, RHODA. In "Forging Ahead," she is the stepdaughter of Benjamin Reilly, whose wife, her mother, persuades him to give Basil Duke Lee a job, on condition he escort Rhoda to social functions. Basil wants to ditch her when Erminie Gilberte Labouisse Bibble comes to town.

"SING HOTCHA-CHA SING HEY-HI NINNY" (1981). Poem. (Characters: Peaches Finney, Peggy Finney, Pete Finney.) Fitzgerald sends a rousing New Year's greeting to his Finney friends.

SINGLETON, THEA. In "One Interne," she is an army officer's daughter, who grew up in the Philippines, and is an anesthetist at the hospital where William Tulliver V studies and then interns. She was in love with John Gresham, who died. She became Dr. Howard Durfee's "girl." She prefers Tulliver, breaks with Durfee upon his engagement, and remains loyal to Tulliver. Her sorrowful past has toughened her but also makes her sympathetic in her relationship with the egocentric Tulliver. In "Zone of Accident," William Tullivers IV remembers her as a former girlfriend now an anesthetist working in New York City.

"SIX OF ONE—" (1932). Short story. (Characters: Ed Barnes, Esther Crosby, H. B. Crosby, Irene Daley, Louis Ireland, Gladys Irving, Kavenaugh, Howard Kavenaugh, Lallette, Beau Lebaume, James Matsko, Larry Patt, Otto Schlach,

Schofield, Charley Schofield, Mrs. Schofield, Wister Schofield, Jack Stubbs, Gordon Vandervere, George Winfield.) In 1920 in Minneapolis, two wealthy friends, Ed Barnes, childless, and his friend Schofield, with sons Charley Schofield and Wister Schofield, disagree as to the advantage of wealth in the future of "rich boys." Schofield points with pride to his sons and their athletic friends—Beau Lebaume, Larry Patt, and the Kavenaugh brothers—also from wealthy families. Barnes decides to return to his Ohio hometown, seek out six deserving boys from poor or middle-class families, send them to good schools, and see whether money after puberty for boys is more beneficial than longtime family wealth. He chooses Louis Ireland, James Matsko, Otto Schlach, Jack Stubbs, Gordon Vandervere, and George Winfield. In the intervening ten years, all but one of the six young men Schofield praised fail, whereas all of Barnes's half-dozen protégés succeed in various ways. Barnes is glad he experimented but would not do so again and concludes that "all that waste at the top" is both American and sad.

SKIGGS, DR. HEPEZIA. In "Pain and the Scientist," he is a Christian Scientist neighbor of Walter Hamilton Bartney, who falls and hurts himself while walking over for a visit. After Skiggs tells him he must tell himself he feels no pain, Bartney gets even by catching Skiggs trepassing and shaking him until he says "ouch."

SKIPPER. In "Head and Shoulders," he is probably the owner of Skipper's Gymnasium, where Horace Tarbox initially works out.

SKOURAS, SPYROS PANAGIOTES (1893–1971). Greek-born movie executive and philanthropist. In *The Last Tycoon*, Skouras, whose last name is given, is probably the person whose phone call Monroe Stahr should return. Skouras's older brother, Charles, and younger brother, George, were also involved in the movie industry.

Bibliography: Memo from David O. Selznick, sel. and ed. by Rudy Behlmer (New York: Viking, 1972).

SLAGLE. In *The Great Gatsby*, he is a criminal whose phone call Nick Carraway takes in Jay Gatsby's home after Gatsby's murder. He begins to implicate Parke in a shady deal but hangs up when he learns Gatsby is dead.

"SLEEPING AND WAKING" (1934). (Characters: Caroline, Essie.) Essay. If insomnia afflicts you, it starts in your late thirties. It comes between sweet first sleep and deep morning sleep. A friend's case started with a mouse nibbling his exposed finger. Fitzgerald's started two years ago in a New York hotel. Now it follows too much work, illness, or worry over drinking. When it hits, he sees misty Baltimore from his porch, eyes piles of papers on his desk, fantasizes about football and army combat, regrets ''waste'' and ''horror'' in his career, and sleeps at last, dreaming of Caroline and other girls he once knew.

"SLEEP OF A UNIVERSITY" (1920). Poem. While Nassau Hall's bells pretend all is well and real life is far away, the towers watch over the foolish dreams of the college. Fitzgerald called this poem a paraphrase of a similar poem by another Princetonian.

SLOANE. In *The Great Gatsby*, he is a person whose arrival at Jay Gatsby's mansion one Sunday afternoon with a drunken woman causes some minor embarrassment.

SLOANE, CARY. In ''The Rich Boy,'' he is the lover of Edna Hunter, who is Anson Hunter's aunt. Anson threatens to tell Cary's father, Moses Sloane, of his philandering son's affair. Feeling hopeless, Cary commits suicide by jumping off the Queensboro Bridge.

SLOANE, FRED. In *This Side of Paradise*, he is a Princeton student with whom Amory Blaine goes to Asbury Park. Fred, described as impatient and supercilious, is a pitcher on the baseball team. He mistreats Phyllis Styles at the prom.

SLOANE, MOSES. In ''The Rich Boy,'' he is mentioned as a rich, retired cotton broker from Alabama. He is rigidly moral and has threatened to stop his son Cary Sloane's allowance if he does not discontinue his vagaries.

SLOCUM. In ''On Schedule,'' he and his wife provide a room for Becky Snyder. Becky takes a bath at René du Cary's house because the Slocums' water runs too slowly.

SLOCUM, MRS. In ''On Schedule,'' she and her husband provide a room for Becky Snyder.

SMIDY. In ''The Mystery of the Raymond Mortgage,'' he is an ''Arab'' lad who helps John Syrel locate Mrs. Raymond in Indianous, a town near Santuka. This enables Syrel to solve the mystery.

"THE SMILERS" (1920). Short story. (Characters: Mrs. Waldron Crosby, Waldron Crosby, Donny, Jerry, Potter, Dr. Shipman, Sylvester Stockton, Tearle, Betty Tearle, Billy Tearle, Clare Tearle.) Sylvester Stockton, a rich, idle New Yorker, thirty, thinks people who smile at him are too stupid to realize life is difficult. When Betty Tearle, a former girlfriend, smiles at him, it is because she is comfortably married with two children. When his friend Waldron Crosby, a broker, smiles at him in a cigar store, it is because he is happily married. And when Jerry, the room waiter in his hotel, smiles at him, it is because of the 50¢ tip. In truth, however, Betty is leaving her husband, the stock market has just cleaned out Crosby, and impoverished Jerry's girlfriend will wait for him no longer. Fitzgerald sold "The Smilers" to H. L. Mencken,* editor of *Smart Set*, for $75.

SMIRKE. In *The Great Gatsby*, Nick Carraway lists Smirke's name on a timetable as one of Jay Gatsby's summer guests. He is from New York.

SMITH. In "He Thinks He's Wonderful," he is the proprietor of a drugstore where Joe Gorman says he and a few others will go for ice cream.

SMITH. In "Pat Hobby's Secret," he is the bitter bouncer at Conk's bar. When R. Parke Woll takes a swing at Pat Hobby but hits Smith, Smith hurls him to the floor and he dies.

SMITH, ADRIAN. In "The Rough Crossing," he is a New York playwright, thirty-one, and the husband of Eva Smith. They have children, one of whom is named Estelle Smith. The Smith family start across the Atlantic from New York to France. Adrian annoys Eva by flirting with Elizabeth D'Amido. The Smiths are reconciled at the end of the rough voyage.

SMITH, DON. In "On the Trail of Pat Hobby." *See* Hobby, Pat.

SMITH, ESTELLE. In "The Rough Crossing," she is the young daughter of Adrian Smith and Eva Smith. When the trip from New York to France is finished, Estelle says she liked the rough voyage better than the French countryside. The Smiths have other, unspecified children. Their children evidently stay in their room during the entire crossing.

SMITH, EVA. In "The Rough Crossing," she is the wife, twenty-six, of Adrian Smith. They have children, including Estelle Smith. During the rough voyage from New York to France, Eva is annoyed when Adrian flirts with Elizabeth D'Amido; so she drinks with Butterworth and contemplates divorce. Once on land again, she and her husband become reconciled.

SMITH, FRANCES SCOTT FITZGERALD LANAHAN ("SCOTTIE") (1921–1986). Daughter of Fitzgerald and Zelda Sayre Fitzgerald.* Born in St. Paul, Minnesota, she frequently moved with her parents during her childhood and was often left with nannies. Fitzgerald was a concerned father, played games with her, but also was too strict and educative. He and Zelda shielded her from their marital squabbles as much as they could. When Zelda was hospitalized in Switzerland in 1930, Scottie was supervised by a governess and attended school in Paris. Only when she was a young teenager did she realize Fitzgerald was an alcoholic. She attended the Ethel Walker School in Simsbury, Connecticut (1936–1938); she was then a kind of foster child of literary agent Harold Ober* and his wife, Anne, who were hospitable and generous to her. Scottie visited Fitzgerald in California (summer 1937). She went there by train with actress Helen Hayes; while she was there Fitzgerald introduced her to Fred Astaire, her idol, and to Sheilah Graham,* who was nice to her and whom she liked. After graduating from Ethel Walker, Scottie studied for admission to Vassar College, vacationed in France, and visited Fitzgerald again in California (summer 1938 and 1939). He made some of her time in college unpleasant by sending domineering, if affectionate, letters. The advice in them concerning reading, study, friendships, and behavior she largely ignored. She attended his funeral and burial at Rockville Union Cemetery. She graduated from Vassar in 1942.

It was difficult for Scottie to emerge from the shadow of being Fitzgerald's daughter. She established a career in journalism and public service. She wrote for the *New York Times*, the *Washington Post*, and the *New Yorker*. She wrote speeches for Adlai Stevenson during his campaign for the presidency (1956). She wrote and directed musical plays to raise money for the Multiple Sclerosis Society. She coauthored *Don't Quote Me! Washington Newswomen and the Power Society* (1970, as Scottie Smith) and also *The Romantic Egoists* (1974), about her parents (as Scottie Fitzgerald Smith). Scottie was married twice. In 1943 she married Samuel Jackson (''Jack'') Lanahan. They had four children: Thomas Addison (''Tim'') Lanahan, Eleanor Anne Lanahan, Samuel Jackson Lanahan, Jr., and Cecilia Scott Lanahan. Scottie obtained a divorce from Lanahan in Mexico (1967). Within a week she married Grove Smith and soon began to drink too much, as he was already doing. Scottie's son Tim, who was mentally unstable, attended Princeton for two years, served in the U.S. Army in Vietnam, joined the navy, and committed suicide (1973). Scottie and Smith were divorced in 1990. She died of esophageal cancer in Montgomery, Alabama. Beginning in 1939 Scottie wrote at least sixteen pieces long and short about her father. His revealing, often poignant letters to his ''Scottie,'' ''Scottina,'' and ''Pie'' are included in *Scott Fitzgerald: Letters to His Daughter*, edited by Andrew Turnbull* (1965).

Bibliography: Eleanor Lanahan, *Scottie: The Daughter of . . . The Life of Frances Scott Fitzgerald Lanahan Smith* (New York: HarperCollins, 1995).

SMITH, "GYPSY." In *The Beautiful and Damned*, he is a person allegedly libeled in Richard Caramel's novel *The Demon Lover*.

SMITH, MRS. In ''Pat Hobby's Secret,'' she is the huge wife of the bouncer Smith. She tells Pat Hobby she will twist his tongue out if he testifies against Smith at the inquest. Pat conveniently draws a blank.

SMITH, PRICILLA. In ''A Man in the Way,'' she is an attractive Hollywood writer whose idea Pat Hobby tries to steal and sell to his boss, Jack Berners. Pat's plan will backfire because Pricilla is Berners' current girlfriend.

SMITH, ROSALIND SAYRE. Fitzgerald's sister-in-law. Her husband was Newman Smith. She attended Fitzgerald's 1920 wedding to her sister Zelda Sayre Fitzgerald* but never forgave him for not having a postceremonial dinner including her. In 1930 she blamed Fitzgerald for Zelda's mental instability and two years later felt he had institutionalized Zelda to get rid of her. Although Fitzgerald regarded Rosalind as neurotic and foolish, he responded with a long, considerate letter (8 August 1934) when she interfered with his plans for Scottie's* education. In 1939 he was upset when the Smiths would not loan Scottie the money to enter Vassar College and in a letter to Zelda (6 October 1939) recalled loaning the Smiths money in 1925 they could ill afford. Marion Peters and her husband, Lincoln Peters, of "Babylon Revisited" are modeled partly on Rosalind and her husband.

SMITH, SHEIK B. In "Rags Martin-Jones and the Pr-nce of W-les," he is a comedian who performs at the nightclub in which John M. Chestnut stages his ruse.

SMITH, WHARTON. In *Thoughtbook*, he is a playful, admiring friend Fitzgerald later regards as a rival.

SMYTHE. In "Majesty," he is one of the guests at the wedding ceremony called off by Emily Castleton.

SMYTHE, JOHN. In "Teamed with Genius," he is a fictitious worker in the British consulate in New York. Pat Hobby sends a letter supposedly from him to René Wilcox to get René out of Hollywood. The plan will fail.

SNELL, RIPLEY. In *The Great Gatsby*, Nick Carraway lists Snell's name on a timetable as one of Jay Gatsby's summer guests. Shortly before going to jail, he was drunk in Gatsby's driveway, and Mrs. Ulysses Swett ran over his hand.

"A SNOBBISH STORY" (1930). Short story. (Characters: John Boynton Bailey, Ed Bement, Blacht, Miss Brereton, Caroline, Clare, Madelaine Danby, Travis de Coppet, Donald, Evelyn, Mrs. Fiske, Lillian Hammel, Elsie Hammerton, Hoftzer, Kelly, Elsie Kerr, Emily Kohl, Jenny McRae, Jim McRae, Oberwalter, Howard Page, Herbert T. Perry, Josephine Perry, Mrs. Herbert T. Perry, Will.) While Josephine Perry is bored watching a summer tennis match at Lake Forest, outside Chicago, socially influential Jenny McRae hints that if she is nice to her nephew, Donald, from Minneapolis she can appear in a vaudeville skit with Travis de Coppet. John Boynton Bailey, a breezy *Chicago Tribune* reporter who writes pro-socialist plays, is covering the tournament, sees Josephine, and invites her to lunch next day. While they are eating at an obscure Chicago restaurant, Josephine is silently disturbed at seeing her father, Herbert T. Perry, lunching with a floozy. Josephine and Bailey go to a theater workshop, where his play is chosen for production if finances can be arranged and where Josephine meets a girl named Evelyn. When Bailey tells Evelyn she will not be in the play, she storms out. He wants Josephine for the part but then admits Evelyn is his wife. Back home, Josephine hints menacingly to her father that she knows he is throwing money around and asks him to back Bailey's play financially. Puzzled, he asks her to invite Bailey to lunch on Saturday. The two men hit it off, and Perry offers $1,000 if matched by others. The police appear: Evelyn has attempted suicide, is in the hospital, and Bailey is wanted there. Josephine, sensing her career as a great actress is lost, starts rebuking her father for lunching with a girlfriend; he laughs and reveals that the mysterious woman is the lover of his wife's brother Will, whom the Perrys are paying to stay away. Josephine rushes to the tennis finals, late but still in time to play up to the winner, Mrs. McRae's nephew. Josephine does not dance with Travis in the vaudeville skit but watches the performance with the rest of the audience, where she sees Bailey in the rear. She decides to cast her lot with the rich and powerful once and for all.

SNOOKS. In *The Vegetable*, he is Jerry Frost's Irish-Polish bootlegger. In the dream sequence, he is the ambassador of Irish Poland.

SNOOKS, MRS. In *The Vegetable*, she is the bootlegger Snooks's wife. Jerry Frost phones her about a delivery.

SNOW BIRD, THE. In ''Babylon Revisited,'' he is a cocaine addict or dealer Charles J. Wales and Duncan Schaeffer and other Americans in Paris knew a while back.

SNYDER, BECKY. In ''On Schedule,'' she is a fine tennis player, nineteen, graduated in 1932 from high school in Bingham, New Jersey, and is a university student in the town where René du Cary, thirty-four, works. The two are in love and plan to marry as soon as he has conformed to the terms of the will of his deceased wife, Edith du Cary. Becky saves René's laboratory experiment.

SODA SAM. In ''The Jelly-Bean,'' he is the owner of the establishment in the Georgia town where young people gather for sundaes and lemonade.

SOFT SHOES. In ''Tarquin of Cheapside,'' he is a rapist in London whose identity is unknown and who evades two pursuers, both called Flowing Boots. He asks his friend Peter Caxter to hide him and, when safe, writes the beginning of ''The Rape of Lucrece.'' Soft Shoes is William Shakespeare.*

SOHENBERG. In *The Beautiful and Damned*, he is the Manhattan landlord who wants to raise the rent on Anthony Patch and Gloria Gilbert Patch to $2,500 a year. This forces them to move.

SOLLINGER, NED. In *The Last Tycoon*, he is Rose Meloney's nephew. She sent him to New York University, where he played football. Having disgraced himself in medical school, he is now Monroe Stahr's office boy.

"SOME INTERRUPTED LINES TO SHEILAH" (1958). Poem. (Character: Sheilah.) Fitzgerald tells Sheilah she once seemed far away when close, then so close distance was nothing. When just now she phoned him late, he insanely felt stood up. In real life, when Sheilah Graham* stood him up once, he went on a long bender.

"SOME STORIES THEY LIKE TO TELL" (1923). Sketch. Fitzgerald reports that his favorite story concerns the toast an unsteady speaker offered after a Victorian banquet: "Gen'lemen—the queal!"

"SONG" (1981). Poem. The poet humorously orders her to wash off her billy-goat smell by bathing. His habit is to continue not bathing.

"SONG—" (1981). Poem. The poet says there is magic near his addressee.

"A SONG NUMBER IDEA" (1981). Poem. The idea concerns trains to Flushing.

SPAULDING, PORTER S. In "The Honor of the Goon," he is one of the students who called Ella Lei Chamoro a goon.

SPEARS, GEORGE. In "The Bowl," he is a Princeton football team player. He is an unpopular Southerner but is a good runner.

SPEERS, ELSIE. *In Tender Is the Night*, she is the mother of Rosemary Hoyt. Mrs. Speers is twice widowed; one husband was a physician. Mrs. Speers, quite permissive, and Rosemary are close. The name Speers may have been suggested to Fitzgerald by that of his friend Dorothy Speare (1898–1951), singer, novelist, and twice-married Hollywood screenwriter. Her *Dancers in the Dark* (1922) is a breezy novel about excitement-seeking flappers in the early Jazz Age days. She received credit for the story line of the 1934 movie *One Night of Love*.

Bibliography: Latham; Dorothy Speare, "Hollywood Madness," *Saturday Evening Post*, 7 October 1933, 26–27, 59–60.

SPENCE, MISS. In *Coward*, she is an etiquette authority cited by Angelina Bangs.

SPIGOT, MISS. In *Assorted Spirits*, she is the aunt of William Chapman, who comes to visit her. She lives at 225 Greenwood Place, near Peter Wetherby, who confusingly lives at 225 Greenbriar Street.

SPINDLE, MISS. In *Coward*, she is an etiquette authority cited by Angelina Bangs.

"THE SPIRE AND THE GARGOYLE" (1917). Short story. An unnamed college student finishes his examination, and the preceptor, who resembles a gargoyle, collects the booklets. The student is worried, because he cut many recitations to visit New York City, and if he fails the exam he will not become a sophomore. The Gothic spire of a tower on campus symbolizes upward striving to him, and he wants to remain in college. He meets the gargoyle that night on campus but is given no information. Five years later, the young man, having flunked out, works in New York and lives in a dingy boardinghouse. At a museum he chances to meet the gargoyle, who tells him over tea he has a family, is teaching at a Brooklyn high school for better pay, but has a brother who is an instructor at their college. Later one rainy evening the young man takes a train to the university town, intending to spend the night there. He encounters the gargoyle, who is going to visit his brother but does not ask the young man to come along. Feeling like a failure, he boards the train to leave. Part of "The Spire and the Gargoyle" found its way into *This Side of Paradise*.

SPIRIT OF SEVENTY-SIX, THE. In " 'Trouble,' " he is a member of the staff at the hospital and plays in a jazz band at the annual turtle race there.

SPRAGUE, ANNABEL FITZGERALD (b. 1901). Fitzgerald's sister. Their age difference prevented their being close. In 1925 she married Clifton Sprague (1896–1955). He had been commissioned an ensign in the U.S. Navy in 1917 and remained in the service. The couple had two daughters, Hazel Courtney Sprague (Mrs. Daniel Vaughan) and Patricia Sprague (Mrs. Travis Reneau). After Fitzgerald's death, Annabel and her daughters continued amiable relations with Scottie.* Clifton Sprague rose to the rank of rear admiral, served with distinction in the Battle of Leyte Gulf (October 1944), and retired as a vice admiral (1951).

"SPRING SONG" (1981). Poem. (Character: Misseldine.) The poet does not mind being punningly giddy because spring is coming at 7:45 P.M. Fitzgerald wrote this poem for Dorothy Bissel.

SQUARE, WASHINGTON. In "The Captured Shadow," he is the lead character in Basil Duke Lee's incomplete play *Mr. Washington Square*.

SQUIRES, JOE. In "Crazy Sunday," he is a man who, according to Nat Keogh, kicked the movie actor nicknamed The Great Lover at Grauman's and got away with it.

SQUIRES, TOM. In "At Your Age," he is a Yale man, rich, alone, and fifty. He has a fling with Annie Lorry and treasures the memories.

STACOMB ("STAC"). In "The Rough Crossing," he is a passenger on the ship going from New York to France. He flatters Adrian Smith and attracts him and his wife, Eva Smith, to his group of young people.

STACY, MISS. In " 'Boil Some Water—Lots of It,' " she is a Red Cross nurse whose absence helps Pat Hobby have lunch with Helen Earle, the new nurse.

STAHR, MINNA DAVIS. In *The Last Tycoon*, she was Monroe Stahr's beautiful wife, recently deceased and unforgotten. He is initially attracted to Kathleen Moore because she resembles Minna. Fitzgerald's mother-in-law, Minerva Machen Sayre,* was nicknamed Minnie.

STAHR, MONROE. In *The Last Tycoon*, he is the Jewish boy genius movie producer, about thirty-five and the "tycoon" of the novel. He left Erie, Pennsylvania, at fifteen, for New York then Hollywood. He thoroughly grasps all aspects of moviemaking, is dictatorial but often tactful with financial backers, writers, producers, directors, and actors and actresses. He cannot forget his deceased wife, Minna Davis Stahr. He falls in love with Kathleen Moore but is reluctant to propose. She goes ahead and marries her fiancé. Stahr has a heart condition which, combined with overwork, will kill him within six months or so. Monroe Stahr is based closely on Irving Thalberg.*

STANDISH, JOHN. In "The Mystery of the Raymond Mortgage," he is a servant, thirty-two, who has worked for the Raymond family for twelve years. When Agnes Raymond rebuffs his advances, he shoots her to death, after which Agnes's mother, Mrs. Raymond, shoots him to death.

STANDISH, JOHN B. In *The Vegetable*, he is one of bootlegger Snooks's customers.

STANLEY ("STAN"). In "No Flowers," he is the university freshman, from the Midwest, whose tuxedo William Delaney Johns takes. When Marjorie Clark hears Stan and his girlfriend, Estelle, lamenting its disappearance, Johns returns it with an easy fib.

STARHEIM, LIZZETTE. In ''No Harm Trying,'' she is a stunningly beautiful foreign actress. Pat Hobby lures her away from producer Carl Le Vigne to participate in his scheme to exploit script boy Eric's fine movie idea. When it is presented to Le Vigne, he reveals Lizzette to be a ''pinhead'' he has on hold because she cannot learn English.

STARK. In ''One Hundred False Starts,'' he is a watchman about whom Fitzgerald cannot write. He may have been involved in a murder one winter.

"THE STAYING UP ALL NIGHT" (1917). Sketch. At first all seems warm, comfortable, and merry. But time passes, some friends leave, wit grows feeble, breakfast is tasteless, and the new day is a failure.

STEARNE. In ''The Cut-Glass Bowl,'' this is the owner of a house Harold Piper, when drunk, tells Clarence Ahearn he ought to consider buying. Another suitable house, he says, belongs to Ridgeway.

STEIN, GERTRUDE (1874–1946). Author and critic. Stein was born in Allegheny, Pennsylvania, lived with her wealthy family in Austria, France, Baltimore, and San Francisco. She attended Harvard (1893–1894) and studied at Johns Hopkins Medical School (1897–1901), but left without a degree. In 1903 she moved to Paris. Alice B. Toklas began to live with her in a lesbian relationship in 1909. Stein lectured on composition at Oxford and Cambridge universities (1926, 1936). She and Toklas leased a house at Bilignin (1929). Stein lectured in the United States (1934–1935). During the Nazi occupation of France, Stein and Toklas lived in or near Bilignin. In 1944 Stein met and delighted many American soldiers and a year later toured U.S. Army bases in occupied Germany and lectured in Belgium. Notable among her more than five hundred publications are *Three Lives* (1909), *Tender Buttons* (1914), *Four Saints in Three Acts* (1929), *The Autobiography of Alice B. Toklas* (1933), *Lectures in America* (1935), *The Geographical History of America* (1936), and *Picasso* (1938). Among her numerous friends, most talented were Sherwood Anderson,* Guillaume Apollinaire, Djuna Barnes, Sylvia Beach, Ernest Hemingway,* Pablo Picasso,* and Virgil Thomson. Stein is controversial—ridiculed as an inaccessible stylist and praised as an apologist for Modernism and an advocate of many innovative writers.

In 1925 Hemingway took Fitzgerald to Stein's Parisian atelier, and the two developed a pleasant friendship. She responded to his charm, praised *This Side of Paradise* for creating the new, postwar generation for readers, and complimented *The Great Gatsby* for its natural sentences and for creating the contemporary world as William Makepeace Thackeray created his. She urged Fitzgerald to write a big novel, and years later he sent her a copy of *Tender Is the Night* as his response. When she was lecturing in the United States, she visited the Fitzgeralds in Baltimore on Christmas Eve 1934. When he invited Stein to accept as a gift a few paintings by Zelda Sayre Fitzgerald,* Stein's choices triggered an argument, partly because Zelda had promised to give to her doctor the two that Stein chose but mainly because Zelda disliked Stein and regarded her conversation as gibberish. Stein accepted two other paintings. Unlike Hemingway, Fitzgerald never argued with Stein but always looked up to her as a sensitive friend. For example, Fitzgerald wrote to her that she had brought her hearth fire that Christmas Eve, because she carries her ''fine'' warmth with her ''wherever you are'' (26 December 1934).

Bibliography: Donald Gallup, ed., *The Flowers of Friendship: Letters Written to Gertrude Stein* (New York: Knopf, 1953); Bruce Kellner, ed., *A Gertrude Stein Companion: Content with the Example* (Westport, Conn.: Greenwood Press, 1988); Linda Wagner-Martin, *''Favored Strangers'': Gertrude Stein and Her Family* (New Brunswick, N.J.: Rutgers University Press, 1995).

STELLA. In *The Great Gatsby*, she is Meyer Wolfsheim's secretary.

STERNER. In ''Dalyrimple Goes Wrong,'' he is a person whose residence Bryan Dalyrimple does not rob.

STERRETT, GORDON ("GORDY"). In ''May Day,'' he is a Yale man, about twenty-four, back from France after World War I. He is an artist, now ill and threatened with blackmail by Jewel Hudson following his foolish affair with her. He goes to Philip Dean, his wealthy former Yale roommate, but is given only $80 instead of the necessary $300. He attends the Yale dance at Delmonico's, sees his former girlfriend, Edith Bradin, is rebuffed because of his depression and drunkenness, drinks more with Jewel, wakes up in the morning realizing he has married her, and shoots himself to death.

STEVE. In ''The Night of Chancellorsville,'' he is a rebel soldier who, with his buddy, enters the train carrying fancy girls to Virginia. His buddy identifies the girls as General Joseph Hooker's ''staff.''

STEWART, DONALD OGDEN (1894–1980). American writer. Born in Columbus, Ohio, he was the son of a lawyer who was later indicted for theft. After graduating from Yale in 1916, Stewart worked for the American Telephone and Telegraph Company in and out of Columbus. After serving in the U.S. Navy (1918–1919), he returned to work for AT&T in Minneapolis. He met Fitzgerald in St. Paul. In 1920 Stewart went to New York, where Fitzgerald recommended his parodies to *Vanity Fair* editors. Acceptance led to *A Parody Outline of History* (1921). Meanwhile, Stewart was socializing with Fitzgerald and Zelda Sayre Fitzgerald.* In 1921 Fitzgerald published ''Reminiscenses [*sic*] of Donald Stewart.'' Pretending in it he and Stewart are old, he recalls their meeting at a St. Paul club, attending dances, and planning a humorous burglary. He adds that

Stewart once projected a photograph of an African revival meeting upside down on a screen and performed as a ventriloquist with a live "doll" on his lap. He complimented friends, threw snowballs, and liked to give college cheers. Now the work of both old men is done. In *Perfect Behavior* (1922) Stewart parodies etiquette books. In 1922 and 1923 he vacationed in Europe, mostly in Paris, where he met John Dos Passos,* Ernest Hemingway,* fellow Yale graduate Gerald Murphy* and his wife, Sara Murphy,* and other colorful people. Stewart's *Aunt Polly's Story of Mankind*, which appeared in 1923, contains satire of a more serious sort. In Europe in 1924, Stewart fished, drank, and attended bullfights with Hemingway in Spain. Stewart's *Mr. and Mrs. Haddock Abroad* (1924) is full of so-called "crazy humor" and led to a lecture tour during which he visited Hollywood. Stewart was in Paris in 1924 and 1925. Fitzgerald, who saw Stewart in Paris in 1925, had come to regard him as pretentious and wrong-headed. Stewart helped get Hemingway's *In Our Time* published in New York in 1925 and became the model for Bill Gorton in Hemingway's *The Sun Also Rises* (1926). Stewart's *Mr. and Mrs. Haddock in Paris, France* (1926) failed to please the public. In 1926 he signed a contract to write a humorous weekly column for the *Chicago Tribune*, married Beatrice Ames, and honeymooned in Paris, where an argument with Hemingway caused a permanent rupture. Stewart acted in Philip Barry's *Holiday* in 1928 and in *Rebound*, his own play, in 1930. Meanwhile, *Father William*, his last funny book, appeared in 1929; its message is that we should laugh because life is purposeless.

After more theatrical writing and travel, Stewart and his family moved in 1932 to Hollywood. He became a screenwriter for Irving Thalberg* and David O. Selznick, making up to $4,600 per week even as he was turning leftist by 1936. In 1938 Fitzgerald was assigned to work with him on MGM's *The Women*. He also worked in 1939 on a Paramount script for *Air Raid*, which Stewart had started but which was never filmed. In 1938 he was divorced and a year later married Ella Winter Steffens. She was Lincoln Steffens's widow, an expert on the Soviet Union, and a translator. Stewart's screenplay of *The Philadelphia Story* won an Oscar in 1940; noteworthy also was his script for *A Woman's Face* (1941), directed by his friend George Cukor. The labor organizer Brimmer in Fitzgerald's *The Last Tycoon* may be partly based on Stewart. Further movie and also stage successes followed for Stewart, until he was blacklisted for refusing in 1949 to give names to the House Un-American Activities Committee of fellow former anti-Nazis and current Communist sympathizers. In 1951 he and his wife moved to London. Until 1960 sympathetic producers hired him to write for the movies uncredited or using a pseudonym. Stewart died in London, and two days later his wife died there.

Bibliography: Tom Dardis, *Some Time in the Sun* (New York: Scribner, 1976); John Dos Passos, *The Best Years: An Informal Memoir* (New York: New American Library, 1966); Latham; Donald Ogden Stewart, *By a Stroke of Luck! An Autobiography* (New York: Paddington Press, 1975).

" 'STICKING ALONG.' THE VOICE SO FAINT SOMETIMES I COULD SCARCELY HEAR IT" (1981). Poem. The persona wonders why he should continue answering the faint old admonition to stick with it.

STINSON, EDDIE. In "A Short Trip Home," he is the narrator, a Yale sophomore home over Christmas vacation in St. Paul. He and several friends go to a hotel dance. When one friend, Joe Jelke, argues with a stranger who seems to be bothering Ellen Baker, the stranger knocks him out with brass knuckles. Eddie, puzzled and determined to protect Ellen, whom he realizes he loves, follows her to Chicago, insists on accompanying her on the train as far as New York, and outfaces her strange nemesis, who turns out to be Joe Varland, already dead. Eddie and Ellen become good friends when they meet in the summer.

STIRLING, GEORGE. In "John Jackson's Arcady," he is the taxi driver who takes John Jackson from the railroad station in Florence to the hotel. Jackson silently recognizes him as a boyhood friend.

STOCKTON, SYLVESTER ("SYLVO"). In "The Smilers," he is a well-to-do, egocentric New Yorker, about thirty, who thinks everyone who smiles at him is too stupid to realize that life is difficult. In reality he misunderstands Betty Tearle, then Waldron Crosby, and finally Jerry—all of whom smile to conceal their problems.

STOCKTON, VIOLET. In *Thoughtbook*, she is Mrs. Finch's pretty niece, ten, from the South. Fitzgerald's high opinion of her changes.

STODDARD, G. REECE. In "Bernice Bobs Her Hair," he is a Harvard law school graduate who attends dances and is a sought-after bachelor.

STONEMAN. In "Diagnosis," he was a Confederate soldier about whom Chevril reminisces.

STRAIN, JIM. In "Bernice Bobs Her Hair," he is a friend of Ethel Demorest. They have been gloomily engaged for three years.

"STRANGE SANCTUARY" (1939). Short story. (Characters: Appleton, Lila Appleton, Charlie Craig, Clarke Cresswell, Angela Duckney, L. P. Duckney, Evelyn, Dodo Gilbert, Dolly Haines, Morton Haines, John Hamilton, Hazeldawn, Birdie or Willie Lukas, Mrs. Martin, Hep J. Morrison, Sidney, Grace Terhune.) Dolly Haines, thirteen, is visiting friends around Baltimore while her father, Morton Haines, is ill in New Mexico. She reports to the home of Lila Appleton and her husband. They are absent, but handsome Clarke Cresswell, fifteen, answers the door. Lila phones to tell them that they are being held up by a car accident. Clarke has left his prep school because of a measles outbreak and is visiting his aunt, Grace Terhune, Dolly's school's assistant headmistress. He is at the Appletons for dinner, which is served to him and Dolly by a servant. Next day her father tells Dolly by letter to report to her uncle, Charlie Craig, who is coming home after ten years in Europe and who has a house down the street from the homes of the Appletons and Miss Terhune. Dolly goes there, only to learn from Charlie's supposed friend, Major Redfern (really Dodo Gilbert, a thief), and his nurse, Willie Shugrue (really Birdie, Willie Lukas, another thief), that Charlie is sick upstairs and they are caring for him. At church Redfern wangles an invitation from Dolly's friend debutante Angela Duckney to a party. Dolly sees a measles sign on Miss Terhune's house and phones Clarke there. He is confined but says they can talk across adjoining skylights. While Redfern dines at Angela's home, Dolly goes to a big Halloween party disguised as a witch. She is shocked to see Clarke there. Detectives suddenly announce a theft. Dolly hears Willie's cackle under a mask. Clarke tells Dolly he does not have the measles after all. The two sneak into an upstairs room in Charlie's house, learn Dolly's uncle is not there, and go to Miss Terhune's for the night with her permission. The children agree to report nothing. Meanwhile, Redfern taxis to Charlie's house empty-handed, having seen a rival thief at the Duckneys' and quickly left. He meets Willie, who has stolen some jewelry at the costume party. Next day Miss Terhune tells Dolly her father wired that he is coming home. Dolly and Clarke go to Charlie's for her suitcase but find a detective and Charlie there. Charlie welcomes her, and her dear daddy walks in. ''Make Yourself at Home,'' the original title of ''Strange Sanctuary,'' seems cleverer. *See also* ''Too Cute for Words.''

STRANGLER. In ''Your Way and Mine,'' he is a polo player mentioned as one of Honoria McComas's undesirable suitors.

STUART. In ''A Letter to Helen,'' he is mentioned as afraid.

STUART, CHARLES DAVID. In ''The Pusher-in-the-Face,'' he is the unmanly little night cashier, about thirty-five, at T. Cashmael's all-night restaurant. After he is acquitted of a charge of pushing the face of Mrs. George D. Robinson, who bothered him at the theater, he boldly pushes the face of a rude restaurant customer who turns out to be a would-be robber. In the aftermath, Stuart becomes a hero.

STUBBS, JACK. In ''Six of One—,'' he is a boy from Barnes's Ohio hometown. Jack lost an arm in a hunting accident but plays sports in high school. Barnes sends him to Princeton, where he is on the tennis team. When he graduates, Barnes takes him into his office, almost as an adopted son. The two get along wonderfully.

STUDEFORD, DR. In "The Love Boat," he is one of eight physicians panicky Bill Frothington thinks he might consult.

STURGIS, SAM. In *Thoughtbook*, he is a club friend.

STURTEVANT, RUTH. In "A Letter to Helen," she is mentioned as someone who should not be told about Elkins. *See also* Ruth in "Ruth," "There was a young lady named Ruth," and "Truth and—consequences."

STUTZ-MOZART. In *The Vegetable*, he is the leader of the orangutan band in the dream sequence. The band is to play at the wedding reception of Joseph Fish and Doris.

STUYVESANT. In "The Captured Shadow," he is a character in Basil Duke Lee's incomplete play *Hic! Hic! Hic!*

STUYVESANT. In *The Evil Eye*, he is so rich that he easily gets Esmerelda Sage away from Mike, who loves her.

STYLES, PHYLLIS. In *This Side of Paradise*, at twenty-five she is regarded as an improper prom-trotter. She tricks Burne Holiday into inviting her to a prom, only to be mistreated by him and his friend, Fred Sloane, when she blithely arrives.

SUMMER, JACK. In "Between Three and Four," he is the son of the widowed Sarah Belknap Summer. She needs a job to help him through Princeton, after which he wants to be a physician.

SUMMER, JOHN. In *The Beautiful and Damned*, he is a character in the movie for which Gloria Gilbert Patch takes a screen test. Summer is reportedly killed in a car accident, and Gloria, his wife, is to react dramatically in the film.

SUMMER, JOHN. In "Between Three and Four," now deceased, he was the husband of Sarah Belknap Summer and the father of Jack Summer.

SUMMER, SARAH BELKNAP. In "Between Three and Four," she applies to be rehired by Howard Butler, who works for the sons of B. S. Sullivan. Out of spite because she married John Sullivan in Rochester, New York, instead of marrying him, Butler released her years ago and now delays instead of giving her a quick answer. She threatens suicide. He thinks she has killed herself but is mistaken.

SUSIE. In *Fie! Fie! Fi-Fi!*, she is liked by Victor but prefers Sam, who likes Mary.

SUTTON, MISS. In ''O Russet Witch!,'' she is mentioned by Merlin Grainger as a South Dakotan interested in William Shakespeare's* sonnets.

SVENSEN. In ''An Alcoholic Case,'' she is a big, strong nurse Mrs. Hixson would like to assign to the alcoholic case, but Svensen is unavailable.

SWANKINS. In ''One Hundred False Starts,'' he is an adventurer about whom Fitzgerald cannot write.

SWANSON. In *Tender Is the Night*, he is a young consulate in Rome whom Collis Clay brings to the jail to help extricate Dick Diver.

SWANSON, GLORIA. (1897–1983). Movie star. She is a passenger aboard the *Majestic*, which has just carried Rags Martin-Jones from Cherbourg and Southampton to New York.

SWANSON, JOHNNY. In *The Last Tycoon*, he is a former cowboy actor now discarded. Cecelia Brady wants Pat Brady, her father, to help him.

SWETT, MRS. ULYSSES. In *The Great Gatsby*, Nick Carraway lists her name on a timetable as one of Jay Gatsby's summer guests. She ran over drunken Ripley Snell's hand in Gatsby's driveway.

"THE SWIMMERS" (1929). Short story. (Characters: Dr. Derocco, Louise, Marston, Choupette Marston, Henry Clay Marston, Madame de Richepin, Walter Ross, Judge Waterbury, Wiese, Charles Wiese.) Henry Clay Marston, thirty-five in 1925, is an old-line Virginian who has worked for eight years in Paris for an American promissory trust company's branch office. Judge Waterbury and a wealthy Southerner named Wiese call on him and ask him to come back to Richmond, but Marston prefers Paris. Marston returns unexpectedly to the apartment he shares with his Provençal wife, Choupette Marston, and their two little boys, finds her with another man, and has a nervous breakdown. Recovered and reconciled, Marston takes his family to St. Jean de Luz, where Choupette comments sarcastically about various Americans there, including a ''thoroughbred'' female swimmer of about eighteen. When this clean-limbed beauty gets cramps in the water, Marston joins a rescue party but fails to do much because he cannot swim. The girl in gratitude teaches him how to swim. Marston moves with his family to Richmond, and three years pass, during which he works for Waterbury's Calumet Tobacco Company, invests well, and makes a small fortune. On learning Choupette is committing adultery again, this time with Wiese's moneyed son Charles, he confronts the pair on the Virginia shore where all are enjoying a summer vacation, reveals his divorce plans, and demands custody of the children. He encounters the lovely, unnamed American swimmer there. Choupette and Marston join Charles on his motorboat to discuss matters while going out to Hampton Roads. Wiese threatens to expose Marston as mentally deranged, having bribed the Parisian physician who treated his nervous condition to certify as much in writing, and hence an unfit parent. The three experience engine failure and drift dangerously out with the tide. Only Marston can swim, and he agrees to swim to a lighthouse a mile away to dispatch rescuers. First, he forces Wiese to state in writing that he and Choupette relinquish rights to the children and that he bribed the physician. Marston puts everything in his waterproof tobacco pouch, swims to shore, sees a launch speeding to the boat, and agrees with its personnel that the boat would have drifted to safety into Peyton Harbor soon anyway. October finds Marston and his sons aboard the *Majestic* bound for Europe. He sees the swimmer yet again and hopes to have dinner with her that evening. In this farfetched story Fitzgerald turns pro-American and anti-French.

SYNEFORTH, CAPTAIN CLAYTON ("CLAY") HARRINGTON. In "Sentiment—and the Use of Rouge," he is the son of Lady Blachford and Lord Blachford and is an idealistic army officer, twenty-two in 1917. At home in London on leave, he again meets Eleanor Marbrooke, the former fiancée of his dead brother Lieutenant Richard Harrington Syneforth, at a dance. She is disillusioned, and the two debate war-altered morals and manners. He is seduced by her, proposes marriage to her, but is rejected. That March he is killed in the war.

SYNEFORTH, CLARA. In "Sentiment—and the Use of Rouge," she is the sister, eighteen, of Captain Clayton Harrington Syneforth. He objects to her overuse of rouge before she is escorted by a navy subaltern to a dance held at Mrs. Severance's home in London.

SYNEFORTH, LIEUTENANT RICHARD ("DICK") HARRINGTON. In "Sentiment—and the Use of Rouge," he was the brother of Captain Clayton Harrington Syneforth, who was engaged to Eleanor Marbrooke, but was killed in World War I.

SYREL, JOHN. In "The Mystery of the Raymond Mortgage," he is a reporter, twenty-three, on the New York *Daily News*. By careful discovery and analysis of evidence, he solves the murder of Agnes Raymond and John Standish at the Raymond home.

T

TAILOR, BARTHOLOMEW. In *Tender Is the Night*, he is a person Dick Diver tells Nicole Diver he saw in Cannes when Tailor, evidently an impressario, was looking over the area for a menagerie show.

TAINE. In ''The Four Fists,'' he is the owner of a New York restaurant where Samuel Meredith and Marjorie meet too often for lunch.

TALBOT, HARRY. In ''A Luckless Santa Claus,'' he is a wealthy New Yorker whose fiancée, Dorothy Harmon, challenges him on Christmas Eve to give away some money instead of wasting it. Her plan backfires when he celebrates with two men to whom he tries to give the money.

TALES OF THE JAZZ AGE (1922). Short story collection.

TALMADGE, CONSTANCE (1898–1973). Silent movie actress. She was born in Brooklyn, New York, the youngest of three daughters; the others were Norma Talmadge (1893–1957) and Natalie Talmadge (1898–1973). All were pushed by their assertive mother into acting careers. Without finishing high school Constance began as a $5-a-day extra in the Vitagraph Motion Picture Studio in Flatbush (1914) and played in comedy shorts for the next two years. Her appearance in D. W. Griffith's *Intolerance* (1916) launched her Hollywood career, and she appeared in seventy movies, mostly comedies, including one with Douglas Fairbanks* (1916) and two with Ronald Colman* (1924, 1925); her last movie was made in 1929. She was married four times, beginning in 1920. She was a beautiful blond, with lovely brown eyes and a vivacious personality. At the height of her popularity, she had her own production company. Her sister Norma starred as a sentimental tragedienne and was married twice, to executive producer Joseph M. Schenck and George Jessel, actor, singer, songwriter, and producer. Norma was the second of his four wives. She died of arthritis aggravated by drug abuse. Natalie Talmadge married the comic actor Buster Keaton, appeared with him in a 1923 movie, and also was her sisters' secretary.

Fitzgerald, who admired Constance, regarded her as a typical screen flapper. When a director at First National Pictures invited him in December 1926 to write a screenplay for her, he welcomed the chance to make some quick money and went west at once. He wrote "Lipstick," about a girl with magic lipstick: when she wears it, every man wants to kiss her. The climax comes when she goes to a prom, defeats a mean debutante, and wins the college lad they both want. Fitzgerald argued with Constance, and the story was never accepted; after two months, he and Zelda Sayre Fitzgerald* returned home. First, however, he met Irving Thalberg,* the film genius whose love interest was then Constance and who later impressed Fitzgerald greatly.

Bibliography: Michael Adams, "Dick Diver and Constance Talmadge," *FH/A 1977*, 61–62; Anita Loos, *The Talmadge Girls: A Memoir* (New York: Viking, 1978).

TANALAHAKA ("TANA"). In *The Beautiful and Damned*, he is the Japanese servant of Anthony Patch and Gloria Gilbert Patch when they live in Marietta. Maury Noble starts a rumor that Tana is really a spy named Lieutenant Emile Tannenbaum. When Fitzgerald and Zelda Sayre Fitzgerald* moved to Westport, Connecticut, in 1920, they engaged a Japanese houseboy named Tana. George Jean Nathan* started the rumor that Tana was a German spy. Zelda gives Tana a brief part in her novel *Save Me the Waltz*.

Bibliography: Eble.

TANNENBAUM, EMILE, LIEUTENANT. In *The Beautiful and Damned*. *See* Tanalahaka.

TANTRUM, GORE, HAM, JAPHET, JEM, JEMINA, MAPPY, AND PAPPY. In "Jemina," these Tantrums are participants, past and present, in the Tantrum-Doldrum feud. Jem, one of the instigators, is now deceased. Mappy and Pappy are the parents of Jemina, sixteen; she falls in love with Edgar Edison and dies with him in a fire.

TAPS AT REVEILLE (1935). Short Story collection. Fitzgerald dedicated *Taps at Reveille* to his literary agent, Harold Ober.*

TARBOX. In "Head and Shoulders," he is Horace Tarbox's father. He is a Princeton professor of economics, and Horace despises him for trying to make him into a prodigy.

TARBOX, HORACE ("OMAR"). In "Head and Shoulders," he is an all-head prodigy, being a Princeton sophomore in 1917 at fifteen and a Yale master's student in philosophy in 1919. He falls in love with Marcia Meadows, a chorus girl good at shaking her shoulders. She nicknames him Omar. They marry and have a baby. Marcia writes a popular, heady novel, and Horace becomes a vaudeville acrobat with strong shoulders.

TARBOX, MARCIA. In "Head and Shoulders," she is the pretty chorus girl Horace Tarbox marries, when he is eighteen and she is nineteen. She quits shaking her shoulders in a shimmy dance and writes an autobiographical novel titled *Sandra Pepys, Syncopated*. Her stage name was Marcia Meadow; her real name, Veronica Meadow.

TARKINGTON, BOOTH (1869–1946). Author. He was born in Indianapolis, Indiana, attended Exeter (1887–1889), and went without obtaining a degree to Purdue University (1890–1891) and Princeton University (1891–1893). At Princeton, he sang in the glee club; founded the Triangle Club in 1893 and wrote for and acted in some of its shows; and was a campus editor and writer. After returning home, he sought publication of his drawings and written work but with no success until he began publishing novels, including *The Gentleman from Indiana* (1899), *Monsieur Beaucaire* (1900), *Penrod* (1914) and its two sequels, *Seventeen* (1916), *The Magnificent Ambersons* (1918), *Alice Adams* (1921), and *Gentle Julia* (1922). He wrote almost sixty more books, including his memoirs, *The World Does Move* (1928). Tarkington married Louisa Fletcher in 1902. He drank too much. Divorced in 1911, Tarkington became a teetotaler and married Susanah Keifer Robinson in 1912.

While at Princeton, Fitzgerald read and admired some of Tarkington's novels. *This Side of Paradise*, by Fitzgerald's own admission, echoes bits from Tarkington. In his 1921 essay titled "Three Cities," he says that reading *Alice Adams* helped him while away some dull hours in Rome. In a 1922 review of *Gentle Julia*, Fitzgerald calls it funny but only in parts and says it repeats some earlier Tarkington material. Fitzgerald reveals detailed knowledge of other novels by Tarkington, who he says writes the best of any living American. In his "10 Best Books I Have Read" Fitzgerald lists *Seventeen* and calls it the funniest book he ever read. Tarkington met Fitzgerald, Zelda Sayre Fitzgerald,* and Ernest Hemingway* in Paris in 1925. Fitzgerald privately opined that Tarkington concentrated too much on black people, children, and dogs.

Bibliography: James Woodress, *Booth Tarkington, Gentleman from Indiana* (Philadelphia: Lippincott, 1954).

"TARKINGTON'S *GENTLE JULIA*" (1922). Review of *Gentle Julia* by Booth Tarkington.*

"TARQUIN OF CHEAPSIDE" (1917). Short story, published as "Tarquin of Cheepside" and expanded as "Tarquin of Cheapside" in 1921. (Characters:

Peter Caxter, Flowing Boots, Soft Shoes.) Soft Shoes evades two armed pursuers, both called Flowing Boots, through dark London streets. He bursts into the room of his friend Peter Caxter, who is reading part of a new work, *The Faery Queene* by Edmund Spencer [*sic*], concerning Chastity. Soft Shoes asks to be hidden. Peter conceals him above a trapdoor just before his pursuers demand entrance. They search his two rooms, find nothing, and say their unidentified quarry just violated a woman. One pursuer is her brother; the other, her husband. When they leave, the fugitive calmly pens the beginning of a poem called ''The Rape of Lucrece.'' Obviously, he is therefore William Shakespeare.* Fitzgerald insisted on including ''Tarquin of Cheapside'' in *Tales of the Jazz Age* even though editor Max Perkins* was reluctant because it concerned rape.

TASKER, CAPTAIN. In ''The Bowl,'' he is the captain of the Yale football team.

TASWELL, CAPTAIN. In ''The End of Hate,'' he is a Union officer in Georgetown, who loves Josie Pilgrim but withdraws when she prefers Tib Dulany.

TATE. In ''A Short Autobiography,'' he was the proprietor of a Seattle drinking place in 1915.

TATE, EMILY. In ''The Camel's Back,'' she is the daughter of Howard Tate and his wife. She reports to her mother the arrival of the camel at the Tates' party.

TATE, HOWARD. In ''The Camel's Back,'' he is a wealthy man in Toledo. He and his wife are giving a party for their daughter Millicent Tate and her school friends when Perry Parkhurst mistakenly enters it dressed as a camel. When Perry is temporarily unmasked, Tate offers him a drink and goes with him to the circus ball.

TATE, MILLICENT. In ''The Camel's Back,'' she is the daughter of Howard Tate and his wife. Their party for her is in full swing when Perry Parkhurst enters.

TATE, MRS. HOWARD. In ''The Camel's Back,'' she is the ''formidable'' wife of Howard Tate, a wealthy Toledo man, and the mother of Emily Tate and Millicent Tate. She was a Chicago Todd before her marriage.

TATNALL, BOB. In ''The Bowl,'' he is a Princeton football team captain.

TAYLOR. In "The Hotel Child," he is an American diplomat traveling in Europe with his wife and Miss Howard, whom he plans to introduce at court in England. They wrongly dislike Fifi Schwartz.

TAYLOR. In "The Jelly-Bean," he is the owner of the car which James Powell empties of gasoline to clean gum off Nancy Lamar's shoe. Later, Nancy loses to Taylor in a crap game, gives him worthless checks, and is saved from embarrassment by Jim.

TAYLOR, DICK. In *Coward*, he is the little brother of Virginia Taylor and brings news that Charles Douglas, a lieutenant, and his unit are returning home, in retreat, in 1861.

TAYLOR, MRS. In "The Hotel Child," she is the snobbish, Europeanized wife of an American diplomat. She is wrongly critical of Fifi Schwartz.

TAYLOR, VIRGINIA. In *Coward*, she is a friend of Lindy Douglas and her family. A romantic girl, she is smitten by Lieutenant Percy Altwater. Fitzgerald is punning on her name, since she is a seamstress living in Virginia.

TAYLOR, WILLIAM DESMOND. In "Pat Hobby's Christmas Wish," he was a movie director who, according to a letter written by Harry Gooddorf and held by Helen Kagle, was murdered by Gooddorf. When confronted, Gooddorf laughs and says Taylor was shot by someone else.

"TEAMED WITH GENIUS." Short story. (Characters: Jack Berners, Boris, Pat Hobby, Katherine Hodge, Consuela Martin, Rita, John Smythe, René Wilcox.) Jack Berners, Pat Hobby's Hollywood boss, orders him to coauthor a script about the Russian ballet with René Wilcox, who is from England. Berners says the idea was ineptly scripted earlier. Wilcox avoids Pat, works alone, and sends him a script. Pretending they worked together, Pat touches it up and sends it to Berners. Pat also forges a letter allegedly from the British consulate in New York urging Wilson to return to England because his two brothers have been killed in the war. He has his secretary, Katherine Hodge, get the letter to Wilcox. But the truth comes out. Wilcox gave Pat the script the studio discarded earlier and knows all about Pat's schemes because Wilson is friendly with Katherine. Wilson, however, is grateful to Pat because he and Katherine had a quarrel earlier, now forgotten because Pat brought them together again. He asks Berners to retain Pat so he can write a play about him. This story reflects Fitzgerald's discontent in 1931 at being ordered by movie-producer Irving Thalberg* to collaborate on a movie script with Marcel de Sano, a Romanian-born movie director and writer.

Bibliography: Latham.

TEARLE. In "The Smilers," he is Betty Tearle's husband, whom she is about to desert. She leaves a letter for him on their bed.

TEARLE, BETTY. In "The Smilers," she is a friend of Sylvester Stockton. They were close a few years earlier, but she disliked his incurable pessimism. When they meet on Fifth Avenue, she seems happy and smiles at him. In reality, however, she is miserable since she is about to abandon her husband and their two children, Billy Tearle and Clare Tearle.

TEARLE, BILLY. In "The Smilers," he is Betty Tearle's little boy, whom she is about to leave.

TEARLE, CLARE. In "The Smilers," she is Betty Tearle's little girl, whom she is about to leave.

TED. In *Thoughtbook*, he is a friend.

TELEVISION, MISS. In "Outside the Cabinet-Maker's," she is a girl who walks by while the man and his daughter are waiting outside. He so names her to his daughter.

TEMPLETON, BROOKS FISH. In "Presumption," he is the tall, suave Harvard 1912 graduate, to whom Noel Garneau is engaged—that is, until San Juan Chandler successfully pursues her to Boston and then New York.

TEMPLETON, CHARLES MARTIN. In "The Rubber Check," he is a wealthy Philadelphian, the husband of V. Templeton, and the father of their daughter, Mercia Templeton. Val Schuyler initially prefers Ellen Mortmain, Mercia's cousin, to Mercia, who likes him. When he names the Templetons as references to cover his rubber check, V. Templeton ruins his reputation by gossiping. In the end, Val works as a gardener for Templeton, whose daughter still wants Val.

TEMPLETON, MERCIA. In "The Rubber Check," she is Ellen Mortmain's cousin. She is persuaded to invite Ellen and Val Schuyler to Philadelphia for a dance. Mercia likes Val, who prefers Ellen; in the end, Mercia is likely to win the financially ruined young man.

TEMPLETON, V. In "The Rubber Check," she is the wife of Charles Martin Templeton and the mother of Mercia Templeton. Offended when Val Schuyler uses the Templetons as references to cover his rubber check, she gossips about him ruinously.

TEMPTATION, LORD. In *Safety First!*, he is named by Ralph as someone the girls should be wary of. At the end, the whole cast bids him goodbye.

TEMPTATION, MISS. In *Safety First!*, she is identified as nice, like Lord Temptation, flirtatious with old, bald men, and charming when dancing.

"10 BEST BOOKS I HAVE READ" (1923). List. Fitzgerald lists books by Samuel Butler, Joseph Conrad,* Anatole France, James Joyce, H. L. Mencken,* William Makepeace Thackeray, and Mark Twain. He regards Conrad's *Nostromo* as the best novel in the last half century and Joyce's *Ulysses* as the great novel of the future.

TENDER IS THE NIGHT (1934). (Original title: *Tender Is the Night: A Romance*.) (Characters: Mrs. Abrams, Apostle Alexandre, Augustine, Tommy Barban, Mlle. Bellois, Ben, Mme. Bonneasse, Earl Brady, Braun, Luis Campion, Janice Caricamento, Casasus, Charlie, Prince Chillicheff, Claude, Collis Clay, Dr. Colazzo, Crawshow, Crowder, Dr. Dangue, William Harrison Dempsey, Van Buren Denby, Diver, Dick Diver, Lanier Diver, Nicole Diver, Topsy Diver, Dr. Dohmler, Dorsey, Dulschmit, Royal Dumphry, Ed Elkins, Emile, Featherstone, Fernand, S. Flesh, Fouquet, Freeman, Gausse, Gisler, T. F. Golding, Dr. Franz Gregorovius, Kaethe Gregorovius, Carly Hannan, Helen, Major Hengest, Herbrugge, Bill Hillis, Holmes, Mr. Horsa, George T. Horseprotection, Rosemary Hoyt, Hunter, Dr. Ladislau, Laura, Pete Livingstone, Longstreet, McBeth, McKibben, Albert McKisco, Violet McKisco, Maria Amalia Roto Mais, Marius, Marmora, Conte Tino de Marmora, Señora Marmora, Corinna Medonca, Mercer, Michelle, Minghetti, Conte Hosain di Minghetti, Contessa Mary North di Minghetti, Lucienne di Minghetti, Tony di Minghetti, Jeanne-Marie Florentine Bourgeois Mistinguet[t], Geneveva de Momus, Morris, Mrs. Morris, Von Cohn Morris, Muchhause, Nellie, Nicotera, Abe North, Princess Orsini, Evelyn Oyster, Lord Paley, Mme. Paragoris, Mme. Pasche, Paul, Slim Pearson, Perrin, Shah of Persia, Jules Peterson, Pablo Picasso, Pierce, Quarterly, Rainy, Francisco Pardo y Cuidad Real, Pardo y Cuidad Real, Sachs, Schaeffer, Lady Caroline Sibly-Biers, Elsie Speers, Swanson, Bartholomew Tailor, Moises Teubel, Seraphim Tullio, Pandely Vlasco, Maria Wallis, Baby Warren, Devereux Warren, Sid Warren, Wilburhazy, Yardly, Yolanda Yosfuglu, Maurice Yvain.)

Book 1. In June 1925, Rosemary Hoyt (born in July 1907), an American movie star and the hit in *Daddy's Girl*, and her widowed mother, Elsie Speers, are vacationing on the French Riviera between Marseilles and Cannes. After meeting Dick Diver (born in April 1889) and his wife, Nicole Diver (born in mid-1900), on the beach, they are invited to a dinner party at the Divers' cliff house at nearby Tarmes. Other guests are Tommy Barban, mercenary; Earl Brady, movie director; homosexuals Luis Campion and Royal Dumphry; Abe North, idle musician, and his wife, Mary; and Albert McKisco, American novelist, and his wife, Violet. Rosemary sweetly announces her instant love for the handsome, considerate, moody Dick. All goes well at the party until Violet sees something untoward upstairs, starts to gossip about it to some guests on their way to their hotel, and is told by Tommy to stop. McKisco argues with Tommy, who slaps him. The two plan a predawn duel at a nearby golf course. Rosemary goes to McKisco's room with Abe, his second, and then goes secretly with Campion to watch the duel. Firing at forty paces, both adversaries miss.

Rosemary, at her mother's urging, goes with the Divers and the Norths to Paris. They enjoy food, drink, and shopping, and visit a battlefield near Amiens. It is revealed that Nicole is the daughter of a wealthy Chicagoan, that Dick is a physician now writing a treatise, and that Abe, soon to return to the United States, and Mary, heading for Salzburg, are sad at Abe's inability to compose. Despite overhearing the Divers whisper their desire for one another, Rosemary, when alone with Dick, begs him to go to bed with her. His gentle refusal shames her—briefly. Next day they go with Nicole, the Norths, and Collis Clay, a vacationing Yale lad who likes Rosemary, to a sceening of *Daddy's Girl*. In a taxi Dick and Rosemary kiss and declare their love. Fragile Nicole, Dick explains, must never be hurt. After a night of drinking around Paris, the group are seeing Abe off by boat train. While Rosemary is at her studio, Collis tells Dick about Rosemary's affair with a Yale man. Upset, Dick goes to her studio but misses her. He and Nicole dine out that evening. The drunken Abe, still in Paris after all, gets involved with Jules Peterson, an Afro-European from Stockholm who tried to help him in a fracas. The two ask Dick, who is with Rosemary in her room, for advice. He tells Peterson to wait outside and tells Abe to sober up. Rosemary finds Peterson murdered on her bed. Dick persuades the hotel owner-manager to bribe the police to deposit the corpse elsewhere, thus saving Rosemary's professional career. They discover Nicole verbosely hysterical in her bathroom.

Book 2. Richard Diver, Yale graduate (spring 1911), Rhodes Scholar at Oxford (1914–1915), and with a medical degree from Johns Hopkins (1916), obtains a postdoctoral degree at the university at Zurich (1918) under Dr. Dohmler, head of a psychiatric clinic, and becomes friendly with pathologist Dr. Franz Gregorovius. Commissioned captain in the U.S. Army, he serves at Bar-sur-Aube in France (1918–1919). Devereux Warren brings his disturbed daughter, Nicole, late in 1917, to Dohlmer for treatment. Warren confesses he committed incest with her after his wife died years earlier. Nicole has a split personality and a fear of men. Dick meets her in 1918 and is intrigued. Multilingual and bright, she sends touching letters to "Mon Capitaine" in France. He visits her, and she falls in love with him. Advised by Dohlmer and Franz, who fear a "push" of her malady, to resist her, he willingly does so.

Out of the army and vacationing in Montreux (July 1919), Dick encounters Nicole, released from the clinic, traveling with her older, unmarried sister, Baby Warren, handsome Conte Tino di Marmora, and his parents. In the dark fog outside their hotel at Caux, Nicole advances toward Dick, and they kiss repeatedly. Baby, who dislikes Dick and flaunts the Warren family wealth, wants to buy a physician to care for Nicole. Succumbing in Zurich, Dick becomes just that and marries Nicole (fall 1919). In 1920 he publishes his successful book, *A Psychology for Psychiatrists*.

In a stream-of-consciousness section, Nicole rambles about events from 1919 to 1925—her condition, her extensive travels with Dick, Tommy's love for her, her two children, and meeting Rosemary.

After Peterson's murder, Dick and Nicole return to the Riviera. In August Dick says goodbye to Rosemary's mother in Cannes without seeing Rosemary—the two are sailing for America—assembles notes for a second publication, is distressed that Nicole's income exceeds his, and wonders whether his coolness toward Nicole is professional or emotional. They vacation over Christmas with Baby at Gstaad, where Franz persuades him to invest Warren money in a mental clinic on the Zugersee.

Dick smoothly makes his rounds at his and Franz's clinic, comforting patients and visiting rooms for therapeutic activities. Nicole accuses him of trying to seduce the daughter of a discharged patient. Denying it, Dick drives her and their two children to a circus. On their way back, Nicole grabs the steering wheel and crashes the car into a ditch but fails to kill anyone (summer 1927).

Leaving Nicole at the clinic, Dick takes time off and flies to Munich. He bumps into Tommy, who introduces Prince Chillicheff, whom Tommy helped escape out of Russia. Tommy mentions Abe was killed in a New York speakeasy (early 1928). Dick hikes in Innsbruck, learns by cable of his father's death, goes home, and accompanies his father's body from Buffalo to Virginia for burial. He returns via Naples and Rome (March), where he encounters Rosemary making a movie there, Collis taking time off from architectural studies in Florence, and Baby. Dick and Rosemary eat and walk together, and in her room she is willingly "taken" by him. The two argue about their separate futures. He alternately criticizes and flatters Baby. He and Collis get drunk in a Roman cabaret. Alone on the street, Dick fights with some taxi drivers and is beaten up by the police and jailed. Baby obtains his release, secures medical aid for him, and feels she has a moral, as well as a financial, hold over the shamed man.

Book 3. Although Dick, back at their clinic, tells Franz he got hurt boxing on shipboard returning from America, Kaethe Gregorovius is observant enough to tell her husband that Dick was "on a debauch." Dick goes to Lausanne to talk to Francisco Pardo y Cuidad Real, a Chilean homosexual alcoholic, but declines to treat him. He learns Nicole's father is a patient in Lausanne with an alcohol-ruined liver, gets Nicole to rush over to see him a final time, but learns he suddenly checked himself out and has left. A week later the irate father of a patient treated for alcoholism withdraws his son on learning Dick also drinks too much. Franz encourages Dick to let him buy out his interest in the clinic (May or June). The Diver family travels with forty-two pieces of luggage toward the Riviera, stop two weeks at the border to be entertained by Mary North, now the Contessa di Minghetti, wife of a papal count traveling with his two sisters and his son by a previous marriage. Dick argues with Mary when his son is bathed in water allegedly contaminated by her sick stepson. The Divers depart for the Riviera.

Back at Tarmes (February 1929), Dick fires his cook in April for sampling his special wine too freely, only to be called by her an excessive drinker himself. He and Nicole crash a party on wealthy T. F. Golding's yacht, aboard which are Tommy and the affected Lady Caroline Sibly-Biers. Ashore, Dick treats Tommy for a cold before watching him go off to Nice. When Rosemary turns up, Dick tries to show off by waterskiing before her admirers but is out of condition and fails miserably. Mary arrives, is pleasant to Nicole and Rosemary, but snubs Dick. Nicole rebukes Rosemary, and Dick drives alone toward Provence. Nicole initiates a calculated affair with Tommy by writing to him; he picks her up, and they drive to a hotel near Monte Carlo (June). On returning, she finds Dick back early; each feels free of the other. Mary telephones Dick from Antibes that she and Lady Caroline have been jailed on charges of lesbianism. He extricates the two by bribing some officials. Lady Caroline pretends the incident was nothing. When Tommy finds Dick and Nicole at a beauty shop (July), the three discuss the advisibility of a Diver divorce, and the couple agree.

On the beach one last time, Dick sees Nicole, Tommy, and Baby in the distance, and talks hypocritically to Mary. Nicole and Tommy get married, and Dick practices general medicine in several upstate New York locations, but not very effectively.

Tender Is the Night evolved in seventeen drafts, accounting for its troubled structure and zigzag time line. It is notable for its skillful handling of major and minor characters and many settings, especially the Riviera and Switzerland. It has scenario-like episodes, is livened by clever, humorous dialogue and startling imagery, and is marked by moral generalizations often morose in nature. Dick Diver's loss of professional success through excessive drinking and indulgent travel echoes Fitzgerald's own slow decline into the early 1930s, while Nicole's schizophrenic behavior owes much to his observation of Zelda Sayre Fitzgerald's* unbalanced thoughts and actions during the same years. In 1934 the novel sold only 15,000 copies, which disappointed Fitzgerald. In April-May 1934 he worked with Charles Marquis Warren* on an adaptation of the novel for the movies, to no avail. Fitzgerald wanted producer Irving Thalberg* to create a film adaptation, but he regarded Fitzgerald as unreliable. A dramatic version was written in 1938 by Cora Jarrett and Kate Oglebay but never produced. In 1962 a movie was released.

Bibliography: Matthew J. Bruccoli, *The Composition of Tender Is the Night: A Study of the Manuscripts* (Pittsburgh: University of Pittsburgh Press, 1963); Matthew J. Bruccoli and Judith S. Baughman, *Reader's Companion to Tender Is the Night* (Columbia: University of South Carolina Press, 1996); Wheeler Winston Dixon, *The Cinematic Vision of F. Scott Fitzgerald* (Ann Arbor: UMI Research Press, 1986); Latham; Charles R. Metzger, *F. Scott Fitzgerald's Psychiatric Novel: Nicole's Case, Dick's Case* (New York: Peter Lang, 1989); Milton R. Stern, *Tender Is the Night: The Broken Promise* (New York: Maxwell Macmillan, 1994).

TENWEATHER, JASON. In "One Hundred False Starts," he is a person about whom Fitzgerald cannot write. He may have been involved in a murder one winter.

"TEN YEARS IN THE ADVERTISING BUSINESS" (1929). Essay. (Character: Cakebook.) Fitzgerald asks uncooperative Cakebook, his boss in the advertising agency, to give him more than $90 a month because he is getting married. Ten years later Cakebook is willing to give him $1,500, not the $1,000 offered at first, to be a judge in a beauty contest. This mordant essay is based on Fitzgerald's low-paid work in 1919 and his receiving $1,500 as a contest judge along with other celebrities.

TERHUNE, GRACE. In "Strange Sanctuary," she is the assistant headmistress at Dolly Haines's school and Clarke Cresswell's aunt. She befriends both.

TERRAL, HENRY W. In *The Beautiful and Damned*, he is a person presumably helped by Sammy Carleton and his "Heart Talks" scheme.

TERRELL, ELAINE. In "Babes in the Woods," she is Isabelle's schoolmate and invites her home during Christmas vacation, mostly so Isabelle can meet Kenneth Powers.

TERRELL, MRS. In "Babes in the Woods," she is Elaine Terrell's mother and the hostess at the dinner party and dance held during Christmas vacation. She behaves impersonally toward Elaine's schoolmate, Isabelle.

TÊTE-À-TÊTE, MADAME. *Fie! Fie! Fi-Fi!*, she is said to drink whiskey straight.

TEUBEL, MOISES. In *Tender Is the Night*, his is a name read in the *New York Herald*.

THALBERG, IRVING (1899–1936). Movie executive and producer. He was born in Brooklyn, New York, was sickly as a child, never graduated from high school, practiced shorthand and typing, and obtained a job with a trading company. In 1918 he became secretary to the assistant of Carl Laemmle, head of the Universal Film Manufacturing Company in New York City, and soon was his confidant at his Broadway headquarters. When Laemmle assigned him in 1919 to Hollywood to head Universal City in Hollywood, Thalberg improved its administration and choice of scripts. In 1923 he displeased Laemmle by declining to marry his daughter, joined Louis B. Mayer's movie company as vice president and production head, and in 1924 became Metro-Goldwyn-Mayer's vice president and production supervisor. In 1927 Thalberg, attracted earlier to actress Constance Talmadge,* married Norma Shearer,* another of his stars. Owing to Thalberg's genius, MGM grew into the most successful and glamorous movie company in the 1930s. One of his best directors was Fitzgerald's friend King Vidor.* It was Thalberg's habit to reshoot scenes, re-edit massively, have sneak previews before unpretentious audiences, and order overhauls when their reactions were negative. In 1932 he suffered a heart attack, traveled a year later in Europe to recuperate, and returned to work in a diminished capacity. He died of pneumonia.

In 1927 Fitzgerald and Zelda Sayre Fitzgerald* went to Hollywood. He was hired by First National Pictures to help write a script, met Thalberg, and was impressed by him. In 1931 Thalberg hired Fitzgerald to work on a movie to star Jean Harlow, at $1,200 a week, for five weeks. Fitzgerald was to collaborate with another writer and thought of objecting to Thalberg about the arrangement, but he was told not to. One Sunday Fitzgerald attended a party at the Thalbergs where he drank too much, made a fool of himself trying to recite a poem, and was taken home by writer Charles MacArthur at Thalberg's request. Norma Shearer eased Fitzgerald's considerable shame by wiring him that she regarded him as an agreeable guest. Fitzgerald's "Crazy Sunday" reflects the Hollywood scene at this time.

Bibliography: Roland Flamini, *The Last Tycoon and the World of M-G-M* (New York: Crown, 1994); Lambert; Bob Thomas, *Thalberg: Life and Legend* (Garden City, N.Y.: Doubleday, 1969).

"THAT KIND OF PARTY" (1951). Short story. (Characters: Dolly Bartlett, Mrs. Bartlett, Mrs. Cary, Miss Cole, Essie, Aunt Georgie, Gilray, Mrs. Gilray, Gladys, Helen, Irma, Kitty, Charlotte Lapham, Albert Moore, Carpenter Moore, Mrs. Moore, Palmer, Fats Palmer, Martha Robbie, Mrs. Robbie, Joe Shoonover, Mrs. Shoonover, Tipton, Mrs. Tipton, Terrence R. Tipton.) It is about 1909, and Terrence R. Tipton has fallen in love with pretty Dolly Bartlett, ten, at a party at the Gilrays' home, where children played a kissing game called Clap-in-and-clap-out. Terrence asks his pal Joe Shoonover to get his mother to have a similar party. Terrence is soon in trouble for sassing his incompetent teacher and bloodying bespectacled Albert Moore's nose in a fight. Terrence and Joe bribe Fats Palmer, the janitor's son, to tell one of his sisters to deliver a fake telegram to Mrs. Shoonover saying her sister is sick out of town, to get her out of the way. Soon after the party starts, Albert's older brother, Carpenter Moore, arrives. Crippled from the waist down and in a wheelchair for five years, he warns Terrence of the trouble he is in for hurting Albert. The game starts, with Mrs. Shoonover, not out of town after all, offering a piano accompaniment. Terrence is named "It," must hide in the hallway until clapped back into the room, but instead secretly tilts Carpenter, wheelchair and all, into a closet and also kisses Dolly. In sudden fury, Carpenter is able to stand —miraculously—and even to take steps in pursuit of his assailant. Home again, Terrence learns that the telegram was delivered to his own mother by mistake, that she has left town, and—most happily—that Dolly has invited him to supper.

This story was to have been part of the series of stories Fitzgerald wrote featuring Basil Duke Lee. When it was evidently rejected by both the *Ladies' Home Journal* and the *Pictorial Review* because it included kissing by ten- and eleven-year-olds, Fitzgerald changed the young hero's name to Terrence R. Tipton and tried to market the result separately, but failed to do so. "That kind of Party" was published posthumously.

THAYER, LOWELL. In "The Rich Boy," he is a wealthy Bostonian whom Paula Legendre marries when Anson Hunter refuses to make a commitment to her. She divorces Thayer and marries Peter Hagerty.

THÉRÈSE. In *The Beautiful and Damned*, she is the peasant girl at whose leg the Chevalier O'Keefe fatally gawks.

"THERE WAS A YOUNG LADY NAMED RUTH" (1979). Poem. (Character: Ruth Sturtevant.) She never failed to phone lies to Yale.

"THERE WAS A YOUNG MAN OF QUEBEC" (1981). Poem. The man froze his neck and shouted he'd be a wreck.

"THE THIRD CASKET" (1924). Short story: (Characters: Galt, Cyrus Girard, Lola Girard, Oswald Jones, Joseph Hardwick Parrish, George Van Buren.) Cyrus Girard, a hard-working businessman, sixty, has a daughter, Lola, but no son to whom to entrust his New York firm, on Wall Street, upon his planned retirement. He asks his three best college friends to recommend successors between twenty-five and thirty. Each suggests his own son, whereupon John Hardwick Parrish, George Van Buren, and Oswald ("Rip") Jones report to Girard. He offers them a fairy-tale challenge. Whoever pleases him most during a three-month trial period will be free not only to take over the firm but also to marry Girard's Lola, who now presents herself—lovely and chuckling. The men work hard, fraternize with Lola, and defeat Girard at golf. After three months, Girard, unable to choose a winner, presents a final challenge. For the next two weeks, each man must act out retirement behavior, to show what Girard might try in his own anticipated leisure. Parrish and Van Buren dash off to pretend they are retired, but Jones distresses Lola by continuing to work. Two weeks later Parrish and Van Buren report to Cyrus: Parrish spent his free time touring England and France, while Van Buren planned an endowment center for archaeologists and historians. But where is Jones? Galt, Girard's general manager, confesses that Rip was restless and wangled a company assignment in Chicago. When asked, Parrish and Van Buren say each proposed to Lola and was turned down. Girard decides to phone her. At that moment Jones phones him from Chicago to explain he is sorry but he doesn't want to stop working. Girard blurts out that he doesn't want to either, names Jones his partner, and suddenly hears Mrs. Jones—that is, Lola—on the phone from Chicago too. The title and action obviously suggest *The Merchant of Venice* by William Shakespeare* as a source.

"THIS BOOK TELLS THAT ANITA LOOS" (1977). Poem. Fitzgerald writes in the guestbook of Anita Loos* that signatures therein reveal her innumerable friendships, with everyone from Zeus to Mother Goose.

"THIS IS A MAGAZINE" (1920). Sketch. Fitzgerald depicts the magazine as a theater. The cover is a many-featured lady, a college with illustrations and advertisements. When the curtain opens, the drama begins. An Edith Wharton* story vies stuffily with a slangy baseball tale. The two talk with a detective story, a British serial, two love poems, a Robert Chambers story, a political article, and a story lacking a family. A melee ensues involving more prose and ads. When a reader approaches, all snap shut into a silent, watchful darkness.

THIS SIDE OF PARADISE (1920). Novel. (Characters: Allenby, Barbara, Barlow, Barton, Bascome, Bispam, Mrs. Bispam, Bistolary, Amory Blaine, Beatrice O'Hara Blaine, Stephen Blaine, Bobby, Boiling Oil, Isabelle Borgé, Mrs. Borgé, Sukey Brett, Cambell, Carling, Carstairs, Clothilde, Phoebe Column, Alec Connage, Cecelia Connage, Leland R. Connage, Mrs. Leland R. Connage, Rosalind Connage, Ted Converse, Captain Corn, Cunizza, Monsignor Thayer Darcy, William Dayfield, Marylyn De Witt, Margaret Diamond, Dibby, Mrs. D'Invilliers, Thomas Parke D'Invilliers, Dr. Dougall, Ferrenby, Jesse Ferrenby, Firebrand, Garvin, Howard Gillespie, Hambell, Thornton Hancock, Harebell, Healy, Burne Holiday, Kerry Holiday, Dean Hollister, Hortense, Dick Humbird, Mrs. Huston-Carmelite, Joe, Kaluka, Marty Kaye, Annette Kellerman, Krogman, Slim Langueduc, Mrs. Lawrence, McDowell, Findle Marbotson, Queen Margherita, Axia Marlowe, Stephen O'Donahue, Olson, O'May, Cardinal O'Neill, Overton, Page, Clara Page, Frog Parker, Paskert, Pompia, Popular Daughter, Rahill, Reardon, Renwick, Richard, Rooney, J. Dawson Ryder, Mrs. St. Clair, Myra St. Clair, Sarah, Eleanor Savage, Ramilly Savage, Shanly, Fred Sloane, Phyllis Styles, Tully, Mrs. Twelve, Tyson, Cardinal Vitori, Miss Waterson, Jill Wayne, Mrs. Weatherby, Sally Weatherby, Jim Wilson, Bishop Wiston, Wookey-wookey, Tanaduke Wylie, Mr. X.)

Book One. Amory Blaine is a handsome lad growing up in and near Minneapolis. His mother, Beatrice O'Hara Blaine, an affected Irish Catholic, pampers him, while his father, Stephen Blaine, rich through inheritance, mainly stays in his private library. Amory, who is bright but indifferently schooled, goes east at fifteen to St. Regis, a Connecticut prep school. His mentor is Monsignor Thayer Darcy, his mother's friend and a hedonist turned priest. Amory offends classmates until he mends show-off ways and becomes a good football player and the editor of the school paper.

Amory enters Princeton, where he appreciates the architecture, the random eating, and friendships with other freshmen, including Burne Holiday, with whom he discusses social levels, and Thomas Parke D'Invilliers, a sincere poet. Amory reads much but drifts with abated ambition. When World War I begins in Europe, it disturbs him little. He tours with a Triangle Club production of *Ha-Ha Hortense!* during Christmas vacation his sophomore year. Toward the end of the holidays, Amory returns to Minneapolis, mainly to meet an acquaintance's cousin, Isabelle Borgé, sixteen and flirtatious. At a party the two regard each other as antagonists, go upstairs to kiss, but are interrupted by noisy friends.

Back at Princeton, Amory cuts classes for two days to go to Asbury Park with some fellow students. They eat at various places, avoid paying through trickery, and sleep free at a casino. Disliking all subjects at school, he remains lazy, writes for the *Princetonian*, corresponds with Isabelle, drinks and smokes and gambles, and takes predawn bicycle rides. He and Tom D'Invilliers analyze their cultivated snobbishness. After an alcoholic adventure in New York, Amory's friend Dick Humbird dies in an automobile accident. Chaperoned by her mother, Isabelle attends the prom, after which Amory is a guest at the Borgés' Long Island summer home. He and Isabelle argue when his shirt stud bruises her during an embrace, and he leaves abruptly next morning.

During his junior year, Amory, though tutored, flunks mathematics and loses his *Princetonian* position. His father dies that fall, and the family finances slide. Amory visits Darcy, who encourages him to worry less about his personality and to become a ''personage.'' He reads widely and publishes a satire of his own, criticizing a professor he labels a ''mental prig,'' in the *Nassau Literary Magazine*. Kerry Holiday, Burne's brother, quits school and joins the Lafayette Esquadrille in France. Amory double-dates with Fred Sloane, a fellow student, and two girls in New York but leaves the apartment of his girl when he fancies he sees Humbird's ghost. Next day, when he returns to Princeton, Tom also sees an apparition, standing outside their room window and gazing at Amory.

In his senior year Amory joins a movement of about a hundred upperclassmen resigning from socially elitist clubs, including his own Cottage Club. He develops respect for the radicalism of Burne, who recommends Walt Whitman and Leo Tolstoy and comments on leadership, willpower, and how to avoid fear of the dark. Amory introduces Burne to Darcy, who gets Amory to visit Clara Page, Amory's young third-cousin widow. She lives in Philadelphia, has two small children, is radiantly beautiful, and is well read. Amory falls half in love with her. She describes him as vain, easily depressed, and enslaved by his imagination, and tells him she won't marry again. Various Princeton students volunteer for military duty, while Burne resolves to be a pacifist. Amory bids farewell to his beloved campus.

In January 1918 Darcy writes to Amory, an infantry lieutenant bound for France, sends him a poem, calls him his spiritual son, and announces he has been assigned to Rome. On 11 March 1919, from Brest, France, Amory writes to Tom, a lieutenant in a Georgia camp, that he is heading home, that his mother has died and left much of the diminished family fortune to the Church, that he laments the death of Kerry and Jesse Ferrenby, and that he is somewhat agnostic.

Book Two. Amory is invited in February to the Manhattan home of fellow-student Alec Connage, his parents, and his sisters, Rosalind and the younger Cecelia. Rosalind, nineteen, is a beautiful, honest, demanding, romantic debutante for whom a coming-out party is in progress. Although her parents want her to accept the hand of any one of several rich suitors, she rebuffs Howard Gillespie and merely chats with J. Dawson Ryder, whereas she and Amory kiss repeatedly and fall in love—she, briefly. Amory, Alec, and Tom room together. Amory writes advertising copy, and Tom is a book reviewer for the *New Democracy*. Five weeks later, in a tear-filled scene, Rosalind tells Amory she will remember their intimate hours but she cannot marry one whose most endearing qualities are those of a failure.

For three weeks Amory is mostly on an alcoholic binge, at the Knickerbocker and the Biltmore bars, at the theater, and in a street fight. He quits his job, and Alec leaves for home. Amory learns of his worsening family finances. Prohibition spells relief from his drinking, and he begins to read again. He and Tom debate literature, politics, and the power of the press. Although Amory gets a short story accepted for publication, he does not try to write more. Through Mrs. Lawrence, who lives on Riverside Drive, he resumes contact with Darcy, who, in Boston now, advises him to keep religion in his romantic approach to life. In August Tom's mother grows ill, and he and Amory sublet their apartment.

Amory visits a Maryland aunt and while walking is caught by a rainstorm and takes refuge in a haystalk, where he meets Eleanor Savage, the aunt's neighbor, who is eighteen or nineteen. She is a beautiful, witchlike atheist. Falling half in love, the two spend three weeks together, ride horses in the moonlight, and part in September. October finds Amory lolling in Atlantic City. He bumps into Alec in a car with a man and two girls, one named Jill Wayne. Later Amory shifts the blame to himself when authorities are about to find Alec in a hotel room with Jill. Amory suspects Alec will drop him because of this very kindness.

In New York in November Amory learns he is reported in the New York newspapers for having a woman in that hotel room, that Rosalind will marry Ryder, that his family income is depleted, and that Darcy has died. Amory smells poverty-stricken people in the subway, takes a bus uptown in the rain, walks by the river, judges himself to be corrupt and cruel, and analyzes various friends and authors. Attending Darcy's funeral, he wants neither admiration nor love but to be needed by others. He hitchhikes to Princeton and is given a ride in a chauffeured car. Its rich owner turns out to be the father of Jesse Ferrenby, killed in the war. The two discuss the grip capitalists have over the press and therefore on art, and then debate the benefits of socialism. Amory visits a Princeton cemetery, in his mind links evil and beauty in various forms, respects the restraints of Catholicism, wonders whether he should work in art or politics or religion, and concludes he knows only himself.

Fitzgerald told friends he wrote *This Side of Paradise* quickly because he wanted to leave something to be remembered by in case he was killed in the war, which he thought likely. He dedicated it to Cyril Sigourney Webster Fay,* on whom he based Monsignor Thayer Darcy. Much of the background of the novel, a considerably autobiographical *Bildungsroman*, is obliquely presented in Fitzgerald's essay ''Princeton.'' The beginning of Book Two is in the form of a play with stage directions and dialogue. Reviews of the novel were generally favorable. It sold 49,000 copies, with twelve printings, in its first year.

Bibliography: Jack Hendriksen, *This Side of Paradise as a Bildungsroman* (New York: Peter Lang, 1993); James L. W. West III, ed., F. Scott Fitzgerald, *This Side of Paradise* (Cambridge, England: Cambridge University Press, 1996).

THOMAS. In ''The Dance,'' he is the black band leader at the country-club dance in Davis, a Southern town. The narrator learns from him that his sister is Katie Goldstien and that she was once Catherine Jones's nurse. This helps the narrator to conclude that Catherine murdered Marie Bannerman.

THOMAS. In ''What Became of Our Flappers and Sheiks?,'' he is the ignorant, well-to-do father, in San Francisco, of Tommy.

THOMAS, MRS. In ''Between Three and Four,'' she is Howard Butler's African American cleaning lady. She says yes through embarrassment at being illiterate when he asks her whether the suicide victim was named in the newspapers as ''Mrs. John Summer.'' He suspects Sarah Belknap Summer has killed herself.

THORNE, VIENNA. In ''The Bowl,'' she is the daughter, sixteen at the beginning of the action, of an American diplomat, dislikes football because her brother was killed playing the sport, but dates Princeton football star Dolly Harlan anyway. She persuades him to quit the game. He does, for a time; when he plays again, the two argue.

THOUGHTBOOK (1965). (Full title: *Thoughtbook of Francis Scott Key Fitzgerald of St. Paul Minn USA.*) Diary. (Characters: T. Ames, Margaret Armstrong, Bachus, Una Bachus, Baker, Alida Bigelow, Donald Bigelow, Biglow, Laurence Boardman, P. Bulham, Elenor Clair, Bob Clark, Caroline Clark, Tom Daniels, Elizabeth Dean, Julia Dorr, Bob Driscoll, D. Driscoll, E. Driscoll, Earl, Egbert, Mrs. Finch, Arthur Foley, Billy Foster, Harriet Foster, Roger Foster, Gardener, Gardener, Ham Gardener, Nancy Gardener, Harriet Gould, Johnny Gown, Dorothy Green, Harold Green, Ben Griggs, Alfred Guson, Bob Harrington, Marie Hersey, Constance James, Enky James, Dorothy Knox, Emil Knox, William Landig, Laurie, Elenor Mitchell, Jack Mitchell, Archie Mudge, Betty

Mudge, Paul, Jim Porterfield, Cecil Read, Reuben, Susan Rice, Robin, Kitty Schultze, Seymour, Honey Shelenton, Sheply, Adolph Shully, Kitty Shully, Bob Shurmer, Wharton Smith, Violet Stockton, Sam Sturgis, Ted, Tim, Marie Touty, Mrs. Townsend, Catherine Trevall, Van Arnumn, R. Warren, R. Washington, Kitty Williams, Margaret Winchester.)

In a private diary, Fitzgerald describes his childhood activities in Buffalo and St. Paul, from November 1905 to 24 February 1911, in entries dated from August 1910 to 24 February 1911. He discusses friendships, games, dances, flirtations, gifts, efforts at becoming popular, arguments, and juvenile club events. Fitzgerald's spelling, especially of names, is atrocious.

Bibliography: John R. Kuehl, ed., *Thoughtbook of Francis Scott Key Fitzgerald* (Princeton: Princeton University Library, 1965).

"THOUSAND-AND-FIRST SHIP" (1981). Poem. (Character: Helena.) The persona remembers Helena promised to take him to a place of never-ending joy but married someone else.

"THREE ACTS OF MUSIC" (1937). Short story. (Characters: Dr. Kelly, Dr. Menafee.) An intern and a student nurse listen to Vincent Youmans music and delay marriage. Years later, he is back from study in Vienna and she is a nurse. They listen to Irving Berlin music and still delay. Finally, after fifteen years, both are middle aged and fat; he is a physician, back from Europe again, and she is moving to a better job. Listening to Jerome Kern music, they conclude romance of the sort in music is not in their lives.

"THREE CITIES" (1921). Essay. Fitzgerald contrasts Paris, Rome, and Oxford. He extols Anatole France but criticizes the warmongering French. He dislikes rude Italian soldiers in Florence, and he and his companion (surely Zelda Sayre Fitzgerald*) while away their time in mosquito-laden Rome by reading. In Oxford he sees ghosts of figures out of British fiction and expresses fear that the English are growing weaker and wonders whether New York will slip next.

"THREE HOURS BETWEEN PLANES" (1941). Short story. (Characters: Donald Bowers, Nancy Holmes Gifford, Walter Gifford, Judge Harmon Holmes, Trudy James, Kitty, Macks, Donald Plant.) Donald Plant, thirty-two and widowered since his wife's death after six years of marriage, has three hours before his flight continues from the Midwestern city in which he grew up. He wonders about Nancy Holmes, a childhood girlfriend he has not seen for twenty years. He phones her parents' home, learns she is Mrs. Walter Gifford, and phones her. Vaguely remembering Donald, she invites him out to her house. He learns her husband, who is probably unfaithful, is off in New York. Donald and Nancy reminisce over drinks and an old photograph album. His long-buried affection for her begins to surface, but when she points out a picture of Donald and coyly asks him to recall their exploration of a cave, he realizes she has confused him with another Donald, namely Donald Bowers, an obviously intimate childhood friend. Plant quickly leaves, catches his plane, and when aloft concludes his lost childhood and his adult worlds mingled briefly before his flawed memory of Nancy fell away.

THROCKMORTON. In "O Russet Witch!," he is a man in whose divorce Caroline is named correspondent.

TICKNOR, EVANGELINE. In "A Nice Quiet Place," she is a "speedy" girl from Philadelphia. News of her arrival at Lake Forest with Ridgeway Saunders distresses possessive Josephine Perry, who kisses Ridgeway at a dance and thus causes Evangeline to leave town.

TILLY. In "The Jelly-Bean," he is the owner of a garage in the sleepy Georgia town where James Powell lives as a lad. Jim enjoys loafing in the garage.

TIM. In *The Last Tycoon*, he is evidently the director of the movie starring Claudette Colbert* and Ronald Colman.*

TIM. In *Thoughtbook*, he is a friend.

TINSLEY, GORDON. In "A Woman with a Past," he is a rich young Chicagoan jaded Josephine Perry sees in the stag line at a Hot Springs dance. When he asks her to go driving the following day, she declines.

TIPTON. In "That Kind of Party," he is Terrence R. Tipton's father.

TIPTON, MRS. In "That Kind of Party," she is Terrence R. Tipton's mother. She fortunately goes out of town.

TIPTON, TERRENCE R. In "That Kind of Party," he falls in love with Dolly Bartlett, sasses his incompetent teacher, slugs Albert Moore in the nose, and at a children's party accidentally enables Carpenter Moore, long in a wheelchair, to walk again.

"TO A BELOVED INFIDEL" (1981). Poem. The poet contends that her having earlier made love with others sweetens present activities with him. Later he should proudly greet those former lovers. The addressee is surely Sheilah Graham.*

"TO ANNE" (1923). Poem. Some day the poet will take by the hand his dream girl Anne, who is mellow, fragrant, wild, and sweet.

"TO CARTER, A FRIENDLY FINGER" (1981). Poem. (Carter Brown.) Fitzgerald sends Carter some macabre lines about his nearly fatal automobile accident. Death tried to touch him; only a tie, a tooth, his spleen, and some gallstones were salvaged.

TOLLIVER, MARY. In "News from Paris—Fifteen Years Ago," she is Bessie Leighton Wing's well-to-do friend, living in Paris and regarded as "soignée." When Bessie takes Henry Haven Dell to her, the three go to an art show.

"TO DOLLY" (1981). Poem. (Character: Dolly.) The poet addresses a sweet message to Dolly.

TOM. In "Image on the Heart," he is a friend, thirty, of Tudy, whom he helped when her husband drowned at Rehoboth Beach during their honeymoon. A year later, he visits her in Avignon, where she is a student. Having corresponded, they have agreed to marry. Despite evidence of her considerable affection for French aviator Riccard, the two do wed; but Tom wonders about Riccard's image on her heart.

TOM. In *Safety First!*, he is the person to whom criminals are sent for incarceration.

TOM. In "A Short Autobiography," he is a person named by Fitzgerald as a drinking companion at Princeton in 1917.

TOMLINSON (TOMMY"). In " 'I Didn't Get Over,' " he is a member of the 1916 class who did get over. He and some of his classmates reminisce at their twentieth reunion.

TOMMY. In "What Became of Our Flappers and Sheiks?," he is a typically spoiled, parasitic youth. Thomas, his father, ignorantly indulges him.

TOMPKINS. In *Coward*, he is a pupil of Lindy Douglas. His mother tells her to punish him if he misbehaves.

TOMPKINS, GEORGE. In "Gretchen's Forty Winks," he is a seemingly successful interior decorator working in New York City and living in a suburb near Roger Halsey and Gretchen Halsey. George boasts of his cleverness and advises Roger to follow his regimen of work and exercise. While Roger works hard, Gretchen and George go out together. When Dr. Gregory treats Gretchen for oversleeping, he reports that George, another of his patients, overexercised, had a breakdown, and is moving west.

TOMPKINS, MRS. In *Coward*, she is the mother of a pupil in Lindy Douglas's class. His mother tells Lindy to punish him if he misbehaves.

"TO MY UNUSED GREEK BOOK (ACKNOWLEDGMENTS TO KEATS)" (1916). Poem. This is a parody of "Ode on a Grecian Urn" by John Keats, Fitzgerald's favorite poet. The student's textbook is unravished because of the abundance of cribs, ponies, and trots. It may be sweet to study, but it is sweeter still not to. If the student leaves the author alone and ignores the editor, the bard will not be wounded by any interlinear misinterpretations, and his voice will remain pure.

TONY. In "The Bowl," he is an attendant in the football dressing room when Jeff visits Dolly Harlan there after Princeton defeats Yale.

TONY. In "The Broadcast We Almost Heard Last September," he is the leader of the band urging the soldiers to charge.

TONY. In *Safety First!*, he is the greaseball whose habits, including smoking, lured Bridget Kelly away from Ralph.

"TOO CUTE FOR WORDS" (1936). Short story. (Characters: Bryan Bowers, Gwen Bowers, Campbell, Dizzy Campbell, Mrs. Campbell, Clara Hannaman, Helen Hannaman, Harry, Marion Lamb, Dr. Parker, Thomas Pickering, Esther Ray, Mrs. Charles Wrotten Ray, Tommy Ray.) By November widower Bryan Bowers has settled into a new apartment (perhaps in or near New York). However, the room of his daughter, Gwen Bowers, thirteen, is a mess. A peppy girl who currently calls everything "cute," Gwen is allowed to go by train with Dizzy Campbell and Clara Hannaman, two friends, to Princeton to attend a private dance given in her home by Mrs. Charles Wrotten Ray, Dizzy's aunt, before the Princeton-Harvard football game, for which Bryan and Gwen have tickets. When the girls arrive, they find Mrs. Ray called to Albany by her mother's illness, and only Mrs. Ray's children—Esther Ray, twenty, and Tommy Ray, sixteen and shy—are left to welcome them to the Ray house. Disappointed that the dance has been canceled, Gwen, Dizzy, and Clara dress up like older teenagers and plan to crash the pregame prom for Princeton students and their dates, including Esther. In the parking lot of the gymnasium where the dance is in full sway, they happen upon Marion Lamb, an older girl from their school, and Harry, her amorous date, in a car. The girls blackmail the embarrassed couple into helping them find a perch near the indoor track of the gym, to spy on the dancers. Meanwhile, Tommy, having received a telegram addressed to Esther, is trying to find her at the dance. Gwen, noticing Tommy's good looks, suggests approaching Esther by dancing with him right up to her. Gwen's father, sitting with Clara's attractive mother, Helen Hannaman, in the chaperones' box, spies his daring daughter. Next day, Bryan, while attending the football game, is joined by Gwen, who left her game ticket at home but is sneaked in by Tommy, one of the ticket takers. Revealing that he saw Gwen and Tommy at the dance, Bryan easily tells her she looked "too cute for words."

"Too Cute for Words" was the first of a planned series of stories featuring Gwen Bowers, based on Scottie,* born in 1921. The others were "Make Yourself at Home," "Inside the House," and "The Pearl and the Fur." "Make Yourself at Home" evidently became "Strange Sanctuary" (1939); "Inside the House" was published (1936); and "The Pearl and the Fur" was sold but never released.

TOOLE. In "The Bowl," he is a sophomore guard on the Princeton football team.

TORRENCE. In "The Scandal Detectives," he is Margaret Torrence's father.

TORRENCE, ELIZABETH. In "The Woman from Twenty-one," she is the half-Javanese wife of Raymond Torrence. When he decides to return quickly from New York to their home in Java, she is disappointed at not seeing more of the United States but thinks he misses their children back home.

TORRENCE, JANICE. In "The Woman from Twenty-one." *See* Janice.

TORRENCE, MARGARET. In "The Scandal Detectives," she is Basil Duke Lee's girlfriend, thirteen. When he asks, she gives him back his ring. In "He Thinks He's Wonderful," she is fourteen; when Basil neglects her, she criticizes him for regarding himself as wonderful. In "The Captured Shadow," Basil rejects her as a replacement actress in his play *The Captured Shadow* when Imogene Bissel drops out.

TORRENCE, MRS. In "The Scandal Detectives" and "He Thinks He's Wonderful," she is Margaret Torrence's mother.

TORRENCE, RAYMOND ("RAY"). In "The Woman from Twenty-one," he is a successful author living in Java with his half-Javanese wife, Elizabeth Torrence, and their children. The couple visit New York so he can confer with his publisher. He is so disgusted when a woman—designated as Mrs. Richbitch—spoils a play he is attending with his wife by talking loudly that he decides he and Elizabeth should return at once to Java, a more civilized place than New York.

TOSTOFF, VLADIMIR. In *The Great Gatsby*, he is the composer of *Jazz History of the World*, a musical composition Gatsby orders played at one of his parties. The obscene last name derives from that of Toby Tostoff, an imaginary character in James Joyce's *Ulysses*.

"TO THE RING LARDNERS" (1981). Poem. (Characters: Ellis Abbott Lardner, Ring Lardner.) Since the Lardners failed to send the Fitzgeralds a decent gift but only a poem, Fitzgerald is returning the cursed verses.

"TOUCHDOWN SONG BASED ON" (1981). Poem. The basis is Princeton's victory.

TOUTY, MARIE. In *Thoughtbook*, she is a friend of Kitty Williams.

TOWNSEND. In ''The Camel's Back,'' he is a wealthy resident of Toledo. He and his wife host the circus ball which Perry Parkhurst enters as the front end of a camel.

TOWNSEND, MRS. In ''The Camel's Back,'' she is the wife of a wealthy man in Toledo. Dressed as a plump bareback rider, she is the hostess of the circus ball.

TOWNSEND, MRS. In *Thoughtbook*, she is a dance teacher.

TRACY. In *Fie! Fie! Fi-Fi!*, he sings about the turnabout lovers.

TRACY, SPENCER (1900–1967). Movie actor. He starred in gangster roles before moving into character roles. He was in nine movies with Katharine Hepburn and won Academy Awards for performances in *Captains Courageous* (1937) and *Boys' Town* (1938). In *The Last Tycoon*, Monroe Stahr praises Tracy's vigorous action in a fight scene.

"THE TRAIL OF THE DUKE" (1913). Short story. (Characters: Allen, Dodson Garland, Duke of Matterlane, Walmsley, Mirabel Walmsley.) One hot July evening in New York City, Dodson Garland strolls over to call on Mirabel Walmsley, his fiancée. She and her millionaire father are in town to receive a visit from the Duke of Matterlane. Greeting Garland in great distress, Mirabel explains the Duke has wandered out and may get lost. Garland goes out, buys a newspaper to find a photograph of his quarry, checks in bars and alleys and theaters, and seizes a man who resembles the picture. The fellow, a jailbird, warns him away. Garland, drenched in sweat, returns to Mirabel, who holds up Dukey, her poodle, safely home again. The other duke is expected tomorrow.

TREADWAY. In ''The Freshest Boy,'' he is Basil Duke Lee's roommate at St. Regis. When Basil asks him, as well as Bugs Brown and William (''Fat'')

Gaspar, to go to town with him, all refuse; Treadway even moves out to room with Brick Wales.

TRENHOLM. In "The Rich Boy," he is a person whose wedding Nick the Plaza Hotel bartender mentions to Anson Hunter. Hunter curtly replies that he does not know Trenholm.

TRESSIGER, LADY PAULA. In "New Types." *See* Jorgensen, Paula.

TRESSIGER, LORD ERIC. In "New Types," he is the husband of Paula Jorgensen, who is therefore Lady Paula Tressiger. He was wounded in the war, came to New York to learn banking, became an alcoholic, and is paralyzed and dying. To gain money for an operation for him, Paula models. Once she has the necessary $500, the surgery is performed, but Eric soon dies.

TREVALL, KATHERINE. In *Thoughtbook*, she is an admiring friend.

TREVELLION, BUGS. In " 'Send Me In, Coach,' " he is in the play he and other boys rehearse.

"TRIBUTE" (1981). Poem. The poet presents a harmless little Paternoster and Ave Maria.

TRIMBLE. In "One Hundred False Starts," he is a person about whom Fitzgerald cannot write. Nor can he write about Trimble's wife. They settle for the second best instead of trying to change things.

TRIMBLE, LOUIS. In "The Lost Decade," he is a formerly distinguished architect recovering from a ten-year bout with alcoholism beginning in 1928. Orrison Brown, subeditor of a news weekly, takes Trimble to lunch at the request of Brown's boss, and admires Trimble's sensitivity.

TRIMBLE, MRS. In "One Hundred False Starts," she, just like her husband, is a person about whom Fitzgerald cannot write.

TROP, COUNT DE. In *Fie! Fie! Fi-Fi!*, his name is linked by gossip to that of Major Voe.

TROUBLE. In " 'Trouble.' " *See* McClurg, Glenola.

" 'TROUBLE' " (1937). Short story. (Characters: Dr. Compson, Dr. Donowska, Doofus, Luke Harkless, Mrs. Johnston, Glenola McClurg, Phillips, Haile Selassie, The Spirit of Seventy-six, Dr. Dick Wheelock, Winslow, Frederic Winslow, Mrs. Winslow.) Glenola McClurg, a dedicated nurse, is called "Trouble" because her beauty flutters interns' hearts. During the annual turtle race held at the hospital, she accidentally falls from her vantage point on a sun deck, sprains her ankle, and winds up in the arms of nearby handsome Dr. Dick Wheelock. She falls in love with him. For six months Trouble has been caring for Frederic Winslow, an alcoholic whose rich mother amiably asks her why she has thrown him over. Trouble explains: when Fred threatened to drink again if she saw any other men, she told him to go ahead and drink; furthermore, the Winslow wealth is no attraction to her. While Dr. Wheelock examines Trouble's ankle, her new supervisor, Mrs. Johnston, enters and orders her to come to attention. She slips, breaks her ankle, and blurts out at Mrs. Johnston, who gets her fired. Seeking Dr. Wheelock's support, Trouble, now in a cast, sees him drive off on a vacation with an adoring blond. She thinks of applying for work elsewhere, but Fred telephones with an invitation to visit the Winslow home in Virginia. She accepts. His parents are pleasant. A storm forces her to stay overnight. She agrees to marry Fred the following week. He has promised to quit drinking, but when he drops Trouble off at the hospital to collect some belongings, he drinks some more while waiting outside. He sees a rival in Dr. Wheelock, who has just returned and has been looking for Trouble, and he starts a fight. She orders him to wait outside. Dr. Wheelock says he should operate on her badly neglected ankle. She drives with Fred to see his mother, announces her disengagement, and returns by taxi to her favorite environment—the hospital. " 'Trouble' " was the last Fitzgerald story published by the *Saturday Evening Post*. He subsequently submitted seven more, but all were rejected.

TRUBY, MISS. In "Emotional Bankruptcy," she is the person in charge of the New York finishing school attended by Lillian Hammel and Josephine Perry.

"THE TRUE STORY OF APPOMATTOX" (1934, 1971). Short story. (Characters: Ulysses Simpson Grant, Robert E[dward] Lee, Captain X.) Captain X can divulge the truth at last. General Grant was offering to surrender to General Lee at Appomattox when he broke the pencil with which he was writing his "submission." He asked Lee for his sword to sharpen it. When Lee did so, photographers and radio reporters caught the scene; the rest is history.

Bibliography: [Joan Crane], "The True 'True Story of Appomattox': A Fitzgerald Fable Verified," *American Book Collector* 5 (September-October 1980): 8–11.

TRUMBLE, MRS. In "At Your Age," she is a friend of Annie Lorry's mother and Caroline, and is Annie's aunt. Tom Squires sees all three older women at the College Club in St. Paul.

"TRUTH AND—CONSEQUENCES" (1981). Poem. (Characters: Bill, Bobby, Ruth.) Avoid playing this game honestly.

TUDY. In ''Image on the Heart,'' she is a widow, nineteen, whose husband drowned at Rehoboth Beach during their honeymoon, and who a year later is studying in Avignon. She agrees to marry Tom, thirty. He helped her during the Rehoboth calamity, corresponded with her for a year after that, and now comes to France. Although she seems to like Riccard, French aviator, she marries Tom; he wonders, however, about Riccard's image on her heart.

TULLIO, SERAPHIM. In *Tender Is the Night*, his is a name read in the *New York Herald*.

TULLIVER, WILLIAM ("BILL") V. In ''One Interne,'' he is an intern at the hospital. He helps his classmate George Schoatze, joins in the roast of medical faculty members, and falls in love with Thea Singleton. He correctly, if inefficiently, diagnoses the ailments of Senator Billings, Doremus, and Paul B. Van Schaik. Tulliver shows his egocentricity when he resists having surgery for a dangerous volvulus, which Dr. Howard Durfee, his rival for Thea, finally performs.

TULLIVERS, WILLIAM ("BILL") IV. In ''Zone of Accident,'' he is the young intern at the Baltimore hospital when actress Loretta Brooke is brought in with a stab wound. He remembers a former girlfriend named Thea Singleton but has Amy for a current girlfriend. Loretta replaces Amy in his affections, especially when Amy prefers an acting career to him and Loretta prefers him to a continued acting career. William Tullivers is undoubtedly the earlier William Tulliver.

TULLY. In *This Side of Paradise*, he is a companion of Alec Connage during an Atlantic City escapade, along with Miss Waterson and Jill Wayne.

TUNTI. In ''The Bowl,'' he is a person whom Carl Sanderson out of frustration and jealousy names to Vienna Thorne. Carl reminds her she met Tunti in Boston and talked about living on the Riviera.

TURNBULL, ANDREW (1921–1970). Biographer and teacher. He was born in Baltimore. His parents rented La Paix, outside Baltimore, in 1922 and 1923 to the Fitzgeralds, and Fitzgerald befriended Turnbull when he was a boy and later talked football with him and took him to some Princeton games. Turnbull idolized Fitzgerald. Fitzgerald met T. S. Eliot when both were guests at the Turnbull home in 1933. Andrew Turnbull received his B.A. from Princeton in 1942, served in the U.S. Navy (1942–1946), and earned his M.A. (1947) and his Ph.D. (1954), in European history, at Harvard. He married Joanne Tudhope Johnson in 1954, and they had two children. Turnbull taught at the university level intermittently in the eastern United States and in France (1954–1970), working also as a freelance writer part of that time. He wrote *Scott Fitzgerald:*

A Biography (1962) and *Thomas Wolfe* (1967), and edited *The Letters of F. Scott Fitzgerald* (1963) and *Scott Fitzgerald: Letters to His Daughter* (1965). His work on Fitzgerald is notable for detailed research, information gathered from interviews of Fitzgerald's friends, and keen analysis of Fitzgerald's romantic character and personality. The Turnbulls attended Fitzgerald's funeral service at Bethesda, Maryland. Long chronically depressed, Turnbull committed suicide. Turnbull is mentioned in "Momishness."

TWELVE, MRS. In *This Side of Paradise*, she is a cleaning woman at the dormitory where Amory Blaine lives during his freshman year at Princeton.

"TWO FOR A CENT" (1922). Short story. (Characters: Abercrombie, Burling, Deems, Harlan, Henry W. Hemmick, Nell Hemmick, Hoyt, Bill Kennedy, Mieger, Moody.) Abercrombie returns from New York to an Alabama town to see the house he grew up in. He got into trouble and left at seventeen. Near the house he chances to meet Henry W. Hemmick, who explains that he and his family rented the house for years. The two men reminisce. Hemmick says he would have left town but for an incident: twenty-five years ago, as a bank runner, he collected $300.86 owed on a note by a man named Harlan, but he dropped a penny of the sum on the walk back to the bank. He retraced his steps to look for it at an army recruiting station near the railway station where he thought it might be. He was seen there by Deems, the chronically suspicious vice president of the bank, grew hysterical, and was fired. He remained in town, cleared his name, got married, had four children, and never left. Abercrombie explains how he did leave town. He saw an army recruiting poster explaining that for $3.42 one could take the train to Atlanta and sign up. He counted his money and was a penny short, but he found a penny near the station, joined the army, and later rose to prominence.

"TWO OLD-TIMERS" (1941). Short story. (Characters: Bill Corker, Allan Dwan, Mrs. Gaspar, Sergeant Gaspar, Pat Hobby, Phil Macedon.) Pat Hobby, forty-nine and down on his luck as a film writer, is driving a repossessed car when he collides with a car driven by a former friend, Phil Macedon, a conceited but still-handsome retired movie star. Since both men smell of alcohol, Sergeant Gaspar arrests them but at the station is courteous only to Macedon, because Gaspar, a combat veteran, was thrilled by Macedon's acting in a shell-hole scene in *The Final Push*, a 1925 silent war movie. Pat, irate that Macedon has been snubbing him, tells Gaspar that Macedon did not want to do the scene and was shoved crying into the hole, and that the director turned it to his advantage by titling the sequence so that in his role Macedon laments a buddy's death. Gaspar holds Macedon and gives Pat a lift to a hotel room. Pat says Macedon should not have ignored him, since both men are old-timers. The director is based on King Vidor,* who shoved actor John Gilbert* into a hole in a combat scene in *The Big Parade* (1925).

"TWO WRONGS" (1930). Short story. (Characters: Ames, Aronstael, Bill, Brancusi, Cadorna, Georgia Berriman Campbell, Miss Colahan, Lady Sybil Combrinck, Lord Combrinck, William Harrison Dempsey, Donilof, Sir Humphrey Dunn, Gouverneer Haight, Harris, Hopkins, Hubbel, Easton Hughes, Jimmy, Joe, Dr. Kearns, Sol Lincoln, Frank Llewellen, Billy McChesney, Emmy Pinkard McChesney, William McChesney, Paul Makova, Irene Rikker, Alan Rogers, Ned Wayburn.) William (''Bill'') McChesney, a New York drama producer, combines showing off to his associate Brancusi and displaying generosity in hiring Emmy Pinkard, eighteen, beautiful, and from South Carolina, when she asks for a chance on the stage. Bill is engaged to actress Irene Rikker. The troupe is opening a new play in Atlantic City. Bill insults handsome Frank Llewellen, who seems too attentive to Emmy during rehearsal and who punches Bill. She admires Bill's going ahead anyway with the play, which is a success. Three years later, about 1926, Bill and Emmy, now his wife, and their son Billy, are in London, where he is a theatrical and a social success though now an alcoholic. When Bill declines to accept Brancusi's criticism of Bill's recent work in America, the two part company. Bill associates too much with Lady Sybil Combrinck, which distresses patient, now-pregnant Emmy. He crashes a party in Mayfair that Lady Sybil has not invited him to, is thrown into the street by her servants, and gets drunk. He learns too late that Emmy, going to the hospital alone, has delivered a still-born baby. In New York again, Emmy at twenty-six throws herself obsessively into studying ballet while Bill produces artistic but unprofitable shows. Just as she is offered a debut at the Metropolitan, he learns that excessive smoking has ruined a lung and he must recuperate in the Adirondacks or—better—Denver. He wants her to accompany him but has character enough to encourage her to dance in New York. She offers to go with him to Denver, decides to stay in New York, and rationalizes her decision by recalling his conduct in London. On the train heading west, he feels sure she will come ''at the end.''

TYSON. In *This Side of Paradise*, his is the theater where Amory Blaine goes and drinks during his New York binge.

U

"UNDER FIRE" (1923). Review of *Through the Wheat* by Thomas Alexander Boyd.*

UNGER. In ''The Diamond as Big as the Ritz,'' he is John T. Unger's indulgent, golf-playing father. His home is in Hades, on the Mississippi River.

UNGER, JOHN T. In ''The Diamond as Big as the Ritz,'' he is the central character. At sixteen, he goes to St. Midas' School near Boston, two years later is invited by Percy Washington to visit his uniquely rich father in Montana, and is lavishly entertained there. He falls in love with Percy's younger sister, Kismine Washington, and escapes the fiery end of the diamond mountain with her.

UNGER, MRS. In ''The Diamond as Big as the Ritz,'' she is John T. Unger's fatuous mother.

"THE UNSPEAKABLE EGG" (1924). Short story: (Characters: C.T.J. Calhoun, Fifi, Dr. Roswell Gallup, Estelle Holliday, Cal Marsden, Josephine Marsden, Percy, George Van Tyne, Walters.) The New York papers announce the marriage of Fifi and George Van Tyne, but Van Tyne's family founded the pre–Civil War Society for the Preservation of Large Fortunes, and Fifi breaks the engagement. George may be perfect, but he is dull. While visiting her ultra-proper aunts on Montauk Point, Long Island, and enjoying rugged sand dunes, Fifi drags in a hairy, savage-looking derelict called Hopkins from the beach to dinner. Calling him an ''unspeakable egg,'' the aunts try to be courteous until Fifi hints she might go to the Australian bush with the hoarse, uncouth fellow. The aunts summon psychiatrist Dr. Roswell Gallup to query the wayward girl. When he hears a commotion outside, he arms himself and leads the three females to the water. There is George—not Hopkins after all—tended by several sailors from his nearby yacht, carefully shaving, dressing tidily, and in all ways making himself immaculate and suave. He explains that Fifi knew about the ruse from the outset but agreed to let him prove how imaginative his antisocial antics could be.

UPDIKE. In ''Sentiment—and the Use of Rouge,'' he is a minister and an Oxford graduate. Perhaps imaginary, he is mentioned by Sergeant O'Flaherty shortly before he dies.

UTSONOMIA. In ''Forging Ahead,'' he is a Japanese student at Minnesota State University. He is a friend of Eddie Parmelee, who persuades him to substitute for Eddie as unpopular Rhoda Sinclair's date. Utsonomia is happy because he wants to observe American social customs.

V

"VALENTINE" (1981). Poem. The poet wishes he were a saint, to deserve to be with the one he misses so.

VALENTINO, RUDOLPH (1895–1926). Silent movie actor. In *The Last Tycoon*, Cecelia Brady recalls that Valentino attended her fifth birthday party.

VAN ARNUMN. In *Thoughtbook*, he is a dance teacher.

VAN ASTOR. In "The Freshest Boy," he is a character in the Broadway matinee Basil Duke Lee attends and enjoys.

VAN BAKER, LEILIA. In "The Captured Shadow," she is a character in Basil Duke Lee's incomplete play *Mr. Washington Square* and in his play *The Captured Shadow*. The part in the latter is taken by Evelyn Beebe when Imogene Bissel becomes ill.

VAN BAKER, VICTOR. In "The Captured Shadow," he is Leilia Van Baker's brother in Basil Duke Lee's play *The Captured Shadow*.

VAN BECK, AMY. In "What a Handsome Pair!," she is Helen Van Beck Oldhorne's mother and Mrs. Cassius Ruthven's friend. Helen and her husband, Stuart Oldhorne, frequently park their children with her mother.

VAN BECK, BETTY ("BET"). In "What a Handsome Pair!," she is an Irish waitress in New York City whom musician Teddy Van Beck, a little younger than she, marries on the rebound after Helen Van Beck breaks their engagement.

VAN BECK, JOSIE. In ''What a Handsome Pair!,'' she is the daughter of Betty Van Beck and Teddy Van Beck.

VAN BECK, TEDDY. In ''What a Handsome Pair!,'' he is a competent New York pianist and musical composer. When his cousin, Helen Van Beck, breaks her engagement with him and marries Stuart Oldhorne, Teddy marries Betty on the rebound. They have a daughter named Josie. Teddy enjoys a musical career, continues to love Helen—usually from a distance—is something of a philanderer, but returns to tolerant, homeloving Betty. Teddy remains friendly with Stuart.

VAN BUREN, GEORGE. In ''The Third Casket,'' he is a young city man, about thirty, who fails to take over Cyrus Girard's Wall Street firm and marry his daughter Lola Girard. His plan for leisure is an endowed center for history and archaeology.

VAN CAMP, MAX. In ''Your Way and Mine,'' he is Henry McComas's business associate whose way is different from McComas's and more acceptable. McComas advises his daughter, Honoria McComas, to marry Max.

VANCE, T. G. In ''The Bridal Party,'' he is evidently a successful financier who offered financially impaired Hamilton Rutherford a job at $50,000 a year just minutes before Rutherford's marriage ceremony to Caroline Dandy.

VANDERVERE. In ''In the Holidays,'' he is one of three gunmen Joe Kinney relishes thinking about in connection with the planned murder of Griffin. The others are Flute Cuneo and Oaky.

VANDERVERE, GORDON. In ''Six of One—,'' he is the handsome, popular son of a minister in Ed Barnes's Ohio hometown. Barnes sends him to Andover for two years and then Princeton. After graduating, he does little but court Esther Crosby, the rich banker H. B. Crosby's only daughter. The pair fall patiently in love, wear down Crosby's opposition, and are permitted to marry. They plan to go into the diplomatic service in Paris. Barnes laughs at the news and agrees Vandervere has succeeded.

VAN DYKE, MIKE. In *The Last Tycoon*, he is a gag man Monroe Stahr orders to perform a comedy dance to loosen up stiff British writer George Boxley.

VAN SCHAIK, PAUL B. In ''One Interne,'' he is a wealthy patient, about forty, from Washington, D.C. William Tulliver V orders too many tests and fibs about contrary symptoms, but correctly diagnoses him as simply having a hangover.

VAN SCHELLINGER. In ''A Night at the Fair,'' he is Gladys Van Schellinger's rich father. With Mrs. Van Schellinger, they sit in their state fair family box to watch the fireworks. Basil Duke Lee joins them.

VAN SCHELLINGER, GLADYS. In ''A Night at the Fair,'' she, fourteen, invites Basil Duke Lee to watch the fireworks from their state fair family box. He contrasts their families: his is comfortable; hers, rich. He feels they have a common bond through their both leaving soon for school in the East. He goes to the family box late and is pleased by Gladys until she asks him to bring Hubert Blair to visit her next day. In ''He Thinks He's Wonderful,'' Gladys joins other children on Imogene Bissel's veranda but feels a bit superior through having gone east to school. In ''The Captured Shadow,'' she acts in Basil Duke Lee's play *The Captured Shadow* until her mother makes her withdraw because it is about criminals.

VAN SCHELLINGER, MRS. In ''A Night at the Fair,'' she welcomes Basil Duke Lee to their family box, with her husband and their daughter, Gladys, at the state fair to watch the fireworks. In ''The Captured Shadow,'' she is the mother of Gladys, whom she forces to withdraw from Basil Duke Lee's *The Captured Shadow*, his play about criminals.

VAN TYNE. In ''Jacob's Ladder,'' he is a member of the law firm of Read, Van Tyne, Biggs & Company, with which Jacob C. K. Booth threatens Jenny Prince's would-be blackmailer Scharnhorst.

VAN TYNE, GEORGE. In ''The Unspeakable Egg,'' he is Fifi's respectable fiancé, from a wealthy, conservative New York family. The probability of his becoming dull makes Fifi decide to challenge him to be uncouth to Cal Marsden and Josephine Marsden, her proper Long Island aunts. He does so, brilliantly.

VAN VLEEK, MARTIN. In ''Dice, Brassknuckles & Guitar,'' he is a supercilious lad, twenty-one, from a wealthy family. He sneaks liquor into James Powell's summer school, is expelled, and helps cause the closure of the school.

VARLAND, JOE. In ''A Short Trip Home,'' he is the eldritch stranger, seemingly about thirty-five, with a sneer and a soundless laugh. Dogging Ellen Baker, he weaves an evil spell over her until Eddie Stinson outfaces him on the train carrying them from Chicago to New York. Eddie sees a small hole in the man's forehead and later learns that Varland, who preyed on girls on trains, was killed some time ago by a policeman in Pittsburgh.

THE VEGETABLE (1923). (Full title: *The Vegetable; or from President to Postman.*) Play. (Characters: Doris, Joseph Fish, Judge Fossile, Charlotte Frost, Horatio Frost, Jerry Frost, Mrs. Richard Barton Hammond, Jones, Alec Martin,

Pushing, Roxanna, Snooks, Mrs. Snooks, John B. Standish, Stutz-Mozart.) Jerry Frost, a railroad clerk, thirty-five, tells Charlotte Frost, his bickering wife, thirty, that when his superiors had him psychoanalyzed he revealed his whilom desire to be a postman and also president of the United States. His father, Horatio (''Dada'') Frost, deaf, senile, and eighty-eight, dodders in for his Bible. Charlotte's sister, Doris, enters and reveals her engagement to an Idaho undertaker's son, Joseph Fish, twenty-four. When Doris leaves, Snooks, Jerry's bootlegger, enters. He mixes up and flavors two gallons of ''gin''; Charlotte sniffs and goes upstairs. Snooks receives $16 and leaves. Sampling his purchase, Jerry phones ''Information'' and asks who has been nominated for president, but is hung up on. Doris returns, with Fish, and goes upstairs to Charlotte. Fish declines Jerry's offer of a drink. Jerry hears a crowd approach, although Fish does not. A man calling himself the politician Jones bursts in and praises Jerry as Republican candidate for president.

Jerry is now president and in the White House, where almost everything is white. He complains about the numerous requests he gets. Fish, a senator from Idaho, hopes Idaho's demand for Jerry's resignation won't spoil his wedding ceremony to Doris. When Major-General Pushing demands Jerry declare war against any suitable country, Jerry says Dada, now secretary of the treasury, can't afford it. Charlotte encourages Jerry not to resign. Fish reports that Idaho wants Judge Fossile of the Supreme Court to move for Jerry's impeachment. Snooks enters, now the ambassador from Irish Poland. To be rid of Fish, Jerry wants to buy the Buzzard Islands, which Snooks owns, and give him Idaho. When Dada says he has destroyed all the money in the treasury, Snooks offers an even trade. Stutz-Mozart brings in his band for Doris's wedding reception. Fossile starts Idaho's impeachment proceedings, until Jerry says Fish of Idaho is now an nonvalid foreigner. Doris is glad to be disengaged. Pushing wants to declare war on the Buzzard Islands. Fossile plans to seize Jerry, who says he never wanted to be president.

Back at the Frost house a week after the first scene, Jerry, who was drinking a lot, is missing. Doris tells Charlotte that they should check dives and the morgue. A detective enters, but he has not found Jerry, and leaves with Pushing, Jerry's real-life boss, when he angrily reports that Jerry is fired and offers to show Jerry's psychoanalytical report. Doris tells Charlotte she married Fish three days ago but now wants to dump him. Charlotte wishes Jerry were home again. Fish arrives. While he and Doris are disputing, the postman arrives. It is Jerry, so trim, erect, and neat that Doris and Fish fail to recognize him. He calls himself the best postman ever and says he wants to give people letters that will make them happy. All leave. Snooks rings, seeks Jerry, but departs when Charlotte, criticizing his wood alcohol, tells him Jerry is missing. A storm erupts. Hidden under a drenched cape, Jerry returns with a letter that will delight Charlotte. It is from Jerry, who says he has a joyful job. Charlotte says she would like Jerry to know she is proud of him. He leaves. Dada goes upstairs with his Bible. The postman whistles. Charlotte becomes rapturous.

The Vegetable was published in April 1923, opened in Atlantic City as a tryout in November 1923, but closed after a week. It was designed to satirize the stupidity and the spoils-system corruption of politicians during President Warren G. Harding's criminal administration, with stress on the Interior, Justice, and State departments and on the Veterans Bureau. Providing what became the title of *The Vegetable*, H. L. Mencken,* in his essay ''On Being an American'' (*Prejudices: Third Series*, 1922), says, ''Here is a country in which it is an axiom that a businessman shall be . . . a vegetable.'' Much of the humor in the play derives from lengthy stage directions. Fitzgerald was of the opinion that *Of Thee I Sing* (1931) by George Gershwin, George S. Kaufman, and Morrie Ryskind was partly plagiarized from *The Vegetable* and briefly considered filing a lawsuit.

VELANCE, PEPPY. In ''Inside the House,'' she is a movie actress who is Gwen Bowers's ideal. Ed Harrison, who knows her and regards her as stupid, participates in arrangements for Gwen to meet her. The actress's real name is Schwartze, and she is from New Mexico. She may be based on movie actress Lupe Velez (Guadalupe Velez de Villalobos, 1908–1944). She was born in a suburb of Mexico City, was in show business beginning in 1924, went in Hollywood in 1926, starred with Douglas Fairbanks* in *The Gaucho* in 1928, was the lover of many actors, married Johnny Weissmuller in 1933, divorced him in 1938, during an unhappy affair became pregnant, and committed suicide.

Bibliography: James Robert Parish, *The Hollywood Celebrity Death Book* (Las Vegas: Pioneer Books, 1993).

VENSKE, GUS. In ''The Homes of the Stars,'' he advertises himself as a guide to Hollywood stars' homes. When he leaves his umbrella-shaded stand for lunch, Pat Hobby takes his place for any money he can grab.

VICTOR. *Fie! Fie! Fi-Fi!*, he likes Susie, but she prefers Sam.

VIDOR, KING (1894–1982). Movie director. Born in Galveston, Texas, he was a Hollywood scriptwriter and newsreel cameraman before becoming an independent producer in 1918. He worked for Metro in 1922 and, when it merged in 1924 with Goldwyn studios, was an MGM senior director under Irving Thalberg.* Vidor's credits include *The Big Parade* (1925), which was the first big movie about World War I and which started actor John Gilbert* on his road to fame; *Hallelujah* (1929), which was Vidor's first sound film and which had an all-black cast; *The Champ* (1931); *Our Daily Bread* (1934); *The Wedding Night* (1935); *Stella Dallas* (1937); *The Citadel* (1938); *Northwest Passage* (1940); *Duel in the Sun* (1946); *The Fountainhead* (1949); and *War and Peace* (1956). Vidor was married three times: to actress Florence Alto in 1915 (divorced 1924);

actress Eleanor Boardman in 1926 (divorced 1933); and writer Elizabeth Hill in 1937.

In 1928 Fitzgerald and Zelda Sayre Fitzgerald* were fellow passengers while sailing to France with Vidor and Eleanor Boardman. Fitzgerald showed Vidor around Paris and introduced him to Gerald Murphy* and André Chamson,* among others. Murphy, knowledgeable about spirituals, advised Vidor on *Hallelujah* in Hollywood (1928–1929). Vidor's *Our Daily Bread* so closely resembled Champson's *The Road* (1929) that he might been have sued for plagiarism. Meanwhile, back in Hollywood, Fitzgerald had observed arguments between Vidor and Eleanor and used them as the basis of the squabble between Miles Calman and Stella Calman in "Crazy Sunday." Vidor got even with *The Wedding Night*, a movie based on Fitzgerald's marital problems with Zelda. Though named Tony and Dora Barrett in the movie, the husband and wife were called Scott and Zelda Fitzpatrick in the original script. "Two Old-Timers" is based in part on Vidor's directing of Gilbert in *The Big Parade*.

Bibliography: Raymond Durgnat and Scott Simmon, *King Vidor, American* (Berkeley: University of California Press, 1988).

VILLEGRIS, MADAME. In "The Intimate Strangers," she is a friend of Marquise Sara de la Guillet de la Guimpé in Paris.

VIOLET. In "The Cruise of the Rolling Junk," she is a witness, with her friend Morgan, when the Junk's wheel rolls loose down a Baltimore street.

VIONNET. In "On Your Own," this is the name of a dress designer, one of whose lush creations Evelyn Lovejoy wears to the New York dinner party she is invited to attend by George Ives. The unusual name Vionnet may derive from that of Madame Marie de Vionnet in Henry James's *The Ambassadors*.

VIRGINIE. In "The Intimate Strangers," she is the girl Paul Pechard did not marry. He married Margot, a servant of Marquise Sara de la Guillet de la Guimpé.

VITORI, CARDINAL. In *This Side of Paradise*, he is an important Catholic Amory Blaine's mother knew in Rome before her marriage.

VIVIAN. In "Imagination—and a Few Mothers," she is a person for whom Mrs. Paxton did not organize a family orchestra.

VIVIAN. In "One Hundred False Starts," she is a person about whom Fitzgerald cannot write. She, her husband Donald, and their child were shipwrecked on a barren island.

VLASCO, PANDELY. In *Tender Is the Night*, his is a name read in the *New York Herald*.

VOE, MAJOR. *Fie! Fie! Fi-Fi!*, his name is linked by gossip to that of Count de Trop.

VOGEL, AUGUSTUS. In "Zone of Accident," he is a Baltimore artist and one of the judges of the beauty contest.

VOLTAIRE, WILLIE. In *The Great Gatsby*, Nick Carraway lists Voltaire's name on a timetable as one of Jay Gatsby's summer guests. He is from East Egg.

VON BOODLEWADEN. In "The Prince of Pests," he helps prepare the Kaiser to be photographed.

VON MUNCHENNOODLE. In "The Prince of Pests," he advises the Kaiser to destroy Belgium.

VON NICKLEBOTTOM. In "The Prince of Pests," he leads the cheers when the Kaiser mentions Nietzsche.

"VOWELS" (1967). Poem. This is a rhyming translation of Arthur Rimbaud's poem "Voyelles."

W

WADE, MARYLYN. In ''The Ice Palace,'' she is one of Sally Carrol Happer's friends in Tarleton, Georgia. In ''The Jelly-Bean,'' she associates with Joe Ewing and Nancy Lamar, among others.

WAGGONER, DUTCH. In ''No Harm Trying,'' he is a movie director in Hollywood, under contract but not working. Pat Hobby lures him away in his scheme to exploit script boy Eric's fine movie idea. When they present it to Carl Le Vigne, that canny producer sees through the scheme, will make the movie, but tells Waggoner he cannot direct it because he is a drug addict.

WAINWRIGHT, BARBARA. In *The Beautiful and Damned*, she is a character, that of a secretary, in the movie for which Gloria Gilbert Patch makes a screen test.

WAINWRIGHT, WARD. In ''Pat Hobby's Preview,'' he is the well-dressed, conceited movie scriptwriter Pat Hobby worked with briefly. When Pat wants to take his new girlfriend, Eleanor Carter, to the preview of the movie but has the wrong tickets, Wainwright gives them his tickets because the show is so poor he is walking out early.

WAITE. In ''Basil and Cleopatra,'' he is a Yale freshman football team player, who misses a game while taking a test.

"WAIT TILL YOU HAVE CHILDREN OF YOUR OWN!" (1924). Essay. Young parents today, most of whom want their children to be better than they were, should avoid burdening them with useless ideas. The 1890s had ideals and optimism; but the 1920s, full of inexplicable wrongs, brought corruption causing fatigue and cynicism. A friend of Fitzgerald's said she hoped her baby daughter would become a beautiful fool. Fathers in the 1890s urged their sons to be materialistic. Fathers today should want their sons to grow up clean, decent, honest, and informed, and avoid cheap patriots and ill-informed teachers. Such sons, aware that life is vast and merciless, should be world citizens, learn about the human body, hate pretense, distrust the establishment, and value loneliness over fellowship. Most people now between forty and sixty are dull and less cultured than either their parents or their offspring. Fitzgerald vilifies specified pseudo-heroes and praises real heroes who have made their dreams come true, made life fuller and freer. As for present-day women, he downgrades coeds and country-club members and praises working girls who make men the successes they are, but he fears such girls' conformity and advises them to profit from contact with bright men and avoid ruinously stupid ones. He dares to add, however, that stern fathers should exert a greater influence than soft mothers over boys. His sad conclusion: let kids grow up and get burned but also warmed by fire. May they love their parents a little and be polite. Expect them to regard those parents as wrong and leave them in peace.

WAIZE, GUS. In *The Great Gatsby*, Nick Carraway lists Waize's name on a timetable as one of Jay Gatsby's summer guests. He is in theater work.

WAKEMAN. In ''Majesty,'' he is the organist who plays on and on before learning Emily Castleton has called off her wedding ceremony.

WALES, BRICK. In ''The Freshest Boy,'' he is a student at St. Regis. Basil's roommate, Treadway, moves out in order to room with Brick. Later, during a basketball scrimmage, Brick calls Basil ''Lee-y,'' which thrills him and may replace his hated nickname ''Bossy.'' In ''Basil and Cleopatra,'' Brick is one of Basil Duke Lee's roommates at Yale, along with George Dorsey.

WALES, CHARLES (''CHARLIE'') J. In ''Babylon Revisited,'' he is an American businessman, thirty-five, in Prague. After an argument about three years earlier in Paris—before the Crash—he locked his alcoholic, flirtatious wife, Helen Wales, out, and she caught cold and died. He was institutionalized for alcoholism and surrendered custody of their daughter, Honoria Wales, to Helen's sister, Marion Peters. On the wagon for a year and a half, Charlie returns to Paris and seeks custody of Honoria, but he loses out when his former drinking friends Duncan Schaeffer and Lorraine Quarles burst in on the Peters and embarrass Charlie.

WALES, HELEN. In ''Babylon Revisited,'' she is the deceased wife, from Vermont, of Charles J. Wales and the mother of Honoria Wales. Her sister, Marion Peters, has custody in Paris of Honoria and despises Charlie for his former alcoholism and his money.

WALES, HONORIA. In ''Babylon Revisited,'' she is the sweet little daughter of Charles J. Wales. She lives in Paris with her aunt, Marion Peters, and her family, but wants to return to her adored father.

WALES, MISS. In ''Zone of Accident,'' she has been the chief nurse in the Baltimore hospital accident ward for ten years and knows William Tullivers IV well.

WALES, THE PRINCE OF. In ''Rags Martin-Jones and the Pr-nce of W-les,'' he is the person Cedric impersonates. *See* Cedric.

WALKER, STELLA. In ''Crazy Sunday.'' *See* Calman, Stella Walker.

WALLIS, MARIA. In *Tender Is the Night*, she shoots a Britisher in the Paris railroad station. Nicole Diver knows her sister Laura.

WALLY. In ''Emotional Bankruptcy,'' he is a friend Josephine Perry and Lillian Hammel plan to meet, along with Joe, at the Ritz.

WALLY. In ''The Ice Palace,'' it is at Wally's pool, in Tarleton, Georgia, that Sally Carrol Happer and her friends go swimming.

WALMSLEY. In ''The Trail of the Duke,'' he is the millionaire father of Mirabel Walmsley.

WALMSLEY, MIRABEL. In ''The Trail of the Duke,'' she is Dodson Garland's fiancée. She sends him out after the Duke. He seeks the Duke of Matterlane, not realizing that Mirabel's Dukey is her poodle.

WALTERS. In ''The Unspeakable Egg,'' he is one of George Van Tyne's courteous sailors from his yacht.

WARBURTON. In ''The Camel's Back,'' he is Perry Parkhurst's friend who advises Perry to get a marriage license, be macho, and tell Betty Medill she must wed him now or never.

WARD. In ''One Interne,'' a dispensary in the hospital has been named for him.

WARD, CHAUNCEY. In ''Last Kiss,'' he is an experienced but inept British actor in Hollywood. Pamela Knighton makes him a kind of business manager and foolishly accepts his advice to be uncompromising with vicious movie men. When dying, she names him as the person to be notified.

WARDEN, MRS. TEAK. In ''The Rich Boy,'' she is the wife of Anson Hunter's friend. She openly said Anson was a bad influence on her husband.

WARDEN, TEAK. In ''The Rich Boy,'' he is a friend at whose home in Manhattan Anson Hunter and Dolly Karger used to rendezvous. Warden took to drink. When lonely Anson later drops by, he is told the Wardens are away.

WARE, MAURICE DE. In ''The Honor of the Goon,'' he is one of the students who called Ella Lei Chamoro a goon.

WARNER, DAN. In ''A Freeze-Out,'' he is the owner of the house Chauncey Rikker and his family rent when they return to Minnesota.

WARREN. In ''First Blood,'' this is the name of a family Constance Perry and Anthony Harker visit.

WARREN, BABY. In *Tender Is the Night*, she is Nicole Diver's older, unmarried sister, born in 1894. Her real name is Beth Evan Warren. She controls the Warren family money, dislikes Dick Diver, and holds her money and an awareness of his moral and psychological weaknesses as a threat to him.

WARREN, CHARLES MARQUIS (c. 1913–1990). Movie producer, director, and author. He was born in Baltimore, was befriended by Fitzgerald, contributed material to the *Saturday Evening Post*, and after service in the U.S. Navy in World War II succeeded in the movie and television industry. He directed numerous Westerns, wrote the pilot and five later teleplays for the television series *Gunsmoke* (1955), created the television series *Rawhide* (1958), and wrote three popular novels. Warren claimed he helped Fitzgerald write part of *Tender Is the Night*.

WARREN, DEVEREUX. In *Tender Is the Night*, he is the wealthy, widowed father of Baby Warren and Nicole Diver and was educated in Germany. When she was eleven, he committed an incestuous act with Nicole, which occasioned her psychological problems. He places her in a Swiss clinic when she is sixteen. He checks himself into a clinic in Lausanne for an alcohol-damaged liver condition but leaves without completing much treatment. Fitzgerald considered giving Warren the name Charles Warren, because of Fitzgerald's friendship with Baltimore writer Charles Marquis Warren.*

WARREN, LIEUTENANT. In ''The Last of the Belles,'' he is mentioned as a fellow officer of Lieutenant Andy and Lieutenant Bill Knowles at the base outside Tarleton, Georgia.

WARREN, R. In *Thoughtbook*, he is a boy who likes Marie Hersey.

WARREN, SID. In *Tender Is the Night*, he is mentioned as the horse-trading, legendary founder of the Warren's Chicago financial empire.

WASH. In ''The End of Hate,'' he is a Confederate soldier under General Jubal Early and is killed by advancing Union troops.

WASHINGTON. In ''The Diamond as Big as the Ritz,'' he was the indiscreet, alcoholic brother of Braddock Tarleton Washington, who felt obliged to silence him by murdering him.

WASHINGTON, BRADDOCK TARLETON. In ''The Diamond as Big as the Ritz,'' he is Fitz-Norman Culpepper Washington's son, inherits the diamond mountain, and develops it and the attendant fortune. At forty, he blows up the mountain and dies with his wife and their son, Percy Washington.

WASHINGTON, FITZ-NORMAN CULPEPPER. In ''The Diamond as Big as the Ritz,'' he was Braddock Tarleton Washington's father. At the close of the Civil War, he went west with his ignorant slaves and discovered and exploited the Montana diamond mountain by conducting canny overseas sales. He died in 1900.

WASHINGTON, JASMINE. In ''The Diamond as Big as the Ritz,'' she is Braddock Tarleton Washington's daughter and Kismine Washington's older sister. She escapes with Kismine and her boyfriend, John T. Unger.

WASHINGTON, KISMINE. In ''The Diamond as Big as the Ritz,'' she is Braddock Tarleton Washington's daughter, sixteen, falls in love with John T. Unger, and escapes with him and her older sister, Jasmine Washington.

WASHINGTON, MRS. BRADDOCK TARLETON. In ''The Diamond as Big as the Ritz,'' she is the mother of Jasmine Washington, Kismine Washington, and Percy Washington. She perishes in the ruin of the diamond mountain.

WASHINGTON, PERCY. In ''The Diamond as Big as the Ritz,'' he is Braddock Tarleton Washington's son and the brother of Jasmine Washington and Kismine Washington. He invites his fellow student at St. Midas School John T. Unger to visit his father's diamond mountain. Percy dies in the explosion.

WASHINGTON, R. In *Thoughtbook*, he is a male friend.

WASHMER, ELAINE. In ''Forging Ahead,'' she is named by Rhoda Sinclair as her best friend. Elaine is a guest at Benjamin Reilly's dull dinner party, which Basil Duke Lee must attend.

WATCHMAN, BILL. In " 'Send Me In, Coach,' " he is Dick Playfair in the play he and other boys rehearse. Bill learned earlier of his father Cyrus K. Watchman's suicide. Bill wants to stay with the Old Man and Rickey and grow up to resemble them.

WATCHMAN, CYRUS K. In " 'Send Me In, Coach,' " he was Bill Watchman's father. Though acquitted in a court case, he committed suicide.

WATERBURY, ERNEST. In "A Woman with a Past," he is a Yale student and the nephew of Miss Brereton, proprietress of the school attended by Josephine Perry. When he visits the school, Josephine accidentally slips because her shoes are wet and falls into his unwilling embrace. When he does not explain, she is expelled.

WATERBURY, JUDGE. In "The Swimmers," he is a proud Virginian who calls on Henry Clay Marston in Paris and invites him to return to Richmond to make more money than he can in France. Waterbury introduces him to Wiese, a wealthy Southerner. When Marston goes home, he works for Waterbury's Calumet Tobacco Company.

WATERSON, MISS. In *This Side of Paradise*, she is a member of Alec Connage's bunch having fun in Atlantic City.

WATTS. In "Dalyrimple Goes Wrong," she is one of two or more persons whose residences Bryan Dalyrimple does not rob.

WAYBURN, NED. In "Two Wrongs," he is a dance instructor from whom, according to Emmy Pinkard, her dance instructor, Georgia Berriman Campbell of Delaney, South Carolina, took lessons.

WAYNE, JILL. In *This Side of Paradise*, she is part of Alec Connage's group having fun in Atlantic City. When she is about to be caught by hotel guards in Alec's room, Amory Blaine takes the blame.

WEATHERBEE, PERCY B. In *The Beautiful and Damned*, he is an architect Anthony Patch tries to sell "Heart Talks" shares to. Weatherbee quickly dismisses him.

WEATHERBY, MRS. In *This Side of Paradise*, she is Sally Weatherby's mother, who makes Isabelle Borgé welcome in her Minneapolis home.

WEATHERBY, SALLY. In *This Side of Paradise*, she is Amory Blaine's childhood friend in Minneapolis. The name Sally is spelled "Sallee" in a love poem he writes. He meets Isabelle Borgé when she is a guest in the Weatherbys' home.

WEAVER, BETTE. In ''Her Last Case,'' she is the nurse whom Dr. Harrison, her associate in Baltimore, recommends to become Ben Dragonet's private nurse in Virginia, as her last case before her marriage to Dr. Howard Carney of New York City. She falls in love with Ben, likes his little daughter, Amalie Eustace Bedford Dragonet, and is happy when Amalie's mother, Ben's ex-wife, leaves the child with Ben and departs. Bette writes to Howard to the effect that her last case will last a lifetime.

WEAVER, JOHN V. A. (1893–1938). (Full name: John Van Alstyn Weaver.) Editor and writer. Born in Charlotte, North Carolina, he earned an A.B. at Hamilton College (1914) and did editorial work in Chicago and Brooklyn (1916–1924). He married actress Margaret (''Peggy'') Wood in 1924 and freelanced until 1928. He was a Paramount-Famous-Lesky screenwriter (1928–1931). He freelanced in Hollywood (1931–1938) and was drama critic for *Esquire* (1932–1935). He wrote six books of verse, beginning with *In American* (1921), which contains twenty-one poems in slang. He also wrote six novels, beginning with *Margey Wins the Game* (1922), and coauthored a play (1926). He was a idealistic humorist who wrote about the concerns of ordinary people.

Soon after Weaver published his interview of Fitzgerald in the *Brooklyn Eagle* (25 March 1922), Fitzgerald reviewed *Margey Wins the Game*. He begins by trying to summarize the plot in what Fitzgerald calls Weaver's own uniquely humorous ''semi-dialect prose,'' gives up, identifies the heroine as a wealthy wallflower, praises Weaver's handling of Chicago and Chicagoans, and hopes for more such fiction from Weaver. In letters to closer friends, however, Fitzgerald expressed a distaste for both Weaver and his writing.

WEBB. In ''Babylon Revisited,'' he was a young man at a party in Paris attended by Charles J. Wales and his wife, Helen Wales. Her kissing Webb caused Charlie to return home alone and lock her out.

WEEKS-TENLIFFE, MRS. In ''The Rubber Check,'' she is a person who was killed in an airplane crash. Val Schuyler pretends he was at Deauville with her and might have taken the same airplane.

WEEMS, WEASEL. In ''The Freshest Boy,'' he is bully Dan Haskins's toady on the St. Regis football team, or perhaps only in Basil Duke Lee's imagination.

WEICKER. In ''The Hotel Child,'' he is the hotel manager. He is wrongly critical of Fifi Schwartz and rightly suspicious of Count Stanislas Karl Joseph Borowki.

WEINSTEIN, NATHAN. *See* West, Nathanael.

WELLES, ORSON (1915–1985). (Full name: George Orson Welles.) Movie actor and director. Born in Kenosha, Wisconsin, he was an actor in Dublin's Gate Theatre in 1931, directed and starred in *Macbeth* in 1936, cofounded the Mercury Theatre in 1937, and adapted H. G. Wells's* *The War of the Worlds* in a scary radio broadcast aired in 1938. In 1941 came *Citizen Kane*, his first and finest movie, after which he did much more work both in the United States and in Europe. A genius given to posturing, Welles demeaned his talent by narrating documentaries and doing commercials. In ''Pat Hobby and Orson Welles,'' he is announced as coming to the movie set. Pat Hobby, made up to look like Welles as a joke, upsets the crowd awaiting the real Welles.

Bibliography: Frank Brady, *Citizen Welles: A Biography of Orson Welles* (New York: Scribner's, 1989).

WELLS, H. G. (1866–1946). English novelist, historian, and sociologist. He was born in Bromley, Kent. After being apprenticed to a pharmacist and then a draper, he graduated in 1890 from a normal school in science, taught until 1893, and became a versatile author. He wrote science fiction, humorous novels, and dystopian, sociopolitical problem works. His best-known titles include *The Time Machine* (1895), *The Island of Doctor Moreau* (1896), *The Invisible Man* (1897), *The War of the Worlds* (1898), *Kipps* (1905), *Tono-Bungay* (1909), *The History of Mr. Polly* (1910), and *An Experiment in Autobiography* (1934). In a review in 1917 of Wells's *God, the Invisible King*, Fitzgerald says that Wells, along with other specified writers, has rediscovered God, adds little to our knowledge, but neatly calls God both creator and redeemer. In 1917 Fitzgerald regarded *The New Machiavelli* (1911) by Wells as the best English novel of the century. Early in his career, Fitzgerald was subject to two influences from Wells, who saturated his novels with details and whose heroes are often in quest of something. These influences are both notable in *This Side of Paradise*. In his 1921 review of *Three Soldiers* by John Dos Passos,* Fitzgerald decries Wells's influence on younger writers. In ''College of One'' Fitzgerald makes significant use of Wells's *The Outline of History* (1920).

Bibliography: Richard Hauer Costa, *H. G. Wells* (New York: Twayne, 1967); Michael Frost, *H. G.: The History of Mr. Wells* (Washington, D.C.: Counterpoint, 1995).

WELLS, MRS. In ''Family in the Wind,'' she is a woman who, along with the Red Cross, temporarily cares for little Helen Kilrain after the first tornado killed the girl's father.

WENDELL, PETER BOYCE. In ''Head and Shoulders,'' he is a columnist who praises Marcia Meadow's theater act and thus gives her a break. Later, he writes a rave review of her autobiographical novel.

WEST, JEBBY. In "The Bridal Party," she is a friend of Michael Curly and Caroline Dandy. She gives a tea party in Paris to honor Caroline before Caroline's marriage. Both Michael and Caroline attend.

WEST, NATHANAEL (1903–1940). Novelist and screenwriter. Born Nathan Weinstein in New York City, he attended public schools indifferently and never graduated from high school. In 1921 he used an altered transcript and entered Tufts College (now Tufts University), but flunked out after one term. He transferred to Brown University by using the transcript of another Nathan Weinstein and graduated in 1924 with a Ph.B. A close friend at Brown was S. J. Perelman, later West's brother-in-law, a versatile author, a Hollywood scriptwriter, and an acquaintance of Fitzgerald's. Weinstein worked on construction for his father and in 1926 legally changed his name to Nathanael West. He was in Paris briefly (October 1926–January 1927), but his father's slumping business required his return home. He was a hotel manager in New York (1927–1932), during which time he made friends with Lillian Hellman, William Carlos Williams, and other writers and published *The Dream Life of Balso Snell* (1931), a parody of Western ideals. In 1933 he published *Miss Lonelyhearts*, featuring an advice columnist confronting a chaotic world; he also edited the satirical magazine *Americana* for a few months and then went to Hollywood as a contract scriptwriter. In 1934 he published *A Cool Million: The Dismantling of Lemuel Pitkin*, an anti–Horatio Alger exposé of the spurious American Dream. In Hollywood again (1935–1940), he wrote scenarios for low pay, was occasionally unemployed and ill, coauthored an antiwar play, *Good Hunting*, which closed on Broadway after two performances (1939), enjoyed hunting trips with William Faulkner and other writers in Hollywood, and wrote at high pay for various studios. He published *The Day of the Locust* (1939), a bitter view of the underside of Hollywood replete with gangsters, illegal boxing matches and cockfights, and Mexican smugglers. In April 1940 he married Eilen McKenney and in December, while returning from a hunting trip in Mexico, caused an automobile accident near El Centro, California, that killed his wife and himself—one day after Fitzgerald died.

Fitzgerald, in his Introduction to the Modern Library reprint of *The Great Gatsby* praised West, who therefore, although he had not yet met Fitzgerald, wrote to him on 11 September 1934 requesting a letter of recommendation to accompany his application for a Guggenheim fellowship. Fitzgerald sent a letter (25 September) to the Guggenheim trustees defining West as having the potential to lead in the field of American fiction. Despite letters also from Malcolm Cowley* and Edmund Wilson,* West did not receive a grant. Both *Miss Lonelyhearts* and *The Day of the Locust* show the influence of *The Great Gatsby*. Fitzgerald, who relished *The Day of the Locust*, wrote to Perelman (7 June 1939) to praise it. His comments were quoted on the dust jacket of a 1950 reprint of the novel. By late 1940 Fitzgerald, Sheilah Graham,* and the Wests were congenial friends.

Bibliography: Rita Barnard, *The Great Depression and the Culture of Abundance: Kenneth Fearing, Nathanael West, and Mass Culture in the 1930s* (Cambridge, England: Cambridge University Press, 1995); Robert Emmet Long, *Nathanael West* (New York: Ungar, 1985); Jay Martin, ''Fitzgerald Recommends Nathanael West for a Guggenheim,'' *FH/A1971*, 302–4.

WESTGATE. In ''The Passionate Eskimo,'' he is Edith Cary's friend. They argued when his father was sued for breach of promise and the young man pretended he was the one being sued. It took a while for him to pay off the resulting debts. Pan-e-troon locks the two young people in a room, where they become reconciled.

WETHERBY, CECILE. In *Assorted Spirits*, she is Peter Wetherby's daughter. She loves and will marry William Chapman.

WETHERBY, PETER. In *Assorted Spirits*, he is the father of Richard Wetherby and Cecile Wetherby and the brother of Amelia Hendrix, who calls herself Madame Zada the medium. They live at 225 Greenbriar Street, near Miss Spigot, who lives at 225 Greenwood Place. Peter must sell his house for $10,000 to save his business. He hires Madame Zada to rid his house of ghosts so that Josephus Hendrix, who wishes to buy it, will not force him to lower the price because of any alleged ghosts.

WETHERBY, RICHARD (''DICKIE''). In *Assorted Spirits*, he is Peter Wetherby's son. He is supposedly writing a play called *The Dappled Dawn*. Second Story Salle pretends to be interested in it so she can rob him of the $10,000 with which Josephus Hendrix has entrusted him. Dickie's speech is comical because he has hay fever. He says his pen name is Richard Cartridgebelt Wetherby.

WHALEY, MARICE. In ''First Blood,'' she is Anthony Harker's casual friend who lives in an unprepossessing home.

WHALEY, MISS. In ''The Rubber Check,'' she is a worker in Percy Wrackham's office. When Val Schuyler is snubbed at dances, she no longer reads about him in society columns.

WHARTON. In ''The Scandal Detectives'' and ''A Night at the Fair,'' this is the name of the family in whose yard the boys and girls gather socially.

WHARTON, EDITH (1862–1937). Author. She was born Edith Newbold Jones into a rich, reserved family in New York City. She led a sheltered life there, in Newport, Rhode Island, and abroad, was tutored, became a debutante at seventeen, and in 1885 married an unstable Boston socialite, Edward

(''Teddy'') Robbins Wharton. Disliking the life of a high-society wife, she turned for therapy in the 1890s to writing short stories. Immediate success followed. Her early novels include *The Valley of Decision* (1902), *The House of Mirth* (1905, a best-seller), *Ethan Frome* (1911), *The Reef* (1912), and *The Custom of the Country* (1913). After a secret love affair or two and because of her otherwise deteriorating marriage, she obtained a divorce from Teddy, neurasthenic and also unfaithful, in Paris in 1913. She had established a permanent residence in France three years earlier. Wharton devoted great energy to relief work during World War I. Later novels such as *The Age of Innocence* (1920, perhaps her finest work) and *A Son at the Front* (1923) show great power. In her best work she skewers the leisure class, satirizes the vulgarity of the newly rich, and dramatizes how marriage can trap and suffocate people, especially women. Among her forty-seven books are nonfiction accounts of travel in France, Italy, and Morocco; *The Writing of Fiction* (1923), a handbook; and *A Backward Glance* (1934), a memoir. She numbered among her friends Bernard Berenson, Walter Berry, Paul Bourget, Morton Fullerton, William Dean Howells, Henry James, and Percy Lubbock.

Fitzgerald long admired Wharton's work. In 1920, when he first met her in the office of Scribner's, their publisher, he knelt at her feet and intoned admiration for the author of *Ethan Frome*. In 1923 he wrote titles for the silent movie based on *The Glimpses of the Moon* by Wharton (1922). In June 1925 she wrote to Fitzgerald to commend *The Great Gatsby* but deplored its not presenting the hero's early life more completely. The following month she invited Fitzgerald and Zelda Sayre Fitzgerald* to tea at her home just outside Paris. Zelda declined, saying Wharton would patronize them; but Fitzgerald went, found the event stiff and dull, and tried to liven it by an anecdote about an American couple spending a night in a brothel by mistake. He probably did not say he and Zelda were that couple, as often alleged. Wharton is mentioned in ''This Is a Magazine.''

Bibliography: R.W.B. Lewis, *Edith Wharton* (New York: Harper and Row, 1975).

WHARTON, ELSIE. In ''The Adolescent Marriage,'' she is George Wharton's ineffectual wife and Lucy Wharton Clark's mother.

WHARTON, GEORGE. In ''The Adolescent Marriage,'' he is a Philadelphia businessman, Elsie Wharton's husband, and Lucy Wharton Clark's father. Wharton asks his influential friend Chauncey Garnett to persuade Llewellyn Clark and Lucy to prevent gossip by remaining married. When Garnett, failing to do so, appears to have arranged for an annulment, the Whartons announce their daughter's impending marriage to George Hemmick, Wharton's representative in Chicago.

"WHAT A HANDSOME PAIR!" (1932). Short story. (Characters: Anne, Celie, Gus Meyers, Joe Morgan, Oldhorne, Helen Van Beck Oldhorne, Stuart

Oldhorne, Mrs. Cassius Ruthven, Amy Van Beck, Betty Van Beck, Josie Van Beck, Teddy Van Beck.) In 1902 in New York City, well-to-do Helen Van Beck breaks her engagement to her cousin, Teddy Van Beck, saying they are too unlike to get married, since she likes riding horses, tennis, and golf, while he is a musician. He is afraid of horses, and she has a tin ear. In 1903 she marries her new friend Stuart Oldhorne, a Yale athlete, former Rough Rider, and adept polo, golf, and tennis player. One day Helen calls on Teddy and finds him married to Betty, an agreeable Irish girl, a little older than he and formerly a waitress. After the 1907 panic, during which Stuart loses his patrimony, he turns to managing a racing stable. Teddy, something of a philanderer, advances as a concert pianist and composer. One day Helen's polo game is shortened so the men's match can start on time. Infuriated, she lets Teddy, there watching her, drive her to New York to the theater. Stuart follows, goes to Teddy's home, meets Betty and agrees with her that incompatibility is a good basis for marriage, learns Helen and Teddy are at his studio, and proceeds to go there. Betty phones Teddy to get his story straight for Stuart and then come home—quietly so as not to awaken their child, Josie. Teddy returns and assures Betty of his abiding if moderate love. By the time World War I has started, Stuart is a professional at an exclusive golf club, Helen is winning amateur golf tournaments, and the two park their children in New York schools and often house-sit for the rich and idle. Trying to conceal his jealousy at her success, Stuart volunteers in 1915 for the Canadian air force but is rejected because a duffer's stray golf ball injured his left eye earlier. Meanwhile Helen, thinking he is going to France, joins the Red Cross and does go, leaving him lonely. Teddy gives a concert at Carnegie Hall, sees Stuart on the street, and invites him home to a party, where Stuart lectures Mrs. Cassius Ruthven, a moralistic guest, that cooperative marriages end up being competitive. In 1918 Stuart died in combat, presumably with American forces, in France.

This story has autobiographical tinges. Fitzgerald and his wife, Zelda Sayre Fitzgerald,* competed as writers, with Zelda remaining the clever amateur. Fitzgerald may have partly patterned Teddy Van Beck after Theodore Chanler, an American pianist and composer he met in the 1920s, and partly patterned Stuart Oldhorne after Tommy Hitchcock, a World War I war hero and a fine American polo player.

Bibliography: James L. W. West III, " 'What a Handsome Pair!' and the Institution of Marriage," Bryer, *New Essays*, 219–31.

"WHAT BECAME OF OUR FLAPPERS AND SHEIKS?" (1925). Essay. (Characters: Madame Glynn, Marjorie, Thomas, Tommy.) Fitzgerald says life has changed. Young ladies don't check their corsets before a dance, as rumored. Boys of fourteen don't aspire to unusual careers. He traces the early life of Tommy, from driving his girlfriend Marjorie about (no doubt harmlessly) to prep school to tutoring school to knowing chorus girls in New York to flunking out at Yale or Princeton to returning home at twenty—healthy, polished, "fast," and parasitic. Over the hill now, Fitzgerald likes food more than music, prefers old-fashioned dance steps, and watches life's comedy from a chaperone's vantage point. In parallel columns of this essay, Fitzgerald wife, Zelda Sayre Fitzgerald,* wrote about flappers.

"WHAT I THINK AND FEEL AT 25" (1922). Essay. (Character: Percy.) An old family friend asks Fitzgerald why he writes pessimistically when he is young, happy, and successful. The friend leaves when Fitzgerald starts to explain. A reporter asks why he and his wife plan to commit suicide at thirty and wonders if "petting parties" menace the Constitution, but leaves as Fitzgerald begins to say no. Three years ago he was invulnerable to friends' problems and public disasters; at twenty-five, he is wounded by criticism of his family. In prep school he wasted time trying to impress a dullard fellow student named Percy. In the army he was called morbid for writing a novel but was praised when *This Side of Paradise* succeeded. He plans to work hard until sixty, then write a Ben Franklin–like autobiography, but wishes he could loaf now. If you try hard for what you want, you will get it and be happy after twenty-five; if you do not, others will exploit you until you die, but you will have fun before twenty-five. Don't avoid fun now by planning too far ahead. Revealing a mean streak, he confesses a dislike of old people for professing to have benefited from their experiences when most of them have had few experiences and have gained nothing from them. Women of thirty, called lucky to be wives and mothers, are really more vulnerable than when they were younger. After thirty, spouses lack spontaneity. Children are hurt by conceited, domineering, self-sacrificial parents. Yet marriage is our best institution. Whereas allegedly experienced elders run things, only the young matter.

"WHAT I WAS ADVISED TO DO—AND DIDN'T" (1922). Though advised to give up writing ill-paying short stories and stick to his job in the copy department, Fitzgerald declined.

"WHAT KIND OF HUSBANDS DO 'JIMMIES' MAKE?" (1924). Essay. (Characters: Eddie, Jimmy, Mrs. Jimmy, Jimmy Worthington.) A typical "Jimmy" is Jimmy Worthington, the alcoholic son of a man enriched by wartime food hoarding. Welcome at French restaurants for his money, Jimmy talks only about his binges, is conservative politically, and gets out of scrapes because his father bribes the police. Jimmy's wife must go along or leave. By the time they have three half-wanted children, he is already playing around. Hypocritically critical of his children, he sends them to ruinous private schools, is a show-off spender, and cannot hold a job. Unlike the strong British leisure class, rich American families lack a sense of responsibility and devolve from riches to weakness and poverty. Wealthy American women are not idealistic but are social climbers, demean the less well-to-do, and weaken their sons. Typical Jimmies grow selfish, careless with money, and sinful. Whereas the British leisure class had produced leaders in many fields, the best American inventors, politicians, and writers have sprung from poor families. Flashy girls, gamblers, and criminals are the main recipients of the lost wealth of American moneyed families. When will our Jimmies become responsible and stop ruining their sons?

WHAT'S-HER-NAME. In "On a Play Twice Seen," she is a character in the play. She faints in the arms of Mr. X when he defends divorce.

WHEELOCK, DR. DICK. (Full name: Dr. R[ichard]. H. Wheelock.) In " 'Trouble,' " he is the handsome resident in orthopedics, twenty-eight, at the hospital where Glenola McClurg is a nurse. She falls in love with him. He treats her broken ankle. Unknown to her, he gets her reinstated when she is fired. She breaks her engagement to Frederic Winslow, after which Dr. Wheelock will operate on her neglected ankle.

WHEELOCK, MRS. In "Fate in Her Hands," she is a dean's wife whose phone call to Carol Kastler contributes to Carol's saving her husband Benjamin Kastler's life.

"WHEN WE MEET AGAIN" (1981). Poem. The persona knows they will forget what they experienced together, although they once thought their love would last.

WHILOMVILLE, GEORGE. In "Strange Sanctuary," this is an alias of Dodo Gilbert. *See* Gilbert, Dodo.

WHISPER. In "Her Last Case," he is Ben Dragonet's big, loyal African American servant.

WHITBY, HARRY. In "Indecision," he is a Cambridge University hockey player and a member of Tommy McLane's party that goes sleighing to Doldorp one evening.

WHITE, SAM. In "Basil and Cleopatra," he was evidently a successful football player at Princeton.

WHITE, TARZAN. In "Pat Hobby's Secret," he was evidently a boxer. Smith, the bouncer at Conk's Los Angeles bar, went an hour with him.

WHITE, WYLIE. In *The Last Tycoon*, he is a screenwriter, about thirty, for Monroe Stahr. White is clever but alcoholic and would like to become intimate with Cecelia Brady, who puts him off but uses him.

WHITEBAIT, S. B. In *The Great Gatsby*, Nick Carraway lists Whitebait's name on a timetable as one of Jay Gatsby's summer guests. He is over sixty.

WHITEHEAD, JACK. In "The Bowl," he is a Princeton football team player, at end.

WHITNEY, KNOWLETON. In "Myra Meets His Family," he is the young scion Myra Harper decides would do as a husband, and they fall in love. When he suspects her eye is on his family fortune, he hires actors to impersonate his unattractive parents in the Whitney family mansion in Westchester County to scare her off. She discovers his plot; and although he confesses, apologizes, and professes his true love, she tricks him into a sham marriage and deserts him on their honeymoon train.

WHITNEY, LUDLOW. In "Myra Meets His Family," he is the real father of Knowleton Whitney and is evidently a successful Wall Street financier.

WHITNEY, MRS. LUDLOW. In "Myra Meets His Family," she is the real mother of Knowleton Whitney, through whom Myra Harper learns the mother wants a titled daughter-in-law.

"WHO'S WHO—AND WHY" (1920). Essay. Fitzgerald says he scribbled on his school books, went to boarding school, saw a musical comedy, and wrote an operetta for the Triangle Club at Princeton. Beginning in 1917 he was an infantry officer and started a novel called "The Romantic Egoist." After the war he wrote advertising copy, revised his novel as *This Side of Paradise* back home in St. Paul, wrote numerous short stories, and got married.

" 'WHY BLAME IT ON THE POOR KISS IF THE GIRL VETERAN OF MANY PETTING PARTIES IS PRONE TO AFFAIRS AFTER MARRIAGE?' " (1924). Essay. (Characters: Augustus, Clara, Georgianna, Harry.) Most of us are silently hypocritical about morals. Maybe four-fifths of married couples are faithful. Monogamy, unnatural and falsely propped up as it is, may be our best solution even though its very security makes some husbands bullies, some wives shrews, and infidelity frequent. Harry and Georgianna, though tempted to stray, are happily wed and faithful to each other—more firmly because each orders the other not to fool around. Two dangers to marriage are alcohol and large age differences. Premarital physical contacts should be commended as natural, romantic, and historically established precedents to good marriages. We should not blame juvenile petting for infidelity in young wives, since they were probably born oversexed anyway. Amorously experienced girls may make the most faithful wives. Conclusions? Fitzgerald favors early marriages, easy divorces, and more than one child per couple. Rare but uniquely blessed in our wretched world is a truly joyful marriage.

WIDDLE, JOSEPH. In ''On Your Own,'' he is mentioned as a passenger aboard the ship taking Evelyn Lovejoy and others to New York. He is accompanied by his wife and their six children.

WIDDLE, MRS. JOSEPH. In ''On Your Own,'' she, with her husband and their six children, is mentioned as aboard the ship taking Evelyn Lovejoy and others to New York.

WIDDLESTEIN, R. MEGGS. In *The Beautiful and Damned*, he is the author of a booklet titled ''Success as a Writer Made Easy'' which Anthony Patch consults before writing unsuccessful short stories.

WIESE. In ''The Swimmers,'' he is a wealthy Southerner to whom Judge Waterbury introduces Henry Clay Marston in Paris. When Marston returns to Richmond to work for Waterbury, he and his wife, Choupette Marston, meet Wiese's tricky son, Charles Wiese.

WIESE, CHARLES. In ''The Swimmers,'' he is Judge Waterbury's friend Wiese's son in Richmond, reputedly worth $40 million. Some time after Henry Clay Marston, his wife Choupette Marston, and their two young sons return from Paris, so that Marston can work for Waterbury, Choupette and Charles become lovers. When Marston demands a divorce and custody of the boys, Charles boasts that money is power and produces a medical document he obtained by bribery certifying Marston as an unfit parent. Marston threatens to let Charles and Choupette drown—all three are in a boat with a motor gone dead, and only he can swim to alert rescuers—until they legally relinquish custody.

WIESS, MISS. In ''Between Three and Four,'' she is one of Howard Butler's office workers.

WIGGINS. In ''Family in the Wind,'' he was the proprietor of the Bending hospital Dr. Forrest Janney orders broken open so he can treat persons injured by the first tornado.

WILBURHAZY. In *Tender Is the Night*, she is a woman Dick Diver, while in Innsbruck, imagines sleeping with on the Riviera.

WILCOX, RENÉ. In ''Teamed with Genius,'' he is the British writer with whom Pat Hobby's boss, Jack Berners, teams Pat. Wilcox avoids Pat for a while, writes alone, and sends him a discarded script, pretending it is his. Unknown to Pat, Wilcox and Katherine Hodge, Pat's newly assigned secretary, like each other and she was in on Wilcox's scheme. Berners likes Wilcox's new script. Wilcox wants Berners to keep Pat around because Wilcox wants to write a play about him.

WILKINS. In *Coward*, he was a Confederate Army commissary officer. When he was shot, Lieutenant Charles Douglas replaced him.

WILKINSON, DR. HARVEY. In "A Full Life," he is the physician who treats Gwendolyn Davies after her leap from the skyscraper. He follows her career; when he is forty in 1937, he finds her in a Long Island circus and dies with her when she blows up.

WILKINSON, MRS. HARVEY. In "A Full Life," she is the physician's wife, described as practical.

WILL. In "A Snobbish Story," he is the brother of Mrs. Herbert T. Perry, whose husband pays off a floozy to stay away from him. He can now return home from Hawaii.

WILLARD, KEN. In *The Last Tycoon*, he is a character in a movie Monroe Stahr criticizes before ordering changes.

WILLIAM. In "More Than Just a House," he is the Gunthers' fat black servant. Lew Lowrie rescues him after a tree falls on his lean-to near the Gunther mansion during a storm.

WILLIAM II (Kaiser Friedrich Wilhelm Viktor Albert). In "The Prince of Pests." *See* Kaiser.

WILLIAMS, KITTY. In *Thoughtbook*, she is Fitzgerald's special friend. They kiss often and dance together happily.

WILLINGS, PRIVATE. In *Coward*, he is a Union soldier, along with Private Barkis. Jim Holworthy scares Willings away from pillaging by offering to play a kind of Russian roulette with him.

WILLOUGHBY. In "Dalyrimple Goes Wrong," he is a person whose residence Bryan Dalyrimple does not rob.

WILLOUGHBY. In "One of My Oldest Friends," he is a movie-writing friend of Marion and Michael. They plan to invite him and his wife to their party for Charley Hart.

WILLOUGHBY, MRS. In "One of My Oldest Friends," she is the actress-wife of Willoughby. Marion and Michael plan to invite them to their party for Charley Hart.

WILSON. In *The Beautiful and Damned*, he is the president of the bond firm of Wilson, Hiemer and Hardy, where Anthony Patch works briefly.

WILSON, BIG JACK. In '' 'Boil Some Water—Lots of It,' '' he is a director at the movie studio where Pat Hobby works.

WILSON, EDMUND (1895–1972). Literary and social critic. He was born in Red Bank, New Jersey, and attended Princeton University, where he edited the *Nassau Literary Magazine*, met Fitzgerald, John Biggs, Jr.,* and John Peale Bishop* among other talented men, and graduated in 1916. He was a *New York Evening Sun* reporter (1916–1917) and served in the army in the United States and France (1917–1919). He was the managing editor of *Vanity Fair* (1920–1921), a contributor to and an editor of the *New Republic* (1921–1940), literary editor of the *New Yorker* (1943–1948) and an occasional contributor to the *New Yorker* then and later, and a versatile writer. Wilson disputed with the Internal Revenue Service, which in 1958 charged him for failing to file tax returns and for not paying taxes from 1946 to 1955. In 1960 the IRS froze his sources of income. Entirely in the wrong, Wilson paid but turned the episode into a clever book. His major titles are *Axel's Castle: A Study in the Imaginative Literature of 1870–1930* (1931), *The American Jitters: A Year of the Slump* (1932), *The Triple Thinkers: Ten Essays on Literature* (1938, enl. ed. 1948), *To the Finland Station: A Study in the Writing and Acting of History* (1940), *Memoirs of Hecate County* (1946, rev. 1958), *The Shores of Light: A Literary Chronicle of the Twenties and Thirties* (1952), *The Scrolls from the Dead Sea* (1955, enl. eds. 1969, 1978), *Patriotic Gore: Studies in the Literature of the American Civil War* (1962), *The Cold War and the Income Tax: A Protest* (1963), *The Twenties: From Notebooks and Diaries of the Period* (1975), and *The Sixties: The Last Journal, 1960–1972* (1993). Wilson was married four times: to Mary Blair (1923, divorced 1928), to Margaret Canby (1930, widowered 1932), to Mary McCarthy (1938, divorced 1946), and to Elena Thornton (1946).

Fitzgerald, who met Wilson in 1915, called him by his nickname, Bunny. They collaborated with Bishop on *The Evil Eye: A Comedy in Two Acts*, a 1915–1916 Triangle Club musical. Fitzgerald asked for and obtained Wilson's useful if sarcastic comments on the manuscripts of *This Side of Paradise* and *The Beautiful and Damned*. In the latter, the admirable critical writing of Eugene Bronson is consciously parallel to Wilson's. Wilson liked much of Fitzgerald's work, envied him his financial success, warned him against remaining popular and hence shallow, and decried the abuse of his talent and his alcoholic lifestyle. Wilson punned on ''This Side of Paralyzed by F. Scotch Fitzgerald.'' He overvalued Fitzgerald's *The Vegetable* but rightly lauded *The Great Gatsby*. Fitzgerald felt intellectually inferior to Wilson, debased himself before Wilson, and boozily brooded over their relationship. In ''Handle with Care,'' Fitzgerald calls Wilson his ''intellectual conscience.'' After Fitzgerald's death, Wilson edited both *The Crack-Up* and *The Last Tycoon*. He authorized his fee for rather careless work on the latter to be sent to Zelda Sayre Fitzgerald* and Scottie.* *The Shores of Light* contains "A Weekend at Ellerslie," a revealing essay about the Fitzgeralds as hosts.

Bibliography: Milton A. Cohen, "Fitzgerald's Third Regret: Intellectual Pretense and the Ghost of Edmund Wilson,*" *Texas Studies in Literature and Language* 33 (Spring 1991): 64–88; Jeffrey Meyers, *Edmund Wilson: A Biography* (Boston: Houghton Mifflin, 1995).

WILSON, GEORGE B. In *The Great Gatsby*, he, in his mid-thirties, is a garage mechanic in a gas station between West Egg and New York. He and his wife, Myrtle Wilson, have lived there for eleven years. Thinking Jay Gatsby drove the car that killed Myrtle, Wilson kills Gatsby and then himself.

WILSON, JIM. In *This Side of Paradise*, he is a Princeton man Amory Blaine remembers, or pretends to remember, during a New York binge.

WILSON, MYRTLE. In *The Great Gatsby*, she is George B. Wilson's heavily sensual wife, in her mid-thirties. She is Tom Buchanan's mistress and consorts with him in a New York apartment, where they meet by pretending she is visiting her sister Catherine. Myrtle is killed when Tom's wife, Daisy Fay Buchanan, driving Jay Gatsby's car, hits her and speeds away. Daisy and Tom let Gatsby take the blame.

WILSON, WAVELINE. In "The Honor of the Goon," he is one of the students who called Ella Lei Chamoro a goon.

WINCHESTER, MARGARET. In *Thoughtbook*, she is a dancing friend.

WINEBRENNER. In *The Great Gatsby*, he is the owner of a New York poolroom where Meyer Wolfsheim says he first saw Jay Gatsby, then looking for work.

WINFIELD, GEORGE. In "Six of One—," he, nineteen, lives in Ed Barnes's Ohio hometown. When Barnes learns George left school at his father's death, supported his family four years, and returned to finish high school, Barnes sends him to Yale, where he does well until he meets Beau Lebaume, Howard Kavenaugh, and Wister Schofield. When the four are involved in a drunk-driving accident, George is expelled. Wister Schofield recommends George to his father, for whom George and Wister's younger brother Charley work conscientiously and whose family business they now run.

WING, BESSIE LEIGHTON. In "News from Paris—Fifteen Years Ago," she is a family friend of Henry Haven Dell. When they chance to meet in Paris, she says she foolishly married at sixteen, is divorced, is going to break her engagement at lunch, and hopes to see him thereafter. They go to her apartment and then with her friend, Mary Tolliver, to an art show. Bessie is the ex-wife of Hershell Wing.

WING, HERSHELL. In ''News from Paris—Fifteen Years Ago,'' he is the ex-husband of Bessie Leighton Wing.

WINLOCK, BOMAR. In ''The Honor of the Goon,'' he is able to fall down stairs dramatically. When he stages such a fall in college, Ella Lei Chamoro is so frightened and sympathetic that he calls her a goon. Her relative Lei Chamoro avenges her honor by having him beaten.

WINSLOW. In '' 'Trouble,' '' he is Frederic Winslow's rich and pleasant father. The Winslows live in Virginia.

WINSLOW, CHARLOTTE. In ''A Freeze-Out,'' she is Pierce Winslow's wife and the mother of Forrest Winslow and Eleanor Winslow. Their parents' hypocritical snobbishness delays Forrest's romance with Alida Rikker.

WINSLOW, ELEANOR. In ''A Freeze-Out,'' she is the daughter, eighteen, of Pierce Winslow and Charlotte Winslow.

WINSLOW, FORREST. In ''A Freeze-Out,'' he is the son of wealthy Pierce Winslow and Charlotte Winslow. A Yale graduate, he has returned to Minnesota to work in his father's fur business. Snobbish at first, he drops Jane Drake in favor of delightful Alida Rikker. His decision to marry Alida, whose father has a criminal past, upsets his hypocritical parents. His best ally is Mrs. Hugh Forrest, his great-grandmother.

WINSLOW, FREDERIC (''FRED''). In '' 'Trouble,' '' he is nurse Glenola McClurg's alcoholic patient, falls in love with her, proposes to her, and is accepted. He breaks his promise not to drink excessively any more, and he is so jealous of Dr. Dick Wheelock that he fights with him and loses his bride-to-be.

WINSLOW, MRS. In '' 'Trouble,' '' she is alcoholic Frederic Winslow's mother. She admires nurse Glenola McClurg, who cared for her unbalanced son for six months. She wants them to get married but sadly understands when Glenola cancels plans to do so.

WINSLOW, PIERCE. In ''A Freeze-Out,'' he is Charlotte Winslow's wealthy husband and the father of Forrest Winslow and Eleanor Winslow. Rationalizing his hypocrisy, he attends the wedding ceremony uniting his son and Alida Rikkers, whose father has a shady past but valuable business connections.

"WINTER DREAMS" (1922). Short story. (Characters: Devlin, Green, Dexter Green, Hart, T. A. Hedrick, Hilda, Judy Jones, Mortimer Jones, Mrs. Mortimer Jones, Krimslich, McKenna, Martha, Sandwood, Scheerer, Irene Scheerer, Mrs. Scheerer, Lud Simms.) Dexter Green, fourteen, lives in Black Bear and caddies at the Sherry Island Golf Club in Minnesota, near Black Bear Lake. When pouty, oddly smiling Judy Jones, eleven, wants him to caddy for her but calls him "boy," he quits. He dreams of love and life with her. He graduates from a fine Eastern university, returns to the big city near the lake, and borrows money to buy a laundry partnership. When Dexter is twenty-three, an admiring businessman invites him to play golf with two businessmen, one of whom Judy hits in the stomach with a carelessly driven golf ball. Dexter notes her unique beauty. That evening he swims out on the lake to a float, near which Judy drives her motorboat. She invites him to dinner the following evening. After saying she has broken off with a man who told her he was poor, she gets Dexter to admit he is doing well in business, and the two enjoy a surfeit of kisses. She drives him to a picnic, goes off with another young man, and lies about it. They make up, and he asks her to marry him—unsuccessfully. Fitzgerald explains that no disillusion about Judy's world can cure Dexter's illusion of her attractiveness. After a year and a half of slights from Judy, who travels and is briefly engaged, Dexter proposes marriage to sweet, plump Irene Scheerer, whose parents respect him, and plans a June wedding with her. One evening in May Judy reappears, weaves her fiery magic, and proposes to Dexter. She leaves, and ten years pass, during which Dexter served in the army in World War I and became a great success in New York. He learns from Devlin, a visiting businessman from Detroit, that Judy's husband—Dexter had heard she was married—is an irresponsible alcoholic named Lud Simms, that she has children, has faded, and is not beautiful at all. Alone after Devlin leaves, Dexter weeps—not for Judy but for himself, because he no longer cares, because something in him is gone forever. In some ways "Winter Dreams" is a rehearsal for *The Great Gatsby*, as Fitzgerald noted in a letter to Max Perkins* (1 June 1925).

Bibliography: Kuehl.

WISE, BERNIE. In "Last Kiss," he is a shrewd Hollywood producer who dumps Pamela Knighton when she proves unable to act and troublesome.

WISKITH, SAMUEL K. In "Pat Hobby's College Days," he is the dean of students at the University of the Western Coast. Through Louie, Jim Kresge, and Kit Doolan, Pat Hobby is able to meet Wiskith. While Pat is trying to persuade him to arrange for a movie about campus life, Pat's secretary, Evylyn Lascalles, brings him back his empty liquor bottles in a pillow case.

WISTON, BISHOP. In *This Side of Paradise*, he is a Catholic Beatrice O'Hara Blaine appeals to for attention in an affected way.

WITCHCRAFT, SIR HOWARD GEORGE. In "Rags Martin-Jones and the Pr-nce of W-les," he is the captain of the *Majestic*, which transported Rags Martin-Jones from Cherbourg and Southampton to New York.

WOLCOTT, PERCY. In *The Beautiful and Damned*, he is a former boyfriend of Gloria Gilbert Patch. A Cornell athlete, he got fresh with Gloria, and she pushed him over an embankment. Later Gloria's friend Barley beat him up.

WOLF, CAPTAIN. In *The Beautiful and Damned*, he is a man Rachael Jerryl Barnes dates while her husband, Rodman Barnes, a captain, is overseas. Gloria Gilbert Patch dislikes seeing them kiss.

WOLFSHEIM, MEYER. In *The Great Gatsby*, he is a criminal associate of Jay Gatsby and boasts to Nick Carraway that he "made" Gatsby. One of Wolfsheim's many enterprises is called the Swastika Holding Company. Gatsby tells Nick that Wolfsheim fixed the 1919 World Series. He declines to attend Gatsby's funeral. Wolfsheim, whose name is spelled Wolfshiem in the manuscript, is based on Arnold Rothstein, a gambler, racketeer, and unsolved murder victim in 1928. Fitzgerald said he once met Rothstein.

Bibliography: Bruccoli, *Gatsby*; Dalton Gross and Mary-Jean Gross, "F. Scott Fitzgerald's American Swastika: The Prohibition Underworld and The Great Gatsby," *Notes and Queries*, n.s. 41 (September 1994): 377.

WOLL, R. PARKE. In "Pat Hobby's Secret," he is a Hollywood playwright. At a bar Pat tricks the drunken Woll into revealing the secret ending to his script. When Woll realizes the fact, he aims a blow at Pat but instead hits the bouncer, who then accidentally kills him.

"THE WOMAN FROM TWENTY-ONE" (1941). Short story. (Characters: Janice, Jidge, Mrs. Jiggs, Hat Milbank, Mrs. Richbitch, Elizabeth Torrence, Raymond Torrence.) Raymond Torrence, a successful writer, and his wife, Elizabeth Torrence, having lived in Java five years, return to New York to see his publisher. They lunch at the Stork Club, see Hat Milbank, an old friend, and attend a William Saroyan play. The performance is spoiled when a loud woman—designated as Mrs. Richbitch—keeps suggesting to her friends that they return to the Twenty-one Club. She is rude to him when he complains. Torrence decides he and Elizabeth should return home to their children in more civilized Java the next morning.

"A WOMAN WITH A PAST" (1930). Short story. (Characters: Ed Bement, Sergeant Boone, Miss Brereton, Book Chaffee, Miss Chambers, Jack Coe, Adele Craw, George Davey, Lillian Hammel, Dudley Knowleton, Miss Kwain, Herbert T. Perry, Josephine Perry, Ridgeway Saunders, Gordon Tinsley, Ernest Waterbury.) In February, Josephine Perry and Lillian Hammel, students at Miss Brereton's school, visit New Haven with their friend Adele Craw, and with Miss Chambers along as a chaperone. Josephine and Lillian meet Miss Brereton's nephew, Ernest Waterbury, and Adele's longtime friend, Dudley Knowleton. Both are Yale students, and Dudley is a school leader and star athlete. Adele and Dudley have leadership roles at the Yale prom being held at the armory. Josephine ignores her escort, Ridgeway Saunders, gets her hometown friend Ed Bement, also a Yale student, to dance her over toward Dudley, and makes an unsuccessful play for him by complimenting Adele. She is happy when Dudley drives her to her room to replace a stocking she tore, tries to get him to kiss her, but is merely returned to the dance. Another young man, Book Chaffee, sensing her willingness, takes her into a friend's room in the armory; but when someone locks them in, she requires Chaffee to help her escape through a window. At the Brereton school annual dance in March, Josephine is asked to be agreeable to Ernest but accidentally slips on the chapel steps, falls into his unwilling embrace, is seen, and is expelled from school. Her father, on business in New York, takes her to a family vacation at Hot Springs, where she plays golf and meets a Princeton dropout. At a dance they encounter Dudley, at Hot Springs for baseball practice. She plays up to him and suggests some horseback riding by moonlight—until he says Adele will be arriving tomorrow. Rebuffed and lonely, she knows her pride, not her heart, has been wounded. She eyes rich young Chicagoan Gordon Tinsley among the stags, concludes it is a mistake to exploit a man for quick pleasure and thus render unlikely a serious possibility later, but then strolls with the Princeton dropout to a moonlit bower outside.

WOODLEY. In "Your Way and Mine," he is Henry McComas's boss in the Broadway office. He fires McComas for taking too much time typing.

WOOKEY-WOOKEY. In *This Side of Paradise*, she is a deaf housekeeper at St. Regis when Amory Blaine is a student there.

WOOLEY. In "Family in the Wind," he is a person living outside Bending, Alabama. Dr. Forrest Janney asks someone to drive to the Wooley house for emergency medical supplies after the first tornado.

WORDEN, MRS. In "The Rough Crossing," she is Elizabeth D'Amido's chaperone. Since she is seasick during the voyage, she cannot supervise the girl's irresponsible conduct.

WORDSWORTH, CHARLIE. In "The Debutante," he is to be a guest at Helen Halycon's coming-out party. John Cannel, Helen's whilom boyfriend, is jealously aware that Helen now prefers Wordsworth to him.

WORTHINGTON, JIMMY. In ''What Kind of Husbands Do 'Jimmies' Make?,'' he is a typical wastrel son of wealth. He becomes a selfish husband and a neglectful, hypocritical father.

WRACKHAM, PERCY. In ''The Rubber Check,'' he is a New York broker, for whom Val Schuyler works for about two years. He is a Princeton man, and when Princeton has a bad football season he fires Val.

WRENN. In *The Beautiful and Damned*, he is a member of the firm of Wrenn and Hunt. Adam Patch boasts of having sent three members of the firm to the poorhouse.

WYLIE, TANADUKE. In *This Side of Paradise*, he is a puzzling poet in the Princeton sophomore class during Amory Blaine's senior year.

WYMAN, JOE. In *The Last Tycoon*, he is an employee Monroe Stahr orders to find the footage in which the actor Morgan's fly is unacceptably open.

X

X, CAPTAIN. In "The True Story of Appomattox," he is the officer who first divulges the fact that General Grant (*see* Grant, Ulysses Simpson) was offering to surrender to General Lee (*see* Lee, Robert E.) when the latter offered his sword to sharpen the former's broken pencil. Photographers and radio reporters captured the "surrender" scene.

X, MONSIGNOR. In "A Short Autobiography," he offered Fitzgerald a drink in New York City in 1917. He is probably Monsignor Cyril Sigourney Webster Fay.*

X, MR. In "On a Play Twice Seen," he is a character in a play which the poet sees. When Mr. X defends divorce, What's-Her-Name faints in his arms. (Is she happy or sad?) In *This Side of Paradise*, he is a character who defends divorce in a poem Amory Blaine writes during his senior year at Princeton.

Y

YARDLY. In *Tender Is the Night*, he is a person to whom Paul the Ritz concessionaire explains that Abe North is leaving France by ship the next day.

YOKE, MRS. In ''Does a Moment of Revolt Come Some Time to Every Married Man?,'' she is a person Mr. Egg thinks his wife can converse with uncontroversially, hence safely.

YOSFUGLU, YOLANDA. In *Tender Is the Night*, his is a name read in the *New York Herald.*

"YOU'LL BE RECKLESS IF YOU" (1981). Poem. The poet says that although you risk danger doing or not doing, you will be happy wooing but not happy not wooing.

"YOU'LL NEVER KNOW" (1981). Poem. The persona says you will not understand the spring within him.

"YOUR WAY AND MINE" (1927). Short story. (Characters: Russel Codman, Mrs. Corcoran, Mollie Drinkwater, Theodore Drinkwater, McComas, Henry McComas, Honoria McComas, Stella McComas, McTeague, Rose, Strangler, Max Van Camp, Woodley.) Henry (''Mac'') McComas, a big, healthy man of independent ways, is twenty-one in 1900. He is fired by Woodley from a Broadway brokerage office when he takes too long to type a letter. Mac marries Stella, his hometown sweetheart, in Utica, New York, in 1905. They have a son and also a daughter named Honoria. Mac, who has gained weight by 1907, goes into partnership with Theodore (''Ted'') Drinkwater in a New York exporting business. They do well, even though Ted as president of the company disapproves of Mac's seemingly lazy office hours. Ted is plodding, while Mac has intuitive commercial savvy. Mac, Stella, Ted, and his wife, Mollie, socialize but are never close. Stella fusses about Mac's weight. During the early years of World War I, the company does well, and the McComases think of buying a Long Island summer house. Ted tells Stella that if she can make Mac keep better office hours the firm will prosper more. He even recommends running up bills to motivate Mac to work harder. She pays $9,000 toward the summer house, which forces Mac to buckle down but also makes him nervous. One summer evening in 1916, while Ted is away on a business trip and Stella and the children are in the country, Mac has arranged for some foreign agents to meet at his New York home to finalize a huge purchase. He suffers a stroke in his bedroom and cannot summon the deaf housekeeper. The agents ring the doorbell in vain and depart. Ted dissolves his partnership with Mac, who takes until 1919 to recover, after which he starts a thriving business for himself, largely in a chain of hardware stores. By 1926 he is a millionaire, with two main associates, Russel Codman, Mac's righthand man, and Max Van Camp, less reliable but handsome. Both would like to marry Mac's lovely daughter Honoria, who is now nineteen. Mac offers a bonus to whoever competes better in six weeks against McTeague, a rival who is cutting into their efforts in Ohio, where Codman is to proceed, and in Indiana, which is Max's challenge. Codman does well by making plodding transactions while Max tries a daring scheme that fails. Honoria says Codman proposed to her in words echoing those Mac used on Stella, whereas Max was spontaneous. Mac advises her to marry Max, because Codman's way was Mac's and never his own. He says he did not show his liking for Max whereas Honoria did. Their ways are different. Although Fitzgerald wrote to his literary agent, Harold Ober,* (March 1926) that this was a lousy story, Ober sold it to the *Woman's Home Companion* for $1,750.

"YOU'VE DRIVEN ME CRAZY" (1981). Poem. Since the unbalanced addressee has disturbed him, he will disturb her in return.

YVAIN, MAURICE (1891–1965). French musical composer. In *Tender Is the Night*, Nicole Diver says the man who wrote *Pas sur la bouche* (Yvain's 1925 operetta in three acts) came to the Riviera one summer.

Z

ZAVRAS, MRS. PETE. In *The Last Tycoon*, she and her husband have given up their house, and she is ill.

ZAVRAS, PETE. In *The Last Tycoon*, he is a cameraman. When the false rumor was circulated that he was going blind, he became unemployed and grew disconsolate. He jumps off a building to commit suicide but only breaks his arm. Monroe Stahr, who admires his work, sends him to his oculist, and soon all is well. Zavras is so grateful that he offers to murder any enemy Stahr names. In one manuscript, Zavras was named Pedro Garcia.

ZELLER. In ''Magnetism,'' she is a crazy woman actor George Hannaford remembers sought to blackmail him.

ZIGLER, DR. In ''One Interne,'' he is a physician in the hospital. During the roast, when he is called Herpes Zigler, his laugh almost hides his wince.

"ZONE OF ACCIDENT" (1935). Short story. (Characters: Amy, Bach, Boone, Loretta Brooke, Willard Hubbel, Jacoby, Minnie the Moocher, Minska, Dr. Moore, E. P. Poole, George Schoatze, Thea Singleton, Dr. William Tullivers IV, Augustus Vogel, Miss Wales.) Handsome Dr. William Tullivers IV, accident room resident in a Baltimore hospital, is sad when his girlfriend, Amy, grows ambitious to have a Hollywood screen test. A man named Bach, who lives in Baltimore, brings in his daughter, Loretta Brooke, a rising movie star, with a knife wound down her back. They insist on no ruinous publicity. A disgruntled dance partner, during her visit in New York City, followed her to her father's home, demanded a job, and, when rebuffed, stabbed her and disappeared. Dr. Moore closes the wound while Bill donates blood for a transfusion. Loretta grows fond of Bill, who asks her to meet Amy and tell her a movie career is not glamorous. She does so. Bill contrasts Amy's dark, pictorial, and tiresome beauty with Loretta's ever-changing and fascinating beauty. Still ambitious, Amy tells Bill she is entering a pre-movie beauty contest. Influenza hits the city, resulting in a punishing caseload for Bill. When Loretta develops a fever, Bill puts off her worried producer, Minska, when he phones from Hollywood. One night she offers Bill a screen test and kisses him. Two days later he catches her heating her thermometer to continue her "fever" and thus prolong her hospital stay. Disgusted, he storms out to Amy's place, only to find her in an embrace with her Hollywood contact. Disgusted, he returns to the hospital, only to learn Loretta has checked out. Amy tells Bill her intimacy with the agent was to induce the fellow to put her dishonestly ahead of a beauty contestant from Washington. Bill, though indifferent, reads that the regional beauty contest is being held in a Baltimore hotel and Loretta is one of the three judges. He rushes to the hotel just in time to treat Amy's agent, slugged by the irate Washington beauty's escort. Returning to the contest, he sees the judges tallying their votes. Beckoning him aside, Loretta says her vote will break the tie, she will vote for Amy if he wishes, and she herself is tired of making movies. He asks her to vote for Amy. Loretta announces Amy's victory and catches Bill's ecstatic eye.

Bibliography

Bruccoli, Matthew J. *Some Sort of Epic Grandeur: The Life of F. Scott Fitzgerald*. New York: Harcourt Brace Jovanovich, 1981.

Bruccoli, Matthew J., ed. *As Ever, Scott Fitz—: Letters Between F. Scott Fitzgerald and His Literary Agent Harold Ober 1919–1940*. Philadelphia: J. B. Lippincott, 1972.

———. *F. Scott Fitzgerald: A Life in Letters*. New York: Charles Scribner's Sons, Macmillan Publishing, 1994.

———. *The Price Was High: The Last Uncollected Stories of F. Scott Fitzgerald*. New York: Harcourt Brace Jovanovich, 1979.

Bruccoli, Matthew J., and Jackson R. Bryer, eds. *F. Scott Fitzgerald in His Own Time, a Miscellany*. New York: Popular Library, 1971.

Bruccoli, Matthew J., and Margaret M. Duggan, eds. *Correspondence of F. Scott Fitzgerald*. New York: Random House, 1980.

Dixon, Wheeler Winston. *The Cinematic Vision of F. Scott Fitzgerald*. Ann Arbor: UMI Research Press, 1986.

Fryer, Sarah Beebe. *Fitzgerald's New Women: Harbingers of Change*. Ann Arbor: UMI Research Press, 1988.

Higgins, John A. *F. Scott Fitzgerald: A Study of the Stories*. Jamaica, N.Y.: St. John's University Press, 1971.

Kuehl, John, and Jackson R. Bryer, eds. *Dear Scott/Dear Max: The Fitzgerald-Perkins Correspondence*. New York: Charles Scribner's Sons, 1971.

Lanahan, Eleanor. *Scotty: The Daughter of . . . The Life of Frances Scott Fitzgerald Lanahan Smith*. New York: HarperCollins, 1995.

Lehan, Richard D. *F. Scott Fitzgerald and the Craft of Fiction*. Carbondale: Southern Illinois University Press, 1966.

Le Vot, André. *F. Scott Fitzgerald: A Biography*. Translated by William Byron. Garden City, N.Y.: Doubleday, 1983.

Mangum, Bryant. *A Fortune Yet: Money in the Art of F. Scott Fitzgerald's Short Stories*. New York: Garland Publishing, 1991.

Mellow, James R. *Invented Lives: F. Scott and Zelda Fitzgerald*. Boston: Houghton Mifflin, 1984.

Meyers, Jeffrey. *Scott Fitzgerald: A Biography*. New York: HarperCollins, 1994.

Milford, Nancy. *Zelda: A Biography*. New York: Harper & Row, 1970.

Miller, James E., Jr. *F. Scott Fitzgerald: His Art and His Technique*. New York: New York University Press, 1964.

Mizener, Arthur. *The Far Side of Paradise: A Biography of F. Scott Fitzgerald*. 2d ed. Boston: Houghton Mifflin, 1965.

Perosa, Sergio. *The Art of F. Scott Fitzgerald*. Translated by Charles Matz and Sergio Perosa. Ann Arbor: University of Michigan Press, 1965.

Petry, Alice Hall. *Fitzgerald's Craft of Fiction: The Collected Stories, 1920–1935*. Ann Arbor: UMI Research Press, 1989.

Phillips, Gene D. *Fiction, Film, and F. Scott Fitzgerald*. Chicago: Loyola University Press, 1986.

Piper, Henry Dan. *F. Scott Fitzgerald: A Critical Portrait*. New York: Holt, 1965.

Potts, Stephen W. *The Price of Paradise: The Magazine Career of F. Scott Fitzgerald*. San Bernardino, Calif.: Borgo Press, 1993.

Seiters, Dan. *Image Patterns in the Novels of F. Scott Fitzgerald*. Ann Arbor: UMI Research Press, 1986.

Sklar, Robert. *F. Scott Fitzgerald: The Last Laocoön*. New York: Oxford University Press, 1967.

Stern, Milton. *The Golden Moment: The Novels of F. Scott Fitzgerald*. Urbana: University of Illinois Press, 1970.

Turnbull, Andrew. *Scott Fitzgerald*. New York: Charles Scribner's Sons, 1962.

Turnbull, Andrew, ed. *The Letters of F. Scott Fitzgerald*. New York: Charles Scribner's Sons, 1963.

Index

Note: Peripheral and incidental references, including nonsubstantive ones to spouses and titles of works that did not evidently influence Fitzgerald, are omitted. Page references to main entries are in boldfaced type.

Abbot, Hamilton (''The Love Boat''), **1**
Abbot, The (''In the Darkest Hour''), **1**
Abbott, Charley (''Diamond Dickey and the First Law of Woman''), **1**
Abby (''The Intimate Strangers''), **1**
Abdul (''Indecision''), **1**
Abercrombie (*The Beautiful and Damned*), **1**
Abercrombie (''The Dance''), **1**
Abercrombie (''Two for a Cent''), **1–2**
Abercrombie, Bill (''The Dance''), **2**
Abrams, Mrs. (*Tender Is the Night*), **2**
Abrams, Stonewall Jackson (*The Great Gatsby*), **2**
Abrisini, Prince (''A Penny Spent''), **2**
'' 'Les Absents Ont Toujours Tort,' '' **2**
''Absolution,'' **2–3**, 279, 298
Acomba (''The Cameo Frame''), **3**
Act of Darkness (Bishop), 34
Adams, Henry, 129
''The Adjuster,'' **3**
''The Adolescent Marriage,'' **3–4**
''Afternoon of an Author,'' **4**, 69
Aggie, Prince (*The Last Tycoon*), **4**
Aggie, Prince of Denmark, 4
Ahearn, Clarence (''The Cut-Glass Bowl''), **4**
Ahearn, Mrs. Clarence (''The Cut-Glass Bowl''), **4**
''Ah May, Shall I splatter my thoughts in the air,'' **4**
Albrucksburger (*The Great Gatsby*), **4**
''An Alcoholic Case,'' **4–5**
Alcoholism in Fitzgerald, **5**, 112, 238, 239, 243, 321, 323, 376, 390–91
''Aldous Huxley's Crome Yellow,'' **5**, 200
Alexandre, Apostle (*Tender Is the Night*), **5**
Alfonso (''One Interne''), **5**
Alice (''The Family Bus''), **6**
Alice Adams (Tarkington), 407
Alix (''Babylon Revisited''), **6**
Allen (''The Trail of the Duke''), **6**
Allenby (*This Side of Paradise*), **6**
Allerdyce, Thomas (''O Russet Witch!''), **6**
Allison, Parker (*The Beautiful and Damned*), **6**
''All the girls and mans,'' **6**
All the Sad Young Men, **6**, 239, 334

Altwater, Percy, Lieutenant (*Coward*), **6**
The Ambassadors (James), 268, 440
Ambler, Joe (''The Cut-Glass Bowl''), **6**
American Mercury, 206, 278, 279, 297, 298
Ames (''Two Wrongs''), **6**
Ames, Ellsworth (''The Love Boat''), **6**
Ames, Mrs. Ellsworth (''The Love Boat''), **7**
Ames, T. (*Thoughtbook*), **7**
Amy (''The Hotel Child''), **7**
Amy (''Zone of Accident''), **7**
Anderson, Sherwood, **7–8**, 196, 253, 269, 278, 281, 384, 397
André (''Gods of Darkness''), **8**
Andros, Ede (''The Baby Party''), **8**
Andros, Edith (''The Baby Party''), **8**
Andros, John (''The Baby Party''), **8**
Andy, Lieutenant (''The Last of the Belles''), **8–9**
Anna (''John Jackson's Arcady''), **9**
Anne (''Babes in the Woods''), **9**
Anne (''Martin's Thoughts''), **9**
Anne (''To Anne''), **9**
Anne (''What a Handsome Pair!''), **9**
''Answer to a Poem,'' **9**
Anthony Adverse (Allen), 39
Antoinette (''Martin's Thoughts''), **9**
''The Ants at Princeton,'' **9**
''Apology to Ogden Nash,'' **9**
Appleton (''Basil and Cleopatra''), **9**
Appleton (''Strange Sanctuary''), **9**
Appleton, Lila (''Strange Sanctuary''), **9**
Appleton, Warren (''Myra Meets His Family''), **10**
Aquilla (''On Schedule''), **10**
Archie (*Fie! Fie! Fi-Fi*), **10**
Armstrong, Margaret (*Thoughtbook*), **10**
Aronstael (''Two Wrongs''), **10**
Arrot, Ben (''The Ice Palace''), **10**
Art (*The Last Tycoon*), **10**
Ashton, Cecilia (*Coward*), **10**
Ashton, John (*Coward*), **10**
Assorted Spirits, **10–11**
Astaire, Fred, 391
Atkins, Tommy (*Fie! Fie! Fi-Fi!*), **11**
''At Your Age,'' **11**
Auerbach, Hubert (*The Great Gatsby*), **11**
Augustine (*Tender Is the Night*), **11**
Augustus ('' 'Why Blame It on the Poor Kiss If the Girl Veteran of Many Petting Parties Is Prone to Affairs After Marriage?' ''), **11**
Aunty (''The Ants at Princeton''), **11**
''Author's House,'' **11–12**
''An Author's Mother,'' **12**, 134
Autumn in the Valley (Chanler), 243–44
Avery, Helen Tompkins (''Magnetism''), **12**, 286

Babbitt (Lewis), 138, 279
''Babes in the Woods,'' **13**, 279, 298
''Babylon Revisited,'' 5, **13–14**, 290, 293, 392
Babylon Revisited, 14, 377
''The Baby Party,'' **14**
Bach (''A Man in the Way''), **14**
Bach (''Zone of Accident''), **14**
Bachus (*Thoughtbook*), **14**
Bachus, Una (*Thoughtbook*), **14**
Backhysson (*The Great Gatsby*), **14**
Bacon, Dr. (''The Freshest Boy,'' ''The Perfect Life''), **15**
Badenuff (''The Prince of Pests''), **15**
Baedeker (*The Great Gatsby*), **15**
Baer, Dr. Bill (*The Last Tycoon*), **15**
Bailey, Buzz (''Basil and Cleopatra''), **15**
Bailey, John Boynton (''Emotional Bankruptcy,'' ''A Snobbish Story''), **15**
Bailey, Miss (''The Curious Case of Benjamin Button''), **15**
Baily (''The Camel's Back''), **15**
Baird, Tudor (*The Beautiful and Damned*), **15**
Baker (*Thoughtbook*), **15**
Baker, Bicker (''The Rich Boy''), **16**
Baker, Eddie (''Crazy Sunday''), **16**
Baker, Ellen (''A Short Trip Home''), **16**
Baker, George (''Discard''), **16**
Baker, Jordan (*The Great Gatsby*), **16**
Baker, Mrs. (''A Short Trip Home''), **16**
Baldwin (''Family in the Wind''), **16**
Bales, Dr. (''Crazy Sunday''), **16**
''The Baltimore Anti-Christ,'' **16**, 279
Bangs, Angelina (*Coward*), **16**
Bangs, Georgie (*Coward*), **17**

Banizon ("Pat Hobby's Secret"), **17**
Bankland ("How to Live on $36,000 a Year"), **17**
Bankland, Mrs. ("How to Live on $36,000 a Year"), **17**
Bannerman Marie ("The Dance"), **17**
Baptiste (*The Beautiful and Damned*), **17**
Barban, Tommy (*Tender Is the Night*), **17**
Barbara (*This Side of Paradise*), **17**
Barber, Ralph Henry ("The Bowl"), **17**
"The Barber's Too Slick," **17**
Barbour, Carl ("Jacob's Ladder"), **17**
Barkis, Private (*Coward*), **17**
Barks, Major ("The Rubber Check"), **17**
Barley (*The Beautiful and Damned*), **18**
Barlow ("May Day"), **18**
Barlow (*This Side of Paradise*), **18**
Barnes ("No Harm Trying"), **18**
Barnes, Ed ("Six of One—"), **18**
Barnes, Rachael Jerryl (*The Beautiful and Damned*), **18**
Barnes, Rodman (*The Beautiful and Damned*), **18**
Barnett, Dr. ("One Interne"), **18**
Barney, Charles ("On Your Own"), **18**
Barney, Mrs. Charles ("On Your Own"), **18**
Barnfield, Teddy ("The Captured Shadow"), **18**
Barr, Bert, 25
Barrows, Colonel ("A Debt of Honor"), **19**
Barthelmi ("The Count of Darkness"), **19**
Bartholomew ("May Day"), **19**
Bartlett, Dolly ("That Kind of Party"), **19**
Bartlett, Mrs. ("That Kind of Party"), **19**
Bartney, Walter Hamilton ("Pain and the Scientist"), **19**
Bartollo ("On Your Own"), **19**
Barton (*This Side of Paradise*), **19**
Bascome (*This Side of Paradise*), **19**
"Basil and Cleopatra," **19–20**
The Basil Duke Lee and Josephine Perry Stories, **20**
Bates ("The Perfect Life"), **20**
Battles, Johanna ("I Got Shoes"), **20**
Beach, Sylvia, 68
Beard, the ("Shaggy's Morning"), **20**
The Beautiful and Damned, 5, **20–24**, 136, 137, 249, 279, 289, 298, 334, 459
Beauty Boy ("Dearly Beloved"), **24**
Beaver, Edgar (*The Great Gatsby*), **24**
Bebé ("Gretchen's Forty Winks"), **24**
"Because," **24**
Becker (*The Great Gatsby*), **25**
Becker, Chester (*The Great Gatsby*), **25**
Becker, Gwen ("Magnetism"), **25**
Becker, Joe ("Last Kiss"), **25**, 276
Bedros (*The Beautiful and Damned*), **25**
Beebe, Evelyn ("The Captured Shadow"), **25**
Beebe, Ham ("The Captured Shadow"), **25**
Beebe, Mrs. ("Dalyrimple Goes Wrong"), **25**
Beecher, Miss ("Basil and Cleopatra"), **25**
Beef ("Head and Shoulders"), **25**
Beerbohm, Max, 200
"Beg You to Listen," **25**
Behrer, Bill ("No Harm Trying"), **25**
Behrer, Dr. ("Family in the Wind"), **26**
Being Respectable (Flandrau), 138
Belcher, S. W. (*The Great Gatsby*), **26**
Bell ("Crazy Sunday"), **26**
Bell, Mrs. ("The Hotel Girl"), **26**
Bellamy ("The Ice Palace"), **26**
Bellamy, Gordon ("The Ice Palace"), **26**
Bellamy, Harry ("The Ice Palace"), **26**
Bellamy, Mrs. ("The Ice Palace"), **26**
Bellamy, Myra ("The Ice Palace"), **26**
Bellois, Mlle (*Tender Is the Night*), **26**
Beloved Infidel (Graham), 159
Beltzer ("Crazy Sunday"), **26**
Beltzman ("The Freshest Boy"), **26**
Beluga (*The Great Gatsby*), **26**
Bemberg (*The Great Gatsby*), **27**
Bement, Ed ("Emotional Bankruptcy," "First Blood," "A Nice Quiet Place," "A Snobbish Story," "A Woman with a Past"), **27**
Bement, Howard ("The Bowl"), **27**
Ben ("The Jelly-Bean"), **27**
Ben ("A Short Autobiography"), **27**

Ben (*Tender Is the Night*), **27**
Benbower, Miss (''First Blood''), **27**
Bendiri, Samuele (*The Beautiful and Damned*), **27**
''Benediction,'' **27–28**, 100, 316
Bennett, Jim (''Inside the House''), **28**
Benny (''No Harm Trying''), **28**
Benson, Edward Frederic, **28**
Benson, Robert Hugh, 129
Bergson (*Porcelain and Pink*), **28**
Berl (''Reade, Substitute Right Half''), **28**
Berlin, Irving, 422
Berme, Comte de (''Flight and Pursuit''), **28**
Berners, Jack (''A Man in the Way,'' ''Mightier Than the Sword,'' ''On the Trail of Pat Hobby,'' ''Pat Hobby and Orson Welles,'' ''Pat Hobby Does His Bit,'' ''Pat Hobby, Putative Father,'' ''Pat Hobby's College Days,'' ''Pat Hobby's Preview,'' ''A Patriotic Short,'' ''Teamed with Genius''), **28–29**
Bernice (''Bernice Bobs Her Hair''), **29**
''Bernice Bobs Her Hair,'' **29–30**
Bernie (*The Last Tycoon*), **30**
Berry (''A Change of Class''), **30**
Berry, Ralph (''The Hotel Child''), **30**
Bertram de Villefranche (''The Kingdom in the Dark''), **30**
Betts, Mary (''At Your Age''), **30**
Betty (*Safety First!*), **30**
Betty, Russell (*The Great Gatsby*), **30**
''Between Three and Four,'' **30**
Bibble (''Forging Ahead''), **31**
Bibble (''Forging Ahead,'' ''He Thinks He's Wonderful''), **31**
Bibble, Erminie Gilberte Labouisse (''Basil and Cleopatra,'' ''Forging Ahead,'' ''He Thinks He's Wonderful,'' ''The Perfect Life,'' **31**
Bibble, Miss (''Forging Ahead''), **31**
Bibble, Mrs. (''Forging Ahead,'' ''He Thinks He's Wonderful''), **31**
Bibelick (''The Cruise of the Rolling Junk''), **31**
Bickle (''Majesty''), **31**
Bieman (''Design in Plaster''), **31**
''The Big Academy Dinner,'' **32**, 79
Bigelow, Alida (*Thoughtbook*), **32**, 133
Bigelow, Donald (*Thoughtbook*), **32**
Biggs (''Jacob's Ladder''), **32**
Biggs, John, Jr., **32**, 233, 307, 335, 459
Biglow (*Thoughtbook*), **32**
Bill (*Fie! Fie! Fi- Fi!*), **32**
Bill (''The Freshest Boy''), **33**
Bill (''A Luckless Santa Claus''), **33**
Bill (''The Rubber Check''), **33**
Bill (*Safety First!*), **33**
Bill (''Truth and—consequences''), **33**
Bill (''Two Wrongs''), **33**
Billings, Senator (''One Interne''), **33**
Billy (''Family in the Wind''), **33**
Billy (''Myra Meets His Family''), **33**
Bisby, Mrs. Caxton (''The Intimate Strangers''), **33**
Bishop, John Peale, **33–34**, 107, 459
Bispam (''Basil and Cleopatra''), **34**
Bispam (*This Side of Paradise*), **34**
Bispam, Mrs. (*This Side of Paradise*), **34**
Bissel (''The Captured Shadow''), **34**
Bissel, Dorothy (''Spring Song''), **34**
Bissel, Imogene (''The Captured Shadow,'' ''He Thinks He's Wonderful,'' ''The Scandal Detectives''), **34–35**
Bissel, Mrs. (''The Captured Shadow,'' ''He Thinks He's Wonderful''), **35**
Bistolary (*This Side of Paradise*), **35**
Bixby, the Honorable Howard (''The Pierian Springs and the Last Straw''), **35**
Blachford, Lady (''Sentiment—and the Use of Rouge''), **35**
Blachford, Lord (''Sentiment—and the Use of Rouge''), **35**
Blacht (''A Snobbish Story''), **35**
Black, Joseph (*The Beautiful and Damned*), **35**
Blackbuck (*The Great Gatsby*), **35**
Blaine, Amory (*This Side of Paradise*), **35–36**
Blaine, Beatrice O'Hara (*This Side of Paradise*), **36**

Blaine, Stephen (*This Side of Paradise*), **36**
Blair ("Majesty"), **36**
Blair ("Majesty"), **36**
Blair, Gardiner, Jr. ("Majesty"), **36**
Blair, Gardiner, Sr. ("Majesty"), **36**
Blair, George P. ("The Scandal Detectives"), **36**
Blair, Hubert ("The Captured Shadow," "He Thinks He's Wonderful," "A Night at the Fair," "The Scandal Detectives"), **36–37**
Blair, Master Gardiner, III ("Majesty"), **37**
Blair, Miss Gloria ("Majesty"), **37**
Blair, Mrs. George P. ("The Scandal Detectives"), **37**
Blair, Mrs. Potter ("Majesty"), **37**
Blair, Mrs. Princess Potowski Parr ("Majesty"), **37**
Blair, Olive Mercy ("Majesty"), **37**
Blair, William Brevoort ("Majesty", **37**
Blake ("A Freeze-Out"), **37**
Bliss, Dr. ("Her Last Case"), **37**
Bloeckman, Joseph. *See* Black, Joseph
Blondell, Joan, 217
Blossom (*Fie! Fie! Fi-Fi*), **37**
"A Blues," **37**
Blum, Carmel Myers ("Lines on Reading through an Autograph Album," "Orange pajamas and heaven's guitars"), **38**
Blum, Ralph ("Lines on Reading through an Autograph Album"), **38**, 293
Blutchdak ("Rags Martin-Jones and the Pr-nce of W-les"), **38**
Bly, Nellie, 225
Boardman, Eleanor, 57, 85, 440
Boardman, Laurence (*Thoughtbook*), **38**
Bob ("The Love Boat"), **38**
Bob ("One Hundred False Starts"), **38**
Bobbé ("How to Live on Practically Nothing a Year"), **38**
Bobby (*This Side of Paradise*), **38**
Bobby ("Truth and—consequences"), **38**
Bodman ("A Freeze-Out"), **38**
Boileau (*The Evil Eye*), **38**
Boiling Oil (*This Side of Paradise*), **38**
" 'Boil Some Water—Lots of It,' " **38–39**
Boldini, Jeff ("Pat Hobby and Orson Welles"), **39**
Bologna, Iona (*Safety First!*), **39**
Bonaparte, Prince ("The End of Hate"), **39**
Bonneasse, Mme (*Tender Is the Night*), **39**
"A Book of One's Own," **39**
Boone ("Zone of Accident"), **39**
Boone, Joe (" 'I Didn't Get Over' "), **39**
Boone, Sergeant ("A Woman with a Past"), **39**
Boopsie Dee ("One Hundred False Starts"), **39**
Booth, Jacob ("Jacob's Ladder"), **40**
Booth, John Wilkes ("The Room with the Green Blinds"), **40**
Bordley, Bob ("Last Kiss"), **40**
Bordon, Dolly ("Discard"), **40**
Borgé, Isabelle (*This Side of Paradise*), **40**, 230
Borgé, Mrs. (*This Side of Paradise*), **40**
Borgia, John Alexander ("The High Cost of Macaroni"), **40**
Boris ("Teamed with Genius"), **40**
Borowki, Stanislas Karl Joseph ("The Hotel Child"), **40**
Bounds (*The Beautiful and Damned*), **41**
Bourne, Mark H. ("More Than Just a House"), **41**
Bovine, Mrs. (*Fie! Fie! Fi- Fi*), **41**
Bowers, Bryan ("Inside the House," "Too Cute for Words"), **41**
Bowers, Donald ("Three Hours between Planes"), **41**
Bowers, Gwen ("Inside the House," "Too Cute for Words"), **41–42**
"The Bowl," **42**
Bowman, Tom ("The Popular Girl"), **42**
Bowman, Yanci ("The Popular Girl"), **42**
Boxley, George (*The Last Tycoon*), **43**, 200
Boyd, Calvin (*The Beautiful and Damned*), **43**
Boyd, Margaret Woodward, **43**

Boyd, Thomas Alexander, **43–44**, 78, 433
The Boy Grew Older (Broun), 48
"The Boy Who Killed His Mother." *See* "In a dear little vine-covered cottage"
Braden, Carty ("The Popular Girl"), **44**
Bradin, Edith ("May Day"), **44**
Bradin, Henry ("May Day"), **44**
Bradlee ("The Love Boat"), **44**
Bradley ("The Rich Boy"), **44**
Brady, Cecelia (*The Last Tycoon*), **44**, 243
Brady, Earl (*Tender Is the Night*), **44**
Brady, Eleanor (*The Last Tycoon*), **44**
Brady, Jeanne ("Absolution"), **45**
Brady, Mrs. Pat (*The Last Tycoon*), **45**
Brady, Pat (*The Last Tycoon*), **45**, 243
Braegdort ("O Russet Witch!"), **45**
Brain, the ("Shaggy's Morning"), **45**
Brancusi ("Two Wrongs"), **45**
Brancusi, Constantin, 45
Brass (Norris), 304, 342
Braun (*Tender Is the Night*), **45**
Bray, Mrs. ("First Blood"), **45**
Breen, Joe (*The Last Tycoon*), **45**
Brent, Evelyn (*The Last Tycoon*), **45**
Brent, George, 209
Brereton, Miss ("A Snobbish Story," "A Woman with a Past"), **45–46**
Brett (*The Beautiful and Damned*), **46**
Brett, Sukey (*This Side of Paradise*), **46**
Brewer (*The Great Gatsby*), **46**
Brian, Brother ("The Count of Darkness," "In the Darkest Hour," "The Kingdom in the Dark"), **46**
Brian, Friar. *See* Brian, Brother
"The Bridal Party," **46–47**
Bridgebane, Dr. ("Crazy Sunday"), **47**
Brimmer (*The Last Tycoon*), **47**, 399
Brinson, Marjorie Sayre, **47**, 135, 372
Broaca, John (*The Last Tycoon*), **47**
"The Broadcast We Almost Heard Last September," **47**
Brokaw, Bill ("A Short Trip Home"), **47**
Bronson ("The Cut-Glass Bowl"), **47**
Bronson, Ed ("Hot and Cold Blood"), **47**
Bronson, Edgar ("The Family Bus"), **48**
Bronson, Eugene (*The Beautiful and Damned*), **48**, 459
Bronson, Will ("Pat Hobby's Christmas Wish"), **48**
Brooke, Loretta ("Zone of Accident"), **48**
Broun, Heywood, **48–49**, 98, 322
Brown, Ben ("A Patriotic Short"), **49**
Brown, Bugs ("The Freshest Boy"), **49**
Brown, Captain. *See* Hibbing, Captain
Brown, Carter ("Pilgrimage"), **49**
Brown, Delia ("Pat Hobby, Putative Father"), **49**
Brown, Mary (*The Evil Eye*), **50**
Brown, Midget ("The Freshest Boy"), **50**
Brown, Orrison ("The Lost Decade"), **50**
Brown, Satterly ("Inside the House"), **50**
Bruccoli, Matthew J., 243
Brune, Dr. ("One Interne"), **50**
Brune, Eddie ("Diagnosis"), **50**
Buchanan, Daisy Fay (*The Great Gatsby*), 16, **50**, 137, 230
Buchanan, Pammy (*The Great Gatsby*), **50**
Buchanan, Tom (*The Great Gatsby*), **50**
Buck ("Pat Hobby's Christmas Wish"), **51**
Buckner, Mrs. Riply, Sr. ("A Night at the Fair," "The Scandal Detectives"), **51**
Buckner, Riply, Jr. ("The Captured Shadow," "Forging Ahead," "He Thinks He's Wonderful," "A Night at the Fair," "The Scandal Detectives"), **51**
Buckner, Riply, Sr. ("A Night at the Fair"), **51**
Bulge, Miss ("The Diamond as Big as the Ritz"), **51**
Bulham, P. (*Thoughtbook*), **51**
Bull, Francis (*The Great Gatsby*), **51**
Bunker ("The Bowl"), **51**
Bunsen (*The Great Gatsby*), **51**
Burch, Dr. Edwin ("Dearly Beloved"), **51**
Burke, Geraldine (*The Beautiful and Damned*), **51**

Burling ("Two for a Cent"), **52**
Burne-Dennison, the Hon. Martha ("The Intimate Strangers"), **52**
Burns, Phyllis ("Discard"), **52**
Burt, Mrs. (*The Evil Eye*), **52**
Burton (*The Last Tycoon*), **52**
Busch, Arthur ("Magnetism"), **52**
Bushmill, Hallie ("A Penny Spent"), **52**
Bushmill, Jessie Pepper ("A Penny Spent"), **52**
Bushmill, Julius ("A Penny Spent"), **52**
Bustanoby ("A Short Autobiography"), **53**
Butler ("The Room with the Green Blinds"), **53**
Butler, Howard ("Between Three and Four"), **53**
Butler, Vernard ("The Honor of the Goon"), **53**
Butterfield, Warren ("The Camel's Back"), **53**
Butterworth ("The Ice Palace"), **53**
Butterworth ("The Rough Crossing"), **53**
Button ("The Curious Case of Benjamin Button"), **53**
Button, Benjamin ("The Curious Case of Benjamin Button"), **53**
Button, Hildegarde Moncrief ("The Curious Case of Benjamin Button"), **53**
Button, Mrs. Roger ("The Curious Case of Benjamin Button"), **53**
Button, Roger ("The Curious Case of Benjamin Button"), **54**
Button, Roscoe ("The Curious Case of Benjamin Button"), **54**

Cable (*The Beautiful and Damned*), **55**
Cable, Joe ("The Dance"), **55**
Cadmus ("The Kingdom in the Dark"), **55**
Cadorna ("Two Wrongs"), **55**
Caesar's Things (Z. Fitzgerald), 137
Cahill ("The Rich Boy"), **55**
Cakebook ("Ten Years in the Advertising Business"), **55**
Cale ("Lo, the Poor Peacock!"), **55**
Calhoun, Ailie ("The Last of the Belles"), **55–56**
Calhoun, Belle Pope ("The Offshore Pirate"), **56**
Calhoun, C.T.J. ("The Unspeakable Egg"), **56**
Calhoun, Mrs. ("The Last of the Belles"), **56**
Calkins (*Porcelain and Pink*), **56**
Callaghan, Morley, **56–57**, 112, 181
Calman, Miles ("Crazy Sunday"), **57**, 440
Calman, Mrs. ("Crazy Sunday"), **57**
Calman, Stella Walker ("Crazy Sunday"), **57**, 384, 440
Cambell, (*This Side of Paradise*), **57**
Cambell, D. B. ("At Your Age"), **57**
Cambell, Randy ("At your Age"), **57**
"The Camel's Back," **57–58**
"The Cameo Frame," **58**
Campbell ("Babylon Revisited"), **58**
Campbell ("Too Cute for Words"), **58**
Campbell, Dizzy ("Too Cute for Words"), **58**
Campbell, Georgia Berriman ("Two Wrongs"), **59**
Campbell, Mrs. ("Too Cute for Words"), **59**
Campion, Luis (*Tender Is the Night*), **59**
Canby, Carleton ("The Cut-Glass Bowl"), **59**
Canby, Horace, Lieutenant ("The Last of the Belles"), **59**
Canisius, John ("The Guest in Room Nineteen"), **59**
Cannel, John ("The Debutante"), **59**
Cannon ("Financing Finnegan"), **59**
Capps-Karr, Lady ("The Hotel Child"), **59**
"The Captured Shadow," **59–60**
The Captured Shadow, **60**
Caramel, Richard (*The Beautiful and Damned*), **60**
Carey, Martha ("Bernice Bobs Her Hair"), **60**
Carhart, Peter ("The Four Fists"), **60–61**
Caricamento, Janice (*Tender Is the Night*), **61**
Carl ("The Rich Boy"), **61**
Carleton, Mrs. ("A Freeze-Out"), **61**

Carleton, Sammy (*The Beautiful and Damned*), **61**
Carling, Miss (''Forging Ahead''), **61**
Carling (*This Side of Paradise*), **61**
Carlson, Miss (''Financing Finnegan''), **61**
Carlton (''A Debt of Honor''), **61**
Carlyle, Curtis (''The Offshore Pirate''). *See* Moreland, Toby
Carmatle (''The Room with the Green Blinds''), **61**
Carmatle (''The Room with the Green Blinds''), **61**
Carmel (''Crazy Sunday''), **61–62**. *See also* Blum, Carmel Myers
Carney, Howard, Dr. (''Her Last Case''), **62**
Caroline (''At Your Age''), **62**
Caroline (''O Russet Witch!''), **62**
Caroline (''Sleeping and Waking''), **62**
Caroline (''A Snobbish Story''), **62**
Caros Moros, Count de (''Indecision''), **62**
Carrage, Estella (''The Captured Shadow''), **62**
Carraway (*The Great Gatsby*), **62**
Carraway, Nick (*The Great Gatsby*), **62–63**, 340, 357
Carroll, Peter (''Babes in the Woods''), **63**
Carry, Peggy, 230
Carson, (''The Adolescent Marriage''), **63**
Carson (''Basil and Cleopatra''), **63**
Carson, Miss (''Lo, the Poor Peacock!''), **63**
Carstairs (*This Side of Paradise*), **63**
Carstairs, Bill (*The Beautiful and Damned*), **63**
Carter (''A New Leaf''), **63**
Carter, Dr. (''An Alcoholic Case''), **63**
Carter, Eleanor (''Pat Hobby's Preview''), **63**
Carter, Gerald (''Benediction''), **63**
Carton, James (''The Rough Crossing''), **63**
Cartwright-Smith (*The Beautiful and Damned*), **64**
Cartwright-Smith, Mrs. (*The Beautiful and Damned*), **64**
Caruse, Madame (*Assorted Spirits*), **64**
Caruthers, Miss (''Diamond Dick and the First Law of Woman''), **64**
Carver (''The Freshest Boy''), **64**
Cary ('' 'The Sensible Thing' ''), **64**
Cary, Colonel (''On Your Own''), **64**
Cary, Daisy (''The Bowl''), **64**
Cary, Edith (''The Passionate Eskimo''), **64**
Cary, Esther (''A New Leaf''), **64**
Cary, Harriet (''The Jelly-Bean''), **64**
Cary, Jonquil ('' 'The Sensible Thing' ''), **64**
Cary, Miss (''One Interne''), **65**
Cary, Mrs. (''The Scandal Detectives,'' ''That Kind of Party''), **65**
Cary, Mrs. R. B. ('' 'The Sensible Thing' ''), **65**
Cary, Walter (''The Scandal Detectives''), **65**
Casasus (*Tender Is the Night*), **65**
Case, Harold (''The Bowl''), **65**
Cashmael, T. (''The Pusher-in-the-Face''), **65**
Cass (''The Guest in Room Nineteen''), **65**
Cassius ('' 'Send Me In, Coach' ''), **65**
Castle (''Magnetism''), **65**
Castleton (''Majesty''), **65**
Castleton, Emily. *See* Petrocobesco, Princess Emily
Castleton, Harold, Jr. (''Majesty''), **65**
Castleton, Harold, Sr. (''Majesty''), **66**
Castleton, Mrs. Theodore (''Majesty''), **66**
Castleton, Theodore (''Majesty''), **66**
Cates (''On an Ocean Wave''), **66**
Cathcart ('' 'Send Me In, Coach' ''), **66**
Cathcart, Jim (''A Short Trip Home''), **66**
Cather, Willa, 141, 278
Catherine (*The Great Gatsby*), **66**
Catherine (''A Short Trip Home''), **66**
Catlip (*The Great Gatsby*), **66**
Cato (''The Cruise of the Rolling Junk''), **66**

Caxter, Peter (''Tarquin of Cheapside''), **66**
Cecil (''The Love Boat''), **66**
Cedric (''Rags Martin-Jones and the Pr-nce of W-les''), **67**
The Celt and the World (Leslie), 249
Celeste (*Fie! Fie! Fi-Fi!*), **67**
Celie (''What a Handsome Pair!''), **67**
''Censorship or Not,'' **67**
Chaffee, Book (''Emotional Bankruptcy,'' ''A Woman with a Past,''), **67**
Chambers ('' 'The Sensible Thing' ''), **67**
Chambers, Miss (''A Woman with a Past''), **67**
Chambers, Robert, 418
Chamoro, Ella Lei (''The Honor of the Goon''), **67**
Chamoro, Lei (''The Honor of the Goon''), **67**
Chamson, André, **67–68**, 440
Chandelle, Jaques (*Shadow Laurels*), **68**
Chandelle, Jean (*Shadow Laurels*), **68**
Chandler (''Presumption''), **68**
Chandler, Cora (''Presumption''), **68**
Chandler, Mrs. (''Presumption''), **69**
Chandler, San Juan (''Presumption''), **69**
''A Change of Class,'' **69**
Chanler, Margaret, 129, 243
Chanler, Theodore, 453
Chaplin, Charlie, 295–96
Chapman, William (*Assorted Spirits*), **69**
Charley (*The Captured Shadow*), **69**
Charlie (''A Short Autobiography''), **69**
Charlie (*Tender Is the Night*), **70**
Chase (''No Flowers''), **70**
Chase, Reynold (''A Freeze-Out''), **70**
Château (*Tender Is the Night*), **70**
Cheadle (*The Great Gatsby*), **70**
''A Cheer for Princeton,'' **70**
Cheever, Bessie Belle (''Basil and Cleopatra''), **70**
Chestnut, John B. (''Rags Martin-Jones and the Pr-nce of W-les''), **70**
Chevril (''Diagnosis''), **70**
Chilicheff (''The Rich Boy''), **70**
Chillicheff, Prince (*Tender Is the Night*), **70**
Cholmondely (*Fie! Fie! Fi- Fi!*), **70**
The Chorus Girl's Romance, 93, 179
Choynski, Mrs. (''Jacob's Ladder''), **70**
Christopher (''The Passionate Eskimo''), **71**
Chrome (*The Great Gatsby*), **71**
Chrystie, Mrs. (*The Great Gatsby*, **71**
''City Dusk,'' **71**
Civet, Webster, Dr. (*The Great Gatsby*), **71**
''The Claims of the *Lit*,'' **71**
Clair, Elenor (*Thoughtbook*), **71**
Clan-Carly, Lord (''The Rubber Check''), **71**
Clancy, Miss, (''Hot and Cold Blood''), **71**
Clara ('' 'Why Blame It on the Poor Kiss If the Girl Veteran of Many Petting Parties Is Prone to Affairs After Marriage?' ''), **71**
Clare (''A Snobbish Story''), **71**
Clarence (''Imagination—and a Few Mothers''), **71**
Claris (*The Last Tycoon*), **71**
Clark (''No Flowers''), **72**
Clark, Amanda Rawlins (''No Flowers''), **72**
Clark, Bob (*Thoughtbook*), **72**
Clark, Caroline (*Thoughtbook*), **72**
Clark, Jesse (''The Adolescent Marriage''), **72**
Clark, Llewellyn (''The Adolescent Marriage''), **72**
Clark, Lucy Wharton (''The Adolescent Marriage''), **72**
Clark, Marjorie (''No Flowers''), **72**
Claude (*The Evil Eye*), **72**
Claude (*Tender Is the Night*), **72**
Clavine (''Shadow Laurels''), **72**
Clay, Collis (*Tender Is the Night*), **72**
''Clay Feet,'' **73**
Clayhorne (''Diagnosis''), **73**
Clayhorne, Ben (''Diagnosis''), **73**
Clayhorne, Charlie (''Diagnosis''), **73**
Clayhorne, Dicky (''Diagnosis''), **73**
Clayhorne, Pete (''Diagnosis''), **73**
Clayton (''Hot and Cold Blood''), **73**
Cleopatra (*Safety First!*), **73**

Clos d'Hirondelle, Marquis de la (''One Trip Abroad''), **73**
Clothilde (''New Types''), **73**
Clothilde (*This Side of Paradise*), **73**
Cloud, Marion (''The Camel's Back''), **73**
Clover (*Fie! Fie! Fi-Fi!*), **74**
Codman, Russel (''Your Way and Mine''), **74**
Cody, Dan (*The Great Gatsby*), **74**
Coe, Jack (''A Woman with a Past''), **74**
Cohan, George M., 296
Cohen, Clyde (*The Great Gatsby*), **74**
Cohen, Dr. (''Family in the Wind''), **74**
Cola, Capone (''Indecision''), **74**
Cola, Mrs. (''Indecision''), **74**
Colahan, Miss (''Two Wrongs''), **74**
Colazzo, Dr. (*Tender Is the Night*), **74**
Colbert, Claudette, **75**, 76, 423
Colby (''One Trip Abroad''), **75**
Colby, Mrs. (''One Trip Abroad''), **75**
Cole, Miss (''That Kind of Party''), **75**
Coleman, Mrs. Henry (''Dalyrimple Goes Wrong''), **75**
Coles, Joel (''Crazy Sunday''), **75**
''College of One,'' 158, 449
Collins, Captain (*The Beautiful and Damned*), **75**
Collins, Marjorie (''The Bridal Party''), **75**
Collins, Miss (''In the Holidays''), **75**
Colman, Ronald, **75–76**, 188, 191, 286, 359, 405, 423
Colmar, Mme de (''Flight and Pursuit''), **76**
''Colors has she in her soul,'' **76**
Colum, Mary, 182
Column, Phoebe (*This Side of Paradise*), **76**
Combrinck, Lady Sybil (''Two Wrongs''), **76**
Combrinck, Lord (''Two Wrongs''), **76**
''Come in! Come in!,'' **76**
Comerford, R. R. (''The Popular Girl''), **76**
Compson, Dr. ('' 'Trouble' ''), **76**
Comstock, Mrs. (''Benediction''), **76**
''Confessions,'' **77**
Conk (''Pat Hobby's Secret''), **77**
Conklin, Cuckoo (''The Perfect Life''), **77**
Connage, Alec (*This Side of Paradise*), **77**
Connage, Beverly (*The Captured Shadow*), **77**
Connage, Cecelia (*This Side of Paradise*), **77**
Connage, Dorothy (*The Captured Shadow*), **77**
Connage, Hubert (*The Captured Shadow*), **77**
Connage, Leland R. (*This Side of Paradise*), **77**
Connage, Mrs. Beverly (*The Captured Shadow*), **77**
Connage, Mrs. Leland R. (*This Side of Paradise*), **77**
Connage, Rosalind (*This Side of Paradise*), **77–78**
Conrad, Joseph, **78**, 138, 238, 279, 281, 288
Constance (''Emotional Bankruptcy''), **78**
Consuela (*The Great Gatsby*), **79**
''Contemporary Writers and Their Work, A Series of Autobiographical Letters—F. Scott Fitzgerald,'' **79**
Converse, Ted (*This Side of Paradise*), **79**
Cook, Dr. (*Safety First!*), **79**
Cooley, James (''Not in the Guidebook''), **79**
Cooley, Milly (''Not in the Guidebook''), **79**
Coolidge, Calvin, **79**
Cooper, Gary, **79**
Coots, Mrs. (''Not in the Guidebook''), **80**
Coppet, Travis de. *See* de Coppet, Travis
Corcoran (''A Penny Spent''), **80**
Corcoran, Caroline Martin (''Flight and Pursuit''), **80**
Corcoran, Dexter (''Flight and Pursuit''), **80**
Corcoran, George (''Flight and Pursuit''), **80**

Corcoran, Mrs. (''Flight and Pursuit''), **80**
Corcoran, Mrs. (''Your Way and Mine''), **80**
Corey, Martha, 60
Corker, Bill (''Two Old- Timers''), **80**
Corliss, John (''No Flowers''), **81**
Corn, Captain (*This Side of Paradise*), **81**
Cornhill, Mrs. (*The Last Tycoon*), **81**
Corrigan (*The Great Gatsby*), **81**
Cortelyou, Henry (''Diagnosis''), **81**
Costello (''The Offshore Pirate''), **81**
Costello, Bill (''A Man in the Way''), **81**
''Counter Song to the 'Undertaker,' '' **81**
''The Count of Darkness,'' **81**
Courru, Pierre (''Shadow Laurels''), **82**
Cowan, Kenneth (*The Beautiful and Damned*), **82**
Cowan, Lester, 14, 290
Cowan, Mary (''A Freeze-Out''), **82**
Coward, **82**
Cowley, Malcolm, **82–83**, 380, 450
Coy, Ted (''The Bowl''), **83**
Coyne, Countess (*Fie! Fie! F-Fi!*), **83**
''The Crack-Up,'' **83–84**
The Crack-Up, 5, **84**, 112, 153, 173, 182, 325, 459
Craddock ('' 'The Sensible Thing' ''), **84**
Craig (''Dalyrimple Goes Wrong''), **84**
Craig, Charlie (''Strange Sanctuary''), **84**
Craker, Captain (''The Last of the Belles''), **84**
Cramner, H. P. (''The Scandal Detectives''), **84**
Crane, Stephen, 43, 78, 112
Craw, Adele (''A Woman with a Past''), **84**
Crawford (*The Beautiful and Damned*), **85**
Crawford, Jason (''Inside the House''), **85**
Crawford, Joan, 217, 253, 296
Crawshaw (''On Your Own''), **85**
Crawshow (*Tender Is the Night*), **85**
''Crazy Sunday,'' 5, **85–86**, 384, 416, 440
''The Credo of F. Scott Fitzgerald,'' 279. *See also* ''Public Letter to Thomas Boyd''
Cresswell, Clarke (''Strange Sanctuary''), **86**
Crisler, Fritz (''The Ants at Princeton''), **86**
Critchtichiello (''The Diamond as Big as the Ritz''), **86**
Croirier (*The Great Gatsby*), **86**
Croirier (''Image on the Heart''), **86**
Crome Yellow (Huxley), 200
Cromwell, George (''The Lees of Happiness''), **86**
Cromwell, Harry (''The Lees of Happiness''), **86**
Cromwell, Kitty Carr (''The Lees of Happiness''), **86**
Crosby, Esther (''Six of One—''), **86**
Crosby, H. B. (''Six of One—''), **87**
Crosby, Mrs. Waldron (''The Smilers''), **87**
Crosby, Waldron (''The Smilers''), **87**
Crowder (*Tender Is the Night*), **87**
''The Cruise of the Rolling Junk'' **87–88**
Crum, Hector (''Forging Ahead''), **88**
Crum, Lewis (''Forging Ahead,'' ''The Freshest Boy,'' ''He Thinks He's Wonderful''), **88**
Crusoe, Joe (''On Your Own''), **88**
Cukor, George, 290, 399
Cullum (''Basil and Cleopatra''), **88**
cummings, e. e., 43, 196
Cummings, Edith, 16, 230
Cuneo, Flute (''In the Holidays''), **88**
Cunizza (*This Side of Paradise*), **88**
Cuomo, Victoria (''One Hundred False Starts''), **88**
Cupp, Miss (''The Rubber Check''), **88**
Cupps, Walter (''Family in the Wind''), **88**
''The Curious Case of Benjamin Button,'' **89**
Curly, Michael (''The Bridal Party''), **89**
Curtain, Jeffrey (''The Lees of Happiness''), **89**
Curtain, Roxanne Milbank (''The Lees of Happiness''), **90**

Cushman ('' 'Boil Some Water—Lots of It' ''), **90**
''The Cut-Glass Bowl,'' **90**
Cynthia (*Safety First!*), **90**

Da Fontano (*The Great Gatsby*), **91**
Dahlgrim (''No Flowers''), **91**
''Daisy Miller'' (James), 194
Dale, Dick (''Mightier Than the Sword''), **91**
Dale, Miss (''The Rubber Check''), **91**
Daley, Irene (''Six of One—''), **91**
Daly (*The Beautiful and Damned*), **91**
Dalyrimple, Bryan (''Dalyrimple Goes Wrong''), **91–92**
''Dalyrimple Goes Wrong,'' **92**
Dame Rumor (Graham), 158
D'Amido, Elizabeth (''The Rough Crossing''), **92**
Dana, Lord. *See* Gilbert, Dodo
Dana, Viola, **92–93**, 179, 308
Danby, Madelaine (''A Snobbish Story''), **93**
''The Dance,'' **93**
Dancie (*The Great Gatsby*), **93**
Dandy, Caroline (''The Bridal Party''), **93**
Dandy, Mrs. (''The Bridal Party''), **93**
Dane, Oscar (''One Trip Abroad''), **94**
Dangue, Dr. (*Tender Is the Night*), **94**
Daniels, Tom (*Thoughtbook*), **94**
Danski, Mrs. (''The Adjuster''), **94**
Danzer, Abe, Lieutenant ('' 'I Didn't Get Over' ''), **94**
Danziger (''Basil and Cleopatra''), **94**
Darcy, Jack (*The Girl from Lazy J*), **94**
Darcy, Thayer, Monsignor (*This Side of Paradise*), **94**, 244, 421
Dare, Alicia (''O Russet Witch!''). *See* Caroline
The Dark Cloud (T. Boyd), 43
Darrow, Clark (''The Ice Palace,'' ''The Jelly-Bean''), **95**
Davey, George (''A Woman with a Past''), **95**
David Blaize (E. Benson), 28
Davidson (''First Blood''), **95**
Davies (''A Full Life''), **95**
Davies, Connie (''Basil and Cleopatra,'' ''The Captured Shadow,'' ''He Thinks He's Wonderful,'' ''The Scandal Detectives''), **95**
Davies, Gwendolyn. *See* Frejus, Comptesse Gwendolyn de
Davies, Mrs. (''A Full Life''), **95**
Davis (''The Freshest Boy''), **95**
Davis (*Porcelain and Pink*), **95**
Davis, Annie Lee (''Lo, the Poor Peacock!''), **95**
Davis, Jason (''Lo, the Poor Peacock!''), **95**
Davis, Josephine (''Lo, the Poor Peacock!''), **96**
Davis, Katherine (''Magnetism''), **96**
Davis, Owen, 290
Davis, Sam (''The Scandal Detectives''), **96**
Davis, Tad (''The Bowl''), **96**
Day, Helen (''One Internet''), **96**
Day, Mrs. Truby Ponsonby (''One Internet''), **96**
Dayfield, William (*This Side of Paradise*), **96**
Dean (''The Offshore Pirate''), **96**
Dean, Elizabeth (*Thoughtbook*), **96**
Dean, Mrs. Francis, 10
Dean, Philip (''May Day''), **96**
''Dearly Beloved,'' **96–97**
''The Death of My Father,'' **97**, 122, 134
De Bec, Mayall (''The Captured Shadow''), **97**
Debris, Percy B. (*The Beautiful and Damned*), **97**
''A Debt of Honor,'' **97**, 247
''*The Debutante*,'' **97–98**
Decker, Mary (''Family in the Wind''), **98**
de Coppet, Travis (''First Blood,'' ''Emotional Bankruptcy,'' ''A Snobbish Story''), **98**
Deems (''Two for a Cent''), **98**
Deering, Humphrey (''The Passionate Eskimo''), **98**
Deering, Jeff (''The Bowl''), **98**
''The Defeat of Art,'' **48–49**, 98
De Ferriac, Mrs. (''The Four Fists''), **98**

Deglen, Joris (''Design in Plaster''), **98**
Deglen, Marianne (''Design in Plaster''), **99**
De Jong (*The Great Gatsby*), **99**
De Koven, Reginald (''Mightier Than the Sword''), **99**, 188, 197
Delauney, Madame Noel (''One Trip Abroad''), **99**
Delehanty, Jenny. *See* Prince, Jenny
Delihant, Thomas. **99–100**, 226, 316
Dell, Floyd, 48
Dell, Henry Haven (''News from Paris—Fifteen Years Ago''), **100**
Del Monti (*Fie! Fie! Fi-Fi!*), **100**
de Martel, Dr. (''The Love Boat''), **100**
De Mille, Cecil B., **100**
Demming (''Dalyrimple Goes Wrong''), **100**
Demorest, Ethel (''Bernice Bobs Her Hair''), **100**
Dempsey, William Harrison (*Tender Is the Night*, ''Two Wrongs''), **100**, 323
Dempster, Emily Hope (''Imagination—and a Few Mothers''), **100**
Dempster, Paul (''Emotional Bankruptcy''), **100**
Denby, Van Buren (*Tender Is the Night*), **100**
Dennicker (*The Great Gatsby*), **100**
Dent (''Dalyrimple Goes Wrong''), **101**
Denzer, Catherine (''On an Ocean Wave''), **101**
Derehiemer (''Flight and Pursuit''), **101**
Derocco, Dr. (''The Swimmers''), **101**
de Sade, Gilles. *See* Patch, Anthony
de Sano, Marcel, 289, 409
Deshhacker, Mrs. (''Lo, the Poor Peacock!''), **101**
''Design in Plaster,'' **101**
Deslys, Gaby (*Porcelain and Pink*), **101**
Deslys, Miss (*The Evil Eye*), **101**
Destage (''Shadow Laurels''), **102**
DeTinc (''Fun in an Artist's Studio''), **102**
Devereaux (''The Bowl''), **102**
De Vinci, Leonard Edward Davies (''The Perfect Life''), **102**
de Vinci, Mark (''One Hundred False Starts''), **102**
Devineries (''May Day''), **102**
Devlin (''Winter Dreams''), **102**
Devlin, Estelle Hobby (''No Harm Trying''), **102**
Devlin, Jack (''The Bowl''), **102**
Dewar (*The Great Gatsby*), **102**
De Witt, Marylyn (*This Side of Paradise*), **102**
Deyo, Draycott (''Bernice Bobs Her Hair''), **102**
Deyo, Mrs. (''Bernice Bobs Her Hair''), **102**
''Diagnosis,'' **103**
''The Diamond as Big as the Ritz,'' **103–4**
''Diamond Dick and the First Law of Woman,'' **104**
Diamond, Margaret (*This Side of Paradise*), **104**
''The Diary of a Sophomore,'' **104**
Dibby (*This Side of Paradise*), **104**
''Dice, Brass Knuckles & Guitar,'' **104–5**
Dicer, Captain Edward (''Emotional Bankruptcy''), **105**
Dicer, Christine (''Emotional Bankruptcy''), **105**
Dicer, Mrs. (''Emotional Bankruptcy''), **105**
Dick (*The Last Tycoon*), **105**
Dick (''A Nice Quiet Place''), **105**
Dickey (''Diamond Dickey and the First Law of Woman''), **105**
Dickey, Breck (''Diamond Dickey and the First Law of Woman''), **105**
Dickey, Diana (''Diamond Dickey and the First Law of Woman''), **106**
Dickey, Harry (''Fate in Her Hands''), **106**
Dickey, Mrs. (''Diamond Dickey and the First Law of Woman''), **106**
Diffendorfer (''Majesty''), **106**
Dignanni, Princess (''Fun in an Artist's Studio''), **106**
Dillinger, Professor (''Head and Shoulders''), **106**
Dillon (''Emotional Bankruptcy''), **106**

Dillon, Jackson (''First Blood''), **106**
Dillon, Mrs. (''Emotional Bankruptcy''), **106**
Dillon, Roberta (''Bernice Bobs Her Hair''), **106**
D'Invilliers, Mrs. (*This Side of Paradise*), **106**
D'Invilliers, Thomas Parke (*This Side of Paradise*), 34, **106–7**
''A Dirge (Apologies to Wordsworth),'' **107**
''Discard,'' **107**
The Disenchanted (Schulberg), 360, 376
Distant Friends and Intimate Strangers: Stories (East), 208
Diver (*Tender Is the Night*), **107**
Diver, Dick (*Tender Is the Night*), **107**, 205, 293, 315
Diver, Lanier (*Tender Is the Night*), **107**
Diver, Nicole (*Tender Is the Night*), **108**, 137, 293
Diver, Topsy (*Tender Is the Night*), **108**
Divine, Babe (''The Offshore Pirate''), **108**
Divine, Rodney (*Mister Icky*), **108**
Dixon, Leslie (''New Types''), **108**
Dizzy (''Inside the House''), **108**
Dodd, Martha (*The Last Tycoon*), **108**
Dodge, Mack (*The Beautiful and Damned*), **108**
''Does a Moment of Revolt Come Sometime to Every Married Man?,'' **108**
''Dog! Dog! Dog!,'' **109**
Dohmler, Dr. (*Tender Is the Night*), **109**
Doldrum, Boscoe, Hartsum, Heck, and Jem (''Jemina''), **109**
Dollard, Professor (''On an Ocean Wave''), **109**
Dolly (''To Dolly''), **109**
Dolores (''Magnetism''), **109**
Dominique (''Rags Martin-Jones and the Pr-nce of W-les''), **109**
Donahue (''Dalyrimple Goes Wrong''), **109**
Donald (''One Hundred False Starts''), **109**
Donald (''A Snobbish Story''), **109**
Doncastle, Lady (''The Rubber Check''), **109**
Donilof (''Two Wrongs''), **110**
Donnelly, Pop, Sergeant (*The Beautiful and Damned*), **110**
Donny (''The Smilers''), **110**
Donovan (''Magnetism''), **110**
Donovan, Margaret (''Magnetism''), **110**
Donowska, Dr. ('' 'Trouble' ''), **110**
''DONT EXPECT ME . . . ,'' **110**
''Don't you worry I surrender,'' **110**
Doofus ('' 'Trouble' ''), **110**
Doolan, Catherine (*The Last Tycoon*), **110**
Doolan, Kit (''Pat Hobby's College Days''), **110**
Doolan, Mrs. Kit (''Pat Hobby's College Days''), **111**
Doremus (''One Interne''), **111**
Doris (''The Diary of a Sophomore''), **111**
Doris (*The Vegetable*), **111**
Dorothy (''Martin's Thoughts''), **111**
Dorr, Julia (*Thoughtbook*), **111**
Dorrance, Charles (''A Nice Quiet Place''), **111**
Dorrance, Sonny (''A Nice Quiet Place''), **111**
Dorsey (''On Your Own''), **111**
Dorsey (''The Perfect Life''), **111**
Dorsey (*Tender Is the Night*), **111**
Dorsey, George (''The Perfect Life''), **111**
Dorsey, Jobena (''Basil and Cleopatra,'' ''The Perfect Life''), **111–12**
Dorsey, Mrs. (''The Perfect Life''), **112**
Dos Passos, John, **112–13**, 153, 292, 399, 449
Dougall, Dr. (*This Side of Paradise*), **113**
Doubleday, Frank Nelson, 78
Dougherty, Joe (''The Bowl''), **113**
Dougie (''Pat Hobby, Putative Father''), **113**
Douglas (''Magnetism''), **113**
Douglas, Arthur, Judge (*Coward*), **113**
Douglas, Charles (*Coward*), **113**
Douglas, Clara (*Coward*), **113**
Douglas, Lindy (*Coward*), **113**

Douglas, Mary (*Coward*), **113**
Douglas, Tommy (*Coward*), **113**
Doyle, Conan ("The Rich Boy"), **113**
Dragonet, Amalie Eustace Bedford ("Her Last Case"), **114**
Dragonet, Ben ("Her Last Case"), **114**
Dragonet, Mrs. Ben ("Her Last Case"), **114**
Drake, Fred ("Hot and Cold Blood"), **114**
Drake, Jane ("A Freeze-Out"), **114**
Dreiser, Theodore, 43, 278, 297
Drinkwater, Mollie ("Your Way and Mine"), **114**
Drinkwater, Theodore ("Your Way and Mine"), **114**
Driscoll, Bob (*Thoughtbook*), **114**
Driscoll, D. (*Thoughtbook*), **114**
Driscoll, E. (*Thoughtbook*), **114**
Driscoll, William ("Not in the Guidebook"), **114**
Drummon (*The Last Tycoon*), **115**
du Cary, Edith ("On Schedule"), **115**
du Cary, Noël ("On Schedule"), **115**
du Cary, René ("On Schedule"), **115**
Du Chene, Margureta (*Assorted Spirits*), **115**
Duchman ("Fun in an Artist's Studio"), **115**
Duckney, Angela ("Strange Sanctuary"), **115**
Duckney, L. P. ("Strange Sanctuary"), **115**
Duckweed, George (*The Great Gatsby*), **115**
Dudley, Thorton Hart (*The Captured Shadow*), **115**
Duke (*The Great Gatsby*), **115**
Duke, Basil W., 246
Duke, Eubert M. ("The Honor of the Goon"), **116**
Dulany, Tib ("The End of Hate"), **116**
Dulcette (*Fie! Fie! Fi-Fi!*), **116**
Dulcinea ("The Evil Eye"), **116**
Dulschmit (*Tender Is the Night*), **116**
Dumbella, Paola ("The High Cost of Macaroni"), **116**
Dumbella, Princess ("The High Cost of Macaroni"), **116**
Dumphry, Royal (*Tender Is the Night*), **116**
Duncan, Miss ("Magnetism"), **116**
Dunn ("The Freshest Boy"), **116**
Dunn, Sir Humphrey ("Two Wrongs"), **116**
Dunning, Captain (*The Beautiful and Damned*), **116**
Dunois ("A Change of Class"), **116**
Dupont, Pere ("Sentiment—and the Use of Rouge"), **117**
Dureal, Leon (*The Captured Shadow*), **117**
Durfee, Dr. Howard ("One Interne"), **117**
Dwan, Allan ("Two Old-Timers"), **117**
Dyer ("Bernice Bobs Her Hair"), **117**

Earl ("The Passionate Eskimo"), **118**
Earl (*Thoughtbook*), **118**
Earle, Helen (" 'Boil Some Water—Lots of It' "), **118**
Early, Jubal [Anderson], General, 97, **118**
"Early Success," **118**
"The Earth Calls," **118**
East, Charles, 208
Easby, H. P. ("Indecision"), **119**
"East of the sun, west of the moon," **119**
Eberhardt, Mrs. (*The Great Gatsby*), **119**
"Echoes of the Jazz Age," **119**
Eckhaust (*The Great Gatsby*), **119**
Eckleburg, Dr. T. J. (*The Great Gatsby*), **119**
Eddie ("What Kind of Husbands Do 'Jimmies' Make?"), **119**
Eddington ("Between Three and Four"), **119**
Eddington, B. B. ("Between Three and Four"), **120**
Eddington, George ("Between Three and Four"), **120**
Edgar (*The Great Gatsby*), **120**
Edison, Edgar ("Jemina"), **120**
Edna (The Last Tycoon), **120**

Edwards, Big Bill (''The Ants at Princeton''), **120**
Egan (''The Mystery of the Raymond Mortgage''), **120**
Egbert (*Thoughtbook*), **120**
Egg, Mr. (''Does a Moment of Revolt Come Some Time to Every Married Man?''), **120**
Egg, Mrs. (''Does a Moment of Revolt Come Some Time to Every Married Man?''), **120**
Eisenhaur (''Dalyrimple Goes Wrong''), **120**
Elenor (''Martin's Thoughts''), **120**
Elgin, Paul (Fitzgerald pseudonym), 311
Eliot, T. S., 430
Elkins (''A Letter to Helen''), **120**
Elkins, Arthur (''Myra Meets His Family''), **120**
Elkins, Ed (*Tender Is the Night*), **121**
Elkins, Lilah (''Myra Meets His Family''), **121**
Ellen (*Coward*), **121**
''Ellerslie,'' **121**, 135, 181, 380, 460
Ellinger (*The Beautiful and Damned*), **121**
Elliot, Emily (''Indecision''), **121**
Ellis, Walter, 36
Elsa (''The Rubber Check''), **121**
Elsie (''One Hundred False Starts''), **121**
Em (*The Last Tycoon*), **121**
Emil (''The Perfect Life''), **121**
Emile (*Tender Is the Night*), **121**
Emma (''Fate in Her Hands''), **121**
Emma Kate (*The Captured Shadow*), **121**
''Emotional Bankruptcy,'' **122**
Endive, Clarence (*The Great Gatsby*), **122**
''The End of Hate,'' **122–23**
Engalitcheff, Prince Vladimir N., 363
Engels, Crenshaw (''The Fiend''), **123**
Engels, Friedrich, 123
Engels, Mark (''The Fiend''), **123**
Engels, Mrs. Crenshaw (''The Fiend''), **123**
The Enormous Room (cummings), 43, 196
Eric (''Indecision''), **123**
Eric (''No Harm Trying''), **123**
Essie (''Sleeping and Walking''), **123**
Essei (''That Kind of Party''), **123**
Este, Charles, Lord (''Rags Martin-Jones and the Pr-nce of W-les''), **123**
Estelle (''No Flowers''), **123**
Esther (*The Last Tycoon*), **123**
Esther (''Love in the Night''), **123**
Ethan Frome (Wharton), 452
Etherington, Sara (''Diagnosis''), **124**
Etty (*The Great Gatsby*), **124**
Eugénie (''How to Live on Practically Nothing a Year''), **124**
Europe, Jim (''No Flowers''), **124**
Ev (''Family in the Wind''), **124**
Evarts, Gertrude (''Sentiment—and the Use of Rouge''), **124**
Evelyn (''A Snobbish Story''), **124**
Evelyn (''Strange Sanctuary''), **124**
Everett, Tom (''Dalyrimple Goes Wrong''), **124**
''Everytime I blow my nose I think of you,'' **124**
The Evil Eye, **124–25**, 459
Ewing, Joe (''The Ice Palace,'' ''The Jelly-Bean''), **125**
Exile's Return: A Narrative of Ideas (Cowley), 83

Fairbanks, Douglas (*The Last Tycoon*), **126**, 236, 242, 252, 293, 405, 439
Fairboalt, Mrs. (''The Cut-Glass Bowl''), **126**
''The Family Bus,'' **126–27**
''Family in the Wind,'' 5, **127–28**
Farnham (''The Offshore Pirate''), **127**
Farnham, Ardita (''The Offshore Pirate''), **128**
Farrelly, Billy (''Jacob's Ladder''), **128**
''Fate in Her Hands,'' **128**
Fay, Cyril Sigourney Webster, 94, **128–29**, 244, 249, 421, 466
Fay, Ted (''The Freshest Boy''), **129**
Fay, Teeny (''I Got Shoes''), **129**
Featherstone (*Tender Is the Night*), **129**
Fenwick, Larry (*The Beautiful and Damned*), **129**
Fernand (*Tender Is the Night*), **129**

Ferrenby (*This Side of Paradise*), **129**
Ferrenby, Jesse (*This Side of Paradise*), **130**
Ferret, James B. (*The Great Gatsby*), **130**
Fessenden, Claude (''Babylon Revisited''), **130**
Fido (''Pilgrimage''), **130**
Fie! Fie! Fi-Fi!, **130–31**
Fielding, Cyrus (*The Beautiful and Damned*), **131**
The Fiend (''The Fiend''), **131**
''The Fiend,'' **131**
Fifi (''The Unspeakable Egg''), **131**
Fi-Fi (*Fie! Fie! Fi- Fi*), **131**
''Financing Finnegan,'' **131–32**, 307, 335
Finch, Miss (*Coward*), **132**
Finch, Mrs. (*Thoughtbook*), **132**
Fingarson (''The Honor of the Goon''), **132**
Fink, Hymie (''Discard''), **132**
Finnegan (''Financing Finnegan''), **132**, 307
Finney, Peaches, Peggy, and Pete (''SING HOTCH-CHA SING HEY-HI NINNY''), **132**
Firebrand (*This Side of Paradise*), **132**
''First a hug and tease and a something on my knees,'' **132**
''First Blood,'' **132–33**
''1st Epistle of St. Scott to the Smithsonian,'' **133**
Fish, Joseph (*The Vegetable*), **133**
Fishburn, John J. (''The Ice Palace''), **133**
Fishguard (*The Great Gatsby*), **133**
Fiske, Minnie Maddern (*Assorted Spirits*), **133**
Fiske, Mrs. (''A Snobbish Story''), **133**
Fitzgerald, Annabel. *See* Sprague, Annabel Fitzgerald
Fitzgerald, Cecilia Ashton Scott, 133, 135
Fitzgerald, Edward, 97, 122, **133–34**, 135
Fitzgerald, Frances Scott. *See* Smith, Frances Scott Fitzgerald Lanahan
Fitzgerald, Mary McQuillan, **134–35**, 266
Fitzgerald, Michael, 133, **135**
Fitzgerald, Zelda Sayre, 3, 5, 79, 89, **135–37**, 158, 159, 278, 335, 406, 416, 422, 454, 460; and family, 47, 246, 265, 278, 321, 334, 338, 372, 390, 392; in Fitzgerald's writings, 87, 195, 196, 203; and friends and acquaintances, 32, 34, 38, 112, 181, 238, 249, 279, 286, 291, 298, 307, 323, 355, 363, 380, 398, 406, 440, 452; illness, 135–36, 204, 254, 313, 384, 414; as model for Fitzgerald's characters, 64, 78, 174, 326, 453; written work, 24, 83, 136–37, 153, 454
Fitz-Hugh, Major Sir Reynolds (''A Penny Spent''), **137**
Fitzpatrick, Al (''The Love Boat''), **137**
Fitzpatrick, Mae Purley (''The Love Boat''), **137**
Fitz-Peters, Ardita (*The Great Gatsby*), **137**
Flandrau, Grace C. Hodgson, 43, **137–38**, 283
Flappers and Philosophers, **138**, 333
Flesh, S. (*Tender Is the Night*), **138**
Flieshacker, Mort (*The Last Tycoon*), **138**
''Flight and Pursuit,'' **138**
Flink, Maurice A. (*The Great Gatsby*), **139**
Flint, Bill (''The Family Bus''), **139**
Florence (''Love in the Night''), **139**
Flowing Boots (''Tarquin of Cheapside''), **139**
Floyd, Charles Arthur, **139**, 346
Flynn, Dr. (''The Love Boat''), **139**
Foley, Arthur (*Thoughtbook*), **139**
Foley, Phil (*Thoughtbook*), **139**
Foley, R. A., Sergeant (*The Beautiful and Damned*), **139**
''Football,'' **139**
''For a Long Illness,'' **140**
''For Dolly,'' **140**
Forel, Dr. Oscar, 135–36
''Forging Ahead,'' **140**
''For Mary's Eighth Birthday,'' **140**
Forney, Edward (''The Honor of the Goon''), **140**
Forrest, Mrs. Hugh (''A Freeze-Out''), **140**
Forrester, Frank (''Indecision''), **141**
''For 2nd Stanza Baoth Poem,'' **141**

''For Sheilah, a Beloved Infidel,'' 159
''For Song—Idea—He's just a friend he said. But,'' **141**
''For the lads of the village triumph,'' **141**
''For the time that our man spent in pressing your suit,'' **141**
Fossile, Chief Justice (''The Curious Case of Benjamin Button''), **141**
Fossile, Judge (*The Vegetable*), **141**
Foster, Billy (*Thoughtbook*), **141**
Foster, Harriet (*Thoughtbook*), **141**
Foster, Roger (*Thoughtbook*), **141**
Foulke, Dr. (''The Cut-Glass Bowl''), **141**
Fouquet (*Tender Is the Night*), **142**
''The Four Fists,'' **142**
Fowler (''John Jackson's Arcady''), **142**
Fowler, John Jackson (''John Jackson's Arcady''), **142**
Fowler, Ludlow, 47, 199
Fowler, Powell, 47
Fragelle, Lady (''One Trip Abroad''), **142**
Fragelle, Sir Evelyne, General (''One Trip Abroad''), **142**
France, Anatole, 138, 422
''Frances Kroll,'' **142**
Franklin, Ike (*The Last Tycoon*), **143**
Fraser (''Dalyrimple Goes Wrong''), **143**
Fraser (''Majesty''), **143**
Fraser, Alfred J. (''Dalyrimple Goes Wrong''), **143**
Freddie (''Discard''), **143**
Frederico (''A Penny Spent''), **143**
Freeman (*Tender Is the Night*), **143**
''A Freeze-Out,'' **143**
Frejus, Compte René de (''A Full Life''), **144**
Frejus, Comptesse Gwendolyn de (''A Full Life''), **144**
''The Freshest Boy,'' **144**
Freud, Sigmund, 119
Froilich (''A Letter to Helen''), **144**
''From Scott Fitzgerald,'' **144**
Frost, Charlotte (*The Vegetable*), **145**
Frost, Horatio (*The Vegetable*), **145**
Frost, Jerry (*The Vegetable*), **145**
Frothington (''The Love Boat''), **145**
Frothington (''The Love Boat''), **145**
Frothington, Bill (''The Love Boat''), **145**
Frothington, George (''The Love Boat''), **145**
Frothington, Mrs. (''The Love Boat''), **145**
Frothington, Stella (''The Love Boat''), **145–46**
Fry, ''Fish-eye'' (*The Beautiful and Damned*), **146**
''F. Scott Fitzgerald and the Roaring Twenties! After the whoopee came sadness . . . ,'' **146**
''F. Scott Fitzgerald Is Bored by Efforts at Realism in 'Lit,' '' **146**
Fulham (''The Pierian Springs and the Last Straw''), **146**
Fulham, Myra (''The Pierian Springs and the Last Straw''), **146**
''A Full Life,'' **146–47**
''Fun in an Artist's Studio,'' **147**

Gaffney, Miss (''O Russet Witch!''), **148**
Gager, Theodora, 5
Gallup, Dr. Roswell (''The Unspeakable Egg''), **148**
Galsworthy, John, 334
Galt (''The Third Casket''), **148**
Gamble, Hotsy (''No Flowers''), **148**
Garavochi (''Gods of Darkness''), **148**
Garbo, Greta, **148**, 296
Gardener (*Thoughtbook*), **148**
Gardener, Ham (*Thoughtbook*), **148**
Gardener, Nancy (*Thoughtbook*), **149**
Gardner (''The Love Boat''), **149**
Gardner, George. *See* Gardener
Garland, Dodson (''The Trail of the Duke''), **149**
Garneau, Harold (''Persuasion''), **149**
Garneau, Mrs. Clifton (''Dice, Brassknuckles & Guitar''), **149**
Garneau, Mrs. Harold (''Persuasion''), **149**
Garneau, Noel (''Persuasion''), **149**
Garnett, Chauncey (''The Adolescent Marriage''), **149**

Garrod, H. G. (''Gretchen's Forty Winks''), **150**
Garvin (*This Side of Paradise*), **150**
Gaspar, Mrs. (''Two Old-Timers''), **150**
Gaspar, Sergeant (''Two Old-Timers''), **150**
Gaspar, William (''Basil and Cleopatra,'' ''The Freshest Boy''), **150**
Gatsby, Jay (*The Great Gatsby*), 5, **150**, 164
Gatz, Henry C. (*The Great Gatsby*), **150**
Gausse, (*Tender Is the Night*), **150**
Gautier (''The Count of Darkness''), **151**
Gedney, Fred (''The Cut-Glass Bowl''), **151**
Geer, Betty (''Forging Ahead''), **151**
Gehrbohm (''Lo, the Poor Peacock!''), **151**
Gentle Julia (Tarkington), 407
George (''The Passionate Eskimo''), **151**
Georgi, Dr. (''One Interne''), **151**
Georgianna ('' 'Why Blame It on the Poor Kiss If the Girl Veteran of Many Petting Parties Is Prone to Affairs After Marriage?' ''), **151**
Georgie, Aunt (''That Kind of Party''), **151**
Gerald (''O Russet Witch!''), **151**
Germaine (''Rags Martin-Jones and the Pr-nce of W-les''), **151**
Gifford, Nancy Holmes (''Three Hours between Planes''), **151**
Gifford, Walter (''Three Hours between Planes''), **151**
Gilbert, Catherine (*The Beautiful and Damned*), **151–52**
Gilbert, Dodo (''Strange Sanctuary''), **152**
Gilbert, Gloria. *See* Patch, Gloria Gilbert
Gilbert, John, 85, **152**, 163, 263, 286, 431, 439
Gilbert, Russel (*The Beautiful and Damned*), **152**
Gile, Bean (''The Bowl''), **152**
Gillespie, Dr. (''One Interne''), **152**
Gillespie, Howard (*This Side of Paradise*), **152**
Gilman, Edward, 74, 225
Gilray (''That Kind of Party''), **152**
Gilray, Mrs. (''That Kind of Party''), **152**
Ginevra (''A Letter to Helen''). *See also* King, Ginevra
Gingrich, Arnold, 84, 94, **152–53**, 311, 329
Girard, Cyrus (''The Third Casket''), **153**
Girard, Lola (''The Third Casket''), **153**
The Girl from Lazy J, **154**
''Girls Believe in Girls,'' **154**
Gisler (*Tender Is the Night*), **154**
Giuseppe (*Fie! Fie! Fi-Fi!*), **154**
Giuseppi (''Imagination—and a Few Mothers''), **154**
Given, Dr. (''The Love Boat''), **154**
Gladys (*Fie! Fie! Fi-Fi!*), **154**
Gladys (''The Hotel Child''), **154**
Gladys (''A Nice Quiet Place''), **154**
Gladys (''That Kind of Party''), **154**
Gleason, Miss (''In the Holidays''), **155**
Glimpses of the Moon (Wharton), 117, 289, 452
Glock, Doctor (''The Bowl''), **155**
Gloria (*The Great Gatsby*), **155**
Glucose, Israel (''Dice, Brassknuckles & Guitar''), **155**
Glynn, Madame (''What Became of Our Flappers and Sheiks?''), **155**
''A god intoxicated fly,'' **155**
''Gods of Darkness,'' **155**
God, the Invisible King (Wells), 449
Goebel, Eva (''Crazy Sunday''), **155**
Goldberg (''The Offshore Pirate''), **155**
Goldberg, Rube, **156**
Golden (''Gretchen's Forty Winks''), **156**
Goldgreaves (''In the Darkest Hour''), **156**
Golding, T. F. (''One Trip Abroad,'' *Tender Is the Night*), **156**
Goldstein, Louis, 25
Goldstien, Katie (''The Dance''), **156–57**
Gone with the Wind, 289–90
Gonzoles, Tony (*The Girl from Lazy J*), **157**
Gooddorf, Harry (''Pat Hobby's Christmas Wish,'' ''Pat Hobby's Preview''), **157**

Gorman, Herbert Sherbert (''All the Girls and Mans''), **157**
Gorman, Joe (''The Captured Shadow,'' ''He Thinks He's Wonderful''), **157**
Gotrocks (''A Snobbish Story''), **157**
Gottlieb, Captain (''The Bowl''), **157**
Gould, Harriet (*Thoughtbook*), **157**
Govan, Ben (''The Family Bus''), **157**
Governor of California, the (*The Last Tycoon*), **157**
Gown, Johnny (*Thoughtbook*), **157**
Grace (''A Short Autobiography''), **158**
Grady, Henry ('' 'Send Me In, Coach' ''), **158**
Graham (''Myra Meets His Family''), **158**
Graham, Sheilah, **158–59**, 204, 232, 230, 233, 240, 243, 249, 286, 307, 335, 391, 394, 423, 450
Grainger, Arthur (''O Russet Witch!''), **159**
Grainger, Merlin (''O Russet Witch!''), **159**
Grainger, Olive Masters (''O Russet Witch!''), **159**
Granby, Alec (''The Perfect Life''), **159**
Granby, John (*The Beautiful and Damned*), **160**
Granby, Mrs. Alec (*The Beautiful and Damned*), **160**
Granby, Peter (*The Beautiful and Damned*), **160**
Grange, Harold Red, 160
Grange, Red (''No Flowers''), **160**
Granny (''The Count of Darkness''), **160**
Grant, Cary, **160**
Grant, Ulysses Simpson, **160**, 247
Granville, Bonita, **160**, 205
Grayson, Miss (*Coward*), **160**
The Great Gatsby, 78, 106, **160–63**, 181, 208, 279, 335, 450; friends' response to, 112, 279, 323, 334, 380, 397, 452, 459; models for characters and places in, 137, 230, 239; and related works, 2, 164, 340, 357, 462
The Great Gatsby (movie), 32
The Great Gatsby (play), 290
Great Lover, the (''Crazy Sunday''), **163**
Green (''The Offshore Pirate''), **163**
Green (''Winter Dreams''), **164**
Green, Dexter (''Winter Dreams''), **164**
Green, Dorothy (*Thoughtbook*), **164**
Green, Harold (*Thoughtbook*), **164**
Green, Mrs. (''Winter Dreams''), **164**
Gregg, Allen (''Dalyrimple Goes Wrong''), **164**
Gregg, G. P. (''Dalyrimple Goes Wrong''), **164**
Gregorovius, Dr. Franz (*Tender Is the Night*), **164**
Gregorovius, Kaethe (*Tender Is the Night*), **164**
Gregory, Dr. (''Gretchen's Forty Winks''), **164**
Gregory, Walter (''Myra Meets His Family''), **165**
Gregson (''The Mystery of the Raymond Mortgage''), **165**
Gresham, John (''One Interne''), **165**
''Gretchen's Forty Winks,'' **165**
Griebel, Louis (''Pat Hobby and Orson Welles''), **165**
Griffin (''In the Holidays''), **166**
Griffin, Bob (''Last Kiss''), **166**
Griggs, Ben (*Thoughtbook*), **166**
Griselda, Countess (''The Kingdom in the Dark,'' ''Gods of Darkness''), **166**
Grit (movie), 289
Gross, Dr. (''The Love Boat''), **166**
Guescelin (''The Count of Darkness''), **166**
Guesculin (''The Kingdom in the Dark''), **166**
''The Guest in Room Nineteen,'' **166**
Gugimoniki, R. (*The Beautiful and Damned*), **166**
Guillet de la Guimpé, Comte Paul de la (''The Intimate Strangers''), **167**
Guillet de la Guimpé, Marquis Eduard de la (''The Intimate Strangers''), **167**
Guillet de la Guimpé, Marquis Henri de la (''The Intimate Strangers''), **167**
Guillet de la Guimpé, Marquise Sara de la (''The Intimate Strangers''), **167**
Guillet de la Guimpé, Miette de la (''The Intimate Strangers''), **167**

Guillet de la Guimpé, Noel de la (''The Intimate Strangers''), **167**
Guise, the Hon. Elinor (''The Rubber Check''), **167**
Gulick (*The Great Gatsby*), **167**
Gunter (*The Beautiful and Damned*), **167**
Gunther (''More Than Just a House''), **168**
Gunther, Amanda (''More Than Just a House''), **168**
Gunther, Bess (''More Than Just a House''), **168**
Gunther, Jean (''More Than Just a House''), **168**
Gunther, Mrs. (''More Than Just a House''), **168**
Guson, Alfred (*Thoughtbook*), **168**
Guthrie, Laura, 128
Guyenne, Duke of (''The Kingdom in the Dark''), **168**
Gwen (*Fie! Fie! Fi- Fi!*), **168**
Gygsum (''The Diamond as Big as the Ritz''), **168**
Gyp the Blood (''The Rough Crossing''), **168**

Haag, Miss (*The Great Gatsby*), **169**
Haedge (''The Popular Girl''), **169**
Hagerty, Paula Legendre Thayer (''The Rich Boy''), **169**
Hagerty, Peter (''The Rich Boy''), **169**
Haggin (''New Types''), **169**
Haggin, Mrs. (''New Types''), **169**
Haight (*The Beautiful and Damned*), **169**
Haight, Gouverneer (''Two Wrongs''), **170**
Haight, Marjorie (''The Jelly-Bean''), **170**
Haines, Dolly (''Strange Sanctuary''), 41, **170**
Haines, Morton (''Strange Sanctuary''), **170**
Halbird, June (''The Rubber Check''), **170**
Halbird, Mrs. (''The Rubber Check''), **170**
Hale, Musidora (''The Dance''), **170**
''Half-and-Half Girl,'' **170**
Halklite (''Lo, the Poor Peacock!''), **170**
Hallam (''Majesty''), **170**
Halliburton, Miss (''The Captured Shadow''), **170**
Halloran (*The Beautiful and Damned*), **171**
Halogen (*Precaution Primarily*), **171**
Halsey, Gretchen (''Gretchen's Forty Winks''), **171**
Halsey, Maxy (''Gretchen's Forty Winks,'' **171**
Halsey, Roger (''Gretchen's Forty Winks''), **171**
Halycon (''The Debutante''), **171**
Halycon (''The Debutante''), **171**
Halycon, Cecilia (''The Debutante''), **171**
Halycon, Helen (''The Debutante''), **171**
Halycon, Mrs. (''The Debutante''), **171**
Hambell (*This Side of Paradise*), **172**
Hamil (''The Four Fists''), **172**
Hamilton (''Majesty''), **172**
Hamilton, John (''Strange Sanctuary''), **172**
Hammel, Lillian (''First Blood,'' ''A Nice Quiet Place,'' ''A Woman with a Past,'' ''A Snobbish Story,'' ''Emotional Bankruptcy''), **172**
Hammerhead (*The Great Gatsby*), **172**
Hammerton, Elsie (''A Snobbish Story''), **172**
Hammond, Mrs. Richard Barton (*The Vegetable*), **172**
Hamn (''Majesty''), **172**
Hancock, Thornton (*This Side of Paradise*), **172**
''Handle with Care,'' **173**, 325, 459
Hannaford, George (''Magnetism''), **173**
Hannaford, Kay (''Magnetism''), **173**
Hannaman, Clara (''Too Cute for Words''), **173**
Hannaman, Helen (''Too Cute for Words''), **173**
Hannan, Carly (*Tender Is the Night*), **173**
Hannan, Helen (''A Freeze-Out''), **173**
Hannan, Walter (''A Freeze-Out''), **174**
Hanson (''Dalyrimple Goes Wrong''), **174**
Hanson (*The Last Tycoon*), **174**

Hanson, Claud ("On an Ocean Wave"), **174**
Happer, Sally Carrol ("The Ice Palace"), 79, **174**
Harding, Warren G., 297, 439
Hardt, George ("Babylon Revisited"), **174**
Hardy (*The Beautiful and Damned*), **174**
Harebell (*This Side of Paradise*), **174**
Harker, Anthony ("Emotional Bankruptcy," "First Blood"), **174**
Harkless, Luke (" 'Trouble' "), **174**
Harlan ("Two for a Cent"), **175**
Harlan, Dolly ("The Bowl"), **175**
Harlan, Genevieve ("Dice, Brassknuckles & Guitar"), **175**
Harlan, Madison ("Dice, Brassknuckles & Guitar"), **175**
Harlan, Mrs. ("The Bowl"), **175**
Harlan, Ronald ("Dice, Brassknuckles & Guitar"), **175**
Harland, Alice ("John Jackson's Aracady"), **175**
Harland, George ("John Jackson's Aracady"), **175**
Harley (*The Last Tycoon*), **175**
Harley, Ellen ("The Popular Girl"), **175**
Harlow, Jean (*The Last Tycoon*), 175, 416
Harmon, Ned (" 'Boil Some Water—Lots of It' "), **176**
Harmon, Dorothy ("A Luckless Santa Claus"), **176**
Harper, Billy ("Persuasion"), **176**
Harper, Myra ("Myra Meets His Family"), **176**
Harrington, Bob (*Thoughtbook*), **176**
Harris (*The Evil Eye*), **176**
Harris ("Two Wrongs"), **176**
Harris, Ellen ("New Types"), **176**
Harris, George ("Magnetism"), **176**
Harris, Martin ("Design in Plaster"), **176**
Harris, Mary ("Design in Plaster"), **176–77**
Harris, Mike ("Last Kiss"), **177**
Harrison, Dr. ("Her Last Case"), 5, **177**
Harrison, Ed ("Inside the House"), **177**
Harry ("Too Cute for Words"), **177**
Harry (" 'Why Blame It on the Poor Kiss If the Girl Veteran of Many Petting Parties Is Prone to Affairs After Marriage?' "), **177**
Hart ("The Curious Case of Benjamin Button"), **177**
Hart ("The Family Bus"), **177**
Hart ("Winter Dreams"), **177**
Hart, Charley ("One of My Oldest Friends"), **177**
Harvey ("Bernice Bobs Her Hair"), **177**
Harvey, Josephine ("Bernice Bobs Her Hair"), **177**
Harvey, Marjorie ("Bernice Bobs Her Hair"), **178**
Hasbrouk ("A Full Life"), **178**
Hasbrouk, Cornelius B. ("A Full Life"), **178**
Hasbrouk, Gwendolyn. *See* Frejus, Comptesse Gwendolyn de
Haskins, Dan ("The Freshest Boy"), **178**
Hasylton, Morris ("Love in the Night"), **178**
Hat ("Head and Shoulders"), **178**
Hatman, Mabel ("Mightier Than the Sword"), **178**
Hattie ("An Alcoholic Case"), **178**
Haughton, Ad ("The Love Boat"), **178**
Haupt, Mary ("He Thinks He's Wonderful"), **178**
Hawkins ("Dalyrimple Goes Wrong"), **179**
Hawkins, Mrs. ("Dalyrimple Goes Wrong"), **179**
Hawks, Gretta ("An Alcoholic Case"), **179**
Hayes, Helen, 391
Hazeldawn ("Strange Sanctuary"), **179**
Hazelton, Miss (*Coward*), **179**
"Head and Shoulders," 93, **179**
Healy (*This Side of Paradise*), **179**
Hearst ("Reade, Substitute Right Half"), **179**
"Heart of Darkness" (Conrad), 78
Heatherly ("The Freshest Boy"), **180**
Heck ("The Diary of a Sophomore"), **180**
Hecksher ("Jacob's Ladder"), **180**

Hedrick, T. A. (''Winter Dreams''), **180**
Helen (''A Letter to Helen''), **180**
Helen (''Martin's Thoughts''), **180**
Helen (*Tender Is the Night*), **180**
Helen (''That Kind of Party''), **180**
Helena (In ''Thousand-and-First Ship''), **180**
Helena Something-or-Other, Lady (''Myra Meets His Family''), **180**
Hélène (''News from Paris—Fifteen Years Ago''), **180**
Hemingway, Ernest, 132, 153, **180–82**, 259, 339, 380; relationships with others, 7, 33, 56–57, 78, 82–83, 112, 239, 260, 323, 376, 379, 397, 398, 399, 407; writings, 8, 196, 334
Hemmick, George (''The Adolescent Marriage''), **182**
Hemmick, Henry W. (''Two for a Cent''), **182**
Hemmick, Nell (''Two for a Cent''), **182**
Hemple, Charles (''The Adjuster''), **183**
Hemple, Chuck (''The Adjuster''), **183**
Hemple, Luella (''The Adjuster''), **183**
Henderson, Dick (''The Family Bus''), **183**
Henderson, Mrs. T. R. (''The Family Bus''), **183**
Henderson, Ralph (''The Family Bus''), **183**
Henderson, T. R. (''The Family Bus''), **183**
Hendrix, Amelia (*Assorted Spirits*), **183**
Hendrix, Josephus (*Assorted Spirits*), **183**
Hengest, Major (*Tender Is the Night*), **183**
Henriette (''The Intimate Strangers''), **184**
Henry (*Safety First!*), **184**
Henry, O., 39
Herbrugge (*Tender Is the Night*), **184**
''Her Last Case,'' **184**
Herrick, Walter ('' 'Boil Some Water—Lots of It' ''), **184**
Hersey (*The Great Gatsby*), **184**
Hersey, Marie (*Thoughtbook*), **185**
Hersey, Mary, 230
Hertzog (''A Change of Class''), **185**
Hesse (''Dalyrimple Goes Wrong''), **185**
''He Thinks He's Wonderful,'' **185**
Hibben, John Grier, 186
Hibbing, Captain ('' 'I Didn't Get Over' ''), **185–86**
Hicks (''The Perfect Life''), **186**
Hiemer (*The Beautiful and Damned*), **186**
Higgins, Sybil. *See* Knighton, Pamela
''The High Cost of Macaroni,'' **186**
Hilda (''The Cut-Glass Bowl''), **186**
Hilda (''A Freeze-Out), **186**
Hilda (''A Night at the Fair,'' ''He Thinks He's Wonderful,'' ''The Captured Shadow''), **186**
Hilda (''The Scandal Detectives''), **186**
Hilda (''Winter Dreams''), **186**
Hillebrand (''The Ants at Princeton''), **186**
Hilliard, George (''Pat Hobby Does His Bit''), **187**
Hillis, Bill (*Tender Is the Night*), **187**
Hilma (''The Popular Girl''), **187**
Himmel, Peter (''May Day''), **187**
Hip, Claudia (*The Great Gatsby*), **187**
Hirst (''The Hotel Girl''), **187**
Hitchcock, Tommy, 453
Hixson, Mrs. (''An Alcoholic Case''), **187**
Hobby, Estelle. *See* Devlin, Estelle Hobby
Hobby, John Brown. *See* Indore, Prince John Brown Hobby
Hobby, Pat ('' 'Boil Some Water—Lots of It,' '' ''Fun in an Artist's Studio,'' ''The Homes of the Stars,'' ''A Man in the Way,'' ''Mightier Than the Sword,'' ''No Harm Trying,'' ''On the Trail of Pat Hobby,'' ''Pat Hobby and Orson Welles,'' ''Pat Hobby Does His Bit,'' ''Pat Hobby, Putative Father,'' ''Pat Hobby's Christmas Wish,'' ''Pat Hobby's College Days,'' ''Pat Hobby's Preview,'' ''Pat Hobby's Secret,'' ''A Patriotic Short,'' ''Teamed with Genius,'' ''Two Old-Timers''), **187–89**
Hodge, Katherine (''Teamed with Genius''), **189**
Hoffman, Phil (''A New Leaf''), **189**

Hoftzer (''A Snobbish Story''), **189**
Hogue, Madeleine (''Bernice Bobs Her Hair''), **189**
Hoker (''The Family Bus''), **189**
Holcome, Stuart (*The Beautiful and Damned*), **189**
Holiday, Burne (*This Side of Paradise*), **189**
Holiday, Kerry (*This Side of Paradise*), **190**
Holliday, Emily (''New Types''), **190**
Holliday, Estelle (''The Unspeakable Egg''), **190**
Hollister, Dean (*This Side of Paradise*), **190**
Holmes (*Tender Is the Night*), **190**
Holmes, Harmon, Judge (''Three Hours between Planes''), **190**
Holt, Jerry ('' 'The Sensible Thing' ''), **190**
Holworthy, Jim (*Coward*), **190**
Holworthy, Ned (*Coward*), **190**
Holyoke (''Persuasion''), **190**
Holyoke, Miss (''Persuasion''), **191**
Holyoke, Mrs. (''Persuasion''), **191**
''Homage to the Victorians,'' 191, **249**
''The Homes of the Stars,'' **191**
''The Honor of the Goon,'' **191**
Hood, Gilly (''The Four Fists''), **192**
''Hooray,'' **192**
Hopkins (*The Beautiful and Damned*), **192**
Hopkins (''Two Wrongs''), **192**
Hopkins, Sarah (''Bernice Bobs Her Hair''), **192**
Hopman, Red (''The Bowl''), **192**
Hopp (''The Love Boat''), **192**
Hopper, Joe (''Pat Hobby's Christmas Wish''), **192**
Hopper, Sally Carrol (''The Jelly-Bean''), **192**
Horatio (*Safety First!*), **192**
Hornbeam (*The Great Gatsby*), **192**
Horrick, Stella (''A Freeze-Out''), **192**
Horsa, Mr. (*Tender Is the Night*), **192**
Horseprotection, George T. (*Tender Is the Night*), **192**
Hortense (''Hortense—To a Cast-Off Lover''), **193**
Hortense (*This Side of Paradise*), **193**
''Hortense—To a Cast-Off Lover,'' **193**
Horton (''The Lees of Happiness''), **193**
Horton, Edward Everett, 329
Horton, George (''More Than Just a House''), **193**
Horton, Mrs. (''Not in the Guidebook''), **193**
Hoskins, Dead Shot. *See* Gonzoles, Tony
''Hot and Cold Blood,'' **193**
''The Hotel Child,'' **194**
Hotesane, Colonel (''Sentiment—and the Use of Rouge''), **194**
''The Hours (Bishop), 34
Howard (''Benediction''), **194**
Howard (''The Family Bus''), **195**
Howard (''No Flowers''), **195**
Howard (*Safety First!*), **195**
Howard, Lady Mary Bowes (''Majesty''), **195**
Howard, Miss (''The Hotel Child''), **195**
Howard, Mrs. Sigourney (*The Great Gatsby*), **195**
Howard, Sidney (*The Last Tycoon*), **195**
Howden (''Family in the Wind''), **195**
''How I Would Sell My Book If I Were a Bookseller,'' **195**
Howland (*The Beautiful and Damned*), **195**
''How the Upper Class Is Being Saved by 'Men Like Mencken,' '' 279, 347. *See also* ''Public Letter to Thomas Boyd''
''How to Live on Practically Nothing a Year,'' **195–96**
''How to Live on $36,000 a Year,'' **196**
''How to Waste Material—A Note on My Generation,'' 181, **196**
How to Write Short Stories (Lardner), 238, 334, 359
Hoyt (''May Day''), **196**
Hoyt (''Two for a Cent''), **197**
Hoyt, Rosemary (*Tender Is the Night*), **197**, 205, 252, 286
Hubbard, Spud (''The Ice Palace''), **197**
Hubbel (''Two Wrongs''), **197**

Hubbel, Willard (''Zone of Accident''), **197**
Hudson, E. Brunswick (''Mightier Than the Sword''), **197**
Hudson, Jewel (''May Day''), **197**
Hughes, Easton (''Two Wrongs''), **197**
Hughes, Leonora (''Not in the Guidebook''), **197**
Hugo (''Dice, Brassknuckles & Guitar''), **197**
Hulda (*Assorted Spirits*), **198**
Hull, Joe (*The Beautiful and Damned*), **198**
Hull, Perry (''The Rich Boy''), **198**
Hulme, Miss (*The Beautiful and Damned*), **198**
Hulme, Mrs. (*The Beautiful and Damned*), **198**
Humbird, Dick (*This Side of Paradise*), **198**
Hume, Charles (''On Schedule''), **198**
Hume, Delores (''On Schedule''), **198**
Hunt (*The Beautiful and Damned*), **198**
Hunter (''The Rich Boy''), **198**
Hunter (*Tender Is the Night*), **198**
Hunter, Anson (''The Rich Boy''), 47, **199**
Hunter, Edna (''The Rich Boy''), **199**
Hunter, Miss (''In the Holidays''), **199**
Hunter, Mrs. (''The Rich Boy''), **199**
Hunter, Robert (''The Rich Boy''), **199**
[Hunter?], Schuyler (''The Rich Boy''), **199**
[Hunter?], Tom (''The Rich Boy''), **199**
Hupp, Von, Count (*Fie! Fie! Fi-Fi!*), **199**
Hupp, Von, Madame (*Fie! Fie! Fi-Fi!*), **199**
The Husband Hunter (movie), 295
Huston-Carmelite (*This Side of Paradise*), **200**
Huysman, Joris Karl, 129
Huxley, Aldous, 43, **200**, 253, 289
Hype, Peter (''The Diary of a Sophomore''), **200**

''The Ice Palace,'' 79, **201**
Icky (*Mister Icky*), **201**
Icky, Charles (*Mister Icky*), **201**
Icky, Ulsa (*Mister Icky*), **202**
'' 'I Didn't Get Over,' '' **202**
''I Don't need a bit of assistance,'' **202**
''If Hoover came out for the N.R.A.,'' **202**
''If you have a little Jew,'' **202**
''I Got Shoes,'' **202**
''I hate their guts,'' **202**
Ike (''Pat Hobby and Orson Welles''), **203**
Ikey (''Emotional Bankruptcy''), **203**
''Image on the Heart,'' **203**
''Imagination—and a Few Mothers,'' **203**
''In a dear little vine-covered cottage,'' **203–4**
Income for Fitzgerald, 13, 14, 85, 132, 153, 179, **204**, 277, 304, 333–34, 357, 390
''Indecision,'' **204–5**
Indore, Prince John Brown Hobby (''Pat Hobby, Putative Father''), **205**
Indore, Raj Dak Raj (''Pat Hobby, Putative Father''), **205**
''Infidelity,'' **205**
Ingersoll (''A Short Trip Home''), **205**
Ingles, Miss (''The Pusher-in-the-Face''), **205–6**
''In Literary New York,'' **206**
In Our Time (Hemingway), 181, 196
''Inside the House,'' **206**, 426
''An Interview with F. Scott Fitzgerald,'' **206**
''In the Darkest Hour,'' **206–7**
''In the Holidays,'' **207**
''The Intimate Strangers,'' **207–8**
''Introduction,'' **208**
Ireland, Louis (''Six of One—''), **208**
Irene (''The Cut-Glass Bowl''), **208**
Irma (''That Kind of Party''), **208**
Irving, Gladys (''Six of One—''), **208**
Isabelle (''Babes in the Woods''), **208**
Ismay (*The Great Gatsby*), **209**
Ives, George (''On Your Own''), **209**
Ives, Mrs. (''On Your Own''), **209**
Ives, Mrs. Horace J., Jr. (''The Homes of the Stars''), **209**

Jaccy (''I Got Shoes''), **210**
Jack (''My Own New England Homestead on the Erie''), **210**
Jack (''A Penny Spent''), **210**
Jackson (''Rags Martin-Jones and the Pr-nce of W-les''), **210**
Jackson, Ellery Hamil (''John Jackson's Arcady''), **210**
Jackson, John (''John Jackson's Arcady''), **210**
Jackson, Mary (''First Blood''), **211**
Jackson, Mrs. (''Love in the Night''), **211**
Jackson [Thomas ''Stonewall''], General, **211**
''Jacob's Ladder,'' **211**, 286
Jacoby (''Zone of Accident''), **211**
Jacques (*The Evil Eye*), **211**
Jacques (''The Count of Darkness,'' ''Gods of Darkness,'' ''In the Darkest Hour,'' ''The Kingdom in the Dark''), **211–12**
Jadwin, Cecil (''A Change of Class''), **212**
Jadwin, Philip (''A Change of Class''), **212**
Jaggers, George (''Financing Finnegan''), **212**, 335
James (*The Captured Shadow*), **212**
James (''The Mystery of the Raymond Mortgage''), **212**
James, Constance (*Thoughtbook*), **212**
James, Enky (*Thoughtbook*), **212**
James, Henry, 78, 184, 194, 268, 440, 452
James, Trudy (''Three Hours between Planes''), **212**
Janice (''The Woman from Twenty-one''), **212**
Janierka (''Majesty''), **212**
Janney, Butch (''Family in the Wind''), **212–13**
Janney, Dr. Forrest (''Family in the Wind''), **213**
Janney, Edith (''Family in the Wind''), **213**
Janney, Eugene (''Family in the Wind''), **213**
Janney, Pinky (''Family in the Wind''), **213**
Janney, Rose (''Family in the Wind''), **213**
Jansen (''At Your Age''), **213**
Jaqueline (*The Great Gatsby*), **213**
Jaques. *See* Jacques
Jaques, Leland (''At Your Age''), **213**
Jarvis (''Benediction''), **214**
Jarvis, Mrs. (''Benediction''), **214**
''The Jazz Age,'' 119
Jeanne (''How to Live on Practically Nothing a Year''), **214**
Jeff (''Family in the Wind''), **214**
Jefferson (*Coward*), **214**
Jelke, Joe (''A Short Trip Home''), **214**
Jelly-bean. *See* Powell, James
''The Jelly-Bean,'' **214**
''Jemina,'' **214–15**
Jenkins ('' 'Send Me In, Coach' ''), **215**
Jenks, Ed (''Family in the Wind''), **215**
Jennings, Hughie (*Precaution Primarily*), **215**
Jerome, James (''Discard''), **215**
Jerry (''The Freshest Boy'), **215**
Jerry (''The Smilers''), **215**
Jerryl, Rachael. *See* Barnes, Rachael Jerryl
Jessie (''Head and Shoulders''), **215**
Jewett, Dr. (''The Lees of Happiness''), **215**
Jewett, P. (*The Great Gatsby*), **216**
Jidge (''The Woman from Twenty-one''), **216**
Jiggs, Mrs. (''The Woman from Twenty-one''), **216**
Jim (''The Diary of a Sophomore''), **216**
Jim (*The Girl from Lazy J*), **216**
Jim (''A Luckless Santa Claus''), **216**
Jim (''May Day''), **216**
Jim, Uncle (''Fate in Her Hands''), **216**
Jimmy (''Benediction''), **216**
Jimmy (''Two Wrongs''), **216**
Jimmy (''What Kind of Husbands Do 'Jimmies' Make?''), **216**
Jimmy, Mrs. (''What Kind of Husbands Do 'Jimmies' Make?''), **216**

Jinks, Jerry (*The Beautiful and Damned*), **216**
Jinks, Judy (*The Beautiful and Damned*), **216**
Jinnie, Aunt (''Lo, the Poor Peacock!''), **216**
Jo (''The Rich Boy''), **217**
Joan (''Crazy Sunday''), **217**
Joe (''The Diary of a Sophomore''), **217**
Joe (''Emotional Bankruptcy''), **217**
Joe (''Pat Hobby and Orson Welles''), **217**
Joe (*This Side of Paradise*), **217**
Joe (''Two Wrongs), **217**
''John Jackson's Arcady,'' **217–18**
Johns, William Delaney (''No Flowers''), **218**
Johnson (''The Bridal Party''), **218**
Johnson, Capone (''The Family Bus''), **218**
Johnson, Earl (''A Change of Class''), **218**
Johnson, Jack (''Crazy Sunday''), **218**
Johnson, Justine (*The Beautiful and Damned*), **218**
Johnson, Miss (''Your Way and Mine''), **218**
Johnson, Owen, 112
Johnson, Passion (''He Thinks He's Wonderful''), **218**
Johnson, Private (*Coward*), **218**
Johnson, Violet (''A Change of Class''), **219**
Johnston (*The Beautiful and Damned*), **219**
Johnston (*The Captured Shadow*). *See also* Dudley, Thorton Hart
Johnston, Hamilton T. (''An Author's Mother''), **219**
Johnston, John (''An Author's Mother''), **219**
Johnston, Mrs. (''An Author's Mother''), **219**
Johnston, Mrs. ('' 'Trouble' ''), **219**
Jones (''The Rubber Check''), **219**
Jones (*The Vegetable*), **219**
Jones, Bill. *See* Blair, Hubert
Jones, Catherine (''The Dance''), **219**
Jones, Dr. (''The Cruise of the Rolling Junk''), **219**
Jones, Hiram ('' 'Send Me In, Coach' ''), **219**
Jones, Judy (''Winter Dreams''), **220**, 230
Jones, Mortimer (''Winter Dreams''), **220**
Jones, Mrs. Mortimer (''Winter Dreams''), **220**
Jones, Oswald (''The Third Casket''), **220**
Jones, Sam (''Pat Hobby and Orson Welles''), **220**
Jones, William (*The Evil Eye*), **220**
Jordan (''Head and Shoulders''), **220**
Jordan, Dr. (''A Change of Class''), **220**
Jordan, Peter (''Dalyrimple Goes Wrong''), **220**
Jordan, William (*The Beautiful and Damned*), **220**
Jorgensen, Paula (''New Types''), **220**
José (*The Girl from Lazy J*), **221**
Josephe (''Gods of Darkness''), **221**
Joyce, James, 7, 138, 259, 260, 427
Jozan Édouard, 135, 203, 355
Jubal (''Basil and Cleopatra''), **221**
Judkins (''Imagination—and a Few Mothers''), **221**
Judkins, Anita (''Imagination—and a Few Mothers''), **221**
Judkins, Clifford (''Imagination—and a Few Mothers''), **221**
Judkins, Mrs. (''Imagination—and a Few Mothers''), **221**
Judy (*The Great Gatsby*), **221**
Julia (''Diagnosis''), **221**
Jumbo (''The Camel's Back''), **221**
June (''Crazy Sunday''), **221**
June (*The Great Gatsby*), **221**
Jung, Carl Gustav, 119

Kagle, Helen (''Pat Hobby's Christmas Wish''), **222**
Kahler (*The Beautiful and Damned*), **222**
Kaiser (''The Prince of Pests''), **222**
de Kalb, Marquis (''One Trip Abroad''), **222**

de Kalb, Marquise (''One Trip Abroad''), **222**
Kaluka (*This Side of Paradise*), **222**
Kaly (''A Short Autobiography''), **222**
Kamp, Dr. (''In the Holidays''), **223**
Kampf, George (''He Thinks He's Wonderful,'' ''The Perfect Life''), **223**
Kampf, Mrs. George (''He Thinks He's Wonderful,'' ''The Perfect Life''), **223**
Kampf, William S. (''The Captured Shadow,'' ''Forging Ahead,'' ''He Thinks He's Wonderful,'' ''The Perfect Life,'' ''The Scandal Detectives''), **223**
Kane, Frank (''The Bowl''), **223**
Kane, Garland (''Majesty''), **223**
Kane, Muriel (*The Beautiful and Damned*), **223**
Kapper (*The Last Tycoon*), **223**
Karger (''The Rich Boy''), **223**
Karger, Dolly (''The Rich Boy''), **223**
Karger, Mrs. (''The Rich Boy''), **224**
Karr, Alphonse (''The Adjuster''), **224**
Karr, Ede (''The Adjuster''), **224**
Kasper (''Pat Hobby and Orson Welles''), **224**
Kastler, Benjamin (''Fate in Her Hands''), **224**
Kastler, Carol (''Fate in Her Hands''), **224**
Kastler, George (''Fate in Her Hands''), **224**
Kastler, Jean (''Fate in Her Hands''), **224**
Kate, Emma (*The Captured Shadow*), **224**
Katie (*The Last Tycoon*), **224**
Katspaugh (*The Great Gatsby*), **224**
Katzby, Martha (''Dice, Brassknuckles & Guitar''), **224**
Katzby, Mrs. Poindexter (''Dice, Brassknuckles & Guitar''), **225**
Kaufman, George S., 439
Kavenaugh (''Six of One—''), **225**
Kavenaugh, Howard (''Six of One—''), **225**
Kaye (''A Freeze- Out''), **225**
Kaye, Ella (*The Great Gatsby*), **225**
Kaye, Marty (*This Side of Paradise*), **225**
Kearns, Dr. (''Two Wrongs''), **225**
Keats, John, 425
Keatts, Lily (''Pat Hobby Does His Bit''), **225**
Kebble, Freddy (''Benediction''), **225**
Kebble, Maury (''Benediction''), **226**
Keene (''The Bowl''), **226**
Keene, Dr. (''The Curious Case of Benjamin Button''), **226**
''Keep the watch!,'' **226**
Keith (''Benediction''), **226**
Keith, Jean (''Her Last Case''), **226**
Kelleher (*The Great Gatsby*), **226**
Kellerman, Annette (*This Side of Paradise*), **226**
Kelley, Florence (*The Beautiful and Damned*), **226**
Kelly (''Myra Meets His Family''), **226**
Kelly (''A Snobbish Story''), **226**
Kelly, Bridget (*Safety First!*), **227**
Kelly, Dr. (''Three Acts of Music''), **227**
Kelly, Nelson (''One Trip Abroad''), **227**
Kelly, Nicole (''One Trip Abroad''), **227**
Kelly, Sonny (''One Trip Abroad'), **227**
Kendall, George (*The Girl from Lazy J*), **227**
Kendall, Mrs. George (*The Girl from Lazy J*), **227**
Kennedy, Bill (''Two for a Cent''), **227**
Kennedy, Craig (''The Evil Eye''), **227**
Kennedy, Dr. John (*The Last Tycoon*), **227**
Kenyon, Mary (''Fate in Her Hands''), **227**
Keogh, Nat (''Crazy Sunday''), **228**
Kern, Jerome, 422
Kerr, Elsie (''A Snobbish Story''), **228**
Kerr, Robert, 74, 225
Key, Carrol, Private (''May Day''), **228**
Key, Francis Scott, **228**
Key, George (''May Day''), **228**
Key, John, 228
Key, Philip, 228
Keyes, Dr. (''The Love Boat''), **228**
Keyster, Dr. (''Lo, the Poor Peacock!''), **228**
Kibble, Mrs. Albert, Jr., 12
Kilgallen, Dorothy, 228
Kilkallow, Bopes, Marquis (''The Hotel Child''), **228**

Killian, Cedric ("The Intimate Strangers"), **228**
Killian, Dorothy ("The Intimate Strangers"), **228**
Killian, Sara. *See* Guillet de la Guimpé, Marquise Sara de la
Kilrain ("Family in the Wind"), **229**
Kilrain, Helen ("Family in the Wind"), **229**
Kimball, Ed ("The Bowl"), **229**
Kimberly, Scott ("The Popular Girl"), **229**
Kincaid, Charley ("The Dance"), **229**
Kincaid, Mrs. Charley ("The Dance"), **229**
King, Clara (*Assorted Spirits*), **229**
King, George ("The Long Way Out"), **229**
King, Ginevra, 16, 128, 220, **229–30**, 233, 252, 337
King, Mrs. George ("The Long Way Out"), **230**
King, W. F. ("How to Live on Practically Nothing a Year"), **230**
"The Kingdom in the Dark," **230–31**
Kingsley ("Gretchen's Forty Winks"), **231**
Kinney, Joe ("In the Holidays"), **231**
Kippery, Lady ("The Rubber Check"), **231**
Kirby, Carter (*The Beautiful and Damned*), **231**
Kirstoff (*The Last Tycoon*), **231**
Kitty ("Martin's Thoughts"), **231**
Kitty ("A New Leaf"), **231**
Kitty ("That Kind of Party"), **231**
Kitty ("Three Hours between Planes"), **232**
Klipspringer, Ewing (*The Great Gatsby*), **232**
Knighton, Pamela ("Last Kiss"), 159, **232**, 276
Knowles, Bill, Lieutenant ("The Last of the Belles"), **232**
Knowles, Gladys ("On Your Own"), **232**
Knowleton, Dudley ("A Woman with a Past"), **232**
Knox, Dorothy (*Thoughtbook*), **232**
Knox, Emil (*Thoughtbook*), **232**
Kohl, Emily ("A Snobbish Story"), **232**
Kohler, Thurston ("He Thinks He's Wonderful"), **233**
Kohlsaat, Herman Henry, 233
Kohlsatt ("The Love Boat"), **233**
Koven, Reginald de. *See* De Koven, Reginald
Kracklin, Thomas ("Author's House"), **233**
Kreisler, Fritz, 86
Kresge, Jim ("Pat Hobby's College Days"), **233**
Kretching, Lieutenant (*The Beautiful and Damned*), **233**
Krimslich. *See* Green, Mrs.
Krogerman (*This Side of Paradise*), **233**
Kroll, Frances, 142, **233**, 239
Krupsadt ("Dalyrimple Goes Wrong"), **234**
Krutch ("Basil and Cleopatra"), **234**
Kurman ("No Flowers"), **234**
Kwain, Miss ("A Woman with a Past"), **234**

La Borwitz, Jaques (*The Last Tycoon*), **235**
Lacy (*The Beautiful and Damned*), **235**
Lacy, Edward ("Hot and Cold Blood"), **235**
Lacy, Miss ("Hot and Cold Blood"), **235**
Lacy, Mrs. (*The Beautiful and Damned*), **235**
Ladislau, Dr. (*Tender Is the Night*), **235**
Lafarge, Miss ("Jemina"), **235**
Lafouque ("Shadow Laurels"), **236**
Lahaye, Sidney ("Flight and Pursuit"), **236**
Lallette ("Six of One—"), **236**
Lamar, Bob (*The Beautiful and Damned*), **236**
Lamar, Dr. ("The Jelly-Bean"), **236**
Lamar, Lucius Quintus Cincinnatus, 236
Lamar, Nancy ("The Jelly-Bean," "The Last of the Belles"), **236**
Lamarque ("Shadow Laurels"), **236**
La Marr. *See* La Marr, Barbara

La Marr, Barbara, **236–37**
Lamb, Marion (''Too Cute for Words''), **237**
Lamb, Nancy (''The Rubber Check''), **237**
Lambert (''He Thinks He's Wonderful''), **237**
''Lamp in a Window,'' **237**
Lanahan, Frances Scott Fitzgerald. *See* Smith, Frances Scott Fitzgerald Lanahan
Lanclerc, Count Hennen de (''Discard''), **237**
Lanclerc, Countess de. *See* Bordon, Dolly
Landig (*Thoughtbook*), **237**
Landor, Walter Savage, 307
Lane, Dr. (''One Interne''), **237**
Langueduc, Slim (*This Side of Paradise*), **237**
Lapham, Charlotte (''That Kind of Party''), **238**
Lardner, Ellis Abbott, 283, 427
Lardner, Ring, 78, 112, 156, **238–39**, 278, 283, 304, 323, 334, 358, 380, 427
Larkin (''The Ice Palace''), **239**
Larned, Leticia (*The Girl from Lazy J*), **239**
Larrabee, Ceci (*The Beautiful and Damned*), **239**
Lascalles, Evylyn (''Pat Hobby's College Days''), **239**
''Last Kiss,'' 159, 237, **239–40**, 276, 459
''The Last of the Belles,'' **240–41**
''*The Last of the Tycoons*, 241
The Last Tycoon, 112, 159, 182, 200, 204, 233, 240, **241–43**, 323, 335, 376, 384, 388, 399, 427
Laura (*Tender Is the Night*), **243**
Laurie (*Thoughtbook*), **243**
Laurier, Anton (''Head and Shoulders''), **243**
Lawrence, Miss (''One of My Oldest Friends''), **243**
Lawrence, Mrs. (*This Side of Paradise*), **243–44**
Lawson ('' 'Send Me In, Coach' ''), **244**
Leacock, Stephen, 215
Leam, Max ('' 'Boil Some Water—Lots of It' ''), **244**
Leaming, Elwood (''Forging Ahead,'' ''He Thinks He's Wonderful,'' ''A Night at the Fair,'' ''The Scandal Detectives''), **244**
Leanbaum (*The Last Tycoon*), **244**
Lebaume, Beau (''Six of One—''), **244**
Lee (''A Night at the Fair''), **244**
Lee, Alice Riley (''The Captured Shadow,'' ''Forging Ahead,'' ''The Freshest Boy,'' ''He Thinks He's Wonderful,'' ''A Night at the Fair''), **244**
Lee, Basil Duke (''Basil and Cleopatra,'' ''The Captured Shadow,'' ''Forging Ahead,'' ''The Freshest Boy,'' ''He Thinks He's Wonderful,'' ''A Night at the Fair,'' ''The Perfect Life,'' ''The Scandal Detectives''), 12, **245–46**, 417
Lee, Biffy (''The Ants at Princeton''), **246**
Lee, Fitzhugh, General (''A Patriotic Short''), **246**
Lee, Margery (''The Ice Palace''), **246**
Lee, Mrs. (''The Captured Shadow,'' ''Forging Ahead,'' ''The Freshest Boy,'' ''He Thinks He's Wonderful,'' and ''A Night at the Fair''), 246
Lee, Mrs. Kracklin (''Author's House''), 233, **246**
Lee, Robert E(dward), 19, 22, 118, **246–47**
Leech (*The Great Gatsby*), **247**
''The Lees of Happiness,'' **247**
Legendre, Mrs. (''The Rich Boy''), **247**
Legendre, Paula. *See* Hagerty, Paula Legendre Thayer
Legoupy (''Salesmanship in the Champs-Elysées''), **247**
Legros (*The Great Gatsby*), **248**
Leigh, Barton (''A Night at the Fair''), **248**
Lemmon, Mrs. (''A Change of Class''), **248**
Le Moyne, Littleboy (''Basil and Cleopatra''), **248**
Leonard, Jim (''Last Kiss''), **248**

Le Poire (''Gods of Darkness,'' ''In the Darkest Hour''), **248**
Le Poire, Becquette (''Gods of Darkness''), **248**
Leslie, Shane, 24, 129, **248–49**, 298, 333
''Lest We Forget (France by Big Shots''), **249**
Letgarde (''The Count of Darkness''), **249–50**
The Letters of F. Scott Fitzgerald (Turnbull, ed.), 431
''A Letter to Helen,'' 230, **250**
Letts, Courtney, 230
Le Vigne, Carl (''No Harm Trying''), **250**
Lew (*The Last Tycoon*), **250**
Lewis, Sinclair, 138, 278, 279
Libby, Malcolm (''A Nice Quiet Place''), **250**
''Life's too short to,'' **250**
Lightfoot, Claude (''The High Cost of Macaroni''), **250**
Lilly, Ernest (*The Great Gatsby*), **250**
Lilymary (''Dearly Beloved''), **250**
Lincoln, Abraham, 133, 340
Lincoln, Sol (''Two Wrongs''), **250**
Lindbergh, Charles, 119
Lindsay (''Forging Ahead''), **250**
''Lines on Reading Through an Autograph Album,'' 62, **250–51**
Linquist (''The Adolescent Marriage''), **251**
''Lipstick,'' 289, 406
''Listen to the hoop la,'' **251**
''Little by little,'' **251**
Livingstone, Pete (*Tender Is the Night*), **251**
Livingstone, Warren (''I Got Shoes''), **251**
Llewellen, Frank (''Two Wrongs''), **251**
Lockheart, Andy (''The Captured Shadow''), **251**
Loey (''Martin's Thoughts''), **251**
Logan, Josh (''The Bowl''), **251**
Lois (''Benediction''), **251**
Lois (''Crazy Sunday''), **251–52**
Lombard, Carole (*The Last Tycoon*), **252**
Long, Jimmy (''The Popular Girl''), **252**
Long Shadows (Leslie), 249
Longstreet (*Tender Is the Night*), **252**
''The Long Way Out,'' **252**
Loos, Anita, **252–53**, 418
Lord Jim (Conrad), 78
Lorenzo (''Jacob's Ladder''), **253**
Lorraine, Lillian (''The Bowl''), **253**
Lorry (''At Your Age''), **253**
Lorry, Annie (''At Your Age''), **253**
Lorry, Mabel Tollman (''At Your Age''), **253**
''The Lost Decade,'' 5, **253–54**
A Lost Lady (Cather), 141
''Lo, the Poor Peacock!,'' **254**
Louie (''The Cruise of the Rolling Junk''), **254**
Louie (also Lou) (''Fun in an Artist's Studio,'' ''A Man in the Way,'' ''No Harm Trying,'' ''On the Trail of Pat Hobby,'' ''Pat Hobby and Orson Welles,'' ''Pat Hobby Does His Bit,'' ''Pat Hobby's College Days,'' ''Pat Hobby's Preview,'' ''Pat Hobby's Secret''), **254–55**
Louis the Stammerer, King (''The Kingdom in the Dark''), **255**
Louise (''Rags Martin-Jones and the Pr-nce of W-les''), **255**
Louise (''The Swimmers''), **255**
''The Love Boat,'' **255–56**
''Love in the Night,'' **256**
The Love Legend (Boyd), 43
Lovejoy (''On Your Own''), **256**
Lovejoy, Dr. (''On Your Own''), **257**
Lovejoy, Evelyn (''On Your Own''), **257**
Lovely Thing, the. *See* Battles, Johanna
Lovett, Bug Face (''The Honor of the Goon''), **257**
Lowrie, Jessie Piper (''The Cut-Glass Bowl''), **257**
Lowrie, Lew (''More Than Just a House''), **257**
Lowrie, Tom (''The Cut-Glass Bowl''), **258**
''A Luckless Santa Claus,'' **258**
Lucy (''No Flowers''), **258**
Lukas, Birdie (also Willie) (''Strange Sanctuary''), **258**

Lupin, Arséne (''The Scandal Detectives''), **258**
Luther (''No Flowers''), **258**
Lytell, Pete (*The Beautiful and Damned*), **258**

McAllister, Ward, 325
McAlmon, Robert Menzies, 56, **259–60**, 265
McArthur, Mary (''For Mary's Eighth Birthday,'' ''Oh papa—''), **260**
McBeth (*Tender Is the Night*), **260**
McCaffray (''The Family Bus''), **260**
McCarthy, Gyp (''Pat Hobby Does His Bit''), **260**
McCarty, Arthur (*The Great Gatsby*), **260**
McChesney, Billy (''Two Wrongs''), **260**
McChesney, Emily Pinkard (''Two Wrongs''), **260**
McChesney, William (''Two Wrongs''), **261**
McClenahan, Benny (*The Great Gatsby*), **261**
McClurg, Glenola ('' 'Trouble' ''), **261**
McComas (''Your Way and Mine''), **261**
McComas, Henry (''Your Way and Mine''), **261**
McComas, Honoria (''Your Way and Mine''), **261**
McComas, Stella (''Your Way and Mine''), **262**
McCoy, Horace Stanley, 144, **262**
McCracken, Miss (''O Russet Witch!''), **262**
McCrary, Miss (''Lo, the Poor Peacock!''), **262**
McCutcheon (''Lo, the Poor Peacock!''), **262**
McDonald, Joe (''The Bowl''), **262**
MacDonough, Blaine (''The Debutante''), **262**
McDougall, Dr. ('' 'Send Me In, Coach' ''), **263**
McDowell (*This Side of Paradise*), **263**
MacDowell, Thomas J. (''John Jackson's Arcady''), **263**
Macedon, Phil (''Two Old-Timers''), **263**
McFarland, Packy (*The Beautiful and Damned*), **263**
McFiddle, Poke (''The Broadcast We Almost Heard Last September''), **263**
McGinness (*The Captured Shadow*), **263**
McGlook, Minnie (*The Beautiful and Damned*), **263**
McGovern, Miss (*The Beautiful and Damned*), **263**
McGowan, Pop ('' 'I Didn't Get Over' ''), **263**
McGregor (''Majesty''), **263**
McGregor, ''Curly'' (*The Beautiful and Damned*), **264**
McIlvaine, Bee (''On the Trail of Pat Hobby''), **264**
McIntosh, Dean (''Oh Schedule''), **264**
McIntosh, Mrs. (''On Schedule''), **264**
McIntyre (''The Four Fists''), **264**
McIntyre, Charlie (*The Beautiful and Damned*), **264**
MacIntyre, Warren (''Bernice Bobs Her Hair''), **264**
McKee, Chester (*The Great Gatsby*), **264**
McKee, Lucille (*The Great Gatsby*), **264**
McKenna. *See* Kinney, Joe
McKenna (''Winter Dreams''), **264**
McKibben (*Tender Is the Night*), **264**
MacKie, Elizabeth Beckwith, 110
McKinley, William, 188, **265**
McKisco, Albert (*Tender Is the Night*), **265**
McKisco, Violet (*Tender Is the Night*), **265**
Macks (''Three Hours between Planes''), **265**
McLane, Carter (''No Flowers''), **265**
McLane, Tommy (''Indecision''), **265**
McPhee, Hank (''Our American Poets''), **265**
McQuillan, Annabel, 134
McQuillan, Louisa Allen, 134, **265**
McQuillan, Philip T., 134 **265–66**
MacRae, Bessie (''Bernice Bobs Her Hair''), **266**
McRae, Bruce (*Safety First!*), **266**
McRae, Jenny (''First Blood,'' ''A Snobbish Story''), **266**

McRae, Jim (''A Snobbish Story''), **266**
McTeague (''Your Way and Mine''), **266**
McVitty (''The Love Boat''), **266**
Macy, Martin (''The Camel's Back''), **266**
Macy, Theron G. (''Dalyrimple Goes Wrong''), **266–67**
Madame Bovary (Flaubert), 9
''Magnetism,'' **267**, 281
Mahan (''The Love Boat''), **267**
Maine, Duke of (''Gods of Darkness,'' ''The Kingdom in the Dark''), **267**
Mais, Maria Amalia Roto (*Tender Is the Night*), **268**
Maisie (''Imagination—and a Few Mothers''), **268**
''Majesty,'' **268**
''Make Yourself at Home'' (unpublished story), 426
Makova, Paul (''Two Wrongs''), **268**
Malone (*The Last Tycoon*), **268**
Mamie, Aunt (''The Jelly-Bean''), **268**
Manfred, Jeff (''No Harm Trying''), **269**
''A Man in the Way,'' **269**
Mankiewicz, Joseph L., 289, 322
Manly, Esther (''The Rubber Check''), **269**
Many Marriages (Anderson), 7–8, **269**, 281, 384
Many Thousands Gone (Bishop), 34
Maples, Miss (''Financing Finnegan''), **269**
Maplewood (''The Freshest Boy''), **269**
Maranda (''A Patriotic Short''), **269**
Marbotson, Findle (*This Side of Paradise*), **269**
Marbrooke, Eleanor (''Sentiment—and the Use of Rouge''), **269**
Marbrooke, Katherine (''Sentiment—and the Use of Rouge''), **269**
Marchbanks, Captain (''Majesty''), **270**
Marchbanks, Ted, Baron (''Rags Martin-Jones and the Pr-nce of W-les''), **270**
''Marching Streets,'' **270**
Marcus (*The Last Tycoon*), **270**
Marcus, Harold (''The Homes of the Stars,'' ''On the Trail of Pat Hobby''), **270**
Margery, Nell (''I Got Shoes''), **270**
''Margey Wins the Game,'' **270**, 446
Margherita, Queen (*This Side of Paradise*), **270**
Margot (*The Evil Eye*), **270**
Marie (''Martin's Thoughts''), **270**
Marie (''My Very Very Dear Marie''), **270**
Mario (''Pat Hobby and Orson Welles''), **271**
Marion (''One of My Oldest Friends''), **271**
Marius (''The Kingdom in the Dark''), **271**
Marius (*Tender Is the Night*), **271**
Marjorie (''The Four Fists''), **271**
Marjorie (''What Became of Our Flappers and Sheiks?''), **271**
Markey, Billy (''The Baby Party''), **271**
Markey, Joe (''The Baby Party''), **271**
Markey, Mrs. Joe (''The Baby Party''), **271**
Markham (''Dalyrimple Goes Wrong''), **271**
Markham, Josephine (''An Alcoholic Case''), **271**
Markoe, Bill (''An Alcoholic Case''), **272**
Marlowe, Axia (*This Side of Paradise*), **272**
Marmora (*Tender Is the Night*), **272**
Marmora, Conte, Tino de (*Tender Is the Night*), **272**
Marmora, Señora (*Tender Is the Night*), **272**
Marquand (*The Last Tycoon*), **272**
Marquand, Mrs. (*The Last Tycoon*), **272**
Marsden, Cal (''The Unspeakable Egg''), **272**
Marsden, Josephine (''The Unspeakable Egg''), **272**
Marshall (''The Offshore Pirate''), **272**
Marshall, Howard (''May Day''), **272**
Marston (''The Swimmers''), **272**
Marston, Choupette (''The Swimmers''), **273**
Marston, Henry Clay (''The Swimmers''), **273**

Martha ("The Cut-Glass Bowl"), **273**
Martha ("Discard"), **273**
Martha ("Winter Dreams"), **273**
Marthe ("How to Live on Practically Nothing a Year"), **273**
Martin ("A Debt of Honor"), **273**
Martin ("A Freeze-Out"), **273**
Martin ("Martin's Thoughts"), **273**. *See also* Amorous, Martin
Martin, Alec (*The Vegetable*), **273**
Martin, Consuela ("Teamed with Genius"), **274**
Martin, Dr. ("The Cut-Glass Bowl"), **274**
Martin, Jenny (*The Beautiful and Damned*), **274**
Martin, Mrs. ("Strange Sanctuary"), **274**
Martin-Jones, Rags ("Rags Martin-Jones and the Pr-nce of W-les"), **274**
"Martin's Thoughts," **274**
Marvis, Julie (*Porcelain and Pink*), **274**
Marvis, Lois (*Porcelain and Pink*), **274**
Marx ("The Cut-Glass Bowl"), **274**
Marx, Karl, 123
Mary. *See* MacArthur, Mary
Mary (*Fie! Fie! Fi-Fi!*), **274**
Mason, Jim ("Diagnosis"), **274**
Masters, Edgar Lee, 246
Masters, Mrs. ("O Russet Witch!"), **275**
Masters, Olive. *See* Grainger, Olive Masters
Matezka, Gloria ("The Honor of the Goon"), **275**
Mather, James ("Hot and Cold Blood"), **275**
Mather, Jaqueline ("Hot and Cold Blood"), **275**
Matsko, James ("Six of One—"), **275**
Matterlane, Duke of ("The Trail of the Duke"), **275**
Maude (*The Last Tycoon*), **275**
Maxim ("Forging Ahead"), **275**
Maxwell, Elsa, **275–76**
Mayburn, Helen (*The Captured Shadow*), **276**
"May Day," **276–77**
Mayer, Louis B., 243
Meadow, Marcia. 179. *See* Tarbox, Marcia
Meadow, Veronica. *See* Tarbox, Marcia
Mears, Gaston (*The Beautiful and Damned*), **277**
Medill, Betty ("The Camel's Back"), **277**
Medill, Cyrus ("The Camel's Back"), **277**
Medonca, Corinna (*Tender Is the Night*), **277**
Meigs, Hal ("At Your Age"), **277**
Meloney, Rose (*The Last Tycoon*), **277**, 323
Melon-Loper, Jan ("The Family Bus"), **277–78**
Melon-Loper, Jannekin ("The Family Bus"), **278**
Melon-Loper, Kaethe ("The Family Bus"), **278**
Melon-Loper, Mrs. ("The Family Bus"), **278**
Menafee, Dr. ("Three Acts of Music"), **278**
Mencken, H. L., 16, 78, 196, 206, 207, 252, **278–79**, 297, 298, 334, 390, 439
Mendicant, Count ("Love in the Night"), **279**
Mercer (*Tender Is the Night*), **279**
The Merchant of Venice (Shakespeare), 418
Mercy, Carl ("Majesty"), **280**
Mercy, Live. *See* Blair, Olive Mercy
Meredith ("The Family Bus"), **280**
Meredith ("The Four Fists"), **280**
Meredith, Mrs. ("The Four Fists"), **280**
Meredith, Samuel ("The Four Fists"), **280**
Meridien, François ("Shadow Laurels"), **280**
Merriam, Constance Shaw (*The Beautiful and Damned*), **280**
Merriam, Eric (*The Beautiful and Damned*), **280**
Merrill, Mimi ("The Offshore Pirate"), **280**
Merritt, Ogden ("The Jelly-Bean"), **280**

Merriweather, Rosemary (''Indecision''), **281**
Merry, Osborne (*Safety First!*), **281**
Meyers, Gus (''What a Handsome Pair!''), **281**
Michael (''One Interne''), **281**
Michael (''One of My Oldest Friends''), **281**
Michaelis, Mavro (*The Great Gatsby*), **281**
Michaud (*The Beautiful and Damned*), **281**
Michelle (*Tender Is the Night*), **281**
Mieger (''Two for a Cent''), **281**
''Mightier Than the Sword,'' **281–82**
Mike (*The Evil Eye*), **282**
Milbank, Hat (''The Woman from Twenty-one''), **282**
Miles, Cardine (''One Trip Abroad''), **282**
Miles, Liddell (''One Trip Abroad''), **282**
Miller (''Outside the Cabinet-Maker's''), **282**
Miller, Carl (''Absolution''), **282**
Miller, Glen (*The Last Tycoon*), **282**
Miller, Mrs. Carl (''Absolution''), **283**
Miller, Rudolph (''Absolution''), **283**
Minerlino, Roderigo (''Rags Martin-Jones and the Pr-nce of W-les''), **283**
Minghetti (*Tender Is the Night*), **283**
Minghetti, Conte Hosain di (*Tender Is the Night*), **283**
Minghetti, Lucienne (*Tender Is the Night*), **283**
Minghetti, Mary North, Contessa di (*Tender Is the Night*), **283**
Minghetti, Toni di (*Tender Is the Night*), **283**
''Minnesota's Capital in the Rôle of Main Street,'' 138, **283**
Minnie the Moocher (''Zone of Accident''), **283**
Minska (''Zone of Accident''), **284**
Mirliflore, Mme (*The Evil Eye*), **284**
Misseldine (''Oh Misseldine's, dear Misseldine's,'' ''Spring Song''), **284**
''The Missing All'' (Bishop), 34
''Mr. Berlin wrote a song about forgetting to remember,'' **284**
Mister Icky, **284**
Mistinguett, Jeanne-Marie Florentine Bourgeois, **284**
Mitchell, Elenor (*Thoughtbook*), **284**
Mitchell, Jack (*Thoughtbook*), **284**
Mizener, Arthur, 335
Mollat (''A Short Autobiography''), **284**
''Momishness,'' **285**, 431
Momus, Geneveva de (*Tender Is the Night*), **285**
Moncrief, General (''The Curious Case of Benjamin Button''), **285**
Monroe (''Myra Meets His Family''), **285**
Monte (''Rags Martin-Jones and the Pr-nce of W-les''), **285**
Moody (''Two for a Cent''), **285**
Moon, Charlie (''Head and Shoulders''), **285**
Moon Calf (Dell), 48
Moon, Dr. (''The Adjuster''), **285**
Moon, Miss (''The Rubber Check''), **285**
Moore, Albert (''That Kind of Party''), **285**
Moore, Carpenter (''That Kind of Party''), **285**
Moore, Charley (''Dalyrimple Goes Wrong''), **286**
Moore, Dr. (''Zone of Accident''), **286**
Moore, Kathleen (*The Last Tycoon*), 159, 240, 243, **286**
Moore, Mrs. (''That Kind of Party''), **286**
Moran, Lois, 197, 251–52, **286**, 346
Moreland, Colonel (''The Offshore Pirate''), **286**
Moreland, Toby (''The Offshore Pirate''), **286–87**
''More Than Just a House,'' **287**
Morgan (''The Cruise of the Rolling Junk''), **287**
Morgan (*The Last Tycoon*), **287**
Morgan, Holly (''Persuasion''), **287**
Morgan, Joe (''What a Handsome Pair!''), **287**
Morgan, Musidora, 246
Morris (*Tender Is the Night*), **288**

Morris, Mrs. (*Tender Is the Night*), **288**
Morris, Von Cohn (*Tender Is the Night*), **288**
Morrison, Hep J. (''Strange Sanctuary''), **288**
Mortmain (''The Rubber Check''), **288**
Mortmain, Ellen (''The Rubber Check''), **288**
Mortmain, Mrs. (''The Rubber Check''), **288**
Morton, Junie (''The Ice Palace''), **288**
Mose, Trombone (''The Offshore Pirate''), **288**
Moses (''The Dance''), **288–89**
Moskin. *See* Maranda
''The Most Disgraceful Thing I Ever Did: 2. The Invasion of the Sanctuary,'' **289**
''Mother taught me to—love things,'' **289**
A Moveable Feast (Hemingway), 181, 182
Movie work by Fitzgerald, 179, 200, 204, **289–90**
Mridle (''Reade, Substitute Right Half''), **290**
Muchhause (*Tender Is the Night*), **290**
Mudge, Archie (*Thoughtbook*), **290**
Mudge, Betty (*Thoughtbook*), **290**
Muldoon (*The Great Gatsby*), **290**
Muldoon, Ed (''A Short Autobiography''), **290**
Muldoon, G. Earl (*The Great Gatsby*), **290**
Muldoon, Rastus (''Dice, Brassknuckles & Guitar''), **291**
Mulkley, Oates (''The Honor of the Goon''), **291**
Muller (''Between Three and Four''), **291**
Mulligan (*Assorted Spirits*), **291**
Mulligan (''The Captured Shadow''), **291**
Mullins (''The Bowl''), **291**
Mulready (*The Great Gatsby*), **291**
Mumble, Mr. (*The Great Gatsby*), **291**
Munn, Martin (''Emotional Bankruptcy''), **291**
Murdock, Evelyn (''Flight and Pursuit''), **291**
Murphy (''Outside the Cabinet-Maker's''), **291–92**
Murphy, Baoth, 141, 292–93
Murphy, Gerald, 112, 141, 158, 181, 291, **292–93**, 323, 335, 390, 440
Murphy, Honoria, 291
Murphy, Sara, 112, 141, 158, 181, 291, **293**, 323, 390
Myer, Lester (*The Great Gatsby*), **293**
Myers, Carmel, 38, 62, **293**, 316
''My First Love,'' **293**
''My Generation,'' **293**
''My Lost City,'' 129, **294**
''My mind is all a-tumble,'' **294**
''My Old New England Homestead on the Erie,'' **294**
''Myra Meets His Family,'' **294–95**
''The Mystery of the Raymond Mortgage,'' **295**
''My Ten Favorite Plays,'' **295–96**
''My Very Very Dear Marie,'' **296**

Nana (''The Curious Case of Benjamin Button''), **297**
Narry (''The Debutante''), **297**
Nash, Norma (''A Freeze-Out''), **297**
Nassau Literary Magazine, 71, 146
Nathan, George Jean, 24, 206, 278, 279, **297–98**, 301, 334, 406
Necrawney (''Family in the Wind''), **298**
Ned (''The Broadcast We Almost Heard Last September''), **298**
Negrotto, Claude (''The Honor of the Goon''), **298**
Nell (''The Night of Chancellorsville''), **298**
Nellie (*Tender Is the Night*), **298**
''A New Leaf,'' 5, **298–99**
The New Machiavelli (Wells), 449
''News of Paris—Fifteen Years Ago,'' **299**
''New Types,'' **299–300**
''A Nice Quiet Place,'' **300**
Nick (''No Harm Trying''), **300**
Nick (''The Rich Boy''), **300**
Nicotera (*Tender Is the Night*), **301**
The Nigger of the ''Narcissus'' (Conrad), 78, 288

"A Night at the Fair," **301**
"The Night of Chancellorsville," **301**
Noble, Maury (*The Beautiful and Damned*), **301**
Noel ("The Intimate Strangers"), **301**. *See also* Guillet de la Guimpé, Noel de la
"No Flowers," **302**
"No Harm Trying," 237, **302–3**
Nolak ("The Camel's Back"), **303**
Nolak, Mrs. ("The Camel's Back"), **303**
Nora ("The Night of Chancellorsville"), **303**
Normand, Mabel, **303**
Norris, Charles Gilman, **303–4**, 342
Norris, Frank, 212, 303
North, Abe (*Tender Is the Night*), 239, **304**
North, Mary. *See* Minghetti, Mary North
Norton, Dr. ("One Interne"), **304**
Nosby, Claude ("A Penny Spent"), **304**
Nostromo (Conrad), 78
"Not in the Guidebook," **304–5**
"Now is the time for all good men to come to the aid of the party," **305**
"Now your heart is come so near," **305**

Oakey, Mrs. ("Family in the Wind"), **306**
Oaky ("In the Holidays"), **306**
Obaloney, Prince Paul ("The Broadcast We Almost Heard Last September"), **306**
Ober, Anne Reid, 306, 307, 391
Ober, Harold, 93, 132, 146, 158, 204, **306–7**, 335, 386, 391, 406, 468
Oberwalter ("A Snobbish Story"), **307**
"Obit on Parnassus," **307**
O'Brien (*The Last Tycoon*), **307**
O'Brien, Father ("Sentiment—and the Use of Rouge"), **307**
O'Brien, Faustina (*The Great Gatsby*), **307**
O'Connor, Helen ("Flight and Pursuit"), **307**
O'Day, Henry (*Precaution Primarily*), **307**
O'Donahue, Stephen (*This Side of Paradise*), **308**
O'Donavan, Horace (*The Great Gatsby*), **308**
"The Offshore Pirate," 93, **308**, 351
The Offshore Pirate (movie), 93, 308
O'Flaherty, Sergeant ("Sentiment—and the Use of Rouge"), **308**
O'Flarity (*Assorted Spirits*), **308**
Of Thee I Sing (Gershwin, Kaufman, Ryskind), 439
"Of wonders is Silas M. Hanson the camp," **309**
Ogden, Dr. ("The Love Boat"), **309**
O'Hara ("The Captured Shadow"), **309**
"Oh Misseldine's, dear Misseldine's," **309**
"Oh papa—," **309**
"Oh, Sister, Can You Spare Your Heart," **309**
"Oh where are the boys of the boom-boom-boom," **309**
O'Kane ("On an Ocean Wave"), **309**
O'Keefe ("Majesty"), **309**
O'Keefe, Chevalier (*The Beautiful and Damned*), **309**
O'Kelly, George (" 'The Sensible Thing' "), **309–10**
Oldhorne ("What a Handsome Pair!"), **310**
Oldhorne, Helen Van Beck ("What a Handsome Pair!"), **310**
Oldhorne, Stuart ("What a Handsome Pair!"), **310**, 453
Old Man, the (" 'Send Me In, Coach' "), **310**
Ole (*Assorted Spirits*), **310**
Olive ("A Night at the Fair"), **310**
Oliver ("The Last of the Belles"), **310**
Olsen ("A Freeze-Out"), **310**
Olson (*This Side of Paradise*), **310**
Omar ("Heat and Shoulders"), **311**
O'May (*This Side of Paradise*), **311**
"On an Ocean Wave," **311**
"On a Play Twice Seen," **311**
"On Being an American" (Mencken), 439
"One Hundred False Starts," **311**

O'Neill, Cardinal (*This Side of Paradise*), **311**
''One Interne,'' **311–12**
''One of My Oldest Friends,'' **312**
''One Southern Girl,'' **313**
''One Trip Abroad,'' 5, 45, **313–14**
O'Ney (*The Last Tycoon*), **314**
''On Schedule,'' **314**
''On the Trail of Pat Hobby,'' **314–15**
''On Watching the Candidates in the Newsreels,'' **315**
''On Your Own,'' **315**
Oppidan (Leslie), 249
Oral, Mrs. (''The Popular Girl''), **315**
''Orange pajamas and heaven's guitars,'' 293, **316**
Orchid, Newton (*The Great Gatsby*), **316**
''The Ordeal,'' 28, 100, **316**
Ordway (*The Great Gatsby*), **316**
O'Reilly (''Bernice Bobs Her Hair''), **316**
Ormonde, Genevieve (''Bernice Bobs Her Hair''), **316**
Ormonde, Otis (''Bernice Bobs Her Hair''), **316**
Ormsby, Captain (*Coward*), **316**
O'Rourke, Jerry (''The Popular Girl''), **317**
''Orphan Annie,'' 39
Orsini, Princess (*Tender Is the Night*), **317**
''O Russet Witch!, **317–18**
Oscar (''The Rich Boy''), **318**
O'Sullivan, Eddie (''On Your Own''), **318**
Oswald (*Safety First!*), **318**
Otis (*The Beautiful and Damned*), **318**
''Our American Poets,'' **318**
''Our April Letter,'' **318**
The Outline of History (Wells), 449
''Outside the Cabinet-Maker's,'' 293, **318**
Overton (*This Side of Paradise*), **318**
Owl-Eyes (*The Great Gatsby*), **319**, 323
Oyster, Evelyn (*Tender Is the Night*), **319**

Packman, George (''The Bridal Party''), **320**
Page (*This Side of Paradise*), **320**
Page, Clara (*This Side of Paradise*), **320**
Page, Howard (''First Blood,'' ''A Snobbish Story''), **320**
''Pain and the Scientist,'' **320**
''La Paix,'' 136, 430
Paley, Lord (*Tender Is the Night*), **320**
Palmer (''That Kind of Party''), **321**
Palmer (''That Kind of Party''), **321**
Palmer, Clothilde Sayre, 73, 135, **321**, 372
Palmer, Fats (''That Kind of Party''), **321**
Palmer, Miss (''Author's House''), **321**
Palmetto, Henry L. (*The Great Gatsby*), **321**
Pan-e-troon (''The Passionate Eskimo''), **321**
Papa Jack (''Rags Martin-Jones and the Pr-nce of W-les''), **321**
Paragoris, Mme (*Tender Is the Night*), **321**
Paramore, Frederick E. (*The Beautiful and Damned*), 289, **321–22**
Parke (*The Great Gatsby*), **322**
Parker (*Porcelain and Pink*), **322**
Parker, Dr. (''Too Cute for Words''), **322**
Parker, Dorothy, 98, 277, 292, **322–23**
Parker, Frog (*This Side of Paradise*), **323**
Parkhurst, Perry (''The Camel's Back''), **323–24**
Parks, Allen (''More Than Just a House''), **324**
Parmelee, Eddie (''Forging Ahead''), **324**
Parr, Emily (''The Rubber Check''), **324**
Parrish, Joseph Hardwick (''The Third Casket''), **324**
Parsons, Jim (*The Beautiful and Damned*), **324**
Parsons, Louella Oettinger (*The Last Tycoon*), **324**
Pasche, Mme (*Tender Is the Night*), **324**
Paskert (*This Side of Paradise*), **324**
''The Passionate Eskimo,'' **324–25**
''Pasting It Together,'' 173, **325**
Pat (*The Beautiful and Damned*), **325**
Pat (''The Bridal Party''), **325**
Patch, Adam (*The Beautiful and Damned*), **325**

Patch, Adam Ulysses (*The Beautiful and Damned*), **325**
Patch, Alicia Withers (*The Beautiful and Damned*), **326**
Patch, Annie (*The Beautiful and Damned*), **326**
Patch, Anthony (*The Beautiful and Damned*), **326**
Patch, Gloria Gilbert (*The Beautiful and Damned*), 137, **326**
Patch, Henrietta Lebrune (*The Beautiful and Damned*), **326**
Paterson ('' 'Boil Some Water—Lots of It' ''), **326**
''Pat Hobby and Orson Welles,'' **327**, 449
''Pat Hobby Does His Bit,'' **327**
''Pat Hobby, Putative Father,'' **327**
''Pat Hobby's Christmas Wish,'' **328**
''Pat Hobby's College Days,'' **328**
''Pat Hobby's Preview,'' **328**
''Pat Hobby's Secret,'' **329**
The Pat Hobby stories, 5, 153, 204, 233, **329**
''A Patriotic Short,'' **329**
Patt, Larry (''Six of One—''), **329**
Patton, Roger (''The Ice Palace''), **330**
Paul (''Babylon Revisited''), **330**
Paul (*Tender Is the Night*), **330**
Paul (*Thoughtbook*), **330**
Paulson, Charley (''Bernice Bobs Her Hair''), **330**
Paulson, Charlie (''Head and Shoulders''), **330**
Paxton (''Imagination—and a Few Mothers''), **330**
Paxton (''Imagination—and a Few Mothers''), **330**
Paxton, Mrs. (''Imagination—and a Few Mothers''), **330**
Paxton, Prudence (''Imagination—and a Few Mothers''), **330**
Paxton, Speed (''A Night at the Fair''), **330**
Payson (''No Flowers''), **331**
''The Pearl and the Fur'' (unpublished story), 41, 426
Pearson, Slim (*Tender Is the Night*), **331**
Peat (''Head and Shoulders''), **331**
Pechard, Margot (''The Intimate Strangers''), **331**
Pechard, Paul (''The Intimate Strangers''), **331**
Pedro (''Pat Hobby's Christmas Wish''), **331**
Peebles, Claude (''Not in the Guidebook''), **331**
Peebles, Mrs. Claude (''Not in the Guidebook''), **331**
Peltzer (''Family in the Wind''), **331**
''A Penny Spent,'' **331–32**
Pepin, George (''The Rubber Check''), **332**
Pepin, Mrs. George (''The Rubber Check''), **332**
Pepys, Sandra (''Head and Shoulders''), **332**
Percy (*Safety First!*), **332**
Percy (''The Unspeakable Egg''), **332**
''The Perfect Life,'' **332–33**
Perimont, Countess (''A Penny Spent''), **333**
Perkins, Max, **333–35**; biographical details, 333, 335; Fitzgerald's agent and friend, 8, 24, 43, 44, 132, 142, 181, 238, 260, 298, 307, 333–35, 339, 408, 462; model for character, 212; and other authors, 34, 43, 56, 68, 182, 238–39, 249, 376, 380
Perrin (*Tender Is the Night*), **335**
Perry (''Crazy Sunday''), **335**
Perry (''First Blood''), **335**
Perry, Constance (''First Blood,'' ''A Nice Quiet Place''), **335**
Perry, Herbert T. (''Emotional Bankruptcy,'' ''First Blood,'' ''A Nice Quiet Place,'' ''A Snobbish Story,'' ''A Story with a Past''), **335–36**
Perry, Josephine (''Emotional Bankruptcy,'' ''First Blood,'' ''A Nice Quiet Place,'' ''A Snobbish Story,'' ''A Woman with a Past''), 20, 230, **336–37**
Perry, Mrs. (''Crazy Sunday''), **337**
Perry, Mrs. Herbert T. (''Emotional Bankruptcy,'' ''First Blood,'' ''A Nice

Quiet Place,'' ''A Snobbish Story''), **337**
Pershing, John Joseph, General, 348
Persia, Shah of (*Tender is the Night*), **337**
Pete ('' 'I Didn't Get Over' ''), **337**
Peter (*Fie! Fie! Fi-Fi!*), **337**
Peter (*Mister Icky*), **337**
Peters, Birdy (*The Last Tycoon*), **337**
Peters, Elsie (''Babylon Revisited''), **337**
Peters, Lincoln (''Babylon Revisited''), **337**
Peters, Marion (''Babylon Revisited''), **338**, 392
Peters, Richard (''Babylon Revisited''), **338**, 392
Peterson, Jules (*Tender Is the Night*), **338**
Petrocobesco, Emily Castleton (''Majesty''), **338**
Petrocobesco, Prince Gabriel (''Majesty''), **338**
Philippe, Count of Villefranche (''The Count of Darkness,'' ''Gods of Darkness,'' ''In the Darkest Hour,'' ''The Kingdom in the Dark''), **338–39**
The Philippe stories, **339**
Phillips ('' 'Trouble' ''), **339**
The Philosophy of Friedrich Nietzsche (Mencken), 279
Picasso, Pablo, **339**, 397
Pickering, Thomas (''Too Cute for Words''), **339**
Pickman, Josephine (''The Bowl''), **339**
Pierce (*Tender Is the Night*), **339**
''The Pierian Springs and the Last Straw,'' **339–40**
Pierre (''The Kingdom in the Dark,'' ''Gods of Darkness''), **340**
Pilgrim, Dr. (''The End of Hate''), **340**
Pilgrim, Josie (''The End of Hate''), **340**
''Pilgrimage,'' **340**
Pinkard, Emmy. *See* McChesney, Emily Pinkard
Piper, Donald (''The Cut-Glass Bowl''), **340–41**
Piper, Evylyn (''The Cut-Glass Bowl''), **341**
Piper, Harold (''The Cut-Glass Bowl''), **341**
Piper, Jessie. *See* Lowrie, Jessie Piper
Piper, Julie (''The Cut-Glass Bowl''), **341**
Piper, Milton (''The Cut-Glass Bowl''), **341**
Pirie, 230, 233, 252
Pirie, Dr. (''The Long Way Out''), **341**
Pistachio (''The Prince of Pests''), **341**
The Pit: A Story of Chicago (F. Norris), 212
Pitou (''Shadow Laurels''), **341–42**
Plant, Donald (''Three Hours between Planes''), **342**
Playfair, Dick ('' 'Send Me In, Coach' ''), **342**
Poe (''The Ants at Princeton''), **342**
Poindexter, Jo (''Presumption''), **342**
Poindexter, Morton (''Presumption''), **342**
Poitiers, Count of (''The Kingdom in the Dark''), **342**
Pole (*The Great Gatsby*), **342**
Pompia (*This Side of Paradise*), **342**
Poole, E. P. (''Zone of Accident''), **342**
Poore (''The Bowl''), **342**
''Poor Old Marriage,'' 304, **342**
''The Pope at Confession,'' **343**
Popolous, Joe (*The Last Tycoon*), **343**
Popular Daughter (*This Side of Paradise*), **343**
''The Popular Girl,'' **343**
''Popular Parodies—No. 1,'' **343**
Porcelain and Pink, **344**
Porter (''For the time that our man spent in pressing your suit''), **344**
Porter, Cole, 141, 292
Porterfield, Jim (*Thoughtbook*), **344**
Potter (''The Smilers''), **344**
Potterfield-Swiftcormick, Miss (''A Snobbish Story''), **344**
Powell, Alice (''The Jelly-Bean''), **344**
Powell, Amanthis (''Dice, Brassknuckles & Guitar''), **344**
Powell, James (''The Jelly-Bean,'' ''Dice, Brassknuckles & Guitar''), **344–45**
Powers, Kenneth (''Babes in the Woods''), **345**
Prayle (''A Debt of Honor''), **345**

Precaution Primarily, **345**
Prejudices, Second Series (Mencken), 16, 279
Prejudices, Third Series (Mencken), 439
Prendergast, Elsie ("The Popular Girl"), **345**
Preston, Killy ("The Last of the Belles"), **345**
"Presumption," **345–46**
"Pretty Boy Floyd," 139, **346**, 365
Prince, Jenny ("Jacob's Ladder"), 286, **346**
"The Prince of Pests," **346**
"Princeton," 34, 189, **347**
"Princeton—The Last Day," **347**
Prissy, Aunt ("Discard"), **347**
"The Prizefighter's Wife," **347**
Pruit, Miss (*Coward*), **347**
Prunier ("A Short Autobiography"), **347**
"Public Letter to Thomas Boyd," 279, **347**
Pulpat ("O Russet Witch!"), **347**
Pumpkin, Professor ("The Captured Shadow"), **347**
Purley ("The Love Boat"), **348**
Purley ("The Love Boat"), **348**
Purley, Mae. *See* Fitzpatrick, Mae Purley
Purley, Mrs. ("The Love Boat"), **348**
"The Pusher-in-the-Face," **348**
Pushing (*The Vegetable*), **348**

Quarles, Lorraine ("Babylon Revisited"), **349**
Quarrels, Madeline ("The Rubber Check"), **349**
Quarterly (*Tender Is the Night*), **349**
Quill, Moonlight ("O Russet Witch!"), **349**
Quill, Mrs. Moonlight ("O Russet Witch!"), **349**
Quinn, (*The Great Gatsby*), **349**

Radamacher ("The Fiend"), **350**
Raffino ("Jacob's Ladder"), **350**
Raffles (movie), 290
Ragland, Dick ("A New Leaf"), **350**
"Rags Martin-Jones and the Pr-nce of W-les," **350–51**
Rahill (*This Side of Paradise*), **351**
"Rain Before Dawn," **351**
Raines, Marston ("Diagnosis"), **351**
Rainy (*Tender Is the Night*), **351**
Raj, Sir Singrim Dak ("Pat Hobby, Putative Father"), **351**
Ralph ("Emotional Bankruptcy"), **351**
Ralph (*Safety First!*), **351**
Ralston, Mrs. ("John Jackson's Arcady"), **351**
Ramsay, Dr. ("The Love Boat"), **351**
Randall, Louie ("Emotional Bankruptcy"), **352**
Randolph, Eddie (*Coward*), **352**
Ransome (*The Last Tycoon*), **352**
"The Rape of Lucrece" (Shakespeare), 393, 408
Rapf, Maurice, 243
Ratoni, Al ("The Bowl"), **352**
Raudenbuch, Miss ("Pat Hobby, Putative Father"), **352**
Rawlings, Marjorie Kinnan, 335
Ray, Esther ("Too Cute for Words"), **352**
Ray, Mrs. Charles Wrotten ("Too Cute for Words"), **352**
Ray, Tommy ("Too Cute for Words"), **352**
Raycroft, Dorothy (*The Beautiful and Damned*), **352**
Raycroft, Mrs. (*The Beautiful and Damned*), **352**
Raymond ("The Mystery of the Raymond Mortgage"), **353**
Raymond, Agnes ("The Mystery of the Raymond Mortgage"), **353**
Raymond, Mrs. ("The Mystery of the Raymond Mortgage"), **353**
Raymond, Robert Calvin ("The Room with the Green Blinds"), **353**
Read ("Jacob's Ladder"), **353**
Read ("The Love Boat"), **353**
Read, Cecil, 51, **353**
Reade ("Reade, Substitute Right Half"), **353**
"Reade, Substitute Right Half," **353**
Real, Francisco Pardo y Cuidad (*Tender Is the Night*), **353**

Real, Pardo y Cuidad (*Tender Is the Night*), **353**
Reardon (*This Side of Paradise*), **354**
Reardon, Eltynge (*The Beautiful and Damned*), **354**
Red ("The Love Boat"), **354**
The Red Badge of Courage (Crane), 43, 78, 112
Redfern, Major. *See* Gilbert, Dodo
Reece, Lady ("The Rubber Check"), **354**
Reed, Carl (*Thoughtbook*), **354**
Reffer, Marty (*The Beautiful and Damned*), **354**
"Refrain for a Poem. How to Get to So and So," **354**
Regan ("Benediction"), **354**
Reilly ("Forging Ahead," "He Thinks He's Wonderful"), **354**
Reilly, Benjamin ("Forging Ahead"), **354**
Reilly, Everett ("Forging Ahead"), **355**
Reilly, Mrs. Benjamin ("Forging Ahead"), **355**
Reina (*The Last Tycoon*), **355**
Reisenweber (*The Beautiful and Damned*), **355**
Remarque, Erich Maria, 289
"Reminicenses [*sic*] of Donald Stewart by F. Scott Fitzgerald (in the Manner of . . ."). *See* Stewart, Donald Ogden
Renaud ("The Count of Darkness"), **355**
René ("How to Live on Practically Nothing a Year"), **355**
Rennard, Jules ("Magnetism"), **355**
Renwick (*This Side of Paradise*), **355**
Reuben (*Thoughtbook*), **355**
Riccard ("Image on the Heart"), **355**
Rice, Susan (*Thoughtbook*), **356**
Rich ("The Last of the Belles"), **356**
Richard (*This Side of Paradise*), **356**
Richards ("The Passionate Eskimo"), **356**
Richbitch, Mrs. ("The Woman from Twenty-one"), **356**
"The Rich Boy," 47, 182, **356–57**
Richepin, Madame de ("The Swimmers"), **357**
Rickey ("'Send Me In, Coach'"), **357**
Ridgeway ("The Cut-Glass Bowl"), **357**
Ridingwood, Red (*The Last Tycoon*), **357**
Rienmund, Joe (*The Last Tycoon*), **358**
Riggs, Billy ("Fate in Her Hands"), **358**
Rikker, Alida ("A Freeze-Out"), **358**
Rikker, Cathy Chase ("A Freeze-Out"), **358**
Rikker, Chauncey ("A Freeze-Out"), **358**
Rikker, Irene ("Two Wrongs"), **358**
Rikker, Teddy ("A Freeze-Out"), **358**
Rimbaud, Arthur, 441
"Ring," 239, **358–59**
Rita ("Teamed with Genius"), **359**
Rivers (*The Beautiful and Damned*), **359**
Robbie, Martha ("That Kind of Party"), **359**
Robbie, Mrs. ("That Kind of Party"), **359**
Robbins, Jubal Early ("On Your Own"), **359**
Roberg, George ("The Love Boat"), **359**
Robert the Frog ("In the Darkest Hour"), **359**
Robin (*Thoughtbook*), **359**
Robinson ("One Interne"), **359**
Robinson, Deering R. ("The Homes of the Stars"), **359**
Robinson, Mrs. Deering R. ("The Homes of the Stars"), **360**
Robinson, Mrs. George D. ("The Pusher-in-the-Face"), **360**
Robinson, Robby (*The Last Tycoon*), **360**
Roebuck, Cecil (*The Great Gatsby*), **360**
Rogers, Alan ("Two Wrongs"), **360**
Rogers, Orrin ("The Popular Girl"), **360**
Rogers, Mrs. Orrin ("The Popular Girl"), **360**
Rogers, Pete ("The Popular Girl"), **360**
Rolf ("The Kingdom in the Dark"), **360**
Rollins, George. *See* O'Kelly, George
The Romantic Egotists (Smith), 391
Romberg ("Absolution"), **360**
Rombert ("The Pierian Springs and the Last Straw"), **361**
Rombert, George ("The Pierian Springs and the Last Straw"), **361**
Rombert, Miss ("The Pierian Springs and the Last Straw"), **361**

Rombert, Mrs. George. *See* Fulham, Myra
Rombert, Mrs. Thomas ("The Pierian Springs and the Last Straw"), **361**
Rombert, Thomas ("The Pierian Springs and the Last Straw"), **361**
"The Room with the Green Blinds," **361–62**
Rooney ("The Freshest Boy"), **362**
Rooney (*This Side of Paradise*), **362**
Rooney, Miss (*The Beautiful and Damned*), **362**
Roosevelt, Mrs. Claude (*The Great Gatsby*), **362**
Roper, Bill ("The Bowl"), **362**
Roreback, Anthony ("John Jackson's Arcady"), **362**
Rose ("Your Way and Mine"), **362**
Rose, Aunt ("Lo, the Poor Peacock!"), **362**
Rose, Gus, Private ("May Day"), **362–63**
Rosen, Sidney ("Forging Ahead"), **363**
Rosenthal, Herman, 363
Rosenthal, Rosy (*The Great Gatsby*), **363**
Ross, Julia ("A New Leaf"), **363**
Ross, Walter ("The Swimmers"), **363**
Rostoff, Prince Paul Serge Boris ("Love in the Night"), **363**
Rostoff, Princess ("Love in the Night"), **363**
Rostoff, Prince Val ("Love in the Night"), **363**
Rostoff, Prince Vladimir ("Love in the Night"), **364**
Rothstein, Arnold, 463
"The Rough Crossing," **364**
Rousseau, Miss ("Between Three and Four"), **364**
Rowe, Lynwood Thomas, 346, **365**
Roxanna (*The Vegetable*), **365**
Rubber ("The Bowl"), **365**
"The Rubber Check," **365–66**
Rudd, Chinaman ("The Captured Shadow"), **366**
Rudd, Chinyman (*The Captured Shadow*), **366**
Ruff, Dr. ("One Interne"), **366**
"A Rugged Novel," 43, **366**
Rus ("The Camel's Back"), **366**
Russel, Elaine ("Diamond Dick and the First Law of Woman"), **366**
Ruth. *See* Sturtevant, Ruth
Ruth ("A Short Autobiography"), **366**
Ruth ("There was a young lady named Ruth"), **367**
Ruth ("Truth and—consequences"), **367**
"Ruth," **367**
Rutherford ("The Bridal Party"), **367**
Rutherford, Hamilton ("The Bridal Party"), **367**
Rutherford, Mrs. ("The Bridal Party"), **367**
Ruthven, Mrs. Cassius ("What a Handsome Pair!"), **367**
Ryder, J. Dawson (*This Side of Paradise*), **367**
Ryskind, Morrie, 439

Sable, Willa (*The Beautiful and Damned*), **368**
The Sacco-Vanzetti case, 49, 112, 322
Sachs (*Tender Is the Night*), **368**
"Sad Catastrophe," **368**
Sady. *See* Fi-Fi
Safety First!, **368–39**
Sage ("Indecision"), **369**
Sage, Esmeralda (*The Evil Eye*), **369**
St. Claire, Mrs. (*This Side of Paradise*), **369**
St. Claire, Myra (*This Side of Paradise*), **369**
The St. Paul Daily Dirge, **369**
St. Raphael ("Rags Martin-Jones and the Pr-nce of W-les"), **369**
Sal (*Safety First!*), **370**
"Salesmanship in the Champs-Élysées," **370**
Salisbury, Viscountess ("Imagination—and a Few Mothers"), **370**
Salt (C. Norris), 304
Saltonville, Cabot ("The Ants of Princeton"), **370**
Sam ("Diagnosis"), **370**
Sam (*Fie! Fie! Fi-Fi*), **370**
Sam ("The Perfect Life"), **370**

Sampson, Wash (''The Bowl''), **370**
Sanderson, Carl (''The Bowl''), **370**
Sanderson, John (''A Debt of Honor''), **370**
Sandwood (''Winter Dreams''), **370**
Sano, Marcel de. *See* de Sano, Marcel
''The Saraha of the Bozart'' (Mencken), 16
Sarah (''She lay supine among her Pekinese''), **371**
Sarah (*This Side of Paradise*), **371**
Sarnemington, Blatchford. *See* Miller, Rudolph
Sarolai, Count Chiki (''One Trip Abroad''), **371**
Saunders, Ed (''The Rich Boy''), **371**
Saunders, Miss (''The Captured Shadow''), **371**
Saunders, Miss (*The Captured Shadow*), **371**
Saunders, Ridgeway (''Emotional Bankruptcy,'' ''A Nice Quiet Place,'' ''A Woman with a Past''), **371**
Savage, Eleanor (*This Side of Paradise*), **371–72**
Savage, Phil (''No Flowers''), **372**
Savage, Ramilly (*This Side of Paradise*), **372**
Save Me the Waltz (Z. Fitzgerald), 83, 136–37, 298, 334, 372, 406
Sayre, Anthony Dickinson, 135, 326, **372**
Sayre, Anthony, Jr., 135, 326, 372
Sayre, Minnie Buckner Machen, 135, **372–73**, 396
Scandalabra (Z. Fitzgerald), 137
''The Scandal Detectives,'' **373**
Schaeffer (*Tender Is the Night*), **373**
Schaeffer, Duncan (''Babylon Revisited''), **373**
Schaeffer, Edna (''The Pusher-in-the-Face''), **373**
Schaffer, May (''The Love Boat''), **373**
Scharnhorst (''Jacob's Ladder''), **374**
Scheer (''On an Ocean Wave''), **374**
Scheer, Gaston T. (''On an Ocean Wave''), **374**
Scheer, Minna (''On an Ocean Wave''), **374**
Scheerer (''Winter Dreams''), **374**
Scheerer, Irene (''Winter Dreams''), **374**
Scheerer, Mrs. (''Winter Dreams''), **374**
Schemmerhorn, Austin (''John Jackson's Arcady''), **374**
Schenzi (''The Hotel Child''), **374**
Schlach, Otto (''Six of One—''), **374**
Schmiel, Rosemary (*The Last Tycoon*), **374–75**
Schneider (''The Cruise of the Rolling Junk''), **375**
Schnlitski, Gus (''In a dear little vine-covered cottage''), **375**
Schnlitzer-Murphy, Gwendolyn (''The Diamond as Big as the Ritz''), **375**
Schnlitzer-Murphy, Vivian (''The Diamond as Big as the Ritz''), **375**
Schoatze, George (''One Interne,'' ''Zone of Accident''), **375**
Schoen, Cecil (*The Great Gatsby*), **375**
Schoen, Earl, Lieutenant (''The Last of the Belles''), **375**
Schofield, Charley (''Six of One—''), **375**
Schofield, Irene. *See* Irving, Irene
Schofield, Mrs. (''Six of One—''), **376**
Schofield, Wister (''Six of One—''), **376**
Schraeder, O.R.P. (*The Great Gatsby*), **376**
Schroeder (*The Beautiful and Damned*), **376**
Schroeder, Pete (''Magnetism''), **376**
Schulberg, Budd, 16, 50, 243, 254, 290, 360, **376–77**
Schultze (*The Great Gatsby*), **377**
Schultze, Kitty (*Thoughtbook*), **377**
Schuneman, Willy (''Bernice Bobs Her Hair''), **377**
Schuyler. *See* [Hunter?], Schuyler
Schuyler (''The Rubber Check''), **377**
Schuyler, Mrs. Martin (''The Rubber Check''), **377**
Schuyler, Val (''The Rubber Check''), **377**
Schwane (''A Freeze-Out''), **377**
Schwartz, Adolphus, Father (''Absolution''), **378**
Schwartz, Fifi (''The Hotel Child''), **378**

Schwartz, John ("The Hotel Child"), **378**
Schwartz, Mrs. ("The Hotel Child"), **378**
Schwartze. *See* Velance, Peppy
Schwartze ("A Night at the Fair"), **378**
Schwartze, Don S. (*The Great Gatsby*), **378**
Schwartze, Dr. ("One Interne"), **378**
Schwartze, Mannie (*The Last Tycoon*), **378**
Scott, Cecilia Ashton, 135
Scott Fitzgerald: A Biography (Turnbull), 430–31
Scott Fitzgerald: Letters to His Daughter (Turnbull, ed.), 391, 431
"Scott Fitzgerald so they say," **378**
Scottie. *See* Smith, Frances Scott Fitzgerald Lanahan
Scribner, Charles, III, 333
Scully (*The Great Gatsby*), **378**
A Second Flowering: Works and Days of the Lost Generation (Cowley), 83
Second Story Salle (*Assorted Spirits*), **379**
The Secret Agent (Conrad), 281
Sedgewick ("The Pierian Springs and the Last Straw"), **379**
Sedgewick, Earl ("The Family Bus"), **379**
Ségur, Mlle ("On Schedule"), **379**
Selassie, Haile (" 'Trouble' "), **379**
Selby, Mrs. ("The Intimate Strangers"), **379**
Seldes, Gilbert, 153, 239, 289, 292, **379–80**
Selznick, David O., 289–90, 376, 399
Semple ("The Popular Girl"), **380**
" 'Send Me In, Coach,' " **380–81**
Seneca, Old ("Lo, the Poor Peacock!"), **381**
Seneca, Young ("Lo, the Poor Peacock!"), **381**
" 'The Sensible Thing,' " **381**
"Sentiment—And the Use of Rouge," **381–82**
Serpolette ("How to Live on Practically Nothing a Year"), **382**
Seventeen (Tarkington), 407
Severance (*The Beautiful and Damned*), **382**
Severance, Mrs. ("Sentiment—and the Use of Rouge"), **382**
Seymour (*Thoughtbook*), **382**
Shadow, the ("The Captured Shadow"), **382**
Shadow, the. *See* Dudley, Thorton Hart
Shadow Laurels, 5, **382**
Shaggy ("Shaggy's Morning"), **383**
"Shaggy's Morning," **383**
Shakespeare, William, 39, **383**, 393, 403, 408, 418
Shalder ("A Change of Class"), **383**
Shalder, Howard ("A Change of Class"), **383**
Shalder, Irene ("A Change of Class"), **383**
Shanly (*This Side of Paradise*), **383**
Shaver, Harmon ("No Harm Trying"), **383**
Shearer, Norma, 57, 75, 85, 253, **383–84**, 415–16
Sheilah ("Some Interrupted Lines to Sheilah"). *See* Graham, Sheilah
"She lay supine among her Pekinese," **384**
Shelenton, Honey (*Thoughtbook*), **384**
Sheply (*Thoughtbook*), **384**
Sheridan ("On Schedule"), **384**
Sheridan, Mrs. ("On Schedule"), **384**
Sherman, Esther ("One Trip Abroad"), **384**
Shermy (*Safety First!*), **384**
"Sherwood Anderson on the Marriage Question," 7–8, 281, **384**
Shevlin ("The Curious Case of Benjamin Button"), **384**
Shinkey ("Family in the Wind"), **385**
Shipman, Dr. ("The Smilers"), **385**
Shoonover, Joe ("That Kind of Party"), **385**
Shoonover, Mrs. ("That Kind of Party"), **385**
"A Short Autobiography (With Acknowledgments to [Jean George] Nathan)," 129, 181, 239, 293, **385**

''A Short Retort'' (Scottie Fitzgerald), 293
''A Short Trip Home,'' **385–86**
Shorty (''A Short Trip Home''), **386**
Shugrue, Miss Willie, **386**. *See also* Lukas, Birdie
Shully, Adolph (*Thoughtbook*), **386**
Shully, Kitty (*Thoughtbook*), **386**
Shurmer, Bob (*Thoughtbook*), **386**
Shuttleworth, Edward (*The Beautiful and Damned*), **386**
Sibley-Biers, Lady Caroline (''Two Wrongs''), **386**. *See also* Combrinck, Lady Sybil
Sidney (''Strange Sanctuary''), **386**
Silvé (''Image on the Heart''), **386**
Silvé, René, 355
Silverstein, Dave (''Crazy Sunday''), **387**
Simmons, Rabbit (''The Captured Shadow''), **387**
Simmons, Rabbit (*The Captured Shadow*), **387**
Simms, Lud (''Winter Dreams''), **387**
Simone (''Last Kiss''), **387**
Sinclair (''The Diary of a Sophomore''), **387**
Sinclair, Rhoda (''Forging Ahead''), **387**
''SING HOTCHA-CHA SING HEY-HI NINNY,'' **387**
Singleton, Thea (''One Interne,'' ''Zone of Accident''), **387**
''Six of One—,'' **387–88**
Skiggs, Dr. Hepezia (''Pain and the Scientist''), **388**
Skipper (''Head and Shoulders''), **388**
Skouras, Spyros Panagiotes, **388**
Slagle (*The Great Gatsby*), **388**
''Sleeping and Waking,'' **388–89**
''Sleep of a University,'' **389**
Sloane (*The Great Gatsby*), **389**
Sloane, Cary (''The Rich Boy''), **389**
Sloane, Fred (*This Side of Paradise*), **389**
Sloane, Moses (''The Rich Boy''), **389**
Slocum (''On Schedule''), **389**
Slocum, Mrs. (''On Schedule''), **389**
Smidy (''The Mystery of the Raymond Mortgage''), **389**
''The Smilers,'' **389–90**
Smirke (*The Great Gatsby*), **390**
Smith (''He Thinks He's Wonderful''), **390**
Smith (''Pat Hobby's Secret''), **390**
Smith, Adrian (''The Rough Crossing''), **390**
Smith, Don. *See* Hobby, Pat
Smith, Estelle (''The Rough Crossing''), **390**
Smith, Eva (''The Rough Crossing''), **390**
Smith, Frances Scott Fitzgerald Lanahan, **390–91**, 460; biographical details, 135, 195, 233, 293, 307, 335, 373, 390–92, 395; and Fitzgerald, 146, 202, 204, 206, 391–92; model for characters, 41, 44, 206, 243, 293, 426; writings, 293, 391
Smith, ''Gypsy'' (*The Beautiful and Damned*), **391**
Smith, Mrs. (''Pat Hobby's Secret''), **391**
Smith, Newman, 337–38, 392
Smith, Pricilla (''A Man in the Way''), **391**
Smith, Rosalind Sayre, 135, 337–38, 372, **392**
Smith, Sheik B. (''Rags Martin-Jones and the Pr-nce of W-les''), **392**
Smith, Wharton (*Thoughtbook*), **392**
Smythe (''Majesty''), **392**
Smythe, John (''Teamed with Genius''), **392**
Snell, Ripley (*The Great Gatsby*), **392**
''A Snobbish Story,'' **392–93**
Snooks (*The Vegetable*), **393**
Snooks, Mrs. (*The Vegetable*), **393**
Snow Bird, the (''Babylon Revisited''), **393**
''The Snows of Kilimanjaro'' (Hemingway), 153, 182, 334
Snyder, Becky (''On Schedule''), **393**
Society as I Have Found It (McAllister), 325
Soda Sam (''The Jelly-Bean''), **393**
Soft Shoes (''Tarquin of Cheapside''), **393**
Sohenberg (*The Beautiful and Damned*), **393**

Sollinger, Ned (*The Last Tycoon*), **394**
"Some Interrupted Lines to Sheilah," **394**
"Some Memories of Scott Fitzgerald" (Leslie), 249
"Some Stories They Like to Tell," **394**
"Song," **394**
"Song—," **394**
"A Song Number Idea," **394**
Spaulding, Porter S. ("The Honor of the Goon"), **394**
Speare, Dorothy, 394
Spears, George ("The Bowl"), **394**
Speers, Elsie (*Tender Is the Night*), **394**
Spence, Miss (*Coward*), **394**
Spigot, Miss (*Assorted Spirits*), **395**
Spindle, Miss (*Coward*), **395**
"The Spire and the Gargoyle," **395**
Spirit of Seventy-Six, the (" 'Trouble' "), **395**
Sprague, Annabel Fitzgerald, 134, **395**
"Spring Song," **395**
Square, Washington ("The Captured Shadow"), **395**
Squires, Joe ("Crazy Sunday"), **396**
Squires, Mildred, 136
Squires, Tom ("At Your Age"), **396**
Stacomb ("The Rough Crossing"), **396**
Stacy, Miss (" 'Boil Some Water—Lots of It' "), **396**
Stahr, Minna Davis (*The Last Tycoon*), **396**
Stahr, Monroe (*The Last Tycoon*), **396**, 427
Standish, John ("The Mystery of the Raymond Mortgage"), **396**
Standish, John B. (*The Vegetable*), **396**
Stanley ("No Flowers"), **396**
Starheim, Lizzette ("No Harm Trying"), **397**
Stark ("One Hundred False Starts"), **397**
"The Staying Up All Night," **397**
Stearne ("The Cut-Glass Bowl"), **397**
Stein, Gertrude, 7, 83, 180, 259–60, **397–38**
Stella (*The Great Gatsby*), **398**
Sterner ("Dalyrimple Goes Wrong"), **398**
Sterrett, Gordon ("May Day"), **398**
Steve ("The Night of Chancellorsville"), **398**
Stewart, Donald Ogden, 47, 292, 322–23, **398–99**
" 'Sticking along,' The voice so faint sometimes I could scarcely hear it," **400**
Stinson, Eddie ("A Short Trip Home"), **400**
Stirling, George ("John Jackson's Arcady"), **400**
Stockton, Sylvester ("The Smilers"), **400**
Stockton, Violet (*Thoughtbook*), **400**
Stoddard, G. Reece ("Bernice Bobs Her Hair"), **400**
Stoneman ("Diagnosis"), **400**
Strain, Jim ("Bernice Bobs Her Hair"), **400**
"Strange Sanctuary," **400–401**, 426
Strangler ("Your Way and Mine"), **401**
Strater, Henry Hyacinth, 189
Stuart ("A Letter to Helen"), **401**
Stuart, Charles David ("The Pusher-in-the-Face"), **401**
Stubbs, Jack ("Six of One—"), **401**
Studeford, Dr. ("The Love Boat"), **402**
Sturgis, Sam (*Thoughtbook*), **402**
Sturtevant, Ruth ("A Letter to Helen"), **402**
Stutz-Mozart (*The Vegetable*), **402**
Stuyvesant ("The Captured Shadow"), **402**
Stuyvesant (*The Evil Eye*), **402**
Styles, Phyllis (*This Side of Paradise*), **402**
Summer, Jack ("Between Three and Four"), **402**
Summer, John (*The Beautiful and Damned*), **402**
Summer, John ("Between Three and Four"), **402**
Summer, Sarah Belknap ("Between Three and Four"), **402**
The Sun Also Rises (Hemingway), 182
Surratt, Mary, 133
Susie (*Fie! Fie! Fi- Fi!*), **402**
Sutton, Miss ("O Russet Witch!"), **403**
Svensen ("An Alcoholic Case"), **403**

Swankins (''One Hundred False Starts''), **403**
Swanson (*Tender Is the Night*), **403**
Swanson, Gloria, **403**
Swanson, Johnny (*The Last Tycoon*), **403**
Swett, Mrs. Ulysses (*The Great Gatsby*), **403**
''The Swimmers,'' **403–4**
Swinburne, Algernon Charles, 129
Syneforth, Captain Clayton Harrington (''Sentiment—and the Use of Rouge''), **404**
Syneforth, Clara (''Sentiment—and the Use of Rouge''), **404**
Syneforth, Lieutenant Richard Harrington (''Sentiment—and the Use of Rouge''), **404**
Syrel, John (''The Mystery of the Raymond Mortgage''), **404**

Tailor, Bartholomew (*Tender Is the Night*), **405**
Taine (''The Four Fists''), **405**
Talbot, Harry (''A Luckless Santa Claus''), **405**
Tales of the Jazz Age, 277, 334, **405**, 408
Tales of the Wayside Inn (Longfellow), 39
Talmadge, Constance, 252, 289, **405–6**, 415
Tana, 298
Tanalahaka (*The Beautiful and Damned*), **406**
Tannenbaum, Emile, Lieutenant. *See* Tanalahaka
Tantrum, Gore, Ham, Japhet, Jem, Jemina, Mappy, and Pappy (''Jemina''), **406**
Taps at Reveille, 307, 334, 406
Tarbox (''Head and Shoulders''), **406**
Tarbox, Horace (''Head and Shoulders''), **406–7**
Tarbox, Marcia (''Head and Shoulders''), **407**
Tarkington, Booth, **407**
''Tarkington's *Gentle Julia*,'' **407**
''Tarquin of Cheapside,'' **407–8**
Tasker, Captain (''The Bowl''), **408**
Taswell, Captain (''The End of Hate''), **408**
Tate (''A Short Autobiography''), **408**
Tate, Emily (''The Camel's Back''), **408**
Tate, Howard (''The Camel's Back''), **408**
Tate, Millicent (''The Camel's Back''), **408**
Tate, Mrs. Howard (''The Camel's Back''), **408**
Tatnall, Bob (''The Bowl''), **408**
Taylor (''The Hotel Child''), **409**
Taylor (''The Jelly-Bean''), **409**
Taylor, Cecilia Delihant, 99–100
Taylor, Deems, 98, 322
Taylor, Dick (*Coward*), **409**
Taylor, Dwight, 75
Taylor, Mrs. (''The Hotel Child''), **409**
Taylor, Virginia (*Coward*), **409**
Taylor, William Desmond (''Pat Hobby's Christmas Wish''), **409**
''Teamed with Genius,'' **409**
Tearle (''The Smilers''), **410**
Tearle, Betty (''The Smilers''), **410**
Tearle, Billy (''The Smilers''), **410**
Tearle, Clare (''The Smilers''), **410**
Ted (*Thoughtbook*), **410**
Television, Miss (''Outside the Cabinet-Maker's''), **410**
Temple, Shirley, 39, 188, 191, 359
Templeton, Brooks Fish (''Persuasion''), **410**
Templeton, Charles Martin (''The Rubber Check''), **410**
Templeton, Mercia (''The Rubber Check''), **410**
Templeton, V. (''The Rubber Check''), **410**
Temptation, Lord (*Safety First!*), **411**
Temptation, Miss (*Safety First!*), **411**
''10 Best Books I Have Read,'' 78, 279, 407, **411**
Tender Is the Night, 5, 34, 76, 78, 83, 112, 134, 137, 186, 205, 211, 227, 239, 256, 286, 293, 315, 334, 339, 380, 397, **411–14**, 445
Tenweather, Jason (''One Hundred False Starts''), **415**

"Ten Years in the Advertising Business," **415**
Terhune, Grace ("Strange Sanctuary"), **415**
Terral, Henry W. (*The Beautiful and Damned*), **415**
Terrell, Elaine ("Babes in the Woods"), **415**
Terrell, Mrs. ("Babes in the Woods"), **415**
Tête-à-Tête, Madame (*Fie! Fie! Fi-Fi!*), **415**
Teubel, Moises (*Tender Is the Night*), **415**
Thalberg, Henrietta Heyman, 57
Thalberg, Irving, 57, 75, 85, 243, 253, 289, 383, 384, 396, 399, 406, 409, **415–16**, 439
"That Kind of Party," 20, 373, **416–17**
That Summer in Paradise (Callaghan), 57
Thayer, Lowell ("The Rich Boy"), **417**
Thérèse (*The Beautiful and Damned*), **417**
"There was a young lady named Ruth," **417**
"There was a young man of Quebec," **417**
"The Third Casket," **417–18**
"This book tells that Anita Loos," 253, **418**
"This Is a Magazine," **418**, 452
This Side of Paradise, 5, 49, 94, 98, 118, 129, 135, 206, 230, 249, 279, 304, 333, 347, 395, 397, 407, **418–21**, 449, 454–55, 459, 466
Thomas ("The Dance"), **421**
Thomas ("What Became of Our Flappers and Sheiks?"), **421**
Thomas, Mrs. ("Between Three and Four"), **421**
Thorne, Vienna ("The Bowl"), **421**
Thoughtbook, **421–22**
"Thousand-and-first-ship," **422**
"Three Acts of Music," **422**
"Three Cities," 407, **422**
Three Comrades (movie), 289, 322
Three Comrades (Remarque), 289
"Three Hours Between Planes," **422–23**
Three Soldiers (Dos Passos), 112, 449
Throckmorton ("O Russet Witch!"), **423**
Through the Wheat (T. Boyd), 43–44, 78, 433
Ticknor, Evangeline ("A Nice Quiet Place"), **423**
Tilly ("The Jelly-Bean"), **423**
Tim (*The Last Tycoon*), **423**
Tim (*Thoughtbook*), **423**
Tinsley, Gordon ("A Woman with a Past"), **423**
Tipton ("That Kind of Party"), **423**
Tipton, Mrs. ("That Kind of Party"), **423**
Tipton, Terrence R. ("That Kind of Party"), 417, **423**
"To a Beloved Infidel," **423**
"To Anne," **423**
"To Carter, a Friendly Finger," **424**
Tolliver, Mary ("News from Paris—Fifteen Years Ago"), **424**
Tom ("Image on the Heart"), **424**
Tom (*Safety First*), **424**
Tom ("A Short Autobiography"), **424**
Tomlinson (" 'I Didn't Get Over' "), **424**
Tommy ("What Became of Our Flappers and Sheiks?"), **424**
Tompkins (*Coward*), **424**
Tompkins, George ("Gretchen's Forty Winks"), **424**
Tompkins, Mrs. (*Coward*), **425**
"To My Unused Greek Book (Acknowledgments to Keats)," **425**
Tony ("The Bowl"), **425**
Tony ("The Broadcast We Almost Heard Last September"), **425**
Tony (*Safety First!*), **425**
"Too Cute for Words," 206, **425–26**
Toole ("The Bowl"), **426**
Torrence ("The Scandal Detectives"), **426**
Torrence, Elizabeth ("The Woman from Twenty-one"), **426**
Torrence, Janice. *See* Janice
Torrence, Margaret ("The Captured Shadow," "He Thinks He's Wonderful," "The Scandal Detectives"), **426**
Torrence, Mrs. ("He Thinks He's Wonderful," "The Scandal Detectives"), **426**

Torrence, Raymond (''The Woman from Twenty-one''), **426**
Tostoff, Toby, 427
Tostoff, Vladimir (*The Great Gatsby*), **426–27**
''To the Ring Lardners,'' 239, **427**
''Touchdown song based on,'' **427**
Touty, Marie (*Thoughtbook*), **427**
Townsend (''The Camel's Back''), **427**
Townsend, Mrs. (''The Camel's Back''), **427**
Townsend, Mrs. (*Thoughtbook*), **427**
Tracy (*Fie! Fie! Fi-Fi!*), **427**
Tracy, Spencer, **427**
''The Trail of the Duke,'' **427**
Treadway (''The Freshest Boy''), **427–28**
Trenholm (''The Rich Boy''), **428**
Tressiger, Lady Paula. *See* Jorgensen, Paula
Tressiger, Lord Eric (''New Types''), **428**
Trevall, Katherine (*Thoughtbook*), **428**
Trevellion, Bugs ('' 'Send Me In, Coach' ''), **428**
''Tribute,'' **428**
Trimble (''One Hundred False Starts''), **428**
Trimble, Louis (''The Lost Decade''), **428**
Trimble, Mrs. (''One Hundred False Starts''), **428**
Trop, Count de (*Fie! Fie! Fi-Fi!*), **428**
Trouble. *See* McClurg, Glenola
'' 'Trouble,' '' **428–29**
Truby, Miss (''Emotional Bankruptcy''), **429**
''The True Story of Appomattox,'' **429**
Trumble, Mrs. (''At Your Age''), **429**
''Truth and—consequences,'' **429**
Tudy (''Image on the Heart''), **430**
Tullio, Seraphim (*Tender Is the Night*), **430**
Tulliver, William V (''One Interne''), **430**
Tullivers, William IV (''Zone of Accident''), **430**
Tully (*This Side of Paradise*), **430**
Tunti (''The Bowl''), **430**
Turnbull, Andrew, 285, 391, **430–31**
Twain, Mark, 89
Twelve, Mrs. (*This Side of Paradise*), **431**
''Two for a Cent,'' **431**
''Two Old-timers,'' 117, **431**, 440
''Two Wrongs,'' **431**
Tyson (*This Side of Paradise*), **431**

Ulysses (Joyce), 427
''Under Fire,'' 43, **433**
Unger (''The Diamond as Big as the Ritz''), **433**
Unger, John T. (''The Diamond as Big as the Ritz''), **433**
Unger, Mrs. (''The Diamond as Big as the Ritz''), **433**
''The Unspeakable Egg,'' **433–34**
Updike (''Sentiment—and the Use of Rouge''), **434**
Utsonomia (''Forging Ahead''), **434**

''Valentine,'' **435**
Valentino, Rudolph (*The Last Tycoon*), **435**
Van Arnumn (*Thoughtbook*), **435**
Van Astor (''The Freshest Boy''), **435**
Van Baker, Leilia (''The Captured Shadow''), **435**
Van Baker, Victor (''The Captured Shadow''), **435**
Van Beck, Amy (''What a Handsome Pair!''), **435**
Van Beck, Betty (''What a Handsome Pair!''), **435**
Van Beck, Josie (''What a Handsome Pair!''), **436**
Van Beck, Teddy (''What a Handsome Pair!''), **436**
Van Buren, George (''The Third Casket''), **436**
Van Camp, Max (''Your Way and Mine''), **436**
Vance, T. G. (''The Bridal Party''), **436**
Vandervere (''In the Holidays''), **436**
Vandervere, Gordon (''Six of One—''), **436**
Van Dyke, Mike (*The Last Tycoon*), **436**

Van Schaik, Paul B. (''One Interne''), **436**
Van Schellinger (''A Night at the Fair''), **437**
Van Schellinger, Gladys (''The Captured Shadow,'' ''He Thinks He's Wonderful,'' ''A Night at the Fair''), **437**
Van Schellinger, Mrs. (''The Captured Shadow,'' ''A Night at the Fair''), **437**
Van Tyne (''Jacob's Ladder''), **437**
Van Tyne, George (''The Unspeakable Egg''), **437**
Van Vleek, Martin (''Dice, Brassknuckles & Guitar''), **437**
Varland, Joe (''A Short Trip Home''), **437**
The Vegetable, 196, 206, 334, **437–39**, 459
Velance, Peppy (''Inside the House''), **439**
Velez, Lupe, 439
Venske, Gus (''The Homes of the Stars''), **439**
Verses in Peace and War (Leslie), 249
Victor (*Fie! Fie! Fi-Fi!*), **439**
Vidor, King, 44, 57, 68, 85, 292, 416, 431, **439–40**
Villegris, Madame (''The Intimate Strangers''), **440**
Violet (''The Cruise of the Rolling Junk''), **440**
Vionnet (''On Your Own''), **440**
Virginie (''The Intimate Strangers''), **440**
Vitori, Cardinal (*This Side of Paradise*), **440**
Vivian (''Imagination—and a Few Mothers''), **440**
Vivian (''One Hundred False Starts''), **440**
Vlasco, Pandely (*Tender Is the Night*), **441**
Voe, Major (*Fie! Fie! Fi- Fi!*), **441**
Vogel, Augustus (''Zone of Accident''), **441**
Voltaire, Willie (*The Great Gatsby*), **441**
Von Boodlewaden (''The Prince of Pests''), **441**
Von Munchennoodle (''The Prince of Pests''), **441**
Von Nicklebottom (''The Prince of Pests''), **441**
''Vowels,'' **441**
''Voyelles'' (Rimbaud), 441

Wade, Marylyn (''The Ice Palace,'' ''The Jelly-Bean''), **442**
Waggoner, Dutch (''No Harm Trying''), **442**
Wainwright, Barbara (*The Beautiful and Damned*), **442**
Wainwright, Ward (''Pat Hobby's Preview''), **442**
Waite (''Basil and Cleopatra''), **442**
''Wait Till You Have Children of Your Own!'', 100, **442–43**
Waize, Gus (*The Great Gatsby*), **443**
Wakeman (''Majesty''), **443**
Wales, Brick (''Basil and Cleopatra,'' ''The Freshest Boy''), **443**
Wales, Charles J. (''Babylon Revisited''), **443**
Wales, Helen (''Babylon Revisited''), **443**
Wales, Honoria (''Babylon Revisited''), 293, **444**
Wales, Miss (''Zone of Accident''), **444**
Wales, the Prince of, **444**. *See also* Cedric
Walker, Stella. *See* Calman, Stella Walker
Wallis, Maria (*Tender Is the Night*), **444**
Wally (''Emotional Bankruptcy''), **444**
Wally (''The Ice Palace''), **444**
Walmsley (''The Trail of the Duke''), **444**
Walmsley, Mirabel (''The Trail of the Duke''), **444**
Walters (''The Unspeakable Egg''), **444**
Wanger, Walter, 204, 290, 376
Warburton (''The Camel's Back''), **444**
Ward (''One Interne''), **444**
Ward, Chauncey (''Last Kiss''), **444**
Warden, Mrs. Teak (''The Rich Boy''), **445**
Warden, Teak (''The Rich Boy''), **445**

Ware, Maurice de (''The Honor of the Goon''), **445**
Warner, Dan (''A Freeze-Out''), **445**
Warner, Eltinge F., 297, 354
Warner, Reuben, 37
Warren (''First Blood''), **445**
Warren, Baby (*Tender Is the Night*), **445**
Warren, Charles Marquis, 414, **445**
Warren, Devereux (*Tender Is the Night*), **445**
Warren, Lieutenant (''The Last of the Belles''), **445**
Warren, R. (*Thoughtbook*), **445**
Warren, Sid (*Tender Is the Night*), **446**
Wash (''The End of Hate''), **446**
Washington (''The Diamond as Big as the Ritz''), **446**
Washington, Braddock Tarleton (''The Diamond as Big as the Ritz''), **446**
Washington, Fitz-Norman Culpepper (''The Diamond as Big as the Ritz''), **446**
Washington, Jasmine (''The Diamond as Big as the Ritz''), **446**
Washington, Kismine (''The Diamond as Big as the Ritz''), **446**
Washington, Mrs. Braddock Tarleton (''The Diamond as Big as the Ritz''), **446**
Washington, Percy (''The Diamond as Big as the Ritz''), **446**
Washington, R. (*Thoughtbook*), **446**
Washmer, Elaine (''Forging Ahead''), **446**
The Wasted Generation (Johnson), 112
Watchman, Bill ('' 'Send Me In, Coach' ''), **447**
Watchman, Cyrus K. ('' 'Send Me In, Coach' ''), **447**
Waterbury, Ernest (''A Woman with a Past''), **447**
Waterbury, Judge (''The Swimmers''), **447**
Waterson, Miss (*This Side of Paradise*), **447**
Watts (''Dalyrimple Goes Wrong''), **447**
Wayburn, Ned (''Two Wrongs''), **447**
Wayne, Jill (*This Side of Paradise*), **447**
Weatherbee, Percy B. (*The Beautiful and Damned*), **447**
Weatherby, Mrs. (*This Side of Paradise*), **447**
Weatherby, Sally (*This Side of Paradise*), **447–48**
Weaver, Bette (''Her Last Case''), **448**
Weaver, John V. A., 270, **448**
Webb (''Babylon Revisited''), **448**
The Wedding Night (movie), 440
Weeks- Tenliffe, Mrs. (''The Rubber Check''), **448**
Weems, Weasel (''The Freshest Boy''), **448**
Weicker (''The Hotel Child''), **448**
Weinstein, Nathan. *See* West, Nathanael
Welles, Orson, 39, 188, **449**
Wells, H. G., 78, **449**
Wells, Mrs. (''Family in the Wind''), **449**
Wendell, Peter Boyce (''Head and Shoulders''), **449**
West, Jebby (''The Bridal Party''), **450**
West, Nathanael, 259, **450–51**
Westgate (''The Passionate Eskimo''), **451**
Wetherby, Cecile (*Assorted Spirits*), **451**
Wetherby, Peter (*Assorted Spirits*), **451**
Wetherby, Richard (*Assorted Spirits*), **451**
Whaley, Marice (''First Blood''), **451**
Whaley, Miss (''The Rubber Check''), **451**
Wharton (''A Night at the Fair,'' ''The Scandal Detectives''), **451**
Wharton, Edith, 117, 289, 418, **451–52**
Wharton, Elsie (''The Adolescent Marriage''), **452**
Wharton, George (''The Adolescent Marriage''), **452**
''What a Handsome Pair!'', **452–53**
''What Became of Our Flappers and Sheiks?'', **453–54**
''What I Think and Feel at 25,'' **454**
''What I Was Advised to Do—And Didn't,'' **454**
''What Kind of Husbands Do 'Jimmies' Make?'', **454–55**
What's-Her-Name (''On a Play Twice Seen''), **455**
Wheelock, Dr. Dick ('' 'Trouble' ''), **455**

Wheelock, Mrs. (''Fate in Her Hands''), **455**
''When We Meet Again,'' **455**
Whilomville, George. *See* Gilbert, Dodo
Whisper (''Her Last Case''), **455**
Whitby, Harry (''Indecision''), **455**
White, Sam (''Basil and Cleopatra''), **455**
White, Tarzan (''Pat Hobby's Secret''), **455**
White, Wylie (*The Last Tycoon*), 243, **455**
Whitebait, S. B. (*The Great Gatsby*), **456**
Whitehead, Jack (''The Bowl''), **456**
Whitney, Knowleton (''Myra Meets His Family''), **456**
Whitney, Ludlow (''Myra Meets His Family''), **456**
Whitney, Mrs. Ludlow (''Myra Meets His Family''), **456**
''Who's Who—and Why,'' **456**
'' 'Why Blame It on the Poor Kiss If the Girl Veteran of Many Petting Parties Is Prone to Affairs After Marriage?' '', **456**
Widdle, Joseph (''On Your Own''), **457**
Widdle, Mrs. Joseph (''On Your Own''), **457**
Widdlestein, R. Meggs (*The Beautiful and Damned*), **457**
Wiese (''The Swimmers''), **457**
Wiese, Charles (''The Swimmers''), **457**
Wiess, Miss (''Between Three and Four''), **457**
Wiggins (''Family in the Wind''), **457**
Wilburhazy (*Tender Is the Night*), **457**
Wilcox, René (''Teamed with Genius''), **457**
Wilkins (*Coward*), **458**
Wilkinson, Dr. Harvey (''A Full Life''), **458**
Wilkinson, Mrs. Harvey (''A Full Life''), **458**
Will (''A Snobbish Story''), **458**
Willard, Ken (*The Last Tycoon*), **458**
William (''More Than Just a House''), **458**
William II. *See* Kaiser
Williams, Kitty (*Thoughtbook*), **458**
Willings, Private (*Coward*), **458**
Willoughby (''Dalyrimple Goes Wrong''), **458**
Willoughby (''One of My Oldest Friends''), **458**
Willoughby, Mrs. (''One of My Oldest Friends''), **458**
Wilson (*The Beautiful and Damned*), **459**
Wilson, Big Jack ('' 'Boil Some Water—Lots of It' ''), **459**
Wilson, Edmund, 33, 84, 132, 158, 242–43, 278, 294, 298, 321, 323, 335, 380, 450, **459–60**
Wilson, George B. (*The Great Gatsby*), **460**
Wilson, Jim (*This Side of Paradise*), **460**
Wilson, Myrtle (*The Great Gatsby*), **460**
Wilson, Waveline (''The Honor of the Goon''), **460**
Winant, Cornelius W., 304
Winchester, Margaret (*Thoughtbook*), **460**
Winebrenner (*The Great Gatsby*), **460**
Winesburg, Ohio (Anderson), 7–8
Winfield, George (''Six of One—''), **460**
Wing, Bessie Leighton (''News from Paris—Fifteen Years Ago''), **460–61**
Wing, Hershell (''News from Paris—Fifteen Years Ago''), **461**
Winlock, Bomar (''The Honor of the Goon''), **461**
Winslow ('' 'Trouble' ''), **461**
Winslow, Charlotte (''A Freeze-Out''), **461**
Winslow, Eleanor (''A Freeze-Out''), **461**
Winslow, Forrest (''A Freeze-Out''), **461**
Winslow, Frederic ('' 'Trouble' ''), **461**
Winslow, Mrs. ('' 'Trouble' ''), **461**
Winslow, Pierce (''A Freeze-Out''), **461**
Winter Carnival (movie), 290, 360, 376
''Winter Dreams,'' 230, **462**
Wise, Bernie (''Last Kiss''), **462**
Wiskith, Samuel K. (''Pat Hobby's College Days''), **462**
Wiston, Bishop (*This Side of Paradise*), **462**
Witchcraft, Sir Howard George (''Rags Martin-Jones and the Pr-nce of W-les), **463**

Wolcott, Percy (*The Beautiful and Damned*), **463**
Wolf, Captain (*The Beautiful and Damned*), **463**
Wolfsheim, Meyer (*The Great Gatsby*), 239, **463**
Woll, R. Parke (''Pat Hobby's Secret''), **463**
''The Woman from Twenty-One,'' **463**
''A Woman with a Past,'' **464**
Woodley (''Your Way and Mine''), **463–464**
Wookey-wookey (*This Side of Paradise*), **464**
Wooley (''Family in the Wind''), **464**
Worden, Mrs. (''The Rough Crossing''), **464**
Wordsworth, Charlie (''The Debutante''), **464**
Worthington, Jimmy (''What Kind of Husbands Do 'Jimmies' Make?''), **465**
The Women (movie), 289–90
Wrackham, Percy (''The Rubber Check''), **465**
Wrenn (*The Beautiful and Damned*), **465**
Wylie, Tanaduke (*This Side of Paradise*), **465**
Wyman, Joe (*The Last Tycoon*), **465**

X, Captain (''The True Story of Appomattox''), **466**
X, Monsignor (''A Short Autobiography''), **466**
X, Mr. (''On a Play Twice Seen,'' *This Side of Paradise*), **466**

A Yank at Oxford (movie), 289
Yardly (*Tender Is the Night*), **467**
Yoke, Mrs. (''Does a Moment of Revolt Come Some Time to Every Married Man?''), **467**
Yosfuglu, Yolanda (*Tender Is the Night*), **467**
You Know Me Al (Lardner), 358
''You'll be reckless if you,'' **467**
''You'll never know,'' **467**
Youmans, Vincent, 422
''Your Way and Mine,'' **467–68**
''Youth'' (Conrad), 78
''You've driven me crazy,'' **468**
Yvain, Maurice, **468**

Zavras, Mrs. Pete (*The Last Tycoon*), **469**
Zavras, Pete (*The Last Tycoon*), **469**
Zeller (''Magnetism''), **469**
Zigler, Dr. (''One Interne''), **469**
''Zone of Accident,'' **469–70**

About the Author

ROBERT L. GALE is Professor Emeritus of English at the University of Pittsburgh. His numerous publications include *A Herman Melville Encyclopedia* (1995), *A Cultural Encyclopedia of the 1850s in America* (1993), *The Gay Nineties in America: A Cultural Dictionary of the 1890s* (1992), *A Nathaniel Hawthorne Encyclopedia* (1991), and *A Henry James Encyclopedia* (1989), all available from Greenwood Press.

ISBN 0-313-30139-5
90000>
EAN
9 780313 301391
HARDCOVER BAR CODE